MAGILL'S
LITERARY ANNUAL
2003

MAGILL'S LITERARY ANNUAL 2003

Essay-Reviews of 200 Outstanding Books
Published in the United States during 2002

With an Annotated Categories List

Volume One
A-M

Edited by
JOHN D. WILSON
STEVEN G. KELLMAN

SALEM PRESS
Pasadena, California   Hackensack, New Jersey

PUBLISHER'S NOTE

Magill's Literary Annual is celebrating its fiftieth year of publication; the series began in 1954. Critical essays for the first twenty-two years were collected and published in the twelve-volume *Survey of Contemporary Literature* in 1977; since then, yearly sets have been published. Each year, *Magill's Literary Annual* seeks to evaluate critically 200 major examples of serious literature, both fiction and nonfiction, published during the previous calendar year. The philosophy behind our selection process is to cover works that are likely to be of interest to general readers, that reflect publishing trends, that add to the careers of authors being taught and researched in literature programs, and that will stand the test of time. By filtering the thousands of books published every year down to 200 notable titles, the editors have provided the busy librarian with an excellent reader's advisory tool and patrons with fodder for book discussion groups and a guide for choosing worthwhile reading material. The essay-reviews in the *Annual* provide a more academic, "reference" review of a work than is typically found in newspapers and other periodical sources.

The reviews in the two-volume *Magill's Literary Annual, 2003*, are arranged alphabetically by book title. A complete alphabetical list of all covered titles can be found at the beginning of volume 1, followed by an annotated list arranged by category that provides readers with the title, author, page number, and a brief description of the particular work. Every essay is approximately 2,000 words, or four pages, in length. Each one begins with a block of reference information in a standard order:

- Full book title, including any subtitle
- *Author:* name, with birth and death years
- *First published:* Original foreign-language title, with year and country, when pertinent
- Original language and translator name, when pertinent
- Introduction, Foreword, etc., with writer's name, when pertinent
- *Publisher:* company name and city, number of pages, retail price
- *Type of work:* chosen from standard categories

Anthropology	Film	Media
Archaeology	Fine arts	Medicine
Autobiography	History	Memoir
Biography	History of science	Miscellaneous
Current affairs	Language	Music
Diary	Law	Natural history
Economics	Letters	Nature
Education	Literary biography	Novel
Environment	Literary criticism	Novella
Essays	Literary history	Philosophy
Ethics	Literary theory	Poetry

Psychology	Short fiction	Theater
Religion	Sociology	Travel
Science	Technology	Women's issues

- *Time:* period represented, when pertinent
- *Locale:* location represented, when pertinent
- Capsule description of the work
- *Principal characters* [for novels, short fiction] or *Principal personages* [for biographies, history]: list of people, with brief descriptions

The text of each original essay-review analyzes and presents the focus, intent, and relative success of the author, as well as the makeup and point of view of the work under discussion. To assist the reader further, essays are supplemented by a list of additional reviews for further study in a bibliographic format. Every essay includes a sidebar offering a brief biography of the author or authors. Thumbnail photographs of the book covers and the authors are included as available.

Four cumulative indexes, which list titles reviewed in annuals between 1977 and 2003, can be found at the end of volume 2:

- Biographical Works by Subject: Arranged by subject, rather than by author or title. Readers can locate easily a review of any biographical work published in the Magill annuals since 1977—memoirs, diaries, and letters in addition to biographies and autobiographies—by looking up the name of the person covered.
- Category Index: Groups all titles covered from 1977 to 2003 into subject areas such as current affairs and social issues, ethics and law, history, literary biography, philosophy and religion, psychology, and women's issues.
- Title Index: Lists all works reviewed from 1977 to 2003 in alphabetical order, with relevant cross references.
- Author Index: Lists, beneath each author's name, all of his or her books covered in the Magill annuals since 1977. Next to each title, in parentheses, is the year of the annual in which the review appeared, followed by the page number.

In all four indexes, titles that appeared in *Magill's History Annual* (1983) and *Magill's Literary Annual, History and Biography* (1984 and 1985) are indicated parenthetically by an *H*, followed by the year of the annual in which the review appeared.

Our special thanks go to the editors for their expert and insightful selections: John Wilson is the editor of *Books and Culture* for *Christianity Today*, and Steven G. Kellman is a professor at the University of Texas at San Antonio and a member of the National Book Critics Circle. We also owe our gratitude to the outstanding writers who lend their time and knowledge to this project every year. The names of all contributing reviewers are listed in the front of volume 1, as well as at the end of their individual reviews.

LIST OF TITLES

TITLES BY CATEGORY

ANNOTATED

TITLES BY CATEGORY

FICTION

POETRY
DRAMA

LITERARY CRITICISM
LITERARY HISTORY
LITERARY THEORY

ESSAYS

LITERARY BIOGRAPHY

AUTOBIOGRAPHY
MEMOIRS
DIARIES
LETTERS

Blinded by the Right: The Conscience of an Ex-Conservative—
   David Brock 83
   A memoir of journalist Brock's role in conservative politics, especially his contro-versial books and articles on Anita Hill, Hillary Rodham Clinton, and President Bill Clinton which fueled the acrimonious and partisan atmosphere of American political life in the 1990's

The Bullet Meant for Me: A Memoir—*Jan Reid*. 119
   After Reid is shot and paralyzed by robbers in Mexico City, he goes through a long process of rehabilitation, during which he maintains his friendship with a young Chi-cano boxer and comes to a mature understanding of the nature of masculinity

The Dressing Station: A Surgeon's Chronicle of War and Medicine—
   Jonathan Kaplan 238
   The compelling account of Kaplan's extraordinary adventures working as a field surgeon, filmmaker, and journalist in remote trouble spots of the world

Flotsam and Jetsam—*Aidan Higgins* 307
   A collection of short fiction, autobiographical excerpts, and travel pieces, mostly published between 1960 and 1989, by an award-winning Irish memoirist and fiction writer

Girl Meets God: On the Path to a Spiritual Life—*Lauren F. Winner* 330
   A spiritual autobiography that recounts Winner's journey from Judaism to Chris-tianity

Lazy B: Growing Up on a Cattle Ranch in the American Southwest—
   Sandra Day O'Connor and *H. Alan Day*. 460
   Lazy B, the huge cattle ranch overseen for 113 years by three generations of the Day family, provides the backdrop for this intimate memoir by the first woman to be named a justice in the United States Supreme Court and her brother

A Life in Letters, 1914-1982—*Gershom Scholem* 475
   A collection of letters documenting the life and ideas of Gershom Scholem, scholar of Jewish mysticism, that includes correspondence with his family and with important European intellectuals of the twentieth century

A Life in Pieces: The Making and Unmaking of Binjamin Wilkomirski—
   Blake Eskin. 480
   Spurred by the German writer Daniel Ganzfried's 1997 announcement that Bin-jamin Wilkomirski's award-winning Holocaust memoir was a fraud, Eskin investi-gates the authenticity of the counterfeit memoirist to whom his family at one time be-lieved they were related

BIOGRAPHY

TITLES BY CATEGORY

TITLES BY CATEGORY

CURRENT AFFAIRS
SOCIAL ISSUES

SCIENCE
HISTORY OF SCIENCE
TECHNOLOGY

NATURE
NATURAL HISTORY
ENVIRONMENT

PHILOSOPHY
RELIGION

TITLES BY CATEGORY

TITLES BY CATEGORY

PSYCHOLOGY

SOCIOLOGY
ARCHAEOLOGY
ANTHROPOLOGY

TRAVEL

WOMEN'S ISSUES

CONTRIBUTING REVIEWERS FOR 2003 ANNUAL

Michael Adams
*City University of New York
Graduate Center*

Andrew J. Angyal
Elon University

Bryan Aubrey
Independent Scholar

Philip Bader
Independent Scholar

Carl L. Bankston III
Tulane University

Dan Barnett
Butte College

Chuck Berg
University of Kansas

Nathan Berg
University of Texas at Dallas

Milton Berman
University of Rochester

Cynthia A. Bily
Adrian College

Margaret Boe Birns
New York University

Pegge Bochynski
Salem State College

Steve D. Boilard
Independent Scholar

Harold Branam
Savannah State University

Gerhard Brand
*California State University,
Los Angeles*

Peter Brier
*California State University,
Los Angeles*

Jeffrey L. Buller
Mary Baldwin College

Thomas J. Campbell
Pacific Lutheran University

Edmund J. Campion
University of Tennessee

Mary Ellen Campion
Independent Scholar

Sharon Carson
University of North Dakota

Dolores L. Christie
*CTSA/John Carroll
University*

C. L. Chua
*California State University,
Fresno*

Richard Hauer Costa
Texas A&M University

Mary Virginia Davis
Independent Scholar

Frank Day
Clemson University

Bill Delaney
Independent Scholar

Francine A. Dempsey
College of St. Rose

M. Casey Diana
*University of Illinois,
Urbana-Champaign*

Margaret A. Dodson
Independent Scholar

Robert P. Ellis
Independent Scholar

Thomas L. Erskine
Salisbury University

Rebecca Hendrick Flannagan
Francis Marion University

Roy C. Flannagan
Francis Marion University

Robert J. Forman
St. John's University

Ann D. Garbett
Averett University

Janet E. Gardner
*University of Massachusetts,
Dartmouth*

Leslie E. Gerber
Appalachian State University

Karen Gould
Independent Scholar

Hans G. Graetzer
*South Dakota State
University*

Miriam Graetzer
Independent Scholar

Diane Henningfeld
Adrian College

Theodore C. Humphrey
*California State University,
Pomona*

Jeffry Jensen
Independent Scholar

Leslie Ellen Jones
*University of California at
Los Angeles*

Eileen A. Joy
Francis Marion University

Steven G. Kellman
*University of Texas at San
Antonio*

Grove Koger
Boise, Idaho, Public Library

James B. Lane
*Indiana University,
Northwest*

Eugene Larson
Los Angeles Pierce College

Leon Lewis
Appalachian State University

Thomas Tandy Lewis
Independent Scholar

R. C. Lutz
University of the Pacific

Janet McCann
Texas A&M University

Mark McCloskey
Independent Scholar

Philip McDermott
Independent Scholar

David W. Madden
*California State University,
Sacramento*

Lois A. Marchino
*University of Texas at El
Paso*

Patricia Masserman
Microsoft Press

Mira N. Mataric
Independent Scholar

Charles E. May
*California State University,
Long Beach*

Laurence W. Mazzeno
Alvernia College

Kenneth W. Meadwell
University of Winnipeg

Robert A. Morace
Daemen College

Daniel P. Murphy
Hanover College

Robert J. Paradowski
*Rochester Institute of
Technology*

David Peck
*California State University,
Long Beach*

Cliff Prewencki
Independent Scholar

Maureen J. Puffer-
Rothenberg
Valdosta State University

Edna B. Quinn
Salisbury University

R. Kent Rasmussen
Independent Scholar

Rosemary M. Canfield
Reisman
*Charleston Southern
University*

Joseph Rosenblum
*University of North Carolina
at Greensboro*

John K. Roth
*Claremont McKenna
University*

Kelly Rothenberg
Independent Scholar

Marc Rothenberg
Smithsonian Institution

Irene Struthers Rush
Independent Scholar

J. Edmund Rush
Independent Scholar

Barbara Kitt Seidman
Linfield College

Carroll Dale Short
Independent Scholar

R. Baird Shuman
*University of Illinois at
Urbana-Champaign*

Thomas J. Sienkewicz
Monmouth College

Charles L. P. Silet
Iowa State University

Roger Smith
Independent Scholar

Ira Smolensky
Monmouth College

A. J. Sobczak
Independent Scholar

George Soule
Carleton College

August W. Staub
University of Georgia

Paul Stuewe
St. Jerome's University

James Sullivan
*California State University,
Los Angeles*

Jack E. Trotter
Trident College

William Urban
Monmouth College

John Wilson
Independent Scholar

Michael Witkoski
University of South Carolina

Scott Yarbrough
*Charleston Southern
University*

MAGILL'S
LITERARY ANNUAL
2003

ACHILLES

Author: Elizabeth Cook (1952-   )
First published: 2001, in Great Britain
Publisher: Picador USA (New York). 116 pp. $16.00
Type of work: Novel
Time: 1184 B.C.E. (the final year of the Trojan War);
    1821 (the last year of John Keats's life)
Locale: Troy; England

~

*A prose poem that retells the story of Achilles, yet actu-
ally meditates on the nature of heroism, vulnerability, and
human frailty*

~

Principal characters:
ACHILLES, the title character and Greek hero, son of Thetis and Peleus
THETIS, daughter of Oceanus
PELEUS, king of the Myrmidons, mortal husband of Thetis
ZEUS, chief of the Olympians, who arranges the marriage of Thetis and
    Peleus
AGAMEMNON, king of Mycenae, chief among the Greek warriors at Troy
ODYSSEUS, king of Ithaca, who with Agamemnon recruits Achilles for
    the Trojan expedition
PATROCLUS, protégé and beloved of Achilles, who is killed at Troy
PENTHISELEIA, queen and commander of the Amazons, who is killed by
    Achilles
CHIRON, the wise centaur, teacher of Peleus and Achilles
DEIDAMIA, daughter of Lycomedes, Achilles' first female lover and
    mother of Neoptolemus

The title page of Elizabeth Cook's *Achilles* indicates that it is a novel, yet this is not
an entirely accurate description. The work is also not a simple retelling of the life of
Achilles, as it emphasizes the vulnerability of its title character and by extension the
vulnerability of humanity in general. The expected elements appear: Thetis's fate is to
bear a child destined to overthrow Zeus, and Zeus's determination is to redirect her to
a mortal whose offspring would not pose him a threat. Even from this early stage,
therefore, the vulnerability motif is plain, although it is Zeus's vulnerability that first
draws attention. By marrying Thetis to the mortal Peleus, Zeus sets Achilles' fate.

When Thetis tries to obviate her son's fate, which is to live either a short but glorious life or a long but undistinguished one, her plan to confer immortality upon him by
submerging him in the flaming underworld river Styx nearly kills him. Furthermore,
the immortality Achilles receives through this procedure does not extend to his heel,
the one part of his body that remained untouched by the river. Homer's epithet for

~

*Elizabeth Cook edited the works
of John Keats for the Oxford
University Press and has written
scholarship on Renaissance
literature as well as short fiction,
poetry, and works for television
and theater. She was born in
Gibraltar and raised in Nigeria
before moving to Britain; she lives
in London.*

~

Achilles, the "swift-footed," thus has an irony that touches as much on that hero's mortality as it does on his prowess in battle.

Not content with her precaution, Thetis sees to it that Chiron the centaur raises Achilles to keep him from the eyes of those who might entice her boy to an early death. In contrast to the centaur Nessos, who attempts to rape Heracles' wife and is ultimately responsible for that hero's death, Chiron is an educator. Since he is part beast, he can understand the bestial, and since he is part human, he can understand what it means to be humane. Thetis then brings her son to the court of King Lycomedes and bribes the king to raise Achilles among his daughters. This does not last long, for Agamemnon and Odysseus soon recruit Achilles as their most promising prospect for the immanent war to be fought at Troy.

The theme that emerges in Cook's retelling of Achilles' story is the ultimate futility of elaborate safeguards against the inevitable. Achilles can no more resist the need to join the Trojan expedition than he can refuse to respond by reentering the battle once Hector has killed his beloved protégé Patroclus. Fate ordains that Lycomedes' daughter Deidamia will bear Achilles' son Neoptolemus. The birth of Neoptolemus will provide Achilles with an agent of revenge after the weak-willed Trojan warrior Paris, he who had started the war through his abduction of Helen, aims his unfailing arrow at Achilles' foot.

Zeus, Thetis, Deidamia, Patroclus, and Achilles are all in some way vulnerable to inevitable pain. Cook's conception of the situation is similar to that expressed by William Butler Yeats in his poem "Leda and the Swan" (1924). The narrator of this poem asks whether Leda, the mother of Helen, realized the spirals of death that would follow from Zeus's rape. Cook, like Yeats, is really talking about the gyres of history, series of events that inevitably cause others, all in some way tragic. Ten years of war at Troy and countless deaths, many of them foolish, follow directly from an act of lustful love. At this point the reader's mind may move to T. S. Eliot's poem "The Love Song of J. Alfred Prufrock" (1915) and his rhetorical question, "Was it worth it after all?"

With postmodern abruptness, Cook breaks her narrative to focus first on the two mythic characters who clearly loved Achilles most of all: his mother Thetis and his teacher Chiron. Cook calls these parallel narratives "relays," by which she apparently means the gyred history that produces chains of comparable events. Ironically, Thetis hastened her son's death by securing new armor for him, forged by the artisan deity Hephaestus, which allowed Achilles to reenter the battle after Patroclus's death. Achilles himself bore some responsibility for Patroclus's death; had Achilles refused his protégé permission to fight, wearing Achilles' armor, the Trojan Hector would never have challenged and killed the young man, for Hector believed that he was challenging Achilles. Nevertheless, Achilles had to grant the permission, for he was

Patroclus's teacher, and a teacher must eventually surrender his charge, and Hector had to challenge the warrior he believed was Achilles, since this was his own destiny.

Cook re-creates the scene in Homer's *Odyssey* (725 B.C.E.) in which Odysseus journeys to the underworld and speaks to his mother Antikleia; however, Cook focuses on Achilles' ghost standing beside that of Patroclus. Focusing by implication on the epithet "great-hearted" that Homer applies to Achilles, Cook notes the silence of the two heroes that contrasts so profoundly with the clamor of the shades that gather around Odysseus's sacrificial offering. Despite, or likely because, of their silence, the greater ability of Achilles to love is plain. It is a measure of his great-heartedness, the generosity of spirit that characterizes human heroism in every sphere of endeavor. In Homer's *Iliad*, Achilles' great-heartedness emerges in the threnody of mourning with which he commemorates Patroclus's death, but it is seen even more tenderly in his courteous return of Hector's body to Priam, the king of Troy and the young man's father, after he has killed him.

In the same way as Achilles had mourned Patroclus, so Chiron laments Achilles. Chiron had taught Achilles the arts of life and the arts of war. That he is half man, half horse allows him to see both the human and animal aspects essential to the process of living, yet he mourns as profoundly for that process as he does for his former student. Thetis mourns too. She picks up the bones of her son from the funeral pyre on which they had been incinerated and they become dust in her hands. Only the skull remains, a triumph of enduring intellect as much as a symbol of inevitable death.

Cook's third "relay" abruptly turns to the life of the English poet John Keats (1795-1821). Her own experience as general editor of Keats's works for Oxford University Press leads her to this logical mimesis. Keats is presented as attending while Astley Cooper (1768-1841), the noted British surgeon, performs one of his careful autopsies. Cooper's most famous work, *Surgical Essays* (1818), anticipated modern surgical techniques and curiously enough appeared the same year as Mary Shelley's *Frankenstein*, a story of a monster created from the assembled pieces of dead human bodies.

One could surmise that the year of Keats's imagined appearance in Cooper's surgical rooms would have been 1819 or 1820, one year before his own death from tuberculosis. Tuberculosis was a curse for the entire Keats family; it struck both of his parents and his siblings. Keats was an unprepossessing hero, barely five feet, two inches in height. He was a young man who loved deeply, yet could never actually love because of his knowledge of his inevitable fate. He thus faced alternatives comparable to those of Achilles: to die unrecognized but with the chance of a prolonged existence free from work, or to use his final months to produce some of the finest poetry ever written in the English language. Keats chose the latter, even though his excessive work in Rome certainly shortened his life and caused him to die, like Achilles, in a foreign land.

The Achilles-Keats relay also seems anchored through Keats's association with George Chapman's famous translation of Homer (1611). Keats's poem "On First Looking into Chapman's Homer" describes this encounter with Greek epic as a journey though untraveled realms. This was certainly true for Keats, who had none of the aristocrat's educational opportunities available to his contemporary Percy Bysshe Shelley (1792-1822). Even so, to anyone who knows the English Romantics, the aesthetic differences between Keats and Shelley were just as dramatic as those between Achilles and Agamemnon.

Shelley favored confrontation, political engagement, atheism, and radical democracy; Keats longed for rest, peace, and quiet departure after hard work. Shelley eloped with William Godwin and Mary Wollstonecraft's daughter while still married to Harriet Westbrook. Keats refused to commit himself to his beloved Fanny Browne because he was all too aware of his immanent fate. While Shelley and Keats never publicly fought, the differences in the way they lived their lives and the oppositions in their poetry underscore the differences in the men themselves. Perhaps this is the real magic of Cook's *Achilles*. She directs the reader into this kind of meditation through pure suggestion and without explanation in her text.

One cannot help but feel that Cook also thinks of herself as she contemplates the story of Achilles. Her hero lives the days of his life aware that his time is running past as surely as the water streams through the double rivers that surround Troy. Cook preserves the present tense throughout her narrative as if to argue that her words are limited, that they need to be paid out quickly because they are her own life's blood and therefore are so finite. The result is an epic that is hardly more than one hundred pages, yet one that seems to privilege the role of the creative artist as much as the hero about whom she writes.

Robert J. Forman

Sources for Further Study

The Atlantic Monthly 289 (February, 2002): 102.
The New Yorker 78 (April 8, 2002): 89.
Publishers Weekly 248 (December 17, 2001): 63.
The Spectator 286 (March 17, 2001): 36.

AFTER THE QUAKE

Author: Haruki Murakami (1949-   )
First published: Kami no kodomo-tachi wa mina odoru,
   2000, in Japan
Translated from the Japanese by Jay Rubin
Publisher: Alfred A. Knopf (New York). 181 pp. $21.00
Type of work: Short fiction
Time: February, 1995
Locale: Japan

∼

Six stories about characters indirectly affected by the
1995 earthquake in Kobe, Japan

∼

Principal characters:
> KOMURA, an electronics salesman whose wife leaves him
> SHIMAO, a friend of the sister of Komura's colleague
> JUNKO, a young woman building a bonfire on a beach
> MIYAKE, another fire-builder
> YOSHIYA, a man pursuing a man he believes to be his biological father
> SATSUKI, a woman on a business trip to Thailand
> KATAGIRI, a man who is recruited by a super-frog to save Tokyo from an
>   earthquake
> JUNPEI, a short-story writer
> SAYOKO, his college love, now divorced
> SALA, Sayoko's young daughter

In the early morning hours of January 16, 1995, a 7.2 earthquake hit the port city of Kobe, Japan, killing over five thousand people, causing billions of dollars worth of damage, and putting 300,000 out of their homes, including the parents of writer Haruki Murakami. Two months later, the radical Aum Shinrikyo cult carried out a gas attack on the subway system in Tokyo, killing eleven and crippling many others for life. Because of these twin terrors, Murakami, who had lived in the United States for several years, returned to Japan to research and write a series of newspaper articles on the terrorist attack, later published as *Underground: The Gas Attack and the Japanese Psyche* (2001), filled with accounts of the lives of both survivors and cult members. In Murakami's new book, *After the Quake*, six stories explore the seemingly tangential, yet very real, effect of the earthquake on several Japanese characters in February, 1995, the month between the two disasters.

The first story, "UFO in Kushiro," begins with a woman who has spent five days after the quake in front of the television. On the sixth day, when her husband Komura, a salesman at an electronics store in Tokyo, comes home, she has disappeared,

A best-selling novelist in Japan, with works that have been translated into twenty-seven languages, Haruki Murakami has been a visiting fellow in Eastern Asian Studies at Princeton University. Among his many awards in Japan, he is the recipient of the Yomiuri Literary Prize.

leaving him a note saying that although he is good, kind, and handsome, living with him is like living with a "chunk of air." As usual with Murakami's characters, Komura does not make any emotional reactions to his wife's departure. He takes a week off from work, and one of his colleagues says that if he will deliver a small package for him to his younger sister in the city of Kushiro he will pay for his airfare and hotel.

When the sister, Keiko, along with a friend, Shimao, meet Komura at the airport, he has the strange impression that he is witnessing some moment from the past. He also feels he has not come far even though it was a long journey. These impressions create a transition from everyday life into a mysterious realm of reality typical of many of these stories. When Komura says he does not think his wife's departure had anything to do with the earthquake, Shimao says she wonders if things like that are nonetheless connected somehow. When Komura and Shimao try to have sex, he fails several times because he has been seeing images of the earthquake. He tells her about his wife's note, and she asks if it is true that there is "nothing" inside him. When he asks what "something" inside of him could be, she tells him that the box he brought contains the "something" inside of him and that he will never get it back. At the end of the story, the most pessimistic in the collection, Komura understands the emptiness inside himself.

The second story, "Landscape with Flatiron," focuses on a young woman named Junko and an older man named Miyake building bonfires on the beach. As Junko watches, she thinks of the story "To Build a Fire," by Jack London (1876-1916), about a man traveling alone in the Alaskan wilderness who cannot get a fire started and freezes to death. She is convinced that the man actually wanted death, even though he fought to stay alive. Junko has always felt a "certain something deep down" as she watches bonfires. Miyake, who is obsessed with the fires, tells her that getting such a feeling while looking at a fire shows a deep, quiet kind of feeling inside a person.

Like Komura in the first story, Junko says she is empty, to which Miyake replies that he is an expert on emptiness. After talking about committing suicide together when the fire goes out, Junko goes to sleep and Miyake tells her that when the fire goes out she will feel the cold and wake up whether she wants to or not. In spite of the sense of emptiness, characteristic of other stories in this book, there is also a sense of communion between the two characters at the end. This mutual understanding suggests that it is possible that when the fire goes out, the two will still have each other.

The story "All God's Children Can Dance" begins with a man named Yoshiya following a mysterious man with a missing earlobe. Interspersed with accounts of Yoshiya following the man are flashbacks to Yoshiya's childhood, when his mother told him that his father was the Lord, and that one day he will show himself to him if he keeps his faith. Yoshiya is convinced the man with a missing earlobe must be his biological father. When the man gets off the train in an industrial area, he walks like a mechanical doll being drawn by a magnet. The fact that there is no sign of human life and the place looks like an imaginary stage set in a dream is another indication, typical of these stories, that the main character has entered some alternate dream reality. When Yoshiya follows the man into an empty baseball field, he disappears, and Yoshiya's acts seem to have no meaning to him; in fact, meaning itself seems to have broken down, never to be the same again. Kneeling on the pitcher's mound, Yoshiya gives himself up to the flow of time, saying aloud, "Oh God." Once again, Murakami's story ends with a sense of emptiness and loneliness; however, because Yoshiya calls out the name of his absent father at the end, there is some ambiguity about whether his discovery is positive or negative.

In "Thailand," a woman named Satsuki goes to a professional conference in Bangkok, Thailand, and decides to vacation there for a week with the help of a limousine driver and guide named Nimit. The alternate reality theme is introduced when the limousine arrives looking like an object from another world, as if it had dropped from someone's fantasy. When Nimit asks Satsuki if her hometown of Kyoto, which is not far from Kobe, was much damaged by the quake, she thinks of an unnamed "he" who lives in Kobe. Nimit takes Satsuki to a poor village to meet an eighty-year-old woman fortune-teller who tells Satsuki that there is a stone inside her body and that she must dream of a snake that will remove it or she will die. The old woman also tells Satsuki that the unnamed man in Kobe, obviously a man who jilted Satsuki in the past, is not dead. Satsuki now recognizes that it is she who is headed toward death. She even thinks that the earthquake may be her fault because she wished for it to kill the man. As she flies home, she wishes for sleep so her dream will come. Once again, a character is reminded of the emptiness inside the self, but once again also there is some ambiguity about the implications of this realization. If Satsuki has her dream, will she be saved from the hardness of her heart?

The most surreal story in the collection is "Super-Frog Saves Tokyo," which begins, Kafka-like, with a man named Katagiri finding a giant frog in his apartment who tells him he has come to save Tokyo from destruction from an earthquake. Frog says that he and Katagiri must go underground to do mortal combat with a creature named Worm, who gets larger as he absorbs hatred. Frog, quoting the nineteenth century German philosopher Friedrich Nietzsche, says Katagiri must cheer him on, for fighting is not something he likes to do. When Katagiri tells Frog that he is even less than ordinary and does not see how he can help save Tokyo, Frog says he is trying to save Tokyo for good, ordinary people just like him. However, on the day they are to go underground Katagiri is shot by a man in the street and wakes up in a hospital, only to find out there has been no earthquake and that he was not shot at all. Like other characters in these stories, Katagiri has no idea of what is true anymore. When Frog comes to the hospital and tells Katagiri that he did a great job in his dreams, the strange creature begins to break out in boils, out of which come maggots, centipedes, worms, and bugs, which fill the room and crawl all over Katagiri. When he wakes up, he knows that Frog saved Tokyo at the cost of his life, for he went back to the mud and will never come again. Then Katagiri falls into a restful, dreamless sleep. Although this is certainly the most Kafkaesque story in the book, it is also one of the most optimistic, for it ends with Katagiri no longer troubled by strange dreams, peaceful in his very ordinariness.

Perhaps the most hopeful story in the book is "Honey Pie," which begins with a man named Junpei telling a story to a child named Sala about a bear named Masakichi, who has no friends and is especially hated by a tough bear named Tonkichi. The child's mother, Sayoko, has called Junpei, a writer and a friend, to come and help her because Sala is having hysterical fits in which she believes someone called the Earthquake Man is trying to put her in a little box.

When Junpei, Sayoko, and her husband Takatsuki were close friends at the university, Junpei felt that Sayoko was the girl he had been looking for, but because he could never bring himself to express his feelings to her, Takatsuki was the first one to declare his love. After graduation, Junpei became a successful short-story writer, while Takatsuki got a job with a newspaper and married Sayoko. Just before Sala's second birthday, Takatsuki and Sayoko divorce and Junpei thinks about asking Sayoko to marry him but cannot make up his mind. When Junpei and Sayoko take Sala to a zoo to see the bears, he tells the little girl a story about Tonkichi who trades salmon with Masakichi for his honey, eventually making them best friends. When the salmon disappear, Tonkichi ends up being sent to the zoo.

That evening after dinner, Junpei and Sayoko embrace as if nothing has changed since they were nineteen. During the night Sala comes into the bedroom and says the Earthquake Man came and told her that he has a box for everyone. Junpei sleeps on the sofa and looks at the television, musing that they are inside the television waiting for the box to open. He thinks that as soon as Sayoko wakes up he will ask her to marry him. He also thinks of a conclusion for the story for Sala; he has Tonkichi bake honey pies, which Masakichi takes to town and sells so they can live as best friends forever. Thinking he now will keep watch over this woman and little girl and never let anyone put them in that crazy box, not even if the earth should crack open, Junpei decides he wants to write stories different from those he has written so far; he wants to write about people who dream and wait. Indeed, this final story in Murakami's collection is precisely that kind of story—a story that ends with fullness and unity instead of emptiness and separation. Thus, although these stories seem distinct entities, they are interconnected not only by the effect of the Kobe earthquake, but also because they move from meaninglessness to final hope.

Charles E. May

Sources for Further Study

Booklist 98 (July, 2002): 1821.
The Hartford Courant, September 15, 2002, p. H5.
Library Journal 127 (June 15, 2002): 99.
Los Angeles Times Book Review, August 25, 2002, p. 13.
Milwaukee Journal Sentinel, August 18, 2002, p. 10E.
The New York Times, August 20, 2002, p. E8.
The New York Times Book Review 107 (August 18, 2002): 5.
Publishers Weekly 249 (July 29, 2002): 53.

ALGERNON BLACKWOOD
An Extraordinary Life

Author: Mike Ashley (1948-   )
First published: Starlight Man: The Extraordinary Life of Algernon Blackwood, 2001, in Great Britain
Publisher: Carroll & Graf (New York). 395 pp. $28.00
Type of work: Literary biography
Time: 1869-1951
Locale: United Kingdom, Germany, France, Canada, United States, Switzerland, Hungary, Russia, Egypt, Austria, and Italy

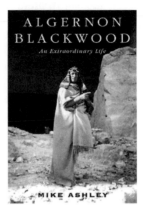

∼

Remembered today for a handful of supremely frightening stories, Algernon Blackwood lived a truly extraordinary life, traveling extensively, writing prolifically, and befriending many of the most important figures of his day. The fruit of twenty-three years of research, Mike Ashley's pioneering biography resurrects one of the key figures of supernatural literature

∼

Principal personages:
ALGERNON BLACKWOOD (1869-1951), short-story writer and novelist
STEVENSON ARTHUR BLACKWOOD, his father
GEORGE ARTHUR BIGGE, a confidence man who befriended Blackwood
ALFRED H. LOUIS, a lawyer and philosopher whose counsel inspired Blackwood
MAYA KNOOP (née Mabel Stuart-King), Blackwood's close friend for many years

Although the many stories and novels that Algernon Blackwood produced in his later years are distinguished by their spiritual character, it was a spirituality far different from that he knew as a child. Blackwood's father, Stevenson Arthur Blackwood, was a zealous albeit loving evangelist, and Blackwood grew up fearing that his parents' grim beliefs were true. Dreamy and impractical, he failed repeatedly at school. An institution maintained by the Moravian Brotherhood in Germany's Black Forest offered a more positive experience, although surely it is significant that when he used a similar school for the setting of a story years later, Blackwood turned the Brothers into devil-worshipers.

Throughout his biography, Ashley proceeds in this manner, relating Blackwood's stories and novels to particular places and events in his life, and in turn deducing the man's mental and emotional states from the works. Some guesswork is involved here, for although Blackwood published a memoir of his early years, *Episodes Before*

Thirty (1923), his memory for dates was unreliable and his reticence considerable. For instance, he omitted almost all mention of the several mystical and supernatural experiences he refers to obliquely in other contexts.

Blackwood senior must have despaired of his son, who was ill equipped for a life in business, but the parent never gave up. Thinking that greater opportunities might lie in Canada, where he owned

～
English writer Mike Ashley has written or edited more than sixty volumes devoted to supernatural literature and other genres, including Who's Who in Horror and Fantasy Fiction *(1976).*
～

land, Stevenson toured the dominion with his son and introduced him to potentially useful contacts. However, Algernon's investments in a dairy business and (to his father's horror) a bar proved disastrous. Yet a job as secretary and copy editor with the *Canadian Methodist Magazine* led to the young man's first published writings. Among other subjects, they dealt with his sojourn in the Black Forest. A few dreamy poems also appeared—under a pseudonym—in other Canadian magazines.

By this time Blackwood had long since thrown off his father's stultifying beliefs. Although he was later to become closely involved in the Hermetic Order of the Golden Dawn through the auspices of Irish poet William Butler Yeats (1865-1939), he first dabbled in Buddhism and Theosophy. This latter movement was the religio-philosophical creation of Madame Helena P. Blavatsky (1831-1891), who believed in universal brotherhood and claimed to be in touch with certain Eastern spiritual masters. Ashley identifies the core of Blackwood's beliefs in Franz Hartmann's Theosophical work *Magic, White and Black* (1884), which Blackwood read in Canada. Hartmann theorized that "every living being is an organism in which the magic power of life acts," and went on to suggest that the man who learns to employ this "magic" consciously rather than submitting to it unconsciously is a "magician."

It was to be some years before Blackwood became that "magician." He eventually quit Canada for New York City, but the metropolis frightened the nature-lover, who "hated the concentration of humanity." Blackwood's attempts at journalism brought in little remuneration at first, and he quickly fell into the clutches of amiable confidence man George Arthur Bigge. An abscess in Blackwood's side left him increasingly debilitated, but the ensuing delirium generated ideas—for instance, the striking concept of a crack between one day and the next that might lead to the paradise lying beyond the drab veneer of everyday reality. That crack would appear years later in *The Education of Uncle Paul* (1909). It was also at this time that Blackwood befriended Alfred H. Louis, a cosmic philosopher and social dropout whose vibrant attitudes and beliefs buoyed the young man during many of his darkest moments.

After many trials, Blackwood became a successful journalist with *The New York Times* but, ever restless, he left after sixteen months to become private secretary to a banker. During this period he spent several summers at the Muskoka Lakes in the Canadian woods, out of which experience came the first recognizable "Blackwood" story, "A Haunted Island" (1899). Trips farther north and deeper into the wilderness bore richer fruit, including "The Wendigo" (1910), an elaboration of an Algonquin Indian legend and one of his greatest works.

By the time Blackwood returned to England in 1899, he had begun publishing a few of his stories, but it was a friend who submitted a selection of his stories to a book publisher. At first alarmed when the manuscript was accepted, Blackwood relented and the collection appeared in 1906 as *The Empty House, and Other Ghost Stories*. A second collection, *The Listener, and Other Stories* (1907), followed, and included Blackwood's first masterpiece, "The Willows" (1907). Both were critical and popular successes, and Blackwood was launched as a writer. A third collection, *John Silence, Physician Extraordinary*, appeared in 1908 and featured an occult detective as its central character. The collection was advertised widely on London omnibuses and billboards and cemented Blackwood's reputation. Its high point was an account of a werewolf on a remote island in the Baltic Sea entitled "The Camp of the Dog."

Blackwood had already begun and set aside a longer, magical novel of childhood, but now seemed the time to resurrect it. This was *Jimbo: A Fantasy*, which appeared in 1909. His second novel, *The Education of Uncle Paul*, looked at childhood from the vantage point of an adult, "Uncle" Paul Rivers. Among its admirers was C. S. Lewis (1898-1963), who himself grew up to become a popular and acclaimed writer for children and adults. A thematic sequel, *A Prisoner in Fairyland (The Book That "Uncle Paul" Wrote)*, appeared in 1913, but by then that particular spell was broken. Far more successful was *Julius Le Vallon: An Episode* (1916), whose protagonist remembers a previous incarnation on another planet. Once again a sequel, *The Bright Messenger* (1921), followed, but once again Blackwood found it hard to live up to his original inspiration.

A man of few possessions, Blackwood traveled widely and almost compulsively, sooner or later incorporating most of the places he visited into what he wrote. If he had a single "subject," it was perhaps the forces of nature, but in his best stories and novels those forces are linked to specific places. As a child he had visited the Isle of Skye off the coast of Scotland with his family. School had taken him to Germany and France, and as a young man he lived in Canada (setting of "The Wendigo") and the northeastern United States. Later came boating expeditions down the Danube, destined to be the setting of "The Willows," an outstanding story in which two men are stranded on a tiny island that is a gateway to another, frighteningly malignant world. Other trips took him to Egypt and to the Caucasus. This mountainous region lying between the Black and Caspian Seas became the setting of what is perhaps his best novel, *The Centaur* (1911), a work that showed the full "Face of Nature." A fine skier, Blackwood spent his winters in the Alps whenever possible.

Along the way Blackwood formed an intense if celibate relationship with Maya Knoop, the wife of a Russian industrialist. Maya inspired many of Blackwood's works and introduced him to such figures as German poet Rainer Maria Rilke (1875-1926), who himself had an interest in centaurs. Among other aspects of Blackwood's extraordinary life, he ran spy networks in Switzerland for the British during World War I, collaborated with English composer Edward Elgar (1857-1934) on a musical production entitled *The Starlight Express* (1915), and befriended such noted fellow writers as Hilaire Belloc (1870-1953) and Compton Mackenzie (1883-1972). Although his best work had appeared in the early years of the twentieth century, he survived long enough into that century's middle years to become a fixture on British Broadcasting Corporation (BBC) programs. He even made memorable storytelling appearances on television, and his face, "lined like a walnut," became a familiar one to thousands of viewers.

Blackwood was often haunted by guilt, although the ultimate source of that guilt is unclear. As a child in a narrowly religious household, he felt compelled to confess to wrongs he had not committed. In New York City he felt guilty for having George Arthur Bigge arrested and later still relived the guilt by writing about the event at length in *Episodes Before Thirty*. Upon the death of his father in 1893, he was consumed with guilt over never having lived up to his parent's expectations. As an old and respected man, he panicked when he thought that a policeman was shadowing him. (It turned out that the policeman had simply recognized him from his television broadcasts.) Ashley wonders whether repressed homosexuality may have been at the root of Blackwood's guilt, but he concludes that Blackwood repressed all of his sexual impulses after his betrayal by George Arthur Bigge in New York City. Throughout his life Blackwood would number many men as close friends, and women were drawn to him like moths to the proverbial flame—although none was immolated. Perhaps it was the magician at work.

It is no exaggeration to say that Mike Ashley has written the book on Algernon Blackwood. In fact, before the publication of his biography, only two other books had been devoted to Blackwood, one of them being Ashley's own *Algernon Blackwood: A Bio-Bibliography* (1987). The product of twenty-three years of research and writing, the biography is rounded out with twenty-two pages of notes and references, an appendix devoted to Blackwood's family tree, substantial bibliographies of primary and secondary sources, and an analytical index. Although some gaps remain in the account, it is hard to imagine at this late date that they will ever be filled. It is unfortunate that Ashley's occasional infelicities of style were not improved in the editorial process, but by most standards this biography is worthy of its subject. Its portrait of a fascinating figure and its elucidation of his works may well spark a revival of interest among adventurous readers.

Grove Koger

Sources for Further Study

Booklist 98 (January 1-15, 2002): 794.
Choice 39 (April, 2002): 1417.
Kirkus Reviews 69 (November 1, 2001): 1525.
Library Journal 126 (December, 2001): 122.
Publishers Weekly 248 (December 17, 2001): 76.
The Spectator 287 (December 1, 2001): 46.
The Times Literary Supplement, November 30, 2001, p. 6.

AMBLING INTO HISTORY
The Unlikely Odyssey of George W. Bush

Author: Frank Bruni (1964-   )
Publisher: HarperCollins (New York). 278 pp. $23.95
Type of work: Current affairs
Time: Summer, 2000, through fall, 2001
Locale: The United States

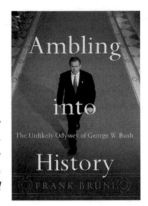

∾

A New York Times *correspondent who followed the 2000 presidential campaign of George W. Bush offers behind-the-scenes glimpses of the future president, putting his portrait of Bush into the context of the emerging challenge of the September 11, 2001, attack on the United States and subsequent war on terrorism*

∾

Principal personages:
> GEORGE W. BUSH, forty-second president of the United States
> KARL ROVE, Bush's chief campaign strategist
> KAREN HUGHES, director of communications in Bush's presidential campaign
> GEORGE H. W. BUSH, fortieth president of the United States, George W. Bush's father
> BARBARA BUSH, George W. Bush's mother

In *Ambling into History: The Unlikely Odyssey of George W. Bush*, Frank Bruni offers a behind-the-scenes account of Bush the candidate as he completed the home stretch of his quest for the presidency in the 2000 election. As *The New York Times* correspondent covering the Bush campaign, Bruni is able to present numerous glimpses which, in the end, add up to a thought-provoking overall portrait of the future president. This portrait is based on access not available to ordinary Americans. For most people, presidential candidates are figures presented through the filter of mass media. Bruni and other correspondents got to see Bush face-to-face on a daily basis. While Bruni does not go so far as to suggest that this gives him knowledge of the "real" George W. Bush, he does believe that he has valuable insights to offer as to Bush's personality and motivations. These insights, of necessity, throw light on Bush's most important advisors and allies as well, including key Bush family members. Bruni's book also includes a modest attempt to augment his portrait of George W. Bush with helpful commentary about the nature of presidential politics in the United States. Finally, Bruni opens and closes his book with a brief assessment of President Bush's performance during the early days of the war on terrorism following the September 11, 2001, attacks on the World Trade Center in New York City and

the Pentagon in Washington, D.C., often referred to as 9/11 (which took place about
eight months after Bush took office).

The George W. Bush revealed in Bruni's
book is neither the magnanimously compassionate conservative and strong leader portrayed by Bush publicists nor the total bumbler
and dunce portrayed by late-night comedians
and some of Bush's less subtle critics. He
cuts, instead, a more complex figure, one
which is less easily cast simply as hero, villain, or court jester.

To be sure, Bush is neither an eloquent
extemporaneous speaker nor an impressive

~

*Frank Bruni is a reporter for the
Washington Bureau of* The New York
Times. *He is a former winner of the
Polk Prize for Metropolitan Reporting
and has appeared on* Nightline *and
other news programs to share his
expertise on the Bush campaign and
presidency. He is the coauthor of*
Consumer Terrorism *(1997) and* A
Gospel of Shame *(1993), both with
Elinor Burkett.*

~

thinker with a clear focus on issues of public policy. Bruni makes it clear that the frequent "Bushisms" one sees quoted are not isolated incidents which have been magni-
fied by the media. Left to fend for himself, Bush produces a never-ending abundance
of malapropisms, which, in turn, have contributed to his image as an intellectual and
rhetorical lightweight. Also feeding this image is the fact that Bush is not particularly
knowledgeable about any topic outside sports. In short, despite holding a bachelor's
degree from Yale and a master's degree in business administration from Harvard,
Bush has never been a distinguished student of ideas. This image of Bush is not re-
futed in Bruni's book.

It does not, however, tell the whole story. Bruni reports that Bush's SAT scores
were well above average. (In addition, Bruni deflates the intellectual credentials of Al
Gore and John McCain, Bush's chief rivals in the 2000 campaign.) Moreover, Bush
has shown, both during the 2000 campaign and subsequent to his election, the ability
to deliver effectively speeches written by staff members. Bruni argues convincingly
that this is an indication that Bush is willing and able to put in sufficient time and effort to understand complex issues. Thus, the image of Bush as disinterested and even
lazy must be tempered if one is truly to understand the man. For example, Bruni
thought, during the campaign, that Bush handled the education issue with an acceptable level of authority.

This is not to say that Bush lives and breathes "compassionate conservatism."
Rather, for Bush, that credo appears, for the most part, to be a convenient and effective formula for political success, with the conservative element cementing the allegiance of the powerful right wing of the Republican Party (including the "religious
right") and the compassionate part appealing to moderates among Republicans, as
well as Independents and some potential crossover Democratic voters. Perhaps because his emergence from alcoholism in the 1980's was linked to religious beliefs,
Bush does have a more than convenient affinity for issue positions held by the religious right, including those on the question of abortion. This does not, however, keep
him from pursuing more moderate or centrist stances in order to win elections and
keep his political persona in line with public opinion. Indeed, this application of the

Ronald Reagan formula for success also suggests that Bush is focused and adequately intelligent when it comes to the bottom line of political campaigns—victory. Put another way, Bush may be seen as a talented and hard-working political opportunist.

What is left after one has eliminated the misleading positive and negative images of Bush? It adds up to a person who can, with some accuracy, be called capable and, at least in some settings, charming. Based on Bruni's book, however, one could not by any means describe Bush as a charismatic leader or political visionary.

None of this should come as much of a surprise, since it mirrors the early perceptions of President George W. Bush held by the public as a whole. This is clear from the results of the 2000 presidential election and subsequent public opinion polls. Though Bruni passes over the results of the election rather quickly, the fact is that Bush was not immediately popular with the American electorate. He suffered some early defeats at the hands of the underfunded and underorganized Arizona senator John McCain in the Republican primaries. In the general election, he came very close to defeat at the hands of Vice President Al Gore, a candidate with heavy baggage and one who, in the opinion of most expert observers, ran a lackluster campaign. Bush actually did lose the popular vote. In short, Bush did not exactly sweep to a convincing victory, indicating that the American people had their doubts about him.

After the election's litigious and chaotic conclusion, Americans clearly threw their collective support to the new president, but in a way that affirmed the legitimacy of the republic, rather than deep-seated belief in Bush himself. Even after the attacks of September 11, 2001, when the president's approval rating shot to record high levels, public support was limited to Bush's role as war leader, not as overall policymaker for the nation. Polls showed consistently that Americans wished to show a united front behind the commander-in-chief, but were willing to differ with the president on a whole range of domestic issues. Taken as a whole, through the first half of Bush's term in office, the American public has seen the president as having sufficient ability to man the ship of state in troubled times. Supreme confidence in Bush's personal abilities has yet to be demonstrated. Nor has Bush been provided with a deep mandate in terms of his overall policy agenda.

In seeking a fuller picture of George W. Bush, Bruni also looks at key people— handlers and family—around Bush, in turn shedding more light on Bush himself. Bush campaign (and later White House) staff members Karl Rove and Karen Hughes are portrayed as single-mindedly dedicated to Bush and—for the most part—highly competent. Indeed, they overtly attempt to conceal and compensate for Bush's more than occasional lack of a serious demeanor. Bush's parents are also subject to a lengthy interview. They come off as intensely loyal to their son and surprisingly bitter (to the point of ungraciousness) about outgoing president and First Lady, Bill and Hillary Clinton, as well as Al Gore. George H. W. Bush (George W. Bush's father) was defeated by Clinton in his campaign for a second presidential term in 1992. Bruni sees this as a prime motivator for George W. Bush in 2000. As indicated by the book's title ("ambling") and subtitle ("unlikely odyssey"), Bruni sees Bush as a somewhat reluctant candidate for the nation's highest office. It is the desire to please his family, both avenging his father's defeat in 1992 and erasing his image as the family clown, that drives Bush on, according to Bruni. (On the other hand, Bruni sometimes interprets Bush's rhetorical strategy and image-building effort during the campaign as conscious attempts to avoid making the mistakes that led to his father's defeat in 1992.)

While Bruni's book presents a useful portrait of Bush, it is far less successful in its commentary on the nature of contemporary presidential campaigns. Bruni does include some interesting snippets of the wild and crazy experiences of correspondents on the Bush beat during the heat of the campaign, but his half-hearted effort to explore the role of the media in making and breaking campaigns (if indeed they have that power) is not well enough developed to advance discussion on the issue. Clearly, there is a triangular relationship in which candidates, reporters, and voters are accomplices in making campaigns superficial and unsatisfying. Bruni's occasional criticisms and confessions merely whet the reader's appetite for penetrating analysis of the issue and perhaps even some fresh insight and helpful suggestions.

Likewise, Bruni's attempt to put his book into the dramatic context of the war on terrorism feels like a gimmick for selling more books or perhaps even achieving the proper measure of political correctness. The book went to press far too early to cover Bush's response to 9/11 in any depth or detail. Beyond the fact that Bush did not, on one hand, turn tail and run, or, on the other, simply "nuke" every alleged ally of terrorists, Bruni really has very little of value to contribute to the matter. Since Bruni stopped covering Bush after he was elected, he has no firsthand information to share with the reader.

Bruni's book has other weaknesses as well. There is something highly questionable about Bruni's decision to divorce observations of Bush's behavior and personality from his policy proposals and political vision. For example, when it is asserted by his father that George W. Bush has read the entire text of the Bible twice, one would like an analysis of how that experience is reflected in Bush's policy agenda. Bruni does not even raise the question. Nor does he critically consider the reliability of the glimpses he is permitted of the "behind the scenes" Bush. For example, Bush and his cronies were constantly indicating that the candidate was an avid reader, something Bruni had disputed in an early piece he wrote for *The New York Times*. Bruni accepts the evidence that he was mistaken and, at least partially, withdraws the notion that Bush is a confirmed nonreader. Yet Bush never goes into depth in his discussion of these books, nor is it clear that Bush would have read them if he had not wanted to change Bruni's opinion. On this and other matters, Bruni sometimes seems to overestimate the reliability of his data, forgetting that, even behind the scenes, reporters are privy only to what candidates let them see. Bruni did get a front row seat to the show behind the show. How close this comes to reality is something that is hard to assess. In order to know for sure, one would have to peel away another layer or two of facade and get to the guts of the campaign itself. This Bruni is not able to do. Despite these limitations, Bruni's book is worthwhile for its readability and the light it casts on the personality, strengths, and limitations of the United States' forty-second president, George W. Bush.

Ira Smolensky

Sources for Further Study

The American Prospect 13 (May 20, 2002): 33.
Business Week, April 15, 2002, p. 20.
The Economist 362 (March 23, 2002): 100.
Library Journal 127 (March 15, 2002): 95.
The New York Times Book Review 107 (March 31, 2002): 8.
The New Yorker 78 (April 1, 2002): 93.
Publishers Weekly 249 (February 11, 2002): 174.
The Village Voice 47 (March 19, 2002): 64.
The Weekly Standard 7 (March 11, 2002): 35.

AMERICAN BABEL
Literatures of the United States from Abnaki to Zuni

Editor: Marc Shell
Publisher: Harvard University Press (Cambridge, Mass.).
   Illustrated. 520 pp. $49.95; paperback $24.95
Type of work: Literary history

≈

Twenty-five essays by different scholars examining the complex multilingual traditions which help define the breadth and depth of American literature from its very beginnings

≈

The essays in *American Babel*, Marc Shell informs readers in his brief preface, originated in a three-day seminar on "The Non-English Literatures of the United States" held in Mexico during the annual meeting of the American Comparative Literature Association in 1997. Most of the essays in this resulting collection focus on non-English expressions and traditions in American literature (such as Arabic, Yiddish, and Vietnamese) and explore the theoretical issues which inform the study of American literary history in general and often place American literature in a wider global context.

Shell does not spell out the organizational plan for this large volume, but he has assembled the essays into six different sections: "Introduction" contains two essays, a longer one by Shell ("Babel in America") and a second, shorter piece by the Algerian writer Alexander Del Mar ("The Name of America") originally written in 1911. The body of the volume is contained in the middle four parts of the book, in sections on "Resistance and Assimilation" (five essays), "Authoritative and Nonauthoritative Languages" (five), "Loss and Gain" (five), and "Nationalism and Internationalism" (seven). The volume concludes with an "Afterword," an essay by Shell on Mark Twain's famous short story "The Jumping Frog of Calaveras County"(1865) and its translation into French and back, an analysis which tries to tie together metaphorically some of the themes touched on in earlier essays.

As with any collection of this size and scope, there is a great range in the value and quality of the different contributions, and little overall consistency or continuity. There are, for example, three essays on Chinese American literature, three on German American literature, and three on Welsh language and literature in America, but none at all on Slavic or Italian American contributions to American literature, and only glancing looks at African American and Latino literatures. (Although he does not say so, Shell and his contributors may intend to focus on those literatures which have not been studied as systematically in the past.) The contents can also be intimidating:

~

Marc Shell is Irving Babbitt Professor of Comparative Literature and professor of English at Harvard University. With Werner Sollors, he founded the Longfellow Institute for the Study of Non-English Language and Literatures of the United States in 1994.

~

While the writing is on the whole accessible, these are academic essays; one runs to thirty pages and has eighty footnotes. What Shell establishes in this collection, however, in spite of its unevenness and its scholarly apparatus, is the significance of non-English works in the development of American literature from its very beginnings.

The movement to open up the American literary canon to diverse literary traditions grew in the last quarter of the twentieth century, and peaked with the 1990 publication of *The Heath Anthology of American Literature* (edited by Paul Lauter and others, and now in its fourth edition), which added hundreds of pages of non-European writers to the "canon" of American literature for the first time. What the Heath anthology established—and all other anthologies of American literature in the 1990's rushed to echo—was the linguistic and cultural diversity of American literature from its beginnings in Native American oral traditions through slave narratives and the literature of immigration in the nineteenth century, to the popular ethnic writers in fiction, poetry, drama, and nonfiction in the late twentieth. (In "Carved on the Walls: The Archaeology and Canonization of the Angel Island Chinese Poems" in this volume, Te-Hsing Shan shows the dangers implicit in placing ethnic literatures into the literary mainstream through volumes like the Heath anthology.)

American Babel is an important addition to the scholarship which has been closely trailing this popular and academic rediscovery of American literary diversity. The volume shows that criticism is nowhere close to the full recognition of the immense contribution of ethnic literatures to the literary cultures of the United States. In particular, *American Babel* argues for greater examination of what Shell calls "American multilingualism," the polyglot linguistic traditions which have been in America since before its discovery by Europeans. German literature written in German in the United States—to take just one example—has a long history; Benjamin Franklin established the first German-language newspaper in North America in 1732, and the "German language remained a strong, unofficial presence in the United States throughout the nineteenth century." The German department at any reputable American university studies mainly literature from Germany, however, and departments of English generally consider only American literature written in English. Literary works published in this country in German—or in any other language but English—may fall between the cracks of these exclusive academic provinces and often drop from sight. As Steven Rowan proves in his essay in this collection, for example, Baron Ludwig von Reizenstein's 1854 novel *Die Geheimnisse von New-Orleans* (the mysteries of New Orleans) is an important and overlooked work in both the gothic and American-exotic traditions of early nineteenth century romantic literature. Werner Sollors does a similar reevaluation of Ferdinand Kurnberger's novel *Der Amerika-Mude* (1855). In an ethnic investigation into another important multilingual tradition, Ala Ayres's opening essay recovers the "Autobiography of Omar Ibn Said" penned in 1831, the only extant slave narrative written in Arabic. Finally, Lawrence Rosenwald establishes that "Alfred Mercier's Polyglot Plantation Novel of Louisiana" (*L'Habitation Saint-Ybars*, published in 1881) may be "the only systematically bilingual novel in American literature," using as it does both standard spoken French and Louisiana French Creole. *American Babel* identifies many such literary works, and in the process confirms "the full magnitude of multilingualism in the United States" and lays out many new areas for future scholarly study in American literary history.

The essays deal with more than linguistic issues, however; several of the best ones get to the complexity of American political and social history. As Shell writes in his long introductory essay, language often becomes the prism through which citizens come to understand racial and national issues. Kenneth Nilsen's essay on "Irish Gaelic Literature in the United States," for example, gets at the complicated area of social class in the nineteenth century—use of the Irish language in this country was often a signal of poverty and ignorance—and the bifocal vision of the Irish living in America, torn between two countries; the essay uncovers some wonderful poetry written in the United States in Irish Gaelic during both the nineteenth and twentieth centuries. Esther Whitfield's "*Mordecai and Haman:* The Drama of Welsh America" studies how a traditional Welsh festival (*eisteddfod*) in Scranton, Pennsylvania, at the end of the nineteenth century reflected the changing interests of an immigrant community. Yota Batsaki's essay on Greek American literature at the beginning of the twentieth century ("Unfaithful Translation: Bilingual Versions as Greek-American Strategies of Concealment") reveals the social and political complexity which characterizes any serious study of multilingual literature, here how Greek language and literature became crucial tools of immigrant survival. At the same time that nineteenth century immigrants were losing their native language and culture, they were gaining American language and nationality. This development was never smooth, however, and varied from ethnic group to ethnic group, even within individual groups. *American Babel* gets at some of the complexity of this transitional process, and at how literary and linguistic questions often turned out to be matters of national and political identity as well.

Other essays focus on the value of the non-Anglophone American literary traditions themselves. In "Written in Sound: Translating the Multiple Voices of the Zuñi Storyteller," Dennis Tedlock analyzes one oral narrative from west-central New Mexico and shows the artistic complexity of the different voices in the tale: "The result is a multivocal discourse of a kind that never existed—or so we have been solemnly told—until European novelists invented it" at the beginning of the twentieth century. The dominance of Anglo-American literary traditions through the twentieth century, in short, has obscured multilingual American literary contributions like the Zuñi. Stephen G. Kellman, in "Translingualism and the American Literary Imagination," summarizes how many modern writers have worked in two or more languages: Vladimir Nabokov in Russian and then English, Joseph Conrad and Jerzy Kosinski in Polish and English, Gloria Anzaldua and Rolando Hinojosa in Spanish and English, and so on. Some of the greatest Modernist monuments of the earlier twentieth century—T. S. Eliot's *The Waste Land* (1922), Ezra Pound's *Cantos* (1925-1968), and James Joyce's *Finnegans Wake* (1939), to name just three—are works which transcend the limitations of single languages. American culture, meanwhile, continues to labor under the myth and limitations of monolingualism. As Shell reminds readers in his introduction, the harsh truth is "that a country once polyglot, with thousands of bilingual schools, has become unilingual, if barely literate, in the twenty-first century."

One of the best essays in the collection explores this complex multilingual interaction. James Loeffler, in "'Neither the King's English nor the Rebbetzin's Yiddish': Yinglish Literature in the United States," explains the relationship between Yiddish and English languages in the United States, and the "Yinglish" dialect that was the result of this linguistic exchange. The two languages enriched each other and helped to create a third, hybrid mix of the two, and Loeffler shows how writers such as Abraham Cahan, Leo Rosten, Philip Roth, and others benefited from this rich exchange.

Toward the end of his essay, Loeffler writes that "Some 80 percent of the world's Yiddish speakers were murdered during the Holocaust," and readers are suddenly brought back to where *American Babel* nearly always returns, to the interchange of language, culture, history, and politics. As Loeffler quotes the Yiddish linguist Max Weinreich in a footnote to his essay, "A language is a dialect with an army and a navy." In other words, and as Marc Shell makes clear in his introductory essay and most of his contributors corroborate, language is never "pure" but always mediates among issues of national identity, cultural conflict, and political power. The same thing is true of American literatures. During all the years of the dominant "melting pot" theory of American history, ethnic literatures—Native American and African American literatures as well as the literatures of immigration and exile—were often ignored or viewed as exceptions which proved the monolithic cultural rule. All literatures, according to this conservative ideological stance, were aiming for consensus, assimilation, "Americanness." Now the academic pendulum has swung the other way, and non-Anglophone literature is being recognized for its uniqueness and its crucial contribution to the diversity of the American landscape. *American Babel*—in essays on Haitian literature and Vietnamese literature in the United States, pidgin pastoral poetry in Hawaii, or German Jewish women poets writing in exile in this country—confirms this in a number of essays of originality and value. The book is a major corrective to the monolingual view of American culture.

David Peck

Source for Further Study

Library Journal 127 (September 1, 2002): 174.

AMERICAN JIHAD
The Terrorists Living Among Us

Author: Steven Emerson (1954-   )

Publisher: Free Press (New York). 262 pp. $26.00

Type of work: Current affairs and history

Time: 1988-2001

Locale: Oklahoma City, Oklahoma; Ontario, California; New York City; Richardson, Texas; other sites in the United States and worldwide

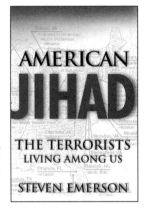

∼

A survey of Islamic fundamentalists, terrorists, and jihadists who have been living (and plotting and acting) in the United States since the late 1980's

∼

Principal personages:

MAHMUD ABOUHALIMA,

MOHAMMED A. SALAMEH,

RAMZI AHMED YOUSEF, and

EYAD ISMOIL, involved in the 1993 bombing of One World Trade Center

SAMI AL-ARIAN, a Palestinian professor of engineering at the University of South Florida, founder of the Islamic Committee for Palestine, chairman of the World and Islam Studies Enterprise, and editor of *Inquiry*

SEIFELDIN ("SEIF") ASHMAWY, Egyptian-born Muslim and peace activist whose *Voice of Peace* exposed the extremist views of various U.S.-based Muslim organizations

MUHAMMAD AL-ASI, Iranian American imam of various schools and centers in the United States, strongly pro-Iranian yet linked to Hamas and other extremist organizations

ABDULLAH AZZAM, a Palestinian mullah who called for worldwide jihad; killed in 1989

HUDAIFA AZZAM, Abdullah's son and guerrilla warrior in Peshawar, Pakistan

KHALID DURAN, Arabic scholar and Emerson's translator

WADIH EL-HAGE, naturalized American citizen from Lebanon who worked for al-Qaeda and for Osama bin Laden

SHEIKH MUHAMMAD HISHAM KABBANI, a moderate, who testified that 80 percent of all mosques and Muslim charities in the United States are controlled by "extremists"

MUSA ABU MARZOOK, resident of Virginia and Louisiana and a Hamas leader, who organized terrorist operations for fifteen years from the United States

RAMADAN ABDULLAH SHALLAH, former adjunct professor at the University of South Florida, secretary-general of the Palestinian Islamic Jihad

*Before becoming executive director
of the Investigative Project, Steven
Emerson was a journalist who wrote
for* The Wall Street Journal, The
New York Times, The Washington
Post, The New Republic, *and* U.S.
News & World Report. *He is the
coauthor of several books on
terrorism, and his 1994 documentary*
Jihad in America *won the George
Polk Award for Excellence in
Journalism and the Investigative
Reporters and Editor's Award for
best national investigation into
criminal activity.*

Steven Emerson directs the Investigative Project, which claims to be the largest intelligence and data-gathering center in the world monitoring militant Islamic activities. This book is based on his active, full-time investigation of these activities since 1993 and reveals how large numbers of terrorists, perhaps thousands of them in dozens of organizations, have infiltrated American society. This book argues that the September 11, 2001, terrorist attacks on the World Trade Center and the Pentagon, often referred to as 9/11, were not isolated or random events but were the results of coordinated efforts by organizations and individuals who live, work, and plot in such American locations as Brooklyn and New York City; Chicago; Oklahoma City; Omaha; Ontario, California; and Tampa, Florida. Extremist Muslim leaders such as Abdullah Azzam have called on Muslims to "carry out jihad no matter where they were, even in America. . . . The word 'jihad' means fighting only, fighting with the sword." Indeed, after Emerson's Public Broadcasting System documentary *Jihad in America* aired in 1995, he says U.S. officials informed him that a South African Islamist death squad was looking for him and that he should "go underground."

Emerson traces the activities of a host of Islamic militant organizations: the Muslim Arab Youth Association (MAYA), Hamas, the Muslim Brotherhood, Palestinian Islamic Jihad, Council on American-Islamic Relations (CAIR), American Muslim Council (AMC), the Republican Brotherhood, Alkhifa Refugee Center (also known as the Office of Services for the Mujahideen, which was the predecessor organization to al-Qaeda), El-Sayeed Nosair, the Holy Land Foundation for Relief and Development (which has given millions of dollars a year to support Hamas activists), and the Advice and Reformation Committee (ARC). To support his claims, he takes his readers inside the meetings of many of these organizations, at which they may hear repeated calls for the extinction of Israel and the destruction of the United States—for jihad. Even organizations that appear on the surface to be engaged in charitable fundraising to help Palestinians in refugee camps emerge in Emerson's research as covers for providing funds and supplies to terrorist organizations.

On the other hand, as Emerson acknowledges, "militant Islamist views are confined to a relatively small slice of American Muslims." He profiles several "courageous" Muslim heroes in this country such as Seifeldin Ashmawy, Khalid Duran, and Sheikh Muhammad Hisham Kabbani. Ashmawy has provided strong evidence of militant extremist infiltration of the United States. Kabbani, testifying before the State Department, provided insight into "the Wahhabism movement that has given birth to many of today's extremists." Beginning in the seventeenth and eighteenth centuries but flourishing only after 1920, as a result of the fall of the Ottoman Empire,

Wahhabism is a fiercely puritanical and iconoclastic belief, the religion of the al-Saud family (the rulers of Saudi Arabia), and firmly tethered to Islamic militancy and the idea that Islam must be reformed with the sword. It is this connection that may result in a "struggle within the United States" according to Sheikh Kabbani. Emerson claims further that Islamic extremists may have taken over 80 percent of the more than twelve hundred mosques in the United States, most of which are funded by Saudi money and most of which subscribe to Wahhabism, which "supports the spread of Islam through violence." Emerson argues that the militant fundamentalists pose a grave threat "not only to American institutions and lives, but also to moderate Muslims" everywhere.

Emerson provides several appendices to support and elaborate his principal claims. One of the most fascinating is Appendix C, titled "The Terrorists' Support Networks: The Sea in Which the Fish Swim." In this section Emerson details the nature, operations, and funding of nine separate militant Islamic networks operating within the United States under the wide protections granted in this country to organizations for research, charitable work, or civil rights activities. These nine groups provide significant support for terrorist organizations and are thoroughly radicalized. The nine include the Muslim Arab Youth Association (MAYA) formed in 1977; the American Islamic Group (AIG), now defunct; the Islamic Cultural Workshop (ICW), based in Walnut, California, from 1992 to 1999; and the Council on American-Islamic Relations (CAIR), which publicly condemns terror and defends the civil rights of Muslims in America against racial profiling while defending the actions of suicide bombers and developing connections with Hamas. CAIR stands accused by the Federal Bureau of Investigation (FBI) of being tethered to a platform that supports terrorism. The American Muslim Council (AMC) was created in 1990 as a tax-exempt educational organization dedicated to explaining Islam to the public. Emerson argues that the AMC supports radical Islamist causes, champions Hamas terrorists and Middle Eastern terrorist regimes, supports Hezbollah, and routinely issues anti-Semitic and anti-American statements. Islamic Circle of North America (ICNA) was established in 1972; it comprises mostly Muslim supporters who are of South Asian descent and is allied with Jamaat-e-Islamiya in Pakistan and Bangladesh. The Muslim Public Affairs Council (MPAC), founded in 1988 as a nonprofit social welfare organization complete with a 501(c)(4) tax status, sponsored a rally in Washington, D.C., in 2000 supporting the Al-Aqsa *intifada* between Palestinians and Israelis and in support of Hamas and Hezbollah, the principal organizers of terrorist attacks on Israel. Its leaders also participated in several other rallies that proclaimed death to all Jews and celebrated attacks on American installations and the suicide bombings in Israel. The American Muslim Alliance (AMA) was incorporated as a nonprofit organization in California in 1994 and operates as a political action committee, its leaders appearing in support of Hamas and openly supporting violence against Israel. The Islamic Society of North America (ISNA) operates out of Plainfield, Indiana. Founded in 1981, it serves as an umbrella organization for hundreds of Islamic organizations in the United States, according to Emerson. Muzammil Siddiqi, as president of the Islamic Society of Orange County in California, served as the president of the Board of Directors of ISNA until November, 2001; he made statements supporting radical Islam, "glorifying the jihad in Afghanistan," and condemning America for its support of Israel. ISNA has held large conferences to raise funds for the terrorist groups.

Emerson's work at times seems to depend more on labels and loaded terms such as "radical" and "militant" than close analysis and argument, but his descriptions of the activities, speeches, and public and private statements of these organizations and their leaders make it clear that a significant number of Muslims in this country are hostile to Israel, opposed to the Jewish presence in the Middle East, support the violent actions of the Palestinians and other makers of jihad, and are hostile to U.S. interests and activities in the Middle East. Appendix A, "Current and Recent Militant Islamist Groups in the United States," maps the locations and activities of such groups as al-Qaeda, Hamas, Hezbollah, Islamic Jihad, and other groups in the United States. Appendix B: "Current and Recent Terrorist Front Cells and Groups with Direct Association with Terrorists," lists each organization, such as al-Qaeda, with its supporting or originating organization, its principal U.S. offices, and any offshoots or cells that Emerson has discovered.

Emerson's book is disquieting for a number of reasons, partly because it appeared after 9/11 and partly for its sweeping claims about the infiltration of Islamic terrorist and extremist groups into the United States. It is disquieting as well to anyone who may be fearful of the sort of witch-hunt mentality that humans periodically exhibit. His strategy is to support his claims by quoting the speeches, texts, Web sites, and other documents emanating from various Muslim organizations and individuals to show specifically how they defame and revile Jews, call for the destruction of Israel, attack U.S. support of Israel, and call for jihad (with "the sword") against both Israel and the United States. The responses to Emerson's work, especially in the form of press releases, hostile reviews, and Muslim Web sites are largely ad hominem, very shrill, and capitalize on some embarrassing mistakes that Emerson made prior to this work, especially in his erroneously attributing the bombing of the Alfred P. Murrah Federal Building in Oklahoma City in April, 1995, to militant Islamic groups. Another problem lies with his associations with rather right-wing radio and TV talk shows, whose full-voiced support of Emerson's warnings and the airtime they have given him in the post-9/11 environment raises cautionary flags for the suspicious reader. Those caveats aside, what Emerson says in this book makes for chilling reading.

Certainly history is full of writers and orators who have raised their voices in warning and exhortations but were ignored and decried as racists and warmongers; one thinks, for example, of British statesman Winston Churchill (1874-1965). History is also full of demagogues like the communist-baiting senator Joseph McCarthy (1908-1957) and members of the vigilante Ku Klux Klan. Emerson, however, seeks to sift the terrorists from the general populace of U.S. Muslims and to show that not all Muslims either here or abroad are terrorists. Indeed, he devotes a section of the book to celebrating some Muslim heroes. Even so, the book is not a dispassionate, scholarly analysis or a cool, evenhanded presentation. It is itself a jihad, a call to arms for every

American citizen to be alert, a posting of danger signs widely over the face of the country and in its cultural and social life. His subtitle asserts that there are "terrorists among us," and he makes an alarming case for their numbers. Readers must ask how to protect themselves from such terrorists and their acts on one hand, and how to protect the freedoms of innocent Muslims—and themselves—in an open-armed culture on the other. However, discernment and fairness are always hard sells when war is the business of the day. Emerson's book will be better judged by history than by the current perspective, which is surely influenced by post-9/11 anger and hysteria. Americans have a history of culturally and politically induced myopia and hysteria—such as the genocide of the American Indians, the World War I phobia against anything German, and the incarceration of West Coast Japanese Americans during World War II. It is important to keep in mind that for every Muslim terrorist living in the United States today, there are thousands of Muslims who are innocent of any conspiracy against their country.

Theodore C. Humphrey

Sources for Further Study

Commentary 113 (March, 2002): 77.
The New York Times Book Review 107 (March 17, 2002): 10.
The Weekly Standard 7 (February 25, 2002): 39.

AMERICAN SCOUNDREL
The Life of the Notorious Civil War General Dan Sickles

Author: Thomas Keneally (1935-   )
Publisher: Nan A. Talese/Doubleday (New York). 397
   pp. $27.50
Type of work: Biography and history
Time: 1819-1914
Locale: The United States and Britain

◈

*A vigorous retelling of the life of New York congress-
man Dan Sickles, an inveterate womanizer, who murdered
his wife's lover in 1859, was acquitted, and later achieved
fame as a Union general at the Battle of Gettysburg*

◈

Principal personages:
> DANIEL EDGAR SICKLES, congressman (1857-1861 and 1893-1895) and
>   Civil War general
> TERESA BAGIOLI, Sickles's first wife
> JAMES BUCHANAN (1791-1868), president of the United States, 1857-1861
> PHILIP BARTON KEY, Teresa's lover
> JAMES TOPHAM BRADY, defense attorney at Sickles's murder trial
> ABRAHAM LINCOLN (1809-1865), president of the United States, 1861-
>   1865
> MARY LINCOLN, wife of Abraham, friend of Sickles
> JOSEPH HOOKER (1814-1879), Civil War general, Sickles's commander
>   and friend
> GEORGE GORDON MEADE (1815-1872), general in command at the Bat-
>   tle of Gettysburg
> ANDREW JOHNSON (1808-1875), president of the United States, 1865-1869
> ULYSSES S. GRANT (1822-1885), president of the United States, 1869-1877
> CAROLINE DE CREAGH, Sickles's second wife
> ISABELLA II (1830-1904), deposed queen of Spain, Sickles's mistress

Novelist Thomas Keneally became fascinated by the lurid life of Dan Sickles
while researching the Civil War for a previous book. He uses novelistic techniques to
provide a lively portrait of Sickles, his young wife, and New York and Washington
society in the mid-nineteenth century.

Daniel Edgar Sickles was born in New York City on October 20, 1819, the son of
George Garrett Sickles, a lawyer and sixth generation descendant of Dutch settlers of
New Amsterdam, who became wealthy by speculating in real estate. Keneally tells
the reader that Dan was a wild teenager whose parents arranged for him to receive special tutoring and live in the house of Lorenzo Da Ponte, Mozart's librettist,

who had immigrated to America in 1805 and now taught Italian at Columbia College. Da Ponte's granddaughter, Teresa Bagioli, three years old when Sickles arrived, admired their handsome young boarder. In 1852, when she was fifteen and Sickles nearly thirty-three, she accepted his proposal of marriage.

Tammany, Manhattan's corrupt political machine, also found the young lawyer attractive, despite rumors that he cheated clients and his known fondness for prostitutes and barrooms. Sickles was elected to the New York State Assembly in 1847; in 1853 he was appointed corporation counsel of New York City, leaving that position before the end of the year to become first secretary of the American legation in London. There Sickles assisted James Buchanan, the American minister, in his failed attempt to purchase Cuba from Spain. Sickles demonstrated his wild streak and scandalized New York society by leaving Teresa and his infant daughter at home in America while taking a well-known prostitute with him to London and presenting her at court to Queen Victoria.

Australian novelist Thomas Keneally is best known for Schindler's List *(1982), which won the Booker Prize and was later made into a powerful award-winning film. In addition to his many novels, he also wrote* The Great Shame *(1998), which describes the experiences of several generations of Irish people, sentenced in the mid-nineteenth century by the British to transportation to Australia, who lived lives of distinction there and in the United States.*

Returning to the United States, Sickles was elected to Congress the same year that Buchanan won the presidency. On the floor of the House of Representatives, Sickles strongly supported the efforts of Buchanan to prevent secession by appeasing the South. Teresa's vivacious, youthful beauty made her a favorite of Washington society. Sickles busied himself with congressional duties and sexual adventures with married women. Teresa began spending her time with Washington district attorney Philip Barton Key, son of the composer of "The Star-Spangled Banner." The two were soon engaged in a passionate affair that became a matter of gossip known to all Washington society except Sickles.

Informed of the affair in an anonymous letter, Sickles became furious and angrily extorted a detailed, written confession from Teresa. Seeing Key near his house the next day, Sickles confronted him with three pistols, shot him in the leg, and continued shooting his fallen foe until he killed him, then surrendered to the police. The case fascinated the nation's press, which covered the ensuing trial in detail; it became the 1859 equivalent of the O. J. Simpson murder trial of 1995. Sickles's friends assembled a team of eight lawyers to defend him, headed by leading New York criminal lawyer James Topham Brady. Acquitting a husband who killed his wife's lover was not uncommon in the nineteenth century. However, Brady felt the situation was dangerous for Sickles since his actions had all the marks of premeditated murder. He had stalked and shot down an unarmed man, firing three times at a victim who begged Sickles not to kill him. Brady entered a plea of temporary insanity which, Keneally states, was the first use of that defense in the United States. After twenty-two days, during which Sickles's attorneys acted as though Key and Teresa were on trial for adultery rather than Sickles for murder, the jury acquitted Sickles.

Keneally uses the trial to demonstrate the mid-nineteenth century double standard toward women. Females were not permitted in the courtroom for fear that the case might corrupt them. Yet when the defense leaked Teresa's raunchy confession to the press, newspapers across the country reprinted it. In contrast, evidence of Sickles's habitual sexual misconduct was never presented to the jury or the public. One defense attorney even argued that "the personal body of the wife was the property of the husband" and therefore Key's sexual relations with Teresa constituted a direct assault on Sickles which he was justified in repelling by force.

After the trial, when word spread that Sickles had forgiven Teresa and resumed relations with her, his supporters were infuriated. Keneally notes that "if the world had been divided in response to his murder of Key, the world was universally outraged by his reconciliation with Teresa." Despite facing public opprobrium, Sickles returned to Washington for his final session of Congress in early 1861. Although Sickles had been in favor of granting every Southern demand in order to avoid secession, news of Southern seizures of post offices and forts infuriated him; he now clamored for a military response.

Keneally describes the way the Civil War revived Sickles's reputation, turning him into a national hero. Although he had no previous military experience, Sickles raised a five-regiment brigade of New York troops, earning himself the rank of brigadier general of volunteers. His brigade was part of General Joseph Hooker's division in the Army of the Potomac. Sickles proved an above-average political general and soon became a drinking companion of West Point graduate Hooker. As Hooker moved up the chain of command, Sickles advanced in his wake, becoming a major general in 1862 and commanding a division during the battle of Fredericksburg. After Hooker took command of the Army of the Potomac, Sickles was given the Third Corps, which he led effectively at Chancellorsville.

At Gettysburg, July 2, 1863, Sickles disliked the position General George Gordon Meade assigned him and, against Meade's explicit orders, moved his corps forward where they were attacked and driven back to the Cemetery Ridge line that Meade had specified. Sickles claimed that moving his men forward caused the Confederate attack and set the stage for their ultimate defeat. Meade believed the action endangered the entire army and was reputed to have said that if Sickles had not lost his leg at Gettysburg, he would have been court-martialed. During the battle a cannonball had smashed Sickles's right leg, which had to be amputated above the knee. His wound made him a national hero. Sickles believed he looked particularly impressive on crutches and all his life preferred to use them rather than his prosthetic leg. In 1897 Sickles finally received a belated Congressional Medal of Honor for his bravery at Gettysburg.

Sickles became a favorite of the Lincolns. The president liked Sickles's aggressive military stance and his battlefield behavior. Mary Lincoln treated him as a personal friend, inviting him to the séances she held to communicate with her dead children. However, when Sickles asked to return to active command, Lincoln would not order Grant or Meade to appoint him. Instead, the president, in 1864, sent Sickles on a tour of the occupied South to report on the progress of Reconstruction and, in 1865, on a diplomatic mission to Colombia, South America.

After Lincoln's death, President Andrew Johnson appointed Sickles military governor of South Carolina in 1865. His active defense of blacks and repression of Confederate resistance groups led to Southern demands for his removal, and in August, 1867, Johnson relieved him of his command.

While Sickles was in the South, Teresa came down with tuberculosis and died in February, 1867. Keneally is fascinated by Teresa and presents a much more favorable picture of her than the three other authors who have dealt with Sickles's life and murder trial. He portrays her as a naïve young girl (she was barely thirty-one years old at her death), very much in love with her older husband, and driven to an affair with Key as a result of Sickles's blatant womanizing and lack of attention to her. Keneally criticizes Sickles for ignoring Teresa after their reconciliation, effectively exiling her to a farm in rural Upper Manhattan, far from her friends, during the last eight years of her life.

Keneally loses interest in Sickles after Teresa's death and covers the last forty-seven years of Sickles's life (he died in 1914, aged ninety-three) in twenty-six summary pages. Those years were hardly without interest or dramatic incidents. W. A. Swanberg's standard life, *Sickles the Incredible* (1956), devotes over a quarter of his biography to the last half of Sickles's life. Sickles actively aided the failed attempt to impeach and remove Johnson from the presidency. President Ulysses S. Grant rewarded Sickles's help in the campaign of 1868 by appointing him minister to Spain, a post he held until 1874. While there, he unsuccessfully maneuvered to purchase Cuba for the United States. In 1871 he married Caroline de Creagh in Madrid and fathered two more children. While courting his second wife, Sickles met the deposed Queen Isabella II of Spain in France. He began a notorious sexual liaison with her that had him commuting between Madrid and Paris and earned him the derisive nickname, "Yankee King of Spain." While still minister to Spain, Sickles returned briefly to New York in 1872 and directed the forcible removal of Jay Gould from the presidency of the Erie Railroad. In 1892 he again won election to the House of Representatives as a Democrat. Defeated for reelection in 1894, he returned to the Republican Party and in 1896 toured the country by rail speaking in favor of William McKinley's bid for the presidency. From 1886 to 1912 he was chairman of the New York Civil War Monuments Commission, until he was removed amid charges that he had embezzled Commission funds.

Keneally makes effective use of manuscript and printed sources of information on Sickles's active life. The author's use of novelistic technique permits him to add to the descriptive material in his sources and convincingly speculate about what the characters in his narrative thought and felt. The publisher's unfortunate decision to omit illustrations—the other three books on Sickle include many portraits and cartoons of the day—denies readers of this volume many graphic insights into nineteenth century life. However, Keneally's vivid prose provides an intriguing and smoothly readable account of the picaresque adventures of a mid-nineteenth century rogue and hero.

Milton Berman

Sources for Further Study

Booklist 98 (February 1, 2002): 906.
Los Angeles Times, June 20, 2002, p. E2.
The New York Times Book Review 107 (April 14, 2002): 11.
Publishers Weekly 249 (January 14, 2002): 47.
St. Louis Post-Dispatch, April 2, 2002, p. F12.
The Washington Post Book World, April 14, 2002, p. 2.
The Washington Times, June 8, 2002, p. B3.

THE ART OF THE COMMONPLACE
The Agrarian Essays of Wendell Berry

Author: Wendell Berry (1934-   )
Edited, with an Introduction, by Norman Wirzba
Publisher: Counterpoint (Washington, D.C.). 330 pp.
 $26.00
Type of work: Autobiography, essays, nature, philosophy,
 and religion

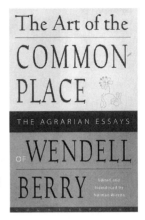

≈

A representative collection of Wendell Berry's agrarian essays, which advocate the adoption of economic democracy, a lifestyle in which local, sustainable use of resources replaces specialized extractive industries and their concomitant damage to personal, familial, and cultural integrity

≈

As this retrospective volume of essays demonstrates, Wendell Berry is a unique and gifted contributor to American literature and culture. Recognized early on as a poet, Berry soon developed as an essayist focusing on an agrarian vision of a healthy society. His persuasive, sometimes caustic, arguments have given him an almost prophetic stature among readers seeking to reduce personal anxieties and to avoid cultural breakdown. According to its supporters, agrarianism will reduce such ills as alienation, waste, crime, and environmental degradation. Only the restoration of the vital connections between people and their local environment and the reestablishment of the nurturing role of farming will lead to physical and spiritual wellness. In Berry's case, his choice to leave a successful teaching and writing career in New York and to return to his homeland in Kentucky has enabled him to live as he advocates, combining the roles of writer, farmer, and family member in an agrarian setting.

The essays in the volume *The Art of the Commonplace* have been arranged thematically into five sections, but because Berry has maintained an unwavering belief in the same principles throughout his career, all overlap in content. Over time he may have expanded his vision and refined its application, but the fundamentals of his beliefs involve a woven fabric of life in which no element can be ignored. Sections of the collection may thus contain essays from varied time periods. However, part 1, "A Geobiography," contains only the single essay "A Native Hill," excerpted from *The Long-Legged House* (1969). It serves as an introduction to Berry's essential beliefs.

As Berry makes clear in "A Native Hill," his life and career are founded on his ongoing relationship with the land. For this reason his daily experiences include episodes of wonder and authenticity. His life is rooted in the soil and in his understanding of the historical relationships between the land and his forebears. His philosophy fur-

~

Wendell Berry has been recognized as an accomplished poet, essayist, and fiction writer, having published more than thirty books. He has received a number of honors, including the T. S. Eliot Award and recognition from the National Institute of Arts and Letters and the Lannan Foundation.

~

ther requires responsible behavior, an element that he found sorely lacking in twentieth century culture.

Berry's family has occupied a segment of land in Henry County near the Kentucky River since his great-grandfather emigrated from Ireland. It is here that young Berry came to learn important, traditional values from the last of an older generation. He also learned these values from the living ecosystem of the place itself. Through this knowledge he came to know a host of human qualities such as compassion, happiness, stubbornness, and their opposites—a knowledge essential to creating health in and for the earth as a whole. Berry quotes an autobiographical passage written by a young Methodist minister while he assisted in a road-building project in 1797. The violence of the men toward the land and each other supports Berry's assertion that American settlers squandered resources, never learning to be a part of the land. This pattern has continued as generations of Americans have used resources primarily for commercial gain.

Although Berry's own ancestors clearly engaged in soil-eroding farming practices, he relates to their influence in his life more positively. He describes how slopes that are now heavily eroded should never have been plowed. According to Berry, this kind of mistake results from an assumption that what is good for human beings is also good for the land. The reckless loss of topsoil despoils an element of earth that Berry believes to be Christ-like in its combination of peacefulness and energy. He is most troubled that people presume to impose their ideas and wishes on the land, using up its resources and then moving on, rather than attempting to understand its fundamental nature. Yet interspersed with these dour musings, Berry describes the beauty of the natural world as it persists. These revelations are triggered by seemingly ordinary events such as a heavy fog or the view through the window opening of an uninhabited old cabin. In the poetic ending of his "geobiography," Berry relates how he is able to lie down upon the ground and feel himself to be a part of the earth, thus finding himself reborn when he arises.

Part 2 of the collection, "Understanding Our Cultural Crises," elaborates the basic tenets of Berry's philosophy in his many roles, including that of a member of a household economy. "The Unsettling of America," which is taken from the 1977 book of the same title, charges that the United States' national history is one of exploitation. This has resulted in a kind of corporate totalitarianism that continues to exhaust the land and results in social disruptions.

Berry's defense of agrarianism is not only a product of his independence and critical abilities. In the early history of America, Thomas Jefferson advocated an agrarian economy based on educated small landholders producing their means of survival from the soil and practicing responsible citizenship. His legacy solidified as agriculturists from the South later supported President Andrew Jackson in his opposition to the newly rich industrialist class and their efforts to solidify power and wealth in the hands of an upper class. As late as the 1930's, agriculture played a key role in the Southern economy, although its decline in the face of industrialization had been threatened to such an extent that a group of Southerners banded together to defend the agrarian lifestyle. Publishing a small literary magazine called *The Fugitive*, Robert Penn Warren, Allen Tate, and other future literary greats advocated the protection of workers and their connection to the soil. In "The Agrarian Manifesto," they opposed the early stages of what would come to be known as "agribusiness," in which machines actually replaced workers rather than easing their work. The industrial agriculture Wendell Berry condemns grew exponentially after the Depression, in spite of the widespread discussion of agrarian ideals stimulated by the writers.

Other essays in part 2 discuss how cultural problems such as race and gender inequities result from exploitive practices. Political power as it is tied to wealth reduces everything to its market value and thus destroys democracy. Dependence on the idea of freedom as spending power enslaves everyone. Households become units of consumers in which couples make use of each other. Personal independence is impossible without community, and community requires safety for the air, water, plants, and animals as well as human inhabitants. Berry urges people to think carefully about expenditures, to "Think Little," as the title of the last essay in this section suggests. He mistrusts big ideas and questions the true effectiveness of the civil rights, peace, and environmental movements, deeming them oversimplified and faddish.

Parts 3 and 4, "The Agrarian Basis for an Authentic Culture" and "Agrarian Economics," further explain how an agrarian life functions to develop healthy people in moral relationships with each other and with the land that supports them. As Berry portrays the situation in "Sex, Economy, Freedom, and Community," development has been falsely heralded as progress. The growth of mechanized agriculture has gone hand in hand with the dispossession of small landowners, making them "subject" to the wealthy classes and urban dwellers. In fact, Berry likens this pattern of operation to colonialism, the practice in which one area or region is sacrificed for the benefit of people living elsewhere. In the agrarian view, this is an entirely immoral undertaking.

In "People, Land, and Community" Berry charges that society acts foolishly in unleashing technology that is surely dangerous and then imagining that it will be possible to overcome the disastrous results. This kind of shortsightedness ranges from using up water in the Ogallala Aquifer with no replacement water in sight, to developing atomic weapons with faulty activation systems that may result in unintentional holocaust. Berry believes that when the link between humans and the land is weakened, the resulting fallacies, such as the idea that a "public" future can be planned for, endanger everyone.

Embroidering upon this point, Berry explains the enormous difference between a "public" society that is "free" to pursue unlimited profit and a "community" wherein there is a sense of responsibility in using resources, a commitment not only to other members of the community but also to future generations who stand to inherit healthy resources. Such planning for the future avoids reliance on skewed statistical studies that leave out expenses such as the costs of maintaining clean air. In "Solving for Pattern," Berry recounts the story of a farmer who realized his land was overused and chose to sell half his herd, thus reducing his dependence on cash purchases and allowing his lands to regenerate. The farmer achieved not only a more profitable status but also increased peace of mind.

In Berry's view, health ultimately derives from healthful land-use practices. Thus there is a need for a change of direction in the medical industry, in which specialization has resulted in the practice of treating illness without regard to its origin. As Berry states in "Health Is Membership," health professionals ignore other anomalous practices. For example, the use of tobacco is a target of governmental regulation but the use of antibiotics and other poisons in the production of meat remains a standard practice. Ultimately the doctors and the community will be more successful at achieving health when all become citizens in a true community. Similarly, specialization in the workplace denigrates body and soul, another theme Berry consistently employs. He explains in "Economy and Pleasure" that the only road to physical and spiritual health is through work that is healing in nature. Employment that demands machine-like activity leads to a life of suffering.

In the 1983 essay "Two Economies," Berry recounts a conversation in which the economic ruin of farming as a personal endeavor was likened to an attack on the Kingdom of God. Berry rejects the commonly held Christian view that condones environmental despoliation in fulfillment of a commandment supposedly giving humans "dominion" over the earth. Several essays in "Agrarian Religion," the fifth and final part of the collection, including "The Pleasures of Eating" and "The Gift of the Good Land," explain the religious foundations of agrarianism.

Throughout his writing, Berry uses a variety of literary references to establish what he believes is the true nature of humankind and to prove that the agrarian life is the only reasonable choice for humanity. He includes passages from sources such as the Bible, Homer's epic *Odyssey* (725 B.C.E.), and William Shakespeare's play *King Lear* (pr. c. 1605-1606). Among more recent figures, he quotes novelist Thomas Hardy and poet Ezra Pound. These and similar sources add dignity and a timeless authority to Berry's arguments that spiritual, physical, and environmental well-being are inseparable.

Margaret A. Dodson

Sources for Further Study

America 187 (September 30, 2002): 27.
Library Journal 127 (May 1, 2002): 125.
The Nation 275 (July 1, 2002): 35.

AT THE END OF AN AGE

Author: John Lukacs (1924-   )
Publisher: Yale University Press (New Haven, Conn.).
    230 pp. $22.95
Type of work: History, philosophy, and science
Time: 1500 to the present
Locale: Europe and North America

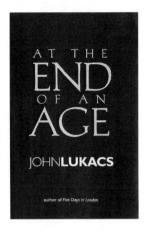

～

An extended essay on the origins, development and passing of the modern age, focusing especially upon its central characteristic: the emergence of historical consciousness as the condition of all human knowledge, including the scientific

～

The Hungarian-born John Lukacs has always eschewed the tendency toward narrow specialization practiced by most academic historians. He has written histories of the Cold War, of the age of the bourgeoisie, and of *fin-de-siècle* Budapest, as well as several works that defy the usual descriptive labels. *At the End of an Age* is one of these, and it is in some respects an extended footnote to several earlier books, including his *Historical Consciousness: Or, The Remembered Past* (1968), a work whose central conundrum may be stated simply: What does it mean to write history in an age in which the very conditions of understanding have themselves become historical? *At the End of an Age* reconsiders a number of answers to this question, among them the claim that historical understanding, governed as it is by the principle of indeterminacy, can be neither purely objective nor purely subjective, but is necessarily relational or participatory.

Lukacs begins with a chapter that seeks to justify the claim that the present is, indeed, the end of an age. The age in question is the modern age, which began some five hundred years ago and which still lingers on. Lukacs is convinced, nonetheless, that however prolonged its expiration, the modern age is passing, soon to be replaced by a new civilizational phase. What this new age may look like, Lukacs is hesitant to say. The current moment is the interregnum, but precisely whom does it affect? The modern age is, first of all, a European phenomenon, and thus a distinct period in the ongoing development of Western civilization. However, European expansionism meant that the typical institutions and cultural assumptions of its modern age were carried throughout the world, and thus the end of the modern age is a global concern.

Lukacs insists that the passing of the modern age is not synonymous with the decline of the West. He makes a convincing case that the modern age is, thus far, the most illustrious age in the history of the West, a complex mosaic of ages, none of which can be said to be more essential to its character than any other. The modern age

John Lukacs is the widely known author of more than twenty books of history, including A Thread of Years *(1998),* The Duel *(1991),* The Last European War *(1976), and the best-seller* Five Days in London *(1999).*

is, however, primarily a bourgeois age, which was first of all the age of the State (here understood as the sovereign nation-state). Allied at first with the absolute monarchies of western Europe, the bourgeoisie emerged in the seventeenth and eighteenth centuries as the ruling class of most of the nation-states of Europe and North America. The modern age was also the age of money and industry. Money, while not the invention of the bourgeoisie, has certainly been a distinctive sign of its mode of power, and it was under the hegemony of the bourgeoisie that, by 1900, money reached the greatest extent of its value and the Industrial Revolution became the engine of an unprecedented prosperity and mobility.

Lukacs offers a brief but illuminating discussion of the bourgeois invention of privacy—a phenomenon he associates with the age of the family, a period in which the idea of "home" was associated with a heightened interior life and a new respect for the privacy of individuals within the matrix of familial ties. Only later, growing out of this initial recognition of an almost sacred zone of privacy, did the panoply of individual rights begin to be recognized and sanctioned by a growing body of law. It must also be noted that the bourgeois family was an urban family—the bourgeoisie represent the first ruling class in Western history to be identified almost exclusively with city life. Thus, the modern age is also the age of the town, and Lukacs notes the irony that the many great metropolitan centers that developed under the auspices of the bourgeoisie had, by the late twentieth century, become the breeding grounds of millions of autonomous, deracinated individuals for whom the bourgeois cult of privacy had become virtually meaningless. Instead, the denizens of the modern city in its decline crave not privacy but recognition, not concealment but exposure.

Modern science appeared in the seventeenth century, and is popularly assumed to be the quintessential product of the modern age. However, as Lukacs argues in chapter 2, "The Presence of Historical Thinking," a more important development occurred at roughly the same time: the emergence of historical consciousness. As late as the Renaissance, the past was understood much as the classical Greeks and Romans had understood it: as a reservoir of types or models of virtue and vice, as a source of moral or political instruction, but never as the story of how the present came to be what it is. Only at the beginning of the seventeenth century does a break occur, suggesting a new understanding of the past as historical development. Thus, Francis Bacon, in 1600, was the first to use the term "progress" to mean not progress in space but in time. Throughout the seventeenth and eighteenth centuries, the popular interest in historical narrative grew enormously, but even the historical understanding of the Enlightenment, Lukacs argues, was deficient by modern standards. It required the Romantic revolution to usher in a fully developed mode of historical understanding, one at first allied with the growth of national consciousness and a concern for the particularities of cultural inheritance.

However, as Lukacs frequently cautions, the understanding that the present is linked to the past by an essential continuity should not be confused with the deterministic idea of progress that seized so powerfully upon the thinkers of the eighteenth century. In Lukacs's view, the idea of progress is one of the great myths of the modern age, and has in fact retarded the development of true historical understanding. The progressive view of history understands historical development as a linear or dialectical movement toward the perfection of human society, the slow but inexorable triumph of human reason over ignorance and superstition. Lukacs, while not denying the fact of human progress, rejects the notion that history is determined, whether by ideal or material causes. Instead, he insists upon the Judeo-Christian (and commonsense) view that historical development, progressive or otherwise, is ultimately not a mere product of "forces" but the outcome of free human choices. The record of the past is never simply what happened, but also what might have happened. Thus, the job of the conscientious historian is "always to maintain toward his subject an indeterminist point of view. He must constantly put himself at a point in the past at which the known factors still seem to permit different outcomes."

As a result of the professionalization of history in the nineteenth century, history came to be understood as a science, and to the degree that this meant a heightened concern for accuracy and verification, such a change was welcome. All too often, however, professional historians fell under the sway of a false objectivism, the assumption that an absolutely objective and indisputable record of the past was possible and that the productions of history could have the same certainty as those of applied science. In chapter 4, "The Question of Scientific Knowledge," Lukacs examines the revolutionary implications of German physicist Werner Heisenberg's (1901-1976) so-called uncertainty principle, suggesting that Heisenberg's scientific theorem, properly understood, also undermines the claims of academic historians to be capable of achieving objectivity. In 1925, Heisenberg demonstrated that "the act of the physicist's observation [of subatomic particles] . . . interfered either with the movement or with the situation of the object." If that were so, then no purely objective view of the object was possible. Classical Newtonian physics was no longer reliable, at least at the extremes of scientific knowledge. More important, the very act of observing alters the nature of the object.

From Lukacs's perspective, what is essential here is the realization that what is true of scientific observation in the most extreme cases is a fortiori true of historical observation in typical cases, for the object of historical observation is not matter but human society. To be purely objective, that is, removed from the object of observation, the historian would have to be something other than human. In historical understanding, the act of observation always alters the nature of the object. While Lukacs admits that the objectivist mode of thought in academic history has largely become discredited in theory, it nonetheless lingers on in practice, or it has been replaced by an equally mistaken subjectivism, the view that historians' own historical and social environments wholly determine their perspective. However, Lukacs denies that this recognition of historical uncertainty amounts to an endorsement of subjectivism. Again, he weighs in against all determinisms.

Historical understanding, argues Lukacs, is emphatically the understanding of human beings by human beings and is therefore not achieved by antiseptic detachment from its object but through participation, "which is always, and necessarily, incomplete." In chapter 4, "An Illustration," Lukacs explores a historical phenomenon that he has written about extensively, the rise of Hitlerism in Germany. He attempts to show the inadequacy of the scientific model of history for understanding Hitler himself, his anti-Semitism and its relation to his political and military actions, or his popularity among the German people. Regarding the latter, Lukacs notes that there can be no satisfying method of understanding Hitler's standing with the Germans by purely objective means. Lukacs notes that if a historian, after extensive research into whatever quantifiable information is available, were to conclude objectively that "only 20 percent of the German people . . . were unquestioning adherents of Hitler, this [would] not mean that 80 percent were his potential (let alone actual) opponents." The reverse would also hold. Such purely scientific approaches to historical study are often superficial. In Lukacs's view, a more profound historical understanding of Hitler's popularity would necessarily involve attempting a participatory understanding of the minds and hearts of the German people; it would mean refusing to make Hitlerism an absurdly unique phenomenon and placing Hitler's appeal to the people within the context of the ongoing popularity of German nationalism (which long preceded Hitler), among other factors.

In a short concluding chapter titled "At the Center of the Universe," Lukacs makes a startling claim: Contrary to the prevailing opinion of most modern thinkers, human beings do occupy the center of the universe. While not denying the strictly scientific accuracy of the discoveries of Nicolaus Copernicus (1473-1543) or Galileo (1564-1642), Lukacs insists that in a far more significant sense, the principle of indeterminacy enables humans to recover the position of centrality that was earlier thought to be lost. Indeterminacy proves the priority of mind over matter, thus reversing René Decartes's (1596-1650) dictum *cogito, ergo sum* ("I think, therefore I am"); instead, argues Lukacs, "*sum, ergo cogito, ergo sum*. I exist; therefore I think; and the consciousness of my thinking gives another dimension to my existence." At the end of the modern age it is no longer possible to deny "the inseparability of our thinking from matters around us, of what we can see and observe." In spite of the narrow accuracy of scientific claims, the universe does not in the most important sense exist apart from human knowledge of and participation in it.

Readers coming to Lukacs's work for the first time may find this slim volume inadequate for a full understanding of his argument. Such readers may find an acquaintance with his earlier books, especially *Historical Consciousness*, helpful. It should be noted as well that *At the End of an Age* is a work that assumes a rather demanding knowledge of modern history and a wide familiarity with the leading intellectual currents of the nineteenth and twentieth centuries, such as Marxism, scientism, positivism, Freudianism, and so on. Some may also object to the rather freewheeling style of composition in this book; its ideas are not developed systematically and the examples provided, while often interesting, are not always transparently apt. Finally, there are bound to be critics of this work who will dismiss it as merely reactionary. That would be a mistake. Lukacs's thought balances a number of conflicting perspectives impressively. Neither a conservative (in the usual sense of the word) or a progressive, Lukacs is the kind of historian who is needed more than ever: one whose vision of the past is not limited by either reactionary nostalgia or progressivist distortion.

Jack E. Trotter

Sources for Further Study

The Chronicle of Higher Education, April 26, 2002, p. B7.
First Things: The Journal of Religion and Public Life, May, 2002, p. 55.
National Review 54 (June 3, 2002): 52.
Publishers Weekly 249 (March 25, 2002): 58.
The Spectator 288 (May 4, 2002): 41.
The Weekly Standard 7 (June 17, 2002): 39.

ATONEMENT

Author: Ian McEwan (1948-   )
Publisher: Nan A. Talese/Doubleday. 351 pp. $26.00
Type of work: Novel
Time: 1935, 1941, and 1999
Locale: Surrey, Dunkirk, and London

∼

A subtle exploration of how the themes of mendacity, guilt, and art work themselves out in the lives of a privileged English family before, during, and after World War II

∼

Principal characters:
    BRIONY TALLIS, a novelist and perjurer
    CECILIA TALLIS, Briony's older sister
    ROBBIE TURNER, Cecilia's lover
    GRACE TURNER, Robbie's mother, the Tallis family's housekeeper
    LEON TALLIS, Briony's older brother
    LOLA QUINCEY, a cousin to Briony, Cecilia, and Leon
    EMILY TALLIS, the neurasthenic mother of Briony, Cecilia, and Leon
    PAUL MARSHALL, a chocolate magnate and friend of Leon
    PIERROT and JACKSON QUINCEY, twin cousins of Briony
    SISTER DRUMMOND, the tyrannical head nurse at the London hospital
      where Briony works

It was commonplace in the nineteenth century English novel that the author was God—omniscient and omnipotent within the fictional universe that exists between the covers of a book. Novelists such as William Makepeace Thackeray (1811-1863) and George Eliot (1819-1880) exercised their divine privilege through overt intrusions into the narrative to arrange the lives of their characters and to tell the reader what to think. Rejecting that model and metaphor, modernism assigns novelists a more modest role—to transcribe their characters' states of consciousness.

Early in her illustrious literary career, Briony Tallis, dominated by the influence of Virginia Woolf, writes a novella, *Two Figures by a Fountain*, that fulfills her modernist ambition: "To enter a mind and show it at work, or being worked on, and to do this within a symmetrical design—this would be an artistic triumph." However, Cyril Connolly, the legendary editor of *Horizon*, rejects Briony's manuscript, complaining that it "owed a little too much to the technique of Mrs. Woolf" and is weak in narrative interest.

In her seventies, Briony, now a literary celebrity, reworks the same material into a much more complicated book with a strong story line, one that, because it draws directly on actual incidents and people, cannot be published during her own lifetime.

That novel, *Atonement* itself, reverts to the model of nineteenth century fiction, in which a narrative deity controls everything. The text of *Atonement* is an attempt to rewrite history. It is Briony's bid to repair a terrible wrong that she committed when she was thirteen. Though the book will be her gesture of atonement, Briony recognizes that atonement is submission to an external authority and that, for a sovereign author whose imagination is supreme, such submission is impossible to achieve. In her final sentences, while vascular dementia begins to deplete her memory and defeat her imagination, seventy-seven-year-old Briony asks: "How can a novelist achieve atonement when, with her absolute power of deciding outcomes, she is also God? There is no one, no entity or higher form that she can appeal to, or be reconciled with, or that can forgive her. There is nothing outside her." There is, nonetheless, another author, Ian McEwan, as well as a reader outside Briony Tallis, and *Atonement*, which she despairs of as a mere attempt at impossible atonement, succeeds despite itself.

∽

Ian McEwan received the Somerset Maugham Award for his short-story collection First Love, Last Rites *(1975), the Whitbread Novel of the Year Award for* The Child in Time *(1987), and the Booker Prize for his novel* Amsterdam *(1998). His other novels include* The Cement Garden *(1978),* The Comfort of Strangers *(1981),* The Innocent *(1990),* Black Dogs *(1992),* The Daydreamer *(1994), and* Enduring Love *(1999).*

∽

The novel starts with and arises out of thirteen-year-old Briony's actions during a hot summer day in 1935. On her family's country estate in Surrey, Briony conscripts her three cousins, fifteen-year-old Lola Quincey and Lola's nine-year-old twin brothers, Pierrot and Jackson, to perform a silly play, *The Trials of Arabella*, that she herself has written. The cousins, troubled by their parents' divorce, are not very cooperative, and the production is aborted. The imperious young playwright, described as "one of those children possessed by a desire to have the world just so," fabricates another script that reconstructs the world for everyone around her. In Briony, McEwan examines the ambiguity of his own art—the storyteller as both creator and prevaricator. Robbie Turner, the handsome, brilliant son of the Tallis family's housekeeper, has recently graduated from Cambridge University with financial support from Briony's father. Despite the social chasm separating them, Robbie dares to love Cecilia, Briony's older sister, also a recent Cambridge graduate. Briony senses, without understanding it, a powerful bond between the two, but she is confirmed in her assessment that Robbie is a "maniac" when he asks her to deliver to Cecilia a lewd, sealed note that she opens and reads. Robbie had written another, less blunt letter of affection and does not realize that he has inadvertently put his crude expression of sexual longing into the envelope that he hands to Briony.

When, later in the evening, amid a confused search for the missing twins, Lola reports that she was sexually molested, Briony concocts a story in which Robbie is the culprit. Lola does not contradict her, and Robbie is arrested, convicted, and imprisoned. Though literary fiction is a creative, generally benign distortion of the truth, in this case a promising young life is blighted by the misuse of imagination. "Liars! Liars!" shouts Grace Turner, as the police take her son, manacled, away. Everyone else acquiesces in the lie, including Briony's easygoing older brother, Leon, and Leon's visiting friend, Paul Marshall, who plans to make a fortune selling a candy bar to the military.

In the second of four sections that constitute *Atonement*, Cecilia, furious that her snobbish family supported Briony's obvious perjury, breaks with them and goes off on her own to work as a nurse in London. Though she writes regularly to Robbie, she is unable to be with him. After three and a half difficult years in prison, he is mustered into the British Expeditionary Force as a private. Much of section 2 is a wrenching account of the frantic British retreat from Dunkirk. Amid the frenzied, violent rout that follows Germany's defeat of France, all that sustains Robbie in his struggle for survival is the thought of reunion with Cecilia.

In section 3, Briony suffers pangs of conscience for her false testimony against Robbie. Rejecting the advantages of her social class, she follows her estranged sister into nursing. Briony embraces the discipline of Sister Drummond, tyrannical head nurse of the military hospital in London where, as secular penance for her misdeed, she takes on the most humiliating and arduous tasks. When the hospital fills with casualties from the debacle at Dunkirk, Briony throws herself into the job of caring for the critically wounded.

In section 4, Briony is an aging literary luminary who is honored on her seventy-seventh birthday with a performance of *The Trials of Arabella*, the play she wrote at thirteen and was intending to mount on the fateful day in 1935 when she also presumed to write the real-life script for Robbie and Cecilia. Acutely aware of the disparity between her version of the sexual assault on Lola and what actually happened that evening, she has finally finished creating a richer, more reliable account. Yet it is one that, for all of its scrupulousness, also insists on imagining alternative destinies for the wronged lovers, Robbie and Cecilia. Though Briony cannot publish her revised account as long as Lola's influential and litigious rapist lives, she recognizes that, after writing it, "My fifty-nine-year assignment is over."

Though the reader is supposed to assume that Briony is the author of the entire narrative, one of the most remarkable features of the book is how convincingly it manages to represent the states of mind of several characters—not only of Briony but also of Robbie, Cecilia, and even her mother, Emily Tallis, a woman whose recurring migraines shield her from having to deal with the fact that her absentee husband, a government official, is unfaithful and deceitful. Briony represents her own progress as a writer and a human being in her increasing ability to vary points of view. It is a significant moment in her artistic and ethical development when Briony realizes that, "It wasn't only wickedness and scheming that made people unhappy, it was confusion and misunderstanding; above all, it was the failure to grasp the simple truth that other people are as real as you. And only in a story could you enter these different minds and show how they had an equal value." At thirteen, dreamy Briony suffers from a lack not of imagination but of imaginative sympathy, the ability to acknowledge the emotional autonomy of others. Her artistry is peremptory; through clever combinations of words, she presumes to impose her personal designs on the lives of other human beings. Fifty-nine years later, Briony demonstrates that she has grown far beyond the megalomaniacal fantasies of her early artistic efforts. Her mature writing is the product of research, not merely adolescent fancy. Like McEwan himself, she has spent many hours in the archives of the Imperial War Museum at Lambeth, immersing herself in the letters, journals, and memoirs of British nurses and soldiers who served during the retreat from Dunkirk. The result is remarkably successful in representing not only the genteel society in which Briony grew up but also the experiences of working-class nurses and military conscripts. Through her work, Briony transcends the narrow limits of her background and interests, and McEwan enters the mind of a woman born to privilege twenty-six years before he came into the world. The novel is a triumph of empathy if not atonement.

Throughout his career, McEwan has found and shared pleasure in excavating the horror that lurks beneath placid surfaces. All is not well at the lovely country house occupied by the Tallises, just as visitors to Venice rely at their peril on the comfort of strangers in McEwan's 1981 novel of that name. His first book, a collection of short stories called *First Love, Last Rites* (1975) which won the Somerset Maugham Award, immediately served notice that he was a writer worth watching. His novel *Amsterdam* (1998) won the prestigious Booker Prize. As soon as it was published, *Atonement* jumped onto the best-seller lists and stayed there for several months, while numerous reviewers, in both Britain and the United States, resorted to the word "masterpiece" to describe it. *The Washington Post*'s Jonathan Yardley hailed McEwan's novel as the magnum opus of the foremost living Anglophonic writer: "Certainly it is the finest book yet by a writer of prodigious skills and, at this point in his career, equally prodigious accomplishment. It confirms me in the belief that there is no one now writing fiction in the English language who surpasses McEwan, and perhaps no one who equals him." One could quibble over the names of McEwan's contemporaries who surpass him in breadth of experience, range of tone, or verbal dexterity, but what cannot be denied is that the author of *Atonement* has nothing to regret.

Steven G. Kellman

Sources for Further Study

The Atlantic Monthly 289 (March, 2002): 106.
Booklist 98 (November 15, 2001): 523.
The Economist 360 (September 22, 2001): 1.
Library Journal 126 (November 15, 2001): 97.
The New Republic 226 (March 25, 2002): 28.
The New York Review of Books 49 (April 11, 2002): 24.
The New York Times, March 7, 2002, p. E1.
The New York Times Book Review 107 (March 10, 2002): 8.
The New Yorker 78 (March 4, 2002): 80.
Newsweek 139 (March 18, 2002): 62.
The Washington Post Book World, March 17, 2002, p. 1.
The Weekly Standard 7 (April 29, 2002): 43.

THE AUTOGRAPH MAN

Author: Zadie Smith (1975-   )
Publisher: Random House (New York). 347 pp. $24.95
Type of work: Novel
Time: 1986 and 2001
Locale: Mountjoy, a suburb in England; New York
City

~

Smith's second novel satirically examines the nature of fame from the point of view of Alex-Li Tandem, dealer of autographs

~

Principal characters:

ALEX-LI TANDEM, a twenty-seven-year-old British autograph collector and dealer who worships 1940's film star Kitty Alexander
LI-JIN TANDEM, Alex-Li's father who died of cancer when his son was twelve
KITTY ALEXANDER, an aging movie star living in retirement in New York City
MAX KRAUSER, the president of the Kitty Alexander fan club
ADAM JACOBS, Alex-Li's frequently stoned friend, who is interested in Jewish mysticism
JOSEPH KLEIN, Alex-Li's friend, an insurance agent who bears a strong resemblance to writer Franz Kafka
BRIAN DUCHAMP, an older autograph trader who is hospitalized for cancer
ESTHER, Alex-Li's frequently estranged girlfriend
MARK RUBINFINE, Alex-Li's friend, a rabbi
HONEY RICHARDSON, a New York autograph dealer who had her moment of fame when she was caught having sex with a movie star

When, in her mid twenties, Zadie Smith wrote the sprawling, Dickensian, multi-racial London novel *White Teeth* (2000), she found herself a best-selling novelist praised by the critics as a hot new voice of the twenty-first century. Written in the comedic vein of Salman Rushdie with hip-hop-influenced cultural savvy, her first novel combined a lively immigrant cast showcased by two oddball middle-aged friends, Archie Jones and Samad Iqbal, as they weathered mutinying teenage children, suicide attempts, the seeping loss of their cultural heritage, Jehovah's Witnesses, Islamic political movements, and a genetically enhanced mouse, among other things. Smith herself characterized the novel as the "literary equivalent of a hyperactive, ginger-haired, tap-dancing ten-year-old," but her fictional debut, begun while she was attending Cambridge University as an English major, is assured,

funny, and polyphonic, blending the voices of disparate generations and cultures in a distinc tively
British potpourri. With the novel's success in both
Great Britain and the United States, Smith found
herself famous and obliged to fulfill the second half
of her publisher's two-book contract.

Smith's next novel, *The Autograph Man* (2002),
differs from its predecessor in its scope, its themes,
and in its intended audience. A more narrowly focused study of one young man's career in autograph
dealing, the novel is also darker in tone. While
White Teeth embraced multiple generations, *Autograph Man* is chiefly concerned with youth, specifically people in their twenties. Thematically, the
novel revolves around Jewish mysticism and the insidious effects of fame on modern life. In an interview with *Entertainment Weekly* magazine, Smith
claimed that the novel grew out of her year-long attempt to write a rabbi joke as well as a comment by
actor Marlon Brando in the *Guardian* newspaper
about being famous: "I haven't had an honest moment with a person in forty-one years." That comment struck a chord with Smith, since she had al-

Zadie Smith's fictional debut
White Teeth *(2000), winner of*
the Whitbread First Novel
Award and a finalist for the
National Book Critics Circle
Award, was one of the most
enthusiastically received novels
in recent years, both in Great
Britain and in the United States.
The Autograph Man *(2002) is*
her second novel.

ready felt the dislocations and vertiginous effects of being instantly renowned. Her
youthful good looks, exotic lineage (her father is white and British while her mother is
a black Jamaican), and Bret Easton Ellis-style savvy about youth culture made her a
marketer's dream, and *The Autograph Man* reflects her disenchantment with both the
machinery of fame and the slavish hero-worship that it breeds in consumers.

The book begins with a flashback prologue set in 1986, when the protagonist,
Alex-Li, was twelve years old. He is traveling to the Royal Albert Hall with his father and two friends, Rubinfine and Adam, to a professional wrestling match star-
ring a wrestler called "Big Daddy." While the children talk the esoteric language
of television shows and wrestling trivia, Smith's narrator reflects upon the de-
evolution through the years of the Royal Albert Hall from an arts and sciences center celebrating the love of Prince Albert and Queen Victoria to its manifestation
as a scene for a wrestling bout. The evening's canned entertainment summarizes
many of the elements that Smith finds deplorable in popular culture: The spectacle is visually crude, preprogrammed, and geared primarily for children. Li-Jin
(Alex's Chinese father) and Alex meet Joseph Klein, an autograph-collecting boy
who resembles Franz Kafka, and his appropriately philistine father Herman Klein,
a dealer of fancy-goods for women (Joseph Klein subsequently leads Alex-Li into
his career as an autograph collector and dealer). After the wrestling bout, they all
go backstage to ask Big Daddy for his autograph; in the crush of the crowd Li-Jin
suffers a seizure related to cancer that causes him to collapse and die amidst the

throng. As Smith concludes the chapter: "He [Li-Jin] sees people. Many, many people. Nobody famous, though. No one familiar or friendly. No one to help. No one he knows."

From this point on, Smith's rhetorical agenda becomes clear. Beginning with Li-Jin's death, the novel explores the destructive effects of fame, both in the way it distorts and corrupts human relationships and in the way it feeds the popular imagination with images of "stars" who both substitute for religion and fuel resentment for those who benefit from fame's often arbitrary largesse—its ability to cheat death through electronic substitution, magnification, and repetition. Those who are not famous live acutely conscious of fame's effects in a bereft, secondhand world of gestures and phrases derived from movies and television. Alex-Li grows up both a worshiper of obscure screen idols and a dealer in the "tinny, cheap, reflected light"of fame through autographs. After the prologue, the novel jumps to a twenty-seven-year-old Alex-Li recovering from an extended acid trip during which he wrecked his car, hurt his long-standing relationship with his girlfriend Esther, and mysteriously received a rare signed picture of his favorite 1940's screen idol, Kitty Alexander. As Alex-Li meanders around London, one gets an idea of his listless, rather passive lifestyle, running into Rubinfine (who has now become a rabbi), getting stoned and discussing Jewish mysticism with Adam, dealing autographs, and masturbating to pornography on his computer. He finds that he has absentmindedly booked a flight to New York for an Autographicana Fair during the time when Esther will be undergoing surgery for the installation of a new pacemaker, and much of the latter half of the novel concerns his quest to finally meet his idol—the aging screen star Kitty Alexander, who lives in semireclusion in New York.

As a send-up of the emptiness of fame, the novel succeeds handsomely, but it has difficulty getting the reader engaged with the characters. For one thing, Smith often fails to generate much suspense, preferring a whimsical sense of plotting that often as not immediately satisfies Alex-Li's desires without much conflict. For a time, the shift to New York City energizes the novel. At the Autographicana Fair convention Alex-Li befriends Honey Richardson, an African American autograph dealer clearly modeled on the real-life prostitute who earned a moment of fame when she was caught having sex with film star Hugh Grant. Her role emphasizes the arbitrariness of celebrity, since she enjoys her fifteen minutes of fame, visits the various talk shows, works on a film deal, and then immediately drops out of the public's attention. She realizes that her autograph is only worth something when it is surreptitiously united with the film star's on the same sheet of paper without his knowledge. Honey helps Alex-Li track down Kitty Alexander, who proves to be a sweet old lady, and Alex-Li convinces her to fly back with him to England on the earnings of her autographs. Once there, there is a hint of conflict when Kitty realizes that her manager back in the United States, Max Krauser, had angrily announced her death to the media, thereby allowing Alex-Li to sell off her autographs in an auction at inflated prices, but she ultimately forgives Alex-Li for that as well. While Alex-Li is in New York, Joseph Klein magically replaces his wrecked car with insurance money (like Kafka, he works in an insurance firm). The long-neglected Esther reconciles with him. Even Alex-Li's cat Grace gets along with Kitty Alexander's dog Lucia. Even though Alex-Li repeatedly gets drunk, sloppy, and belligerent, he does not suffer any major consequences for his actions, perhaps due to the comedic nature of the novel.

In reply to the arbitrary nature of the plot, Smith consistently has her characters meditate on Jewish mysticism. Alex-Li's mother is Jewish, and the novel has several illustrated Kabbala diagrams interspersed through the first half—the first one supplies a framework for the opening paragraphs and it includes figures such as Jimmy Stewart representing Beauty, Bette Davis representing Eternity, and John Lennon standing in for Splendor. Another ironic Kabbala appears depicting all the major figures in Elvis Presley's life, including the man who sold Elvis his first guitar. Earlier on, when Alex-Li smokes marijuana with Adam, they meditate in front of a more serious diagram of the ten Sefirot and the twenty-two foundation letters of the Hebrew alphabet, although Alex-Li is too lost in a "marijuana fug" to feel much sense of transcendence. Even as this emphasis on Judaism provides interesting insights about the nature of the godhead and the Lenny Bruce-influenced cultural distinctions between Jewishness and goyishness, this effort at profundity can seem forced and inorganic. Occasionally, Alex-Li runs into Rubinfine and two other rabbis, who repeatedly and humorously try to force an item of furniture into the trunk of a car. *The Autograph Man* concludes with Alex-Li publicly praying a Kaddish for his deceased father, a means to come to terms with his death and bring the narrative to a close.

The Autograph Man becomes the sort of novel one appreciates more for its insights than for its characterization or sense of plot. As in the case of Bret Easton Ellis's equally funny fiction, the theme of the shallowness of contemporary culture can lead to shallow characters just as a book about the hollowness of fame can seem hollow itself. Not sharing in her level of fame, the reader of *The Autograph Man* may have difficulty sympathizing with Smith's disdain for it, but her depiction of what it is like to become famous is chilling. Late in the novel, Alex-Li experiences some of its effects when the autographs that he sells earn him some notoriety among his peers. As he realizes, "he could feel himself transforming, in the eyes of this audience, into a symbol of his century's collective dream: *He'll never work again*." Even this small amount of attention gives Alex-Li a "new order of fraudulence" in his relations with others and a "new type of loneliness"—the sense that people see him with envy more as an emblem of their projected desires than as a complex individual. Given Alex-Li's lifelong hero-worship of celebrity, this serves as the final irony of the book. Even though the storyline ends happily, one remembers Smith's bitter take on her themes, especially the drugged, soporific nature of people's addiction to entertainment. As Alex-Li notes, watching the passengers on the jet zoning out in front of their televisions as they cross the Atlantic, "Everything in this plane is an interface, like the windows on his computer. . . . Pretty, pretty pictures. Lovely, distracting stories we tell each other." As he looks down the aisle, he notices "this private experience he is meant to be having is replicated as far as the eye can see."

Roy C. Flannagan

Sources for Further Study

The Atlantic Monthly 290 (October, 2002): 143.
Booklist 99 (October 1, 2002): 276.
Esquire 138 (October, 2002): 40.
Library Journal 127 (October 15, 2002): 95.
The New York Times, September 25, 2002, p. B1.
The New York Times Book Review 107 (October 6, 2002): 13.
Publishers Weekly 249 (September 30, 2002): 47.
The Times Literary Supplement, September 27, 2002, p. 21.

BAD BLOOD
A Memoir

Author: Lorna Sage (1943-2001)
First published: 2000, in Great Britain
Publisher: William Morrow/HarperCollins (New York).
   281 pp. $24.95
Type of work: Memoir
Time: The 1930's to the 1960's
Locale: Hanmer, a small village in Flintshire, Wales;
   Whitchurch, Shropshire, England

≈

*Literary critic Sage's memoir of her girlhood in north-
ern Wales traces the source of her "bad blood" back to her
scandalous maternal grandfather, offering a meditation on
the nature of marriage and partnership, family dysfunc-
tion, and social constraints on sexuality*

≈

Principal personages:
> GRANDPA, a priest in the Church of England, embittered by the scandal-
>   ous consequences of his affair with a nurse in 1933-1934
> GRANDMA, a malicious, manipulative woman who blackmailed her hus-
>   band for years over his infidelities
> MOTHER, an otherworldly woman who rebelled against her dysfunc-
>   tional family through household incompetence
> FATHER, owner of a trucking company, the high point of whose life had
>   been his service in World War II
> LORNA, a rebellious teenager who manifested her grandfather's "bad
>   blood" by becoming pregnant at age sixteen but nonetheless pursued
>   her academic dreams
> VIC, Lorna's first boyfriend and the father of her child

Lorna Sage was considered by many to be a "lipstick feminist," an academic who
wrote perceptively on women's literature and advocated intellectual and social equality for women, but who also refused to reject the typically feminine accoutrements of
make-up, high heels, and beauty. James Fenton's essay on *Bad Blood* in *The New
York Review of Books*, for instance, was not so much a review of the book as his own
memoir of Sage's enormous personal charm and attractiveness. To more radical feminists, who regard such qualities and habits as signs of complicity in patriarchal oppression, Sage might have appeared a sellout; as her memoir of a truly dysfunctional
childhood in North Wales in the 1940's and 1950's shows, however, Sage came by
her orneriness naturally, growing up in a family that refused to conform to standard

~

Lorna Sage was a renowned feminist literary critic and professor of English at the University of East Anglia in Britain. She first came to public attention in 1964, when she and her husband, Vic Sage, became the first married couple of ordinary student age in Britain to graduate simultaneously in the same subject with first-class degrees. Sage went on to write Women in the House of Fiction *(1992),* The Cambridge Guide to Women's Writing in English *(1999), and* Moments of Truth *(2001), published after her death from emphysema in January, 2001.*

~

social roles yet also refused to rebel by merely reversing those roles.

Although the memoir is narrated through Sage's own experience, the book is divided into three sections focusing successively on her grandparents' marriage, her parents' marriage, and her adolescence culminating in her own marriage. These divisions also correspond to temporal and geographical eras in Sage's life. As a small child during World War II, she, with her mother, lived with her mother's parents in the Hanmer vicarage while her father was in the army; after his return and the death of Sage's grandfather (and thus the loss of his house, since it was attached to the church living and therefore was passed on to the next incumbent), the family moved to a brand new housing estate on the edge of the village; finally, during Sage's teenage years, when she was attending school in Whitchurch, just over the border in England, the family purchased a home nearby. Superficially, the narrative appears to be merely an account of the life of a decidedly eccentric family, but as it nears its conclusion it becomes clear that Sage's purpose all along has been to explore the different ways in which couples may deal with the vicissitudes that life hands them.

The most outrageous characters are Sage's grandparents. They are first presented through the memories of Sage herself, a child who sees no need to delve into the reasons why family members behave as they do because family is a given. Her grandparents lived in a state of constant war, marked by "murderous rows" when they were still talking to each other, nonstop vilification to anyone within earshot after direct communication had ceased. Grandpa bore a scar on his face from the time his wife had gone at him with the carving knife when he came home drunk. Grandma refused to interact with anyone in the village; when the doorbell rang, she would scuttle into her own room while her daughter frantically, futilely tidied the visible sections of the house and then led the caller to Grandpa's study. Both of Sage's grandparents felt exiled in Hanmer, her grandfather because a small village in Flintshire offered no scope for his intellectual talents, her grandmother because a small village in Flintshire offered none of the creature and social comforts she had enjoyed growing up.

Outweighing the grandparents' intellectual mismatch was their sexual mismatch. Sage comments that her grandmother

thought men and women belonged to different races and any getting together was worse than folly. The "old devil," my grandfather, had talked her into marriage and the agony of bearing two children, and he should never be forgiven for it. She quivered with rage whenever she remembered her fall.

Even more unforgivable was his infidelity. Years after the deaths of both grandparents, after the death of her own mother, Sage asked her father if the family legend were true, that her grandmother had blackmailed her grandfather into turning over a large part of his stipend—so much of it that the family could not afford to keep the house in anything more than minimally livable condition—by threatening to turn over to the bishop certain damning diaries of his. Sage had assumed that this story was simply part of her family's self-aggrandizing Gothicity. Much to Sage's surprise, her father confirmed that it was true: He had the diaries. Their entries reveal the story of Grandpa's affair with Nurse Burgess, begun in the months when he lived in Hanmer alone, before his wife and daughter joined him from St. Cynon's in the Rhondda, his previous living. The affair continued even after the family was reunited and eventually came to light when Grandpa, laid up with a leg injury, used the nurse's visits to his very bedroom as a cover for their liaisons.

Having alienated his wife, Grandpa proceeded to alienate his daughter by having an affair with her best friend, Marjorie. The intensified fighting that ensued from the discovery of that affair proved so distracting that Sage's mother was able to slip through her own little rebellion in the form of dating and eventually marrying the local haulier's son, a young man with brains and ambition but decidedly lower on the social scale than the vicar's daughter.

Whereas Sage's grandparents to a certain extent mirrored the social chaos and economic depression of the 1930's, Sage's parents made their best effort to accommodate the stricter mores of social conformity of the 1950's. After leaving the vicarage, the family settled in a council estate:

> My mother . . . had mysteriously forgotten how to ride a bicycle now that they had a home of their own. . . . But her new-found helplessness didn't seem as odd as it might have, since this was, of course, the time when married women, having been sent back home en masse, were encouraged in every possible way to stay there—first demobilized and then immobilized. . . . My mother's acquired ineptitude fitted this post-war pattern. And she did, as the propaganda said, try to turn herself into a housewife, although she was very bad at it. Quite how bad only became clear once we'd moved into the council house . . . she had a kind of genius for travesty when it came to domestic science.

Years of hopeless rearguard action against the "Gothic grime and disorder" of the vicarage had ingrained in Sage's mother a kind of learned helplessness regarding housework; her culinary skills were even more useless. Furthermore, she inherited her mother's dogma that a pride in housework was a sign of a "coarse-grained nature." The increasing postwar availability of convenience foods and labor-saving devices was a godsend to her. Sage perceptively notes that her parents' relationship worked because each bolstered the other's psychological needs: Her mother's helplessness allowed her father to show off his competence, while her father's bent for bossiness gave her mother the attention and support she had never received from her parents, wrapped up as they were in their all-consuming hatred. Nonetheless, their mutual dependence entwined them so tightly that there was as little space for Sage and her brother in their parents' emotional world as there had been for Sage's mother and uncle in their parents' marital war zone.

Sage, meanwhile, had grown into an intellectually precocious troublemaker. The village school was dedicated to the proposition that no one who lived in a backwater like Hanmer was ever going anywhere where education would be needed; Sage had acquired a taste for reading from her grandfather, and the unexpected side effect of a case of chronic sinusitis was permission to stay up as late as she pleased at night, reading whatever she could get her hands on. Sage passed her eleven-plus (the qualifying examination for grammar school, potentially leading to university) and was enrolled in Whitchurch Girls' High School.

Grammar school was enlightening for Sage in many ways. The shadow of her family's eccentricity was less eclipsing in the new environment. Teachers who were actually dedicated to educating their students gave validity to Sage's "private currency" of reading. Above all,

> Latin, the great dead language that only existed in writing, would compensate for my speechlessness, vindicate my sleepless nights and in general redeem my utter lack of social graces. Latin stood for higher education . . . it was the sign of being able to detach yourself from here and now, abstract your understanding of words, train your memory, and live solitary in your head with only books for company. So it was meant to be hard, but I found it wonderfully easy, for just those reasons. I fell in love with Latin. It was the tongue the dead spoke, *ergo* Grandpa's language, of course.

Adolescence also meant boys. At her very first dance, Sage found herself, to her dismay, monopolized by "Victor Sage, his mother's pride but no-one else's"; encountering him again later in the year, Sage, convinced that he was hardly boyfriend material, made him her friend. She discovered that his family was as mad as hers: His father (also from South Wales, indeed from the next valley over from Tonypandy, Grandma's home) was a paranoid schizophrenic convinced that he was receiving secret messages from some Alien Command. Companionship turned into sexual exploration, and although Sage did not admit to herself what was happening, at the age of sixteen she found herself pregnant. She had proved herself her grandfather's progeny to the core.

This was an era when girls with children did not go to university; reproduction condemned them to a life of the body rather than the mind. Convention dictated that Sage be immured in a Home for Unmarried Mothers until she gave birth to a child who would be promptly adopted while she returned home to disgrace and a job as a typist, if she were lucky. Vic, for his part, contemplated running away to sea. Instead, the two decided that they would marry, have their baby and, by hook or by crook, get themselves into university. Sage hid her pregnancy for one term of school, the two were married at the Christmas holiday, and Sage gave birth to a daughter shortly before she was scheduled to sit for her A-levels, the examinations that would qualify her for university. She had to fight the nurses to be allowed to leave in time, but by this time it was clear that Lorna Sage was going to live her life the way she wanted. The young couple managed both to be accepted at the University of Durham, while their daughter, Sharon, was cared for by Sage's parents.

In some ways, Sage can be seen as a predecessor of the late twentieth century Supermom, the woman who has it all, family and career, refusing to make an either/or choice between intellect and reproduction. Yet it is difficult to see Sage as a paradigm for anyone's life but her own, and perhaps this is, indeed, the ultimate goal of feminism.

Leslie Ellen Jones

Sources for Further Study

The Atlantic Monthly 289 (April, 2002): 137.
Los Angeles Times, April 15, 2002, p. E3.
The New York Review of Books 49 (June 13, 2002): 21.
The New York Times, March 29, 2002, p. E42.
The New York Times Book Review 107 (April 21, 2002): 12.
The New Yorker 78 (April 1, 2002): 93.
Publishers Weekly 249 (January 21, 2002): 75.
The Times Literary Supplement, September 21, 2001, p. 28.
The Washington Post Book World, March 24, 2002, p. 1.

BAUDOLINO

Author: Umberto Eco (1932-   )
First published: 2000, in Italy
Translated from the Italian by William Weaver
Publisher: Harcourt (New York). 528 pp. $27.00
Type of work: Novel
Time: 1142-1204
Locale: Italy, Paris, and Constantinople

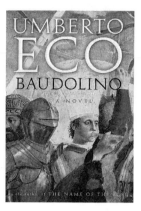

❧

Eco's story of Baudolino and his life and times, which mixes medieval history and myth in the quest for the legendary Prester John

❧

Principal characters:
> BAUDOLINO, a young Italian peasant with a vivid imagination
> FREDERICK BARBAROSSA (c. 1123-1190), Holy Roman Emperor and Baudolino's patron
> NIKETAS CHONIATES (c. 1140-1213), an important official of the Byzantine Empire during the sack of Constantinople in 1204
> BEATRICE OF BURGUNDY (1145-1184), the young wife of Frederick Barbarossa
> PRESTER JOHN, mythical Christian king in the east
> ZOSIMOS OF CHALCEDON, a corrupt Orthodox monk
> COLANDRINA, Baudolino's young wife
> ARDZROUNI, an Armenian nobleman
> GAVAGI, a skiapod, a mythical creature with only a single leg
> DEACON JOHANNES, ruler of the mythical city of Pndapetzim
> HYPATIA, a mythical beast, half-human and half-goat, Baudolino's true love

It is rare that a university academic becomes a popular novelist, but Umberto Eco's first novel, *Il nome della rosa* (1980; *The Name of the Rose*, 1983), was an international best-seller as well as a popular motion picture. The novel, a detective story set in the Middle Ages, was more challenging than the movie, and Eco's second novel, *Il pendolo di Foucault* (1988; *Foucault's Pendulum*, 1989), was even more difficult, but it, too, achieved best-seller status. *Baudolino*, Eco's fourth novel, is his most accessible fictional work for the general reader.

The author, a professor of semiotics at Italy's University of Bologna, is a specialist in medieval history, and the setting for *Baudolino* is the twelfth and early thirteenth centuries. The Dark Ages have ended, trade and commerce have revived, cities have been reestablished, and universities founded. It is also the era of the crusades, or Christian holy wars dedicated to the recovery of the Holy Land from Islam. The crusaders were motivated not only by religion but also by economic greed, political ambition, and the love of violence for its own sake.

Baudolino is a young Italian peasant, born about 1142. In the year 1204 he finds himself in Constantinople, the capital of the Byzantine Empire and the greatest city in Christendom. It is during the Fourth Crusade, famous not because Jerusalem was recaptured from the Muslims but because (Orthodox) Christian Constantinople was seized and put to the sack by (Roman Catholic) Christian crusaders from Western Europe. During the bloody chaos, Baudolino rescues Niketas Choniates, a Byzantine official and historian, from imminent death. In an effort to understand his life, Baudolino relates his many adventures to Niketas. The difficulty, according to Baudolino, was that "[T]he problem of my life is that I've always confused what I saw with what I wanted to see."

Umberto Eco, professor of semiotics at the University of Bologna and a expert on medieval history, has been the recipient of numerous academic degrees and other awards for his academic accomplishments and for his several novels, including The Name of the Rose *(1983) and* Foucault's Pendulum *(1989).*

Eco's Baudolino is a person whose stories might or might not be true. Some must be accurate. Assuming his claim to a peasant background is authentic, by 1204 he has become both literate and highly knowledgeable and he has a facility with languages, both spoken and written. He tells Niketas that the Holy Roman Emperor Frederick Barbarossa was forced to spend the night with Baudolino's family during a military siege and took Baudolino with away with him, becoming his foster father and subsequently providing him with numerous opportunities. Baudolino's story may have some basis in fact, or perhaps it does not.

Baudolino, whatever the truth of the chief character's own words, is a marvelous pastiche of medieval history. Eco's account of Frederick's involvement in Italy's interminable wars reflects the papal-imperial rivalries of the era as well as the attempts of urban merchants and artisans to achieve their own freedom from external control. One event in the novel is the founding of the city of Alesandria, near where Baudolino was born, which for reasons of diplomacy and defense rather than for religious piety was named after the reigning pope, Alexander III. Eco's description of the convoluted considerations—geographic, economic, and political—underlying the establishment of Alesandria gives the reader insight into the era's history. Eco was born in a city called Alesandria, but whether the author's account of the origins of *Baudolino*'s Alesandria reflects the beginnings of the historical Alesandria is more problematic. Eco is not writing history as it occurred but a fictional history, similar to Baudolino's own imagined and untruthful stories.

In addition to the historical imperial and papal conflict, Baudolino also becomes enmeshed in two of the most popular legends of the Middle Ages, those of Prester John and of the Holy Grail. The origins of the former possibly evolved from the tradition that St. Thomas, one of Jesus's disciples, preached Christianity in the Indian subcontinent during the first century C.E. By the twelfth century, the legend had taken root in Europe and many believed that Prester John ruled a great Christian kingdom somewhere in Asia. In the novel, Baudolino and his student colleagues in Paris avidly fantasize about Prester John, and Baudolino composes a fictional letter from Prester John to Frederick Barbarossa in an attempt to involve the emperor in a quest for the legendary eastern ruler. (The authentic medieval legend was propelled by just such a letter.)

Eco also skillfully incorporates the legend of the Holy Grail into the story of Baudolino. In many medieval legends associated with King Arthur, the Grail was the cup or chalice which held the wine Jesus consecrated at the Last Supper and which was subsequently used by Joseph of Arimathea to catch Jesus's blood when he was hanging on the cross. Purportedly it possessed miraculous powers. Holy relics, particularly those associated with Jesus or his mother, Mary, played a major role in the popular religion of the Middle Ages, and Eco incorporates the multiple heads of St. John the Baptist and other fake relics into the novel. As a potential gift from Frederick to Prester John, Baudolino produces the Grail, or Grasal, which was in fact his father's plain wooden wine cup. By returning the Grasal to Prester John, supposedly its true custodian, Frederick would become renowned throughout Christendom as the new Joseph of Arimathea. Baudolino justified his falsification of the Grasal by claiming, "We believe that we, only we, need God, but often God needs us. At that moment I believed it was necessary to help him."

In 1187, the Muslim warrior Saladin recaptured Jerusalem. The response of Christendom was to launch a new crusade, the Third Crusade. Frederick, along with Richard the Lionheart of England and France's Philip Augustus, took up the crusading cross. After recapturing Jerusalem, Frederick planned to then continue east with the Grasal to the court of Prester John. While still on the road to Jerusalem, Frederick, along with Baudolino and his friends, rest at the castle of Ardzrouni, an Armenian nobleman. Baudolino discovers that Ardzrouni is fabricating relics, notably seven heads of John the Baptist which he intends to sell to gullible buyers. In addition, Ardzrouni claims to have designed a bedroom from which air can be extracted, creating a complete vacuum, a concept which appeared either magical or impossible to the medieval mind. During the night, although secure in the locked room, Frederick dies, and fearing they would be blamed for the emperor's death, Baudolino and his cohorts place Frederick's body in a nearby river where his death will appear to be the result of accidental drowning. During the course of events the Grasal vanishes, and all quickly conclude that Frederick was murdered by someone eager to have the Grail. Between Frederick's death and the rivalry between the French and English kings, the Third Crusade failed to regain Jerusalem, which eventually led to the Fourth Crusade and the novel's beginning.

After the emperor's demise, Baudolino and his companions continue the quest for Prester John, posing as the twelve magi kings of tradition. In their journey to the east they come across numerous peoples of differing religions and philosophies, including the Greek-speaking "gymnosophists," who practice nakedness and vegetarianism and who have abandoned desire and the belief in a creator God, something entirely foreign to the Christians from the west, and perhaps an allusion by Eco to Indian Hinduism. Other mythical creatures appear, including a basilisk, a chimera, and a manticore. Finally they reach the Sambatyon, a river of stone rather than water, across which, according to legend, God had relocated the Ten Lost Tribes of Israel.

Entering a province headed by Deacon Johannes but ruled by eunuchs, they are forced to wait in the capital, Pndapetzim, for authorization to continue to the kingdom of Prester John. There Baudolino's band come across many strange sentient beings. Skiapods have only one leg and blemmyae have no heads. There are also ponces, giants, panotians, tongueless, nubians, eunuchs, and satyrs-who-are-never-seen. However, the various groups identify themselves not by their shape or appearance but by which version of Christianity they practice, with Eco cleverly including references to various Christian heresies, such as the belief that Jesus was adopted by God and not of the same substance and that Jesus was pure spirit, issues which had divided Christianity since its inception.

While in Pndapetzim, Baudolino attempts to locate the never-seen satyrs. While searching, he discovers a beautiful young woman named Hypatia, who was a hypatia (all hypatians were named Hypatia), philosophical descendants of Hypatia of Alexandria, a Neoplatonist mathematician who was murdered by Christians about 415. As Baudolino's Hypatia elucidates at length her Neoplatonist ideas about God and reality, Baudolino falls in love for the third time. His first love was Frederick's wife, Beatrice, and reflected the courtly love of the Middle Ages. His second was his young wife Colandrina, who died in childbirth, an example of medieval marriage patterns. Hypatia represents for Baudolino both carnal love and romantic love, or true love. When finally sexually consummated, Baudolino discovers that Hypatia is a female satyr, but her goat legs and feet do not deter either his love or his passion. She becomes pregnant, but before they can return to the west, the White Huns invade the Deacon's lands. The satyrs and the hypatians flee into the mountains, the eunuchs cross into the kingdom of Prester John, destroying the road so that no one can follow, and Baudolino and his remaining comrades turn west. They have further adventures during the next seven years until they finally reach Constantinople in 1204, the last part of the journey flying on the backs of giant rocs.

Back in Constantinople, Baudolino discovers that he has unknowingly carried the Grasal in one of the several heads of John the Baptist ever since Frederick's death. One of the remaining members of the party takes the Grasal back to Alesandria, where it will become the great holy relic of the city, famous throughout Christendom even though it is in reality a peasant's wooden drinking cup. Baudolino also discovers that Frederick had not been murdered and that he did not die in Ardzrouni's castle. Instead, the emperor was overcome by fumes from the fireplace, only appearing to be dead, and he was still alive when Baudolino threw his body into the river. Thus, Baudolino was the accidental murderer of his foster father. In an act of contrition and to atone for his sin, Baudolino mounts a high pillar, much as the Christian hermit Simeon Stylites had done centuries earlier, and like Simeon, he gains fame as saintly figure. Popular approval can be fickle, and Baudolino abandons his perch and once again sets off to the east to find Prester John and Hypatia. On an earlier occasion Baudolino commented that "Faith makes things become true. . . . The Kingdom of the Priest is real because I and my companions have devoted two-thirds of our life to seeking it." This was the Middle Ages.

As a novel, *Baudolino* succeeds on several levels. Eco has written an exciting adventure story, a search or quest for something larger than mundane reality. The work is also a well-written historical novel, reflecting the events and ethos of the High Middle Ages. *Baudolino* is also a challenging intellectual work, with its discussion of numerous religious and philosophical ideas and assumptions. Ultimately, reflecting his own discipline of semiotics, Eco is also asking about the relationship between words and objective reality: Baudolino is a consummate liar, but he and others come to believe his own lies even when they know his statements are false, suggesting that words do not reflect reality, but instead they create reality.

Eugene Larson

Sources for Further Study

Booklist 98 (July, 2002): 1794.
Library Journal 127 (July, 2002): 116.
Los Angeles Times Book Review, October 27, 2002, p. 6.
The New York Times Book Review 107 (November 3, 2002): 14.
The New Yorker 78 (December 2, 2002): 111.
Publishers Weekly 249 (July 1, 2002): 44.

BENJAMIN FRANKLIN

Author: Edmund S. Morgan (1916-   )
Publisher: Yale University Press (New Haven, Conn.).
    Illustrated. 339 pp. $24.95
Type of work: Biography
Time: 1706-1790
Locale: Philadelphia and London

≈

Drawing on Franklin's voluminous writings, Morgan examines Franklin's contributions to the political life of eighteenth century America

≈

Principal personages:
> BENJAMIN FRANKLIN (1706-1790), printer, scientist, inventor, and politician
> DEBORAH READ FRANKLIN, his wife
> WILLIAM FRANKLIN (1731-1813), his illegitimate son, royal governor of New Jersey
> JOHN ADAMS (1734-1826), politician
> PETER COLLINSON, Quaker merchant and scholar; friend of Franklin
> ISAAC NORRIS (1701-1766), important Pennsylvania political figure
> CHARLES GRAVIER, COMTE VERGENNES (1719-1787), French foreign minister during the American Revolution

If Edmund S. Morgan's volume had a subtitle, it would be "An Appreciation." The phrase fits for two reasons. The first is that Morgan admires Franklin, though he does so as Ben Jonson did William Shakespeare, this side of idolatry. The other is that Morgan does not attempt a full biography of his subject. This book offers a sketch rather than a detailed portrait. However, Morgan's research background is more voluminous than any other Franklin biographer can claim; as chair of the administrative board overseeing the publication of Franklin's papers (thirty-six volumes of which have been published to date), Morgan has read virtually everything Franklin ever wrote, as well as everything ever written to him.

Instead of beginning with Franklin's birth or ancestry, Morgan in his first chapter explores what he regards as some of Franklin's ruling passions, as the eighteenth century would have called them. The first of these, and the one that Morgan regards as controlling Franklin's life, is utility. Morgan notes that while Franklin was in England for the first time, in the mid-1720's, the young colonial published a pamphlet claiming that whatever is, is right. Good and evil, Franklin here maintained, are meaningless terms because whatever happens must have the sanction of an omnipotent deity. After two of Franklin's acquaintances to whom he had lent money used his argument

Edmund S. Morgan has published many books on American history, including Inventing the People: The Rise of Popular Sovereignty in America *(1988), which won the Bancroft Prize, and* American Slavery, American Freedom *(1975), which received both the Francis Parkman Prize and the Albert J. Beveridge Award. Sterling Professor Emeritus of History at Yale University, Morgan received the National Humanities Medal in 2000.*

to justify failing to repay him, Franklin concluded that while his contention may have been philosophically sound, it was not useful. Franklin thus erected a morality based on practicality.

Morgan generally avoids recapitulating the ground covered in Franklin's own *Autobiography* (first published in 1791, covering the period 1706-1759), but he does pause over one of the most famous parts of that work: Franklin's list of thirteen virtues. As Morgan observes, these qualities all have utilitarian values. Under "Silence," for example, Franklin wrote, "Speak not but what may benefit others or your self." For Franklin, chastity meant, "Rarely use Venery but for Health or Offspring; Never to Dulness, Weakness, or the Injury of your own or another's Peace or Reputation." Absent from Franklin's list is the triad of cardinal Christian virtues of faith, hope, and charity, as are courage and wisdom from the classical quartet. At the head of Franklin's list is temperance. In the first *Poor Richard's Almanak* (1732) Franklin explained that moderation in diet would prolong life and moderation in drink would save money as well as reputation.

Nonetheless, Morgan denies the common accusation that Franklin's chief aim was the accumulation of wealth. He acknowledges that Franklin did warn repeatedly against debt and that poverty was his version of his Puritan ancestors' conception of hell. Franklin modeled his *Autobiography* on John Bunyan's *The Pilgrim's Progress* (1678); Franklin's retelling shows a poor youth rising to affluence and influence. According to Morgan, however, Franklin's conception of heaven was not riches but rather contentment. Had Franklin merely sought to amass a fortune, Morgan writes, he would not have retired at the age of forty-two.

Instead, Morgan argues, Franklin's overriding desire was to be useful to others. When Cadwallader Colden wrote that he intended to retire from politics to pursue scientific research, Franklin protested this decision. Morgan shows that Franklin made the opposite choice: Throughout his long life, Franklin benefitted others. In the 1720's he organized some dozen friends into the Junto, a social club that used its weekly meetings to improve the minds and fortunes of its members. As part of their effort at self-improvement, the Junto members brought books to their meeting place. Because the number of volumes was small, Franklin suggested that they establish a subscription library, which survives as the Free Library of Philadelphia. Franklin conceived of Philadelphia's first volunteer fire department, the city's first fire insurance company, and its first public hospital. His argument for creating what became the University of Pennsylvania was again utility. Education would teach students to serve their communities, country, and world.

For all his contributions to his adopted city of Philadelphia and colony of Pennsylvania, the British Empire was Franklin's first love. Morgan shows how Franklin devoted some two decades to trying to preserve an Anglo-American connection. Morgan places Franklin's Albany Plan of Union in this context. For Morgan, this idea as proposed by Franklin was not an early bid for colonial independence but rather the reverse. In 1754, delegates from the various colonies met in Albany, New York, to forge an alliance with Native Americans at the outset of the French and Indian War. Franklin proposed doing more than meeting for a single negotiation: He recommended the creation of a Grand Council, with representatives from each colony, to negotiate with the tribes. Since such a council would infringe on the authority of the individual colonial assemblies, Franklin hoped to persuade the English parliament to establish such a body without the assemblies' approval. The British Board of Trade rejected the idea, fearing that the colonies thus united would seek independence.

Franklin's vision of an Anglo-American empire made him an ideal choice to represent Pennsylvania in its quest to become a royal rather than a proprietary colony. For some fifteen years Franklin lived in England, which he loved and where he even considered settling and running for Parliament. Morgan expresses surprise that even after Parliament began trying to tax the American colonies in the 1760's, Franklin continued to prefer royal to proprietary rule. Yet such a position is consistent with Franklin's vision of America and Britain united with one parliament and one king. Franklin regarded Britain and America as linked by self-interest as well as history. As he told Member of Parliament Richard Jackson, "You cannot hurt us without hurting yourselves."

For Franklin, British infringement on what Americans saw as their rights was, to use a word he applies in his *Autobiography* to what one might see as a moral lapse, an "erratum," or printer's error. Franklin did not judge his own actions or those of Parliament by some abstract scale of right and wrong but rather by his constant touchstone of usefulness. This approach was rational, but it ignored the emotions on both sides of the growing conflict. Although Franklin thought that the 1765 Stamp Act was a mistake, he did not imagine that the colonies would go so far as to refuse to buy stamped paper. In fact, Franklin used his influence to secure the post of stamp commissioner for Pennsylvania for his friend John Hughes in expectation of it being a lucrative position. American protests surprised Franklin. Morgan notes that by 1765 Franklin had lived some eight years in England, having returned only once to Pennsylvania since his arrival in Britain in 1757. Hence, he was out of touch with the sentiments of the colonists, who were growing disaffected with an England and an empire that Franklin still loved.

Franklin's lack of understanding of America's attitude is evident also in his support of the 1767 Townsend Acts. Whereas the Stamp Act had created an internal tax, the Townsend duties were levied on imports and so were an external tax. Franklin expected colonial compliance, not the nonimportation agreements that the colonies drafted. He warned Parliament that retaining a tax on tea while repealing the other duties would not improve matters, yet after the Boston Tea Party (December 16, 1773) Franklin still hoped that the two sides could reconcile their differences. Massachusetts could compensate the East India Company for the lost tea, and England would stop taxing the colonies.

Neither of these events occurred. Even after the First Continental Congress gathered, Franklin's hopes for an Anglo-American empire did not die. He thought that the congress would impose an embargo on British goods that would cause the intransigent North ministry to collapse and bring to power a new British government sympathetic to American concerns. In England he encouraged William Pitt, now Lord Chatham, and the former Lord Chancellor, Lord Camden, to introduce into Parliament measures to remove British troops from Boston and limit Britain's authority over the colonies. The North ministry rejected both motions.

When Franklin returned to Philadelphia in March, 1775, he still believed that reconciliation between Britain and the colonies was possible. Morgan astutely observes, however, that Franklin's letters to his many friends and admirers in England now refer to America as "us" and "we," whereas the British are "you." Despite himself, and perhaps only subconsciously, Franklin had declared his independence from Britain.

Over the next eight years Franklin contributed as much as anyone to making the colonies as a whole independent as well. His greatest achievement was securing French recognition and French funds for the fledgling nation that did not yet know it was one. Individual states competed with Congress to secure loans, offering higher interest rates than Congress was willing to pay. Franklin also had to contend with rivals undermining his efforts. Morgan offers a strong brief defending Franklin against John Adams, Arthur Lee, and Silas Deane, all of whom criticized Franklin's activities and believed themselves better suited to carry on negotiations with France.

Morgan devotes little attention to Franklin's last years, which included helping to draft the U.S. Constitution and serving as president of Pennsylvania's executive council for three years. Franklin also wrote papers about the Gulf Stream, advised engineer Robert Fulton on using steam engines for ships, continued to improve home heating, and designed faster sailing ships. In a 1750 letter to his mother, Franklin had expressed the hope that when he died people would say he had lived usefully. Morgan amply illustrates that Franklin achieved that goal.

Joseph Rosenblum

Sources for Further Study

Booklist 98 (August, 2002): 1916.
Los Angeles Times Book Review, September 22, 2002, p. 12.
The New York Review of Books 49 (September 28, 2002): 43.
The New York Times Book Review 107 (October 20, 2002): 20.
Publishers Weekly 249 (July 1, 2002): 64.
The Washington Post Book World, September 15, 2002, p. 2.

BETRAYAL
The Crisis in the Catholic Church

Author: The Boston Globe Investigative Staff
Publisher: Little, Brown (Boston). 274 pp. $23.95
Type of work: Current affairs and religion
Time: 2002
Locale: Boston

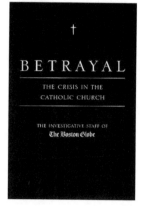

∼

A sequential and sometimes graphic account of the sexual abuse crisis that has plagued the Catholic community in Boston and elsewhere and has shocked the general public since the unprecedented scandal broke early in 2002

∼

Principal personages:
JOHN J. GEOGHAN, former priest of the Boston archdiocese
BERNARD F. CARDINAL LAW, archbishop of Boston
PAUL R. SHANDLEY, former priest of the Boston archdiocese
EDWARD M. CARDINAL EGAN, archbishop of New York

Early in 2002, *The Boston Globe* broke the shocking story of a local pedophile, a former Catholic priest whose extensive abuse of children had been swept delicately under the plush carpets of the Boston diocesan offices and local parishes for many years. Further investigation revealed that the Geoghan case was not an isolated phenomenon but only an extreme instance of a much deeper problem involving scores of other Catholic clergy. Flowing from the newspaper series that exposed the "festering sore on the body of the entire church," this book provides an account of the sexual abuse crisis in the Catholic Church as well as a detailed exposition of many of the specific cases in the Boston archdiocese. The book stands out as the painfully true and sordid story of men of the cloth—promised to celibacy and to the service of the Catholic community—and their superiors who stand convicted of crimes repugnant even to those who do not profess a belief in God or in the importance of a life of service.

The poster boy of the scandals in Boston is former Father John J. Geoghan, a cleric with promise, strong backing from his bishop and a priest-uncle, and a heavily guarded, ugly secret. *The Boston Globe* reporters reveal a litany of evidence and testimony that details Geoghan's extensive abuse of children in the Boston parishes, where the priest had served for over thirty years, a story that eroded Catholic belief and trust in the Church's integrity.

With little to go on initially, the investigative team of *The Boston Globe* set about to search for answers. The story that they wished to write would not be easily revealed, however. It was necessary to unseal the more than ten thousand pages of doc-

The reporters principally responsible for The Boston Globe*'s coverage—Matt Carroll, Kevin Cullen, Thomas Farragher, Stephen Kurkjian, Michael Paulson, Sacha Pfeiffer, Michael Rezendes, and Spotlight Team editor Walter V. Robinson—were supervised by deputy managing editor for projects Ben Bradlee, Jr.*

uments that the diocese had concealed. After a judge allowed access to these records, the work began. Digging by reporters into Geoghan's past not only unearthed Geoghan's activities but also revealed that he was one of many more molesters who had victimized scores of children. Furthermore, the investigation found that the Church had created an effective internal protection system that shielded the accused priests from criminal liability, preserved their positions as active church functionaries, and muffled the voices of victims and their families with discreet financial settlements. After winning the legal challenge to the confidentiality agreements that the archdiocese had extracted from families who had complained and received settlements, the reporters were able to obtain the documents essential to the understanding of the extent of the abuse and cover-up. Many of the documents they discovered are reproduced in the book in a lengthy and revealing appendix. Reading these papers, mainly letters, reinforces the sense of sadness and of horror that pervades the entire book. It buttresses the belief that ecclesial power resides exclusively in the hands of the clerical structure and reveals the degree to which power corrupts even those with a religious calling.

What the investigative team discovered in their search was a series of accusations from both victims and other concerned individuals, a series of priests moved quietly from parish to parish without reservation or censure, and a pervasive climate of willful denial. For some molesting priests, the transfers actually offered upward mobility, positive career moves to more prestigious parishes. For many victims and their families, the archdiocese's handling of their accusations blunted their desire for public justice but not the painful memories of what had been done to them, sometimes many years before.

The book is not simply a compilation of the series of articles that appeared in the newspaper. It is rather a separate project, enriched with considerable detail and background material. Its chapters provide the reader with an in-depth look at the former priest whose activity sparked the investigation, John Geoghan; the long-term cover-up; the unbelievable extent of abuse in the Boston archdiocese; and an account of the poignant stories of the victims. One chapter details the career of Cardinal Bernard Law, who rose "from the buckle of the Bible Belt to preside over the Church's crown jewels." The son of a military father, he learned well the lessons of discipline, adaptation to frequent moves, and singular loyalty to one's "corps." These lessons were applied in his handling of the abuse cases that he inherited when he became the leading prelate of Boston. He apparently managed to oversee an archdiocese without really sinking roots into it and to cover over activities of those inside the institution who victimized children. The final chapters of the book consider the scandal from the point of view of public reaction and its effect both within and outside the greater Catholic community.

John Geoghan's public face as a young priest could have been the model for Bing Crosby's kindly and approachable cleric in the movie *Going My Way* (1944). Although Geoghan was not distinguished either as a scholar or for his maturity in the seminary and suffered from a "nervous condition," he was eventually ordained and began a promising career as a parish priest. He was an outgoing, smiling man, helpful and accommodating especially to needy Catholic mothers trying to raise their children in their faith. Geoghan inserted himself into their families, gaining their trust and the opportunity to exploit those who were especially vulnerable. Although some of his behavior raised questions—he was seen to escort young boys into rectory bedrooms, wrestle with them, buy them ice cream—no red flag was raised high enough to cause serious suspicion about what was going on within these liaisons. Support from an uncle who was also a priest, glowing reports from his superiors (who called him "an outstanding priest"), and a veil of silence cast by those with suspicions kept Geoghan's activity out of the vision of those who might have done something to stop it. By the late 1990's, when he had already been removed from three parishes due to accusations of molestation, Geoghan was still confident enough of his status to request to be made pastor of a plum parish. In the end, after failed treatment for his "problem," Geoghan was offered retirement by the bishop. It was hoped that the difficult problem of his sexual abuse was solved—or so it was believed in 1996.

A look at accusations dating back to the 1980's, however, shows why this would not be the case. Not only did the archbishop of Boston, Bernard Law, knowingly and repeatedly assign the affable Father Geoghan to new parishes, he and other bishops followed the same pattern with other priests documented as having committed abuse. Mixed opinions concerning the seriousness and the curability of pedophilia helped support the continued endorsement of Geoghan and others, although evidence shows that studies indicating the seriousness and irreversibility of the pathology were known and available to bishops as early as the 1980's. Only a flood of accusations that finally emerged in the public arena late in the 1990's broke the dam of secrecy that overflowed onto the pages of *The Boston Globe* in early 2002.

The authors of *Betrayal* were instrumental in making this happen. At the end of 2002, the story was still developing. Cardinal Law publically expressed his regret for the way in which the scandal was handled and finally resigned in December. The Catholic Church responded nationally and internationally with proposals for handling such issues as they arise in the future. Will this reform be successful? Can the Church return to its former public image of credibility? Can a culture of secrecy and protection which has ruled and shaped the culture of Catholic clericalism be changed? It is to be hoped that the honest journalism of a few good reporters will have moved an elderly and often sedentary institution in that direction.

Perhaps the only significant critique of the book is its persistent graphic detailing of the activities of the accused priests with their victims. Peter Steinfels, former religion editor for *The New York Times*, has suggested that the media coverage of the scandal has viewed it mainly through the eyes of the victims' lawyers. This book flows from that coverage. Is it true that sex sells, even in the context of such sordid stories, or rather, is it journalistically necessary to divulge the ugly details to support the allegations, since the story itself is so far from what is commonly accepted as the image of the Catholic cleric? Perhaps only the graphic can guarantee that a concealing cover will not again be pulled over the awful truth. Perhaps only then can the Catholic Church recover, reform, and resume its place as guide on the high road.

The questions of this book are largely those of biography: biography of the archbishop of Boston, Bernard Law, biography of the victims of sexual abuse and their families, biography of the abusers. Perhaps the most important biographical tract in the book is that of the American Catholic Church itself. The final chapter of that biography has yet to be written. Meanwhile, *Betrayal* provides a contemporary snapshot of the erosion of the position of the Catholic Church in America.

One might point out minor flaws in the text. It is rare in a contemporary context, for example, to speak of a priest as "defrocked," a phrase used more than once by the authors. Theologian Charles Curran is wrongly described as having been censured "for teachings deemed out of step with Catholic theology." Although Father Curran was removed from the faculty of the Catholic University of America for alleged dissent from Catholic teaching—an accusation lacking strong supporting evidence—he is widely respected in and beyond the Catholic theological community for his extensive contribution to Catholic theology. Finally, the book makes no attempt to place the scandal in the broader reality, that is, that abuse of the young is neither exclusively nor primarily the problem of Catholic clergy nor of those of homosexual orientation; girls were abused as well as boys. However, to dwell on these issues would indeed be to quibble with a well-written and helpful book.

On the whole *Betrayal* captivates the reader like a good novel. The ingredients of drama, clarity of description, and, indeed, plenty of sex support this claim. The candor and good scholarship that the staff of *The Boston Globe* has contributed to its endeavor are praiseworthy. The book should be required reading for Catholics who care about the Church and wish it to grow, as well as for any who have concern about the victimization of children.

Dolores L. Christie

Sources for Further Study

Editor and Publisher 135 (June 10, 2002): 9.
Knight Ridder/Tribune News Service, July 17, 2002, p. K4518.
Los Angeles Times, July 27, 2002, p. B20.
The New York Review of Books 49 (August 15, 2002): 8.
The New York Times Book Review 107 (July 14, 2002): 8.

BIG IF

Author: Mark Costello (1936-   )
Publisher: W. W. Norton (New York). 315 pp. $24.95
Type of work: Novel
Time: The 1990's
Locale: Center Effing, New Hampshire, and nearby
   towns; suburban Maryland; Hinman, Illinois; Iowa;
   various outposts on the vice president's campaign
   trail

∾

*A glimpse into the lives and characters of Secret Service
agents assigned to guard the life and assure the security of
the vice president of the United States as he campaigns
across the country in his bid for the presidency*

∾

Principal characters:
   Vi Asplund, an unmarried Secret Service agent in her twenties
   Walter Asplund, Vi's father, an insurance adjuster
   Jens Asplund, Vi's brother, a computer geek
   Petulia "Peta" Boyle, Jens's wife, a real estate agent
   Gretchen Williams, a high-ranking Secret Service agent, aged forty-
      eight
   Tevon "Tev" Williams, Gretchen's ten-year-old son
   Lloyd Felker, a Secret Service agent
   Lydia Felker, Lloyd's wife, a former television actress
   Tashmo, a Secret Service agent
   Shirl, Tashmo's wife

Raised in a New Hampshire hamlet nestled between Interstate 95 and the Atlantic Ocean, Vi Asplund and her brother Jens grew up quite routinely. Their father, a Republican, atheist, insurance adjuster, crosses out "God" on United States currency and inks "U.S." into the slogan "In God We Trust." Vi learns investigative techniques early as she accompanies her father to the disaster sites covered by his insurance company's policies: a farming accident resulting in a lost foot, a lightning strike that kills a golf professional, a fire that burns down a building and appears to be arson.

Walter Asplund could sniff out fraud better than anyone else in his field. At his funeral, he was eulogized as someone who could read scorch marks better than any other insurance adjuster. When Walter died, Vi, then about twenty-five, fled Center Effing and joined the Secret Service, first working in the Crime Division tracking down counterfeiters but then, at her own request, moving to the group assigned to protect high government officials and their families.

~

Mark Costello's earlier book, Bag Men *(1997), was published under the pseudonym John Flood. He worked as a federal prosecutor for five years before beginning his writing career. He lives in New York.*

~

Jens, bright and obsessed by computers, graduated from Harvard and went on to the Massachusetts Institute of Technology, which he quit a dissertation short of a Ph.D. He returns to Center Effing to help start BigIf, a computer corporation he hopes will go public so that he can sell his interest in the company and set himself up for life. He is working specifically on constructing a complicated war game whose success and acceptance he considers his passport to financial security.

Big If, a finalist for the National Book Award in Fiction, focuses chiefly on the group that, during the months preceding the presidential election, works together to protect the vice president, now a presidential candidate. The vice president is a phantom figure, glimpsed fleetingly in passing. The book clearly is not about him. In the spotlight is the group of five Secret Service agents assigned to see that nothing catastrophic befalls him during his campaign.

The alienation that demanding jobs cause in human relationships is a controlling theme in this novel, Mark Costello's second major venture into fiction. The Secret Service agents guarding the vice president have families of their own and family responsibilities. Even Vi, who is young and unmarried, has her brother Jens and Peta, his wife, as well as their three-year-old Kai, all of whom are relatively close to Vi. The lead agent, Gretchen Williams, a forty-eight-year-old single mother, has a ten-year-old son, Tevon, whose grandmother looks after him in Beltsville, Maryland.

Tevon has grown increasingly resentful of his mother's constant absences and has begun to act out in ways that signal his distress. He has discovered, via the Internet, that his father, Carlton Imbry, lives in Los Angeles and has taken the initiative in making contact with Imbry. He uses the threat of going to California to be with his father as a feeble club to keep Gretchen in line.

Gretchen's job—which, incidentally, she neither sought nor wanted—tears her in many directions. She was virtually commanded to take the job, which would keep her away from home a great deal, by being told that if she did not take it, she would be reassigned to Los Angeles. This prospect terrified her, presumably because she did not want Tevon to know the identity of his father or to associate with him. Gretchen loves Tevon, but when the telephone rings and she is told she is to fly out of Andrews Air Force Base in two hours, she must go.

Lloyd Felker, clearly the group's intellectual, owns a farm in northern Virginia, where he lives with his beautiful wife, a former television actress, and their son, Jasper Jason. Lloyd carries such a wealth of classified information in his head that losing him would constitute a great security risk. For a time, however, it appears that Felker has indeed been lost.

During a campaign trip, the vice president hears about a raging flood in Hinman, Illinois, and decides that his flight to Washington should be diverted to someplace near Hinman to provide him with a valuable photo opportunity. The situation in

Hinman is grave. Convicts have been brought to town to help the residents build a levee against the swirling waters. Felker tries to rescue people from a mobile home but is swept away by the current. He is presumed dead until charges to his credit cards begin to turn up in various parts of the Southwest. Has he defected in order to use his encyclopedic knowledge of the Secret Service as barter?

Apparently Felker was floating away on a roof when one of the convicts scrambled to the same roof to save himself. The two were catapulted down river and finally washed ashore. The convict, presuming Felker was dead, robbed him, then headed west using Felker's credit cards. Felker, however, was quite alive and, after he regained consciousness, disappeared in the confusion following the flood. He finally reappears, but the Secret Service does not publicize his survival. Rather, he is quietly reassigned to the Technical Assistance Unit of the Data Administration Group of the Personnel Division, Boston station, where he bears the title of Leave Specialist. He and his family move to Massachusetts, where Felker yields to the sexual temptations of Ranger Nguyen and is finally shot and killed by Nguyen's jealous lover.

Before Felker is done in, however, his wife confesses to him that his colleague, Tashmo, whose sexual prowess is legendary, was years earlier involved in an affair with her and that the son that Felker presumed was his own is actually Tashmo's, conceived in Santa Barbara during Ronald Reagan's administration. Felker takes this revelation stoically, but apparently the thought of it consumes him.

Here again the alienation theme is undeniable. The pressures of the job presumably lead to dalliances such as Tashmo's. Tashmo, whose sexual indiscretions are numerous, thinks that he wants to reform. He would like to confess to his wife, Shirley, but as Costello recounts, "He had tried many times in the last few years to say or imply or insinuate that [Shirley] didn't need to worry when he was away, that he was finally faithful, finally settled, finally hers, but she wouldn't let it go, this image of her husband as a stud. No woman wants a man no woman wants. She couldn't see him as a relic of past futures, because what would that make her? Jealousy is vanity eventually, he thought."

The alienation theme exists not only among the Secret Service people in the novel; they, after all, must be so fully committed to protecting the people they are guarding that when trouble erupts, as it does at the end of this novel, they must unquestioningly cry "Gun, gun" and throw themselves on top of the person they are protecting to take any bullets that are fired, risking death, the ultimate alienation. Granted, the agents wear protective kevlar vests, but agents are nonetheless in the line of fire and sometimes are shot when assaults are made on public figures.

Costello could have explored the alienation theme by focusing on occupations other than the Protection Detail of the Secret Service, but people on this detail are committed to their work in ways that few people in other professions are. Not many occupations or professions require the absolute loyalty demanded of those on the Protection Detail.

Jens, Vi's brother, suffers alienation from his father less than two weeks before Walter's death when he tells Walter about the work he does, the programming of war games. Walter considers this work immoral or, at least, amoral. He disapproves of it so strenuously that Jens goes for a week without having any contact with Walter. They have been reunited for less than a week when Jens is called upon to plan Walter's funeral.

Big If is a well-written novel. The author's close observation and recording of physical detail makes his writing exceptionally visual. In describing the headquarters of the Secret Service, for example, he writes, "The quad was a grass oval, big enough for soccer, browned over for the winter. The buildings on the quad—Threats, Plans, Movements, Psych Services, the Weapon School, and Technical Support—were of a set, if not a mind-set, red brick and cream steel, sculptural, abstract, like if you pushed them all together, they would fit and make a giant checkered cube." This passage is typical of much of the physical description Costello employs in the novel—specific, spare, direct.

One might question whether the author loses valuable focus by devoting nearly fifty pages from chapters 9 through 11 to Jens Asplund, his wife Peta, and their child Kai. Certainly the alienation theme is preserved in these pages: Peta dislikes her job of selling mansions to the nouveau riche, working ungodly hours, sacrificing her evenings and weekends to her work, but she is a successful sales person. Much of the information contained in this portion of the book, notably Vi's relationship with her brother, sister-in-law, and nephew, could have been condensed to less than five pages without doing significant damage to the ongoing story. Actually, in these pages are the seeds of another novel, but their inclusion here detracts from the emphasis on the five Secret Service agents who are at the heart of *Big If.*

Costello succeeds in bringing together the two strands of his novel by detailing a critical security problem within the final pages of the text. Vaughn Naubek has been fired from the BigIf Company the day before the vice president's visit to New Hampshire. He is seen and recognized in the crowd milling about to hear the vice president's speech. Oddly, he is dressed in the garb of a Postal Service employee.

Vaughn drops the helmet he has been carrying. Then Vi notices that Vaughn's hand goes into his coat and brings from it a revolver. The anguished cry of "Gun, gun" crackles through the intercom as Agent Bobbie Niles throws herself onto the vice president's chest. The sharp shooters stationed around Market Square fire two rounds. One hits Vaughn in the head, the other in the chest. The latter rips apart a suicide note Vaughn had written and was carrying in his inside pocket.

Vi, knocked down, is splattered with blood and bone fragments. The vice president is also splattered with blood. It is soon determined, however, that neither he nor Vi have sustained injuries. Vaughn's revolver is retrieved. Its magazine is empty, a fact that the Secret Service suppresses. It is clear that Vaughn has engineered a situation that would lead inevitably to his death, which was, therefore, technically a suicide.

R. Baird Shuman

Sources for Further Study

Booklist 98 (June 1-June 15, 2002): 1680.
Fortune 145 (June 10, 2002): 218.
The New York Times Book Review 107 (June 16, 2002): 7.
O. The Oprah Magazine 3 (June, 2002): 956.
Publishers Weekly 249 (April 29, 2002): 39.

THE BLACK HEARTS OF MEN
Radical Abolitionists and the Transformation of Race

Author: John Stauffer
Publisher: Harvard University Press (Cambridge, Mass.).
  367 pp. $29.95
Type of work: Biography and history
Time: 1835-1874
Locale: New York State, Kansas, and Virginia

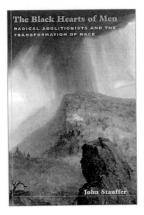

~

A study of four friends and radical opponents of slavery,
two white and two black, during the years before and after
the American Civil War

~

Principal personages:
GERRITT SMITH (1797-1874), wealthy New York abolitionist
JAMES McCUNE SMITH (1811-1865), the first African American professional physician
FREDERICK DOUGLASS (c. 1818-1895), renowned escaped slave and writer
JOHN BROWN (1800-1859), notorious rabble-rousing abolitionist and martyr to its cause

John Stauffer's *The Black Hearts of Men* is a story of social idealism and friendship in nineteenth century America. Its protagonists are four radical opponents of slavery, two black and two white, two major historical figures and two almost forgotten. Gerritt Smith is presented as the central character in the alliance of the four. Smith was a wealthy resident of the state of New York, a U.S. congressman for a time, and an abolitionist. James McCune Smith was a graduate of the University of Glasgow in Scotland and the first black professional physician in the United States. Frederick Douglass was a self-educated escaped slave, author, and orator, one of the renowned heroes of African American history. John Brown was a financial failure who became a prophet of violent slave uprising, a martyr in the eyes of some and a fanatic in the eyes of others after he was hanged for a raid on a federal arsenal at Harpers Ferry. These four men were tied to each other by friendship and by their commitment to ending slavery. Stauffer argues that it was an unusual friendship in the setting of nineteenth century America, not just because it cut across racial lines, but because the two white men, Gerritt Smith and John Brown, identified with the blacks and became black in their hearts.

Although all four were close friends, the only recorded time that they were together in the same place was in June, 1855, at the convention of Radical Abolitionists at Syracuse, New York. The Radical Abolitionists, also known as the Radical Political Abolitionists, differed from other abolitionists such as William Lloyd Garrison (1805-1879). Garrison and his associates favored a chiefly moral opposition to slavery and many favored breaking up the United States to maintain the moral purity of the nonslave portion of the country. In most abolitionist societies, the leaders were all white and blacks played only supporting roles. Colonization, the program of sending freed blacks to Africa, was widely popular among abolitionists. Few argued that freed slaves should become equal citizens in the United States. The Radical Abolitionists, however, favored political action to end slavery and looked forward to an interracial society. James McCune Smith, Frederick Douglass, and other blacks were prominent in the Radical Abolitionist party.

John Stauffer earned his Ph.D. in English from Yale. He is an associate professor of English and American civilization at Harvard University. His research concentrates on American literature and culture around the time of the Civil War and on nineteenth century photography. The Black Hearts of Men *is Stauffer's first book.*

Gerritt Smith's father was self-made man who made money in fur trading, invested in land, and became a partner of John Jacob Astor (1763-1848). The young Smith had uneasy relations with his father. The older man, for much of his life, saw business and the pursuit of wealth as the only worthwhile occupations and he was apparently uncomfortable with close personal relations. Gerritt aspired to be a scholar and a poet in the Romantic tradition of Lord Byron (1788-1824). Raised in prosperity, the younger man wanted to realize high ideals in his life, not to be caught up in the tedium of making money. However, after his father turned to religion, Gerritt was left with no option but to take over the family business.

Gerritt Smith resolved his dilemma by turning his wealth to idealistic ends. He involved himself in temperance reform, a cause that would continue to concern him throughout his life. He also turned to abolitionism, buying slaves and setting them free. He supported Oberlin College, the first American college to make a policy of admitting blacks and an institution strongly associated with the abolitionist cause. Elected to Congress, Gerritt Smith served a largely ineffectual term attempting to promote his causes.

One of Smith's most ambitious acts of philanthropy was his plan to donate land in the Adirondacks for settlement by poor blacks. The members of the community, known as Timbucto by the inhabitants, were expected to be self-sufficient on their farms. Although intended for blacks, one piece of the land was acquired by John Brown, who lived there for a time.

James McCune Smith was Gerritt Smith's close associate. McCune Smith was born a slave in New York City, but was freed by a state emancipation act when he was fourteen. Unable to enter any American universities because of the color of his skin, McCune Smith went to Scotland to become a physician. Stauffer argues that McCune Smith was an admirer of author Herman Melville and that Melville's *Moby Dick* (1851) served as a model for some of the black physician's own writing. If this is true, then James McCune Smith deserves more attention from literary scholars as well as historians. *Moby Dick* was generally regarded as unreadable in the nineteenth century and was only acclaimed to be a masterpiece with the emergence of modernist approaches to literature in the early twentieth century. McCune Smith may have shown extraordinary foresight in his literary judgement.

Gerritt Smith and James McCune Smith between them worked out a view of the world that they referred to as "Bible politics." This view was based on the idea that there should be no difference between principles of divine justice and government on earth. If slavery was contrary to divine justice, then slavery would have to be brought to an end immediately. No compromises were possible and the institution could not continue to exist in any portion of the country. The Bible politics of the Smiths would serve as the philosophy of the Radical Abolition party.

Frederick Douglass and John Brown are familiar to every American student. Douglass was an escaped slave who published two widely read autobiographies, edited his own periodicals, and achieved renown as a public speaker. In a time when it was commonly assumed that blacks were inferior to whites, Douglass served as living evidence of black intelligence and ability.

John Brown was the least admirable and the most influential of the four men. A failure in farming and business, Brown became convinced that God had called him to end slavery, which could be ended only through bloodshed. In 1854, the U.S. Congress gave Brown an opportunity to pursue his crusade when it passed the Kansas-Nebraska Act. The act left the issue of slavery in the territories of Kansas and Nebraska up to popular decision. Proslavery forces poured into Kansas from Missouri and antislavery forces moved in from the North. Supported by the two Smiths and Douglass, Brown and five of his sons moved into Kansas to take part in the armed struggles between the two forces. He became notorious when he and his followers dragged five unarmed proslavery settlers out of their cabins and hacked them to death.

Brown's last and most renowned venture occurred in the summer of 1859, when he led sixteen whites and five blacks in an attack on the federal arsenal at Harpers Ferry in Virginia. Brown was hoping that he would spark a slave rebellion that he could arm with weapons from the arsenal, leading to an uprising and warfare across the South. Instead, after a battle, he was captured by U.S. Marines under the command of Robert E. Lee (1807-1870), tried for treason and murder, and hanged.

Brown's raid was a crisis for the four men. James McCune Smith was the least affected. Frederick Douglass had known about the raid but decided not to participate. Still, he was charged with being part of the conspiracy and had to flee the country. Gerritt Smith had known about Brown's plans and had supported them. Afterward, Gerritt Smith was stricken with regret at the bloodshed for the sake of a failed rebellion. He suffered a mental breakdown and was confined to an institution for a time. When he recovered his faculties, he concluded that his close association with blacks and his support for their causes had led him into error. Despite efforts by James McCune Smith to contact Gerritt, the friendship came to an end.

Stauffer makes intriguing observations about the relationship of the economic panic of 1837 with abolitionism and other forms of moral and political reform. After a period of economic growth, high prices, and easy credit, the year 1837 saw a crash and the beginning of several years of economic depression. Shattered optimism led many to new views on society and morality. For the two white men under consideration in this volume, the changes of 1837 helped to cut psychological connections with established respectability and pushed them to define themselves as outsiders and to identify with enslaved blacks. Gerritt Smith's lands dropped drastically in value and for several years he struggled to pay off mounting debts. Although he managed to become solvent again, he responded to his financial hardships by emotionally devaluing his wealth and property and by committing himself to opposition to alcohol and to radical, uncompromising approaches to abolition. John Brown lost his farm, plunged into business failure, and in 1842 finally had to declare bankruptcy. Having failed at worldly activities, Brown gave himself over to his crusade against slavery.

The life of Frederick Douglass was also affected by the hard times, though in a more advantageous way. Douglass proposed to his master that he be allowed to hire out his own labor at caulking ships, in return for which he would guarantee to the master a regular payment. Falling profits may have inclined the master to accept this proposal, and the slave's control of his own time and the money he earned from caulking appear to have enabled him to escape.

Stauffer makes unique use of the daguerreotypes included with the text. These old photographs do not simply illustrate the text, they are actually part of it. Stauffer points out that the new medium of photography caught on quickly in nineteenth century America and that photographs quickly became ways in which people identified themselves. He interprets and comments on photographic portraits as presentations of self. While some readers might see his interpretations of the daguerreotypes as overly speculative, Stauffer does raise interesting questions about how new media of communication express social and psychological currents in history.

The organization of the book is a bit loose and the author has a tendency to repeat the same themes more than necessary. The chapters on what the four main characters thought about women and American Indians seem to be included because these are trendy academic matters and not because they are relevant to the book's main subjects. Stauffer is also remarkably uncritical of extreme violence, as long as violence is on the side that has his approval. He shows few qualms about John Brown cutting the throats of unarmed civilians during the years in Kansas, but is sorely disappointed with Frederick Douglass for moving toward greater political moderation with age.

Stauffer's sympathy with the unyielding values of his four Radical Abolitionists leads him to present their political perfectionism as an admirable state of integrity and to view Gerritt Smith and Frederick Douglass in their later years as backsliders for shrinking from this perfectionism. Critical readers might ask what the radicals achieved by their radicalism. Gerritt Smith was ineffective as a congressman, founded a utopian community that did not succeed, and was driven to insanity by the consequences of his support for John Brown. Brown practiced terrorism in Kansas and led a senseless raid at Harpers Ferry that freed no slaves and killed a black worker and sixteen other people. William Lloyd Garrison is often criticized for being more concerned with maintaining the moral purity of opposition to slavery than with freeing slaves, but at least Garrison did not slash throats for the sake of his moral posturing.

Carl L. Bankston III

Sources for Further Study

Choice 40 (October, 2002): 344.
The New York Times Book Review 107 (March 24, 2002): 11.
Publishers Weekly 248 (November 21, 2001): 44.
The Virginia Quarterly Review 78 (Autumn, 2002): 122.

THE BLANK SLATE
The Modern Denial of Human Nature

Author: Steven Pinker (1954-   )
Publisher: Viking (New York). 509 pp. $27.95
Type of work: Psychology, science, and sociology

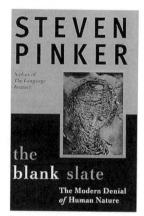

~

Pinker argues scientifically that current understanding of cognitive science and genetics demonstrates that there is a universal human nature and argues philosophically that the existence of this human nature does not defend or excuse moral anarchy

~

With *The Blank Slate: The Modern Denial of Human Nature*, Steven Pinker picks up an idea he began to describe in *The Language Instinct* (1994) and *How the Mind Works* (1997): that there is a set of characteristics hard-wired in all human brains. Pinker proved that language is an instinct because all healthy children learn the logic of language in the same way and because the capacity to use language is found in an identifiable part of the brain. In other words, children do not learn language because adults teach it to them, but because they are genetically wired to do so. In *The Blank Slate*, Pinker presents evidence that humans are not entirely unique or entirely formed by their environment; they share a universal human nature. The idea of a human nature has been explored before by philosophers, artists, psychologists, and ethnographers, and Pinker described their work in his earlier books. Here he builds on and moves beyond the work of the anthropologist Donald E. Brown, who identified a list of "human universals," or behavioral traits observed in all cultures around the world, to identify "deeper universals of mental structure that are revealed by theory and experiments."

Part 1, comprising the first five chapters, is devoted to explaining and debunking three theories or doctrines—the blank slate, the noble savage and the ghost in the machine—that guided common understanding of human cognition and personality before the discoveries of new sciences, including cognitive science, evolutionary biology, and sociobiology. The blank slate is the idea that at birth the human brain is a *tabula rasa*, a blank sheet of paper waiting to be written on, with no innate knowledge or personality traits—no universal human nature. Everything individuals become can be traced to their environment: the way they are raised, their economic situation, illnesses that might befall them, and so on. According to this model, which can be traced back to the seventeenth century philosopher John Locke (1632-1704), all healthy children have the potential to grow up smart, or musical, or kind, or violent, if only they are brought up that way. Locke was arguing against the idea that societies should be shaped by divine right or by hereditary rulers; rather, he argued, all people

Steven Pinker is a professor of psychology and the director of the Center for Cognitive Neuroscience at the Massachusetts Institute of Technology. He has been awarded prizes for his research, his teaching, and his writing. Pinker's best-selling books about science include The Language Instinct *(1994),* How the Mind Works *(1997), and* Words and Rules *(1999).*

started out equal and free, and should have equal chances to develop their talents.

A related idea is the notion of the noble savage, a term that comes from a seventeenth century poem by John Dryden (1631-1700). According to this theory, there is such a thing as human nature, an innate universal personality. This innate nature is good and strong and selfless; any violent or competitive urges humans might feel have been impressed upon them by a cruel modern world. Legends abound of supposedly peaceful societies in the wilds of undiscovered lands, and these stories can be traced back as far as the European explorers in the New World. Unexposed to technology and "civilization," these mythical people live or lived without war, without wage gaps, without greed, and with intact nuclear families. If negative influences (for example, violent song lyrics) could be eliminated, the natural nobility of humans could be recaptured.

A third idea, which Pinker deals with less than with the others, is the ghost in the machine, which Pinker labels a "sacred doctrine." The notion of the ghost in the machine, attributed to seventeenth century scientist René Descartes (1596-1650), splits human beings into two separate parts: the body and the mind or soul. The body is a machine and acts according to physical laws of electricity or chemistry. Within or above that body is the mind, or what some religions would call the soul. It is a distinct thing from the body, and it is what makes humans moral or immoral, and what gives a person "personality."

Pinker draws on examples from several contemporary scientific studies in cognitive science (his own field), sociobiology, and genetics to make the case that the slate is far from blank, that there is indeed a universal human nature. If the mind were truly blank, he reasons, it would not be able to learn from its environment, because there would be no way for it to know how to learn (rather like a computer hard drive that cannot run even the most basic software without a functioning operating system). Science has demonstrated that the brain is a data-processing system, and "the mind is equipped with a battery of emotions, drives, and faculties for reasoning and communicating, and that they have a common logic across cultures . . . were shaped by natural selection acting over the course of human evolution, and owe some of their basic design . . . to information in the genome."

Putting to rest the blank slate and its two companion theories is only part of Pinker's intention in this book. Of greater interest to the author is explaining why so many people have persisted in clinging to the old ideologies in spite of scientific evidence. Frequently, scientists who present evidence that human hard-wiring affects human behavior are denounced as racists, sexists, even Nazis. Pinker believes that the greatest motivation for those who deny the existence of a universal human nature is well-intentioned fear.

If, for example, it were shown incontrovertibly that intelligence is determined by genetics, would that not lead to stratification along race or gender lines? If it could be shown that one race or gender is genetically more or less intelligent than another, would that not sanction various forms of discrimination and undo decades and centuries of movement toward equality? Might it undermine the notion that hard work can lead to reward if a person's status were biologically determined? Pinker tells horrifying anecdotes of scientists in several fields who presented research demonstrating how natural selection might shape human nature or how genetics might shape a human mind, only to be met with angry, fearful, and sometimes violent attacks (primarily from other academics) having much more to do with politics than with science.

Pinker claims that these fears are unjustified for several reasons. For one thing, saying that genetics affects intelligence is not the same thing as saying it determines intelligence. Put another way, biology might make a trait probable, but not inevitable. Further, observations about broad groups of people are not illuminating when considering individuals. Pinker repeats the lesson offered in earlier works that the concept of race is nearly meaningless for geneticists; there is no more observable difference in the genetic code between Caucasians and Africans, for example, than between any two randomly selected individuals. Men and women are genetically different and difference in abilities can be attributed in general terms to the sexes—it can be said that men are better at solving word problems and women are better spellers—but even the casual nonscientific observer knows that some women are better than some men at word problems, and some men spell well.

Most importantly, those who fear that science will uncover a universal human nature must keep in mind the difference between moral and natural. Even if rape or cheating could be shown to be biologically natural, the acts would still be immoral. Equality is a moral value, not something determined by "a factual claim that humans are biologically indistinguishable." As Pinker argues, "Enlightened societies choose to ignore race, sex, and ethnicity in hiring, promotion, salary, school admissions, and the criminal justice system because the alternative is morally repugnant."

Having attempted to dispatch the fear of evolutionary psychology, Pinker maps out the current state of knowledge about human nature and five "hot button" topics: politics, violence, gender, children, and the arts. In these chapters, perhaps the most fascinating in the book, he fiercely takes on gender feminists, the Christian Right, child psychologists, postmodernists, and others, making a plea they not misuse science in an attempt achieve ethical goals. For the generalist reader, the sections of *The Blank Slate* that deal with academic disputes will be either fascinating or baffling, reassuring or pointless. Pinker points out hypocrisy and errors in the writings of other scientists, including James Watson, Richard Lewontin, and the late Stephen Jay Gould. Will readers who have only vaguely heard of the nature/nurture debate find an account of a group of protesters turning violent over a presentation claiming that human nature includes a tendency toward aggression and violence puzzling or ironic?

The Blank Slate demonstrates why Pinker has a large following of readers outside the worlds of social science who simply admire and enjoy the breadth of his knowledge and his humor and wit. To explain complex technical ideas, he finds analogies and examples in such disparate places as Mark Twain's *Adventures of Huckleberry Finn* (1884), John Huston's film *The African Queen* (1951), the comedy of the Marx Brothers, the business philosophy of Walt Disney, *Calvin and Hobbes* comic strips, and the art of Paul Cézanne. Pinker is convinced that a universal human nature is present and scientifically verifiable and writes passionately about the potential harm caused by those who disagree with his position. However, there is no venom in him, and he uses humor to disagree agreeably. "Not to put too fine a point on it," he writes, summing up a section on how parents are encouraged to guide their children toward higher intelligence, "but much of the advice from the parenting experts is flapdoodle."

Still, there is disagreement surrounding these issues and Pinker has drawn his share of criticism for the ideas in this book. Several reviewers have found that Pinker overstates how much science knows about the mind. Also among *The Blank Slate*'s detractors are social scientists whose own research leads them to different conclusions, for example, experts for whom the empirical evidence demonstrates that repeated exposure to television violence does indeed lead to violent behavior in young people. Pinker might disagree with their findings, but he welcomes the conversation so long as it is based on science, not on emotion, ideology, or politics. It is imperative, he explains, "to examine claims about human nature objectively, without putting a moral thumb on either side of the scale." Pinker sees his own book as an early stage in the discussion, not a set of final conclusions. "Human nature is a scientific topic," he argues, "and as new facts come in, our conceptions of it will change."

Cynthia A. Bily

Sources for Further Study

Kirkus Reviews 70 (August 1, 2002): 1105.
New Scientist 175 (September 7, 2002): 56.
New Statesman 131 (September 16, 2002): 52.
New York 35 (September 30, 2002): 85.
The New York Times Book Review 107 (October 13, 2002): 9.
Publishers Weekly 249 (August 12, 2002): 292.
Science 297 (September 27, 2002): 2212.
The Times Literary Supplement, September 27, 2002, p. 10.

BLINDED BY THE RIGHT
The Conscience of an Ex-Conservative

Author: David Brock (1962-   )
Publisher: Crown (New York). 336 pp. $25.95
Type of work: Memoir
Time: The 1980's and 1990's
Locale: Berkeley, California, and Washington, D.C.

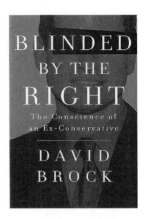

∼

A memoir of journalist Brock's role in conservative pol-
itics, especially his controversial books and articles on
Anita Hill, Hillary Rodham Clinton, and President Bill
Clinton which fueled the acrimonious and partisan atmo-
sphere of American political life in the 1990's

∼

Anyone who took even a passing interest in American politics during the 1990's could not fail to be aware of the acrimonious atmosphere that pervaded national politics. Partisan battles raged as left and right fought to win control over the political and cultural life of the nation. A taste of what was to come occurred in 1991, when the whole nation was riveted to its television screens during the Senate confirmation hearings of Supreme Court nominee Clarence Thomas. Thomas was accused by a law professor, Anita Hill, of sexual harassment, and the hearings contained the kind of lurid detail that is normally confined to supermarket tabloids. Thomas was narrowly confirmed to the Supreme Court, but the vicious infighting that accompanied the process would scar political debate for years to come.

Brock, who made his own contribution to the Thomas affair by writing a book that, he now admits, unjustly smeared Anita Hill, has written a memoir in which he in effect renounces his past. He freely admits to the most damning of sins in a journalist charged with delivering factual information to the public: he lied deliberately, repeatedly, and unashamedly. He was so caught up in his desire to serve the radical right that he lost his integrity in the process. Now he wants to cleanse his soul by confessing the truth. *Blinded by the Right* does not make pleasant reading, since there seem to be no depths of mendacity to which Brock, the right-wing hit man, would not sink in order to further his own journalistic career. He seems now to be genuinely ashamed of many of the things that he did, but given his consistent track record of lying to suit himself, the reader might be forgiven for wondering whether he is indeed telling the truth and nothing but the truth this time around.

Brock began his political life as a liberal; his hero was Democratic icon Robert F. Kennedy. However, when he attended the University of California at Berkeley in the early 1980's, he underwent a conversion experience. Disturbed by what he saw as intolerance on the part of the student left, Brock's misgivings came to a head when

David Brock is the author of The Real Anita Hill *(1993) and* The Seduction of Hillary Rodham *(1996). He has written for* Esquire, New York, Rolling Stone, Talk, The New York Times, *and* The Washington Post *op-ed pages. He appears regularly on television talk shows, and his work has been featured on National Public Radio.*

Jeane Kirkpatrick, the U.S. ambassador to the United Nations, visited the campus. Kirkpatrick was an outspoken supporter of U.S. anticommunist policies in Central America, and when she visited Berkeley, student liberal activists shouted her down and she was unable to deliver even a word of her speech. Shocked by this incident, Brock gravitated toward conservatism and in his remaining undergraduate years forged a reputation for himself as a conservative journalist on the main student newspaper at Berkeley, the *Daily Cal*. In 1986, Brock moved to Washington D.C. and got a job as a news reporter with the conservative *Washington Times* newspaper. He became increasingly devoted to the conservative cause, and for *Insight, The Washington Times'* weekly newsmagazine, he wrote an article in support of the notoriously brutal regime of General Augusto Pinochet in Chile, ignoring the regime's record of torture and other gross human rights abuses. This set the tone for Brock's later work. He saw himself as part of a movement that had declared war on the political left and his job as the prosecution of a war with all the journalistic means he could muster. It was "us" against "them."

In explaining how he got caught up in this way of thinking, Brock writes that he was content to think what everyone else in the conservative movement was thinking. He claims that he never thought deeply about conservative ideology, nor did he see any conflict in his being a homosexual man in the largely antihomosexual Republican party, although he did not publicly disclose his sexual orientation until 1994. During the 1980's, according to Brock, the Republican Party did not show the hostility toward gays that would characterize it a decade later. Nonetheless, as a closeted homosexual, Brock admits that he was an unhappy man, unable to create meaningful personal relationships. He now realizes that it was his personal misery that in part produced his vituperative writings: "A mad dog, an emotional monster, was about to be released."

The first fruit of the "mad dog" was *The Real Anita Hill* (1993), in which Brock tried to prove that Hill's accusation of sexual harassment against Thomas was a liberal conspiracy to frame the nominee. Brock dressed up his theory to create a superficially plausible book, while accepting at face value virtually every salacious rumor about Hill that he could find. Now, Brock, the repentant sinner, can hardly find enough words to repudiate his work and to castigate himself. The book, he writes, was "a witches' brew of fact, allegation, hearsay, speculation, opinion, and invective." It was "sloppy, skewed, slanderous." His famous phrase about Hill ("a little bit nutty and a little bit slutty") was "degraded sarcasm—inexcusable, disgusting." Rarely can an author have repudiated his own work with such loathing, although Brock still claims that at the time he believed his reporting was solid and accurate.

The success of *The Real Anita Hill* boosted Brock's emerging status as a journalistic soldier of the right. It was at this time that a motley collection of right-wing activists, refusing to accept Bill Clinton as the nation's legitimate president, was beginning its long, unscrupulous campaign to bring Clinton down. According to Brock, this effort to dig up scandals relating to both Bill and Hillary Clinton showed a "lack of fidelity to any standard of proof, principle, or propriety." At the time, Brock was as eager as anyone to put his nose in the mud. He accepted money from a Republican activist named Peter Smith to investigate Clinton's past in Arkansas. As he describes his role in this dirty tricks operation, Brook's self-loathing surfaces once more: "I was a whore for the cash," he writes.

This was the origin of "Troopergate." As with the rumors masquerading as facts in *The Real Anita Hill*, none of the accusations against Clinton were anything more than unsubstantiated stories told by state troopers seeking financial reward by turning on their former boss. At the time, Brock did not see it that way and he even chose to publish rumors that the troopers themselves admitted were only their speculations. Brock now condemns this article as a "cruel smear disguised as a thorough 'investigation.'"

Brock's next adventure was to participate in the Arkansas Project, launched by *The Spectator* magazine and financed by the reclusive billionaire Richard Mellon Scaife. The aim was to comb the state of Arkansas searching for scandals that would bring Clinton down. It was this project that gave Brock insight into "the underbelly of Arkansas's political culture, a hotbed of conspiracy and lunacy."

At the same time that he was fishing in the murky waters of Arkansas politics, Brock's journalistic integrity reached its nadir. It came in his response to the book *Strange Justice* (1994) by Jane Mayer and Jill Abramson, two *Wall Street Journal* reporters. The book made it abundantly clear that it was Clarence Thomas, not Anita Hill, who had lied during Senate confirmation hearings. In a desperate attempt to discredit the book, Brock dug up sensitive personal information about one of Mayer and Abramson's sources and threatened to use it against her, just as he "had blackened the reputations of all the other women who had come forward with damaging information about Thomas," unless she cooperated with him. In the negative review he wrote for *The Spectator*, Brock concluded that no evidence existed that Thomas had ever rented a pornographic video (which was an important part of the case against him). Brock now admits that when he wrote those words, he knew they were false. Further, he concludes, "I trashed the professional reputations of two journalists for reporting something I knew was correct. I coerced an unsteady source, I knowingly published a lie, and I falsified the historical record."

Brock's deliberate flouting of journalistic ethics finally brought on a crisis of conscience. In his next book, *The Seduction of Hillary Rodham* (1996), he refused to produce the kind of work that Clinton's enemies were expecting. Instead, the book was a fair-minded, even sympathetic portrait of the First Lady. As a result, Brock's days in the conservative movement were numbered. He had failed to do what was expected of him and he would now see how intolerant and ruthless his former associates, some of them personal friends, could be. He was, as he puts it, blackballed and excommunicated from the movement whose dirty work he had for so long been so willing to do.

How is one to assess such an unusual memoir, one in which the author, instead of burnishing his achievements, consistently denigrates and repudiates them? Certainly Brock deserves some credit for making what must have been a difficult public confession. The book is also startlingly illuminating regarding the lengths to which some activists on the right went in order to attack the Clintons and the unreasoning level of hatred that the political right bore them. However, Brock's book, while often illuminating, is spoiled by its spiteful, gossipy tone. He has not been able to lose his habit of dishing out the dirt. For example, he accuses Richard Mellon Scaife of no less a crime than murder; he attempts to discredit Juanita Broderick, the woman who accused Clinton of raping her; he accuses one of his former friends, a female conservative well known as a television pundit, of anti-Semitism (she left her lawyer's job in New York "to get away from all these Jews"); he sees fit to inform the reader that another former friend and cable television news personality once pulled a gun on a boyfriend after he broke up with her; he gratuitously insults liberal journalist Christopher Hitchens; and, perhaps worst of all, he "outs" a well-known media personality by printing a private e-mail that the man, who has publicly denied being gay, sent to him. It is a pity that Brock did not have an editor who could have advised him against this kind of pointless and mean-spirited disclosure, which serves nobody. In addition, it is ironic that, while Brock's earlier work came complete with all the trappings of scholarship, this book has none. There are no footnotes and no index, and none of the quotations are referenced. One wonders why.

Bryan Aubrey

Sources for Further Study

Commentary 113 (May, 2002): 84.
Library Journal 127 (April 15, 2002): 108.
The Nation 274 (April 8, 2002): 25.
The New York Times Book Review 107 (March 24, 2002): 14.
Publishers Weekly 249 (April 8, 2002): 22.
Time 158 (July 9, 2001): 28.

BLUE SHOE

Author: Anne Lamott (1954-   )
Publisher: Riverhead Books (New York). 304 pp. $24.95
Type of work: Novel
Time: The late 1990's to the early 2000's
Locale: In and around Marin County, California

~

Mattie Ryder, a single mother of two, struggles to deal with her failing mother, confront the unspoken truths of her troubled childhood, and find new love

~

Principal characters:

> MATTIE RYDER, a newly divorced woman in her thirties
> ISA, Mattie's demanding, seventy-one-year-old mother, who is becoming senile
> HARRY, Mattie's six-year-old son
> ELLA, Mattie's two-year-old daughter
> DANIEL, a married carpenter with whom Mattie falls in love
> NICKY, Mattie's philandering former husband, an assistant professor of literature
> AL, Mattie's older brother, a high-school teacher
> ABBY GRANN, a childhood friend of Mattie, who is now mentally unstable and living in squalor
> NOAH, Abby's son

Mattie Ryder, newly separated from her husband, Nicky, has moved back into the home where she was raised after her widowed mother, Isa, moves to The Sequoias, a retirement home. The house is in need of many repairs, and Mattie is especially bothered by the rats she hears in the walls and ceilings. When she calls an exterminator to clear out the rats, the company sends out Daniel. It is his first day on the job and, unable to stand the thought of killing animals, he quits on the spot. Mattie feels sorry for him and offers to pay him to chop wood for her, although she has very little money herself. From that improbable start, Mattie and Daniel become close friends. Daniel often helps Mattie with projects around her house, plays with her children, Harry and Ella, and attends Mattie's small Christian church with her each Sunday. Daniel's wife, Pauline, is a beautiful, zaftig blonde, alternately depressed and passionate, who seldom joins in Daniel and Mattie's activities. Mattie and Pauline have a civil relationship, but soon Mattie begins to wish Pauline were out of the picture so she and Daniel could be more than friends.

Mattie is struggling with several life changes. Having left her emotionally erratic husband, she must adjust to life as a single parent on a more limited income. Her two children, especially Harry, are dealing poorly with their parents' separation. Mattie

Anne Lamott is the author of five earlier novels and three books of essays; she also writes a magazine column and contributes to on-line magazines. She has received a Guggenheim fellowship. She was raised in Tiburon, California, and lives with her son in Fairfax, California.

and the children are all jealous of Nicky's young, blonde girlfriend, Lee. Isa is becoming more forgetful and dependent. Angela, Mattie's closest friend, has moved to Los Angeles with her lover, Julie. Mattie's beloved dog, Marjorie, is in failing health. The one positive factor in Mattie's life is her church and her deep, personal relationship with her God.

Mattie is a spoiled, neurotic woman who has no identity or self-esteem without a man. It seems that she has never had to take responsibility for herself. She has few job skills—her only income is her salary as a part-time clothes model at Sears. She loses even that job after Nicky and Lee's son Alexander is born, because she loses so much weight that she is no longer a size 12—an extreme reaction that demonstrates her addiction to Nicky's attention.

Mattie's only sibling, Al, lives nearby with his girlfriend, Katherine. Al fears that he could never be a good parent but is a loving surrogate father to Harry and Ella. Mattie depends on Al to help her with the increasing demands of their mother. They find a sensitive ally in Isa's new friend Lewis, another resident of The Sequoias, who is kind, devoted, and gentlemanly toward Isa. He also begins to join Mattie and Daniel at church.

Mattie and Al had a tumultuous childhood. Their parents, Isa and Alfred, were part of a group of politically and socially liberal Marin County bohemians, and the children were often left to fend for themselves. Alfred, a lawyer, drank a great deal; Isa worked, cleaned, and nagged. The two fought tumultuously and were generally miserable together. Alfred left town monthly, allegedly on business trips to Washington, D.C. Al was a troubled and aggressive child and began drinking and using drugs as a young teen. Mattie responded to the chaos by trying to be as good as possible. As the two grew older, they became close, and Al achieved sobriety in his twenties after years of therapy.

Among the Ryders' closest friends were Neil Grann, his daughter Abby, and his girlfriend Yvonne Lang. However, Mattie and Al long ago lost touch with their old friends. One day Mattie sees the old Volkswagen bus that her father owned in the 1970's. She learns that the driver had bought it years ago, after her father had sold it to Neil Grann and Abby subsequently wrecked it. The driver still has the odd collection of objects that had been in the glove compartment, including a paint-can opener coated with pale blue paint and a tiny blue plastic tennis shoe, and he gives them to Mattie. Although she has never seen these two items, Mattie begins to keep the blue shoe with her as though it had some magical power and wonders where her father had used the paint-can opener, since they had never had a blue room in their home.

Lonely and jealous of the gorgeous Lee, Mattie had quickly resumed a sexual relationship with Nicky after they separated, often using problems with the children or the house as excuses to have him come over. Although she prays for the strength to resist this temptation, the reader may suspect she has little interest in having her prayers answered. Eventually, Nicky announces that he and Lee are expecting a child, and Mattie's jealousy and guilt both intensify. Still she continues to sleep with Nicky, even after Nicky and Lee are married and their son, Alexander, is born.

Harry is an intelligent child, often asking questions and making comments that are very mature for his years, but he takes out his anger and frustration on his little sister and creates dramatic scenes that leave Mattie shaken. Ella finds quieter ways to express her pain—gnawing on her wrist until it develops a permanent open wound, later chewing her fingernails until they bleed.

While buying sandwiches for a beach picnic at a small market, Mattie sees William, son of the store's owner, Ned. She and William had been classmates in elementary school, and she is surprised that the short, irritating eighth-grader has turned into a tall, handsome, cultured, charming gentleman. They begin dating and become sexually involved, but Mattie realizes that she is using William to inoculate herself against sleeping with Nicky and pining after Daniel. Mattie keeps William at arm's length emotionally, hiding personal information about herself and her family, telling him only what she thinks will flatter her.

Al and Mattie discover boxes of their parents' things in the attic of their childhood home, including several letters from Neil to their father. Recollecting half-forgotten incidents from their teenage years, they begin to wonder about Isa and Alfred's real lives. After Mattie starts working part time for Ned, she learns that Abby lives nearby like a squatter in a dilapidated beach shack, filthy and barely coherent. Her son, Noah, works in the small local library. Mattie and Al soon feel compelled to make contact with Abby and Noah.

Isa's growing mental deterioration becomes obvious to her family after she runs into heavy machinery parked on a highway shoulder, then accuses the police of Gestapo tactics when she is taken in for reckless driving and leaving the scene of the accident. Mattie insists that Isa see a doctor, but at the doctor's office, Isa is charming and relaxed. Nevertheless, the doctor orders a series of tests. Mattie is saddened when she sees her mother's aging, naked body, and concerned that Isa smells unclean and is wearing dirty undergarments. The doctor eventually determines that Isa has had a series of small strokes.

Mattie and William's relationship is collapsing, and he is about to leave her. Although she constantly faults William's personality and character, Mattie is desperate to keep him available to her, so she breaks a confidence with Al and tells William the secret she and Al have uncovered about Abby and Noah. When Al learns what she has done, he withdraws from her completely for weeks. Mattie and William's relationship soon ends anyway, leaving Mattie alone again and more needy than before.

Daniel and Mattie continue their close friendship and his marriage becomes rockier. However, he remains committed to Pauline, and they leave on vacation in the hope of rekindling their feelings for each other. After a few days, Daniel calls Mattie from Idaho, saying that he and Pauline have had an awful fight. Mattie offers to let him stay at her house while he sorts out what he wants to do. After a few days, he agrees to her offer and moves into her laundry room. They settle in together as roommates, maintaining a chaste friendship for many months, even after declaring their love for each other.

As Isa fails more mentally, she becomes as much of a child to Mattie as her children are. Like the rebellious teenager that Harry is quickly becoming, Isa constantly challenges Mattie's plans and suggestions. She is particularly adamant that she will not move into the assisted living wing of The Sequoias, despite the fact that she can no longer live alone. She fires the aides her children hire to help her, badgers Mattie to let her move in with her, and tries to make Mattie feel guilty when she refuses. Isa finally has no choice but to move to the assisted living wing, where she is reunited unexpectedly with a long-lost friend.

Lamott's earlier novels, plus her books of essays, have drawn heavily on her life, including her troubled childhood; her alcoholism, drug addiction, and recovery; her first year as a single mother; and her membership in a small, racially integrated church. Many of these subjects reappear in *Blue Shoe*, plus the new element of her recently deceased mother's bout with Alzheimer's disease. Although many current novels incorporate the problems of middle-aged children caring for deteriorating parents, *Blue Shoe* also features a theme less often seen in mainstream contemporary fiction: a relationship with God. God could be considered a major character in the novel, since Mattie chats with God throughout the novel.

Blue Shoe is narrated by Mattie, so the feelings of the other characters are presented only through her eyes; however, most of the other characters are strongly written and clearly presented. The novel covers a span of four years, but seems more compressed; the main clue to the passing of time is given when Mattie talks about the children's ages.

Lamott's themes will resonate with many contemporary readers: conflicting feelings after a divorce, the trials of single parenthood, the challenges of finding new love, the fears and problems of adults raised by overly permissive parents in the 1960's, dealing with an aging parent who is losing her mental facilities, and even the heartbreak of letting go of a treasured family pet who is dying. The bureaucratic details involved in trying to find Isa the help she needs and the financial burdens that will result for her family are presented with painful accuracy. In spite of her litany of problems, Mattie's story also has many humorous moments and is enlivened by Lamott's wit and rich, descriptive language.

The deteriorating house to which Mattie returns is a metaphor for the life her family lived there—the house's structural flaws have been covered over with paint and wallpaper but never repaired; the rats scurrying in the walls and ceiling whisper the secrets that Mattie finally acknowledges each of them pretended not to know that they knew. When Mattie and Al finally uncover the secrets of the paint-can opener and the blue shoe, they are not surprised and neither is the reader.

Irene Struthers Rush

Sources for Further Study

Booklist 99 (September 1, 2002): 6.
The Christian Science Monitor, September 26, 2002, p. 19.
Library Journal 127 (September 15, 2002): 92.
Los Angeles Times, October 15, 2002, p. E11.
The New York Times Book Review 107 (October 13, 2002): 34.
Newsday, September 27, 2002, p. D32.
Publishers Weekly 249 (August 26, 2002): 40.
St. Louis Post-Dispatch, October 6, 2002, p. G10.

THE BONDWOMAN'S NARRATIVE

Author: Hannah Crafts
Edited by Henry Louis Gates, Jr.
Publisher: Warner Books (New York). 416 pp. $24.95
Type of work: Novel
Time: The 1850's
Locale: The United States

~

A renowned literary scholar resurrects a forgotten manuscript that may prove to be the first novel written by an African American woman and the only known novel by a female fugitive slave

~

Principal characters:
> HANNAH CRAFTS, a young mulatto woman who escapes from slavery
> MRS. VINCENT, a mulatto woman and the wife of Hannah's first master, who accompanies Hannah during her first, unsuccessful flight from slavery
> MR. TRAPPE, a solicitor and an opportunist who specializes in the discovery and enslavement of individuals of African ancestry who pass for white
> MRS. HENRY, a white clergyman's wife who nurses Hannah back to health after her fall from a carriage
> MRS. WHEELER, the wife of a North Carolina senator and Hannah's final mistress prior to her successful escape
> AUNT HETTY, an elderly white woman who teaches the young Hannah to read and with whom Hannah is reunited during her final escape from slavery

Dr. Henry Louis Gates, Jr., an internationally acclaimed literary and cultural critic and director of the W. E. B. Du Bois Center for Afro-American Research, has received considerable attention in the past for his discovery of unknown or neglected works by early African American authors. After finding a copy of Harriet E. Wilson's novel *Our Nig: Or, Sketches from the Life of a Free Black* (1859) in a secondhand bookstore, Gates reissued the long-forgotten novel in 1983 and established Harriet E. Wilson as the first African American woman to publish a novel in the United States, a designation previously reserved for Frances Ellen Watkins Harper, author of the 1892 novel *Iola Leroy.* With the publication of *The Bondwoman's Narrative* in 2002, Gates has once again altered the landscape of American and African American literature.

Gates discovered the handwritten and previously unpublished manuscript in an auction catalog for Swann Galleries, which specializes in "Published & Manuscript African Americana." The catalog described it as "a fictionalized biography, written in an effusive style, purporting to be the story of the early life and escape of one Hannah Crafts, a mulatto, born in Virginia." Furthermore, Dorothy Porter Wesley, a renowned historian and librarian at Howard University's Moorland-Spingarn Research Center, was the seller. These two facts—that the author was reputed to be black and that the manuscript had once been a part of Wesley's private collection—convinced Gates that the item could be of considerable importance.

Henry Louis Gates, Jr., is the chair of the Afro-American Studies department at Harvard University. He is the author of numerous books on African and African American literature and has edited several collections of slave narratives and other works by nineteenth century African Americans.

Gates has published *The Bondwoman's Narrative* with a comprehensive introduction and appendices which comprise nearly a third of the published text, and in which Gates discusses the methods used to examine and authenticate the manuscript. His pursuit of the historical identity of Hannah Crafts reads like a detective story and is, perhaps, as compelling a tale as the one that Crafts depicts in her novel. Relying on internal and external evidence, Gates assembled a convincing theory as to the origins and autobiographical nature of *The Bondwoman's Narrative*; as he suspected, his research indicated that the novel could very well be the first such work written by an African American woman and the only known novel written by a female fugitive slave.

After his initial reading of the novel, as he describes in his introduction, Gates noted several distinctive qualities about the text. Crafts incorporated several styles of writing in her novel, borrowing from such genres as the slave narrative, the gothic novel, and the ubiquitous nineteenth century sentimental novel. The combination of these various styles represented something quite new in the African American literary tradition. "Crafts . . . uses the story of a fugitive slave's captivity and escape for the elements of her plot," Gates explains, "as well as a subplot about passing, two other 'firsts' for a black female author in the African American literary tradition."

Perhaps the most important factor for Gates in determining the racial heritage of Hannah Crafts was drawn from an observation made by Dorothy Porter Wesley, the previous owner of the manuscript. "There is no doubt," Wesley wrote in a letter to Emily Driscoll, the original owner of the manuscript, "that she was a Negro because her approach to other Negroes is that they are people first of all." As Gates notes, nineteenth century white authors such as Harriet Beecher Stowe did just the opposite, by drawing immediate attention to the racial heritage of black characters and by introducing white characters more naturally, with no reference to any distinguishing racial features.

For a more thorough analysis of the manuscript, Gates sought the assistance of two celebrated specialists: Dr. Ken Rendall, who assisted in the analysis of the fraudulent Hitler diaries in the 1980's; and Dr. Joe Nickell, a celebrated skeptic who exposed the Jack the Ripper diary as a hoax. Scientific analysis demonstrated that the manuscript was written before 1860, that the author was a young woman with no formal education, and that the author was largely self-taught and familiar with the popular literary works of her day. Citing the "elegance" of Dr. Nickell's research, Gates appended the full "Authentication Report" to the novel. Having established with reasonable certainty the authenticity of *The Bondwoman's Narrative* as a mid-nineteenth century novel written by a young African American woman, Gates turned to the text for any details that might provide clues to the historical identity of Hannah Crafts and the events in her narrative.

Hannah Crafts begins her narrative by describing the disadvantages of her birth and early life at Lindendale, a large estate in Virginia. "I soon learned what a curse was attached to my race, soon learned that the African blood in my veins would forever exclude me from the higher walks of life," a situation she finds exceedingly difficult to bear "because my complexion was almost white, and the obnoxious descent could not be readily traced." Her prospects improve when an elderly white neighbor, known only as Aunt Hetty in the novel, offers to teach young Hannah to read, against the wishes of her master and the dictates of the law.

In due course, the master of Lindendale, Mr. Vincent, decides to take a bride, of whom Hannah becomes a particular favorite. She eventually discovers that Mrs. Vincent is, in fact, the daughter of a slave, although she is passing for white. Raised by her father to believe that she was his natural daughter, Mrs. Vincent only determines her true origins after her father's death, when Mr. Trappe, the family solicitor and executor of the estate, finds the evidence among her father's personal papers. Mr. Trappe resolves to extort money from Mrs. Vincent and her new husband under the threat of exposing her secret.

Fearful of the consequences of such exposure, Hannah resolves to flee Lindendale with Mrs. Vincent, only to be discovered some months later by Mr. Trappe. Under the strain of learning that her husband has died and that she will be sold as a slave, Mrs. Vincent collapses and dies. Hannah passes briefly through the hands of a slave-trader, Mr. Saddler, whose cart overturns on the way to the home of her new master. Mr. Saddler is killed instantly, but Hannah survives and finds sanctuary in the home of Mrs. Henry, a clergyman's wife, who nurses her back to health.

Through the agency of Mrs. Henry, Hannah becomes the personal maid of Mrs. Wheeler, the wife of a former North Carolina senator and a friend of the Henry's. Initially comfortable in her new situation at the Wheeler's plantation in North Carolina, Hannah soon suffers the vindictiveness of a fellow slave, whom she has supplanted as Mrs. Wheeler's personal maid. Mrs. Wheeler, convinced by deceit that Hannah has betrayed her confidence, banishes her from the house and further punishes her by promising her as a wife to one of the field slaves. Rather than suffer the indignity of a forced marriage and the horrific working and living conditions among field slaves, Hannah resolves to escape. She disguises herself as a young man and, aided by her fair complexion, flees the Wheeler plantation and joins the company of two fugitive slaves whom she meets on her journey north. After the deaths of her two companions, Hannah narrowly escapes drowning while trying to evade pursuers. When she regains consciousness, she reunites with her former teacher, Aunt Hetty, whose cottage provides a safe haven until she is well enough to continue north.

In the final pages of Crafts's novel, Hannah finds freedom and happiness in the North. She settles in New Jersey, opens a school for black children, and marries an honorable and loving man. In contrast, the villainous Mr. Trappe reaps the consequences of his greed and inhumanity when, after acquiring the ownership and planning for the sale of a family of slaves through deceit, he is murdered by his prospective victims. In the fashion of most nineteenth century romances, Crafts's novel ends with rewards for the righteous and punishment for the wicked, a goal that Crafts makes explicit in her preface to the original manuscript.

In his "Authentication Report," Dr. Nickell noted that Crafts initially abbreviated the family name of Wheeler, a common practice in eighteenth and nineteenth century novels. However, Crafts later filled in the full name of Wheeler, suggesting that the Wheelers were indeed actual people with whom Crafts was well acquainted. In the novel, Mr. Wheeler serves as a government official in Washington, D.C., and owns a large plantation in North Carolina. After consulting federal census records from North Carolina and Washington, D.C., Gates found that one man, John Hill Wheeler, matched the circumstances of Mr. Wheeler in the narrative. Gates also made an important discovery about a slave named Jane Johnson who belonged to John Hill Wheeler.

While traveling with John Hill Wheeler to Philadelphia, Pennsylvania, in 1855, Jane Johnson and her two children fled from Wheeler with the assistance of several others. Jane Johnson's escape caused considerable public attention and the consequent court case in which Wheeler tried to regain custody of Jane became one of the first challenges to the Fugitive Slave Act of 1850. Having thoroughly investigated the historical Jane Johnson, the details of which research he includes in his introduction to *The Bondwoman's Narrative*, Gates found a connection between the historical Jane Johnson and a character in Crafts's novel. When the character of Hannah is retained as Mrs. Wheeler's personal maid in chapter 12, she replaces Mrs. Wheeler's former slave, Jane, who had recently escaped.

Under the subheading "Searching for Hannah Crafts" in his introduction, Gates documents his meticulous examination of federal census records for the state of New Jersey, where the character of Hannah settles in the final chapter of *The Bondwoman's Narrative*. Gates also examined records from the Freedman's Bank and the American Methodist Episcopal church (in the novel, Hannah's husband is described as a Methodist minister). While he discovered several promising leads, Gates's research turned up nothing concrete with regard to the historical identity of Hannah Crafts. In the end, the mystery of Hannah Crafts's true identity remains, though the implications of Gates's discovery continue to resonate.

The Bondwoman's Narrative relies heavily on the conventions of traditional nineteenth century sentimental fiction, even cribbing gratuitously in several sections from Charles Dickens's *Bleak House* (1852-1853), as Gates points out in his introduction. Despite its limitations as literature, however, *The Bondwoman's Narrative* is free of the editorial tampering so common with other works by black authors of the nineteenth century. "Between us and them," Gates explains, "between a twenty-first century readership and the pre-edited consciousness of even *one* fugitive slave, often stands an editorial apparatus reflective of an abolitionist ideology." Crafts's unpublished manuscript exhibits no such influences and therefore provides an entirely unique perspective on the life and literature of nineteenth century black authors. "To be able to study a manuscript written by a black woman or man . . . unaided by even the most well-intentioned or unobtrusive editorial hand, would help a new generation of scholars to gain access to the mind of a slave in an unmediated fashion heretofore not possible."

Philip Bader

Sources for Further Study

Black Issues Book Review 4 (May/June, 2002): 39.
Booklist 98 (March 15, 2002): 1189.
Library Journal 127 (June 1, 2002): 147.
The New York Times Book Review 107 (May 12, 2002): 30.
Publishers Weekly 249 (April 1, 2002): 53.

THE BOOK OF ILLUSIONS

Author: Paul Auster (1947-   )
Publisher: Henry Holt (New York). 321 pp. $24.00
Type of work: Novel
Time: 1985-1999
Locale: Vermont, New York, and New Mexico

～

*A middle-aged professor deals with loss by immers-
ing himself in the films of a little-known silent film come-
dian*

～

> *Principal characters:*
> DAVID ZIMMER, widower and professor of comparative literature
> HECTOR MANN, silent film comedian
> FRIEDA SPELLING, his wife
> ALMA GRUND, Mann's biographer

The Book of Illusions is Paul Auster's tenth novel and thirty-fifth book overall. Although long praised as a decidedly literary writer, Auster has more recently achieved
a wider audience. His last novel, *Timbuktu* (1999), narrated by an abandoned dog, became a best-seller, and the anthology *I Thought My Father Was God, and Other
Stories from NPR's National Story Project* (2001) has been widely praised, understandably so given the American public's hunger for "true stories" from oral histories
to so-called reality television. Auster's fiction, however, deals not with the authentically true but with the patently artificial. *The Book of Illusions* represents a return to
Auster's roots in his particular brand of existential metafiction, but with a difference,
one that the pathos of the earlier canine story helps explain.

The narrator-protagonist of *The Book of Illusions* is David Zimmer, who first appeared in Auster's 1989 novel *Moon Palace*. Then Zimmer was a brilliant graduate
student at Columbia University, as well as (for a time) roommate, helper, foil, and al-
ter ego of that novel's main character, the passive quester Marco Stanley Fogg. Now
Zimmer is a professor of comparative literature at the fictitious Hampton College in
Vermont, whose life changes drastically on June 7, 1985. The deaths of his wife,
Helen, and two young sons, Todd and Marco, in a plane crash leave him devastated,
spending much of his time alone, in an alcoholic haze, some of the time dressed in
his wife's clothes in an effort to bring her back from the dead. Even as he slowly ad-
justs to his new life of loss, he still finds it difficult to "know who I was." At this
point, chance once again intervenes. Watching a television documentary on silent film comedy, Zimmer sees a clip from an old Hector Mann film (an actor Zimmer
had never heard of before) and laughs for the first time since the crash. Suddenly, the
scholarly Zimmer, who had previously held film in low regard, becomes intensely,

Paul Auster's novel Timbuktu *(1999) was a national best-seller, as was* I Thought My Father Was God *(2001), the NPR National Story Project radio anthology, which he edited. He lives in Brooklyn, New York.*

even obsessively interested in Mann's films, which become the focus of Zimmer's recently meaningless life. Zimmer's pursuit of Mann (one of Auster's most fascinating and typically elusive characters) largely focuses on the actor's screen persona: a man "not out of step with the world so much as a victim of circumstances."

Several mysteries complicate and facilitate, as well as focus, Zimmer's research, which he finances with the settlement money from his wife and sons' deaths. Hector Mann arrived late to silent film comedy—in the mid-1920's—and disappeared in 1929 at the height of his career, without a trace, and under mysterious circumstances, after making just twelve movies. The handful of newspaper articles that Zimmer locates offer conflicting accounts of Mann's pre-Hollywood days. Nine of the twelve films only became available after 1981, anonymously sent to nine major film archives in Europe and the United States. In a rented flat in Brooklyn Heights (not far from Auster's own Park Slope brownstone), Zimmer writes *The Silent World of Hector Mann*, a study of the films, not of the absent Mann, who is present only in his art. The book is published by the University of Pennsylvania Press "eleven years ago this past March" (that is, in 1988). Three weeks later, Zimmer, now back in Vermont, receives a letter from Frieda Spelling, who purports to be Mrs. Hector Mann. Intrigued but skeptical, Zimmer replies and soon receives an urgent invitation to visit Mann in New Mexico, to which he once again replies, asking for proof that his correspondent is who she claims to be.

Then there is silence, or nearly so, for in the meantime an old friend, Alex Kronenburg, contacts Zimmer to offer his condolences and invite Zimmer to participate in a Library of World Classics series financed by aluminum-siding tycoon Dexter Feinbaum (yet another of the archly allegorical names in Auster's novel). On the basis of a brief remark Zimmer made while the two were graduate students, Kronenburg asks Zimmer to produce a fresh translation of François-René de Chateaubriand's *Memoirs d'outre-tombe* (1849-1850; *Memoirs*, 1902). Thus Zimmer has a new (Sartrean) project to keep him occupied—or would have, had he not come home one night to find Alma Grund waiting for him. Alma ("the feminine form of *almus*, meaning nourishing, bountiful," as Zimmer pedantically notes) is the daughter of Charlie Grund, Hector Mann's cameraman; she is also Frieda Spelling's emissary, arrived (like some earthly Beatrice) to escort Zimmer to the Manns's ranch in Tierra del Sueno, the land of dreams. Nothing in Auster's deceptively straightforward, paratactic fiction is ever quite so simple, however. The purple stain on one side of Alma's face, for example, links her to Georgina in Nathaniel Hawthorne's short story "The Birthmark" (1843), whose scientist husband Aylmer (not Alma or Almus) ends up killing her in an effort to perfect her.

During the plane ride from Boston to New Mexico, Alma takes over the narration, telling Hector's story from shortly before Hector's disappearance to the present, focusing on the essential points and leaving the rest for Zimmer to read at the ranch in the biography she has written. Hector Mann was born Chaim Mandelbaum in the mid-Atlantic, en route from Europe to Argentina. After arriving in Hollywood in 1925 and beginning his film career, he had an affair with a young journalist, Brigid O'Fallon. (Like Alma, Brigid is a Smith College graduate; like all of Auster's novels, *The Book of Illusions* is a book of coincidences and doubles). Brigid becomes pregnant and Hector plans to marry her, even though he does not love her, but then he meets Dolores Saint John, "the next big thing," the next Gloria Swanson or Norma Talmadge. Several contrived but nonetheless compelling plot complications later, Dolores accidentally shoots and kills Brigid. After disposing of the body, Hector disappears, takes on a new name and identity, Herman Loesser (lesser or loser), and a succession of jobs, spending much of his time educating himself, eventually working in a Portland sporting goods store owned by Brigid's father. When Brigid's sister Nora falls in love with him, Hector takes off, ending up in Chicago, where he becomes Sylvia Meers's partner in live sex acts performed for private audiences.

When Sylvia learns who Herman really is, Hector takes to the road again, stopping in Sandusky, Ohio, which had figured prominently in his fictional screen, or "reel," biography and now figures even more prominently in his "real" one. There he unintentionally, perhaps suicidally, foils a bank robbery and, although nearly fatally wounded himself, saves the life of Frieda Spelling, a bohemian artist who is the daughter of a prominent local family and the only person in the bank who recognizes Hector. Hector and Frieda marry, take to the road, and finally settle in New Mexico, where Hector devotes himself to planting trees. The death of their young son leaves Hector severely depressed—as the deaths of his wife and sons had left Zimmer—and so Frieda convinces Hector to resume filmmaking, which he had abandoned after Brigid's death as an act of penance, in another act of penance for his son's death. Hector invites Charlie Grund to come to the ranch to help him, thus unwittingly saving Charlie from his own alcoholic depression. One of the actresses hired for Hector's films—films that will never be shown outside the ranch and that will, as per his instructions, be destroyed upon his death—is the beautiful Faye, who becomes Charlie's wife and Alma's mother.

Having learned all this, Zimmer arrives at the ranch and meets Hector, but only once and even then just briefly, for Hector dies and Frieda destroys the films. Zimmer has time to see just one of the fourteen films, *The Inner Life of Martin Frost*, the shortest of the eleven longer films. Frieda soon goes well beyond the letter of Hector's request and begins destroying everything connected with the films: scripts, notes, scenery. After Zimmer returns to Vermont, where Alma is to join him, Frieda goes even further. She destroys Alma's biography: notes, hard copy, disks, even the computer. Returning to the ranch and seeing the carnage, Alma angrily pushes Frieda, who falls, hits her head, and dies, leaving a distraught, guilt-ridden Alma to compose (and fax) a long letter to Zimmer before taking her own life. Then, as Nick Carraway says in F. Scott Fitzgerald's *The Great Gatsby* (1925), "the holocaust was complete."

Not quite complete, however, because there is still Zimmer, the one left alive (sort of) to tell the tale, as well as to update it, to fill in the reader, briefly, circumspectly, on what happened between 1988, when he returned from the ranch and 1999, when he writes the narrative now being read: his two heart attacks, his no longer living alone, the revival of interest in Hector Mann's work. In a proleptic move, he also foresees his own death: "if and when this book is published, you can be certain that the man who wrote it is long dead." In other words, Zimmer's story is posthumously published, or seems to be. After all, Chateaubriand had planned to publish his memoirs posthumously, too, until financial matters forced him to change his plans.

Auster's novel is certainly postmodern—entertainingly, intriguingly so. Part of its postmodern feel derives from its densely intertextual style, which allows Auster to allude to, draw on, adapt, and in effect translate or rewrite an entire Library of Great Works: Chateaubriand's *Memoirs*, but also Luis Buñuel's memoir *Mon dernier soupir* (1982; *My Last Sigh*, 1983), Dante's *La divina commedia* (c. 1320; *The Divine Comedy*, 1802, 3 vols.), Hawthorne's "The Birthmark" as well as "Wakefield" (1835), a sardonic rewrite of Washington Irving's "Rip Van Winkle" (1819), Edgar Allen Poe's "The Fall of the House of Usher" (1839), Gabriel García Márquez's *Cien años de solidad* (1967; *One Hundred Years of Solitude*, 1970), and a touch of Frieda and D. H. Lawrence as well as Frida Kahlo and Diego Rivera. Hector Mann, who "popped fully formed" into Auster's head in the early 1990's, recalls silent film comedians Charlie Chaplin, Buster Keaton, and Harold Lloyd, and less obviously the French clown Max Linder and the Marcello Mastroianni of *Divorce—Italian Style* (1961) and the plays and fictions of Samuel Beckett, who similarly drew on silent film comedy. Film is more than a point of reference in *The Book of Illusions*; it is also an important element of style. Summaries and descriptions of Hector's films mimic their different cinematic styles, while other passages parody other film genres or even individual films: film noir, *Casablanca* (1942), art-house cinema. As Zimmer says of *The Inner Life of Martin Frost*, the reader may say of *The Book of Illusions:* "The story has shifted into another register."

Part of the genius of this novel derives from Auster's ability to be at once meditative, metaphysical, metafictional, and emotionally engaging as he explores the mystery of identity while creating "the music of chance." As such, *The Book of Illusions* is the latest variation on an autobiographical theme. While at summer camp, the fourteen-year-old Auster saw the boy next to him struck and killed by lightning. This "foundational event . . . gave me a deep sense of the arbitrariness and utter fragility of life, how vulnerable we are to unforeseen events." Thus the emphasis on plot, chance, coincidence, and improvisation, as well as redemption and rebirth, in his work, and more recently (and in *The Book of Illusions*, most compellingly) of death. If on one hand *The Book of Illusions* is a work in which the *mise-en-abime* meets the garden of forking paths while lost in fiction's funhouse, it is also a novel about the pain of loss and about uncertainty in all its forms. Not despite its permutating possibilities but because of them, the Escher-like *Book of Illusions* is Paul Auster's most human, most important, and most affecting novel.

Robert A. Morace

Sources for Further Study

The Atlantic Monthly 290 (September, 2002): 154.

Booklist 98 (January 1-January 15, 2002): 1644.

Esquire 138 (September, 2002): 78.

Library Journal 127 (August, 2002): 138.

Los Angeles Times Book Review, September 8, 2002, p. 3.

The New York Times, October 14, 2002, p. E1.

The New York Times Book Review 107 (September 1, 2002): 6.

The New Yorker 78 (September 23, 2002): 92.

Publishers Weekly 249 (August 26, 2002): 42.

USA Today, September 17, 2002, p. D5.

The Washington Post Book World, September 8, 2002, p. 10.

A BRAIN FOR ALL SEASONS
Human Evolution and Abrupt Climate Change

Author: William H. Calvin (1939-   )
Publisher: University of Chicago Press (Chicago). Illustrated. 341 pp. $25.00
Type of work: Anthropology, archaeology, environment, natural history, and science
Time: Five or six million years ago to the present

∾

Calvin explores the relationship between abrupt climate change and the evolution of the human brain, especially its capacity for adaptation. The mechanism of climate change is thoroughly discussed

∾

This fascinating work is sprinkled with tidbits from archaeology and seasoned with quotations from sources as varied as novelist Mark Twain and physicist Werner Heisenberg. While William H. Calvin's stated agenda is to explain his theory that abrupt climate change influenced the development of the human brain, he focuses much more on explaining the mechanisms that effect climate change in the past and in the present. This is a bit of a disappointment, as a book with such a tantalizing premise, which actually does provide strong factual support for his ideas and brings the discussion within reach of most interested readers, abandons the issue of brain development altogether in its final chapters. The final fourteen chapters of the book, nearly one third of the text, are concerned almost exclusively with explaining abrupt climate change, its possible effects, and what can be done to prevent it. The book jacket reveals that this final third of the book is based on an article he wrote for *The Atlantic Monthly* entitled "The Great Climate Flip-Flop."

The book is divided into thirty-five chapters, and each chapter heading is presented as an e-mail addressed to the "Human Evolution E-Seminar" from Calvin. The chapters also follow an overflight of the globe, and Calvin gives his location in degrees longitude and latitude. In his "Afterthoughts" section, however, Calvin admits that he has never actually given any e-seminars, let alone this one, and that "the present framework is an amalgamation of various European and African trips, meetings, and over-the-pole flights between 1999 and 2001, rearranged to suit thematic development." Whether or not he decided on the e-seminar as an attractive gimmick for modern audiences, it does not intrude much on the reading experience and can be ignored rather easily. Calvin's style is smooth, chatty, and filled with anecdotes. Any reader who is interested in this subject will find his ideas and the way he brings the reader to them easy to comprehend but hardly simple-minded. Calvin is serious about his subject and seeks information from experts in the fields of paleoarchaeology and climatology, which he amply shares with the reader. His sincerity comes through especially in his explanations of the climate phenomena that humans depend upon and his pleas to pay attention while it may still be possible to do something to stabilize the current favorable climate.

    In his "Preamble," Calvin sets out his basic theory. The existence of the ice ages of the past has long been known; however, it has only recently been discovered that the planet's climate has experienced not only gradual changes, but also sudden and drastic "flip-flops" every few thousand years.

    ∼

William H. Calvin teaches at the University of Washington School of Medicine in Seattle, where he is an affiliate professor of psychiatry and behavioral sciences. He has authored or coauthored ten other books on the brain and how it thinks.

    ∼

The examination of ice cores and cores from ocean floors and undisturbed ancient lake beds reveal these worldwide climate changes. The current warm period, during which humankind invented agriculture and built civilizations dependent on its success, has lasted for an unprecedented length of time. Why this uninterrupted good time exists is unknown. Human ancestors were subject to climate changes that caused populations to crash and ecosystems to collapse. Within a single generation, the old ways of sustaining life disappeared and only those who were able to take advantage of the new situations that the climate change brought survived to continue the species.

    The first chapter begins the "journey" of this book at Charles Darwin's country home in Downe, England. Calvin states that most people do not understand the principles of evolution that Darwin wrote about and enumerates five important elements that speed up evolution: speciation; sex (or mating); populations separated into islands; "empty niches" in which competition is absent; and climate fluctuations. Like a committee, Calvin says, these five elements work together to force change.

    The second chapter takes Calvin to France and to an examination of the fossil record. Fossil evidence shows that there was not a single hominid species that led directly from apelike ancestors to *Homo sapiens*, or modern humans. Instead, several different species arose, just as the gorillas, orangutans, and chimpanzees are different branches arising from that more distant ancestor. Once it was thought that Neanderthals were part of the human line, but now it appears that both it and *Homo erectus* were different evolutionary experiments that died out, leaving the ancestors of *Homo sapiens* as the only hominid species to continue to the present day. While researchers are limited in their ability to determine exactly how and why hominid populations crashed, climate change and its effects on local ecologies were crucial.

    The ice ages are generally discussed as though their colder temperatures were their most important factor, but Calvin writes that temperatures worldwide during the ice ages were really only a little cooler than the ages that preceded them. What mattered more was dryness and drought. When the climate changes from wet and warm to cold and dry, plant life struggles to survive. Lightning sparks and high winds contribute to vast fires that consume large expanses of woodlands—and incidentally, woodlands were where humans' apelike ancestors made their homes. This clearing of woodlands created an opportunity for grasses to spread and, following that, grazing herds to expand. What was a "bust" cycle for some species became a "boom" time for others.

Those who lived in the forests and ate the plants of the forests could only survive at a fraction of the previous population size, with no time to shift gradually to other food sources.

In the sixth chapter, "Layover Limbo," whose subject is "IQ and evolution's package deals," Calvin shows that when the brain increases in size, it does not do so "bump by bump." Rather, an increase in size occurs across the entire brain, and one benefit likely comes along with a host of others. Calvin compares this to the package deal one gets when buying an automobile: The leather seats one wants require also taking power windows and a sunroof, even if they were not specifically desired. However, those unrequested extras may turn out to be useful at a later point in time.

Calvin discusses the differences between the skulls of *Australopithecus*, a vegetarian like the gorillas, and human ancestors. Grooves in the skull of *Australopithecus* show the presence of muscles to support the large teeth and chewing action needed to consume quantities of vegetable matter, while the absence of such grooves and presence of smaller teeth indicate that human ancestors were eating something else. Combining these physical differences with habitat conditions of grassland expansion, it can safely be assumed that their diet had shifted to the consumption of meat.

Eating meat was probably not a total innovation to these hominids. Animal protein is an important source of nutrients and fat an important source of energy. Chimpanzees, humans' closest primate relatives, are opportunistic carnivores, meaning that they will consume small, helpless creatures that they come upon as they forage and will even band together at times to kill small creatures to eat. An interesting sideline of this practice is that it leads to chimpanzees sharing for mutual benefits beyond the food consumption of the moment. Whether they do this in the hope of sharing in another chimp's future catch or to influence a sought-after mate, even the existence of "free-loaders" who never reciprocate does not cause sharers to cease this behavior. Early hominids had to learn to work together to capture larger animals and to share the catch that no one individual could consume before the meat spoiled. Those who had meat possibly shared with others who did not participate in the hunt to establish reciprocity in the future. Calvin quotes Frans de Waal, from his book, *Good Natured: The Origins of Right and Wrong* (1996), describing the irony that "human morality is steeped in animal blood":

> When we give money to begging strangers, ship food to starving people, or vote for measures that benefit the poor, we follow impulses shaped since the time our ancestors began to cluster around meat possessors. . . . Given the circle's proposed origin, it is profoundly ironic that its expansion should culminate in a plea for vegetarianism.

Calvin travels down through Africa and examines the sites of ancient lakes and the presence of a common tool of *Homo erectus*, the hand axe. Its use is not completely understood. These stone tools, of a particular, symmetric, leaflike shape that is believed difficult to make, are not particularly suited as any sort of hand tool, being sharpened not only on the cutting edge, but also on the edge "the hand has to wrap around." Many simpler tools would suffice for the uses that have been attributed to it. Calvin considers the hand axe and the congregation of game at shrinking water holes and comes up with a viable explanation, which also explains the presence of so many of these tools in the mud of ancient lake shores. The tools turn out to be an efficient way of bringing down large animals that have come to drink in herds. The momentum of the thrown stone, transferred to the animal, combined with the animal's "pain flexion," can defeat its ability to keep itself upright. The panic of the herd under attack could prevent the animal from getting back on its feet in time to escape the hunters.

The Little Ice Age, which occurred between the early Renaissance and the middle of the nineteenth century, gave rise to weather extremes that ruined harvests and caused famines. Although the average temperature changes were small, they caused colder winters and hotter summers. The famines might even have caused witch hunts, as people tried to understand why they were having trouble making a living as their parents had and looked for someone to blame. Perhaps it was easier to see witches riding the winds with evil intentions than to accept that the impersonal winds were the cause of the droughts that led to starvation.

The mechanism of climate and how it can go wrong is a complex subject. Painstakingly, with numerous charts, graphs, and even aerial photographs, Calvin explains the currents that carry warm water north from the tropics and cold water south in the Atlantic Ocean. This information helps to understand why Europe has such a mild climate even though it is farther north than regions in the United States that suffer through more severe weather. He delineates the physics of upwelling warmer waters and of winds evaporating water from top ocean layers until the salt left behind causes the colder waters to sink, forming a conveyor belt that sustains the current climate. The danger to this system posed by freshwater floods from melting glaciers, caused by global warming, is made clear through Calvin's patient explanations of how global warming can lead to an ice age.

Going further, Calvin poses scenarios to describe the results of a global climate "flip-flop." These possibilities, depending on whether humans do nothing to halt the change or try some of the methods he suggests, range from catastrophic population collapse and human misery to an undertaking that would cost, comparably, less than the construction of a medieval cathedral did in its time. Calvin's assertion that this climate change is inevitable but also preventable raises this book far above the usual warnings of doomsayers who offer no practical solution to a problem once they have delineated it.

Patricia Masserman

Sources for Further Study

Books and Culture 8 (May, 2002): 41.
Choice 40 (October, 2002): 319.
Discover 23 (June, 2002): 78.
Scientific American 287 (July, 2002): 91.
The Seattle Times, May 17, 2002, p. H25.

BREAKING THE SLUMP
Baseball in the Depression Era

Author: Charles C. Alexander (1935-   )
Publisher: Columbia University Press (New York). 352
   pp. $29.95
Type of work: History
Time: 1930-1941
Locale: The United States

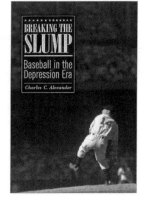

~

A history of baseball in the period when it truly was "the nation's pastime"

~

Principal personages:
> GEORGE HERMAN "BABE" RUTH, JR. (1895-1948), legendary hitter for
> the New York Yankees
> ROGERS "RAJAH" HORNSBY (1896-1963), legendary hitter and manager
> of the Chicago Cubs, St. Louis Cardinals, and St. Louis Browns in the
> 1930's, whose career was dogged by accusations of gambling
> LOU GEHRIG (1903-1941), powerhouse teammate of Ruth who held the
> record for most consecutive games played until 1995; retired due to
> amyotrophic lateral sclerosis, now known as Lou Gehrig's disease, in
> 1939
> HANK GREENBERG (1911-1986), the first Jewish baseball star
> JAY "DIZZY" DEAN (1910-1974), legendary pitcher for the St. Louis
> Cardinals
> TED WILLIAMS (1918-2002), record-holding hitter for the Boston Red
> Sox
> JOE DIMAGGIO (1914-1999), hitter who led the New York Yankees to
> four consecutive World Series titles from 1936-1939

   Professional baseball began in the 1860's as a product of the vogue for "sporting culture" that took many forms in mid-nineteenth century America, ranging from yachting and other sports reserved for the wealthy to more democratic outlets such as hunting and shooting clubs, boxing, and baseball. These were principally male activities that emphasized fellowship and camaraderie. They were largely inspired by British models, but a strong nationalistic spirit pervaded American sporting culture—hence, in the case of baseball, the myth that the game was a pristinely American invention, created by Abner Doubleday in 1839 in Cooperstown, New York.

   In fact, various ball games had been common in America since the colonial era, drawing on British games such as rounders and also no doubt absorbing influences from Native American ball games. In the 1850's, the amateur Knickerbocker Base

Ball club in New York—founded in the previous decade—popularized the variant of baseball that led to the modern game, with foul lines, three outs per inning (as opposed to one per inning in the "Massachusetts" game), and nine innings altogether. From those humble beginnings, baseball has evolved to the multibillion-dollar industry that delights and dismays fans in the early twenty-first century, with major league franchises in thirty cities and a vast and ever-growing archive of history and lore, for no other sport matches the historical self-consciousness of baseball.

The period covered in Charles Alexander's *Breaking the Slump: Baseball in the Depression Era*, is exactly midway between the beginnings of professional baseball and its current incarnation. The formative years of the game had been turbulent in every way, with shifting franchises, rule changes, and financial instability. However, after 1903, when

Charles C. Alexander is Distinguished Professor of History at Ohio University. He is the author of the biographies Ty Cobb *(1984),* John McGraw *(1988), and* Rogers Hornsby *(1995) and of* Our Game: An American Baseball History *(1991).*

an agreement was reached between the warring National League (established in 1876) and American League (the upstart founded in 1901 by crusader Ban Johnson, who was determined to eliminate violence and routine profanity, making the game more appealing to the general public and, not least, to women), with the annual World Series between the champions of the two leagues marking the culmination of the season, baseball enjoyed five decades of exceptional stability. Not until 1953, when the Boston National League franchise moved to Milwaukee, did any of the sixteen teams active in 1903 shift location, nor were there any fundamental rule changes.

Baseball's traditional claim to be known as "the national pastime" sounds merely quaint in the twenty-first century, but as Alexander observes, there was a time when this slogan was the simple truth. From the mid-nineteenth century until well into the twentieth, no other game was so widely played at so many levels, from sandlots and cow pastures to college diamonds. In 1930, the first year of Alexander's chronicle, professional sports in general were in their infancy; not for decades would professional football and basketball begin to rival baseball's appeal, competing with golf and tennis and other sports in the extraordinary surge of spectatorship fueled by television.

In tracing the fortunes of baseball from 1930 to 1941, *Breaking the Slump* shows how the game reflected the story of the nation—from the depths of the Depression through a painfully slow recovery to the onset of a world war—while at the same time looking at baseball during this period for its own sake. Alexander is well equipped to do both. A historian who has published books on the Ku Klux Klan, Project Mercury, and American nationalism, among other subjects, he is best known for his books on baseball, including superb biographies of John McGraw, Ty Cobb, and Rogers Hornsby and a one-volume history, *Our Game* (1991).

For the most part, Alexander tells his story in straight chronological fashion, season by season, with accounts of what happened in each league and in the World Series, intermixed with context-setting reports on events in the larger world. After a quick survey of the state of the game and the nation at the end of the 1920's, he begins with 1930, "The Last Fat Year," when major league baseball enjoyed record attendance totals that would not be repeated for a decade. Though baseball fared well, the impact of the 1929 stock market collapse was already being felt, and a number of baseball players were among those who saw their life savings lost in bank failures. Still, those who were able to make a living as ballplayers were among the fortunate, and as the Depression settled in, it lent an extra edge of ferocious competition as players fought not just to stay in the game but to hold a good job at a time when jobs of any description were increasingly scarce. The result, Alexander suggests, was a certain intensity that lifted the quality of play.

An occasional dose of baseball history should be required reading for historians who seek to turn their discipline into a science—and for all readers, historians or not, who are tempted to forget about the role of the unpredictable, the idiosyncratic, the contingent, and the individual in history. The 1930 season is a case in point. For reasons never satisfactorily explained (though theories abound), that year produced an offensive explosion somewhat comparable to the end of the dead-ball era in 1920 (when, among other things, a livelier ball contributed to a sharp increase in run production) and to the power boom of the late 1990's. *Breaking the Slump* is full of such exemplary cases, though not many are as dramatic as the 1930 explosion.

With the 1931 season, major league baseball began to feel the effects of the Depression with a vengeance. In seasons to come, many players had to accept salary cuts even when their performance was very good. Many were simply glad that they were still employed. Yet even when management lacked the excuse of economic necessity, players could not feel secure. In this era, long before the onset of free agency, players were essentially without recourse; power resided in the hands of the owners.

In some respects, however, economic hard times accelerated change. At the beginning of the 1930's, several minor league teams installed lights and began to play some games at night. Major league franchises were strongly resistant, but declining gate revenues for traditional day games (when many of those people who could afford a ticket were at work) eventually prompted a change, and by 1939 a number of teams were introducing night games for the first time. That was also the year of the first televised game, a Brooklyn-Cincinnati doubleheader on August 26, seen only by a tiny number. Radio coverage of major league baseball had continued to expand, bringing the game to the majority of fans, who had few opportunities to see a game in person. Indeed, it was the ambience of baseball on the radio, perhaps more than any other single factor, that created the lifelong attachment the game enjoyed during its heyday.

Partway through the book, Alexander interrupts his chronological narrative for two thematic chapters. In "Baseball Lives," he offers an overview of the players of the era: the backgrounds (regional, ethnic, and otherwise) from which they were most likely to come, their size, their education (or lack of same), the benefits they enjoyed and the perils and temptations to which they were prone, and more. Included here is an account of the ethnic stereotyping that accompanied the rise of Italian American players. In the accompanying chapter, "Shadowball," Alexander surveys the ups and downs of the Negro leagues in the 1930's, making good use of the growing scholarship on black baseball.

Any interesting history of baseball is to a considerable extent an account of great players and great teams, and Alexander does not disappoint in this respect. *Breaking the Slump* is full of stories of outstanding achievement, not to mention the controversies and oddities, the quirky characters and the litany of names that any fan loves to recite: Hack Wilson and Goose Goslin, Pepper Martin and Frenchy Bordogaray, Dizzy Dean and Dazzy Vance, Satchel Paige and Cool Papa Bell.

Whether beguiled or disgusted by the recent dominance of George Steinbrenner's Yankees after a long spell of mediocrity, readers will find that *Breaking the Slump* offers a reminder of the least remembered of the great Yankee dynasties: the post-Ruth teams that won the World Series four consecutive times from 1936 through 1939—and won again in 1941. (When they won the series in 1939, the Yankees had been victorious in twenty-eight of their previous thirty-one World Series games.) Like the Yankees of recent vintage, this was a team that relentlessly reinvented itself, adding outstanding rookies and key trade acquisitions to a core of veterans. When the indomitable Lou Gehrig was finally slowed by the illness that would soon kill him, there was a young outfielder the Yankees had purchased several years earlier from the minor league San Francisco Seals, Joe DiMaggio, just coming into his prime.

The distance between the Barry Bonds era and the appearance of DiMaggio on the cover of *Time* magazine in 1936 (the first time a ballplayer was so honored) is at least as great as that between DiMaggio's Yankees and the barnstorming Cincinnati Red Stockings of 1869, the first great professional team. Baseball in the early twenty-first century is not by any stretch of the imagination the nation's pastime, and yet it is recognizably the same game. How Bonds, Sammy Sosa, Randy Johnson, and their peers will look in the eyes of a historian seventy or eighty years in the future can only be guessed. Will such a historian be able to count on a living knowledge of the game, or—as seems more likely—will this require the reconstruction of a lost world?

John Wilson

Sources for Further Study

Booklist 98 (March 15, 2002): 1202.
Choice 40 (December, 2002): 666.
Library Journal 127 (March 15, 2002): 86.
Los Angeles Times Book Review, May 5, 2002, p. 7.

BRIGHT EARTH
Art and the Invention of Color

Author: Philip Ball (1962-   )
Publisher: Farrar, Straus and Giroux (New York). 384
  pp. $30.00
Type of work: Fine arts, history of science, and science

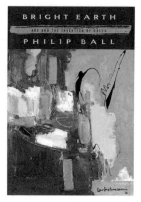

∽

*An examination of the history of art and the history of
science as they have overlapped in the chemical and al-
chemical preparation of artists' pigments and dyes*

∽

In *Life's Matrix: A Biography of Water* (2000), poly-
math Philip Ball gave himself no less challenging a task
than to explain the physics, chemistry, mythology, sociology, psychology, and politics of water from the beginning of time to the present. His goal for his latest book,
Bright Earth: Art and the Invention of Color, is scarcely less ambitious: to trace the
history of Western art from cave painting to the ancient Greeks to the artists working
with computers at the turn of the twenty-first century, and to do it through the lens of
chemistry. Ball looks at color in a painting as a substance that must be produced and
manipulated and shows how many of the choices made by painters through history
were guided not only by aesthetics but by what materials were available at a given
time. Trained in chemistry and physics, Ball is also passionate about art, announcing
early on, "I relish paint and pigment as materials, with appearances, smells, textures,
and names that entice and intoxicate." While the focus of the book is on the chemistry
of color, Ball also delves into "its historical traditions, its psychology, its prejudices,
its religiosity and mysticism."

The word "invention" in the title is not casually chosen. Ball shows how the naming of colors—even the understanding of what is meant by color—is neither universal nor fixed. Before the appearance in common consciousness of the color spectrum, cultures were just as likely to distinguish colors by their intensity, or brightness
or lightness, as they were to choose hue as the primary feature, and many different
systems still exist for naming and distinguishing colors. The ancient Greeks certainly lived in the same world of color that readers of Ball's book inhabit, yet they
mention only four colors in descriptions of their painting: black, white, red, and yellow. The medieval word *sinople* was used to refer to red or to green, with no apparent distinction. Latin has no word for gray. Certain Asian languages do not distinguish between blue and green. On one level, then, the word "invention" refers to
the fact that notion of color itself is a social construct. At what point does red become
orange become yellow? The answer has been invented differently for different cultures.

The other level on which "invention" functions is at the heart of the book. Art and its demands for new pigments and dyes spurred developments in alchemy and chemistry, just as the invention of new pigments and other materials gave rise to innovation in art. The shifting territory between art and science, between creation and invention, is the realm Ball explores in *Bright Earth*. Admirers of Ball's previous work will recognize the theme underlying this volume. His fascination with the history of science, with the story of how certain men of science (and they were mostly men) set about to look for one thing and found another, and with how seemingly small incremental steps have led to sudden leaps, forms

~

Philip Ball, a writer and consulting editor for the British scientific journal Nature, *holds degrees in chemistry and physics. He is the author of five previous books about science for general readers, including* The Self-Made Tapestry: Pattern Formation in Nature *(1998),* Designing the Molecular World: Chemistry at the Frontier *(1994), and* Life's Matrix: A Biography of Water *(2000).*

~

a thread that also runs through *Designing the Molecular World: Chemistry at the Frontier* (1994) and *Life's Matrix*. The idea that art and science inform each other is another repeated theme in Ball's work, and it is the central theme of this book.

Assuming a reader who knows something of art history but little about science, Ball begins his book with a science lesson. The first two chapters explore the changing notions of color and describe from the viewpoint of physics what scientists past and present have understood color to be. He explains the concepts of subtractive mixing (by which red and yellow pigment can combine to form orange) and additive mixing (by which red, blue, and green light can combine to form white light), reviews the rods and cones of the human eye, and wonders where brown and pink, which do not appear on the spectrum, originate. The book's sixty-six color plates and several black-and-white diagrams illustrate the concepts that words alone cannot convey.

With the third chapter, Ball begins a chronological survey of Western art history, beginning with the ancient world. As he moves forward in time, he describes what is known about the materials used in each region and age and how the availability of different materials informed the use of color. The Roman Empire, for example, reserved robes of rich purple for the emperor and others of high rank because purple was difficult and expensive to produce. Purple came to represent royalty because of its rarity, not because of more ethereal associations. Similarly, medieval religious paintings of the Virgin Mary are striking for their conventional use of rich blue for the Virgin's robes. This is not, as might be assumed, because of any symbolic association of blue with purity or the heavens. Rather, blue was chosen because it was the most expensive pigment, and nothing less would have been suitable for the mother of God. The cost of the pigment also explains the shimmering gold haloes that surround the heads of holy figures in these paintings; presumably, if orange or violet had been more costly to produce, saints would have been crowned with haloes of those hues. In fact, there is little pure orange or violet in painting before the nineteenth century, because no one knew how to make it.

Until the nineteenth century, when elements and molecules began to reveal their secrets, pigments and dyes were made exclusively from animal, mineral, and vegetable ingredients. In the 1850's, however, while attempting to make a synthetic form of quinine to treat malaria, young William Henry Perkin accidentally formed a synthetic dye from an aniline compound. This section of the book shows Ball at his best and most enthusiastic, eagerly telling the tale of "how the eighteen-year-old young man launched the chemicals industry, experimenting at home like a teenager in his bedroom." Perkin's work led to a commercially successful mauve dye that not only revolutionized European fashion, but also showed that increasing knowledge of the physical properties of materials could enable scientists to predict the color of new compounds. Several large multinational chemical companies, including Bayer and BASF, got their start in the quest for synthetic dyes.

Another important way that art has changed over the centuries is that artists have become less intimately acquainted with their materials. Medieval and Renaissance painters made their own paints or supervised their making. Pigments were purchased in solid form and ground by hand into fine particles, which were then mixed with binder into the desired consistency. This laborious task, vividly brought to life for the generalist reader by Tracy Chevalier's novel *Girl with a Pearl Earring* (1999), gave the careful artist a great deal of quality control, assuming the sources for the raw materials were reliable. The availability of ready-made paints, Ball shows, gave the artist both more freedom and less control. Landscape painting in the nineteenth century, for example, evolved not only because the Romantics offered new ways to think about the world, but also because the invention of metal tubes made it possible for the first time to carry paints outdoors for hours at a time without their drying out. Painters in the twentieth century could purchase literally hundreds of organic and synthetic colors ready for use, but artists no longer had to know much about their composition. Vincent van Gogh (1853-1890) was among those who eagerly used every new paint that caught his eye, sometimes before they had been tested against time. His 1889 painting *Sunflowers*, Ball explains, is brownish and "a drab, lackluster piece, uncharacteristic of the artist" not because that is what van Gogh envisioned or created, but because "the pigment (chrome yellow) has degraded over time, and we are left with a shadow of the true painting."

In addition to his unhesitating appreciation for beautiful art, another hallmark of Ball's writing is his delight in the etymologies of everyday words. In *Bright Earth*, he explains the derivation of common color names and other terms. For example, his analysis of the Renaissance studio system of masters and apprentices reveals that the term "masterpiece" originally referred to the artwork submitted to the guild by an apprentice who felt ready to become a master—therefore, not an artist's greatest work, but that artist's first competent production. The term "pink" originally designated any pigment made up of an organic colorant with an inorganic base; most of the early pinks were yellow in color, but there were also pinks of green and brown and, eventually, rose. It was not until the nineteenth century that "pink" was used to name the color made by combining red and white. The volume is liberally sprinkled with anecdotes like these, unveiling the surprising histories of "carmine" (named for the insect from which it was made), "miniature" (named for the red pigment minium, which was often used in small paintings), and "scarlet" (at first the name for a particular type of woven cloth, which over time came to be frequently dyed a rich red).

In the final chapters, Ball examines art in the late twentieth century and peers into the future of electronic art. After going back in time to give a brief history of photography, he explains the difficulties of reproducing art in prints, writing straightforwardly of the limitations of his own book's color plates. Even computers, which theoretically can display thousands of colors, have difficulty conveying the brightness of certain colors (particularly rich greens) because of the limitations physics places on the materials from which monitors are made. Ball concludes that there may never be a perfect way to reproduce color, and that "It is by no means obvious at this point that the new technologies will enhance the color range of on-screen images—possibly quite the opposite." Furthermore, while artists who create their work on computers may be exhilarated with the range of colors available to them on-screen, the capabilities of printers continue to lag far behind.

The questions Ball raises in this study are fascinating, and even as he answers them his study raises a host of new questions. What might the same approach yield if applied to the making of stained glass, a completely different way of producing and combining color? What might the fields of psychology or cognitive science add to the discussion of how color is perceived and valued? Do academic art historians have the same view of the development of art as Ball? What will the future bring? The mark of a good book is just this: It leaves the reader satisfied, yet curious and hungry for more.

Cynthia A. Bily

Sources for Further Study

Booklist 98 (January 1, 2002): 788.
Contemporary Review 280 (March, 2002): 191.
Kirkus Reviews 69 (December 1, 2001): 1655.
New Scientist 172 (November 24, 2001): 44.
Publishers Weekly 248 (November 26, 2001): 46.
Science 295 (March 8, 2002): 1841.
Scientific American 286 (March, 2002): 98.
Time International 159 (January 28, 2002): 54.

BROWN
The Last Discovery of America

Author: Richard Rodriguez (1944-   )
Publisher: Viking (New York). 256 pp. $24.95
Type of work: Current affairs, history, and sociology
Locale: The United States

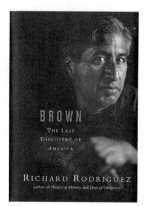

∼

*Lyrically exploring the evidence for his claim that the
United States is "browning," the cultural critic Richard
Rodriguez subverts conventional ethnic and racial classifications by offering an American Dream that emphasizes a
blurring of boundaries and the inclusiveness that may result*

∼

Forecasting a revolution of consciousness that would sweep through the United
States, Charles Reich's *The Greening of America* (1970) soared to best-seller status.
Consciousness III, as Reich called it, promised a rediscovery of selfhood in which the
preciousness of all human life would be affirmed. Within a few months, despite its
claim that this "greening" was inevitable, Reich's book had come and gone.

Thirty years later, Richard Rodriguez announced the "browning" of America. Although *Brown*'s immediate impact did not match *The Greening of America*, Rodriguez's book is likely to have greater validity in the long run. It is doubtful that Rodriguez has identified "the last discovery of America," as his book's inflated subtitle
claims, but he musters considerable evidence to support his thesis that brown—not
the red, white, and blue of the "Stars and Stripes"—is the quintessential American
color.

When Rodriguez says that "the future is brown," his thesis is complex, because he
thinks of brown "not in the sense of pigment, necessarily," but as a color that entails
the mixing of earthy experience. Although Rodriguez hopes that "brown may be as
refreshing as green," that vision has to reckon with the fact that, historically, the dominant American color has been white. Contradicting the "innocence" often associated
with that complexion, white ensures that Americans are not color-blind but color-
conscious. Much of that awareness has manifested itself in black and white, as the African American sociologist W. E. B. Du Bois discerned in *The Souls of Black Folk*
(1903) when he argued that the "color line" would be the twentieth century's decisive
problem. Dubious that America could solve it, Du Bois became an expatriate, leaving
his native United States for Africa in the early 1960's.

Not long before Du Bois's departure, Rodriguez's parents emigrated from their native Mexico to California, where Richard, the third of their four children, was born
in San Francisco and raised in Sacramento. Although American census classifica-

tions have dubbed him "Hispanic," a category he attacks, Rodriguez sometimes underscores the complexity of American identity by contending that he is "Irish," which is his way of paying respect to the formative influence of Irish nuns who taught him English. In its "brown" form, English becomes a language best called "American," and it is to the multiple expressions of that tongue that Rodriguez owes much of his hard-earned optimism.

Hunger of Memory: The Education of Richard Rodriguez (1982) and *Days of Obligation: An Argument with My Mexican Father* (1992) were the first two installments of "a trilogy on American public life and my private life" that *Brown* completes. Emphasizing that Benjamin Franklin is one of Rodriguez's heroes, the latter book shows how profoundly its author has continued to believe in the American Dream of opportunity, mobility, new beginnings, and self-invention. His reasons for doing so include the fact that he has never forgotten the true words that his father impressed upon him. As they polished the secondhand blue DeSoto that was the family car in the 1950's, Rodriguez's father would tell him: "Life is hard, boy, even harder than you think."

Richard Rodriguez is an editor at the Pacific News Service in San Francisco, as well as a contributing editor to Harper's *and the Sunday "Opinion" section of the* Los Angeles Times. *He also appears on* The News Hour with Jim Lehrer *on* PBS. *His books include* Hunger of Memory: The Education of Richard Rodriguez *(1982) and* Days of Obligation: An Argument with My Mexican Father *(1992).*

Ironies, those gaps between expectation and reality that dwell in shortfalls between what Americans preach and practice, are part of what makes life hard in the United States. Rodriguez describes, for example, how it was during the first term (1969-1973) of Richard Nixon's presidency that "I became brown. A government document of dulling prose, Statistical Directive 15, would redefine America as an idea in five colors: White. Black. Yellow. Red. Brown." As artificial as it was racial, as constructed as it was convenient for those who wanted American "minorities" for one reason or another, those color lines tagged Rodriguez not only "brown" but also "Hispanic." That category, Rodriguez shows, is a misguided invention, for only in America are "Hispanics" to be found. They have no reality anywhere else. In Rodriguez's case, however, being a "minority" and eventually "Hispanic" had advantages. These classifications put him on affirmative action's fast track to opportunity. That track, however, did not mean full acceptance and inclusion in America, because white dominance left him tainted "brown." As long as such schemes and classifications persist, Rodriguez contends, American life will be less than it can and ought to be.

Rodriguez does not find "race" to be "such a terrible word for me." Although he acknowledges it to be a "tragic noun" whose implications of superiority and inferiority bear responsibility for immeasurable pain and suffering, Rodriguez stresses that racial differences have been attractions, too. "The word race," he writes, "encourages me to remember the influence of eroticism on history. For that is what race memorializes. Within any discussion of race, there lurks the possibility of romance." Race divides and separates, but in Rodriguez's American vision, it lures and connects as well.

When he says that race memorializes eroticism and romance, Rodriguez suggests that racial differences will end up "brown." Again, autobiography informs his cultural analysis. "I do not have a race," Rodriguez asserts. Already racially mixed, he relishes the mixture and thus insists that so much more than race looms large. Race is real only because social reality has been constructed in its terms. Slowly but surely, American life reveals the absurdity of racial categories. Rodriguez wants to hasten that process: "I write about race in America," he says, "in hopes of undermining the notion of race in America."

While ironies make life hard in the United States, *Brown* argues that they can also be sources of hope to support an American Dream of inclusiveness that blurs the nation's multifaceted lines of ethnicity and color. Standing at the heart of this vision is Rodriguez's conviction that "America is browning." When Rodriguez changes "brown"—the noun or adjective—into the verb-form "browning," it becomes clear that he thinks an unavoidable process is under way. Increasingly, Americans are unable to define—simply, clearly, innocently—where they come from, no matter how detailed their family trees may be. As it creates, continues, and changes American identity, a "browning" process has been taking place for a long time in the history of the United States. Often without awareness, let alone acknowledgment, Americans are becoming more and more "brown." Not fully under American control, this process continues even—often especially—when Americans oppose it. As Rodriguez explores and celebrates the power of "browning," he brings the hidden into view. Rejecting easy optimism about how this process is working, *Brown* sets before Americans the cunning of a history that is destined to make the nation even more "American" than its color-lined consciousness might imagine.

Rodriguez makes his case by "looking for a brown history of America." He finds it by turning to widespread episodes and repeated encounters that "lead off the page" of conventional narratives. In the mid-nineteenth century, for example, the young American historian Francis Parkman took a 1,700-mile trip to explore the Oregon trail. Boarding a riverboat in St. Louis, Parkman noted the diversity of its passengers, but he did not ponder the questions that drew Rodriguez's attention: So very different in terms of what Rodriguez calls the "three isolations" of class, ethnicity, and race, what were those people doing in St. Louis? Where were they going, individually and collectively, literally and figuratively, on that riverboat? Rodriguez suggests that the unwritten history of America, which produces the children that change the nation's face, shows that those folks, in one way or another, were "browning."

Americans, Rodriguez thinks, do not talk about what is "off the page," or at least not enough for their own good. Whatever American identity has been, he contends that it has been mixed, blended, confused, impure. Conflict and resolution drive this tension-filled process. Rodriguez feels it when he hears his name: "I am Richard Rodriguez," he writes. "My baptismal name and my surname marry England and Spain, Renaissance rivals." He sees the same tension when contemplating his mirrored face, a brown blend of south-of-the-border Indian and Conquistador, which like so many akin to it has become part of an American blurring that makes greater inclusivity more unavoidable and therefore more probable.

Testifying on behalf of the latter points, Rodriguez states that the 38 Geary Municipal bus line in San Francisco transports some 47,000 people on a typical weekday. The 38 Geary, he points out, is not a Missouri riverboat, but the comparison is nonetheless valid. The persons traveling on such vessels support Rodriguez's point that people in the United States, with all of their discordant and even dangerous differences, are thrown and brought together so that ethnic, racial, national, religious, and sexual borders do not and cannot hold. Sometimes kicking and screaming, but often erotically and lovingly, Americans are making the nation's motto, *E Pluribus Unum* ("Out of Many, One"), true and good.

Americans may fail to see the beauty and the passion of "browning" because of their individualism. Overlooking how profoundly, how sensuously, "the 'we' is a precondition for saying 'I,'" Americans underplay the very impurity that enriches both the American "I" and "we," a theme that Rodriguez calls his most important. Thus, making the identification his "mestizo boast," Rodriguez gladly describes himself as "a queer Catholic Indian Spaniard at home in a temperate Chinese city in a fading blond state in a post-Protestant nation." Rodriguez makes no mistake in linking the personal to the public and political. The roots of individual American identities, often oppressed and oppressing, are increasingly snarled, entangled, mixed, and mingled, so much so that "righteousness should not come easily to any of us."

In Rodriguez's view, homogenized Americans are not the result. Instead the outcome can be a deeper and better sense of individuality, one that grasps the irony of American history, appreciates the complexity of individual identity, and admits one's dependence on a vast array of social relationships. From the ethnic foods Americans enjoy to the words and dialects they speak, from the religious communities they have formed and reformed to the mixed marriages they have consummated and the ongoing sexual improprieties, transgressions, and "miscegenations" that have climaxed their way through American history, Rodriguez finds the United States embodying the vision of its nineteenth century poet Walt Whitman. That most American of writers who, more than Franklin, is Rodriguez's progenitor, had all Americans in mind, especially those of the future, when he wrote "Of every hue and caste am I," the line with which *Brown* ends.

Rodriguez knows that American color lines persist. The border-crossing decisions and boundary-blurring acts of "browning" do not go unpunished. Rodriguez's gritty response is that "only further confusion can save us." As *Brown* draws to a close, his belief in "browning" finds its deepest expression through allusions to his Catholic Christianity. "God's love comes first," says Rodriguez, "and is not changed. . . . God so loved the world that the Word became incarnate, condescended to mortal clay. God became brown. . . . By brown I mean love." Time will tell whether *Brown* can bear the weight of American history, but as the cunning ways of that process unfold, there is little question that "browning" will play parts as persistent as they are contested.

John K. Roth

Sources for Further Study

Los Angeles Times Book Review, March 24, 2002, p. 10.
The Nation 274 (June 17, 2002): 30.
The New York Times Book Review 107 (April 7, 2002): 1.
The Washington Post Book World, April 21, 2002, p. 2.

THE BULLET MEANT FOR ME
A Memoir

Author: Jan Reid (1945-   )
Publisher: Broadway (New York). 240 pp. $24.95
Type of work: Memoir
Time: The 1950's to the 1990's
Locale: Texas and Mexico

≈

After Reid is shot and paralyzed by robbers in Mexico City, he goes through a long process of rehabilitation, during which he maintains his friendship with a young Chicano boxer and comes to a mature understanding of the nature of masculinity

≈

Principal personages:
  JAN REID, a journalist and novelist
  DOROTHY REID, his wife
  LILA, his stepdaughter
  JESUS CHAVEZ, a Mexican boxer and friend of Reid
  RICHARD LORD, owner of a boxing gym in Austin, Texas, and friend of Reid
  MIKE HALL, editor, musician, and friend of Reid
  JOHN SPONG, a magazine fact checker and friend of Reid
  DAVID COURTNEY, freelance writer and friend of Reid

Jan Reid and three friends were in Mexico City in April, 1998, to watch Reid's friend, a young Mexican boxer named Jesus Chavez, fight. On the evening following the fight, they visited a bar in a rough part of the city, the Plaza Garibaldi. When it was time to leave, they got into a taxi to take them back to their apartment. This was when their nightmare began. The driver took them on a detour, after which they were tailed by another car. Having taken them almost to their apartment, the cabdriver stopped unexpectedly in the middle of a block. From the car behind emerged two gunmen who jumped into the taxi, which sped off onto the freeway. One gunman demanded all their cash and one of Reid's credit cards. Then the taxi stopped and the four men were ordered out of the car. One of them, David Courtney, made a run for it, while Reid angrily threw off the grip of one of the gunmen, whom he calls Honcho. Furious, Honcho advanced toward Reid. Reid, who had had some boxing training, aimed a straight left-handed punch at him, but the punch fell short of its target. Honcho took aim with his gun and pulled the trigger. Reid felt searing pain in his abdomen and spine and as he fell to the ground he cried out, "I'm killed."

Jan Reid is an award-winning writer for Texas Monthly. *He has also contributed to* GQ, Esquire, Men's Journal, *and* The New York Times. *He is the author of* Close Calls: Jan Reid's Texas *(2000), a much-praised collection of his articles. He lives with his wife in Texas.*

This is the opening episode in Reid's engaging memoir, which then goes back in time to describe his childhood and youth in Texas, his later interest in boxing and his friendship with Chavez, and his marriage to Dorothy Browne. This leads to another, more detailed account of the shooting and of his long period of rehabilitation, during which he was convinced, correctly as it turned out, that although diagnosed as a paraplegic he would eventually be able to walk again. During his rehabilitation, he examined what led him to throw that failed punch at the gunman: Was it courage or recklessness? Bravery in the face of mortal danger or a mindless machismo that had been ingrained in him since childhood?

Reid was born in 1945 and grew up in small Texan towns. His family was blue-collar middle class, but Reid went to school in Wichita Falls with the children of oil millionaires. A skinny boy, unsure of himself, he was teased because of his first name. He was not athletic, but even at the age of eight he was fascinated by boxing. However, his mother would not allow him to pursue it. A stint in the Marine Corps reserve toughened him up, and he later got involved in a fight with some local toughs, which he lost. Vocalizing a theme that runs through the book, Reid comments on the futility of the redneck macho culture that equates manhood with hooliganism. Many young Texas men never grow out of it. "But if you're lucky," Reid says, "you become someone else."

In his mid-thirties, Reid was still unmarried, unsuccessful in relationships, and living alone in a rented cabin on a hill overlooking a valley. He worked out on a heavy punching bag, grew marijuana, and hunted rattlesnakes. Then, at a party in Austin, he met Dorothy, who was twice divorced and the mother of one girl, Lila. Courtship and marriage followed, and eventually, after seven years, a move to Austin.

It was in Austin that a friend took Reid to a boxing gym owned by a former boxer named Richard Lord. An old interest was quickly reawakened; Reid sparred and worked out regularly. Thirty years after his mother had banned him from boxing, he was finally learning to fight. At Lord's gym he met Chavez, a twenty-two-year-old Chicano boxer from Chicago. Chavez was an illegal immigrant who had served a prison term for armed robbery. After completing his sentence he had been deported by the Immigration and Naturalization Service (INS) back to Mexico City, but he had quickly made his way back, unauthorized, to the United States.

At the gym, Chavez directed the workouts. He was a hard taskmaster and an excellent teacher for Reid; they became good friends. In spite of his prison conviction, Chavez was a decent young man who wanted to make an honest living through boxing. He also represented all that Reid had wanted to be as an athlete, and gradually Reid came to think of him with affection as a surrogate son. Chavez fought regularly in Austin and became a contender for a world superfeatherweight title; he was well known in the community and was commended by the mayor for his work with youths who were in danger of getting involved in gangs.

However, when Chavez applied for a Texas driver's license, the INS caught up with him. Immigration law in the mid-1990's was harsh and ruthlessly applied, especially to Mexican immigrants. Chavez managed to work out a deal whereby he would be allowed two more fights in the United States before "voluntarily" returning to Mexico. Thus, in October, 1997, Jesus returned to Mexico to live with his grandparents in Chihuahua. In Mexico, Chavez boxed for a fraction of the pay he was used to receiving in the United States, and his chances of a world title fight receded; no one would fight him for a world title in Mexico because there would be no American television money.

When Chavez arranged a fight in Mexico City, Reid and his friends Mike Hall, John Spong, and David Courtney decided to go down to see it. They were unaware that the U.S. State Department had recently added Mexico City to its list of most dangerous foreign destinations. Even had they known this, Reid doubts that it would have stopped them. For male Texans, heading down to Mexico was a ritual they were born to; it was part of a long tradition in the violent relations between the two countries. The danger was part of the appeal.

The night following Chavez's victory, the four men ended up back in the Plaza Garibaldi where they had celebrated the previous night. This was in spite of warnings about the danger of the area from local residents and despite Reid's own misgivings. After the shooting, Reid was rushed by ambulance to the emergency room of the American British Cowdray Hospital. He was in agonizing pain and believed that he was dying. At the hospital, Reid received excellent care, especially from Dr. Roberto Casteñeda, who led the first team of surgeons. Next, neurosurgeons discovered that the bullet had fractured Reid's twelfth thoracic vertebra and had come to rest in the cauda equina, a bundle of nerves at the base of the spinal cord. Reid was paralyzed but, because he could move his toes, there appeared to be some hope. Family and friends rallied around him and soon he was transported from Mexico to Houston Medical Center.

The media got hold of the story, which came at a time when interest was growing in violence against Americans in Mexico. Reid even conducted a press conference from his hospital bed, clips from which were included in ABC's *20/20* program on Mexican violence. Much of the media presented the incident as a case of a brave Texan standing his ground against the gunman, but there were other views. Reid's friend Mike Hall told him that he had been brave but stupid, a view echoed by many of the women in Reid's circle of friends.

Over the following months, Reid underwent unrelenting physical therapy and lived his life from a wheelchair. His greatest fear was not that he would never walk again but that his disability would destroy his marriage. This did not happen, although not surprisingly, given the sudden demands placed on it, the marriage went through periods of great strain.

Step by step, Reid moved from wheelchair to walker to crutches and then to a single crutch. Richard Lord urged him to get back to the gym. At first he resisted, but he eventually went back and got used to punching the heavy bag again. The crutch gave way to a cane. Reid pushed himself hard, ignoring the pains that would shoot through his legs. His goal was to walk down the aisle with his stepdaughter Lila at her wedding.

He was also thinking of his friend Chavez. They talked on the phone and by e-mail. Would Chavez ever be able to return to the United States and fight for a world title? It did not seem likely. Chavez did have one success. In Mexico City he took on the Mexican superfeatherweight champion Julio Alvarez and won a unanimous decision from the judges. This was in defiance of the conventional wisdom that Chavez, who was ridiculed in Mexico City as a gringo—he had grown up in Chicago and spoke Spanish imperfectly—could never win a decision against the popular Mexican.

Keeping up their friendship, Reid made a solitary trip to Mexico to visit Chavez in Chihuahua City. He watched him win another fight, held in a provincial town against a mediocre opponent. In being willing to go back to Mexico, Reid answered in the affirmative a question that had been vexing him: Would he ever be at ease in Mexico again, after what had happened?

The trip to Mexico was the first of a number of healing events that were soon to take place, giving Reid's memoir a happy ending. On New Year's Eve, 1999, he and Dorothy traveled to Paris and watched as ten thousand flashbulbs were set off on the Eiffel Tower at midnight. Meanwhile, a new lawyer had taken up Chavez's case, which paved the way for him to receive permanent U.S. resident status. He had a homecoming bout in Austin (another victory) and hoped for a world title fight. Reid relates a telling incident as he and Chavez walked to his car after a dinner with friends:

> I could tell he debated whether to take my arm as I stepped down from a curb. All the prohibition born of being told what it was to be a man fell away. Beside my car, we stood for a moment hugging each other. He loomed so large in the ring that I often forgot how short he was. I sighed and rested my chin on the top of his head.

Finally, at the invitation of Roberto Casteñeda, the surgeon who first attended him after he was shot, Reid and his wife returned to Mexico City, where he visited the exact spot where he had been shot. He found that he had no regrets about what he did at that fateful moment and realized that in his own way, he had won that fight with the gunman Honcho. It is a fitting reflection on which to end a touching, honest, unpretentious memoir.

Bryan Aubrey

Sources for Further Study

Booklist 98 (February 15, 2002): 976.
Kirkus Reviews 70 (January 1, 2002): 35.
Publishers Weekly 249 (January 28, 2002): 278.

BY THE LAKE

Author: John McGahern (1934-   )
Publisher: Alfred A. Knopf (New York). 336 pp. $24.00
Type of work: Novel
Time: The present
Locale: A rural community in what appears to be County
Leitrim, Ireland, on the edge of a lake

A pair of middle-aged former advertising executives re-locate from London to rural Ireland and become the focus of attention of the local community

~

Principal characters:
JOSEPH RUTTLEDGE, Irishman who returns to his homeland
KATE RUTTLEDGE, Joseph's English-born wife, a former advertising
    executive
JAMESIE MURPHY, neighbor and town gossip
MARY MURPHY, Jamesie's patient, understanding wife
PATRICK RYAN, local handyman
THE SHAH, Ruttledge's uncle, the wealthiest man in the village

Joseph and Kate Ruttledge, advertising executives from London, renounce urban life and move to Ireland seeking quiet and repose. Ruttledge's uncle, the Shah, a self-made success and resident Croesus, arranges their purchase of a twenty-acre farm on the edge of a lake. The novel details the Ruttledges' involvement in the lives of a small circle of local inhabitants as they are repeatedly drawn into their domestic and business affairs and asked to intervene in their minor complications.

Much of the narrative focuses on Jamesie and Mary Murphy, an amusing couple who have lived their lives at the lake and stand as models of people who have perfectly accommodated themselves to the rhythms of rural life. As community gossip, Jamesie is full of stories, history, and hearsay, somehow insinuating his way into everyone's affairs. He constantly visits the Ruttledge house as he and Joe Ruttledge form an endearing bond. Attention shifts to Patrick Ryan, an itinerant handyman who sporadically appears and builds a shed with Ruttledge; the Shah and his erratic attempts to sell his business; Patrick Quinn, the local lothario who works his way through a parade of wives and lovers; and Bill Evans, a spectral figure surviving an orphaned childhood and hardscrabble adulthood.

The novel is largely plotless; while events do occur, the narrative energy emerges from the extended dialogue and the complex characterizations. The novel places Joe Ruttledge at the center of this odd assemblage of personalities, acting as go-between and mediator for the misunderstandings, skirmishes, and complications that invade

John McGahern's style has been compared to that of James Joyce, and he is equally noted for grappling with controversial topics of Irish life such as sexuality, family turmoil, and the Catholic Church. He has written novels, short stories, and radio and television scripts, and he edited the letters of John Butler Yeats, father of the poet William Butler Yeats.

the tranquillity of the lake. One of the most curious events is his intervention on his uncle's behalf in the sale of his business. The Shah would prefer not to deal with strangers, and Ruttledge recommends selling to the Shah's long-standing colleague. However, the man and the Shah have no relationship other than labor; the Shah literally does not know how to talk to Joe Dolan. Ruttledge must intervene, bargaining a price, arranging a payment schedule, even securing the loan itself. He is furthermore called upon to save Jamesie from a seemingly intractable family problem when Murphy's brother in England is laid off from his job and announces his intention to move back to Ireland and live with his brother. Ruttledge writes a letter suggesting the inadvisability of the plan in such a deft fashion that all parties are delighted not to have to deal with one another. Such scenes are not only humorous for their absurd complications but sharply poignant, illustrating the ties that bind as well as separate these lives.

In his capacity as mediator, Ruttledge represents a curiosity. He is a cultural anomaly, an Irishman returned from exile to live among his countrymen once more. His position is decidedly ironic—he is both insider and outsider—and as an outsider he is freed of the rigid conventions and traditions that bind these lives in tight coils. Like an ancient Celtic poet, Ruttledge has complete freedom of passage and is admitted into all the characters' lives, even those who have grudges or enmities and no longer deal with one another.

The lake, the geographical presence that defines and informs all these lives, plays as strong a role as any of the characters. For everyone, it represents a timeless presence, an image of stasis amidst change. The novel charts the events in a year's time, and that temporal span is conveyed through the changing descriptions of the lake's appearance and ecosystem. The seasons begin with summer and cycle through to autumn, when Ruttledge looks across its expanse and sees "Jamesie and Mary . . . framed in the light. . . . They heard coughing and scolding and laughter as Mary, and then Jamesie, disappeared from the sky." The lake accentuates the predictability and timeless rhythms of the life lived on its edges, and most of the book's most luminous passages are devoted to its description.

> The ground had become soft and unpleasant for walking and they did not go further than the hanging hill above the inner lake from where they were able to count the sheep. Several swans were sailing on the lake amid dark clutches of wildfowl. The occasional lone heron flew between the island and the bog. Nothing was sharp. The lanes of watery light that pierced the low cloud from time to time seemed to illuminate nothing but mist and cloud and water. The sedge of Gloria Bog and the little birches had no color. The mountains were hidden.

The lake not only defines difference or recaptures the past, but for its residents it also provides all their material and spiritual needs. What these folks know of life and its stimulations are found at the lake. They constantly journey out to walk its shores or fish its depths; it acts as the ultimate form of entertainment and a powerful source of instruction. Jamesie has never ventured more than a few miles away, and at the novel's close he reflects, only partly ironically, "'I may not have traveled far but I know the whole world,' he said with a wide sweep of his arm. 'You do know the whole world,' Ruttledge said, 'And you have been my sweet guide.'"

McGahern's treatment of the lake represents a modern continuation of a deep and abiding strain in Irish literature extending back to the ancient bardic poets. One of medieval Ireland's most important works is a cycle of poems called "The Madness of Sweeney," in which the hero, a warrior named Sweeney who has been cursed for injuring a saint's acolyte, spends his days leaping from treetop to treetop about Ireland, admiring the countryside and giving loving testimony to the majesty of the natural landscape. McGahern's lake provides the same consolations, as well as life-affirming rituals that create order, purpose, and harmony among its inhabitants.

Against the constancy of the lake are pitted these few lives, and the novel often meditates on the meaning of human existence. At one point a power broker from London arrives to offer Kate her old job back. The temptation of a generous salary and professional challenges is formidable, yet she ultimately declines, choosing the lake's durable presence over the unreality of urban stimulation. While the characters all respond to the sacredness of life, there is a mournful recognition of its fragility and fleetingness. Mary Murphy, thinking of her brother-in-law living in exile, remarks, "People we know come and go in our minds whether they are here or in England or alive or dead. . . . We're no more than a puff of wind out on the lake." Similarly, the Shah, reflecting on turning over the reigns of his business, concludes, "The rain comes down. Grass grows. Children get old . . . . That's it. We all know. We know full well and can't even whisper it out loud."

Against this seeming fatalism, the novel explores what existence may mean. Ruttledge, for instance, cannot believe in an afterlife: "I don't know from what source life comes, other than out of nature, or for what purpose. I suppose it's not unreasonable to think that we go back into whatever meaning we came from." The characters all struggle stoically with their private sorrows—the Ruttledges that they do not have children, the Murphys that their one son lives far away in Dublin and even further from the sensibilities of his parents—yet the novel also ponders the consolations of existence. Human contact, friendships, shared work, love of spouse—all these provide an abiding sweetness for these seemingly backward lives. However, it is the concept of happiness that lies behind the novel's quietly profound meditations. Leo Tolstoy, at the beginning of *Anna Karenina* (1875-1877; English translation, 1886), offers the famous observation, "Happy families are all alike; every unhappy family is unhappy in its own way." McGahern challenges this idea; happiness for his characters is individual and defining, an abstraction that nevertheless proves elusive yet compelling.

When asked at one point if he is happy, Ruttledge can only answer that he is not unhappy, a response that suggests that happiness has no substance of its own. Yet, when listening to his friends talking and recalling the pleasures of another simple day passed,

> with a rush of feeling [Ruttledge] felt that this must be happiness. As soon as the thought came to him, he fought it back, blaming the whiskey. The very idea was as dangerous as presumptive speech: Happiness could not be sought or worried into being, or even fully grasped; it should be allowed its own slow pace so that it passes unnoticed, if it ever comes at all.

Happiness, like the lake, is transitory and evanescent, a fleeting essence that cannot bear too much scrutiny. This idea is as much a pleasure savored in its own right as a form of self-protection, yet Ruttledge is willing to confront its enigma directly. Later he concludes that sometime in the future, when he looks back on these tranquil moments, they will reveal the essence of happiness itself, "all that life could give of contentment and peace." Modern novels rarely concern themselves with such a candid consideration of pleasure itself, yet such consideration is precisely McGahern's challenge to the reader in *By the Lake*.

In an understated way, the novel is quintessentially Irish, concerning itself with classic Irish themes of emigration, exile, colonial oppression, and the yearning for freedom. Indeed, there is an Irish Republican Army man in the town, but his role in the novel is radically limited and he holds almost no influence over Ruttledge and life at the lake. Characters brood on the separation of Northern Ireland from the Republic, and Johnny Murphy's life in England leads Jamesie to one of his few dark pronouncements,

> These people forced into England through no fault of their own were often looked down on—most unjustly looked down upon—by some whose only good was that they managed to remain at home with little cause to look down on anybody. It's always the meanest and poorest sorts who have the need to look down.

As Ireland enjoys the economic advantages of participation in the European Union, the rural life of the lake is quickly passing from view. Ruttledge has seen this future while living in London and he wants none of it. Thus, the novel stands as a paean to a rapidly vanishing Ireland.

By the Lake is McGahern's first novel in twelve years and a triumph. It is by turns subtle, poetic, and delicately nuanced. John McGahern is a writer of remarkable grace and skill, and one unashamed of exploring the territory ignored by other writers.

David W. Madden

Sources for Further Study

Booklist 98 (February 15, 2002): 993.
Europe, May, 2002, p. 31.
Library Journal 127 (April 1, 2002): 141.
The New Leader 85 (March/April, 2002): 26.
The New York Review of Books 49 (May 23, 2002): 10.
The New York Times Book Review 107 (March 17, 2002): 9.
The New Yorker 78 (May 6, 2002): 135.
Newsweek 139 (April 29, 2002): 16.
Publishers Weekly 249 (January 28, 2002): 268.

THE CADENCE OF GRASS

Author: Thomas McGuane (1939-   )
Publisher: Alfred A. Knopf (New York). 238 pp. $24.00
Type of work: Novel
Time: The present
Locale: Montana

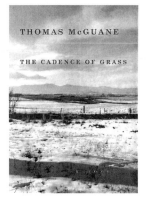

~

When the domineering patriarch of a dysfunctional Montana family dies, he creates further havoc in their lives by willing the family business to his ex-convict son-in-law

~

Principal characters:
> EVELYN WHITELAW, elder daughter of the deceased "Sunny Jim" Whitelaw
> NATALIE WHITELAW, "Sunny Jim's" younger daughter
> ALICE WHITELAW, "Sunny Jim's" widow
> PAUL CRUSOE, Evelyn's estranged husband
> BILL CHAMPION, a neighboring rancher, World War II veteran, and family friend

Tough guys, in fiction as in life, tend not to age well. It is a rule of thumb that inevitably confronts reviewers of an author such as Thomas McGuane, particularly since this new work is his first fiction since 1992's *Nothing But Blue Skies* and comes thirty-three years after McGuane's wildly successful debut novel *The Sporting Club* (1969). Can his outrageous, ultrahip, hard-edged, impulsive, brawling characters still charm the readers of a new millennium? The answer from *The Cadence of Grass* is yes and no.

The story opens, appropriately, at the funeral of one of those larger-than-life types: "Sunny Jim" Whitelaw, head of the dysfunctional Whitelaw family and soda-pop tycoon, is dead, but thanks to his last will and testament, he continues to manipulate and browbeat his heirs from beyond the grave. Specifically, he gives total control of the sinking family business to his slimy, ne'er-do-well son-in-law Paul Crusoe, who has just finished serving time in the state penitentiary for manslaughter. The family could liquidate the bottling plant and split the profits, but there is a small catch: In order to do so, under the terms of the will, Jim's daughter Evelyn, currently separated from Paul, would have to call off her plans for divorce and reconcile with her husband. To Sunny Jim's widow, Alice, and younger daughter, Natalie, this seems a small enough price to pay for getting on with their lives, but Evelyn, finally enjoying the freedom and solitude of running her father's small ranch, wants no part of a marital reunion.

To the untrained eye, there may not seem many directions in which such a story line could go. It is McGuane's sheer madcap inventiveness that comes to the rescue—comes, arguably, to too many rescues, as the energetic plot often veers from satire into farce. The evil Paul naturally has to have an affair with his sister-in-law, as well as another with his probation officer. A bizarre piece of back-story provides the motivation for Sunny Jim's posthumous generosity to Paul. Once, on a business trip together, Jim lured Paul into an encounter with a call girl who drugged him in his hotel room so that a renegade surgeon could steal his kidney, which Sunny Jim desperately needed, not for himself, but . . . it is complicated territory, and a long story. If this sounds like a narrative thread from a novel by Carl Hiassen or Elmore Leonard, it is just a measure of the influence that McGuane's fictional universe, with its weird mix of whimsy and tragedy, has had on a generation of younger writers.

Thomas McGuane is the author of eight novels, including The Sporting Club *(1969),* The Bushwhacked Piano *(1971), and* Ninety-two in the Shade *(1973), as well as a collection of short stories and two collections of essays. He lives in Montana.*

Even throughout the excesses of the book's first half, fans will be cheered by recurring nuggets of phrasing and observation that are solid McGuane. During Sunny Jim's funeral, for instance: "The priest addressed his remarks to the coffin. . . . Evelyn was discomfited to recognize in the sermon whole passages from that year's *Farmer's Almanac*." Natalie reflects on her dependable but hopelessly obtuse husband, Stuart: "It was with a rare lightness of spirit that she resolved to stop seeing Paul at least until she could dump Stuart. It would be like the release of the white doves at the opening of the Olympics."

Part of the problem with the setup of *The Cadence of Grass* is foreshadowed by the writers' workshop adage, "A novel is only as strong as its worst villain." Paul Crusoe's villainy is never in question, but his roundedness as a character is. His probation officer, Geraldine, observes at one point in their liaison, "There was really something infernal about Paul, but it was only this very sulfurousness that made her act so out of character and believe that they were entitled to a harmless good time together." This explanation does not ring true. The reader never gets a sense of Paul's evil as the kind that gives off sparks; as villains go, he is drab and one-note. He is so patently conscienceless, self-serving, and gratuitously cruel (particularly to women) that it is hard for the reader to imagine even his forbidden-fruit aspect as sufficient aphrodisiac for the plain Geraldine, much less to fathom his appeal to Evelyn and Natalie, who have been wounded for years by his faithless escapades. Paul is the proverbial charming rogue minus the charm, and despite Geraldine's evaluation of his "very good looks, his compact physique and fine features, the particular way his black hair was combed in a kind of 1930's look, and his quickness of mind," his physical appearance alone does not seem a convincing enough reason for women to be falling at his feet.

However, just when the reader may be wearying of Paul's initial novelty and the story threatens to founder, McGuane's writerly instincts seem to propel him into a far more fruitful venue, one that makes for most of the novel's finest moments: the developing friendship between Evelyn and neighboring rancher Bill Champion, a fatherly World War II veteran and her father's former business partner, who not only instills in her an old-time custodial feeling for the land but also spins wonderful yarns at the drop of a hat. The interludes between Evelyn and Bill, with the author's lyrical evocations of the Montana landscape as backdrop, give McGuane the chance to show off one of his strong suits: his enduring strength as a prose stylist, most likely the reason he maintains an enthusiastic audience into his fourth decade of publishing while numerous young Turks have burst out and then passed quietly from the scene. This is just one example of McGuane's descriptive style among many:

> When the chinook stopped blowing, it stayed still for two days. Skies were clear and the cattle scattered out to look for patches of bare ground, old grass, and a change of diet. Bill and Evelyn took their horses into the summer pasture, Evelyn riding her colt Cree, crossing drifts until the Crazy Mountains arose like a silver wedding cake to the north. From there, the water courses, tree lines on a white expanse, made spindly courses to the Yellowstone. The Bridgers could be discerned, as well as the bench of Sheep Mountain, the low-humped Deer Creeks and, to the south, the blue crags and high, dark canyons of the Absaroka. This was altogether too much for the colts, who kept trying to turn toward home and were afraid of the crowds of deer at the bottom of every snow-filled bowl. Evelyn was aware of a great weight lifting off her as they rode along. The notion of not ever going back made her smile and think of the trail: Texas to Montana and never once turn your horse around. Her happiness began to be felt by Cree, who looked eagerly in the direction of their travel while Evelyn made plans with Bill for next year, the following year, the next five and ten years. A three-mile cross fence was in the wrong place and should be moved a half mile to the east. Springs needed to be improved, salt grounds moved, pastures rested, loafing sheds built. Somehow the money must be found for the tractor they coveted, a four-wheel-drive New Holland that would let them bale wild timothy for the horses. From the ridges, they could look down into their small valley and see flocks of pigeons trading between the barn and hay sheds, wings sparkling in the brilliant light.

Far from being just an idyllic distraction from the drama's unpleasant business of law offices and courtrooms, Champion's role becomes integral to the plot, as Evelyn has an epiphany regarding his odd long-time friendship with her mother. Bill Champion becomes, almost effortlessly and with a minimum of sentimentality, the much-needed moral center of the novel. The reader relishes his scenes for their warmth and common sense, all the while knowing that, under the laws of literature, this puts him on an inevitable collision course with the world of the story's dark side, Paul.

Although the second half of the book is not free of shaggy-dog plot threads, even these seem to take on a heightened focus and grandeur. It would be hard to imagine a more vintage (darkly hilarious) McGuane set-piece than Evelyn's misadventures when, driving home at night through a blizzard after a disastrous honky-tonk date, her car slides into a ditch. Pursued by thugs through the wilderness snowstorm, she is finally rescued by a backcountry rancher named Torvald Aadfield, whose strange family includes a timid wife, Esther, and a cross-dressing, hard-rocker son, Donald. They are snowed in, Evelyn gradually discovers, with "Grandpa," who is lying as a corpse in his Norwegian naval uniform:

> Evelyn, shivering from the cold, couldn't quite keep her eyes off the corpse, and was tempted to blame it for everything. Donald said he was uncomfortable having it lean up against the wall like cordwood and put it in a small wagon, towing it around the room looking for a better place. "I remember when the damn thing was jumping around barking orders," he said. He looked through the room for a place to park the wagon. "My dreams change every day," Donald was saying. "For years I've also had a great interest in going to Mars. It seems more and more possible. If I could hang on to my share of Grandpa's pension and invest it wisely, I could be on one of the first trips. When I heard they'd found evidence of water there, I thought, *Whoa*, I could have it all: *a hot tub on Mars!* Here, this is good, I think. . . ." He lifted the corpse out of the wagon and stood it in an upended metal stock tank, where it took on the aspect of a roadside shrine down in Mexico.
>
> Evelyn tried to see the merits of hot tubbing on Mars, the plains of the Red Planet all around and the troubled, complicated Earth hanging on the far edge of the void. Donald had put her in a strange mood.

The rest is a long story, but a classic McGuane "digression" that is the equal of any from the early days.

Near the end, as the forces of the book begin to resolve themselves, Champion is slowly but inexorably sucked into an ill-fated business deal with Paul and his cohorts. McGuane renders the violence of the bleak finale in a chilling, tour-de-force narrative sequence that resonates long after the reader closes the cover.

This time out, McGuane's Wild West saga may be wildly uneven, but at its best *The Cadence of Grass* will not only satisfy longtime fans but, ideally, show a new generation of readers what all the fuss was about.

Carroll Dale Short

Sources for Further Study

Kirkus Reviews 70 (March 15, 2002): 361.
Library Journal 127 (May 15, 2002): 126.
The New York Review of Books 49 (June 27, 2002): 21.
The New York Times, May 21, 2002, p. E7.
The New York Times Book Review 107 (May 19, 2002): 12.
The New Yorker 78 (June 3, 2002): 95.
Publishers Weekly 249 (May 6, 2002): 35.

CARAMELO

Author: Sandra Cisneros (1954-   )
Publisher: Alfred A. Knopf (New York). 469 pp. $24.00
Type of work: Novel
Time: The twentieth century
Locale: Mexico and the United States

≈

Cisneros weaves the multigenerational stories of a Mexican American family into a colorful pattern, thematically structured of intricate motifs: passion, betrayal, and ultimate forgiveness

≈

Principal characters:
    CELAYA (LALA) REYES, a young woman who travels between Chicago
        and Mexico City
    SOLEDAD REYES, Celaya's grandmother
    NARCISO REYES, Celaya's grandfather
    INOCENCIO REYES, Celaya's father

Sandra Cisneros, America's most-read Latina, utilizes the rebozo, the traditional Mexican shawl, as her primary metaphor throughout *Caramelo*, the author's first novel since her celebrated *The House on Mango Street* (1984). The eight-foot-long rebozo represents Mexico's ultimate *mestizo*, or mixed article. Spanish in origin, it also enculturates native Indian influences and, in addition to protection from the cold, acts as an apron, a baby carrier, a tablecloth, and can even designate the marital status of a woman. Much like the time-honored rebozo, which features an intricately woven, multifaceted fringe, Cisnero's autobiographical novel elaborately portrays a complicated pattern of family turmoil, tenacity, betrayal, love, and forgiveness that spans three generations.

Every summer Celaya Reyes, an American girl and the youngest of seven, travels in a family parade of cars from Chicago to Mexico City, crossing the border in Texas to "the other side." It is in Mexico City that the young girl first encounters Awful Grandmother Soledad's caramelo (striped) rebozo in the family home on Destiny Street. Caramelo, from which the novel takes its name, is the most highly prized rebozo due to its candy-striped pattern. Awful Grandmother, descended from a renowned clan of shawl makers, has carefully wrapped away her mother's unfinished striped shawl in the family walnut armoire. Only in the glorious cloth's silky embrace does the old woman find comfort, as she remembers her fairy-tale past. When young Celaya, otherwise known as Lala, spies the wonderful cloth, she asks immediately whether she can own it, but she has to wait until Awful Grandmother dies to make it her own. During this visit, the young American girl also meets Candelaria, the daughter of Awful Grandmother's washerwoman. A poor, slightly older girl, whose caramel skin color represents the intermingling of Mexican cultures, the child is carried on her mother's shoulders on three buses to Awful Grandmother's house to wash the family's dirty clothes. At Awful Grandmother's quixotic insistence, Candelaria accompanies the family on an outing to an Acapulco beach but the trip ends miserably in family squabbles. Zoila, Lala's mother, in a fury, insists on being left out of the car and Candelaria disappears. The hazily remembered events of this trip will come to play a meaningful role later on in Lala's life.

Sandra Cisneros was born in Chicago in 1954. Her poetry and fiction have brought her international acclaim as well as numerous awards, including the Lannan Literary Award and the American Book Award, and fellowships from the National Endowment for the Arts and the MacArthur Foundation.

The Americanized Lala and her brothers clash with Awful Grandmother, finding her cold, domineering, and detached. Lala soon realizes that Awful Grandmother loves only Little Grandfather and her son Inocencio, Lala's papa, and disregards her other two sons, Uncle Fat-Face and Uncle Baby, and her daughter, Aunty Light-skin. In addition, she hates her daughter-in-law Zoila for stealing her favorite son. After Little Grandfather dies, Awful Grandmother moves north with her sons but, finding the Chicago winters intolerable, buys a house and sets up a furniture upholstery business for Inocencio's family in warmer San Antonio, Texas. After making her daughter-in-law's life even more miserable, Awful Grandmother suffers a stroke and soon after dies. However, she is hardly out of Lala's life. Suffering great adolescent angst, Lala, who never has had a room of her own, suffers from lack of privacy as well as harassment at the hands of high-schoolers who despise her American ways, especially her correct use of English. The youngster does not know where she belongs. Abandoned on the freeway one afternoon after a beating by Cookie Cantu and her *desperadas*, Lala hears Awful Grandmother's voice calling her and guiding her through the oncoming traffic. A pick-up truck changing lanes barely misses her. Because of her vicious ways, it seems, the old woman remains stuck between Earth and the afterlife. She must repent, make amends, and gain the forgiveness of those who suffered at her hands—and, Lala must be the medium through which this feat will be accomplished.

Awful Grandmother's voice becomes louder and louder inside Lala's head as she advances through her teenage years. At fifteen, she falls in love with Ernesto, her brother's geek friend who arrives to rescue Lala, in fairy-tale prince fashion, in his white pick-up truck. The young couple runs away to Mexico City in an effort to force her family to approve their marriage. After a week of bliss, Lala's lover comes to favor his Catholic upbringing over her own atheist ways and abandons her. Like her grandmother before her, Lala finds comfort in the caramelo rebozo she took time to pack. However, Awful Grandmother coaxes Lala through the resultant period of depression. In time, the older woman's voice wins out and Lala realizes she must write Awful Grandmother's story. Returning to the metaphorical rebozo, Grandmother's story represents only a single thread in the fabric that makes up this fabulous family's history. If removed, the whole would unravel, so other Reyes family stories must similarly be recorded.

The life of Awful Grandmother, whose real name is Soledad, reads like the fairy tale "Cinderella," except that in Cisnero's story the abused kitchen maid turns into the evil stepmother, or as the author describes her, the witch in "Hansel and Gretel." Abandoned by her father after her mother dies and he remarries, Soledad, whose name connotes aloneness, travels to Mexico City to live with her Aunt Fina, the neglectful mother of seventeen children. Soledad, a child who never experiences a childhood, carries her most precious possession with her: the unfinished caramelo rebozo left her by her mother. The enslaved youngster suffers sexual abuse at the hands of Uncle Pio and spends her days cleaning up after children until her prince arrives: her elegant, formal cousin Narciso Reyes, in a cadet uniform. However, instead of bringing her to a castle, he brings her to his own mother's kitchen and, eventually, to his bed. Her future mother-in-law continues to abuse Soledad because the girl's dark skin reminds her of her own despised Indian heritage. She has married a light-skinned musician from Madrid. The poor girl sleeps in uncomfortable quarters attached to the kitchen. In time, Soledad becomes pregnant and the self-serving Narciso, meticulously well named, marries her, in an act of honor, only at his father's insistence. While she cannot believe her good luck, because she passionately loves Narciso, he falls passionately in love with an entertainer who disrespects him and abandons him. He spends the rest of his days whimpering for her and dies on the city streets with her name on his lips. Soledad, who becomes ever more manipulative and malicious as she ages, focuses her pent-up love on her son Inocencio and makes everyone miserable—in particular, her innocent daughter-in-law Zoila. As she ages, she becomes ever more invisible and when she becomes sick, her children forget her.

Sandwiched between these two women is the melancholy Inocencio, Soledad's son and Lala's father. After experiencing adolescent trouble with his father, Inocencio makes his way to relatives in the United States, where he becomes an expert furniture upholsterer. After a great deal of confusion, he winds up in jail one night during World War II. Prompted by a friend, he convinces the police that he wants to enlist, and they gladly escort him to the draft office right around the corner. As a new American citizen, he serves his country with honor and dignity, is honorably discharged, and soon marries. As he says, he becomes the proud father of seven sons, except one of them is a daughter—Celaya—on whom he dotes excessively, like Awful Grandmother, to the exclusion of his other children. Although not as rich a literary character as Awful Grandmother, Inocencio remains an interesting figure who carries, like all the family members, a deep dark secret. Throughout his life, he attempts above all to be true to himself and to be an honorable gentleman, *un caballero.* In his efforts to support his family, he performs upholstery work to the highest possible standards, with high quality materials, and uses his hands to tie each thread, instead of mass-producing popular, shoddy furniture. The resultant stress of working so long and hard, battling the encroachment of new production ideas and continued racism and discrimination, in one case at the hands of the U.S. government which he so honorably served, forces him into ill health, the hospital, and, ultimately, his death bed.

For a reason that remains unclear, Lala's mother Zoila confesses to Lala a family secret before she sees her father in the hospital. It could be that Zoila realizes that only when the whole truth is known can one truly forgive, but she seems angry when she tells her daughter that Inocencio fathered another daughter before Lala was born. This daughter, it turns out, was Candelaria, the housekeeper's daughter, with the lovely caramel-colored skin. Lala experiences a great shock when the story comes out. It means that her father was not, after all, perfect: He ran away from his responsibility, leaving the housekeeper pregnant and abandoning his daughter, another recurring theme that Awful Grandmother knew full well. While this revelation elicits sympathy for Awful Grandmother and highlights the theme of family interconnectedness, it also allows Inocencio to be forgiven—not by the girl he abandoned, but by her sister. Lala orders her mother to give Inocencio a break. However, the family secrets continue to unfold during this time of crisis. Zoila also reminds Lala of the trip the family took years ago to the Acapulco seaside. Her dismay on that sad day, it seems, was brought about by Awful Grandmother's own revelation that Candalaria was Inocencio's daughter. One cannot help wonder whether Awful Grandmother imparted this information to cause a permanent breach in her son's marriage and thus regain his full attention. When the family secrets are revealed, the loose fringe ends of the unfinished candy-colored rebozo, which metaphorically connects the individual family member's histories, are thus tied into place and the pattern completed.

Initially, *Caramelo* overwhelms. It is like a first look into a kaleidoscope, when only chaotic color is visible, before intricate patterns have a chance to emerge. In over eighty chapters, Cisneros focuses primarily on the lives of Soledad, Soledad's favorite child Inocencio, and Lala's bicultural existence in the United States and in Mexico City. Lala Reyes acts as the voice for her family across time and international borders, recalling and retelling the Reyes family's passionate tales of their decline into poverty, their bewilderment over immigration, their military encounters, their passionate attachments, their honor in taking responsibility, their skilled workmanship, their intense passion for unobtainable others, their obsessive love, and the hatred born out of such love, as they travel back and forth following their destinies between Mexico and the United States.

Although the novel is richly spiced with Mexican cultural and historical detail, it can be at times overbearing and sometimes downright distracting. In a tone that can border on anger, Cisneros attempts to exult loudly every aspect of her culture from Emperor Maximilian and Empress Carlota to Raquel Welch. After a while, this emphasis becomes cacophonous and distracting, especially in a novel.

M. Casey Diana

Sources for Further Study

Booklist 98 (August, 2002): 1883.
Library Journal 127 (September 15, 2002): 88.
Los Angeles Times Book Review, September 29, 2002, p. 16.
The New York Times Book Review 107 (September 29, 2002): 24.
Publishers Weekly 249 (August 12, 2002): 275.

CENTURY'S SON

Author: Robert Boswell (1953-   )
Publisher: Alfred A. Knopf (New York). 308 pp. $24.00
Type of work: Novel
Time: The last year of the twentieth century
Locale: A college town in Illinois, population 150,000

∾

An alcoholic, lecherous old expatriate from the Communist Soviet Union creates havoc in his American-born daughter's dysfunctional family when he moves into their home in a conservative Midwestern college town

∾

Principal characters:
> MORGAN, a middle-aged garbage collector and former labor organizer
> ZHENYA MORGAN, his wife, a professor at the local university
> EMMA MORGAN, their twenty-year-old daughter, a university student and unwed mother
> PHILIP MORGAN, their son who committed suicide at the age of twelve and still haunts their lives in flashbacks
> PETER IVANOVICH KAMENEV, Zhenya's father, a dissident Russian intellectual
> DANNY FORD, a young hoodlum who works as Morgan's partner until arrested as an accessory to a gang murder
> ROY OBERLAND, the Morgan family's next-door neighbor, a police officer
> ADRIANA EAST, a socially prominent middle-aged woman, another of the Morgan family's neighbors

The title of Robert Boswell's new novel, *Century's Son*, refers to the fact that the protagonist, Peter Ivanovich Kamenev, claims to have lived throughout the entire twentieth century and to have known many of the most important figures of that turbulent epoch. This earthy old man will remind readers of Boris Yeltsin, former president of Russia, who was a renegade, a heavy drinker, and a notorious bottom-pincher. Kamenev may also remind readers of the actor Akim Tamiroff (1901-1972), the fictional character Zorba the Greek, and possibly a little of novelist Vladimir Nabokov (1899-1977). Kamenev is by far the most interesting character in Boswell's book. Each of its nine chapters is headed by a quotation purportedly from the writings of Peter Ivanovich Kamenev, who provides a philosophical counterpoint to a story about alienation, despair, and guilt in modern middle America. Here are a few examples of his cryptic one-liners:

> Strengths and weaknesses are the same thing, the valuable and the invaluable.
> We record history as if it were a sorrow pageant, each disaster competing with the next to wear the crown.
> Vulgarity is an expression of stupidity, coarseness, or freedom.

~

*Robert Boswell, author of six
previous books, is one of America's
most gifted fiction writers. He is a
professor of English at New Mexico
State University and faculty member
of the influential Warren Wilson
MFA Program for Writers. He has
received two National Endowment
for the Arts Fellowships, a
Guggenheim Fellowship, and other
important awards.*

~

Peter Ivanovich invites himself to move into his daughter Zhenya's house, where he behaves like a barbarian but sets an iconoclastic example that changes the lives of the other three members of his uptight, small-town American family as well as the lives of two of their neighbors. His chief claim to fame is that, in his youth, he had a golden opportunity to assassinate Josef Stalin and declined to do so on philosophical principles, thereby allowing Stalin to live to become the greatest murderer of the twentieth century. Peter Ivanovich speaks in broken English, lies outrageously about his life experiences, and stays drunk most of the time. Yet he is obviously the genuine article, a real intellectual and a genius, as opposed to the dignified portraits of famous men of the twentieth century usually found in reverential biographies and stiffly posed photographs.

The Morgans are a mismatched couple. Zhenya is a political science professor at the local university, while her husband, who goes only by his last name, drives around collecting the town's garbage and trucking it out to the dump. He is sensitive and intelligent, an underachiever who pushes Zhenya to the brink of divorce because he is so apathetic and so indifferent to her upwardly mobile aspirations. Morgan lost interest in life after their son, Philip, committed suicide. The family is haunted by his death. Their daughter, Emma, became pregnant at age fourteen and refused to divulge the name of her son Petey's father. The reader is let in on the secret in chapter 2. The boy's father is none other than the next-door neighbor and good family friend Roy Oberland, a policeman who was twenty-seven at the time of Petey's conception and therefore guilty of statutory rape.

Emma, a university student, is now twenty years old. She and Roy have been carrying on an affair for six years right under her parents' noses. Roy is still consumed with guilt. He is deeply in love with Emma but married a woman he did not really love because he hoped to get over his obsession with a minor. Emma has a beautiful figure. She is on the Hayden University diving team and spends much of her spare time practicing in the family swimming pool. Roy stands on his bed in the second-floor bedroom to watch her surreptitiously. Eventually his wife discovers his guilty secret and divorces him. He is relieved, because he thinks he might be able to marry Emma now that she has reached adulthood. In the interim, however, she has made friends with college youths and is having misgivings about remaining involved with a lover who is already thirty-four.

The secret of Petey's paternity is the most dramatic element in the story and the clandestine trysts between Emma and Roy provide much of the suspense. The reader expects an explosion when Morgan and Zhenya find out that their friend and neighbor is a child rapist. They may be blind to the truth, but the truth does not escape the sharp eyes of Peter Ivanovich, who has a weakness for young girls himself. He understands that Roy's interest in Petey, as well as their physical resemblance, are unmistakable clues that Emma's parents cannot see because they could not believe that their friendly, trusted neighbor—a police officer at that—would have taken advantage of a fourteen-year-old girl.

Morgan further irritates Zhenya by befriending the loutish Danny Ford, using family funds to bail him out of jail and letting him live in their basement. Danny was Morgan's assistant on the garbage truck until he was arrested by Roy for possession of a pistol that had been used in a gang murder. No one can understand why Morgan should have any compassion for this young former gang member, who cannot even function effectively as a probationary apprentice garbage collector. Peter Ivanovich hates him on sight. He sees the overgrown, obnoxious bully as belonging to the same class as the uniformed thugs who mindlessly executed orders to enslave tens of millions in Europe and the Soviet Union. Roy hates him because he recognizes him as a career criminal. Roy is also apprehensive about having an unprincipled young hoodlum living under the same roof as Emma and disapproves of the friendship that springs up between his young son Petey and Danny, whose intelligence quotient is not much higher than that of the little boy.

Danny characteristically expresses his primitive feelings in grunts, glares, and shrugs. In spite of their antipathy, Roy and Zhenya find themselves helping Danny to escape the prison term he richly deserves. Roy destroys his career by stealing the gun that would have been used to convict Danny of being at least an accessory to murder, and Morgan and Zhenya become accessories to the crime themselves by burying the weapon in a nightmarish scene at the city landfill in the dead of night. Danny shows no gratitude, but gratitude is not in his nature. He, too, is a product of the twentieth century, an all-too-common example of the barbarians proliferating in cities, towns, and out among the junkyards, roadhouses, and dilapidated house trailers in the isolated countryside.

Peter Ivanovich, who has learned more from bitter life experiences than from all the books he has read, tries to explain to his daughter Zhenya why her husband concerned himself about Danny's fate. She initially suspected that it was because Morgan had somehow found out that Danny was the father of Emma's child. Since she loathes Danny, this suspicion only makes her the more disgusted with her entire life and the more motivated to terminate her marriage. She goes as far as trying to buy a condo in a new suburban development. She is told, however, that she cannot take title as sole owner as long as she is only contemplating divorce but still legally married. She feels hopelessly entangled with a husband who comes to university functions in smelly work clothes, a daughter who seems content to be a dependent unwed mother, a grandson for whom she became the primary caregiver because her daughter was only a child herself when she gave birth, and a father who seems destined to become a houseguest for all of his remaining years.

Peter Ivanovich was one of the worst fathers a daughter could imagine. He was absent throughout most of her life and never provided the love and understanding she needed. Nonetheless, she knows—and her father knows—that she has an innate compulsion to play the part of the devoted daughter which every Russian father expects.

Having obtained a key to the condo of her dreams—a sepulchrally white set of empty rooms that offer the false promise of a chance to start life all over again—Zhenya goes there in secret to hide from everyone she knows. She even breaks into the unit to sleep on the carpet after the real estate agent has had to change all the locks. Her father finally reveals that the real explanation for Morgan's interest in Danny is that the young man is exactly the same age their son would have been if he had lived. This revelation hardly makes Zhenya feel any better. In fact, she slaps her father's face and orders the astonished old man never to mention that theory again.

Boswell likes symbolism, even though it seems a little out of place in what—at least in its deadpan tone and lackadaisical plot—resembles a minimalist novel. The street where the Morgans live is being widened to make way for the relentless progress that is homogenizing so many American towns with chainsaws, bulldozers, dump trucks, and franchise outlets. All the beautiful trees on Forest Avenue have to be cut down and the symbolism of this event is perhaps a little too reminiscent of Anton Chekhov's play *Vishnyovy sad* (pr., pb. 1904; *The Cherry Orchard*, 1908). Boswell's people, like little people everywhere, are victims of powerful forces that do their insidious work slowly over centuries. They have no choice but to accept their fate and to grab whatever little happiness they can find along the way. To quote French detective novelist Georges Simenon (1903-1989), who saw his share of the twentieth century's troubles, "Nothing is ever pleasant and serene. Nowhere."

Peter Ivanovich has seen so many real troubles in his lifetime, including Stalin's mass murders and two world wars, that he cannot take his family's problems very seriously. Having lived through much of history's cruelest century, he has no illusions about humankind. Americans may expect life to be tranquil, hygienic, and comfortable, but he knows that life everywhere is precarious and unpredictable. He not only disrupts the lives of his daughter and son-in-law but also gets involved with the uptight, prudish Adriana East, who lives in a spotless house on the other side of the now deforested Forest Avenue. She is the type of woman who involves herself with committees and cultural affairs, reading the latest books whether she likes them or not, keeping herself busy to avoid facing her loneliness and sexual frustration. The drunken Russian libertine takes her to bed on the night he first meets her and in a short while, he has made himself quite at home in her home—though he still comes across the street to help himself to his daughter's food and liquor. Mrs. East realizes that her hitherto genteel reputation has been demolished but adopts her lover's hedonistic, amoral, existential attitude. She suddenly seems to be a much better, much more likable person, because she has become real.

All the characters' problems seem to work themselves out at the end, although not to anyone's complete satisfaction. Life drifts on in Hayden, Illinois, as it does everywhere else. The old century comes to an end and a new one begins, offering promises that will never be fulfilled and illusions that will have to be shattered.

Bill Delaney

Sources for Further Study

Booklist 98 (March 15, 2002): 1210.
Kirkus Reviews 70 (February 15, 2002): 203.
Library Journal 127 (March 15, 2002): 106.
The New York Times Book Review 107 (April 21, 2002): 10.
Publishers Weekly 249 (March 18, 2002): 79.

CHARLES DARWIN
The Power of Place

Author: Janet Browne (1950-   )
Publisher: Alfred A. Knopf (New York). 624 pp. $37.50
Type of work: Biography, history of science, natural history, and science
Time: 1858-1882
Locale: England

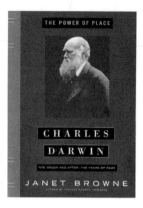

~

This comprehensive narrative of the last third of Darwin's life focuses on the provenance of On the Origin of Species *(1859), the controversies it provoked, and the research and writings it stimulated*

~

Principal personages:
>CHARLES DARWIN (1809-1882), English naturalist who discovered the mechanism of how new species originate
>EMMA (WEDGWOOD) DARWIN (1808-1896), Charles Darwin's first cousin, later his wife, and mother of their ten children
>ALFRED RUSSEL WALLACE (1823-1913), English naturalist who independently proposed the theory of evolution by survival of the fittest
>CHARLES LYELL (1797-1875), English scientist whose *Principles of Geology* (3 volumes, 1830-1833) had a pivotal influence on Darwin
>THOMAS HENRY HUXLEY (1825-1895), English evolutionary biologist who became a principal proponent of Darwinism
>JOSEPH DALTON HOOKER (1817-1911), Darwin's closest friend, who founded and directed the Royal Botanic Gardens at Kew

Charles Darwin: Voyaging (1995), the first volume of Janet Browne's two-volume biography, was highly praised by several knowledgeable critics. That first volume centered on how the voyage of the *Beagle* transformed Darwin from a shiftless student into a focused naturalist with a talent for observation, experiment, and imaginative theorizing. In style and substance Browne's second volume, which deals with Darwin's transformation from a respected rural naturalist to a world-famous biologist, constitutes a complementary continuation of the story and themes she introduced in her first volume.

Unlike biographers who depict Darwin as an isolated recluse, Browne views him, through his family, friends, and fellow scientists, as very much a part of Victorian England and, through his immense correspondence, as very much a part of the world. Her perceptive use of the thousands of letters Darwin wrote freshens familiar stories and deepens the understanding of the origin and development of his ideas. Despite the ongoing spate of books on Darwin, Browne has discovered new things about the man and reinterpreted old things. Drawing on original documents, she has been able to situate Darwin and those who were important in his life in meticulously imagined social, political, and institutional settings.

The framework for her analysis in the second volume is tripartite. In part 1, "Author," her main concern is with the events leading to the publication of Darwin's great work, *On the Origin of Species by Means of Natural Selection: Or, The Preservation of Favoured Races in the Struggle for Life*, and with the subsequent controversies generated by the book's publication. In part 2, "Experimenter," she focuses on Darwin's efforts, largely through his work on the variations of domesticated plants and animals, to provide extensive evidence for the truth of his ideas. In part 3, "Celebrity," she details how Darwin became a world-famous scientist through his various publications and through his adroit use of correspondents, disciples, and the nineteenth century mass media (newspapers, magazines, and journals).

Janet Browne was an editor of Darwin's correspondence and one of the editors of the Dictionary of the History of Science *(1981); her previous books include* The Secular Ark: Studies in the History of Biogeography *(1983) and* Charles Darwin: Voyaging *(1995). She is professor in the history of biology at the Wellcome Trust Centre for the History of Medicine at University College, London.*

The pivotal part is the first, which shows how *On the Origin of Species* changed his life. Browne begins this part by setting the scene with Darwin comfortably ensconced in his large country house, loved by his wife Emma and their children, and cared for by a large staff of servants. By the late 1850's Darwin had produced a number of scientific publications that had garnered for him a reputation as a skilled naturalist. Twenty years earlier, he had conceived the idea of natural selection, and he had begun writing a massive book to prove its validity. However, he was a perfectionist who wanted to overwhelm his readers with evidence. In 1856 his friend Charles Lyell warned him to publish a preliminary account of this theory to avoid some competitor preempting him, but Darwin was happy with his routine of leisurely fact-gathering and writing. With a large private income, he was under no pressure to publish, unlike his academic correspondents.

This state of affairs changed cataclysmically when Darwin received a letter and handwritten essay from Alfred Russel Wallace, who was then living and working on an island in the Dutch East Indies. His essay, "On the Tendency of Varieties to Depart Indefinitely from the Original Type," described a mechanism for the genesis of new species that precisely mirrored the idea that Darwin thought was unique to himself. Darwin resolved the dilemma of what to do with Wallace's article by following a suggestion of Charles Lyell and Joseph Hooker: a presentation of both Darwin's and Wallace's work on natural selection at a meeting of the Linnean Society. However, since Wallace was separated from these scientists geographically (he was half a world away) and socially (he was neither well-born nor wealthy), it was easy for Lyell and

Hooker to manipulate the situation in Darwin's favor. Darwin did not attend the meeting because of the death of one of his children, and on learning what happened he felt shame and guilt because he assumed his work would be subordinated to Wallace's, rather than vice-versa. When Wallace eventually heard from Darwin, he accepted good-naturedly what had been done, but the theory of natural selection would become known as Darwinism, not Wallaceism.

The emotional origin of *On the Origin of Species* was therefore in Darwin's disappointment and guilt. His perfectionism and procrastination were now pushed to the side, and he distilled his piles of data into a book intended for a general audience. He wisely began it with domesticated plants and animals, since he realized that ordinary people were familiar with the creation of domestic varieties by breeders. Having convinced people of the mutability of species, he was then able to use an analogy: Whereas breeders select the variation they desire to preserve, nature acts on all variations, preserving those that help the creature survive, eliminating those that interfere with its survival. Darwin still believed in God while writing this book, but the story he told of the deselection of poorly adapted organisms throughout time was in stark contrast to the spiritual and progressive account of the creation of living things in the Bible.

The publication of *On the Origin of Species* in 1859 transformed Darwin's life. The books and articles he would publish, the friendships he would make and break, and the controversies he and his followers would engage in all grew out of this book's ideas and their verifications. Although *On the Origin of Species* did not sell as well as Charles Dickens's *A Tale of Two Cities*, published in the same year, it sold surprisingly well for an intricately reasoned scientific treatise. Darwin collected nearly 350 reviews, and the issues he raised in this book were widely debated. However, he remained aloof from these public debates, preferring to propagandize his ideas through his correspondence and through such surrogates as Thomas Huxley, Hooker, and Lyell. Browne depicts Darwin as a masterful tactician who advanced his cause by cultivating supporters in the media and in significant institutions. Another way Darwin advanced the theory of natural selection was through publications resulting from his continued observations and experiments. The data he collected on domesticated plants and animals became an important part of *The Variation of Animals and Plants Under Domestication* (1868). During the last two decades of his life he published over sixty articles and ten books, and these enhanced his reputation as England's leading naturalist.

What amazed earlier biographers is that this prodigious creativity came from a very sick man. Many books and articles in the Darwin industry have been dedicated to possible solutions to the mystery of Darwin's illness. Previous authors have attributed his problems to a tropical disease, unresolved emotional difficulties connected with his mother's death, or acute anxiety over becoming a transmutationist. Others think that Darwin was allergic to some of the chemicals he used in his research. Browne's views on this controversial topic are that the multiplicity of Darwin's symptoms (nausea, frequent vomiting, skin disorders such as eczema and boils, and dizziness) indicate that he must have been suffering from a variety of conditions or diseases.

Darwin was deeply concerned that he would pass his health problems onto his children, since he had married his first cousin. He was relieved when his plant experiments showed that the deleterious effects produced by inbreeding were not nearly as pernicious as he had once believed. His interest in the issue of human breeding found an outlet in his book on the origin of human species, *The Descent of Man and Selection in Relation to Sex* (1871). He bluntly stated in this book that no basic difference existed between humans and the higher mammals. He even tried to biologize religious belief, asserting that faith was little more than inherited instinct, much like a monkey's fear of snakes. He also held that moral good and evil were neither absolute nor innate; these value judgments were the consequences of learned behavior.

Many reviewers reacted negatively against Darwin's evolutionary views on humans, and Browne, reflecting her own ideological commitments, points out some of the unacceptable ramifications of Darwin's arguments. For example, he believed in the superiority of males over females. Furthermore, his naturalism meant that races had to be understood biologically, reinforcing ideas then prevalent in his social class about racial hierarchies, with the white race on top and the black race on the bottom. Although these views actually contradict Darwin's constant admonition to himself to avoid any mention of higher and lower when discussing the differentiation of various species, Darwin was emotionally imprisoned in his social class. He simply assumed that the British upper classes possessed the highest moral and cultural principles that had ever emerged in evolutionary history.

Instead of diminishing Darwin's celebrity, his controversial views seemed to enhance it, and in the last years of his life he became very famous, particularly through such popular books as *The Expression of the Emotions in Man and Animals* (1872), which showed the cross-cultural emotional universality of certain facial expressions, and *The Formation of Vegetable Mould Through the Action of Worms* (1881), his final book and, astonishingly, his overall best-seller.

Since his remaining seven children were now adults, he had ample time for his work. Some of his boys chose scientific careers, though none became as successful as their father. A grandchild, Bernard, brought joy to his declining years, and his article, "Biographical Sketch of an Infant," based on his observations of Bernard, had a major influence on developmental psychology. His deteriorating health and the deaths of relatives and friends distressed him but, as Browne points out, Darwin could be selfish, self-indulgent, even ruthless in cutting himself off from events and people that no longer served a useful purpose in his life.

Now extremely wealthy, he could afford the care of four doctors during his final months. When he died on April 19, 1882, he was an unrepentant agnostic. However, his well-known attacks on religion (he had called the Christian God cruel and irrational) did not prevent his being buried, after an elaborate religious service, in Westminster Abbey. Continuing the work of their master, his supporters had secured this honor for him because it would help spread Darwinism.

As a historian and biographer, Browne sees Darwin both as a product of his time and place (Victorian England) and of his life (he made the *Origin* but the *Origin* also made him). Thus she has room for many Darwins in her treatment—the humble and ambitious, the abolitionist and racist, the revolutionary and conservative. With her mastery of a massive number of primary and secondary sources, she is able, through her lucid prose, to capture many of these Darwins and to give the reader a vivid sense of the places and times that nurtured his fascinating intellectual odyssey.

Robert J. Paradowski

Sources for Further Study

Booklist 98 (August, 2002): 1901.
The Christian Science Monitor, September 26, 2002, p. 21.
Discover 23 (October, 2002): 78.
Kirkus Reviews 70 (June 15, 2002): 851.
Library Journal 127 (October 1, 2002): 124.
Nature 419 (October 24, 2002): 781.
The New York Times Book Review 107 (October 6, 2002): 12.
Publishers Weekly 249 (July 22, 2002): 167.
Quarterly Review of Biology, June, 2002, p. 175.
Science 297 (September 13, 2002): 1812.
Scientific American 287 (October, 2002): 103.

CHILD OF MY HEART

Author: Alice McDermott (1953-   )
Publisher: Farrar, Straus and Giroux (New York). 242
   pp. $23.00
Type of work: Novel
Time: The early 1960's
Locale: East Hampton, New York

～

Fifteen-year-old Theresa baby-sits and walks dogs for
East Hampton's rich summer residents, while developing
a loving, protective relationship with her eight-year-old
cousin

～

Principal characters:
> THERESA, an intelligent, beautiful fifteen-year-old girl
> DAISY, Theresa's eight-year-old cousin
> FLORA, Theresa's two-year-old baby-sitting charge
> THE ARTIST, Flora's seventy-year-old father
> ANA, the artist's housekeeper and lover
> DR. KAUFMAN, one of Theresa's baby-sitting and dog-walking clients
> MR. and MRS. RICHARDSON, Theresa's clients

Child of My Heart is a middle-aged woman's reminiscence of her fifteenth summer, when she was in charge of "four dogs, three cats, the Moran kids, Daisy, my
eight-year-old cousin, and Flora, the toddler child of a local artist." Theresa's recollections of that momentous summer possess a dreamlike quality, as if life in early
1960's East Hampton was slightly removed from reality. The youthful characters are
clearly delineated, their daily rounds meticulously described, while the portrayal of
the adult world is sketchy, vague, and short on names. Unfortunately, adult reality im-
pinges upon the idyllic realm of childhood as the teenage Theresa bridges the gap between youth and adulthood.

Theresa's parents, in their mid-forties at her birth and knowing she would be their
only child, moved from Brooklyn to East Hampton, Long Island, when Theresa was
only two. Aware that their daughter possessed an unusual beauty in the mold of Jackie
Kennedy or Elizabeth Taylor, they relocated to this summer enclave of the rich
to maximize her opportunities for success. Being working-class Irish Americans
of limited education, they could envision future success for their daughter only
through an advantageous marriage. To maximize her contacts with the wealthy, they
enrolled Theresa as a day student at a boarding school for the daughters of wealthy
South Americans and Asians during the school year and in the summer encouraged
her to hire herself out to the wealthy as baby-sitter, dog-walker, or mother's helper.

∼

Alice McDermott published her first
novel in 1982. Her second novel,
That Night *(1987), was nominated*
for the Pulitzer Prize and the
National Book Award. She won the
National Book Award for Charming
Billy *(1998). She has taught at the*
University of California at San
Diego and American University, has
been a writer-in-residence at
Lynchburg and Hollins Colleges in
Virginia, and was lecturer in
English at the University of New
Hampshire. Much of her work is
based on her experience growing up
Irish Catholic in Long Island, New
York.

∼

Proving equally popular with adults, kids, and dogs, Theresa became from the age of ten the most sought after baby-sitter in town. Her knack with children and animals was such that they often preferred her company to that of their own parents or owners.

This particular summer, Theresa is charged with the daily care of Flora, the two-year-old daughter of a famous seventy-year-old artist and his much younger fourth wife. She is also dog-walker for Dr. Kaufman, a recently divorced, lonely, middle-aged man, and an older couple, the Richardsons. By default, she often also tends to the severely neglected neighboring Moran children. Most importantly, however, she is companion to her eight-year-old cousin Daisy who, at Theresa's invitation, has come to spend the summer with her, escaping Brooklyn and her seven siblings, strict father, and tired mother.

Daisy accompanies her cousin on the daily round of baby-sitting and dog-walking while the two girls weave a wonderful private fantasy world around themselves as they perform their duties. Entering into this private domain, however, is the increasingly evident fact that something is seriously wrong with Daisy. She has bruises on her feet, back, and arm, suffers from fevers, and appears pale and weak. Theresa, sensing that Daisy's summer idyll will be over once the adults notice her condition, tries to minister to the eight-year-old herself, feeding her liver and spinach and sneaking her children's aspirin.

In Theresa's world, adults appear to have abdicated responsibility for their children. Her own parents are barely a presence in her life, leaving for work early in the morning and returning home late. Even while at home, they seem to form a close bond which does not include Theresa. At breakfast, "when they saw me, my father would pull out the third chair and my mother would stand up to get an extra plate as if I were an unexpected guest." Theresa realizes that she is destined to separate herself from them, as "the best assurance they would have that I had indeed moved into a better strata of society would be my scorn for the lesser one to which they belonged." She notices that in "[t]urning away from me in anticipation of my turning away from them, they left me more alone that summer than perhaps I'd ever been."

Daisy's parents also form a close unit which tends to shut out their children. Theresa notes that in her aunt and uncle's bedroom, rather than pictures of their children, they have only a wedding picture, as if believing that by closing the bedroom door they can deny the existence of their offspring. Theresa's young charge Flora might as well be parentless, as her mother leaves for parts unknown, her father only fitfully notices her, and the housekeeper has no interest in her at all. The neighboring Moran children, as well, are the victims of extreme parental neglect.

Almost from the beginning the reader is privy to the fact of Daisy's impending death, which is prefigured in many ways, casting an air of sadness over the otherwise joyous summer days. For example, when one of the cats she has been caring for dies, Theresa realizes that "It was not Curly anymore, that lifeless thing Debbie had cradled, not in my recollection of it. It was the worst thing. It was what I was up against." In the sight of Daisy carrying a kite on her back one afternoon toward the end of their time together, Theresa cannot help but see "[a] modern art version, it seemed to me, of angel wings." Also running throughout the novel is the metaphor of Daisy's jeweled plastic shoes, the color of which seems to magically reflect her condition at the time. One day, toward the end of the summer, Theresa points out to Daisy that they have turned sky blue, which means she is about to fly.

Daisy's impending death is emblematic of the death of Theresa's childhood. The summer that Daisy begins to die is the summer Theresa leaves childhood behind for good and crosses over into adulthood. She passes all of her childhood stories and fantasies on to Daisy, along with her old clothes, still stored neatly in the attic. Little by little she gives over her childhood to Daisy, who is soon to die. Significantly, Theresa refers to Daisy as the "child of my heart." As Theresa's childhood dies with Daisy, her adult self begins to emerge, beginning with her sexual initiation.

Although the loss of a young girl's virginity is usually accompanied by a loss of innocence, Theresa is already wise beyond her years and in control of her fate. She coolly admits that "my easy-to-admire childish beauty was quickly becoming something a little thinner, and sharper, and certainly more complicated . . . " and she very deftly handles the clumsy behavior of the middle-aged men whose children and pets she tends to. Her sexual initiation with Flora's seventy-year-old father is not so much a seduction by him as a simple experiment on her part. "My advantage was that I knew what he was trying to do—and I was better at it." After sleeping with the artist, she feels that her separation from her parents, and thus her childhood, is complete: "I felt sweet, deep, sorrowful nostalgia for them, and for the days I had been in their care."

McDermott is particularly adept at creating a childlike sense of wonder. Theresa has a special touch in creating magic for the children in her care. Instead of buying one sucker for Daisy at the corner store, she buys one hundred, which they giddily toss all over Daisy's house to the delight and amazement of her siblings. On a day too cold to go to the beach, Theresa, Daisy, and Flora build an elaborate construction-paper city on the porch, in which Flora's missing mother has wondrous adventures. On what is to become their last day together, the three girls attach lollipops and licorice strings to a tree in Flora's yard, creating a marvelous candy tree.

McDermott also excels in depicting the Irish Catholic experience in America which, although only peripheral to this novel, she captures beautifully. She describes Theresa's parents and their friends spending evenings tracing "[c]ircuitous, circumstantial lineages that seemed to encompass all the years of their youth and the breadth of the five boroughs, and were always linked . . . to the names of Catholic parishes, as if no identity of friend or cousin . . . could be truly established without first determining where he or she had been baptized or schooled or married. . . . " Although content with this insular, smothering world themselves, they realize that it will never be enough for their daughter.

Child of My Heart simultaneously inspires admiration and provokes questions. Theresa seems at times too good to be true—too mature for a fifteen-year-old, too in control, too perfect with the children, and her attraction to the seventy-year-old artist is problematic. Similarly, Theresa's motives in keeping Daisy's bruises and fevers from any responsible adults is questionable. Does she really want to preserve Daisy's one last summer of magic, or does she just want to keep her close to preserve her own childhood? "I knew I would have to tell someone, my mother, my father, perhaps Dr. Kaufman himself, and already I felt the loss of her, taken from my arms." Underlying the entire novel is the question of the narrator's reliability. The middle-aged Theresa is a complete cipher, and the reader can only guess at her motives.

Thus, *Child of My Heart*, on the surface a simple reminiscence of a notable summer, is in fact a many-layered, complex novel, dealing with death, childhood, adolescence, loss of innocence, parental responsibility, and much more. The overriding theme, however, is loss, "the inevitable, insufferable loss buried like a dark jewel at the heart of every act of love."

Mary Virginia Davis

Sources for Further Study

Booklist 99 (September 15, 2002): 180.
Library Journal 127 (November 15, 2002): 101.
Los Angeles Times Book Review, November 24, 2002, p. 3.
The New York Times Book Review 107 (November 24, 2002): 11.
Publishers Weekly 249 (October 7, 2002): 51.

THE CITY OF YOUR FINAL DESTINATION

Author: Peter Cameron (1959-   )
Publisher: Farrar, Straus and Giroux (New York). 312
   pp. $24.00
Type of work: Novel
Time: 1995-1996
Locale: Lawrence, Kansas; Ochos Rios, Montevideo,
   Tacuarembo, and Tranqueras, Uruguay; Manhattan

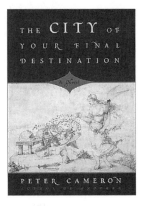

~

*A graduate student seeking to write a biography as his
dissertation finds his life changed by his experiences in
Uruguay*

~

   Principal characters:
   OMAR RAZAGHI, a graduate student at the University of Kansas
   JULES GUND, a recently deceased novelist
   ARDEN LANGDON, Gund's mistress
   CAROLINE GUND, his wife
   ADAM GUND, his brother
   PETE, Adam's lover
   DEIRDRE MCARTHUR, Omar's girlfriend
   PORTIA, daughter of Arden and Jules Gund
   DR. PENI, Omar's physician

Peter Cameron's fourth novel begins as if it will be yet another self-conscious,
postmodern contemplation of the worlds of literature and academics, full of arcane allusions and games-playing. It turns out, however, to be something quite different: an
unsentimental yet moving look at the ways love, identity, and destiny intertwine.

   An Iranian raised in Canada, Omar Razaghi is a graduate student in literature at the
University of Kansas who receives a fellowship to write a biographical study of novelist Jules Gund, a native of Uruguay. Omar has told the fellowship committee he has
been granted cooperation by Gund's estate, but in fact, such approval has been denied. Without access to the writer's papers and interviews with his family, Omar cannot possibly create a biography. A passive fellow, Omar is willing to give up and take
his punishment for lying, but his girlfriend Deirdre, a fellow student, nags him into
going to Uruguay to confront the novelist's literary executors.

   The biography is not opposed by Gund's elderly brother Adam, who lives on the
family estate with his lover Pete, a young Thai he has rescued from a life of prostitu-
tion in Germany. Adam is outnumbered, however, by Caroline, Gund's widow, who
claims her husband told her he wanted no biography, and by Arden Langdon, the
writer's mistress and mother of his only child, the eight-year-old Portia. Arden, an

~

The son of a banker, Peter Cameron grew up in Pompton Plains, New Jersey, and London. After graduating from Hamilton College, he went to work for St. Martin's Press and began publishing short stories. He has published four novels and three collections of stories. He has taught at Oberlin College and Hamilton College and lives in Manhattan.

~

American who met Gund while taking his class at the university in Montevideo, feels that an artist's work should speak for itself. Typical of Cameron's subtle, understated approach is the lack of any hint that anyone sees anything unusual about a man's wife, mistress, and illegitimate child living together after his death. Likewise, no reason is given for Gund's suicide.

Caroline and, especially, Arden gradually soften toward Omar, with the latter developing romantic feelings for the exotically handsome youth. This sympathetic view grows after an unfortunate accident. Helping Pete pick peaches, Omar is stung by a bee, falls, and is temporarily paralyzed. (Nature's indifference to man is one of several minor themes running through the novel.) Deirdre is summoned, and feelings of jealousy arise between her and Arden. Meanwhile, the incapacitated Omar has time to reflect upon what he truly wants to do with his life.

The City of Your Final Destination is essentially about character, mood, and style; the plot and any thematic content are almost afterthoughts. Cameron is concerned with setting up a situation that most readers will expect to go in one direction, only to take it into unexpected areas as the characters discover truths about themselves.

Omar progresses from a timid, uncertain careerist to a more mature, if still unsettled man not afraid to take chances. Initially, Deirdre must take control because Omar cannot. She wants to prevent him from becoming "one of those professors who are always wandering around the halls searching for their office with egg salad spilled down their front." He has long planned the Gund biography but has somehow never gotten around to learning Spanish. Omar is a danger to himself. In care of his Kansas landlady's dog, he not only misplaces it but steps into quicksand while searching for the animal.

When Arden suggests he is using flattery as part of his strategy, Omar replies, "If I had a strategy, I wouldn't be here in the first place." Admitting he is cowed by reality, he promises to "behave like a normal person for as long as I possibly can." Meeting resistance from the executors, he impulsively says he no longer intends to write a standard academic biography and then tries to understand why he would say such a thing. Cameron does not, however, intend Omar—or any of the other characters, for that matter—to be seen as neurotic. Omar is just uncertain of his goals, slightly adrift.

He becomes, briefly, physically paralyzed but is always emotionally and even intellectually paralyzed, a bit like nineteenth century novelist Henry James's international travelers. Displacement is a major theme of *The City of Your Final Destination*. The Gunds are American, French, German, and Thai exiles in South America, and Omar has never had a feeling of home either in Toronto, where he grew up, or Kansas. He is drawn to Gund in the first place because the writer is a half-Jewish European raised as a Catholic in Uruguay. Even in Kansas, Omar is not in Kansas anymore. He is actually more at ease in the Gunds' Ochos Rios, an Oz more like home than Kansas.

Caroline's motives for trying to prevent Omar from writing the biography are selfish, but some of the reasons she gives him are actually valid. "Whatever holds you to writing this biography is not important," she tells him. "Now is your chance to let that all go. This is an opportunity to change your life." Neither he nor the reader understand the truthfulness of her stance at this point. Such is the complexity of Cameron's motivations for his characters. Doing the right thing can result from selfishness, cowardice, or a fluky accident.

People are not psychological stereotypes in Cameron's fictional universe. People are complex. Deirdre is drawn to Omar's goodness, sweetness, and loveliness, while recognizing these are balanced by his foreignness, strangeness, otherness, "all the uncharted regions of him she did not know." Omar begins to find his identity—one of the more significant of Cameron's themes—only after finally standing up to Deirdre following his accident. He is inept because she sees him that way, and he is tired of feeling guilty about his inadequacies.

When Pete tells Omar that Caroline has been lying about Gund's wish that there be no biography, Omar confronts her as well, threatening to pursue the project even without her approval. By finally being aggressive, he learns the truth about her resistance to the biography: She fears she will be portrayed as a monster (because of Gund's unfaithfulness and suicide) regardless of who writes such a book.

Seeing she has no control over her husband's life, Caroline gives in: "Explain it all to us. Explain ourselves to us. How grateful to you we will be." Such a statement is doubly ironic: Not only is Omar unlikely truly to understand this highly unusual group of people, but they actually need someone to help them understand themselves.

Omar's victory, however, has been earned by too much emotional pain, and he feels hollow. The scholar has his rights, but the feelings of those he hurts may matter more. Accepting responsibility for the consequences of one's actions is another theme and perhaps has something to do with Gund's unexplained death. As with the Gund family's flight from Germany and his own from Iran, Omar seeks escape and the hope of personal peace but only after facing down a sense of doom.

While Omar comes to Uruguay as an outsider, Arden is already an outsider within Ochos Rios, despite Portia's love and Adam's sympathy. A former child actor who grew up essentially on her own in Wisconsin, California, and England, Arden always played orphans or sick children in films. Cutting herself off from her father, an alcoholic director, she drifted into Montevideo as a member of a religious musical group, suddenly, in her words, came to her senses, and met and fell in love with the enigmatic Gund. She has generally been at a loss since his death but begins coming back to life after meeting Omar. Cameron's characters find themselves only through being loved by and caring for others.

Adam realizes his selfish love for Pete is suffocating the youth and is willing to set him free. Caroline, for her part, had essentially lost her own identity by stealing Gund from her sister. In Uruguay, she turned from being an artist to being a painter who has lost her belief in her talent, reducing herself simply to copying the works of others. Omar jolts her out of her smug self-pity, and she returns to New York and the home left her by her sister, slowly embracing a new life like the one on which she had turned her back. It is wonderfully ironic that the passive Omar can bring about so many changes for others. The author might be criticized for inflicting pain on Adam and Deirdre, but these characters are more capable of dealing with disappointment than the others. Both joy and pain occur on his characters' endless voyages of self-discovery.

The City of Your Final Destination is a subtle, beautifully written novel that never indulges in showing off. Made up of two-thirds dialogue and one-third short declarative sentences, it resembles a less self-conscious version of Ernest Hemingway's style: Caroline "crossed the room and looked out the other side, out across the tops of trees. She looked up: the sky was still a very pale blue, a tired, ancient blue. There were no clouds. She heard gravel crunching and saw Diego walking down the drive. He had come up from the village to fix the hot water heater. Perhaps they would have hot water tonight. She could take a bath."

Cameron brilliantly follows Hemingway's dictum that what is left out of a work of fiction is often as important as what is left in. It is truly amazing what he can suggest about Jules Gund while revealing only a handful of facts. Gund lives on less in his art than in his effect on those who loved him.

The unforced beauty of Cameron's distinctive style accents the surface languidness of life at Ochos Rios. Cameron's merging of style, strong characterization, gentle, often amusing satire, and unsentimental insights into the quiet desperation of his creations is a masterful achievement. He is a craftsman of highly intelligent, wonderfully compassionate fiction.

Michael Adams

Sources for Further Study

Gay & Lesbian Review 9 (July/August, 2002): 45.
Kirkus Reviews 70 (February 15, 2002): 204.
Library Journal 127 (February 1, 2002): 129.
The New York Times, May 15, 2002, p. E8.
The New York Times Book Review 107 (May 19, 2002): 14.
Publishers Weekly 249 (February 11, 2002): 158.
The Times Literary Supplement, May 3, 2002, p. 21.

COMMONS

Author: Myung Mi Kim (1957-   )
Publisher: University of California Press (Berkeley). 111
   pp. $35.00; paperback $16.95
Type of work: Poetry

≈

Kim's poetry reflects on the very nature by which lan-
guage creates meaning and how individual sounds distin-
guish one word from another; her poems scrutinize the lim-
its of translation and examine to what degree authorship of
a text implies authority on its subject

≈

Myung Mi Kim's fourth collection of poetry, *Commons*, challenges the reader to reflect on the very way in which language operates to create meaning and how free association influences human thought processes. The poems are minimalist and always require attentive reading in order to catch their nuances of meaning. Most are set in the contemporary world in places reminiscent of America or South Korea, or at least of a developing country which has seen its share of bloodshed and hunger. Kim offers the reader a beautiful microcosm of language sounds, word juxtapositions, and associative reflections which carry the persona into fresh cognitive territory. The incorporation of multiple text fragments from the works of other writers reflects the central question behind many poems collected in *Commons:* To what degree can a reader trust the assumed authority of any writer on a given subject?

Commons opens with "Exordium," the fifteen stanzas of which explore the power of free association. Here, Kim's technique is reminiscent of that of the European Surrealists such as Max Ernst (1891-1976) or Jean Arp (1887-1966) in the early twentieth century, who promoted what they called "automatic writing," or writing down ideas just as they came to their minds, as an alternative to classic models of composing poetry. At first glance, Kim's sentences within each stanza appear as unrelated as the stanzas themselves. "Numbers in cell divisions. Spheres of debt. The paradigm's stitchery of unrelated points." Just as the idea of free association is used in classical psychoanalysis to get at core concerns in the subconscious, Kim's sentences do show some relation to each other and possess a unifying idea. Here, the mathematical mode of thinking, which is used by modern, Western-based biological science to derive at some truth and understanding of the work of living cells, is linked to the use of mathematics in modern, Western-based capitalism, where it serves to define and fix the debts afflicting various borrowers. Thus, the third sentence itself comments on the technique of the poem: Apparently unrelated ideas are stitched together to reveal an underlying paradigm, or belief system. The modern Western world relies on mathematics to understand, and to control, all aspects of life ranging from small cells to a nation's debt burden.

Myung Mi Kim was born in 1957 in South Korea and emigrated to America. She is a professor of creative writing at San Francisco State University and has published four well-received volumes of poetry. Her first book, Under Flag *(1991), won the 1991 Multicultural Publishers Book Award, and her poetry has been praised by literary critics.*

"Exordium" continues to reveal insights through free association and juxtaposition of apparently unrelated sentences. Also evident is wordplay and a finely tuned sense for the nuances of language, where the slight alteration of a common phrase can suddenly startle the reader and thus invite new thinking about an issue. "A red balloon and a blackwinged bird at semblance of crossing in a pittance of sky." The sentence may remind a reader of the American poet Wallace Stevens (1879-1955), whose red wheelbarrow and much-analyzed blackbirds form a frame of reference in modern poetry. Kim's look at this sudden juxtaposition of two different yet similar things apparently meeting on the two-dimensional plane of the sky, of which only "a pittance" is visible, invites the reader to reflect on the little things and unexpected observations in life. From here, readers may begin their own investigation into the interaction of all living and created things against the backdrop of a shared nature.

"Lamenta" consists of a long series of numbered poems, most of which occupy exactly one page. In correspondence with the poet's desire to create a fragmented, dislocated, eruptive, and challenging world, most poems are missing in any given range of numbers. The sequence entitled "229 318", which a reader may expect to consist of poems 229 to 318, only offers poems 229, 311, 312, and 314 to 318. It is as though the reader has come across an old book with many pages missing, and the poet invites the reader to use imagination and creativity to fill in her blanks.

Again, *Commons* seems to comment on its own technique in the first lines of poem 229: "The transition from the stability and absoluteness of the world's contents/ to their dissolution into motions and relations." This is ostensibly what the poems are about. A reader's expectation of order is immediately confounded. In *Commons*, all systems of order are suspected of serving the interests of someone else. Order is seen as subjecting that which is ordered to a limited, exploited existence. Thus the poems seek to break up order and substitute it with free associations, fragments, and multiple, disjointed voices. As there are many points of view in life, Kim's poetry strives to reflect this state of existence by being deliberately fragmented, elusive, and self-questioning.

The poems reveal a critical fascination with the sounds and the spelling of the English language. Many of Kim's lines make a critical issue out of words that normally carry quite dissimilar meanings but are either pronounced or written in very similar terms. This fascination links Kim's work to that of the contemporary Chinese American poet Li-Young Lee, whose poem "Persimmons" (in *Rose*, 1992) famously reflects on a creative connection between "sun" and "son," two words that sound exactly the same in English. Like Lee, Kim learned English as a second language. Thus, the two poets may be especially aware of the arbitrary nature of phonetics and the random assignment of meaning to certain speech sounds in all human language.

Poem 314 highlights this underlying play with the arbitrary currents of language: "Money and mourning met/ Sun and sorrow am sent/ For fade and flame." The alliteration of "m" in the first line underlines the similar sound of the two nouns, and invites a creative connection. The poem asks whether money can be linked to mourning in capitalist society and whether the two words are linked causally as well as by the accident of their pronunciation and spelling. The deliberate violation of grammar in the second line serves to jolt the reader to play with a multitude of interpretations. "Sun and sorrow" could be stand-ins for the first-person pronoun "I," which would repair the grammatical flaw to read "I am sent." This would indicate that the persona sees itself as a cosmic force, strongly linking the sustenance of life by the sun with the sorrow which is apparently an inevitable part of life. The purpose of sun and sorrow is to "fade and flame." Here, Kim plays with literal and metaphoric meaning. While the sun literally fades at the end of day and flames in a clear sky, human sorrow does so only as a figure of speech. Ironically, the common sequence of the two activities is reversed by the poet, and sun and sorrow fade before they flame.

Interspersed with the numbered poems of "Lamenta" are three texts by Renaissance scientists reporting their anatomical discoveries. This real analysis of human and animal bodies is juxtaposed to the poems' analysis of the anatomy of language. Kim's examination also goes beyond the English language and includes reflections on the problems of translation. Using her first language of Korean as an example to start her critical inquiry, the poet includes lines in Korean. To highlight the problems associated with translating and transcribing a language that does not use Roman characters, the poems include lines that are written in Korean characters, phonetic transcriptions of Korean sounds in English, and finally show Korean printed according to the official system of transcribing the language using the Western alphabet. In Poem 404, this process is alluded to in a rather stark image:

> Her name and her mother's name
> . . . .
> Carcass of coyote and deer separated by a stream linked by bones
> . . . .
> *sahl-rlim-sah-ri*   house
>   chores

With printed names already seen as dead as animal cadavers, the act of translating the Korean name of the immigrant daughter into English may appear to be like linking them across a stream with a bridge of dry bones. The ensuing phonetic transcription of the Korean language startles the reader, and the association of mother and daughter to household chores is very poignant.

The death of the father has left the poet unable to express herself other than by bracketing all her writing, as if to illustrate the tentativeness of all human efforts and language in the face of death, in Poem 410: "[when my father died and left me nothing]/ [this is how I speak]"

Commons takes its reflection on the look of the spoken word in written language to a final point in its third section, "Works." Here, an anonymous English text is dismembered by the deliberate insertion of blanks, which obliterate part of the original words:

> The lower level of the social hierarchy ====== made up of ====== who tilled and ======== the food

Again, like a European Surrealist poem, a "found sentence" written by someone else is artistically altered to invite the reader to reflect on the everyday use of language, which may itself hide more than it reveals and may also serve the interests of authorities uninterested in social change. Here, the unchallenged reference to a "lower level" of society may implicate writer and reader in the acceptance of such a division. The apparently neutral statement of the fact that such a division exists covers up the alternative position to challenge this division and work for social change. By altering the original line, the poet seeks to encourage the reader to think outside the silent, invisible norms of society, which call for a blind acceptance of official language.

This break-up of an English text is followed by Kim's transcription of the original Korean handwriting of Olga Kim. This woman spent forty years living in Siberia under the former Soviet Union and her fragile Korean characters tell of the experience. The poet does not translate this excerpt, and her non-Korean reading audience is left to behold the writing as inaccessible calligraphy.

While *Commons* contains many allusions to war, strife, hunger, and human suffering, there is also a detailed look at the vegetation surrounding humanity. There is plenty of play with words, and the poet constantly seeks to surprise and challenge the reader. Toward the end of "Works," there is a reflection on the impulse to utter language as an act stemming from the abundance of natural life: "That snapdragon's crimson/ Understood as a potential sound."

Commons closes with a metapoetic reflection on its own creation and describes the poet's motivation for writing. "Pollen Fossil Record" is a succinct self-analysis of the poems that have preceded the final section. The attentive reader can learn of the poet's design for her work, her reasons for using the techniques she employs, and her goals for her art. This self-reflection closes with this powerful line that expresses the poet's purpose for her writing: "To mobilize the notion of our responsibility to one another in social space." Rereading *Commons*, most readers would concur that Myung Mi Kim's poetry has succeeded in this goal.

R. C. Lutz

Sources for Further Study

Publishers Weekly 249 (January 21, 2002): 86.
The Village Voice 47 (May 7, 2002): 121.

THE COMPANY
A Novel of the CIA

Author: Robert Littell (1935-   )
Publisher: Overlook Press (Woodstock, N.Y.). 894 pp.
    $28.95
Type of work: Novel
Time: 1950-1995
Locale: Washington, D.C., Germany, Hungary, Cuba,
    Afghanistan, and the Soviet Union

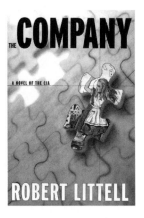

≈

*Littell's magnum opus charts the history of the Central
Intelligence Agency (CIA) in the Cold War, from its beginnings in World War II through the fall of the Soviet Union*

≈

Principal characters:
> HARVEY ("THE SORCERER") TORRITI, the alcoholic head of American
> espionage operations in Berlin, Germany
> JACK ("THE SORCERER'S APPRENTICE") MCAULIFFE, his assistant and
> longtime friend
> E. WINSTROM EBBITT II, another CIA officer
> LEO KRITZKY, a CIA officer and Soviet mole code-named SASHA
> YEVGENY ALEKSANDROVICH TSIPIN, a Soviet spy also known as
> EUGENE DODGSON and GENE LUTWIDGE
> PAVEL (PASHA) SEMYONOVICH ZHILOV, a master of Soviet counter-
> intelligence and known to the CIA only as Starik

Espionage is probably as old as civilization itself. Fictional accounts of the subject have intrigued readers at least since the early nineteenth century, when James Fenimore Cooper's novel *The Spy* (1821) gained its author a loyal following and a lucrative income. In more recent times, renewed interest in the genre came about as a result of tensions between the United States and the Union of Soviet Socialist Republics (U.S.S.R.) following World War II. From 1945 until the fall of the Soviet empire in 1991, the world's two reigning superpowers grappled with a persistent conundrum. Though each nation had its own spheres of influence and both possessed massive military establishments, neither could risk open hostilities because of the risk of nuclear holocaust. Such a war would have incinerated cities and destroyed civilization. This uneasy relationship came to be known as the Cold War, where these determined adversaries employed proxy wars, puppet regimes, propaganda, and espionage as the means of undermining the opposition. The principals in this era of tense international relations are fading from the collective public memory; those who were born after its demise can scarcely comprehend how such a conflict ever came about. Fortunately,

Frequently compared to Graham Greene and John le Carré, Robert Littell has proven himself to be a master of the spy novel. The former Newsweek *reporter's books have been translated into a dozen languages, and one—*The Amateur *(1981)—became a motion picture. His other works include* The October Circle *(1977),* Mother Russia *(1978),* The Once and Future Spy *(1990),* An Agent in Place *(1991),* The Visiting Professor *(1994), and* Walking Back the Cat *(1997).*

there is Robert Littell's novel *The Company* to remind readers what the Cold War was like to those who fought it.

The spy novel, like its close cousin the detective novel, has often been unfairly consigned to the remunerative but déclassé world of the cheap paperback. However, espionage fiction covers a broad spectrum. It runs the gamut from the pure fantasy of Ian Fleming's James Bond to the convincing realism of John le Carré's George Smiley. With several well-received novels in this genre to his credit, Robert Littell is decidedly ranked in the quality end of the spy novel continuum. Littell, like his predecessors, has written extensively about this period, and his novel *The Defection of A. J. Lewinter* (1973) is a fine example of this. What sets *The Company* apart from other works in this genre is the fact that it is nothing less than a comprehensive history of American espionage in the Cold War. It is true that other books have been written about America's spy agency, and the general public has gained some insight into the inner workings of the CIA through the occasional scandal; however, due to the inscrutable nature of its mission—much of its work must always be conducted sub rosa—the public record of the CIA will always remain incomplete. Even more difficult is the problem of cracking the CIA culture, a world closed to those who do not belong to "the Company." As the displaced puzzle piece on the novel's book jacket suggests, this agency is a persistent conundrum. It is only through the medium of fiction—with its seamless blending of the real and the imaginary—that one can supply at least some of the missing pieces.

Undoubtedly, what readers relish most about espionage is the subtlety and complexity of this, the most dangerous of games. This is underscored through Littell's exploitation of two of Lewis Carroll's works, *Alice's Adventures in Wonderland* (1865) and *Through the Looking Glass and What Alice Found There* (1871). These books are essential to Littell's novel both structurally and thematically. In terms of its structure, each of *The Company*'s six major sections is preceded by an epigraph from one of the Carroll works, and each quotation helps to define the theme or content of that section. Thus, in the first part, "Priming the Gun," the metaphor of applying powder to the flash pan of a musket preparatory to firing it alludes to the necessary first steps to be taken in any enterprise. It is also a subtle means of intimating the topic of this particular section, namely the recruitment, training, and early careers of the novel's chief characters. Littell drives home this point with a Carroll quotation where Alice has just initiated her adventures by following the rabbit down the hole: "In another moment, down went Alice after it, never once considering how in the world she was to get out again." In other words, this is one master storyteller invoking the words of another in order to inform the reader that this is a beginning in more ways than one: the CIA, the careers of the protagonists, and, obviously, the story itself.

In the second section, "The End of Innocence," this process continues with another quotation from *Alice's Adventures in Wonderland:* "They're dreadfully fond of be-heading people here: The great wonder is that there's any one left alive!" Again, the demise of innocence functions on multiple levels. There is the debacle of the failed Hungarian Revolution of 1956, which soiled the United States' reputation for having encouraged in theory a revolt it was unwilling to support in practice. It was a loss of innocence, too, for such CIA officers as the fictional E. Winstrom Ebbitt II, who participated in the conflict, and most decidedly for the Hungarians themselves, who continued to suffer under Soviet hegemony. The tone for the third part, "Vicious Circles," is also set by an epigraph from Carroll, where Alice notices that "There was something very queer about the water . . . as every now and then the oars got fast in it, and would hardly come out again."

Against the backdrop of the Cuban Missile Crisis in 1962, the (real-life) CIA chief of counterintelligence, James Jesus Angleton, runs the agency and its operatives in circles in his futile effort to thwart a Soviet mole within the CIA, code-named SASHA. Angleton's search for the mole in the fourth section ("Sleeping Dogs") leads to the detention, torture, and eventual release of CIA officer Leo Kritzky. Confusion still reigns in the fifth section, "Blind Alley," where the quotation's allusion to an undisclosed adversary chasing the White Queen foreshadows the revelation of the mole's identity: "'There's some enemy after her, no doubt,' the King said, without even looking round. 'That wood's full of them.'"

The sixth and final section, "Dead Reckoning," also reveals multiple meanings—a means of navigation at sea and a final reckoning for both the Soviet empire and some of the novel's characters. Again, when Alice wonders in the epigraph "if the game was over," she suggests what will follow, a questioning of whether the game has ended.

What makes this interweaving of Carroll and Littell so effective is the extent to which it defines the book's themes even as it obfuscates particular moments. Taking its cue from the expression that any place that is confusing or contradictory is an "Alice in Wonderland" world, Littell characterizes early on the labyrinthine nature of espionage. According to Harvey Torriti, the earthy head of Berlin base, "A defector who delivers true information could still be a black agent. Which is another way of saying that a black agent also has to deliver a reasonable amount of true information in order to convince us that he is a genuine defector so that we'll swallow the shit he slips in between the true information." It is not for nothing that Torriti likens the process to a "wilderness of mirrors." Deception is the name of this hazardous game—as it is practiced on one's opponents and even upon oneself. For the gritty, alcoholic Torriti, finding the truth is a matter of trusting one's instincts (when his nose begins to twitch) and scorning intellectuals, but even the seemingly straightforward Torriti—surely one of Littell's most entertaining creations—is not above deceiving his closest friends in order to achieve his ends. When an exfiltration, the defection of a Soviet spy, goes awry, Torriti does not hesitate to sacrifice other covert operations in order to trace the problem to its ultimate source, a (real-life) Soviet mole in Britain named Kim Philby. This includes betraying an operation run by his friend and assistant Jack McAuliffe—a fact he repeatedly denies.

The master deceivers in *The Company* are often the characters most susceptible to self-deception. Though American counterintelligence chief Angleton prides himself on his skills, he is unable to accept Philby's culpability even when the evidence is as overwhelming as it is obvious. The twofold nature of deception (clouding both the deceiver and the deceived) also extends to the novel's virtuoso of deception, Zhilov. As Angleton's counterpart at the *Komitet gosudarstvennoi bezopastnosti* (KGB), he drives nearly all of the action in the novel and is a fascinating amalgam of contradictions. Though he is a man of the twentieth century in a sophisticated intelligence organization, he lives in a pre-Revolutionary dacha, dresses as a peasant, quotes Count Leo Tolstoy rather than Karl Marx, and—like Carroll—exhibits a passion for little girls. His actions are both devious and deviant. With a minimum of technology, he is consistently able to mislead the CIA throughout the novel. Zhilov, whom the CIA only know by the name of "Starik" ("the old man"), employs a Soviet spy named Eugene Dodgson as a means of communicating with Philby and SASHA while they are undercover. Again, Littell is invoking *Alice*, for Dodgson was Lewis Carroll's real name. Indeed, Starik also manages to exploit Carroll's works by using passages from them to send coded messages to Dodgson.

Once Philby's treachery is revealed, Starik is expert in his reading of Angleton's character. Knowing that this betrayal by a close friend would exacerbate Angleton's suspicious nature, Starik wreaks havoc in the CIA through Angleton's obsessive search for SASHA. It is this decades-long hunt for the Soviet mole that ties together this sprawling novel and piques the reader's interest. On a fundamental level, *The Company* is a superb whodunit. Even when Angleton's suspicions lead him to imprison CIA officer Leo Kritzky and interrogate him for months without result, Starik's intricate chess moves cause other CIA officers to believe in Kritzky's innocence and force Angleton into retirement. It is only after Kritzky absconds to the Soviet Union that Angleton—now bitter and ill—is vindicated. There is no doubt that Starik has defeated his opponent. Littell makes it clear, though, that Starik deceives himself just as easily as he tricks others. While he easily manages to outwit the CIA, he himself foolishly believes that he can destroy the United States with KHOLSTOMER, his master plan to undermine American currency. Even more important for this truly malevolent character is the fact that, for all his chicanery, he is blind to the bankrupt nature of Soviet ideology and powerless when the Soviet state eventually collapses.

In addition to the intricacy of its construction, *The Company* provides enthralling accounts of some of the most momentous events of the Cold War. When the Hungarian Revolution explodes in 1956, Littell uses fictional CIA officer E. Winstrom Ebbitt II as a means of giving the reader an eyewitness perspective as events unfold—

from his torture by Hungarian Communists to his daring escape to Austria. Littell employs this same approach to good effect in the failed Bay of Pigs invasion of 1961, when American-trained Cuban commandos made a futile attempt to topple President Fidel Castro. This is historical fiction at its best: richly drawn characters breathing life into the stuff of textbooks. Though the CIA's accomplishments may be problematic at best, there is no doubt about Littell's achievement. *The Company* is superb.

Cliff Prewencki

Sources for Further Study

Booklist 98 (February 1, 2002): 927.
The Economist 364 (August 10, 2002): 75.
Kirkus Reviews 70 (January 1, 2002): 11.
Library Journal 126 (December 1, 2001): 173.
The New York Times Book Review 107 (May 12, 2002): 25.
Publishers Weekly 249 (February 18, 2002): 71.

A CONVENIENT SPY
Wen Ho Lee and the Politics of Nuclear Espionage

Authors: Dan Stober and Ian Hoffman
Publisher: Simon & Schuster (New York). 384 pp.
  $26.00
Type of work: Current affairs
Time: 1999-2000
Locale: Los Alamos, New Mexico

~

An investigative report about the discovery and prosecution of an alleged spy at the Los Alamos nuclear weapons laboratory

~

Principal personages:
WEN HO LEE, weapons-code scientist at Los Alamos National Labora-
tory
CHRISTOPHER COX, U.S. Congressional Representative from California,
head of the Cox Committee, which investigated security lapses in
U.S. relations with China
CAROL COVERT, Federal Bureau of Investigation (FBI) Special Agent
assigned to the Lee investigation
JANET RENO, U.S. Attorney General
NOTRA TRULOCK, director of intelligence and counterintelligence at the
U.S. Department of Energy
ROBERT S. VROOMAN, Central Intelligence Agency (CIA) liaison to Los
Alamos National Laboratory

In March, 1999, *The New York Times* printed a front-page story headlined "China
Stole Nuclear Secrets from Los Alamos, U.S. Officials Say." The story followed ear-
lier published accounts that China had somehow obtained secret data on U.S. nuclear
warheads and marked a high point in American concern over China in the post-Cold
War world. It also provided fodder for critics of the foreign and security policies of
President Bill Clinton's administration. When the alleged source of the security
breach was identified as Wen Ho Lee, a Chinese American scientist working at the
Los Alamos Scientific Laboratory, the story took on ethnic and racial dimensions.

A Convenient Spy presents this story in exhaustive detail, providing a short biography of Wen Ho Lee, background information on the Cold War and U.S.-Chinese relations, and a step-by-step account of how the U.S. government discovered, prosecuted,
and unsatisfactorily concluded its investigation concerning an alleged spy at Los
Alamos. Journalists Dan Stober of the *San Jose Mercury-News* in California and Ian
Hoffman of the *Albuquerque Journal* in New Mexico investigated what has come to
be known as "the Wen Ho Lee affair" and lay out their findings in a style reminiscent

of Bob Woodward and Carl Bernstein's magiste-
rial *All the President's Men* (1974). Like the
book on the Watergate scandal, *A Convenient Spy*
builds on a collection of newspaper reports the
authors wrote as the affair unfolded.

*Dan Stober has won a Pulitzer
Prize for his reporting at* The San
Jose Mercury-News. *Ian Hoffman is
a reporter for* The Albuquerque
Journal.

For an issue that has generated enormous controversy in newspapers and magazines and on
the Internet and talk radio, *A Convenient Spy*
provides a definitive account of the affair. The book is based on numerous interviews
(excluding, one suspects, interviews with Wen Ho Lee himself), extensive research
of books and newspapers, hearing transcripts, government documents, and other
sources. Although a "Notes" section is provided at the end of the book, most facts and
assertions are not individually cited. Instead, the section simply identifies the main
sources used for each chapter. Presumably this level of generality is due, in large part,
to the need to protect the anonymity of some sources, but the lack of clearly identified
sources seems inconsistent with the tone of omniscience that permeates the book.

The undisputed point, which serves as the climax of the story, is that Wen Ho Lee
concluded a plea bargain and pleaded guilty to one of the fifty-nine charges brought
against him: using an unsecured computer to download a sensitive document. (Later,
in a way that was ironic—almost surreal—CIA director John Deutch himself was
found to have committed a somewhat similar offense, having edited top-secret documents on his unsecured home computer. Deutch would not be prosecuted. Stober and
Hoffman, perhaps unfairly, suggest this is the case because Deutch is white.) In any
event, the presiding judge dismissed the remaining charges against Lee and sentenced
him to his time served—277 days. The judge then criticized the government's handling of the case and apologized to Lee "for the unfair manner [he] was held in custody by the Executive Branch."

The main axis of debate surrounding the Wen Ho Lee affair was whether Lee was,
in fact, guilty of willfully providing secret weapons data to a foreign power or was an
innocent victim of "racial profiling," singled out for his Chinese heritage. The former
position portrays the issue as one of espionage, while the latter portrays it as one of
civil rights.

In contrast to these views, this book presents the issue primarily as a critique of official efforts to apprehend and prosecute Wen Ho Lee. The authors are quite critical
on this point. The CIA, FBI, Department of Energy, and other entities are portrayed as
somewhat inept, marginally unethical bureaucracies pursuing their own agendas at
the expense of truth and even national interest.

More than this, the authors assert that the Wen Ho Lee affair illustrates a problem
with America's national mood. In the final paragraph, they assert that the case "suggested Americans had lost sight of the true national interest. Nuclear weapons are the
nation's ultimate defence, a supposed tool of last resort for safeguarding democracy.
But H-bombs are never the supreme national interest. . . . Presumably, the national interest lies in the guarantees of freedom that the nation so cavalierly discarded in the
futile search for a spy."

Some of Lee's supporters have interpreted the book as confirming their contention that Lee was unfairly accused by overzealous prosecutors in a latter-day McCarthyite style. Indeed, this point is forcefully and emotionally made in the title and narrative of Lee's own book, *My Country Versus Me: The First-Hand Account by the Los Alamos Scientist Who Was Falsely Accused of Being a Spy* (2002), which was released at about the same time as *A Convenient Spy*. The general point was picked up in the press and a loose consensus developed that the prosecution of Wen Ho Lee was bungled.

Still, Stober and Hoffman hardly provide vindication for Lee's claims of innocence. Indeed, the authors raise serious concerns about Lee's statements, actions, and motives. Most importantly, Lee admitted to committing what the authors describe as "an egregious security offense" (illegally making his own personal tapes of the secret computer codes used to design America's nuclear weapons) which "placed so many of the nation's basic tools of weapons design at such great risk." He "broke the fundamental trust that underlies the weapons world and, in the end . . . seriously eroded America's confidence in the weapons labs and the ability of his colleagues to protect secrets." His explanation for his actions—that he simply wanted to have back-up copies in case the lab's computer crashed—were unconvincing. He had lied on a number of occasions about meetings with Chinese officials and other matters. He had failed polygraph examinations. Earlier he had offered to help a suspected spy against the United States. Why had he deleted files after he was identified as a suspect? What had he done with the tapes, which never were found? (He claimed he had thrown them in the garbage.) Why did he experience so many putative memory lapses about critical events?

In short, the book concludes that the spy case was indeed woefully bungled by the U.S. government, that it exposed serious flaws in the way Los Alamos—and, by extension, the whole U.S. nuclear program—was run, and that it revealed a latent anti-foreigner sentiment that permeates matters of national security among officials and the general public. However, the book specifically does not conclude that "Lee did not do it." After reading the book, readers still do not know the answer to a fundamental question: whether the Chinese government's development of U.S.-style nuclear warheads was facilitated by spies within the United States, by unintentional security lapses on the part of the United States, or simply through diligent Chinese research.

The book is engaging and absorbing, written in a style more like a novel than a treatise on the politics of nuclear espionage. The personalities of the characters are well developed, with considerable attention paid to the appearance, emotions, and presumed motives of the various players. Much of this material appears to be included more for color and entertainment than as part of the effort to elucidate the mystery of Wen Ho Lee's actions. Lee is depicted as a man who was seen by his coworkers as "friendly and capable; to his friends, he was a kind man and a good father." Readers are told that he shared fruit from his trees with his neighbors; that an FBI agent "jokingly referred to [Lee's wife] as 'Madame Sue-eee,' as if he were a farmer calling a pig to dinner;" that Lee did not eat red meat or sugar; that FBI agent Carol Covert "was in her mid-forties, an attractive woman with reddish-brown hair."

Yet the narrative's implicit claims of omniscience, coupled with the vagueness in identifying sources, calls into question how much of the narrative is speculative. When, as the authors relate, Lee looked into Carol Covert's eyes, did she really "remind him a little of his daughter and her college friends"? How do the authors know that Lee "wondered . . . how much they [knew]"? How do the authors know that "Lee believed his job was safe." (The authors indicate they obtained information on this exchange largely through the FBI's interrogation transcripts, which could not include unspoken thoughts.)

All that said, this book offers one of the best, most comprehensive accounts of the Wen Ho Lee affair—a story that has been misrepresented by partisans of various political stripes in public and private discourse. More importantly, the story is important to the understanding of how the United States does, and how it should, balance national security interests with individual rights. This is especially important now, as America redefines its security interests in the post-Cold War world, and particularly after the terrorism of September 11, 2001.

Steve D. Boilard

Sources for Further Study

American Scientist, 90 (July/August, 2002): 371.
Business Week, February 4, 2002, p. 17.
Choice 40 (September, 2002): 186.
Current History 101 (September, 2002): 295.
The New York Times Book Review 107 (February 17, 2002): 9.
Publishers Weekly 248 (November 12, 2001): 46.
The Wall Street Journal, January 16, 2002, p. A14.

THE CRAZED

Author: Ha Jin (1956-   )
Publisher: Pantheon Books (New York). 352 pp. $24.00
Type of work: Novel
Time: 1989
Locale: China

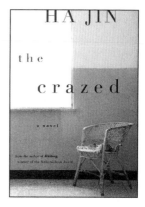

~

Through the prism of a professor crazed by a stroke, award-winning novelist and short-story writer Jin explores the impact of communism on the profession of higher education in post-Maoist China

~

Principal characters:
> PROFESSOR YANG, an English teacher hospitalized as a result of a stroke
> JIAN WAN, a graduate student at the university in Shanning
> MEIMEI, Jian's fiancé and Professor Yang's daughter
> BANPING FAN, a graduate student at Shanning University
> WEIYA SU, a graduate student at Shanning University

Most teachers of writing encourage students to avoid using clichés, largely on the basis that they have become so familiar that they have lost any power to grab the reader's attention. At times, however, a cliché can be appropriate; in the case of novelist Ha Jin, the idea that "necessity is the mother of invention" seems most apt to describe his meteoric rise to prominence in American letters and to suggest something about the power that underlies his second novel, *The Crazed*.

Although the novel is not strictly autobiographical, understanding something of the novelist's life may help illuminate both the story and theme of this work. When Xuefei Jin was fourteen, he joined the Chinese Army. When he was twenty, he left the service to take up a career as an educator. In 1985, after earning his master's degree in China, he obtained a fellowship to Brandeis University in Massachusetts to pursue a doctorate in literature. His plans, as he told John Thomas in a 1998 interview for *Emory Magazine*, were to earn his degree and return to teach in his native country. In 1989, however, events there changed his plans. He and his wife watched on television as the Chinese army quashed the student rebellion in Tiananmen Square. Xuefei Jin realized then that Thomas Wolfe was probably right in his case: He could not go home again.

The necessity to earn a living for his family drove Xuefei Jin to writing and, to risk another cliché, the rest has become literary history. Writing under the pen name Ha Jin, within a little more than a decade the Chinese expatriate produced several collections of short stories and two novels, all of which generated significant praise from reviewers and critics in America. His 1999 novel *Waiting* won the PEN/Faulkner prize and his short story collections were recognized by literary associations for their compelling analysis of human nature. Ha Jin would say they are compelling because they emerge from the blend of experience and imagination that produces fiction which has the ring of authenticity.

The Crazed is such a novel. Set in Shanning, a provincial city, the novel chronicles the struggles of a young graduate student, Jian Wan, who is assigned by the university to care for his adviser, Professor Yang, the victim of a stroke. Jian finds that he must divide time between studying for qualifying examinations that would allow him to be admitted to doctoral study in Beijing and caring for Yang at the local hospital.

Ha Jin, a native of China, emigrated to the United States in 1985 and is a professor of English at Boston University. He is the author of Waiting *(1999), a novel that won the National Book Award, and of several collections of short stories.*

What makes Jian Wan's job difficult is that his mentor seems to have been affected in a strange way by his stroke. From time to time Yang launches into strange ravings that include commentary on religion, literary criticism, political statements about communism and the Chinese Communist Party, and descriptions of sexual exploits. At times he seems jocular, at others deadly serious, and a large portion of his commentary is simply cryptic. The graduate student is not sure how to respond to his teacher's behavior. For example, Jian Wan is confused by Yang's creative restatement of the story of Genesis, the professor's version of which is a fable about how the donkey (a beast of burden) and a monkey (a playful free spirit) both gave up years of their life span to the acquisitive "man"; in this way Yang explains how humankind has been cursed with long life so that people can suffer the infirmities of old age. Yang cries out, too, about the virtues of reading Dante's *La divina commedia* (c. 1320; *The Divine Comedy,* 1802, 3 vols.), telling Jian Wan that it is the one work that can comfort humankind. Both stories leave the young scholar perplexed, since the ideology of both the Christian Bible and Dante's poem are at odds with the pronouncements of communism, which Professor Yang has always seemed to support.

In fact, on more than one occasion Yang launches into long speeches denouncing those who oppose Chairman Mao Zedong and the party, calling for punishment of those who stand in the way of a communist utopia. On the other hand, shortly before he dies, Yang confides to his pupil that he believes his life has been wasted because scholars in China are merely clerks carrying out the commands of a totalitarian government interested more in indoctrinating its people than in promoting real scholarship.

The professor's rantings about his sexual exploits form the center of a mystery for Jian Wan to solve. In this way Ha Jin has an opportunity to create a surprise ending of sorts, something that is characteristic of much of his work. Jian Wan is simultaneously fascinated and repelled by his professor's repeated ravings about sexual liaisons. As the delirious Professor Yang describes his encounters with women, Jian Wan becomes aware that Yang is not speaking of his wife. Who is this other woman? Has there been more than one? The answers surprise Jian Wan but will not necessarily surprise readers, for hints regarding the professor's amorous adventures with at least one woman are there for all—including the obtuse Jian Wan—to see. Far from being a simple plot device, however, the mystery of Professor Yang's love life reveals something of his character and explains much about the relationship between teacher and student. Long accustomed to seeing Yang as some sort of disembodied intellect, Jian Wan learns that his revered teacher is a man like other men, concerned about fulfilling his personal needs. Yang's ravings about his time in a Chinese rehabilitation camp perform a similar function, allowing Jian Wan and readers some insight into the complex personality that lies beneath the inscrutable face of the university professor.

Like all of Ha Jin's work, there is a political subtext in *The Crazed*. In fact, as he has done in previous works, such as the story "Saboteur," Ha Jin uses illness as metaphor: The professor's breakdown mirrors that of post-Maoist China, a country exhibiting signs of schizophrenia as capitalism competes with communism at the end of the twentieth century. Jian Wan is not able to discern whether Professor Yang's ravings are the delusions of a madman or the uninhibited truth-tellings of a man no longer able to live with the hypocrisy of the communist system. So it is with China, Ha Jin suggests: The stresses on the country eventually lead to catastrophe, one manifested in the real-life events of the summer of 1989.

Looming in the background throughout Jian Wan's struggle to understand his professor is the specter of conflict between university students and the government that culminates in the massacres in Tiananmen Square in June, 1989. Being in the provinces, Jian Wan and his colleagues hear rumors of the growing turmoil. Jian Wan gradually becomes aware that many students believe the government's restrictive policies on education have been stifling the country's intellectual growth. Naïvely, these would-be activists believe that once they present their issues to the central government in Beijing, reforms will follow. Confident in their cause, Jian Wan and fellow graduate students agree to chaperone a group of undergraduates who wish to travel to the capital to demonstrate in the Square. The final chapters of the novel describe the horrifying consequences of their miscalculation.

Readers familiar with history know what to anticipate as they complete *The Crazed*, but the brutality exhibited by the army in dealing with the student demonstrators shocks Jian Wan as he experiences it. He is amazed and demoralized to see those he expected to be defending China turn upon its citizens. Ironically, as he moves about Beijing in an effort to escape the army, Jian Wan experiences what might be called an epiphany, allowing him to put into perspective not only the events of his own life but those of the country as well: "Essential personal motives" lie at the root of many political activities. "It's personal interests," he muses, "that motivate the individual and therefore generate the dynamics of history." While the insight may not be revolutionary for readers, it is for the young graduate student who finally realizes that his naïveté and idealism have made him a target for others wishing to advance personal agendas.

The dramatization of such themes has done much to endear Ha Jin to Western critics. Not everyone has been kind to him, however; woven into the generally laudatory commentary on his work are two criticisms raised succinctly by one reviewer of *The Crazed*. "For all its efforts," Gail Caldwell writes, "*The Crazed* contains some awful prose and some shockingly naïve sentiments." Like Caldwell, some have claimed that the praise the Chinese novelist has received is based more on his meteoric rise to competency with the English language; what is celebrated in his work, critics argue, would hardly be noticed in native speakers.

Supporters may dismiss this charge as an issue of style, but Caldwell's second criticism is more stinging: "Jian's running commentary on women, from Mr. Yang's disinhibited sexual shenanigans to his own affections for Meimei and others, is comical in its puerile sensibility; one assumes this effect was not intended." This observation demands response. While it may be true to say that Jian Wan seems puerile, the same need not be assumed about his creator. Assuming the imperceptiveness of a character indicates that the author is similarly limited in his perceptions of human nature seems wrongheaded. Whether Ha Jin shares his character's naïve views about the opposite sex is neither apparent nor relevant. Instead, one should conclude that Jian Wan's inability to understand women—his fiancée, the female professors and graduate students, Dr. Yang's wife—is indicative of his inability to effectively perceive what is happening around him on many fronts. Concentrating on preparing for his doctoral examinations, he is unable to see that he is being manipulated by others: Dr. Yang, the department chair and the political officer associated with the university, his friends, even his fiancée.

When he realizes his predicament, Jian Wan becomes disillusioned, abandoning hopes of studying in Beijing and eventually deciding to give up the study of literature in favor of a career as a bureaucrat. When he faces the soldiers in Tiananmen Square, he is first unable to believe that he has been so deceived by his government, then unable to do anything to help the victims of the army's violent actions. The novel ends on this demoralizing note, creating the mood its author intended. For Jian Wan, and for China, the future is indeed most gloomy.

Laurence W. Mazzeno

Sources for Further Study

Booklist 99 (September 1, 2002): 6.
The Boston Globe, November 3, 2002, p. D6.
Library Journal 127 (September 15, 2002): 91.
The New York Times Book Review 107 (October 27, 2002): 7.
Publishers Weekly 249 (September 30, 2002): 47.

THE CREATION OF PSYCHOPHARMACOLOGY

Author: David Healy
Publisher: Harvard University Press (Cambridge, Mass.).
   469 pp. $39.95
Type of work: History of science and science

∾

Healy details the discovery and development of psychiatric medications, the extremely profitable partnership between psychiatrists and the large pharmaceutical companies, and the frightening consequences for today's culture and society

∾

No one in the United States today could be unaware of the tremendous surge in psychopharmacological drugs. All one has to do is turn on the nightly news or flip through any popular magazine to be bombarded with seemingly innocuous advertisements for feel-good chemicals to cure a hyperactive son, shy daughter, agoraphobic father-in-law, emotionally distant spouse or, indeed, one's own broken heart. David Healy's groundbreaking *The Creation of Psychopharmacology* details the discovery and development of psychotropic medications, the extremely profitable codependent relationship between psychiatrists and pharmaceutical companies, and the subsequent impact on the society and the culture surrounding and supporting them. Healy maintains that the rise of antipsychotic drugs, which flooded the marketplace on the heels of the first antibiotics and antihypertensives just after World War II, is as historically significant in the history of medicine as the discovery of penicillin. He furthermore insists on the absolute necessity for far more research on the effects of these types of medications, more specifically their effect on certain types of patients.

In this ambitious and dramatic work, the first to examine the history of psychopharmacology, Healy unravels the complex story behind the emergence of neuroscientific research and paints a picture, not of heroic scientific conquest, but of a mild-mannered takeover, one of serendipitous accidents leading to discovery. During the early part of the twentieth century, psychiatry tended to follow in the footsteps of psychoanalysts Sigmund Freud (1856-1939) and Jacques Lacan (1901-1981), embracing "talking cures" for the mentally ill. Severely mentally ill patients were called lunatics and locked away in asylums, sometimes with little hope for release. Early chemical treatments, such as lithium (rediscovered in the early 1950's) and insulin shock therapy, were developed for one purpose, with neither the researcher nor the doctor understanding how these treatments worked. This all changed dramatically during the mid-twentieth century.

The common historical view of psychiatry asserts that the invention of chlorpromazine (marketed as Thorazine and Largactil) in 1952, which successfully eliminated delirium, gave rise to a biologically based scientific psychiatry. This extraordinary discovery dramatically revolutionized psychiatry, changing it from a therapeutic area of expertise whose underpinnings were rooted in psychotherapy to one based solidly on biochemistry, and led directly to today's severely problematic changes in health care. Before this vital discovery, mentally ill patients in the throes of delirium were often seen as hopeless and left at the mercy of barbaric treatments. When severely psychotic chlorpromazine patients suddenly gained mental clarity, the drug took on the status of a miracle cure; so began the parade of drugs for treating psychosis, depression, anxiety, compulsive disorder, panic attacks, and myriad other mental disturbances. However, large numbers of perfectly normal people, maybe with an individual quirk or two, now came to be labeled as abnormal.

∾

David Healy is the director of the North Wales department of psychological medicine at the University of Wales College of Medicine in Bangor. A prominent British psychiatrist, he sued the University of Toronto in 2000 for $9.4 million in damages when a job offer was revoked after he gave a lecture on the negative effects of Prozac. In addition to publishing papers on such diverse topics as phenomenology, nosology, and hysteria, he is the author of The Antidepressant Era *(1999),* The Psychopharmacologists: Interviews *(1996), and* Psychiatric Drugs Explained *(2002).*

∾

During the 1960's, the emerging radical antipsychiatry social movement played a role in the surge of psychopharmacological drugs. This group considered psychotherapists such as Freud to be oppressors rather than liberators. By denigrating the study and practice of psychoanalysis through the itemization of its many abuses, this influential movement inadvertently shifted the focus of psychiatry away from psychoanalysis and toward drug consumption. For example, psychoanalysts erroneously, and dangerously, maintained that Parkinson's disease symptoms resulted from patients' deep-seated anger and that a cure would be forthcoming only through intensive (and expensive) psychoanalysis therapy. In the light of the negative outcry from the antipsychiatry radicals, many psychiatrists wholeheartedly embraced the move toward the new antipsychotic medications that followed in the wake of the discovery of chlorpromazine and came to view the pharmaceutical corporations as the saviors of their medical practices.

The market for these new psychotropic drugs seemed limitless. Low levels of serotonin, rather than childhood abuse and abandonment, became the late-twentieth century mantra for the real cause of mental suffering. In addition to psychopaths and schizophrenics, now drug abusers, overweight people, the lovelorn, those suffering from obsessive-compulsive disorders, the lonely, the shy, and even restless children came to be diagnosed with mental disorders and viewed through the medical lens as problem patients whose diseases became manageable only through a lifetime of highly profitable pill consumption. The heart of Healy's book, then, is concerned with the way in which marketing determines culture.

It would seem that with all these chemical "fixes," mental illness should be by now well in decline. However, Healy shows that this assumption is absolutely false and argues that flawed procedures brought about through science, in conjunction with the pharmaceutical companies, developed a large variety of ineffective and dangerous pharmacological remedies. The heavy political interests of medicine enable it to propagate and disseminate information that ensures the absolute necessity of these psychotropic drugs to treat a large part of the populace. The utilization of qualitative models of mental illness that rely on small samples and severely controlled conditions (which has become the *sine qua non* of scientific inquiry), rather than on far more complex clinical experience, contributes greatly to misdiagnosis. Furthermore, admissions to psychiatric wards have continued to multiply by a factor of 15 over the past century, with corresponding rates of detention. Indeed, schizophrenics and those suffering from manic depression were hospitalized far more frequently at the end of the twentieth century than they were at its beginning. Simply put, many of these expensive, omnipresent drugs are overestimated, oversold, and just plain ineffective. Healy maintains that today's society is a "brave new world" shaped and molded by new drugs created in pharmaceutical laboratories.

Healy argues that, increasingly, treatment options for mental sufferers are dependent, not on skilled therapists, but on the pharmaceutical industry, whose primary motivation is financial gain. Once drug companies recognized the enormous monetary potential of antipsychotic medications, they agitated more and more for increased market development. With profit in mind, independent research into treatments for mental illness has been abandoned, and pharmaceutical companies tend to support highly pragmatic, randomized drug trials which focus on quantifiable data (solely because of the resultant large market numbers) instead of qualitative clinical evaluations, in which the practitioner emphatically encounters and treats the suffering human being. This translates, however, into the fact that certain drugs prescribed to treat the symptoms of psychiatric conditions have not necessarily proven effective. A case in point, Healey argues, is the selective serotonin reuptake inhibitor (SSRI) antidepressant Prozac, which has revealed only unpredictable effects. To hammer home his point concerning the subjective effects of seemingly harmless drugs, Healy points out incidents of cab drivers who ran red lights after taking antihistamines. In one particularly chilling example, the author looks back to the Korean War, when chlorpromazine was included as part of U.S. soldiers' medical kits. Lives were lost because the wounded acted indifferently and failed to take the required action to save their own lives. As the author makes clear, there simply is no magic-bullet cure to psychological problems. Healy, himself a physician, ultimately calls for the deregulation of psychoactive drugs, which would empower people suffering from mental illness and force physicians to treat their patients emphatically, in clinical encounters.

Healy maintains that commerce and science have been equal partners in the development of today's ubiquitous, highly questionable psychopharmacological medications. He delineates the distressing power pharmaceutical companies now exert over the whole field of psychiatry and waves a large, red danger flag about the future. He argues that the most effective treatments for mental illness have combined both medical and therapeutic techniques. However, as the United States' corporate-preferred method of "managed care" seeps into health care systems throughout the world, the division between drug-prescribing, highly paid medical physicians and lower priced, hands-on therapists will widen, leaving wretched patients no option except chemical treatment. For instance, workers suffering from work-related stress can have their attitude, or for that matter their personality, changed by popping pills.

Rationality, Healy argues, especially in the United States and Europe, takes a back seat to profit, and as science spins further out of control, it remains imperative to consider the social consequences of this foolishness. For instance, he warns that psychotropic drugs may be the cause of social problems rather than their cure. Indeed, lawsuits by patients who claim to have committed violent acts while under the influence of Prozac are believed to be numerous, and pharmaceutical companies want to keep this information quiet. In addition, the sales rhetoric developed by pharmaceutical companies blinds physicians to preventable deaths and covers up the fact that the life expectancies of their patients are falling and not, as reported, rising. Healy ominously warns that the large pharmaceutical companies in question will own the products developed by the Human Genome Project and especially cautions physicians who prescribe Ritalin for children to look toward the future. The treatment of young children with drugs had been all but prohibited until 1990, and the current mass treatment of youngsters, even preschoolers, with Ritalin (available since 1950) indicates a deep cultural shift that ties in with the development of chlorpromazine.

The Creation of Psychopharmacology is a major contribution to the literature of psychopharmacology, following on the heels of Healy's well-received *The Antidepressant Era* (1999). Healy, the leading international authority on the history of psychopharmacology, is not by any means shrill and does not force his opinions upon the reader; he merely lets his meticulously gleaned facts and figures argue for themselves.

One area in which Healy perhaps wanders a bit too far afield is an unnecessary venture into the theoretical realm. People today, he muses, substitute holiness for concern with health. While the suggestion that intense holiness merely represents immortality insurance for believers and that it correlates with today's frantic obsession with life-prolonging good health is intriguing, it seems out of place and forced, as if Healy were attempting to address and placate critics. His marvelous arguments dealing with historical and economic "hows" stand solidly without forcing tenuous "whys"—economic gain, no doubt, is the real "why." Professionals will fall under the spell of this thought-provoking, serious book and feel either very uneasy or very thankful to find validation in its rock-solid evidence that everything is not quite right with their patients. However, the density of the facts and figures could be at times a bit overwhelming for the average reader who, sadly, might not glean this book's much-needed information. With luck, someone will utilize Healy's findings and put them into a more approachable format that the general public can appreciate. However, it is well worth the effort to read this marvelous and very important book.

M. Casey Diana

Sources for Further Study

Choice 40 (September, 2002): 137.
Library Journal 127 (March 15, 2002): 98.
New Scientist 173 (March 30, 2002): 50.
Science 297 (August 16, 2002): 1125.

CRITICAL TIMES
The History of *The Times Literary Supplement*

Author: Derwent May (1930-   )
Publisher: HarperCollins (New York). Illustrated. 606
   pp. $35.00
Type of work: Literary history
Time: 1902-2002
Locale: Printing House Square, London

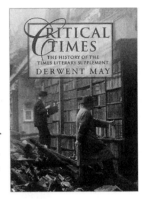

～

Through an examination of one hundred years of files of
The Times Literary Supplement *(TLS), May traces the history of one of the world's most important book-reviewing journals*

～

Principal personages:
> BRUCE RICHMOND, first real editor of the *TLS*, 1903-1937
> CHARLES FREDERIC MOBERLY BELL, managing editor of the London
>   *Times* in 1902
> ALFRED HARMSWORTH, LORD NORTHCLIFFE, longtime owner of the
>   *Times*
> DAVID L. MURRAY, Richmond's successor as editor of the *TLS*, 1938-
>   1945
> STANLEY MORISON, typographer and editor of the *TLS*, 1945-1947
> ALAN PRYCE-JONES, Morison's successor as editor, 1948-1958
> ARTHUR CROOK, assistant editor, and then editor of the *TLS*, 1959-1974
> JOHN GROSS, Crook's successor, 1974-1981
> JEREMY TREGLOWN, Gross's successor, 1982-1990
> FERDINAND MOUNT, novelist, journalist, and editor of the *TLS*, 1991-
>   present

   In 2002, the *TLS* celebrated its hundredth birthday. According to legend, it was envisioned as a temporary publication to carry book reviews displaced from the *Times* by Parliamentary reports, but when the Parliamentary session ended, no one remembered to discontinue it. In fact, May demonstrates that the *Literary Supplement* (as it was known for decades) had been intended by Charles Frederic Moberly Bell, the *Times*'s manager, as a replacement for *Literature*, which had been losing money and which the *Times* had sold to the *Academy* early in 1902. Bell hoped that the free supplement would lure readers to his newspaper.

   The first review in the first issue of the *Literary Supplement* was of *More Letters of Edward Fitzgerald*. The article was written by Augustine Birrell, an educated man of letters and an example of the audience that the *Supplement* hoped to attract. This first issue exemplified the range of the subjects the supplement would discuss throughout

∽
*Both Derwent May and his son
worked for* The Times Literary
Supplement. *May has served as
literary editor of the* Listener,
the Sunday Telegraph, *and the*
European. *Author of four novels
as well as works about Marcel
Proust and Hannah Arendt, he
writes for the London* Times
about books and birds.
∽

its history: In addition to Fitzgerald's letters, it carried reviews of *Scottish Men of Letters in the Eighteenth Century, Scenes of Rural Life in Hampshire, Napoleon's Polish Campaign: 1806-1807,* and *The Lore of Cathay.* Hugh Monro Ross surveyed "Science in 1901" and A. B. Walkley, the *Times* theater critic, published three articles about "The Drama." Three other features appearing in this issue would remain staples for many years: a list of recent publications, notes on forthcoming books, and a chess column that included a problem.

This issue also reflected the range of people who would appear in the pages of the *Supplement:* staff writers for the *Times,* professional reviewers, and academics. May notes that over the years, this last group has increased in prominence as both contributors to and readers of the journal. The cantankerous letters for which the *TLS* is famous also appeared early in its history, with a complaint by the Reverend Alfred B. Beaven about the *Dictionary of Literary Biography* in the second issue and a debate about William Blake's poem "Tyger" running through May, 1902, a debate that prompted a letter from William Butler Yeats.

Yeats was one of many important literary figures to appear in the *Literary Supplement.* In 1905, Bruce Richmond, who would edit the journal almost from its inception to 1937, engaged as a reviewer Miss A. V. Stephen, better known as Virginia Woolf. The titles given her were not always worthy of her mettle but she wrote brilliantly even when the authors she reviewed did not. In her diary, she complained that nothing could be said of W. E. Norris's *Barham of Beltana,* but in her review she wittily and subtly criticized the work. Recognizing her skills, Richmond frequently called upon her to review for him. Altogether she would write some three hundred essays for the *Literary Supplement.* Her contributions enlivened the journal, but May argues that through these pieces she also honed her ideas about writing fiction.

In March, 1908, Alfred Harmsworth, Lord Northcliffe, bought the *Times.* He reduced the size of the *Literary Supplement* from twelve pages to eight. When the *Supplement* continued to lose money, Northcliffe considered eliminating the journal, or at least the editor. The manager and the editor of the *Times* supported Richmond, and both the *Supplement* and Richmond remained. Northcliffe would again consider killing the *Supplement* in 1922, but it was he who died in August of that year, while the journal continued.

By 1922 the *Supplement* was, in fact, a publication separate from its parent newspaper, having gained its independence in 1914. Although in 1914 it cut the fees it paid contributors, it still attracted writers such as Max Beerbohm on imaginary novels mentioned in real ones (March 12, 1914) or Henry James on novels of young writers (March 19 and April 2, 1914). The May 14, 1914, issue carried Edith Wharton's "The Craft of Fiction."

The *Supplement* did not generally address current events, but with the outbreak of World War I it began reviewing books on the subject. It also carried patriotic poems. Arthur Clutton-Brock ran a series of front-page essays supporting Britain's position, and John Galsworthy in 1915 commented on the adverse effect the conflict was having on literature. Reviewers during this period showed little sympathy with the stirrings of high modernism. James Joyce's *Dubliners* (1914), Ezra Pound's *Lustra* (1916), William Butler Yeats's *Responsibilities* (1914), and T. S. Eliot's *Prufrock and Other Observations* (1917) as well his 1919 *Poems* received unfavorable notices. Joyce's *Ulysses* (1922) was not reviewed at all.

Though Eliot's poetry did not excite the *Supplement*'s reviewers, in 1919 Richmond asked Eliot to write for the journal. On November 18, 1919, Eliot contributed an essay on the Renaissance dramatist Ben Jonson, and during the next two years Eliot would publish articles on other important seventeenth century English writers. Both he and Woolf continued to write for Richmond into the 1930's. Richmond also was recruiting new talent, such as the future eminent historian A. L. Rowse and the future Warden of All Souls College, Oxford, John Sparrow.

The Great Depression reduced the readership of the *Supplement* and advertising revenue fell, particularly for deluxe editions and illustrated sets. In an effort to increase circulation, the journal revised its format by reducing the front page from four columns to three and by adding subtitles to articles to make the front page more inviting. On November 2, 1935, the *Supplement* began running illustrations. Richmond's successor, David L. Murray, sought to appeal to a wider audience by adding more news to the journal. He introduced the column "News and Notes" and devoted more space to popular novels. None of these measures improved circulation, but the coming of World War II helped the *Supplement* financially. Paper rationing reduced the size of the journal and hence cut costs. As other newspapers curtailed their reviews, publishers also chose to advertise in the *TLS*.

When Stanley Morison became editor of the *Supplement* in February, 1945, he reversed Murray's attempts to popularize the publication. He eliminated the crossword puzzle and restored the long lead articles that Murray had removed. Morison increased the number of columns per page from four to five, thus adding some thirty-five hundred words to each issue. To fill his pages he recruited a new group of academics, including historians A. J. P. Taylor and Louis Namier, architectural historian Nikolaus Pevsner, and art critic (and Soviet spy) Anthony Blunt. Morison showed less interest in engaging reviewers sympathetic to modern fiction, but his assistant and successor, Alan Pryce-Jones, brought in the author Anthony Powell to write about contemporary novels. In 1947, the *Supplement* for the first time devoted an entire page to a current work of fiction, Ivy Compton-Burnett's *Manservant and Maidservant*, reviewed by another novelist, Rose Macaulay. Ronald Lewin perceptively praised Saul Bellow and Philip Larkin at the outset of their careers.

Under Morison's editorship the *Supplement*'s circulation rose from 23,340 to 30,000 and advertising increased, nearly tripling the journal's weekly profits (from £120 to £330). Because Morison was eager to return to his multivolume history of the *Times*, he resigned in favor of Pryce-Jones in 1948. Among Pryce-Jones's innovations were special issues such as "A Critical and Descriptive Survey of Contemporary British Writing for Readers Overseas" (August, 1950) and the twice-yearly *Supplement* devoted to children's literature. Under Pryce-Jones the *Supplement* showed increased sympathy to modern literature, favorably reviewing Angus Wilson, L. P. Hartley, John Wain, Anthony Powell (who had left off reviewing to write his twelve-volume *A Dance to the Music of Time*), Kingsley Amis, Iris Murdoch, Lawrence Durrell, and John Updike.

Pryce-Jones's successor, Arthur Crook, sought to acquaint British readers with literary developments on the Continent. He introduced a special issue each fall, coinciding with the Frankfurt Book Fair, devoted to foreign writers. He also featured American literature; in November, 1959, he ran a special issue on "The American Imagination." Though the *Supplement* did not always appreciate the books being written across the Atlantic, it did discuss them. Americans reciprocated this interest, accounting for two-thirds of the *Supplement*'s overseas sales in the 1960's. Another of Crook's concerns was structural criticism. The *Supplement* probably provided many of its readers with their first exposure to the literary theories of Umberto Eco and Roland Barthes. Crook also implemented the change of the journal's official name from *The Times Literary Supplement* to simply *TLS* on January 2, 1969.

When John Gross succeeded Crook in 1974, he was at once confronted with the question of whether or not to continue the journal's long-standing practice of anonymous reviewing. The issue had been debated periodically in the pages of the *TLS*, and the Thomson organization, which had acquired the *Times* in 1966, favored abandoning the practice. Gross agreed. The last unsigned review appeared on December 13, 1974. Gross added various light-hearted features, such as "Reputations Revisited" (January, 1977), in which writers nominated the most overrated and underrated authors of the twentieth century. A serious consequence of this column was the rediscovery of Barbara Pym, whose books returned to print and who resumed her writing career after a hiatus of fifteen years. Another delightful feature that Gross introduced was the "Author, Author" quiz, inviting readers to identify the writers of three thematically linked passages that range from the mildly to the excruciatingly obscure. He expanded the "Commentary" section on the arts and introduced "Remainders," a humorous look at books and book-buyers. Gross encouraged the punning headline, such as that for a review of a Brian Aldiss novel: "Aldiss and Heaven Too."

In 1981, Rupert Murdoch bought the *Times*, and in 1982 Jeremy Treglown replaced Gross as editor. He retained many of Gross's features and added "American Notes" by Christopher Hitchins. Treglown's interest in American writers was reflected in the large number of poems by John Ashbery and Joseph Brodsky that appeared in the pages of the *TLS*. Brodsky, a Russian who had moved to the United States, also wrote essays and reviews for Treglown. In an effort to render the *TLS* more popular, Treglown added lighter columns such as "NB," dealing generally with literature and publishing, and "Freelance," by nonacademic writers discussing their interests. At the same time, the *TLS* devoted increasing space to literary theory, which dominated academic discourse in the 1980's.

Treglown's efforts to increase circulation failed. At the end of 1990, he resigned to return to teaching. Ferdinand Mount, who had served in the Margaret Thatcher government, now steered the *TLS* in the direction of the *London Review of Books* and *The New York Review of Books*, which carried articles about current events and issues. The deaths of many prominent authors in history, philosophy, and politics gave Mount the chance to deal with a variety of subjects outside the context of a review. Mount continued the focus on literary theory, publishing a symposium on the topic in July, 1994.

May shows how the *TLS* has evolved over its first hundred years. By concentrating heavily on the reviews that have appeared in its pages, May also provides a literary history of the twentieth century. While the *TLS* sometimes failed to appreciate, or even to review, some works that have emerged as classics, *Critical Times* shows that the journal can be proud of its past accomplishments and can look forward to many more.

Joseph Rosenblum

Sources for Further Study

The Atlantic Monthly 290 (July/August, 2002): 180.
The Boston Globe, April 28, 2002, p. E5.
Choice 39 (May, 2002): 1558.
The New York Review of Books 49 (May 23, 2002): 48.
Publishers Weekly 249 (January 14, 2002): 47.
The Washington Post Book World, March 10, 2002, p. 15.

THE DARTS OF CUPID, AND OTHER STORIES

Author: Edith Templeton (1916-   )
Publisher: Pantheon Books (New York). 312 pp. $23.00
Type of work: Short fiction
Time: The 1920's to the 1990's
Locale: Bathdale, England; Bordighera, Italy; Prague

∼

In these seven stories situated in several European lo-
cales, Templeton traces the vagaries of passion and loss,
both political and emotional

∼

Principal characters:
> EDITH, the first-person narrator of several stories, who comes of age dur-
> ing the course of three of the stories
> EVE PRESCOTT-CLARK, the young assistant at the U.S. War Office in
> Bathdale who has an affair with a married man
> THE MAJOR, Eve's American who cannot commit to, but cannot deny,
> their relationship
> DALIBOR, a painter in Prague
> KONSTANTIN BLONIK, a Russian spy living in Prague
> LOUISE, an older woman retired to Bordighera, Italy, with her much
> older husband
> EDMUND, Louise's physician husband
> MRS. RICHARDS, an elderly widow who must sell the silver her husband
> has in storage
> FORBES, the young clerk who assists at the sale

Though the stories in *The Darts of Cupid, and Other Stories* cover several different decades and cultural milieus, Templeton's style, mood, tone, and use of first-person narration connect the works, as does her persistent interest in loss and its effects on her characters. Given that many of the facts of Templeton's own life parallel details related by the narrators within the collection, one senses that the author might also be using autobiography to inform these stories. Templeton's subjects, set against the backdrop of modern Europe, tend to be bleak. Her characters meet during wartime, then part. One narrator's family loses its family house as a result of the Communist takeover of Bohemia. Another learns of her husband's unfaithfulness as he is dying. Her narrators sometimes take risks, but often do the honorable rather than the most pleasing thing. Most have lost lovers. One gets the sense that even in their happiest moments, these women cast about for something more. Templeton does not let her characters become maudlin and cowering. They are resilient and find themselves sustained by the past rather than destroyed by it. Templeton maintains a precarious balance between that sense of loss and sense of strength.

The collection opens with the title story, "The Darts of Cupid," set during World War II. The narrator, Eve Prescott-Clark, works with a number of other women engaged in relatively mundane secretarial tasks in a medical facility in Bathdale, England. Most of the women are having affairs of one sort or another. Though married, Eve uses her stint in the military to "leave her husband." She meets an American major who takes charge of the facility and adopts a flirtatious interest in the narrator's work methods. Because he does not use the typical lothario approach of the other men, the two develop a very real friendship which then dovetails into love.

Edith Templeton was born in Prague and left to marry an Englishman. While in Great Britain, she worked in the Office of the Chief Surgeon for the U.S. Army and eventually became a captain in the British army. She began publishing short stories in the 1950's, primarily in The New Yorker. *She has also published a number of novels, as well as a nonfiction travel book,* The Surprise of Cremona *(1954). Templeton's second husband was the physician to the king of Nepal. She lives in Bordighera, Italy.*

One could never call "Darts of Cupid" a wartime romance story. Templeton subverts the atmosphere of wartime romanticism by relating very specifically the various sexual peccadilloes of the men and women in the facility. People sleep together regardless of whether the lover is married, and most of those "romances" are affairs of convenience and lust, not emotion. For example, the Major is married to a lovely woman in the United States, yet he is also living with a beautiful English woman ironically named Constance, who is pregnant with his child. In fact, his relationship with his lover is so open that he invites Eve to the house he shares with her. Constance arranges for Eve to have a beautiful nightgown to wear that evening as the Major slips into her bed. The war atmosphere makes sexual relations less important, more perfunctory.

Templeton undercuts the elements of romance, yet her narrator falls in love despite herself. The Major is called away and the two must live without one another. Eve feels a sense of tragedy that their love will remain unfulfilled. Yet, as the story ends, Templeton draws parallels between the narrator's loss and the stories of her many girlfriends who married their wartime boyfriends. One of them, Claudia, comes back at the end of the story and relates how her new husband bored her after all, that sex was all there was, and that eventually one had to get out of bed. Though Eve seems saddened at losing touch with this great love of her life, Templeton suggests that the memory of love might be more gratifying than its reality.

Three stories in the collection involve the coming of age of a first-person narrator named Edith, which again hints at an autobiographical strain in the collection. The first of these stories, "Irresistibly," concerns the narrator's relationship to a painter named Dalibor, who has been asked to do a portrait of the Cardinal Archbishop of Prague. The banter between these characters revolves around the idea of destiny and one's ability to "change one's fate." Philosophically, the young girl does not understand the painter's position until his death some months later. He had, inexplicably, gone to Paris because a fortune-teller told him he would meet his destiny there. He stayed out in a storm and was killed when a tree fell on him. Bystanders felt he had, in some way, caused his own death. The young girl puzzles over the idea that one can choose a fate that might be negative. A family friend, the Professor, suggests an instructive conclusion to young Edith's quandary: "Destiny is what we make ourselves. Because our destiny is always irresistible to us."

After this philosophic coming of age, young Edith begins her sexual awakening in "The Dress Rehearsal." Because of her mother's beauty and spirit, most men use Edith to get closer to her mother. Few seem to realize that Edith wants to be liked on her own terms. She grows disillusioned with most males' patronizing attitudes toward her. During a dress rehearsal for a play, a young man begins to lavish attention on her. He takes off her cap and kisses a part of her hair that has always been covered, symbolically touching her in an exclusive and erotic way. This action arouses her for the first time and she begins to see the importance of undivided attention, even though the act itself does not suggest anything out of the ordinary. Though she knows she will have no further contact with this man, who is much too old for her, she recognizes her self-worth for the first time.

The third story concerning Edith, "The Equality Cake," is the most political in the collection. Told in two sections, the narrative illustrates the changes imposed on Edith's family as a result of the Communist takeover of Bohemia. In the first section, which takes place in Edith's youth, the family gathers in the family castle, discussing fears of an overthrow of their government and that the workers might use their castle for a barn, destroying all it stands for. The family is somewhat impoverished but still clings to its sense of noblesse oblige.

The second section of the story begins with an older Edith journeying back to the castle after the country has become Communist. She has been warned that things will be very different and so she enters the house primed for a sense of loss. She is surprised to find that the young female curator is interested in learning more about the castle from her. Edith also notes that the government has taken better care of the castle than the family had. The murals in several of the rooms have been restored and, overall, the changes have been positive, not negative. As Edith sees the realities of her greatest childhood fear, she comes to the realization that most of the time she had lived in ignorance and fear. Although she feels sad at the family's (and, by extension, the country's) loss, she is also able to feel some joy at the restoration of the castle and the possibilities for the future of the country.

Although "A Coffeehouse Acquaintance," one of the longest stories in the collection, takes on similar political themes, Templeton does not meld the personal and the political as well in this story. The female narrator meets a Russian, Konstantin Blonik, in a Prague coffeehouse. She is on the run from a bad marriage and wants to see the effect of communism on the homeland of her youth. Like her, Blonik seems to be lonely and in need of companionship. The two have an affair that lasts several weeks. Throughout that time, the narrator is puzzled by the man's political allegiances, his apartment (which seems to be borrowed), and many incongruities in his manner. He discusses the political climate of Prague as though he were unconnected to it. As the two discuss the benefits of communism over the old order, the restrictions of communism, and the narrator's former life in pre-Communist Bohemia, the narrator begins to sense camaraderie with Blonik. Yet, eventually, they part. A few years later, the woman comes back to Prague and tries to look up her former lover, partially because she has been unable to categorize him. When she meets him again, she realizes that he is probably a Russian spy and had lied about most of his history. This story exposes some of the more problematic realities of the Communist regime but the narrator's place in that larger political arena is never very clear. Furthermore, the narrator's interpersonal relationship with the Russian seems less realistic than Templeton's other depictions of couples.

The last two stories in the collection seem to concern the same woman, called "Louise" in "The Blue Hour," and "Mrs. Richards" in "Faun & Nymph." Both women marry elderly men, physicians, who die. Both women live in the same area in Italy. In "The Blue Hour," Louise must ignore bizarre sexual advances from a friend's husband. Her own husband refuses to see these advances as problematic and tries to get Louise to ignore them. This attitude becomes indicative of their entire relationship and inadvertently forces Louise to rethink her lengthy marriage to a man who probably does not love her. As a worker at the train station tells her, "[Y]ou cannot understand—you'll never be able to understand—that when you get married to a man you get a husband." This remark seems to free Louise to understand that all marriages might end up similarly, since familiarity seems to create this type of discontent.

In the last story of the collection, "Faun & Nymph," Mrs. Richards, a wealthy widow, no longer dwells on her deceased husband's negative attributes. Rather, she fixates on selling off some silver that he had in storage for many years. In effect, the silver becomes symbolic of his hidden self. As she considers traveling north to negotiate this sale with the clerk Forbes, she realizes that this young man reminds her of her former lover Gordon, who committed suicide prior to her marriage. Though Forbes turns out to be too young to be a paramour, he does talk to her and quell her sense of loneliness. Like the narrator of "The Dress Rehearsal," Mrs. Richards must learn about her self-worth, as well as about the importance of memory in one's life. Strengthened by her conversation and her memories of Gordon, Mrs. Richards returns from her trip a more vibrant and open woman.

In these finely polished stories, Edith Templeton shows the reader the inexplicable ways characters make their own destinies, then accept the consequences of their actions through distance and memory. Though often bleak and spare, the stories resonate with Templeton's realistic portrayals and her ability to create a rich sense of time and place. The narrators' passions and betrayals, their losses and their victories underscore Templeton's genius at creating a mood that allows such drama to take place realistically.

Rebecca Hendrick Flannagan

Sources for Further Study

Book: The Magazine for the Reading Life 21 (January/February, 2002): 74.
Booklist 98 (February 1, 2002): 924.
The New York Times Book Review 107 (March 31, 2002): 9.
Publishers Weekly 248 (December 10, 2001): 48.
Victoria 16 (February, 2002): 38.
Vogue 192 (February, 2002): 173.

DECEMBER 6

Author: Martin Cruz Smith (1942-   )
Publisher: Simon & Schuster (New York). 339 pp.
    $26.00
Type of work: Novel
Time: 1922-1941
Locale: Tokyo and Nanking, China

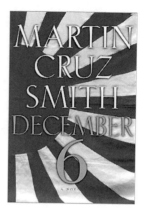

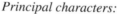

*Harry Niles, an American who has lived most of his life
in Japan and is caught between two cultures, learns of the
impending attack on Pearl Harbor*

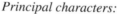

Principal characters:
> HARRY NILES, owner of a Tokyo nightclub
> MICHIKO FUNABASHI, a performer in Harry's club and his girlfriend
> OHARU, a nightclub performer in Harry's past
> KATO, an artist and Harry's mentor
> ISHIGAMI, Harry's nemesis
> GEN YOSHIMURA, a navy pilot and Harry's childhood friend
> LADY ALICE BEECHUM, Harry's married mistress
> ARNOLD BEECHUM, a British diplomat and Lady Alice's husband
> WILLIE STAUB, a German businessman
> IRIS STAUB, Willie's Chinese wife
> AL DEGEORGE, correspondent for *The Christian Science Monitor*
> YOSHITAKI, a shipping magnate
> ADMIRAL YAMAMOTO, commander in chief of the Japanese navy
> ROY HOOPER, an American diplomat and Harry's childhood friend
> ROGER NILES, a missionary, Harry's father
> ORIN NILES, Harry's uncle

Beginning with *Gorky Park* (1981), Martin Cruz Smith has been known for writing thrillers that are both highly entertaining and intelligent. Smith is expert at delineating both contemporary and historical times and settings and usually provides a bit more character depth than such comparable practitioners as Ken Follett. The sophistication of his novels has led to his being called "the John le Carré of thriller writers." Smith's *Stallion Gate* (1986) is a look at the Manhattan Project that contributed to the end of World War II. With *December 6*, he turns to the beginning of that conflict and events surrounding the launch of the Japanese attack on Pearl Harbor.

Harry Niles's parents came to Japan as missionaries when he was very young, and except for a brief period back in the United States, he has lived in Japan ever since. Like Smith's best works, *December 6* is a character study, showing how Niles manages to fit into Japanese society, to a degree, while retaining an essential American

*Martin Cruz Smith was born in
Reading, Pennsylvania, and
graduated from the University of
Pennsylvania. He was a writer and
editor for television stations,
newspapers, magazines, and the
Associated Press before becoming a
full-time novelist. He received
Edgar Award nominations from the
Mystery Writers of America for*
Gypsy in Amber *(1971),* The Midas
Coffin *(1975),* Gorky Park *(1981),
and* Nightwing *(1987), and won the
Hammett Award for* Rose *(1996)
and* Havana Bay *(1999). He lives in
Mill Valley, California.*

personality. Like the hero of Thomas Berger's *Little Big Man* (1964), however, Harry is trapped between two ways of life and can live completely comfortably in neither.

Harry's role as existential outsider is established at the beginning when Smith shows the young Harry playing with Japanese boys whose idea of a good time is to chase him and knock him down. For most of *December 6*, Smith's method is to alternate chapters depicting Harry's childhood in the 1920's with scenes from December 6-8, 1941. When the opening chase leads Harry to seek refuge in a peep show in the Asakusa quarter, he finds his true milieu. This seedy yet glamorous, exotic and erotic neighborhood of bars, theaters, dancing girls, artists, prostitutes, and thieves is the center of the novel, becoming as much a distinctive character as Harry himself.

Without Asakusa, there would be no Harry Niles. Oharu, a dancer in the peep show, takes pity on the *gaijin* (foreigner), and eleven-year-old Harry is hired to run errands. Also hired at Harry's insistence is Gen, who has been one of his tormentors but becomes his best friend. That Harry wants to be Gen's friend but will always be seen as different is established in this opening chapter. Harry's trust in Gen will have tragic consequences in 1941.

The flashbacks are dominated by Harry's love for the teenaged Oharu and by his relationship with the artist Kato, who becomes his mentor, teaching him about the world of Asakusa. Kato is fascinated that "a gaijin could speak like a Japanese, eat like a Japanese, and shoplift cigarettes." That the boy is a missionary's son only heightens Kato's pleasure in Harry's exploits. Harry is able to roam the Asakusa with Oharu, Kato, and Gen because his parents are chasing converts in the countryside and he is in the custody of Orin Niles, his neglectful, drunken uncle. This gaudy paradise begins unraveling, however, when Harry sees Oharu in a pornographic pose for Kato.

The thirty-year-old Harry lives with Michiko Funabashi, who plays records to entertain the customers in the Happy Paris, the club owned by Harry. She also dances alluringly to tunes by such jazz musicians as Count Basie and Artie Shaw. Michiko, twenty, is a communist and feminist but nevertheless a romantic and a devoted reader of *Vogue* magazine. An enigmatic figure and minor Tokyo celebrity, she is as much a mystery to Harry as to anyone else: "What frightened Harry was that he knew

Michiko regarded a double suicide of lovers as a happy ending, but she'd be willing to settle for a murder-suicide if need be." Harry observes that when male radicals are imprisoned, they turn to religion and the emperor, while women like Michiko hang themselves "rather than give their keepers an inch of satisfaction."

Harry sees his parents and their lives as limited and unrealistic and strives to be their exact opposite. In contrast to his Bible-thumping father, "Harry's confidence was in his unrighteousness, his ability to dodge the consequences." Harry is the epitome of the American hustler, doing anything to get ahead of the game and stay that way, forever on the move, always looking for an advantage. While Michiko is unbridled emotion, Harry sees himself as embodying pure reason.

His most pressing dilemma is escape and survival. It is only a matter of time before the war begins, and as an American businessman, Harry must get away before that happens. Obstacles include the two policemen who follow him everywhere and the fact that the only means out of the country is a plane scheduled to leave on December 8. He does everything he can to ensure that he is on the plane along with his mistress, Lady Alice, wife of British diplomat Arnold Beechum. Michiko knows about Alice and knows she will be left behind.

Harry has other problems as well. Willie Staub, a young German businessman Harry meets in China, must leave the country but wants to take along Iris, his new Chinese wife. The Japanese authorities will not approve her exit visa, but Willie knows that Harry is capable of fixing anything and hopes his friend will come through for him. Other friends are more cynical. Al DeGeorge, a correspondent for *The Christian Science Monitor*, suspects Harry is running a pool on when the war will begin. Harry's friends, acquaintances, and enemies watch with suspicion, fear, and amusement to see what he will do to try to manipulate the authorities. As Michiko tells him, he always has an angle.

A larger problem is Ishigami. Wherever Harry goes, he is told the army officer is looking for him. He first meets Ishigami as a boy while delivering pornographic drawings for Kato. Gen goes with him once, and there are hints of a homoerotic attraction between Harry's boyhood friend and the man destined to be his greatest enemy. Harry meets Ishigami again years later in Nanking, China, when he and Willie see Chinese peasants lined up waiting for the officer to chop off their heads with his sword. Harry tries to stop the slaughter in a distinctively Niles kind of way. He bets that Ishigami cannot cut off the heads with only one swing. As soon as he fails, Harry and Willie spirit away five peasants. Ishigami is in Tokyo looking for the five heads he feels he is owed. Any contact with the psychopath will put Harry and his friends at great risk. Just as the opening chapter establishes escape as a major theme, the Nanking episode shows how the Japanese perceive war as a ritual, almost as a game.

Looking for an edge, Harry delivers a passionate—and therefore seemingly anti-American—address in support of Japan to businessmen, government officials, and foreign diplomats at the prestigious Chrysanthemum Club. The speech leads Arnold Beechum to call him "the most despised white man in Asia" and ends any possibility of help from the American embassy. Yoshitaki, owner of a shipping line and one of the country's wealthiest men, is not taken in by Harry's words: "I felt you would say anything to advance yourself. You are a marginal creature, like a crab that feeds neither in the water nor on land but in the rocks between." Yet the head of Nippon Air is impressed and offers Harry a seat on the Hong Kong plane.

Discovering evidence that the Japanese plan to attack the United States naval base in Pearl Harbor, Hawaii, Harry finds his patriotism on the rise. Ironically, he is partly to blame for the impending attack because one of his many schemes has involved making the Japanese believe there are secret American oil tanks on Oahu. He tries to warn the American diplomat, Roy Hooper, another missionary's son whom Harry knew as a boy, but Harry's credibility has completely eroded. Smith's elegantly plotted tale becomes a race for Harry to save himself from Ishigami, to help Willie and Iris, to protect Michiko, to escape from Japan with Lady Alice, and to try to save his country at the same time.

If any of this sounds vaguely familiar, Smith's obvious model is *Casablanca* (1942), the classic Hollywood World War II romance. Like Humphrey Bogart's Rick Blaine, Harry is a nightclub owner at the center of considerable nefarious activity. Like Rick, he poses as a cynical tough guy: "I'm not going to be a sucker, a fall guy, the chump left holding the bag." He is again like Rick in being a sentimentalist at heart, as his efforts on behalf of the Staubs show. Coming upon a fire in a tailor's shop and home, Harry helps the family's young son round up his pet beetles. There is, however, a degree of true cynicism about Smith's hero. His name recalls Harry Lime, Graham Greene's postwar black marketeer in *The Third Man* (1950). Both Harrys are adept at manipulating others to achieve their ends. Smith clearly wants Harry to represent an amalgam of the best and worst qualities of both his nations.

December 6 is full of wonderfully realized scenes such as Harry's rescue of the Chinese peasants and his discovery about Oharu. Others include an encounter with Babe Ruth during an American baseball all-star team's tour of Japan, a visit to the rooftop garden of a Ginza department store, a card game with some dangerous gangsters, a highly unusual meeting with the legendary Admiral Yamamoto, Harry's exposure of a scientific hoax, Michiko's unexpected efforts to save Harry from Ishigami, an encounter with Prime Minister Tojo in a park, and, especially, his conning the Nazis to help the Staubs. Smith also slowly accelerates the suspense about the consequences of Pearl Harbor masterfully.

Harry's mentor Kato has spent time in Paris and longs to paint in the Impressionist styles of Edgar Degas, Claude Monet, and Pierre-August Renoir. Kato is blind to the mediocrity of his French imitations and to the considerable virtues of the Japanese portraits he does only for money. Unlike Kato, Smith recognizes that what he does best is take the conventions of the thriller genre and create something close to art through painstaking attention to details, exemplary plotting, and very distinctive characters.

Michael Adams

Sources for Further Study

Booklist 98 (August, 2002): 1887.
Boston Herald, October 6, 2002, p. E1.
The Economist 365 (October 19, 2002): 109.
Kirkus Reviews 70 (June 15, 2002): 837.
Library Journal 127 (August 15, 2002): 147.
The New York Times Book Review 107 (October 20, 2002): 10.
Publishers Weekly 249 (August 5, 2002): 50.
San Francisco Chronicle Book Review, October 6, 2002, p. 6.
Time 160 (October 7, 2002): 96.
The Washington Post Book World, October 6, 2002, p. 2.

DEEP IN A DREAM
The Long Night of Chet Baker

Author: James Gavin (1964-   )
Publisher: Alfred A. Knopf (New York). 430 pp. $26.95
Type of work: Biography
Time: 1929-1988
Locale: The United States and Western Europe

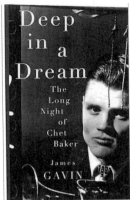

∼

This legendary jazz trumpeter's early promise is not fulfilled, mainly because of his long-time drug addiction

∼

Principal personages:
CHET BAKER, jazz trumpeter and addict
VERA BAKER, his mother
CHARLAINE SOUDER BAKER, his first wife
HALEMA ALLI BAKER, his second wife
CAROL JACKSON BAKER, his third wife
LILIANE CUKIER, his girlfriend
DIANE VAVRA, his girlfriend
RUTH YOUNG, his girlfriend
CHARLIE PARKER, jazz alto saxophone player
GERRY MULLIGAN, jazz baritone saxophone player
DICK TWARDZIK, jazz piano player

Chet Baker was a legendary jazz trumpet player from the 1950's through the 1980's. His legend is paradoxical. He was a romantic artist, breathtakingly handsome, enigmatic, and mercurial. He was gifted with an intuitive knowledge of music and the ability to play his instrument in beautifully melodic and inventive ways that affected the emotions of his audiences. His beauty and charisma attracted almost everyone who knew him, including three wives, his children, many musicians, and a great many girlfriends. On the other hand, he was an ill-educated, unreliable, childish, and totally self-centered man. He became addicted to all sorts of drugs: marijuana, cocaine, heroin, codeine, alcohol, tobacco, and more. Although Baker used drugs to enable him to make beautiful music, it is almost as accurate to say that Baker played music in order to get money to buy drugs.

To tell Baker's story, there cannot be many sources in the United States and in Europe that James Gavin has not consulted: recordings, films, television programs, magazines, newspapers. People who knew Baker were still alive to interview, and the biography is laced with remarks by these people, mainly two of his three wives and a number of his girlfriends. The result is a solid biography that gives both the facts and a number of perspectives. Gavin includes a detailed discography.

Chesney Henry Baker, Jr. (later known as "Chettie" and then "Chet") was born on December 23, 1929, in the small town of Yale, Oklahoma. His father was a guitar and banjo player who idolized Jack Teagarden, the jazz trombonist, and Bix Beiderbecke, the jazz trumpeter (whose life Chet's would resemble). The older Baker's career was thwarted by the Great Depression, which began about the time of Chettie's birth. Gavin emphasizes the bad effects of Baker's childhood. His father was distant and beat him; this, combined with his mother's suffocating love, produced a trauma that drove the young Chet Baker, even though he could not talk about it. Fortunately, Gavin does not pursue this theme too stridently.

James Gavin has written Intimate Nights: The Golden Age of New York Cabaret *(1992), which won ASCAP's* Deems Taylor Award. *He contributes to* The New York Times *and other publications. In 1996, he received a Grammy nomination for his liner notes for* Ella Fitzgerald: The Legendary Decca Recordings.

When he was ten, Chettie and his mother traveled by bus along fabled Route 66 to join his father in Glendale, California. There Baker blossomed. Although he was small for his age and looked very young, he was very handsome. His loving mother made sure he was well dressed. He was good at sports such as swimming, basketball, and track. His sports performance set a pattern that would last his entire life: he excelled apparently without trying. His mother taught him erotic popular songs of the day ("I Had The Craziest Dream") and entered him in a talent contest as a boy soprano. He almost won.

More important, when he was twelve his father bought him a trumpet at a pawnshop. Within two weeks, his mother claimed, Chettie was playing along with the famed trumpeter Harry James's solo on the record of "Two O'Clock Jump." Whether or not this is true, it is consistent with the way Baker played in later life. He could hardly read music, and he did not know many chords. He just played.

An important setback dates from this era. One day after school, someone threw a rock that accentually broke off one of Chettie's front teeth. Without that tooth, Baker found it difficult to play the high screaming notes that have produced big effects for other famous trumpeters. Baker's mature style would necessarily be softer and lower than the others (and tooth troubles were to dog him in later life). Nonetheless, he took up the trumpet with a passion. Instead of reading music, he memorized it after hearing it once. He played in school bands and played along with pop records. He idolized James's flamboyant style.

Baker was growing up. His sexual initiation was quick and ugly. He became wild and rebellious. To escape his parents, he joined the army. He was eventually sent to Berlin, where he joined army bands and discovered Stan Kenton and Dizzy Gillespie on the radio. He fell in love with a German girl and was betrayed, causing (according to Gavin) his paranoid mistrust of women.

Out of the army and back in the United States, he returned to high school. Like almost all the jazz musicians of the day, he smoked marijuana; he tried heroin. He became known for driving fast and stealing. When a judge gave him the choice of jail or going back into the army, he reenlisted and was sent to San Francisco. He married Charlaine Souder. For trying to deceive the army into letting him out, he spent time in the stockade before being discharged again in 1952.

All this while, Baker pursued his musical dreams. He sat in on jam sessions, even with such a famous man as piano player Dave Brubeck. From being an aggressive trumpet player, he gradually became more "cool." He admired the melodic style of Paul Desmond, Brubeck's alto sax player. His big break came when he played with Charlie Parker, the great be-bop alto saxophone player. When Parker praised him, Baker suddenly became a celebrity.

Then followed perhaps the most important of Baker's associations—with Gerry Mulligan. Mulligan, a musically well-educated baritone saxophone player and arranger, formed a quartet with Baker on trumpet and (usually) only a bass player and a drummer to back them up. Their performances and recording sessions through 1952 and 1953 are stunning examples of what was known as "West Coast Jazz." Even though Baker and Mulligan often quarreled, they played perfectly together, complementing each other effortlessly. They loved melody and created fuguelike variations on standard tunes, particularly one that became Baker's theme song, "My Funny Valentine." Baker's trumpet sang beautifully and emotionally, though at the same time it was restrained.

Gavin talks about Baker's place in the pop world: He was the handsome, romantic artist who embodied West Coast cool as well. His demeanor was aloof and detached (probably the result of the drugs he was taking). He said little (probably because he had little to say). On stage, he stared at the floor (probably because he was missing a tooth). Even so, he fit into the rebel mold of the early 1950's, that of actors Marlon Brando, Montgomery Clift, and James Dean.

The association with Mulligan ended when the saxophonist was sent to jail for drug possession. Baker formed his own quartet and began to sing vocals in his rather girlish voice. He recorded an album with strings. His glamorous photographs on album covers got him many female fans and many gay male ones as well. (Gavin often suggests that Baker had some homosexual leanings but does not document these suggestions convincingly.) Baker began to tour across the United States, ending up at Birdland in New York City, where he befriended the dying Charlie Parker. *Time* magazine praised him. He appeared on both *Today* and *The Tonight Show*. He won polls proclaiming him America's best jazz trumpeter. He appeared in a film, *Hell's Horizons* (1955). Even though he was still married, he took his choice of the women who offered themselves. His heroin habit continued.

The story of Baker's rise to the top takes about a hundred pages and is wonderfully detailed and interesting. From this point on, although Gavin's account is just as detailed as before, it is repetitive and depressing. This is because Baker's life itself became repetitive and depressing, a series of short-lived musical triumphs, long musical disasters, trips to Europe and back, two more wives, four children, numberless encounters with women (including at least three serious affairs), and drugs of all varieties. In 1957 he may have been responsible for the drug-induced death of his piano player, Dick Twardzik, and Gavin thinks he was tortured by this event.

Even without that death, Baker had torments aplenty. His music got harder and less lyrical; a reunion with Mulligan was a flop. His brand of jazz became old fashioned. He tried to take cures for his addictions, but the cures did not work. He lived with drug dealers and prostitutes and pimps. The money he got from playing gigs or stealing from his friends was spent on drugs. Even so, his friends tried to help him over and over again. His body became a welter of open sores from his injections. He behaved childishly with his fellow musicians. He fought with his wives and mistresses. Even though there must have been some quiet moments, Gavin describes his life as one of constant tumult.

Even though he was revered in Italy, Baker was sent to prison there for drug possession, but not before informing on his wife. He served time in England, too, and was kicked out of Great Britain, Italy, Switzerland, and Germany. Back in the United States, he was arrested many times for drug possession, and he informed on his friends. In order to keep the Los Angeles police from connecting him to a faked prescription, he burned down a pharmacy. No matter how badly he behaved, he described himself as a victim. In 1965, a drug deal went bad and Baker's upper lip was smashed so badly he could not blow his trumpet. His once-good looks did not so much fade as vanish. The excellent illustrations to Gavin's biography show how he changed. When he is only in his fifties, he looks like a cadaverous eighty-year-old man.

There are some bright moments in this terrible story. Baker worked hard to play again using false teeth. Every once in a while he rallied heroically to produce a good concert or a good radio or television show. The old lyricism and emotion were there— sometimes. Even in 1987, a Japanese tour went well. Filmmaker Bruce Weber engaged Baker in a documentary about his life, which eventually appeared in 1989 as *Let's Get Lost*.

Nonetheless, Baker sensed the end was near. He went to Europe in late 1987 and embarked on a whirlwind of gigs to feed his addiction. He disappeared in Holland, and on May 13, 1988, his body was found on the streets of Amsterdam near its notorious drug zone. He either jumped or was pushed from his hotel window.

Throughout his book, Gavin suggests answers to several related questions: What is the peculiar attraction of Baker's trumpet playing? Despite his terrible behavior, what drew people to him? How could such a despicable man produce such beautiful music?

Although Gavin's answers to the first question will not satisfy jazz professionals, they will help most readers. For one reason or another, Baker generally played softly. Because he did not know chords well, he can be heard to search his way intuitively into the chord as he played, or he simply paused until his way became clear; Baker's silences are as perfectly timed and as expressive as his notes. Even at the very end, a musician marveled that so few notes could express so much.

People were drawn to him because he was a great trumpeter who produced lovely music. Gavin and others suggest that Baker's mind was so vacant and his speech so laconic that people could read into him what qualities they desired. There is no doubt that his dogged energy and persistence gave him a great deal of charisma.

The beautiful music? Gavin surmises that behind all of his terrible behavior there lay a deep desire for beauty that he could not find in reality—except in his music, occasionally with women, and almost always in his experience of drugs. "Deep in a Dream," the song which gives Gavin's book its title, evokes the absolute desire for escape that Gavin thinks drove Baker all of his life.

George Soule

Sources for Further Study

Booklist 98 (May 15, 2002): 1566.
Library Journal 127 (May 15, 2002): 100.
The New York Times, May 10, 2002, p. E42.
The New York Times Book Review 107 (June 30, 2002): 9.
Publishers Weekly 249 (April 22, 2002): 65.
The Washington Post Book World, May 26, 2002, p. 2.

THE DEMON AND THE ANGEL
Searching for the Source of Artistic Inspiration

Author: Edward Hirsch (1950-   )
Publisher: Harcourt (New York). 321 pp. $24.00
Type of work: Fine arts and literary criticism
Time: The nineteenth and twentieth centuries

≈

A series of essays that see the source of artistic inspiration in the concept of duende, the passionate struggle with the artist's inner self, as revealed in the work of art

≈

Principal personages:
FEDERICO GARCÍA LORCA (1898-1936), Spanish poet
RAINER MARIA RILKE (1875-1926), German poet
RALPH WALDO EMERSON (1803-1882), American essayist

"This book essays praise for artistic inspiration, for the dark dictations and struggles that get embodied in works of art. It is a hymn to the irrational triumphs of art, to romantic imagination." With these sentences, the author, Edward Hirsch, summarizes the purpose, content, approach, and presentation of this book, which explores facets of inspiration for artistic creation and expression. Although it is used as a verb in this context, the word "essays" is also descriptive of the book's organization in a series of forty-two short essays. These essays, are, in fact, hymns that probe, praise, and investigate how feelings and ideas emerge from the artist's soul to be embodied in a work of art. Hirsch emphasizes the dark and irrational side of artistic creation. These essays focus on the artistic struggle from which Hirsch believes that "art is born." Hirsch finds romance within the way this soul-searching struggle ignites the imagination.

Hirsch looks at the ways that two types of spirit, the demon and the angel, fuel artistic inspiration. In both cases, the demon and angel are understood as figurative symbols of something deeply personal within each individual. As Hirsch puts it, they are figures that validate and summon to the light "the imaginary realms that dwell deeply within us."

Of the two, this book focuses most intensively on the demon, specifically on the concept of "duende." Hirsch traces the roots of duende to the Greek concept of the *daimon*, a mediating spirit that dwells within each soul but seeks to connect with transcendent realms. It was a supernatural spirit who could be called forth by magic or the occult. Although originally the *daimon* could be good or bad, in the Judeo-Christian tradition it eventually became associated with forces of evil: the demon.

~

*Edward Hirsch is a professor of
English at the University of Houston
and has received numerous awards
and fellowships, including
MacArthur and Guggenheim grants
for his books of poetry and literary
criticism.*

~

In Spanish culture, duende arose, in part, from this demoniac heritage. Duende shares with *daimon* or demon the sense of supernatural possession. It carries powers that can be both troubling and exhilarating. It seems to rise from the earth, to seize a person, to court death. It pushes the imagination to its limit and even beyond.

Throughout the book, Hirsch uses the life, poetry, and literary theories of the Spanish poet Federico García Lorca as the primary exemplar and guide to understanding the meaning of duende. García Lorca was from Andalusia in southern Spain, where the folk culture of the gypsy, the expressive sound and movement of flamenco, and the symbol-laden spectacle of bull fighting combined with the ceremonies, customs, and beliefs of Roman Catholic Christianity to produce an approach to life that embraced the extremes of the human condition from life to death with great intensity. García Lorca imbibed this Spanish spirit of duende. He considered Spain to be a culture that opened the doors on death and brought death into the midst of life. García Lorca himself was obsessed with death, even enacting his death and funeral as a performance on several occasions. His life, poetry, and beliefs all exemplified his view of duende as "artistic inspiration in the presence of death."

Hirsch begins the book by introducing García Lorca's lecture on duende under the published English title "The Play and Theory of Duende." Ideas from this lecture, along with examples of García Lorca's poetry, weave throughout these essays on artistic inspiration. While García Lorca provides the scaffolding for exploring duende, Hirsch examines the works of many other artists including poets, visual artists, and musicians to probe its nuances. For instance, darkness, night, and black depths are the settings where duende resides, where the imaginative encounter occurs. It is not surprising that Hirsch finds the force of duende in the works of several American abstract expressionist painters of the mid-twentieth century such as Jackson Pollock (1912-1956), Robert Motherwell (1915-1991), and Mark Rothko (1903-1970), who cultivated the use of the color black as their expressive vehicle. Rothko, for example, painted a series of large paintings for the Rothko Chapel in Houston, Texas, that are large, simple, rectangles in subtle shades from very dark maroon to pure black. Rothko said that these paintings dealt with "the infinite eternity of death." Their somber quality is imbued with that wellspring of duende that pushes the artist to confront the reality of death and the unfathomable eternity that lies beyond.

By contrast, other artists come to a similar confrontation with death through inspiration that seems to descend from angelic presences who evoke a keen awareness of the distance between the human and the divine. In the preface to this book, Hirsch pairs Ralph Waldo Emerson, the nineteenth century American essayist, with Federico García Lorca. The initial incongruity of this juxtaposition led Hirsch to consider that artistic inspiration could descend from heights as well as spring from demoniac depths. Emerson becomes one of Hirsch's guiding figures in the effort to understand the nature of these angelic forces in artistic inspiration.

Emerson, a Transcendentalist, acknowledged a creative space, an "invisible realm," that was somewhere "between sleeping and waking." Hirsch relates this state or imaginary space to the concept of angels. He examines ideas about the angelic world in Christian, Jewish, and Islamic traditions. Angels seem to inhabit a similarly indefinite space between heaven and earth. They are not necessarily comforting or sustaining spirits. Indeed, people may find themselves wrestling with angels in the manner of Jacob in the Old Testament. As Hirsch discusses this archetypal encounter with an angel, he emphasizes the internal, transformative effects of the struggle on the individual. These experiences are truly "epiphanies" that have "a rupturing intensity that is deep and troubling, even terrifying." The struggle represents a "crisis point" when the artistic imagination can be released.

As with duende, Hirsch utilizes examples of works by a number of artists to illuminate the nature of these encounters with angels and their liberating role in artistic creation. The poems of the German poet Rainer Maria Rilke show the power of angelic inspiration with special clarity. Like many of Hirsch's artistic exemplars of duende, Rilke's poetry is imbued with the prospect of death. In Rilke's work *Die Aufzeichnungen des Malte Laurids Brigge* (1910; *The Notebooks of Malte Laurids Brigge*, 1930), the poet approaches death so closely that the poems "stand on its shore and drink deeply of its waters." One poem called "Death" begins with an image of death as a blue liquid in a cup but turns unexpectedly and dramatically at the end to a shooting star "that fell into my eyes and through my body." It was as though death had entered Rilke's body and suffused him with a mystical vision of "a greater unity." Thus, both the demon and the angel unleash internal struggles, challenge artists to place their very beings at risk, but in the process allow the creative imagination to soar.

While this book provides a penetrating, thought-provoking examination of the enabling impact of duende on artistic expression, two key issues, the impact of historical circumstances on duende and the necessity of duende in the creative process, are less fully treated. Throughout the book, Hirsch looks at the artistic struggle with duende as an essentially internal process that takes place within the individual psyche. At one point, however, he briefly acknowledges that the individual is not alone but is always subject to others, to the currents of history which can put a person at the mercy of "forces much larger and stronger" than the self. Since most of the artists that he discusses lived during the nineteenth and twentieth centuries, it is important to analyze the degree to which duende expresses or perhaps owes itself to the collective cultural outlook of a particular moment in history.

At several points, Hirsch mentions the impact that historical events had on them. García Lorca, for example, was executed in 1936 during the Spanish Civil War. Both world wars, the Holocaust, and the Korean and Vietnam Wars brought dislocation, destruction, and immense suffering. History, however, is replete with wars and with atrocious acts committed by those holding power and authority, but artists do not necessarily respond with the same dark fervor that Hirsch so vividly exposes for the artists that he considers.

The question then arises whether other aspects unique to modern culture have contributed to enhancing the depth of anguished feeling expressed by these artists that Hirsch attributes to duende. The effects of science, technology, high-speed communications, and globalization in the nineteenth and twentieth centuries have been a double-edged sword. All the progress and improvements to the quality of life have been offset by the disorienting effects of rapid change, the sense of alienation from traditional communities and from nature, and some loss of faith in established belief systems. Hirsch evokes these very effects in the penultimate chapter, which focuses on García Lorca's encounter with American urban culture that resulted in a cycle of poems called *Poeta en Nueva York* (1940; *Poet in New York*, 1940). García Lorca reacted to the crowds, the noise, and especially "the tireless, dehumanized character of the city." He was acutely conscious not only of his own suffering but also of the suffering of others in the face of such inhuman conditions. Hirsch considers *Poet in New York*, which he terms "an apocalyptic outcry, a dark, instructive, metaphysical howl of loneliness," to be the "apotheosis" of García Lorca's duende. However, Hirsch does not analyze the ways particular features of modern culture affect or become an integral component of duende in this case or any others.

The second issue is whether duende is necessary or essential for artistic creativity. The consistently dark picture of artistic inspiration through the vehicle of both the demon and the angel that Hirsch portrays leaves little room for relief and few possibilities for other types of artistic vision. Toward the end of the book, however, a few glimpses of other prospects emerge. Two of the essays, "Fending Off the Duende" and "The Existentialist Flatfoot Floogie," treat works that do not court duende. Although Hirsch declares that there is "no hierarchy between works with duende and works without it," the few artistic works that he mentions as lacking duende seem diminished by its absence. When artists fend off duende, it is for "the sake of their sanity" and it contributes to "our artistic health." In Hirsch's account, the absence of duende is sometimes detrimental to the work of art. Art that "lives finely within its means and limits" and seeks "emotional balance and tranquillity" is deeper when one senses the darkness and the demon lurking just beneath, when "one feels the primal murkiness threatening to swell up underneath the geometric clarity."

On balance, the weight of arguments presented in this book lead to a conclusion that, in Hirsch's view, duende is vital to artistic inspiration and heightens the power of a work of art. At one point Hirsch quotes Emerson, who says: "Art is the path of the creator to his work." An equally valid case could be made that artistic inspiration can come from other paths that embrace the joys of life, emotional balance, and tranquil reflection. In his search for the source of artistic inspiration, Hirsch has illumined the powers of one source, duende, with considerable depth and feeling. One hopes that this book will provide its own inspiration to widen the search for sources of artistic inspiration with the high degree of intellectual commitment that Hirsch brings to this study.

Karen Gould

Sources for Further Study

Booklist 98 (February 15, 2002): 985.
Choice 40 (September, 2002): 84.
Library Journal 127 (April 1, 2002): 108.
Los Angeles Times Book Review, May 12, 2002, p. 10.
The Washington Post Book World, April 14, 2002, p. 7.

DESIRABLE DAUGHTERS

Author: Bharati Mukherjee (1940-   )
Publisher: Hyperion/Theia (New York). 320 pp. $24.95
Type of work: Novel
Time: 1879-2000
Locale: The East Bengal jungles, Calcutta, Bombay, and
    Rishikesh, in India; San Francisco; Upper Montclair,
    New Jersey; New York City

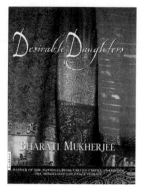

≈

A young Indian American woman solves a mystery and,
in the process, arrives at a fuller understanding of her fam-
ily, her culture, and herself

≈

Principal characters:
>   TARA BHATTACHARJEE, a thirty-six-year-old divorcée, a volunteer in a
>   San Francisco preschool
>   BISHWAPRIYA ("BISH") CHATTERJEE, her former husband, a Silicon Val-
>   ley multimillionaire
>   RABINDRANATH ("RABI") CHATTERJEE, their fifteen-year-old son
>   PADMA ("DIDI") BHATTACHARJEE MEHTA, Tara's oldest sister, a forty-
>   three-year-old artist and television personality living in New Jersey
>   PARVATI BHATTACHARJEE BANERJI, the second sister, a traditional
>   Indian wife, living in Bombay with her financier husband
>   ANDY KAROLYI, Tara's live-in lover, a Zen Buddhist carpenter
>   TARA LATA GANGOOLY, the martyred Bengal activist for whom Tara
>   Bhattacharjee was named

Bharati Mukherjee's writings reflect her preoccupation with three major themes: the status of women, the immigrant experience, and the response to a changing society. As the author has frequently told interviewers, all of her work, including her fiction, is based on her own experiences as a woman caught between two cultures. In her first novel, *The Tiger's Daughter* (1972), Mukherjee described the reactions of a young woman who, like the author, had returned to her native India after an extended stay in the West. What this protagonist discovered was not only that India had changed but also that her own perspective had changed. She now looked at her own country through the eyes of a Westerner. Other Mukherjee heroines are affected in various ways by their confrontation with the New World. In *Wife* (1975), a Bengali woman brought to New York City for an arranged marriage becomes unmoored in her new surroundings, goes mad, and murders her husband. By contrast, in *Jasmine* (1989), as a young Hindu widow travels west, she finds herself less and less influenced by the traditional ideas of a woman's place in the world that she had once ac-

cepted unquestioningly. In her new surroundings, she changes her mind about submitting to
ritual immolation, kills the man who has raped
her, and after settling down for a time in the Midwest, she leaves it and her disabled common-law
husband for a new life in California.

Unlike these earlier novels, which were imaginative extensions of Mukherjee's experiences,
Desirable Daughters began as a memoir. According to an interview in *The Women's Review
of Books*, at first Mukherjee intended the book to
be a study of the three sisters in her own family
and the very different choices they made as to the
directions their lives would take. Although eventually Mukherjee decided that she was not yet
ready to write an autobiography, she did set her
book in Calcutta, where she grew up, and in a
family of Bengali Hindu Brahmins, much like
her own. The "desirable daughters" of the title
are three sisters, and they do choose very different paths. Mukherjee has admitted that her younger sister recognized herself in Parvati Bhattacharjee Banerji, a traditional Indian wife, and
that the character of the westernized, indepen-

*Bharati Mukherjee has written
award-winning nonfiction, novels,
and short fiction. Her collection* The
Middleman, and Other Stories
*(1988) received the National Book
Critics Circle Award for best
fiction. After teaching at various
universities, in 1987 Mukherjee
became a professor at the
University of California, Berkeley.*

dent Padma Bhattacharjee Mehta was based on the author's older sister, a child psychologist living in the United States. Clearly Mukherjee saw something of herself in
the sensitive, thoughtful heroine and narrator, Tara Bhattacharjee, who at the end of
the novel finds herself compelled to write about upper-class Calcutta girls of her own
generation and also about the legendary woman with whose story *Desirable Daughters* begins.

This woman from the past, Tara Lata Gangooly, was the daughter of Jai Krishna
Gangooly, the great-grandfather of the three sisters in Mukherjee's novel. Although
she lived almost a century before them, she, too, had to choose between accepting the
fate a traditional society decreed for her and making her own way, unprotected, in a
world that was rapidly rejecting that established society. The story of Tara Lata introduces two of Mukherjee's major themes: the status of women and the response to a
changing society. Because he did not approve of India's movement toward a secularized society, Jai Krishna moved his family out of a cosmopolitan, urban environment
and into a village in rural Bengal. Then, in keeping with Hindu tradition, he arranged
the marriages of two of his young daughters to suitable boys. As the novel begins, the
youngest of the three sisters, five-year-old Tara Lata, is about to be married to a Bengali Brahmin boy of thirteen. Since the astrologers have given their approval, and he
has made sure that every requirement of his faith has been met, Jai Krishna assumes
that all will go well. However, when the prospective bridegroom dies of snakebite, the

boy's family accuses Jai Krishna of having ignored a sign, omitted a rite, or of attempting to foist off on them a daughter he knew was accursed. The only way that Jai Krishna can save Tara Lata from a lifetime of disgrace and at the same time evade the other family's demands for her dowry is to find another bridegroom immediately. This is how his youngest daughter becomes the bride of a tree.

Up to this point, Tara Lata was a mere puppet, whose fate was in the hands of her father, her family, her society, and her culture. However, as her namesake Tara discovers, because her odd marriage released her from the demands of a flesh-and-blood husband, Tara Lata was able to make a difference in the small village where she lived and even in the greater society. As an untutored nurse and healer and a fearless activist in the cause of Indian independence, she became a local heroine and finally, after being removed from her home by the colonial authorities, a martyr respected by Indians of every faith.

During their childhood in the 1960's, the three Bhattacharjee girls were often told the inspiring story of the Tree Bride. However, they had no idea that they themselves would ever face real danger. As members of Calcutta's highest level of society, they were isolated from the city's poor, protected from criminals, and insulated from any signs that their class and their customs were on the verge of extinction. It is true that women were now educated; however, they were still expected to go docilely into arranged marriages and to spend their remaining years as uncomplaining servants of their husbands.

Of the three sisters, Parvati came closest to fulfilling that ideal. Although she chose her own husband while they were both in American universities, she ended up in Bombay, keeping her house in perfect order while she entertained hordes of houseguests, rearing two sons, providing moral support for her spouse, a harried financier, and lavishing affection on a couple of stray dogs that she had taken in despite his protest.

Patma, or "Didi," also chose her own husband, a non-Bengali businessman, and settled with him in Montclair, New Jersey, where he remains in the background while she shines as a television personality. Didi's attention is focused on the present; she views her heritage as no more than an exotic backdrop for her public appearances and she organizes parties for other Indian immigrants only because they provide a lucrative market for the saris she designs and the jewelry she promotes.

Ironically, the only daughter whose marriage was arranged divorced her husband. Tara had no quarrel with the attractive, ambitious Bishwapriya Chatterjee, or "Bish," but she could not stand being nothing but a rich man's pampered wife. With her son, Rabindranath Chatterjee, or "Rabi," Tara has moved into a modest San Francisco house that is being upgraded and retrofitted by her live-in lover Andy Karolyi.

One reason Tara finds Andy so appealing is that before he achieved serenity through Zen, he was a biker, and for a young woman who has always lived behind guarded gates, protected first by her father and then by her husband, violence has a certain fascination. However, when she encounters a real threat in the person of a man who says he is her nephew and Padma's illegitimate son, Tara does not find the experience pleasant. The fact that the supposed Christopher Dey has struck up a friendship with Rabi makes Tara even more nervous. Her fears are augmented by the letters she receives from Parvati, passing along her husband's warnings about international crime rings. Finally, Tara consults the police, and they identify the supposed nephew as the notorious criminal Abbas Sartar Hai. In the meantime, however, Tara and Rabi have just barely missed being killed, and Bish, who saved their lives, has suffered disabling injuries. The real Christopher Dey, they later learn, was befriended by a stranger, murdered, and his identity stolen soon after his arrival in San Francisco.

Although Dey's fate is hardly typical, Mukherjee does point out that when one leaves a familiar environment, there is usually a price to be paid. A number of the characters in *Desirable Daughters* do very well in the United States. Bish and Padma, for example, find opportunities in their new country that they would never have had in India. However, it is difficult to escape from the culture in which one was reared. The fact that Bish is on the cutting edge in Silicon Valley does not mean that he has advanced ideas about the status of women. He offers his wife a good income and his protection; he cannot understand why Tara would want anything more. However, she does, and she leaves him.

On the other hand, after her brush with death, Tara realizes that the traditional system did have a rationale. She now knows that women pay a price for the freedom the Western world offers them, and that if they live alone, they are especially vulnerable. It is hardly surprising that, as soon as Bish is better, Tara goes back to her family in India, who always made her feel secure.

What Tara finds there, however, is what immigrants returning home generally find: that just because they were absent, time did not stand still. Tara cannot return to the big house in Calcutta, where she and her sisters grew up, because her father has sold it and built a smaller place in the hills. Moreover, her parents are not what they once were. Her mother has grown so frail that she can no longer cook, and her father, once so dynamic, keeps mentioning that according to his horoscope, he has only two or three more years to live.

Tara's stay in India is also troubling because, while previously she had discounted Parvati's accounts of rampant crime there, now she finds that her sister was not exaggerating. The upper classes can no longer be insulated from violence as they were when the sisters were young. Even if she wanted to return to the old ways, which seemed to provide such certainty, Tara could not do so, for she now knows that that way of life is gone forever. What she can do, she realizes, is to capture time in her writing. The book ends with a mystical juxtaposition of moments: Tara Lata at her writing, and Tara, at the Tree Bride's house, hearing the words, seeing the images, recreating the past.

In *Desirable Daughters*, Mukherjee has demonstrated her own power to capture past times. Although this immigrant has made her choice, the New World rather than the Old, in this novel that began as autobiography she pays tribute to her family and to her rich cultural heritage, which continues to provide her with the tales that make her works so spellbinding and with the insights that make them so memorable.

Rosemary M. Canfield Reisman

Sources for Further Study

Booklist 98 (February 1, 2002): 907.
Kirkus Reviews 70 (February 1, 2002): 133.
Library Journal 127 (April 1, 2002): 141.
The New York Times, April 23, 2002, p. E8.
The New York Times Book Review 107 (April 28, 2002): 11.
Publishers Weekly 249 (January 21, 2002): 62.
The Women's Review of Books 19 (July, 2002): 12.

DIRT UNDER MY NAILS
An American Farmer and Her Changing Land

Author: Marilee Foster (1970-   )
Publisher: Bridge Works (Bridgehampton, N.Y.). 175 pp.
   $22.95
Type of work: Environment, essays, and nature
Time: The early 2000's
Locale: Sagaponack, New York

~

Farming in Long Island, New York, as seen through the eyes of an artist, essayist, and farmer

~

Principal personages:
> MARILEE FOSTER, a thirty-one-year-old
>   woman who has returned to farming after college
> DEAN, her brother
> CLIFF, her father

Readers who purchase *Dirt Under My Nails* expecting to learn about the life of a typical farmwoman in the Midwest will be disappointed and perhaps confused. Marilee Foster is not the typical—or stereotypical—farmer. A graduate of Beloit College in Wisconsin, she is a writer and artist as well as a farmer; the land she works is not in the Midwest, but in the ultratrendy Hamptons of Long Island, one hundred miles east of New York City. Her slight book—much of which first appeared in Foster's weekly column for the *Southampton Press*—comprises a series of light, charming essays, arranged by season from winter through fall. It is more than a quarter of the way through before Foster actually discusses the process of growing plants, starting with the vegetable propagation trays in the basement in which she has planted tomato seeds.

Originally, Marilee Foster went to college planning to become a history teacher. Her focus shifted to liberal arts and she studied art, creative writing, and women's studies. Following her graduation in 1994, she spent the summer with her family on the farm on which she grew up. After days and nights of moving irrigation pipes through the potato fields, she decided to join her father and her older brother, Dean, in the family business, living with them on the family's property. There she has built an eclectic life: writing, joining in the regular farm chores, cultivating and marketing exotic and heirloom vegetables, and painting and working on crafts, mainly during the winter.

Dirt Under My Nails is more descriptive of the sights, sounds, and smells of a rural community than a picture of the rigors, trials, and chores involved in farm life. Foster's lovely word pictures may leave city-dwellers with a romanticized view of farm

Marilee Foster is a fifth-generation farmer in Long Island, New York, as well as a writer and painter. She chose to devote her life to farming with her family in 1994, after graduating with a liberal arts degree from Beloit College. Dirt Under My Nails *is her first book.*

life. Although the book is set in the United States, the tone, style, and subjects of Foster's writing should appeal to fans of books such as Peter Mayle's *A Year in Provence* (1989). Foster's whimsical line drawings of plants and animals appear at the start of each section and chapter.

The land making up the Fosters' farm is located in and around Sagaponack (known locally as Sagg), in the Hamptons. Although the ground there is extremely fertile, the Hamptons are now better known as a playground for the rich, glamorous, and powerful than as a farming area. Some of Foster's more serious observations relate to this dichotomy. In one essay, she contrasts her family and their long, deep connection to the land with what she calls the flash-in-the-pan farmer—the white-collar professional who gave up a six-figure income and all of life's superficialities to get a little dirt under his nails and reinvigorate his soul. Sometimes both happen, which suits him just fine until he realizes that he is working harder than he ever did, and with less financial return. What's more, his new occupation is eating into his retirement fund faster than he had calculated. Often the "wanna-be" sells all his equipment, converts or rents his land, and goes back to not-being a farmer, with maybe a not-so-much reinvigorated soul but a wiser one.

In another essay, she reflects on how much she depends on the visiting tourists and semiretired locals to make her cultivation of unusual crops economically successful. While distressed at the way the outsiders have changed her landscape and even her land, she acknowledges that her expensive crops such as heirloom tomatoes—too fragile to be harvested by machine and shipped to supermarkets—only make a profit because the well-to-do are willing to come to her produce stand and pay high prices for what she grows: "The part-time population wants not just [Sagg's] views but its tastes."

After reading an article on the problems of small Midwestern farms in *The New York Times*, Foster contemplates the differences and similarities between her family's farm and family-owned ranches in Nebraska. Both are being threatened by corporate factory farms, legislative decisions that Foster considers shortsighted, and foreign-raised produce. In contrast to Midwestern farmers, however, Foster and many other small farmers in her area can supplement the income from their regular crops with specialty fruits and vegetables. When asparagus from Ecuador was selling in supermarkets for less than $2.00, hers, hand-picked daily, sold for $3.50. She is an honest enough observer and critic to recognize that roadside stands of delicate produce is not "real" farming but a romanticized version thereof. However, in other essays she describes her role on the rest of the farm, where she gets just as sweaty and dirty and tired as any other farmer.

Foster does share one characteristic with many small family farmers: Her land has been in her family for several generations. Her great-great-grandfather, Josiah Foster, bought a plot of land in Sagaponack in 1870, after he tired of the lonely life of a whaling captain. The farm was passed to his son Clifford; to Clifford's sons, Charles and Everett; then to Charles's son Cliff, Marilee and Dean's father. Cliff received the Century Farm Award from the New York State Agricultural Society, an award that honors

> those people who have exhibited the resourcefulness that permits their farms to meet and exceed the demand of an ever-changing market. In addition, the award calls specific attention to a "century farm," a farm that has been in the same family, passed from one generation to the next, for at least one hundred years.

Through the years, the family has acquired more land through purchase and lease, and at the time of her book they were farming 600 acres in and around Sagaponack.

In one section, Foster compares farming and being an artist, and she argues that they "complement each other. Not that they are harmonious so much as they are like old friends, lovingly antagonistic, forcing each other to be honest and contemplative. I do not, in any case, think one would be any good without the other." However, she acknowledges that in at least one way, farming is quite the opposite of creating prose or poetry. In writing, there often are long spells of unproductivity, but "[i]n agriculture, time to ponder is undesirable and resented, even treated with suspicion. Farming is a literal cultivation that demands physical movement, timely responses, and grim determination."

A family farm is both a family and a business. Although the business side of farming is touched on only occasionally, the book is sprinkled with references to the challenges of mixing family with business. The main conflicts seem to occur between her father, Cliff, and her brother Dean. It is obvious that Cliff has trouble accepting his son and former apprentice as an equal partner, a stronger worker, and someone whose ideas should have equal weight with his. As Marilee says, it is a rivalry, and ugly, angry feelings often are vented, but "I know that if my brother can survive this and still want to farm, I'll have a business partner for life."

Although readers learn about Marilee's father and brother, little is said about her mother. Early in the book, Foster speaks briefly of the great differences in her parents' backgrounds—Cliff from a long line of taciturn farmers and laborers, her mother from a much livelier family that once lived in South America and were "long on intellect and short on cash," according to her mother's mother. Marilee's mother grew up in New Jersey and spent summers with her family in Sagg, in a cottage that was little more than a shack on the beach. Her current role in the family or the farm is barely mentioned in *Dirt Under My Nails*.

Foster's life as an artist is evident in the way she writes, as her descriptions often use art-based metaphors and similes. Where others might see and hear only machines tilling soil and dropping seeds, she sees a canvas and hears a symphony. Before the family and hired hands could plant potatoes, piles of debris that had blown into their fields from various construction sites had to be cleared away. "I have come to revere farming as an art form," she complains, "and anything that sullies the landscape, our borrowed canvas, somehow and slowly erodes morale." She calls potato planting an art, one that can be viewed purely for its visual impact, and goes on to rhapsodize over the colors and sounds of the planting:

> I watch as the plow breaks winter's seal. There is the slightest sense of violence when I see the furrow it carves. . . . Then the plow tears through this wavering sheet. It stills it, like a hand over a scream. . . . Potato planting is also a musical feat. The planter itself is like the symphony hall, an acoustic shell. . . . [T]he planter provides a daylong concert of relationship between the seed and the soil. And when I see Jigger there on the back of the machine, I know that he has the unique position of being both the conductor and the dancer.

Foster does discuss weightier issues, if only briefly. A charming recollection of the pond she skated on as a child segues into a discussion of how the local farmers felt they were "skating on thin ice" because of the conflicts between pressure for more development and the attempt to keep the area's rural character, which brings the very people who want to develop it. In another essay, she reflects with amusement on an oversized sport utility vehicle that she watched nearly overturn in a drainage ditch, then reminisces on how twenty years ago she used to join the local children in swimming there. One of her more poignant essays revolves around the lives of the migrant farmworkers who pass through the area during the busiest seasons, although she leaves it to the reader to make the connection between their impoverished lives and the wealthy tourists who are the other seasonal visitors.

Most of the book is cheerful and charming, as she shares with readers the beauty of the landscape around her and recalls the simpler days of her childhood. In the last chapter, however, she sounds an especially bitter note, speaking angrily of the sixty-five-thousand-square-foot mansion being built in Sagaponack by Ira Rennert—the largest house in the United States—and the failure of officials of Southhampton Town to listen to their constituents' pleas for intervention.

Irene Struthers Rush

Sources for Further Study

Booklist 98 (April 1, 2002): 1290.
Library Journal 127 (April 15, 2002): 117.
Los Angeles Times Book Review, May 19, 2002, p. 15.
The New York Times Book Review 107 (April 28, 2002): 11.
Publishers Weekly 249 (April 15, 2002): 55.
Victoria 16 (June, 2002): 45.

THE DIVE FROM CLAUSEN'S PIER

Author: Ann Packer (1959-   )
Publisher: Alfred A. Knopf (New York). 370 pp. $24.00
Type of work: Novel
Time: 2002
Locale: Madison, Wisconsin, and New York City

～

Packer's first novel explores the limits and the respon-
sibilities of love in the story of a young woman whose
fiancé paralyzes himself by diving into a lake, just as she is
about to break the engagement

～

Principal characters:
> CARRIE BELL, a twenty-three-year-old woman from Madison, Wiscon-
> sin, who must decide what to do when her fiancé becomes a quadri-
> plegic
> MIKE MAYER, Carrie's fiancé, who foolishly dives into a shallow lake in
> an attempt to impress Carrie during a picnic with friends
> JAMIE, Carrie's best friend since childhood
> ROOSTER, Mike's best friend since childhood
> SIMON, a gay friend of Carrie who lives in New York
> KILROY, a mysterious older New Yorker with whom Carrie has an affair
> MRS. BELL, Carrie's mother, a single parent

In most novels, there is a moment that irrevocably changes the lives of the characters who inhabit the pages of the book. In high school English classes, that moment is
labeled "the crisis," and usually it takes many pages of exposition to build to this moment. This is not the case in Ann Packer's first novel, *The Dive from Clausen's Pier*.
In this story, the life-changing event takes place in a three-page preface before chapter 1, and everything else that happens in the book is in response to one tragic moment.

Carrie Bell is everybody's girl next door. At twenty-three, she lives in Madison,
Wisconsin, the town where she was born. She gets along with her mother; she has a
great boyfriend, Mike, to whom she is engaged; and she has many friends, the same
friends she has had all of her life. Until very recently, this has been sufficient for
Carrie, but now she has begun to think about the big world and about how much she
wants to experience it. Her frustration is clear:

> [T]he Spartans had been our high school mascot. That we were a year out of college and
> still making Spartans jokes seemed to me to be a symptom of whatever it was we all had,
> whatever disease it was that had us doing the exact same things we'd always done, and
> with the exact same people.

~

*Ann Packer has won several awards
for her short stories, including a
James Michener Award and a
National Endowment for the Arts
fellowship. Her work has appeared
in magazines and was selected to be
included in* Prize Stories, 1992: The
O. Henry Awards. The Dive from
Clausen's Pier *is her first novel.*

~

When she realizes that she has to keep a mental list to remind her what she loves about Mike, she knows that she is going to have to call off the engagement. Before she can do so, however, Mike dives off a pier into shallow water, changing both of their lives forever.

As Mike lingers in a coma for a month, Carrie struggles with her conflicting feelings. Her friends and Mike's family expect her to "be there" for Mike. Rooster, Mike's best friend, is particularly angry with Carrie for not crying or making clear her devotion to Mike. Carrie, on the other hand, who was feeling suffocated before the accident, now finds herself both numbed and panicked that the rest of her life might be devoted to her comatose fiancé. At the same time, her memories of Mike as well as her love for him convince her that there must be something terribly wrong with her that she cannot give what everyone seems to expect and want.

When Mike awakens, things go from bad to worse for Carrie. Mike's mother and his doctor make it clear to Carrie that her presence and unflagging support is necessary for Mike's recovery. Mike is desperate for her love but also knows that she has drifted from him. Carrie's response is to buy fabric and begin sewing. She spends hours and hours making curtains, lingerie, and clothing, anything to occupy her time, her hands, and her body, and to give her an excuse for not visiting the hospital. This response infuriates her friends and mystifies Mike's family.

Carrie herself is mystified. It is as if she is watching herself shift from devoted girlfriend to disinterested stranger and back again. When Mike's sister asks Carrie if she still wants to marry Mike, the question haunts her: "Do you want to? Do you want to? Do you want to? By the time I got home from the hospital that night the question had permeated the very air around me." Indeed, it is this question that forces Carrie to confront the crucial issue: How can she be what everyone (including herself) wants her to be, and yet still have any life of her own?

> I knew I could continue, in Rooster's words, to be there for Mike; I knew I could wait out his sadness or at least that part of it that was the most acute. I could stand by and applaud as he slowly, slowly learned to get around in his wheelchair, how to use what little function he could marshal from his hands to eat, to help dress himself. But what then? Be his caretaker? His cook, nurse, helper, chauffeur, attendant? And his wife, somehow, too? And also myself? Who might that be?

Carrie seems unable to answer this question. When she runs into an old friend, Simon Rhodes, a gay man who now lives in New York, a series of events is set into motion that offer her the escape she longs for. Without saying good-bye to anyone, she packs her car and takes off for New York.

In New York, Carrie moves into the house Simon shares with several other people and begins a new life, far removed from the life she has led until now. She begins an affair with an older man, Kilroy, and takes classes in fashion design. Meanwhile, back in Madison, Mike is devastated and Carrie's friends are furious. Jamie in particular is vicious in her anger with Carrie. Nevertheless, Carrie slowly comes to terms with herself and with Kilroy. It seems as if Carrie has found a new home in New York, a home where her creativity and individuality can blossom. When her fashion design teacher takes special interest in Carrie, the reader begins to imagine a life for Carrie in New York, just as Carrie herself begins to imagine the same thing.

Packer, however, knows that life is much more complicated than that. Her protagonist cannot shake off her first twenty-three years so easily, no matter how much the reader might want her to. When there is an emergency with Jamie, Carrie chooses to go home (because ultimately, home is Madison) and tries to put things right. She reconnects with Mike, in spite of his family's suspicions and anger. Again, Packer demonstrates her understanding of the complexity of life. A lesser writer might have moved her protagonist to a happy ending with Mike, creating a brave young woman who returns to do her duty and finds happiness doing so, or she might have just left Carrie in New York to find her own life, leaving Madison and its restrictions behind her. Packer does neither, choosing the more difficult path by creating a character who is not only complex enough to run away but also compassionate enough to return; not only committed to making a choice, but also conflicted enough to find that neither choice is everything she wants. If Carrie's flight to New York and success there is marred by her ongoing feelings of guilt and love for Mike, in spite of her relationship with Kilroy, her return to Madison is just as ambivalent. She experiences both sadness and loss, and her reconnection with Mike, while genuine, is not the same as falling in love.

Clearly, *The Dive from Clausen's Pier* is not a simple book, nor is Carrie Bell a simple heroine. The book asks its reader to consider, "How much do we owe the people we love?" The answer to this question is not clear-cut. For a considerable part of the first section, it appears that the answer of "Madison Carrie" will be, "Everything." Her escape to New York and her long sojourn there seem to negate that answer, suggesting that the answer of "New York Carrie" might be, "Nothing." The truth is somewhere between total self-sacrifice and complete abandonment of duty, somewhere between putting another person's needs completely before one's own and completely disregarding the other person's needs. In illustrating this truth, Packer has succeeded in a difficult task: She has risked creating a character whom readers might not always like, because Carrie's responses at times might seem uncomfortably close to responses readers might make themselves.

Furthermore, *The Dive from Clausen's Pier* not only offers a serious ethical, moral exploration of love and responsibility, it also offers an interesting psychological portrait of two young people. Mike must learn how to live a life that is far short of his expectations. He must learn how to accept love from people who love him, knowing that he will never live the life he imagined for himself. Packer introduces a cameo appearance here by Mike's counselor, who, if he is unable to offer profound wisdom, is at least able to help Mike through the murky tunnel of quadriplegia. Mike's life is like looking through the wrong end of a telescope: a once-expansive panorama closed into a room, a bed, a chair.

Ironically, just as Mike's world goes through a radical shrinking, Carrie's expands to encompass half a continent and a new culture. Carrie, too, must reach psychological and emotional maturity to bring the book to its resolution. While in Madison, she feels suffocated and alienated; in New York, she often feels isolated and far from home. Even more troubling for Carrie, she continues to behave in ways that seem totally foreign to her. She keeps thinking that she is not the kind of person who would do such a thing—but since she has done it, she must be that kind of person. Moments of intense self-reflection run throughout the book, forcing the reader to feel both anger with and compassion for this conflicted protagonist. It is to Packer's credit that both worlds—Madison and New York—function as realistic spaces where these young people can grow to new understanding.

It is also to Packer's credit that she is able to bring healing to her characters, although, like the rest of the novel, the healing is neither simple nor complete. Although Carrie chooses to stay in Madison, her love for Mike has changed into a friendly love and it is clear they will not marry. Further, her love for Kilroy remains intense, causing her anguish and pain even as she is making her choice. The fashion design career she dreamed of in New York is reduced in scale to fit her circumstances in Madison. It is as though Packer is reminding readers that while they cannot always get everything they want, they can have some of it, and this is sufficient. Surely this is the sign of wisdom and maturity.

The last scene of the novel returns the characters to Clausen's reservoir, at Picnic Point, the place where Mike took his fateful dive. It is clearly not a complete circle, however, because there is still much to be resolved for these characters. Nonetheless, it is a satisfying ending in its incompleteness. Packer's prose, clear and enticing throughout the book, quickly propels readers to this final bittersweet yet hopeful moment, content in the moment itself.

Diane Henningfeld

Sources for Further Study

Chicago Sun-Times, July 14, 2002, p. 17.
Entertainment Weekly, May 3, 2002, p. 80.
Kirkus Reviews 70 (January 1, 2002): 14.
Minneapolis Star Tribune, April 14, 2002, p. 14F.
The New York Times Book Review 107 (May 12, 2002): 11.
Publishers Weekly 249 (March 4, 2002): 54.
School Library Journal 48 (August, 2002): 222.

THE DOCTOR'S HOUSE

Author: Ann Beattie (1947-   )
Publisher: Simon & Schuster (New York). 279 pp.
   $24.00
Type of work: Novel
Time: Around 1970
Locale: New England; Cambridge, Massachusetts

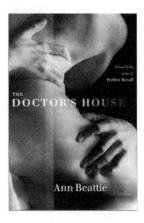

∿

A portrait of a dysfunctional family, exhibiting how the ills of the parents ruin the lives of the children: Disillusioned in marriage by her manipulative, heartless, philandering husband, the wife turns to alcoholism, and both parents neglect the children during their formative years

∿

Principal characters:
   NINA, a shy and introverted loner
   ANDREW, her outgoing, manipulative brother
   MOTHER, their alcoholic mother
   FRANK, father of Nina and Andrew, husband of their mother, and the
      doctor of the title

The structure of *The Doctor's House* is seemingly simple. Instead of intertwining the stories and points of view of the characters simultaneously, as in real life, the novel has three separate first-person narrators: Nina, Andrew, and their mother. In each case, the story offers a personal insight into the individual as well as into other members of the family, with particular focus on the demoniac figure of their tyrannical, abusive father and husband, Frank, "the doctor." In this way, the story of a family life and its members is both directly shown through personal narration and indirectly reflected in other members' narratives. This technique actively involves the reader in the process of decoding the characters' behaviors and thinking processes, which are unusual, deranged, and anomalous. Their thinking processes and their actions, as well as their reactions to the world around them, reveal their characters. What they do not, cannot, or will not see about themselves is scrutinized and depicted by the other two narrators.

Growing up neglected and lonely within a dysfunctional family, with an alcoholic mother and a cold, cruel father, the siblings develop a strong, codependent attachment to each other that carries into adulthood. Andrew is the outgoing, charming, selfish user, Nina the introverted, shy, traumatized loner. Nina devotedly (or rather, compulsively) absorbs, one by one, each of Andrew's numerous relationships, which are forever "on the rocks." She is passive, especially when it comes to her own life, but she tries to help others. While she may be her own worst enemy, her father and brother are actively destructive to others.

Ann Beattie has written seven novels, as well as seven collections of short stories. She is a member of the American Academy of Arts and Letters and a recipient of a Guggenheim Fellowship and the 2000 PEN/Malamud Award of Excellence in Short Fiction, and her work has been included in three O'Henry Award collections and John Updike's Best American Short Stories of the Century. *She is a professor of literature and creative writing at the University of Virginia in Charlottesville.*

The first part of the book is told in Nina's voice, depicting her empty, depressing life following her young husband's tragic death in a car accident. Her brother's life, a string of romantic-sexual conquests, replaces her own. Her life is so empty that listening to the messages on her answering machine counts as an event. Apart from reliving the memories of her gregarious, big, and cuddly husband, Mac, and her boring, homebound job, Nina's days are filled almost solely with her brother's visits to discuss his problems. Occasionally, one of his deserted women calls Nina to find out where Andrew has gone after dropping her or to tell about the abortions he has necessitated. Those women—their names, idiosyncrasies, and stories—float in Nina's memory like icebergs. She does not know all of them, but remembers random details and events. The women befriend her in order to come closer to Andrew; on occasion Nina even baby-sits for them.

Since childhood Nina was endowed with the analytical mind, sharp insight, and imagination of a writer. Ignored by her self-absorbed mother, scorned and belittled by her father, and living in constant terror of his sadomasochistic punishments, Nina's talent for creative writing wilted before it ever developed, ending in an unfulfilling job as a freelance copy editor. However, her mind still has remnants of a sense for the story. She is a thwarted writer. The bits and pieces of her brother's love affairs in Nina's mind are like cut-outs for a multitoned grey-black, sometimes blood red, patchwork. If human psychology is not of interest to the reader, there is not much in Nina's life to make her story entertaining. She is aware that she has "mourned away" her life while her brother "provided cheap thrills." The drudgery of her everyday existence is so well depicted that it flows onto the reader.

The second narrative belongs to Mother. It is the most interesting because it offers a sharp evaluation of her husband's and children's faults as well as the story of her married life. It presents an exciting, colorful sketch of the era of World War II, Vice President Richard Nixon's bribery scandal, Sputnik, the Cold War, and Soviet premier Nikita Khrushchev's "political use" of his shoe. The emphasis, however, is on the woman's world, its social mores and lifestyles. It is a world where a mother does not raise her daughter but rushes her into an early marriage (as her mother had done with her) in the hope of marrying her "well" (to a good profession, not a good man). It shows a mother putting all of her petit bourgeois dreams into designing her daughter's room, ignoring and forgetting in the process both her husband's and daughter's needs and wishes while she is living out her own unfulfilled desires.

Mother confides that, in her youth, her dream was to become a singer like Billy Holiday, a woman of style and transgression, turning her life into a jazz improvisation with her captivating, luscious singing. Mother's narrative is at first alive, picturesquely depicting the fashions, fads, entertainment, dreams, and hopes of the women in her era, allowing gossipy and risqué details to spice the story. About her married life she says, "[L]ife began to evolve out of a boozy swoon in a hotel room, and was christened by my throwing up on the floor." Gradually, her expectations are killed by Frank's too-obvious debauchery. Even their first sexual experience is interrupted by his nurse's call about a faked emergency. She finds out that the nurse is, in fact, his lover, as are his patients, including her personal friend.

In spite of her rampant drinking, Mother's view of Frank is sharp and precise, like a scalpel. She relates that when Andrew was only two, his father proclaimed him a homosexual. Frank does, however, claim to teach Andrew how to be a man, starting when he is five, until Andrew tells him to stop. Andrew proves the adage "Like father, like son" by having even more numerous affairs. Mother admits that she did not know how to raise Nina, a child who always preferred books and fiction to real life. All she knew was that she did not want her daughter to become her own replica. Mostly she ignores her, especially as she drinks to oblivion, sleeping in her own stale vomit. Talking about Nina, Mother diagnoses her correctly: She had inherited her proclivity to misery from her father. Andrew is Mother's only confidant. Dedicated to solitary drinking, she begins inviting him to her bedroom for secret talks late in the night. Throughout her marriage, even though she is secluded in her room, Mother knows what is going on in the outer world and with whom Frank is sleeping. She discovers his technique: billing his patients higher than they can pay, then promising to forget it if the woman "gets together" with him. As her alcoholism progresses, Mother's story loses its spark of life and turns into the bleak ranting of a thwarted mind, more like that of her children.

Andrew's story mostly deals with looking up his old high-school girlfriends to renew sexual liaisons wherever possible (single-minded quests, as Nina calls them). Both Frank and Andrew are capable of sexual performance but unable to feel love. Amoral manipulators and predators, they do not feel the pain of their prey nor do they try to understand it. Andrew's memories shed light on the traumatic events of his and Nina's childhood and adolescence. One special event is directed and staged by Andrew: a teenage, doped, uninhibited orgy of an assumed lesbian nature, filmed by Nina (at his request) and interrupted by their father, who has come to visit his lover. All involved go through an agony of justifiable fear of punishment, with only their father slithering out of it without a scar. The children are terrified enough to promise they will not tell anyone, especially not the police.

Truth is not always pleasant or entertaining, but has to be dealt with. *The Doctor's House* is not an easy, pleasant read. The reader is being admitted into the shady corridors of severely traumatized and deviant minds, both child and adult. The composition of the novel dictates a work driven by character rather than story. It is a bleak and barren land, an emotional desert. The only healthy, vibrant, and warm individual, an oasis of positive, nurturing energy, is Mac, but he dies early in a car crash, so he is seen only through the memories of other people (especially Nina and Andrew). Even those memories are filtered and colored through their minds. Mother, for instance, is never impressed or taken by him. She berates (in her husband's style) his gift of chry-santhemums and misinterprets his asking for a room-temperature water and a vase as his overrating the value of his gift, rather than a sign of caring for the plant. Therefore, to tone him down, she does not thank him. She refuses to be impressed by his career as a doctor or by his good looks. She scoffs at his and her daughter's glow of happiness during the wedding ceremony, which was planned and designed without consulting her. Many others, on the other hand, find a close friend in Mac, whose presence is missed and constantly felt. Without Mac's radiance, the world would be too barren, too bleak, and too impoverished, and life would only be cumbersome, without any meaningful *joie de vivre*. The four main characters live their lives either avoiding con-flicts except for the one that is alive in their own psyche (as in Mother's case) or mini-mizing them through shrinking from life itself (as in Nina's). Those two are passive. Frank and Andrew are active. Where they are, there is conflict. It lives in them and they spread it into the world through their reckless relationships, even thriving on it and leaving broken lives wherever they go.

There is no growth or change in the characters' lives. Depression, trauma, addiction, and illness do not go away or improve without treatment, professional or natural. The afflicted individuals need to recognize the need to assist nature with the healing process, motivated by the presence of a greater force, like love, in some of its abundant forms. This does not happen in *The Doctor's House*. Maybe Mac would have been that catalyst for Nina, had he lived. The doctor himself is not a healer, but a modern version of Doc-tor Jekyll. This novel is here to awaken the reader to the reality in which some people live. That reality is a spreading illness that will not go away unless treated. This is Beattie's social message and her contribution is in calling attention to the symptoms.

Like John Updike, J. D. Salinger, and John Cheever, known for their precision in ex-posing illnesses of family values in her own generation and social class, Ann Beattie once again exhibits her ability to probe into human character with a precision of insight, emotional depth, and lush detail. Long after finishing *The Doctor's House*, readers will retain memory of some outstanding moments, vivid images, and vibrant details that paint a realistic and sobering picture of the mysteries of human character and condition.

Mira N. Mataric

Sources for Further Study

Booklist 98 (December 1, 2001): 605.
Library Journal 127 (January, 2002): 148.
Los Angeles Times Book Review, May 5, 2002, p. 4.
The New York Times Book Review 107 (March 10, 2002): 11.
Publishers Weekly 248 (December 17, 2001): 63.

DOSTOEVSKY
The Mantle of the Prophet, 1871-1881

Author: Joseph Frank (1918-   )
Publisher: Princeton University Press (Princeton, N.J.).
    784 pp. $35.00
Type of work: Literary biography
Time: 1871-1881
Locale: St. Petersburg, Staraya Russa, and Moscow, Russia; Bad Ems, Germany

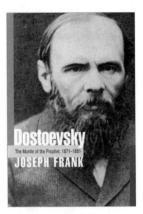

❦

The fifth and last volume of the biography of a great Russian writer as he composes his final masterpiece and becomes for the first time a revered man in his native land

❦

Principal personages:

FEODOR MIKHAILOVICH DOSTOEVSKI, the great Russian writer
ANNA GRIGORYEVNA DOSTOEVSKI, his second wife and business manager
MIKHAIL NIKIFOROVICH KATKOV, editor of *The Russian Messenger*, in which Dostoevski's final novel appeared
COUNT LEO TOLSTOY, another great Russian novelist, who never appears directly but is a presence in Dostoevski's life
IVAN TURGENEV, a Russian novelist and literary rival of Dostoevski

With this fifth volume, appearing twenty-six years after the publication of the first, Joseph Frank brings to a conclusion his distinguished biography of Feodor Dostoevski (1821-1881). The complete work comprises 2,423 pages; this volume, covering the last decade of the author's life is, at 784 pages, by far the longest of the five. Readers familiar with the earlier volumes will find that Frank's procedure remains basically the same. After an introduction summarizing his subject's life to this point, he offers a comprehensive narrative of Dostoevski's activities during the decade, pays much attention to the sociopolitical background of the time, and provides both accounts of his work in progress and commentaries on the finished works, which in this period include mainly his *Podrostok* (1875; *A Raw Youth*, 1916), *Dnevnik pisatelya* (1876-1887, 2 vols.; *The Diary of a Writer*, 1949) and *Bratya Karamazovy* (1879-1880; *The Brothers Karamazov*, 1912).

In 1871, the Dostoevski family returned to their homeland after four years abroad occasioned by Dostoevski's fear of being arrested and imprisoned for debt. At this time, his controversial novel *Besy* (1871-1872; *The Possessed*, 1913) was appearing serially in M. N. Katkov's *The Russian Messenger*, and the payments he received, while not princely, allowed him to stave off the most difficult of his creditors. The

Professor Emeritus at both Princeton and Stanford, Joseph Frank has earned a number of awards for previous volumes of Dostoevsky, *among them the National Books Circle Award for Biography, two Christian Gauss Awards, and two James Russell Lowell Awards of the Modern Language Association.*

family settled in St. Petersburg and were soon able to purchase a summer residence in Staraya Russa, a watering place south of St. Petersburg. Except for periodic business trips to Moscow and several sojourns at Bad Ems, a German spa, where he sought relief from the emphysema which plagued him in his late years, Dostoevski's wandering was over.

The years abroad had increased his xenophobia, and his return elevated his Russian chauvinism to an even higher pitch. These themes, along with the fervent religiosity that was always inextricably bound to his Russian nationalism, find expression in his *The Diary of a Writer*, a personal and independent monthly publication unprecedented in the history of Russian journalism. The *Diary* had grown out of a column in a weekly called *Grashdanin* (the citizen) which Dostoevski agreed to edit in 1872 to provide himself with a regular income but which he soon learned required far too much of his time and energy. Though intensely patriotic, Dostoevski waxed as critical of the political and social realities of czarist Russia as official censorship would permit. His articles paradoxically mingled Christian piety, deep affection for the Russian peasantry, admiration for rebellious young intellectuals, and devotion to Czar Alexander II, whom dissidents, including many of the young rebels, tried repeatedly to assassinate, finally succeeding a month after Dostoevski's own death. In his last years Dostoevski, an ex-convict because of his own youthful revolutionary allegiances, became at the same time a hero of the gun-toting rebels and a counselor to Alexander's young sons. He professed opposition to violence at home, but his pan-Slavic sentiments led him to support enthusiastically the imperialistic Russo-Turkish War of 1877-1878, although in *The Diary of a Writer* he masks his position by assigning it to an interlocutor, while as diarist he opposes bloodshed.

Although not blind to their ignorance and vulnerability, Dostoevski idealized Russian peasantry and Russian society. The serfs, he pointed out, had been freed in the previous decade without the bloodshed characteristic of social revolutions in the West, where oppression at the hands of landowners had simply been exchanged for oppression by entrepreneurs. Now, in the 1870's, he saw industrial expansion threatening to infect his countrymen with a materialistic outlook that had already ruined Western Europe. The liberated serfs seldom possessed enough land to sustain them and had to endure heavy taxation, but Dostoevski insisted that the educated classes would not neglect the welfare of the poor. Basic Christian virtues would prevail in Russia because Eastern Orthodoxy, unlike Western Christianity, had preserved the essence of Christ's teaching. Unfortunately, religious faith often involved religious and ethnic intolerance, and Frank shows that Dostoevski, though sincere in his faith, was far from free of the harsh anti-Semitism prevalent in Russian society.

Dostoevski's fears and hopes for Russian society also pervade his novels. Like other Russian writers of the time, he found it not only convenient but also much safer to develop his social and political ideas through the arguments and interactions of fictional characters. Thus, what might appear to be Frank's excessively "political" reading of Dostoevski's novels is entirely appropriate. Without at least an elementary grasp of the sociopolitical realities of later nineteenth century Russia, the reader is ill-equipped to understand, much less appreciate, these novels. The author's knowledge of Russian society is one of the strengths of this biography.

Nor does Frank neglect his subject's artistry. He depicts the process by which Dostoevski's novels emerged by using whatever information is available, particularly the writer's working notes. Then, in a separate chapter (or, as with *The Brothers Karamazov*, in as many as eight chapters) Frank provides a running commentary on the completed novel, discussing not merely plot but characterization, style, and other aspects of the novel. Although this method is not necessarily as efficient as a more analytical organization, it has several advantages in a literary biography. It serves to remind readers, who may be fairly presumed to have read Dostoevski's major novels, of much in them that they have most likely forgotten. It allows the biographer to incorporate what he considers the most valuable of the critical insights that have accumulated over the years—including, in this case, Frank's own, for it must be remembered that he is not primarily a historian but a professor of comparative literature. In addition, this mode of organization is kinder to the reader, for the narrative as narrative is never lost from sight.

For Frank, *The Brothers Karamazov* is Dostoevski's masterpiece. An enormous fund of the novelist's life experience and his most cherished beliefs went into it. He endows the character of the youngest brother, Alyosha, not just with his own religious piety, love of the land and its people, and an especial fondness for the young, but also with his own concern that reforming fervor would, without Christianity at its core, degenerate into merely ruthless violence against the social order. It is a mark of his artistry that some of the most dubious of Dostoevski's fierce convictions, for instance that an atheist cannot be a truly moral person, become so convincing in characters like Prince Myshkin of *Idiot* (1868; *The Idiot*, 1887) or Alyosha.

The author also continues his depiction of Dostoevski's often ambivalent attitudes toward his great Russian contemporaries in the art of letters. His long-standing feud with Ivan Turgenev (1818-1883), whose literary power he clearly recognized, precipitated a wicked caricature of his rival in Karmazinov in *The Possessed*, installments of which were appearing as this last decade of Dostoevski's life opened. Although he found much to dislike in Turgenev's personality, it was the latter's fondness for things European which most offended Dostoevski's passionate patriotism. The two met publicly in June of 1880 in Moscow at the Pushkin festival sponsored by the Society of Lovers of Russian Literature. In Dostoevski's opinion, Turgenev's speech on June 7 in honor of the poet emphasized far too much Pushkin's affinities with foreign culture, and the next day he responded with a speech of his own in which he turned the "Westerner's" points against him. Pushkin, he argued, appropriated and transformed into truly Russian poetry what was best in the great world writers by means of empathy—a quality possessed most fully by the Russian people. Dostoevski addressed his audience with the intensity of an evangelical preacher, "and the emotions it unleashed," according to Frank, "may be compared with the hysterical effusions typical of religious revival meetings."

Another rivalry, albeit of a different character, developed with Count Leo Tolstoy (1828-1910). Since they came from different ranks of society, the two never met, although in 1878 the author of *Anna Karenina* (1875-1877; English translation 1886) and Dostoevski both attended a lecture by the latter's old friend Vladimir Solovyev in St. Petersburg. When Dostoevski later learned that a mutual friend had accompanied Tolstoy, he chafed over missing the opportunity to at least lay eyes on the man. Although he professed little enthusiasm for *Anna Karenina* when it first began appearing serially, Dostoevski respected the scope and majesty of Tolstoy's novels, so different from the dramatic intensity of his own work. The disparaging remarks about *Anna Karenina* that he sometimes made to friends ineffectually masked an obvious envy of this greatest of his Russian literary contemporaries.

Dostoevski had a difficult life. He lived with the horrid recollection of his trial as a member of the revolutionary Petrashevsky group in 1849, the subsequent experience of being lined up with his companions in front of a firing squad for what turned out to be merely a sham execution, and his four years in a Siberian prison camp (described by Frank in *The Years of Ordeal: 1850-1859*, the second volume of the biography). Periodic epileptic attacks punctuated his adult years, and emphysema severely curtailed his energy as he grew older. Ill-paid for a string of literary accomplishments which the world now regards as brilliant, he struggled for decades with debt compounded by his insistence on assuming also the financial burdens of his extended family—as well as by a weakness for gambling, fortunately overcome by the beginning of his final decade. He suffered much, but all his sufferings inform his work, not only because he was able to depict graphically characters' enduring throes like his own but also because he possessed the ability to empathize with sufferers generally.

His second wife Anna, who suffered herself as only the devoted wife of a loving but extremely difficult husband can, helped alleviate some of these difficulties. Her introduction to his epileptic attacks had occurred in the midst of their postnuptial celebration in 1867; very shortly thereafter she gained painful knowledge of his other weaknesses and shortcomings. In his fourth volume, *The Miraculous Years: 1865-1871*, Frank credited Dostoevski with ending his gambling addiction by sheer force of will, but clearly that effort owed much to his anguished awareness of the toll his habit had taken on his wife. It was Anna who took the initiative to straighten out his jumbled financial affairs. After several years of witnessing her husband's imprudent generosity to his relatives and his deplorable business sense, she functioned effectively as his business manager following their 1871 return to Russia.

The popular success of his *Diary of a Writer*, the fame he gained from his speech at the Pushkin festival, and the crowning achievement of *The Brothers Karamazov* invigorated Dostoevski despite his deteriorating health. He composed careful responses to his many correspondents. He gave public readings for charity which enthralled his audiences. Before he succumbed, the ex-convict had finally become a revered figure, a counselor of the nation who was, in Frank's concluding sentence, "a spiritual leader of the Russian people."

The main fault of this enormous biography is a certain stodginess in both organization and style. It is, however, a fine scholar's work of devotion and an achievement not likely to be supplanted as the definitive life-and-times treatment of its subject.

Robert P. Ellis

Sources for Further Study

Booklist 98 (April 15, 2002): 1376.
Choice 40 (November, 2002): 475.
Los Angeles Times Book Review, May 26, 2002, p. 5.
The New York Times Book Review 107 (June 30, 2002): 11.
Publishers Weekly 249 (April 29, 2002): 53.

THE DOUBLE BOND
Primo Levi: A Biography

Author: Carole Angier (1943-   )
Publisher: Farrar, Straus and Giroux (New York). Illustrated. 898 pp. $40.00
Type of work: Literary biography
Time: 1919-1987
Locale: Turin, Italy, and Auschwitz, Poland

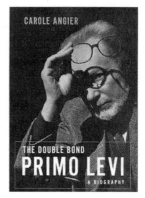

∼

This biography traces the life of Primo Levi through the memories of his friends, his writings, and his experiences as an author, survivor of Auschwitz, and his career as a chemist

∼

Principal personages:
PRIMO LEVI (1919-1987), writer, chemist, and death camp survivor
ANNA MARIA LEVI, his sister
LUCIA MORPURGO LEVI, his wife
RINA LUZZATI LEVI, his mother
CESARE LEVI, his father

Primo Levi would seem a curious subject for a biography, considering how excessively reticent, almost secretive, he was about his personal life, but as Carole Angier notes in her preface, for her as a writer, reserve intrigues—and the extreme reserve exhibited by her subject intrigued her extremely. In spite of her intrigue, however, Angier had to overcome not only Levi's reticence but also his family's high wall of reserve and privacy—made even higher, she discovered, by the traditional diffidence of Turinese—and the tragedy of his death by suicide. As biographer, therefore, Angier found herself confronting a peculiar dilemma, hence the title of her book which she borrowed from Levi's last, incomplete novel: *Il doppio legame*. In Italian, the phrase has a double meaning: the double bonding in chemistry and the double bind in psychology, "a crippling conflict between contradictory or unfulfillable requirements, which you can neither escape nor win." Angier appropriated both meanings in order to take her biography into the personal and inward sides of Primo Levi. To do this, she structured her book on two levels, a rationally known, testable one and an irrational one, felt and imagined. In the end, Angier admits she does not know which turned out to be the more truthful and revealing of her subject, although finally the latter came to seem to her to be of greater significance.

Primo Levi was born on July 31, 1919, on the third floor at Corso De Umberto 75 in a house owned by his mother and in which, except for a year in Milan and one in Auschwitz, he lived for all of his sixty-seven years. His father, Cesare, was an industrial engineer and his mother, Rina, was a typical Italian housewife and mother. His sister, Anna Maria, was born a year and a half later. Although both sides of his family had been observant Jews, Primo's parents had ceased to be religious, as had most Italian Jews who were indebted to the Enlightenment ideas that had freed them to live in a predominantly Christian world. Nevertheless, Primo was bar mitzvahed and for a brief period in his early teens he became intensely involved with his Jewishness; later in life, during the period of persecution by both the Italian and German fascists, he would again become acutely aware of his cultural and religious heritage.

Carole Angier's previous biography of the writer Jean Rhys, published in 1990, won an award for nonfiction from the Writers Guild of Great Britain and was short-listed for the Whitbread Biography Award. She is the Royal Literary Fund Associate Fellow at the University of Warwick and lives in Oxfordshire.

Primo was a slight child, serious and shy, very unlike his sister, who was lively and outgoing. In spite of their differing personalities, she became his closest childhood companion. Primo's schooling started inauspiciously. During his primary years he was frequently absent because of various illnesses, which contributed to the impression that he was somewhat frail, an impression belied by his obvious strength of both body and will that allowed him to survive his experience at Auschwitz. As he progressed through the Italian educational system, he began to flourish, and by the time he attended the Gimnasio Liceo Massimo D'Azeglio, one of the best classical grammar schools in Turin, his intelligence and seriousness made him a model student. He also gradually overcame his shyness, enough at least to develop a number of lasting friendships among his schoolmates. At university, where he was allowed to indulge his passion for chemistry, he blossomed.

Levi's university experience allowed him to exploit his natural intellectual gifts, but Italy's anti-Jewish laws exerted enormous pressures. Jews could not fail a single examination, and they were forbidden to change their areas of interest, so when he grew disillusioned with chemistry and wanted to change to physics, he could not. As he was to write later, this restriction condemned him to a life as a technician rather than as a true research scientist. Angier demurs, suggesting that he chose not to pursue research, and that is what opened the world of letters for him. Levi secured a job as a chemist after graduation, largely because most of the non-Jewish chemists were in the military. His first job was at the mines of Balangero, north of Turin, where he worked on the extraction of nickel. He moved to Milan in July, 1942, to work for a Swiss company, a job that ceased with the armistice in September, 1943, when Italy surrendered to the Allies.

The euphoria that followed the collapse of Mussolini's government was curtailed when the Germans invaded Italy and set up Il Duce as the puppet dictator of the Republic of Salo. The occupation of northern Italy placed Turin and its environs under Nazi control, and unlike the Italian fascists, the Germans strictly enforced the racial laws. Levi, out of a job, joined the partisans—who had already attracted many Italian Jews, some of them his friends—in the Val D'Aosta, and throughout the fall of 1943 and into the new year, he ran guns for the resistance. Then he was picked up by the Gestapo and transported to Fossoli, a central staging point for Italian Jews. The short time he spent in the Fossoli camp, still nominally under Italian control, was relatively benign. However, on February 16 it was taken over by the Germans and on February 22 Levi and the rest of the Jews began their journey to the concentration camps north of the Alps. The year he would spend as a prisoner would be the single most important event of his life.

Primo Levi arrived at Auschwitz on February 26, 1944. In less than ten minutes he had survived the first selection, the culling of those who would be gassed immediately and those who would be allowed to live and work in the camp. Although he was exhausted and weighed only a little over one hundred pounds—he was slightly built and always thin—he was saved from a summary death by the quick thinking of one of his friends, who declared that he and two others, including Levi, were experienced industrial chemists, occupations the Germans needed. Like all the others entering the camp, the Italian Jews who survived the selection were stripped of their clothing, had all of their hair shaved off, were showered, sprayed with disinfectant, and given a striped suit and coat, a shirt, underpants, foot rags, and a pair of wooden clogs. None of it was sized to the individual. Then they were tattooed with their camp number; Levi was number 174517. The process was designed to destroy both their dignity and their human personality, or as he was later to describe it, the demolition of man.

In the camp all the best died and the worst, that is the fittest, survived, he would write in his last book. Angier speculates that by "the best" Levi meant the most civilized, the most delicate, the most innocent. Angier asks, but who was more civilized than Primo Levi? Who was more likely to die of the nakedness, of the bestiality? Who more needed rationality, predictability, faith, and hope? How, then, did he survive? At first he did so through his friendships, by being helped by others in the camp, by fitting himself for starvation, and ultimately by a sheer act of will. He looked on his experience as a chance to learn about human nature and he treated the camp as a laboratory, a large biological and sociological experiment. Finally, by the end of 1943 when all able-bodied Germans were needed for the war machine, slave laborers became more valuable and the conditions in the camps improved slightly. These things kept him alive.

Auschwitz was abandoned by the Germans toward the end of January, 1944, and the prisoners, now free, were left to survive on their own until they were picked up by the invading Soviet Army, who moved many of them to a relocation camp at Katowicz, also in Poland. For the next nine months, Levi would undergo a journey both bizarre and comic that would take him as far north as Minsk, wending its way south to Romania and west through Hungary, Czechoslovakia, Austria, and Germany before he eventually returned to Italy. He arrived back in Turin on October 19, 1945, to find that miraculously both his mother and sister were alive and living in the family home only slightly damaged by the Allied bombing.

Primo Levi returned from the camps a sick and blasted man. All the suffering, grief, and memories he had postponed surfaced and he became seriously depressed, but he also was impelled to talk about his experiences and began to write about them. In the process, he overcame his preoccupation with death and embraced life. First, however, he needed a job, and after months of searching he secured one in January, 1946, as the assistant head of the research laboratory of Duco Avigliana, a manufacturer of paint. For the next thirty years of his life, he worked as an industrial chemist until his retirement as the director general of the SIVA paint company in 1977. During these years, Primo Levi lived two lives: one as an organic chemist and the other as a writer. He also rejoined life in the role of husband when he married Lucia Morpurgo early in December, 1946, and he became a father with the birth of a daughter, Lisa, in 1948 and a son, Renzo, in 1957.

Levi always remarked that if it had not been for Auschwitz, he never would have become a writer. Angier demurs. He was already a writer before the war, but he might not have become a truly great one if his natural Piedmontese reserve had not been overcome by the moral duty he felt to testify to the outrages of the Holocaust. *Se questo è un uomo* (1947; *If This Is a Man*, 1959) and *La tregua* (1963; *The Reawakening*, 1965) were books about his Auschwitz experiences that allowed him to break out as a writer.

In the years immediately before and following his retirement, Levi became world-renowned as a poet, fiction writer, journalist, and translator. If before he had been a respected figure, Angier writes, now he became a famous one with all the accolades and demands that fame demands. He was asked to do interviews by both Italian and foreign journalists; he spoke at schools and conferences; he gave lectures; and he received a growing number of prizes. Increasingly, he was also visited by periodic bouts of depression and his health began to decline. Because he was now famous, he also became embroiled in various causes and controversies, which in turn increased his depression and depleted him physically. In spite of the demands made on him to travel, as Levi grew older, he withdrew more and more into the safety of Corso De Umberto 75. On April 11, 1987, he was found dead at the bottom of the stairway, having fallen from the third floor landing above. The reasons for his death remain obscure: Was he murdered for his political views, was it an accident, or was it, as one Italian newspaper claimed, Auschwitz that claimed him forty years later? Angier believes it was suicide.

The critical reception of *The Double Bond* has been mixed. For example, Janet Maslin, reviewing the book for *The New York Times*, found Angier's literary analysis flimsy and her psychological insights mundane; on the other hand, Richard Elder, writing for *The New York Times Book Review*, described the biography as flawless and remarkable. However one finally judges the book, *The Double Bond* provides an extraordinary read. Although Levi's family refused its cooperation, Carole Angier interviewed an impressive number of those who knew him, many of them from his childhood, and these interviews helped her to construct the composite portrait of her subject. Furthermore, unlike many literary biographers, Angier devotes considerable space to analyzing the writings, often using them to fill in gaps in his life otherwise unavailable. In spite of its flaws, it is difficult to imagine a more challenging study of the life of Primo Levi being written anytime in the near future.

Charles L. P. Silet

Sources for Further Study

Booklist 98 (April 1, 2002): 1296.
Library Journal 127 (April 1, 2002): 104.
The New York Times Book Review 107 (June 23, 2002): 22.
The Wall Street Journal, June 14, 2002, p. W10.

THE DREAM OF SCIPIO

Author: Iain Pears (1955-   )
Publisher: Riverhead Books (New York). 401 pp. $25.95
Type of work: Novel
Time: The mid-fourth century; the fourteenth century;
    1928-1944
Locale: Avignon, France, and its vicinity

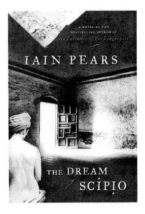

A prismatic narrative that parallels three historical periods during which Western civilization undergoes major changes in its governance and suggests, through the comparable experiences of its three major characters, that individuals either engage, decline to do so, or compromise with those changes

Principal characters:

> JULIEN BARNEUVE, a classicist and disaffected intellectual who becomes
> a functionary in the Vichy government at Avignon
> MANLIUS HIPPOMANES, a fourth century Gallic aristocrat and the subject
> of Barneuve's study; he becomes disaffected with Rome's ability to
> defend southeastern Gaul
> OLIVIER DE NOYEN, a fourteenth century poet and subject of Barneuve's
> study; he becomes disaffected with machinations to return the papacy
> to Rome
> JULIA BRONSEN, a Jewish artist and the fiancé of Barneuve; she is
> betrayed to the Nazi occupiers of Vichy France
> SOPHIA ANAXIA, daughter of Anaxius, the philosopher from whom
> Manlius had taken instruction; she becomes Manlius's platonic love
> and advisor, and ultimately suffers from his intellectual betrayal
> REBECCA, orphan ward of the rabbi Gersonides; she becomes the
> beloved of Olivier, who is ultimately responsible for her and her
> guardian's escape from Avignon

Iain Pears's *The Dream of Scipio* is a novel about the movement of time. In one unalterable moment, a great civilization can cease to be great or an individual seemingly destined for greatness may discover only obscurity and possibly oblivion. Pears's book borrows the famous title of the disquisition on the nature of fame that appears in Cicero's *De republica* (51 B.C.E.; *On the State*, 1817), the Roman rhetorician's own title benignly pilfered from the Greek philosopher Plato. The fourteenth century English poet Geoffrey Chaucer adapted Plato's format to his own discourse on the nature of worldly recognition.

⌒

*Iain Pears was educated at
Wadham College, Oxford. He is
well known as an art historian and
has worked as a journalist and
television consultant. He has written
seven detective novels, a book on
art history, and articles on various
historical subjects. His novel* An
Instance of the Fingerpost *(1999)
received worldwide acclaim.*

⌒

In Cicero's version, Scipio Africanus, conqueror of what would come to be known as Roman proconsular Africa, appears as a spirit to his nephew Africanus Iunior to warn him of the nature of worldly vanity and the transience of power. Chaucer's version retains Africanus but substitutes Geoffrey himself for Iunior. Being an underappreciated courtier was something that Chaucer well understood.

Pears's use of this motif is somewhat more complex. He takes what he considers to be three critical periods in the history of the world—late classical antiquity, the fourteenth century, and the middle years of World War II—and views them in the context of the region surrounding the city of Avignon, France. His link for these three periods is a twentieth century classical scholar and academic named Julien Barneuve. It is Barneuve's interest in late Roman history that leads him to a local bishop of the fourth century to whom he gives the Hellenized name Manlius Hippomanes. Barneuve discovers further references to Manlius in the fourteenth century writings of the poet Olivier de Noyen. This leads him to untangling references to Olivier's beloved, Rebecca, in one of the poet's courtly love poems.

Barneuve soon discovers that the particulars of his own life and those of his two historical predecessors have uncanny resemblances. The most obvious affinity is that all have similar geographic origins within the region of southern France that from the medieval period was called Avignon. In the case of each, there is also a single wise woman who guides and inspires him. There is also a presumed male friend or mentor who disappoints him and fatally influences a tragic outcome.

In Barneuve's case, the betrayal comes from both sides of the political crisis that follows the German occupation of France. His two friends, Bernard Marchand and Marcel Laplace, follow opposite courses in the struggle between the Free and the Vichy French. Marchand takes what on the face of things appears to be the more idealistic path, to join the Resistance. Laplace, on the other hand, sincerely believes that he can do more good by becoming a Vichy administrator in the Avignon region. He ultimately convinces Barneuve to assist him as a minor functionary of the provincial administration. Barneuve's role, combined with the antithetical positions of his two friends, ironically leads to the imprisonment and death of his beloved Julia and his own personal holocaust, the extraordinary narrative with which the novel begins.

At the heart of Pears's aesthetics is the fact that the narrator and his two scholarly preoccupations, Manlius and Olivier, all live at critical periods in the history of the world, moments when civilization changes utterly. The irony is that although the political externals change irrevocably, the lives of those who live within those periods retain almost exactly parallel needs. All require trust and love and at the very least convince themselves that they care for truth. Pears skillfully allows his readers to decide whether the motives of Manlius are as pure as those of Olivier or Barneuve. One suspects that the conclusions reached depend upon preference for a philosophic or a pragmatic standard of goodness.

Manlius, for example, is an aristocrat living in a region of Gaul that Rome can no longer adequately defend. Are the assurances that he receives of Roman assistance against barbarian incursions actually to be trusted? Are the inhabitants of his region ready to sacrifice their material well-being and possibly their lives in order to defend the ideals of Roman law? Should he seek the aid of one of the barbarian armies competing to enter southeastern Gaul by paying tribute? Should he follow the heroic course and fight the barbarians to the last soldier, using only native regional resources?

Manlius's wise advisor, the aptly named Sophia, daughter of his former philosophy master, urges noble resistance, ideological and philosophic if not military. She remains absolutely consistent in her position, even in the face of her patron-beloved's willingness to consort with the Visigoths. This leads to her becoming an outcast both among the natives of the region and by her protector, Manlius. Ironically, Manlius accepts ordination as a Christian bishop not because he has acquired any special convictions about the truth of Christianity, but because he realizes that as a bishop, he will gain a more impressive bargaining position with the barbarians.

In the case of Olivier, the circumstances are parallel, even though the particulars seem markedly different. The papacy had split in the fourteenth century between Rome and Avignon. Annibaldus, Cardinal di Ceccani, a historical personage, leads what amounts to a fifth-column faction to return the papacy to Rome. In Pears's novel, Ceccani uses fears about the bubonic plague to convince the superstitious local population to blame the small Jewish community at Avignon for the plague and to force Gersonides, a scholarly rabbi whose ward Ceccani's protégé Olivier comes to love, to advise the intransigent pope to return to Rome. As events unfold, some Jews convert to Christianity in order to save their lives rather than from any sincere conviction, and Olivier manages, at the cost of his own physical well-being, to spirit Rebecca and Gersonides out of Avignon. The love of Olivier and Rebecca is the only one in Pears's novel that reaches any final resolution, though it is as imperfect as most events in human lives.

Just as Pears explores in three ways the essential nature of truth, so in a literary sense is he also concerned with the relationship between truth and the written text. Indeed, textual concerns are never far away from the novel's narrative. Barneuve writes a text on Manlius. He wonders how this most Roman of all provincial aristocrats could so suddenly have become a Christian bishop. He wonders whether the textual version of the love affair of Olivier and the beloved of his poem was based on the actual events or on an imitation of the fourteenth century Italian poet Petrarch and his Laura. As he untangles the literary tradition against the events of his own historical period and those of his life, he increasingly realizes how difficult it is to approach philosophic truth.

Invariably, what runs through all of Pears's novels is the effect of historical periods that intersect. Time is, therefore, not something linear but gyred. Quantum physics has validated this sense of the world mathematically just as William Butler Yeats has aesthetically, in poems such as "The Second Coming" (1920). Yeats, and clearly Pears as well, holds that at some unpredictable moment the gyre will come full circle and a new order, in some sense resembling the old but importantly different in its overall aspect, will arise. For Yeats, World War I and the changes it wrought in Ireland were paramount. For Pears, the gyre makes its initial, breaking circle at the end of classical antiquity. The Gauls, who had been the dreaded barbarians that Julius Caesar's army managed to control only with difficulty, find themselves the rulers of Romanized Gallic cities like Marsallia (the modern Marseilles) or the Avignon of Pears's novel. The culture reflects the presence of an absence; Rome is there yet definitely not there, though the imminent presence of the Gothic invaders is incontestable. The question is whether to adhere to the hope that Rome will miraculously appear to defend its province and to suffer destruction almost assuredly or to reach some kind of accommodation with the historical conditions that prevail at that time.

As secular classical antiquity receded, the rising moral force was the Catholic Church; the political force was the invading tribes. Manlius Hippomenes combines the secular Roman education he received with a Catholic faith he accepts primarily in order to be able to negotiate with the barbarians as a bishop. His regalia is without any power other than to impress, although that power clearly would not have worked had those in whom power resided at the time still been Romans.

Olivier de Noyen, in serving the Church, realizes, like Manlius Hippomenes, that he does the politically expedient thing because that allows him to continue his education, have access to a fine library and, most of all, continue to write poetry. He is aware of the role Manlius Hippomenes played in the history of the Avignon region, and he is increasingly aware that the dual papacy in Avignon and Rome represents an unhealthy condition for the Church. He also senses that the local Jewish community is likely to be blamed for a periodic outbreak of the bubonic plague. History intersects at the point of Christian Rome's confrontation with Avignon and Avignon's confrontation with the fledgling Jewish community.

This gyred understanding of history, so well understood by Yeats, continues in the novel's third phase, the Vichy occupation during World War II. Again, though with yet another variation, a new center of power meets the old order, and Julien Barneuve, who is well aware of the histories of Manlius Hipponenes and Olivier de Noyen, sees the gyre closing a third time on an era hardly the same yet hardly different from those previous.

Robert J. Forman

Sources for Further Study

Library Journal 127 (May 15, 2002): 127.
The New York Times Book Review 107 (June 23, 2002): 26.
Publishers Weekly 249 (May 27, 2002): 35.

DREAMLAND
Europeans and Jews in the Aftermath of the Great War

Author: Howard M. Sachar (1928-   )
Publisher: Alfred A. Knopf (New York). 385 pp. $30.00
Type of work: History
Time: 1919-1939
Locale: Europe

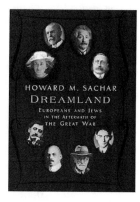

Sachar traces the trajectory of European Jewry from immediate post-World War I prominence and prestige to marginalization and ostracism in many countries by the late 1930's

Principal personages:
    LÉON BLUM (1872-1950), French prime minister 1936-1937, 1938, 1946-1947
    MAX BROD (1884-1968), chairman of the Jewish National Council of Czechoslovakia and Franz Kafka's literary executor
    FRANZ KAFKA (1883-1924), Czechoslovakian author
    BELA KUN (1886-1938), leader of the short-lived Hungarian Soviet government
    ROSA LUXEMBURG (c. 1870-1919), socialist activist
    LOUIS MARSHALL (1856-1929), president of the American Jewish Committee 1912-1929
    JOZEF PILSUDSKI (1876-1935), Polish general and president from 1918 to 1921
    WALTER RATHENAU (1876-1922), German industrialist and foreign minister
    LUCIEN WOLF (1857-1930), first executive director of the Anglo-Jewish Conjoint organization

Howard Sachar takes as his epigraph Lysander's speech in the first act of William Shakespeare's *A Midsummer Night's Dream* (pr. c. 1595-1596) on the fragility of love, which, he says, lasts no longer than a flash of lightning. Similarly, Sachar shows how rapidly in many European nations the Jewish dream of liberty and equality faded in the period between the two world wars.

The Treaty of Versailles in 1919 guaranteed civil rights and cultural autonomy to all Poland's minorities. Jews were granted two additional rights: to administer state funding for Jewish schools and to keep the Jewish Sabbath inviolate. In March, 1921, the Polish senate, the Sjem, enacted legislation consistent with these stipulations, but Sachar shows that the government never fulfilled its promises to any of the country's minorities. Lithuanian, Byelorussian, German, and Ukrainian schools were sup-

Howard M. Sachar has published many books and articles about Jewish history. Among these are A History of Israel from the Rise of Zionism to Our Time *(1976; rev. ed., 1996),* A History of the Jews in America *(1992), and* Israel and Europe: An Appraisal in History *(1999). Professor of modern history at George Washington University, Sachar has served as a Middle East consultant to various government bodies and has lectured widely on Jewish history and the Middle East in the United States and abroad.*

pressed. Germans and Ukrainians were allowed only limited land ownership. Voting districts were designed to limit minority representation. Jews were excluded from civil service posts. Jewish schools were not funded despite the stipulation in the Treaty of Versailles. Throughout the 1920's, Jews were compelled to maintain separate unions, credit cooperatives, health insurance programs, student associations, and health clubs.

The worldwide economic depression of the 1930's further eroded the Jewish situation in Poland. In 1934, as xenophobia and Catholic anti-Semitism grew more pronounced, Poland renounced the Versailles provisions for minorities. Cardinal August Hlond (1881-1948), prelate of Poland, urged an economic boycott of Jewish businesses. This position was echoed in a joint statement by the Union of Polish Catholic Lawyers, the Union of Catholic Writers, the Coordinating Committee of Academic Corporations, and the Union of Technicians and Engineers. Jews were systematically excluded from higher education and their businesses nationalized. In 1935-1937, various parts of Poland witnessed a renewal of pogroms rivaling the dark years of 1919-1920. A three-day pogrom in June, 1937, in Czestochowa, for example, left four Jews dead and hundreds wounded. The government did nothing to check the violence.

In the early post-World War I years, the Polish government had muted its anti-Semitism in an effort to encourage foreign Jewish investment. In 1928, as a means of improving the nation's economy, the Polish consul in New York, Mieczyslaw Marchlewski, urged the Landsmannschaft of Polish Jews in America to support Jewish businesses in Poland. He even organized a Polish-Jewish Goodwill Committee. A decade later, the Polish government was refusing foreign Jewish money unless it would be used to fund Jewish emigration from Poland. The elimination of all Jews from Poland had become the government's goal. Ironically, Poland supported the Zionist movement because this was a means of relocating Jews to another place.

Sachar shows how in Romania, as in Poland, the dream of Jewish emancipation turned to a nightmare of persecution. Article 44 of the 1878 Treaty of Berlin barred religious discrimination in the granting of Romanian citizenship, but before 1914 only 361 of the country's 280,000 Jews had been granted that right. Although the 1923 Romanian constitution granted citizenship to all Jews, this provision was largely ignored as the government set about marginalizing its Jewish population. At the University of Bucharest, the Jewish population fell from 4,200 in 1920 to 1,500 in 1928. By that year, Romania's medical schools were admitting virtually no Jews.

In the 1930's, Romania's political parties vied to outdo each other's anti-Semitism. This stand received the support of the Romanian Orthodox Church. Sachar quotes

Grand Patriarch Doctor Miron Cristea (1868-1939) in a pastoral letter: "One feels like crying with pity for the good Romanian nation, whose very marrow has been sucked from its bones by the Jews." When Octavian Goga (1881-1938) became Romanian prime minister in 1937, he suppressed the nation's three largest newspapers, all Jewish-owned, dismissed those Jews who still held government posts, and threatened to ex-propriate all Jewish-owned land. Although Goga did not act on this last proposal, Romania's peasants did, displacing Jewish landowners. King Carol II (1893-1953) belatedly sought to stem the worst excesses of anti-Semitism, and in 1939 he quashed the ultraright Iron Guard. His efforts proved ineffectual. In 1940, he was forced to flee the country, and Romania became a Nazi client state.

The Austro-Hungarian Empire had a better record of toleration than Romania or czarist-ruled Poland. In 1867, Emperor Franz Josef I (1830-1916) had emancipated the Jews. (In gratitude, many Jewish families named their first-born sons after the Habsburg emperor.) When the empire collapsed at the end of World War I, Hungary emerged as one of its successor states. The first postwar government soon yielded to Bela Kun's Hungarian Soviet. Kun was Jewish, as were many others prominent in his regime.

Still, most Jews opposed Kun, and of the 160 people executed under Kun's regime, 44 were Jews. Yet opposition to Kun's Soviet became linked with anti-Semitism. When Miklos Horthy (1868-1957), wartime commander of the Habsburg navy, as-sumed control of Hungary at the end of 1919, suppressing Kun's communist regime, Horthy gave free reign to reactionary forces, who murdered hundreds of Jews. Under Istvan Bethlen (1874-1947), who assumed the premiership in 1921, the situation of Hungary's Jews improved. However, he did not rescind the government's policy of discrimination in education. In 1910, Jews constituted 40 percent of Hungary's engi-neers. By 1932, that figure had dropped to 16 percent. In 1919-1920, 40 percent of Hungary's medical students were Jewish. In October, 1920, the government ordered this number reduced to 6 percent. Despite such restrictions, Hungarian Jews pros-pered until the late 1930's, when, like its neighbors, Hungary imposed new anti-Semitic measures. In May, 1938, the Hungarian parliament placed employment and salary limits on Jews. Another bill, passed in May, 1939, excluded Jews from the civil service, teaching, theaters, and journalism.

Elsewhere in Europe, Jewish prospects appeared brighter in the 1920's and early 1930's. Sachar suggests that Franz Kafka's stories may be read as indications of Jew-ish helplessness. In *"Josephine die Sängerin, oder Volk der Mäuser"* (Josephine the singer, or the nation of mice), which Kafka completed in the year of his death, 1924, the mouse nation loses its voice. Sachar reads this as a tale of Jewish inability to be heard. If Kafka in fact anticipated the Holocaust, few would have shared his vision in the Czech Republic that emerged from the embers of World War I. Whereas other Eu-ropean nations restricted Jewish access to higher education, Czechoslovakian univer-sities welcomed even foreign Jewish students. Tomas Masaryk (1850-1937), the country's first president, sympathized with Jewish aspirations of full citizenship. The Czech constitution of 1920 guaranteed full citizenship to all minorities, and these rights were granted in fact as well as on paper.

In post-World War I Austria and Germany, Jews also flourished. Both countries had histories of anti-Semitism but both also had served as havens for Jews escaping persecution. In 1890, fifteen Jews sat in the Austrian parliament. In 1900, half of Vienna's physicians were Jewish. Guido Adler (1855-1941), a Jew, held the first chair in musicology at the University of Vienna. According to the popular (Jewish) author Stefan Zweig (1881-1942), nine-tenths of Viennese culture in 1900 was created by the city's Jewish population. The postwar Austrian constitution was drafted by the Jewish law professor Hans Kelson, whose coreligionist Otto Bauer (1881-1938) served as foreign minister in the first postwar government. Of Vienna's lawyers in 1934, 62 percent were Jewish, as were 47 percent of its physicians.

In Germany, Jews were at least as prominent. On the eve of Adolf Hitler's becoming chancellor in 1933, Jews made up only 1 percent of Germany's population but constituted 16 percent of its doctors and lawyers. The Jewish Curt Joël served as minister of justice in 1931-1932. Of the nine German Nobel Prize winners in 1920-1933, five were Jews. The German Higher School for Politics and the Institute for Social Research were largely funded and staffed by Jews. Jews were preeminent in cinema (Ernst Lubitsch and Fritz Lang), the theater (Max Reinhardt), music (Arnold Schönberg and Kurt Weill), and science (Nobel laureates Albert Einstein and Fritz Haber). In 1919, Eugen Fuchs, president of the Jüdische Kulturverein, claimed that in Germany, at least, anti-Semitism had ended with the conclusion of the war. Fuchs was overly optimistic, but given the toleration of the Weimar government one can understand sociologist Franz Oppenheimer (1864-1943) writing in 1931,

> I have been fortunate to have been born and educated in the land of Kant and Goethe, to have their culture, their art, their language, and their knowledge as my own. My Germanism is as sacred to me as my Jewish forefathers. . . . I combine in me the German and Jewish national feeling.

Léon Blum, who served as French prime minister in the late 1930's, felt similarly about his country:

> I was born in France, I was raised in French schools. My friends are French. . . . I have the right to consider myself perfectly assimilated. Well, I nonetheless feel myself a Jew. And I have never noticed, between these two aspects of my consciousness, the least contradiction, the least tension.

As in other parts of Europe, France had its share of anti-Semitism, evident, for example, in the late nineteenth century Dreyfus affair. Throughout the interwar period, the Action Française, led by Charles Maurras (1868-1952), embraced anti-Semitism as part of its ultraright views. Still, in the arts, literature, philosophy, and even politics Jews stood at the pinnacle of success: Sarah Bernhardt, Camille Pissarro, Émile Durkheim, Claude Lévi-Strauss, Marcel Proust, and Blum may serve as metonymies of Jewish achievement in pre-World War II France.

It is a mistake to read history backward and impossible not to do so. In January, 1932, the Jüdische Kulturverein's *Zeitung* argued that, if not for economic problems, Germany would have continued to steer a liberal course. Sachar seems to disagree.

His underlying theme appears to be that, to paraphrase Gershom Scholem's statement about Germans, the Jews loved Europe, but Europe did not love the Jews. Whether or not one shares this view, Sachar's book serves as both a history of this period and a warning for the future, confirming what Albert Camus wrote in *The Plague* (1947): "The plague bacillus never dies or disappears for good; . . . it can lie dormant for years and years . . . ; perhaps the day would come when, for the bane and the enlightening of men, it would rouse up its rats again and send them forth to die in a happy city."

Joseph Rosenblum

Sources for Further Study

Booklist 98 (March 15, 2002): 1208.
Library Journal 127 (February 15, 2002): 162.
The New Leader 85 (March/April, 2002): 18.
Publishers Weekly 249 (March 11, 2002): 67.

THE DRESSING STATION
A Surgeon's Chronicle of War and Medicine

Author: Jonathan Kaplan (1954-   )
Publisher: Atlantic Monthly Press (New York). 320 pp.
   $25.00; paperback $14.00
Type of work: Autobiography and current affairs

   The compelling account of Kaplan's extraordinary adventures working as a field surgeon, filmmaker, and journalist in remote trouble spots of the world

The playwright Anthony Shaffer has been quoted as saying that a man should have a new career e-very five years. Jonathan Kaplan has done just that and more. Forsaking the comfort and security of conventional medical practice, he has pursued his own personal search for a meaningful professional life in remote corners of the globe. He began his extraordinary career as a hospital surgeon, then became a researcher, a field trauma surgeon on the front lines in a number of war zones, a ship's medical officer, a flying doctor, a freelance journalist, a documentary filmmaker, and an occupational health doctor. Chapter headings—"South Africa," "England," "America," "Namibia and Zululand," "Kurdistan," "The South China Sea," "Mozambique," "Burma," "South Africa and Brazil," and "Eritrea"—serve as an itinerary for his odyssey.

Kaplan's reflections on the social and political situations he encounters in his travels, his strong sense of social justice, and his romance with adventure and risk-taking set this well-written book apart from the usual medical autobiography. Moreover, he provides an intimate portrait of what it is like for him to be a doctor. Kaplan is able to communicate his respect for human anatomy and his love for the art and skill of surgery in terms that are often lyrical and sometimes gory. In one passage he tells how he learned to "set fractures, strip out varicose veins, scoop tonsils from little throats, and whip out an inflamed appendix in sixteen minutes from the first incision to the final skin-stitch." In another, he relates how "considerable physical power is needed to wrench an arthritic hip-joint from its socket so that it can be sawed off and a replacement fitted . . . the power-drills hurl pink bone-froth against the face-masks of those around the operating table." However, his compassion for his patients always comes through.

Raised in apartheid-era South Africa, the son of a military surgeon in a respected and privileged family of physicians, Kaplan grew up with the expectation that he would serve. His first experience with trauma medicine came when he was a medical student in Cape Town, treating student casualties at an antiapartheid demonstration. He gained more experience in the accident and emergency department and during his internship at a military hospital near Cape Town soon after the South African army invaded Angola in 1975 and bloody uprisings were spreading across South Africa. However, to avoid the draft, he left for England. Although he admits that cowardice was a factor in his decision, he could not support the politics and violence of the South African government.

In London he studied for the fellowship of the Royal College of Surgeons, working as casualty officer at the cold and run-down East End Hospital, which provided all medical services for the area's "grimy fringe." In some of his best prose, Kaplan describes the patient population. There were drunks, misfits, violent men, drug abusers, black gang members and their victims, "the frankly mad," and the "put-upon patients of the local GPs."

Jonathan Kaplan, born in South Africa, began his medical studies in Cape Town, specialized in the United Kingdom, and did medical research in the United States. The Dressing Station, Kaplan's first book, chronicles his extraordinary career as field surgeon, ship's doctor, and air-ambulance doctor, as well as a journalist and documentary filmmaker.

> All too often the Casualty department here was simply a refuge for the desolate and bereft, those with no one to care about them. In the small hours it hosted the sad teenage girls with their token overdoses of vodka and ten of mum's Valium, their mascara smeared; a whimper for help.

Kaplan's descriptions of the old London hospitals and his insider's view of the National Health System and the British system of surgical training at the time—a kind of "feudal patronage," where networking and connections were more important than skill—are amusing but cynical.

After a series of six-month jobs in various casualty and orthopedic posts and three years as senior house-officer, Kaplan qualified as a senior registrar. His description of losing his first patient at his first post after qualifying is touching. He passed the English fellowship examination and was admitted to the Royal College of Surgeons, but without the proper connections, he found advancing up the career ladder in London difficult. When he failed to qualify for a grant to work on the master's degree in surgery needed to become a consultant (severe budget cuts limited the number of awards), he accepted a research post in a hospital vascular laboratory in the United States. There he was able to write his thesis and earn a Master of Surgery degree.

He spent two years in America, enjoying his work and "the good life," but he was not comfortable with the commercialization of medicine in America. He notes: "The hospital operated as an industry, whose senior staff—its directors—benefitted through salaries, bonuses, and shares. . . . The vascular department, spotting a likely product under development in its laboratory, might invest in it itself, forming a partnership with the company that owned it" in order to share in the financial gains. A thriving company would increase its investment in research, which further benefited the hospital. Kaplan became convinced that most American students go into medicine as a business decision, and he was appalled by the number of unnecessary operations performed annually in the United States.

On his return to hospital work in England, he was troubled by a strange emptiness and lack of emotional energy. He writes, "I felt a great need to step outside the process

for a while, to make a reckoning of what I had achieved and where I might be going."
He left for Johannesburg in search of restoration and visited a friend in Windhoek, the
capital of the old German colony of South West Africa. Together they traveled by
jeep through war zones and minefields to the Namibia-Angola border, patrolled by
United Nations forces after South Africa's withdrawal. Everywhere he saw deprivation and violence. Kaplan decided to work as a sound man for a documentary film
crew on a government survey of Namibian territory, but when it was discovered that
he was a doctor, he ended up treating the sick and injured of the Basarwa ("Bush-
men") there. On his return to South Africa he took a job at a hospital in Zululand. In
describing these excursions, he provides graphic details of tropical diseases and African medicine, with an introduction to the geography of the land and a description of
the lifestyles of those he treats.

Kaplan's need to work outside mainstream medicine led him next to war-torn
Kurdistan, where he worked as a volunteer surgeon for a Paris-based international
medical group, similar to Medécins sans Frontières (Doctors Without Borders) helping the Kurdish rebels in northern Iraq near the Turkish border. (He also worked as a
freelance journalist while there.) When the Gulf War ended in 1991, the Kurds seized
Iraqi garrisons and declared their autonomy, having been led to believe there would
be Western support for their rebellion. There was no support. Saddam Hussein's
forces quickly reclaimed the liberated Kurdish towns, and the plight of the Kurdish
refugees became desperate as Turkish troops tried to turn back the human tide pouring into Turkey. Kaplan found a quarter of a million Kurds crowded into a camp on
the ridged mountainside at the border, huddled under plastic sheet shelters supported
by string and tree branches. With the help of refugee medics, his team dispensed
drugs for dysentery, gastroenteritis, pneumonia, and eye infections before moving on
to set up a treatment center at a fort held by the Kurdish fighters. (Here and elsewhere,
Kaplan was not impressed by the Non-Governmental Organizations that competed
for attention from the press to their relief efforts. In one case he likens them to a
"plague of altruism.") His team arranged for a U.S. Navy cargo helicopter doing a
food drop to the Kurds to put them and their equipment down across the frontier. Unfortunately, their tent, anesthesia box, and packs of surgical instruments and dressings
were dropped by mistake with the food. For the next week, with makeshift supplies,
Kaplan operated on the wounded on a mattress on the floor while the nurse and phys-
iotherapist made tent calls to the crowds of refugees seeking care. Then, suddenly, the
Americans announced the creation of "safe havens" for Kurdish civilians and their
plans to establish a tent hospital near the fort. Kaplan's group moved their dressing
station eastward toward the Iranian border, but his tour was cut short by persistent fever, necessitating his evacuation to England.

Back in London, Kaplan found he was unable to adapt to the discipline and stability of regular hospital work and soon signed on as doctor on a cruise ship in the South
China Sea, treating alcoholics, victims of barroom brawls, sunburns, and salmonella
among the passengers, and venereal disease among the crew. His descriptions of various ports-of-call, life at sea, the passengers, and fellow seafarers—a "pathological society" full of "vengeances, inadequacies and betrayals"—are entertaining.

Next Kaplan traveled to Mozambique, not as a doctor but as a documentary film-maker, hoping to make a difference "on a larger scale." Here he encountered a vicious war and economic devastation. However, his film was not about the suffering, pillage, mutilation, and starvation he witnessed; it was a wildlife documentary about the slaughter of the elephants and plundering of ivory—"No one's interested in just another 'War in Africa' piece," he was told. One day in Mozambique, he visited a small hospital, where he saw the unbearably sad plight of the children, saved a man suffering from a collapsed lung, and performed an emergency cesarean section (too late to save the mother and baby). The following day, filming took him to a marine sanctuary, where he operated on a man bitten by a six-foot crocodile. On his return from the Elephant Farm, he narrowly escaped being killed by a landmine.

Kaplan's next job was that of flying doctor, traveling in light aircraft to remote air-strip clinics in the high mountains of Lesotho, a small isolated kingdom surrounded by South Africa. With another doctor, he usually saw about a hundred patients a day. From this job he went on to work for an aeromedical assistance company, accompanying passengers who had become unwell on holiday back to their homes for treatment. This job took him to interesting places and paid well, while allowing him to work as a freelance journalist between flights.

An international organization recruited Kaplan to lead a medical evaluation team to Burma's southern Shan State, under attack from Burma after declaring its independence. After this assignment, he became involved in occupational health and researched and produced a documentary film about mercury poisoning among workers at a large British manufacturing plant in South Africa. Interest in this field later took him to the Amazon, where he researched mercury poisoning among fishing villagers, who live on fish and other river life contaminated by mercury used in crude gold mining practices. These experiences led Kaplan to specialize in occupational medicine (but not before he treated casualties of the Eritrean-Ethiopian conflict in Eritrea.)

Kaplan describes himself as "just a doctor, with uncertain clinical detachment, the vice of restlessness, and some tarnished shreds of idealism." Those talents have produced a fine book.

Edna B. Quinn

Sources for Further Study

BMJ: British Medical Journal 323 (October 20, 2001): 941.
Booklist 98 (December 15, 2001): 689.
The Economist 362 (February 23, 2002): 85.
Library Journal 126 (December 1, 2001): 158.
The New York Times Book Review 107 (March 3, 2002): 15.
The New Yorker 78 (April 22, 2002): 201.
Publishers Weekly 248 (November 12, 2001): 45.
Time Atlantic 158 (October 8, 2001): 69.

THE DRIFT

Author: John Ridley (1945-   )
Publisher: Alfred A. Knopf (New York). 276 pp. $24.00
Type of work: Novel
Time: The present
Locale: Los Angeles; Spokane, Washington

～

Brain Nigger Charlie, a black man who has left his for-mer life as a successful businessman to ride the rails as a tramp, agrees to try to locate his friend's niece Corina on the notorious High Line, a rail route known for its vicious racist gangs

～

Principal characters:
> CHARLES HARMON (BRAIN NIGGER CHARLIE), a former successful tax
> lawyer who is now a train tramp
> CHOCOLATE WALT, a train tramp who befriends Brain Nigger and
> teaches him how to survive on the rails
> CORINA, Chocolate Walt's seventeen-year-old niece, who leaves home to
> ride the rails
> HAXTON BOOLE, a rail policeman
> KESSLER, leader of a drug-running rail gang
> HESTER (BUZZ CUT), one of Kessler's lieutenants
> FELIX (LIQUID EVIL), one of Kessler's lieutenants
> MATHIAS SMIKLE, an FBI agent
> STUPID BITCH DUMBASS, a young white man who rides the rails
> GUILLERMO, a Mexican man who befriends Corina

No doubt, to most Americans the subculture of tramps and hoboes who spend their lives "riding the rails," is a complete unknown. Perhaps some people might have a vague, romanticized view of the "happy hobo," a man not weighed down by responsi-bility and cares, who is free to travel where he wills, carrying all that he owns on his back. However, if the happy hobo ever existed, he is not to be found in the pages of John Ridley's *The Drift*, which shows the dark reality of the lives of those who choose, or who are forced into, riding the rails. It is not a life to be envied. Violence of the worst, almost unimaginable kind, seems to be routine, as are hunger, fear, and degradation.

This is also a subculture with its own vocabulary. Rail police are "bulls"; local homeless and tramps are "home guard"; the temporary shacks made up of whatever comes to hand is the tramp's "jungle"; clambering aboard a freight train is "catching out"; getting "lifted" is attaining a drug-induced high; "diving" is digging into gar-bage cans for food; "tagging" is giving someone else the nickname by which they are

known on the rails ("San Francisco Mad Boy,"
for example). It is a subculture with its own class
stratifications; hoboes (or 'boes) and tramps are
of a higher order than mere bums or home guard,
largely because the former travel, whereas the
latter just stay where they are.

The reader's guide through this maze of violence, deprivation, and perversion is Brain Nigger
Charlie. Brain Nigger used to be Charles Harmon, a man who would have appeared to have
had everything anyone could want. As a black
man he had succeeded in white society to a degree that most of his race could only envy: He
was a tax lawyer for a Big Eight accounting firm
in Los Angeles; he lived with his attractive wife
Beverly in the affluent suburb of Woodland Hills;
and they possessed all the consumer luxuries that
accompany an upper-middle-class lifestyle. The
trouble came when Beverly got pregnant. Charles
could not face the responsibilities of fatherhood
and was haunted by a recurring nightmare of a
baby with a third, blue eye in its cheek. He took
to drinking, then to designer drugs, and got fired
from his job. Beverly kicked him out of his
home, and before long he was not only homeless
but also penniless. He decided to get out of Los

*John Ridley, who lives in Los
Angeles, is the author of four highly
regarded novels and a former
producer on NBC's* Third Watch
*television series. He wrote and
produced the film* Undercover
Brother *(2002), wrote the story for
the film* Three Kings *(1999), and
wrote and directed* Cold Around the
Heart *(1997). His novel* Stray Dogs
(1996) was made into the film U
Turn *(1997), directed by Oliver
Stone. He is a regular commentator
for National Public Radio.*

Angeles by riding the rails. Staying high on drugs for as long as he could helped him
to avoid sleep, which he dreaded because of the nightmare of the black baby with the
third blue eye.

Several times in the course of the novel, Charles, or Brain Nigger Charlie as he became, refers to that freak blue-eyed baby of his nightmares. Perhaps the significance
of this is that he felt guilty for assimilating so easily into white culture, as if he had betrayed some essential characteristic of his race by doing so. Brain Nigger becomes a
rail rider because he seeks that elusive quality of freedom. In his former life he felt
that he was nothing more than a collection of other people's expectations. His repeated refrain is "Freedom is what the rails are for." The reader might well feel that if
riding the rails is freedom, Brain Nigger is welcome to it. It is hard to imagine anyone
being sufficiently deluded or desperate to think that riding around aimlessly in a
freight car, at the mercy of whatever fate may bring, is a condition of freedom. Yet the
notion occurs repeatedly in the novel. A white teenager, whom Brain Nigger tags Stupid Bitch Dumbass, has just started to ride the rails in search of wider horizons than
his dull existence in Ohio, training to be an auto mechanic, allowed him. He tells
Brain Nigger that his life in Ohio was like living in a tiny box that was getting smaller
and smaller, crushing the life out of him. (Stupid Bitch Dumbass ends up probably

dead, his hand severed by Brain Nigger in self-defense.) The teenage girl Corina, also a new rail rider, has a similar desire to escape the confines of her Milwaukee upbringing. She writes to her uncle, a former rail rider named Chocolate Walt, that on the rails she is lonely, but she gives the term a positive meaning: "It's lonely so I can hear myself think. . . . It's lonely, but in a beautiful way . . . alone is really just being all one. . . . I feel that, out here, I'm all one with me. . . . I feel real good."

Events in the novel will soon undermine this philosophical equilibrium that Corina claims to have discovered, but even a hardened rail policeman like Haxton Boole, with whom Brain Nigger meets up in the course of his travels, cannot free himself from a romanticized view of what riding the rails is like. He contrasts his own life, weighed down by mortgage payments and with a wife to support, with what he imagines Brain Nigger's life to be: "Go where you want, do what you want. See a train, catch out, ride to wherever." In a piece of trite philosophizing, Haxton opines that what a man really wants is not more and more material possessions, but freedom, "Freedom to travel the world or sit on his ass just as equally." Brain Nigger attempts to disabuse him of this notion by informing him that a man obtains his kind of freedom only by walking away from everything in his life and then forever wishing that he could get it all back.

Brain Nigger then gives Haxton his first experience of a drug trip, courtesy of ketamine hydrochloride, an animal tranquilizer known as "Lady K." It gives Haxton a taste of another kind of freedom, a "trip" which Brain Nigger tells him is the equivalent of a near death experience (NDE). Apparently this NDE is a highly pleasurable experience, and Brain Nigger is therefore addicted to his Ladies K and E (the latter is the drug Ecstasy) since they mask the fact that his life as a rail rider, fake philosophizing notwithstanding, is the opposite of free. In fact, it seems to be one long NDE.

It did not take Brain Nigger long to find this out. In his early days as a rail rider, he was regularly raped and beaten up by those stronger and more ruthless than he. This changed, albeit temporarily, when he was befriended by an old black tramp called Chocolate Walt, who taught him essential survival skills. Brain Nigger also acquired a friend in the form of George Plimpton, who is not a person but a four-foot-long "goonie stick" that Brain Nigger uses to devastating effect when occasion demands. George Plimpton looks just like a walking stick made out of wood, but in fact it is lined with metal. It makes a fearsome weapon, and Brain Nigger is soon giving out more punishment than he takes (although in the course of the novel, the score seems to be about even, since Brain Nigger also has to take some merciless beatings, not least at the hands of a nasty little FBI agent armed with a stun gun). By the time he has been a rail rider for some years, Brain Nigger is often on the edge that divides sanity from insanity, and he develops a habit of talking to George Plimpton and even receiving instructions from him. George Plimpton is a goonie stick with a will and a voice of its own.

Brain Nigger's interactions with his chief bodyguard and friend give John Ridley the opportunity for some comic writing—which comes surprisingly often in such a gritty, hard-nosed novel. Here for example, is the novel's opening paragraph: "George Plimpton was up, angry. Doing work. George was a badass. George was a head smacker. And though some tried, George Plimpton was not to be trifled with." It is some time before the reader realizes that George Plimpton is not a man but a stick. Brain Nigger never emerges from the dark shadows of the rail rider's life, although at one point he makes an ill-fated effort to do so. Nevertheless, he is in other ways a changed man as a result of the experiences he goes through. In his quest for Corina, which he undertakes at the request of her uncle, Chocolate Walt, he finds some sense of purpose.

Corina, a light-skinned black girl, has managed to get herself involved with a drug-running gang on the notoriously racist High Line. This is in the northwest of the country, centering on Spokane, Washington. Brain Nigger shows much persistence and considerable physical courage as he pursues his goal of finding her and bringing her home. Eventually he finds out that Corina is a long way from being the sweet little innocent girl he had believed her to be, but this does not matter. At the end of the novel he has found some kind of hope. He still dreams of the child he abandoned, and he still sees the third eye in the baby's cheek, but it is no longer blue but brown. Perhaps this suggests that somehow in the course of his terrifying experiences on the rails, Brain Nigger has become more true to himself than he ever was when he was a tax lawyer for the accounting firm in Los Angeles. He will never be Charles Harmon again, but at least he can be an authentic Brain Nigger.

Bryan Aubrey

Sources for Further Study

Booklist 98 (August, 2002): 1888.
Kirkus Reviews 70 (July 15, 2002): 989.
Library Journal 127 (August, 2002): 145.
Publishers Weekly 249 (August 26, 2002): 41.

EIGHT MEN AND A DUCK
An Improbable Voyage by Reed Boat to Easter Island

Author: Nick Thorpe
Publisher: Free Press (New York). 240 pp. $24.00
Type of work: Travel
Time: February to April, 2000
Locale: Bolivia, Chile, the South Pacific, and Easter Island

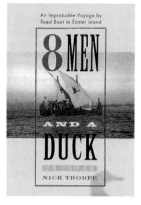

≈

Thorpe recounts an experimental voyage from Chile to Easter Island in a reed boat of traditional design, undertaken in order to test the hypothesis that there was pre-Columbian contact between the island and South America

≈

Principal personages:
> NICK THORPE, the author, a British journalist
> PHIL BUCK, expedition captain, an American mountaineer
> MARCO, Bolivian crew member, Buck's brother-in-law
> JORGE, Chilean crew member
> GREG DOBBS, crew member, a tree surgeon from Texas
> ERIK COTARI, Bolivian crew member, the shipbuilder
> CARLOS MARTÍNEZ, Chilean crew member, a fisherman
> STEPHANE, French crew member

Does this not sound like a script for disaster? An international crew of eight men, most strangers to one another, sails a 64-foot ship made of reeds 2,500 miles from Chile to Easter Island. None has experience navigating on the open ocean or in handling a two-masted vessel. Few, in fact, are sailors. Their communications equipment is unreliable. Their ship, the *Viracocha*, is based upon a traditional Bolivian freshwater boat design and untested at sea. Experts denounce the attempt.

Nevertheless, the experimental voyage succeeded. As Nick Thorpe, one of the crew members, describes it in *Eight Men and a Duck*, however, it sounds as if it were as much a matter of luck in the weather as skill, as much a stunt as a controlled scientific experiment. The book is billed as "travel/adventure" and, to be sure, there is adventure and exotic travel, but what is most striking in Thorpe's treatment is not the daring or the historical background—or even the boat itself—but the human drama among an ill-prepared, cliquish, and sometimes querulous crew.

Thorpe introduces readers to the world of adventurers in maritime anachronism, people who, inspired by Norwegian explorer Thor Heyerdahl's 1947 voyage in *Kon Tiki*, set to sea in frail replicas of ancient craft with the excuse of scientific investigation, but mainly, it seems, just to see if they can do it. Thorpe relates their behavior without the careful prettifying common in previous accounts of anachronistic voyages, and if readers are still as baffled by the *Viracocha* crew's motivation—and success—at the end of the book as at the beginning, he at least puts a believable human face on the "intrepid maverick whose prescience shows the impossible to be possible" caricature that began with Heyerdahl's accounts of his voyages.

Nick Thorpe began his career as a reporter for the Edinburgh Evening News *and* Scotsman *and subsequently worked as a freelancer for such newspapers as* The Times *(London) and for the British Broadcasting Corporation. His travel and feature writing from Africa, the Middle East, and South America earned him several journalism awards.*

In fact, Heyerdahl hovers over the story like an ancient, inscrutable deity. His theories provide the scientific background for the voyage of the *Viracocha*. One important part of Heyerdahl's work involved travel between the South Pacific islands and South America. Specifically, he believed that Easter Island may have received one group of colonists from the Andean region, or vice versa. The proposal is controversial, at best; most scientists dismiss Heyerdahl's theories. Unfortunately, Thorpe relegates his summary of the theories and their critical reception to an appendix, although alluding to both in the text, a source of possible frustration for readers new to the whole topic.

Heyerdahl was a hero and role model to Phil Buck since childhood. Buck conceived of the *Viracocha* expedition to help test Heyerdahl's Easter Island theory. If Buck could sail a reed boat there, then he would demonstrate that communications between the continent and the island had indeed been possible. For the design he chose the type of reed boat used until recently in Lake Titicaca, high in the Andes on the Peru-Bolivia border. There he found Erik Cotari and his family, who preserved the ancient method of building reed vessels. On the Bolivian shore in the village of Huatajata, the team constructed the *Viracocha*, named for an Andean creation god that Heyerdahl believed was identical to the Polynesian Kon Tiki. Thorpe heard of the project while staying in La Paz and went to Huatajata to write an article about it. He became so intrigued by the plan that, in an uncharacteristically reckless impulse, he volunteered for the crew.

Even while the ship was under construction, however, storm clouds of controversy were building on the horizon. For the voyage to be a true experiment, the ship had to use the same materials that were available to ancient shipwrights. In a hurry to get started, Buck and Cotari used synthetic cord instead of natural fiber rope to bind bundles of reeds for an interior core. When a jealous rival adventurer, Spaniard Kitin Muñoz, heard of it, he denounced the whole project as a fraud, giving press conferences and sending around faxes to that effect. Even Thor Heyerdahl dismissed it as unscientific. None of these critics objected to the *Viracocha*'s laptop global positioning system (GPS) receiver, satellite phone, radio, video cameras, cassette player, solar panels, power generator, batteries, maps, or navigation lights, even though ancient Andeans sailed without them; it was the few yards of synthetic cord that condemned the experiment. It is such details as this that reveal to the reader the selectively and vehemently nit-picking mentality of the replica mariner.

Another such detail is the assembling of the crew. They are an accidental mix. Of the eight originally signed up, several quit before the voyage because of the delay in launching or because of conflict with others. Buck appears at first to be an ideal captain, having led mountain climbing expeditions, but his style is to suggest rather than to give orders. This rankles Thorpe, who in his nervousness about the voyage wants clear, firm guidance and structure; he quips that Buck is running a floating focus group rather than a tight ship. Thorpe often grows peevish and bossy himself because of it. This causes grumbles among some South American crew members, who resent British and Americans throwing their weight about. Meanwhile, the Bolivian and Chilean crew members are deeply suspicious of each other, purely because of historical biases. During the voyage itself, tensions arise over food allotment, duty assignments, equipment use, and behavior. Although usually congenial, at times some crewmen display reckless abandon (one even falls overboard while drunk) while others grow sullen and withdrawn. (The duck, Pablo, sole survivor of two ducks, is of more amusement value in the clever title of the book than he is in the story. He is otherwise caged, mean-tempered, and seldom mentioned.)

Delays dog the project. Trucked to a beach near Arica in northernmost Chile and finally ready to launch, the *Viracocha* suffers yet more setbacks. One American, the navigator and chief rigger, suddenly quits in a huff, to be replaced by a volunteer from Arica. The city government, perhaps influenced by the project's critics, turns unhelpful. Buck has to scramble to get more supplies from sponsors. The crew has difficulty sliding the boat over the sand and into the surf. Once they finally manage it, they have difficulty finding a tug to tow them safely offshore. Sometimes comical, sometimes a bit sinister, these contretemps served to heighten the drama of the book, but not by much.

When finally the voyage begins, more minor trouble crops up. The tug fakes engine trouble and leaves them thirty miles from shore, uncomfortably close. The computer navigation system balks. They have communications problems. Nonetheless, they forge on, and here the most engaging portion of the book begins. Although at first the sea is astonishingly empty, which Thorpe blames on factory fishing trawlers, they eventually encounter whales, dolphins, sharks, squid, and a variety of large game fish, such as dorado and marlin. For a while, a fifteen-foot shark shadows them, escalating the consequences of the all-too-possible accident of falling overboard. A Korean freighter nearly hits the *Viracocha* in the night, for a time they are becalmed, and later they fear that the winds may carry them past Easter Island into the vast South Pacific as the boat slowly sinks under them and supplies run out. In the most harrowing episode of the voyage, a storm rips off the ship's mast and leaves them adrift, dangerously close to a rocky islet.

It is the growing interpersonal conflicts among the crew members that produce the greatest drama (and, sometimes, humor) as they struggle to gel as a team. For example, Thorpe finds that his fellow crewmembers are superstitious, sometimes intensely so. When he flouts the superstitions, he nearly makes enemies of some of them and finds himself blamed for bad luck. He overcomes his initial incredulity and learns to respect the beliefs of others, at least while aboard. These passages bring psychological insight and depth to the story. In another instance, he describes how he must face his own fear of death and force himself to function while in danger without further angering his mates. Such episodes are not common in the book, unfortunately, but those that exist enhance its value as travel literature.

The arrival at Easter Island turns out to be anticlimactic. They are greeted indifferently by the residents and are astonished to learn that the Easter Islanders resent attempts to link their heritage to South America, which they regard at a source of repression. Moreover, perhaps because of the vocal critics of the expedition, the local politicians burn the *Viracocha* on the excuse that it might harbor exotic insects. In a truly bizarre scene, the crew rushes back from a picnic to find the boat already afire and the sight bonds them as a single team as never before. Then each goes his separate way.

The book as a whole, however, ends on a positive note. Eight months after leaving Easter Island, Buck and Thorpe make a pilgrimage to the home of Thor Heyerdahl on the Spanish island Tenerife. In preparation, Thorpe discusses more about Heyerdahl's theories than in the rest of the book, but the real point of the episode, as Thorpe well recognizes, is the man himself. He and Buck want his approval for their expedition. After questioning the pair closely about the synthetic cord used inside the *Viracocha*, Heyerdahl satisfies himself the boat was authentically ancient in spirit after all and, reversing himself, grants his approval.

Given Heyerdahl's vast importance to the world of replica voyages, it is a logical note on which to end the book, but still it rings a bit false. True, the reader learns something about South Pacific and Andean archaeology and about the perils of ancient sea voyages, but the emotional heart of the book lies with Nick Thorpe and, to a lesser extent, the other crew members and the internecine competition among crews of rival expeditions. During the prelaunch construction and the voyage, the young author confronts his fears, his biases about others, and his startled realization that the criticisms of him by other crew members, partly personal and partly from national stereotypes, are sometimes justified. The reader witnesses a thoughtful young man grow psychologically. Beyond the theories and thrills, the tale of that growth is the real strength of *Eight Men and a Duck.*

Roger Smith

Sources for Further Study

Booklist 98 (April 15, 2002): 1376.
Forbes 169 (Summer, 2002): 4.
Publishers Weekly 249 (March 18, 2002): 85.
The Washington Post Book World, June 23, 2002, p. 7.

EMBATTLED DREAMS
California in War and Peace, 1940-1950

Author: Kevin Starr (1940-   )
Publisher: Oxford University Press (New York). 386 pp.
  $37.50
Type of work: History
Time: 1940-1950
Locale: California

~

The sixth volume of Starr's history of California covers the pivotal decade of the 1940's, a decade when California became America's dream

~

Principal personages:
RICHARD MILHOUS NIXON (1913-1994), congressman and later president
  of the United States
EARL WARREN (1891-1974), California governor, 1943-1953, and later
  chief justice of the U.S. Supreme Court

In *Embattled Dreams*, Kevin Starr continues his narrative history of California, which he began in 1973 with *Americans and the California Dream, 1850-1915*. In this, the sixth volume, Starr relates the state's history during the 1940's, arguably the most significant decade in California's history not only for the transformations which occurred within the state, but also for the impact California had upon the rest of the United States.

Wars framed the decade of *Embattled Dreams*, beginning with the onset of one war and concluding with the start of another military conflict. Already underway abroad by 1940, World War II was arguably the single pivotal event in California's history. At the end of the decade, America was engaged in a Cold War against communism and Soviet aggression and a "hot war" on the Korean peninsula, both consequences of World War II. Within those parameters, Starr organizes the volume on a chapter-per-year basis, an approach somewhat artificial and limiting: Events have a habit of not confining themselves to a single calendar year.

Given that Starr is primarily a narrative historian, the opening chapter strikes something of a false note in his attempt to give a metaphorical Freudian interpretation to the year 1940, a moment poised between Eros and Thanatos, or the life instinct and the death instinct. However, once past this unsatisfactory interpretative framework, Starr does what he has always done so well: filling his canvas with events and individuals.

In the initial chapter, there is a portrayal of thousands of persons and incidents, or so it seems. Included are President Franklin D. Roosevelt; aviator Charles Lindbergh;

the songs "When You Wish Upon a Star" and
"I'll Never Smile Again"; musicians Duke El-
lington and Glenn Miller; the films *Gone with
the Wind* (1939), *Citizen Kane* (1941), and *Fan-
tasia* (1940); poets Robinson Jeffers and Kenneth Rexroth; *Sunset* magazine; advertisements
for cruises to Japan; newlyweds Ronald Reagan
and Jane Wyman; starlet Jane Russell; the jitter-
bug; spring break at Southern California's Bal-
boa Beach; Stanford University's football team;

*Kevin Starr, in addition to his
highly regarded multivolume history
of California, is also a professor in
the department of history at the
University of Southern California
and is the state librarian of
California.*

University of California physicists Robert Oppenheimer and Ernest Lawrence; Vel-
veeta cheese, Sanka coffee, Lucky Lager beer, and Christian Brothers wine; the
Studebaker and Hudson automobiles; Texaco and Mohawk gasoline stations; Gover-
nor Culbert Olson; baseball player Joe DiMaggio; the San Francisco-Oakland Bay
Bridge; the Santa Fe Super Chief; Pasadena's Rose Parade; Yosemite's Ahwahnee
Hotel; Los Angeles nightspots such as Chasens and 21; the United Airlines DC-3
Mainliner; and much more. Out of all those specifics Starr weaves a mosaic of Cali-
fornia's embattled dream.

Although Starr's technique is encompassing and inclusive, in subsequent chapters
there is a central theme or event which gives focus to each chapter. The second chapter, 1941, relates the beginnings of World War II, including a discussion of the causes
of the war going back to the early twentieth century and the state's prejudiced actions
against Japanese immigrants. An account of the beginning of the war from both an
American and a Japanese perspective is presented: The chapter's title, "Shelling
Santa Barbara," refers to the shelling of an oil field near Santa Barbara by a Japanese
submarine, although the event itself actually occurred in February, 1942. Starr suggests that the war was a California-Japanese war, given the significance of the state
and its past in causing the conflict.

By 1942, California had become, in the words of the third chapter's title, a "Garrison State." Major General George Patton, a native Californian from an elite Pasadena
and San Marino family, trained his tank corps in the deserts near Riverside; Camp
Pendleton became the major Marine Corp base on the Pacific Coast; and other military bases were established throughout the state. By the end of the year, San Francisco
had become the major embarkation and supply port for the Pacific war, and Starr describes wartime San Francisco and its varied entertainments, both legal and illegal.
The garrison state also refers to the incarceration of California's Japanese community
in relocation centers, or concentration camps, an action supported by California officials, including the state's attorney general, Earl Warren.

Starr also focuses on the impact the war had on African Americans and Mexican
Americans. In the zoot suit riots in Los Angeles in 1943, service men on leave
stripped young Latino males of their distinctive garb before the authorities called a
belated halt. Mexican American soldiers were not segregated by race, but the same
could not be said for African Americans. As a group, African Americans made some
limited gains in the defense industries, but as Starr points out, they were generally at

the bottom of the pecking order, a world portrayed in the novels of Chester Himes (1909-1984).

The war transformed the lives of women, particularly those in Southern California who took jobs in the area's burgeoning aircraft industries, such as Douglas and Lockheed. The region had long been a center of aircraft production—Lindbergh's *The Spirit of St. Louis* was built in San Diego—but it was World War II which made Southern California the world's aircraft capital. The defense industry demands and the absence of men, who had gone to war, opened the doors to women. Starr discusses the various issues involved, including the issue of sexuality, which some predicted would lead to a Roman bacchanalia: Norma Jean Baker did move from making parachutes to making pictures as Marilyn Monroe (1926-1962). One of Starr's heroes is Henry J. Kaiser (1882-1967). A builder of ships and steel mills, Kaiser was also a social visionary, creating a prepaid health plan for his workers.

No history of California could ignore Hollywood, and Starr relates the impact of Hollywood on World War II and the impact of the war on Hollywood, from describing the Hollywood Canteen, staffed by movie stars who entertained and danced with service men, to a discussion of the iconic film of the war, *Casablanca* (1942). Some actors experienced combat, such as James Stewart, while others served the military at home, like Reagan. Another star who became an American icon was Bob Hope, who for decades entertained American troops abroad.

The year 1946, subject of chapter 7, was a "Homecoming," except for the 26,000 Californians who died in military service. César Chávez (1927-1993) returned to the agricultural fields of Delano, and Bob Waterfield returned to play professional football and marry his high school girlfriend, Jane Russell, budding movie star of Howard Hughes's *The Outlaw* (1943). Audie Murphy, decorated combat soldier, became a movie star by playing himself. Many other service men who had been in California for military training or in transit elsewhere migrated to the Golden State when discharged. The G.I. Bill allowed veterans to attend college, and they made up nearly 50 percent of the UCLA student body. The growth in population led to the creation of new suburbs, such as Henry Kaiser's Panorama City in the agricultural San Fernando Valley. Not all moved to the suburbs. The controversial author Henry Miller (1891-1980) made Big Sur a bohemian locus of sex and anarchy, according to the tabloids.

One staple of the press was crime, particularly in William Randolph Hearst's Los Angeles newspapers. The year 1947 saw the brutal murder of Elizabeth Short, nicknamed the "Black Dahlia," and the acts of Caryl Chessman, the "red light bandit." It was also the year of the assassination of the gangster Benjamin "Bugsy" Siegel and the accession of Mickey Cohen as Los Angeles's most prominent mobster. Raymond Chandler (1888-1959) brilliantly captured the underside of 1940's Los Angeles through his novels featuring private detective Philip Marlow and in such films as *The Blue Dahlia* (1946) and *Double Indemnity* (1944).

Politics does not dominate *Embattled Dreams*, but politicians have their role. Earl Warren was the premier politician of the era, and Starr devotes more space to Warren than to any other figure. Warren's political success was a reflection of California's growing middle class and its values, and Warren, a very private man, understood, as did the Kennedys later, the political value of having an attractive and energetic family. Elected the state's governor in 1942, Warren was in the Progressive Republican tradition of Hiram Johnson (1866-1945). Distrusted by a few liberal journalists such as Carey McWilliams, Warren was the master of nonpartisanship in a state where political party loyalty was minimal. He was the first state politician to court the support of African Americans and was popular among Mexican Americans, but he also worked with California business interests and political lobbyists. He served as governor for over ten years, ran for the presidency twice, and became chief justice of the U.S. Supreme Court. In contrast to Warren, the Northern California Progressive, Richard Nixon was a staunch Southern California Republican, a representative, Starr suggests, of a more fluid and insecure social environment.

Elected to Congress in 1946, Nixon rose to public prominence during the anticommunist crusade of the early Cold War years. The fear of Communist subversion carried over to Hollywood in violent strikes between the studios and unions. Starr argues that a Communist presence in Hollywood was not simply a fiction, and he discusses the Communist sympathies and connections of various personages, particularly the screenwriter John Howard Lawson (1894-1977), leader of the so-called Hollywood Ten, all of whom were affiliated with the Communist Party.

The Cold War heated up in 1950 when Communist North Korea invaded South Korea. The Korean War aggravated the domestic fear of Communist subversion, which culminated in the University of California loyalty oath controversy, which Starr perceives as a struggle between an older California represented by the Board of Regents and a new California epitomized by the rapidly changing University of California and its faculty. The physicist J. Robert Oppenheimer (1904-1967) was a symbol of the conflict, and in *Embattled Dreams*, Oppenheimer comes across as politically naïve at best. Eventually the regents voted, by a narrow majority, to terminate the thirty-one faculty members who refused to sign the oath. Richard Nixon made the most of the anticommunist fears in his senatorial campaign against the left-leaning Helen Gahagan Douglas, accusing her of Communist sympathies in a series of pink-colored flyers, or Pink Sheets. Already weakened by a divisive primary, Douglas was easily defeated by Nixon, who was elected vice president in 1952.

In his conclusion, Starr states that the 1940's "was perhaps the most ambiguous yet transformative decade in the history of the state," which might be symbolized by its most successful politicians, Earl Warren and Richard Nixon. By the end of the decade, hopes of swimming pools, along with suburban tracts and freeways, had replaced the fears of the Great Depression. A just war had been won and the golden dream of the good life continued.

Embattled Dreams is an engrossing work, filled with many events and portraying the lives of numerous Californians, both famous and obscure. It is also the first book in Starr's multivolume history to cover an era that many of his readers will perhaps remember, thus giving the work an immediacy to some and a sense of nostalgia to others. Whether his focus on so many events and personages always explicates his title is another matter. Critics have argued that Starr's pointillist approach sacrifices the forest for the trees and that he fails to provide sufficient context and analysis. Still, the trees are invariably of compelling interest even if the forest is sometimes obscured.

Eugene Larson

Sources for Further Study

The Atlantic Monthly 289 (May, 2002): 101.
Business Week, May 13, 2002, p. 22.
Los Angeles Times Book Review, April 21, 2002, p. 3.
National Review 54 (August 12, 2002): 46.
Publishers Weekly 249 (April 15, 2002): 52.

EMPEROR OF JAPAN
Meiji and His World, 1852-1912

Author: Donald Keene (1922-   )
Publisher: Columbia University Press (New York). 256
   pp. $39.50
Type of work: Biography and history
Time: 1852-1912
Locale: Japan

≈

*Drawing on a wealth of primary sources translated
from the Japanese, Keene presents a very detailed picture
of the long reign of Japan's first modern emperor*

≈

Principal personages:

MEIJI, first named Sachinomya and called Mutsohito during his life, the
   first modern emperor of Japan who wielded real power
EMPEROR KÔMEI, Meiji's father, who is bitterly opposed to the presence
   of foreigners in Japan
NAKAYAMA YOSHIKO, Meiji's real mother
ICHIJŌ Haruko, Meiji's wife, later called Empress Shôken
PRINCE YOSHIHITO, Meiji's son and successor to the imperial throne as
   Emperor Taishō
TOKUGAWA YOSHINOBU, Japan's last shogun
QUEEN MIN OF KOREA, murdered by the Japanese for her anti-Japanese
   stand
SIR HARRY PARKES, British minister to Japan
SAIGŌ Takamori, leader of a failed rebellion, who committed suicide
ITŌ Hirobumi, trusted minister of Meiji
IWAKURA TOMOMI, nobleman in close contact with Kômei and Meiji

Donald Keene's massive *Emperor of Japan* offers its readers a full, detailed account of the man publicly known as the Meiji Emperor, who ruled as Japan rapidly transformed from a closed, medieval state to an industrialized world power that defeated the Russian empire. The reader with a special interest in the subject will be delighted at the wealth of source material that Keene has made available through his diligent translation from the Japanese and his industrious research. A general reader, however, may feel a bit overwhelmed by the sheer volume of detailed information regarding the players in numerous court intrigues, political maneuvers, and elaborate official ceremonies.

Occasionally, the reader feels as if Keene presents both too much and too little information. The burial of Meiji's father Kōmei, or his marriage to the well-bred and nobly educated Haruko, is retold in a style as elaborate as the original ceremonies.

~

*Donald Keene has written or edited
more than thirty books on Japanese
literature and history in English and
in Japanese. In 1986, the Donald
Keene Center of Japanese Culture
at New York's Columbia University
was founded in his honor. He is
Columbia's Shincho Professor
Emeritus of Japanese Literature.*

~

The same is true for the many palace plots involving the leaders and followers of the two rival factions called "*sonnō jōi*—Respect the emperor and drive out the barbarians!" and "*kōbu gattai*, the union of aristocracy and military," who fought for power at the imperial court of the 1850's and 1860's. Yet there is little by way of a more summary background information guiding a general reader.

For all but the specialist readers, it can be feared, *Emperor of Japan* mirrors the style of the official court record of Meiji's reign, *Meiji tennō ki* (record of the divine emperor Meiji), used by Keene, which amasses a wealth of detail without providing any summaries or narrative commentaries quickly ordering the reported events. Keene mentions the interesting pragmatism of the Japanese aristocracy that solved, for example, marital problems of the imperial family. Since Meiji's mother Nakayama Yoshiko was not the wife of the emperor, the real empress was made his official mother. The same happened a generation later with Meiji's son and crown prince Yoshihito, who "expressed surprise and dismay" when he learned that his true mother was not Meiji's wife Haruko. To make her a bit younger before their marriage, Meiji had also changed Haruko's birthday by one year. Yet in spite of all of Keene's meticulously reported research, readers must often discover general principles uniting different events for themselves.

There is also the unfortunate fact of an apparent lack of editorial work. Even with the confusion arising from the traditional Japanese custom of counting a baby as one year old when it is born, it is still a rather embarrassing oversight when Keene's first chapter misdates the year of Meiji's birth as 1851, when the subtitle as well as most subsequent references has the correct year of 1852. Similarly, there is a confusion of dates when Keene has Shogun Tokugawa Iemochi arrive at the imperial court at Kyoto on April 21, 1863, but has him announce on April 7, clearly the wrong date, that he wants to leave Kyoto now. It is a pity that no editor has caught these unnecessary errors.

The huge number of individuals populating the narrative of *Emperor of Japan* has the potential to intimidate anybody who may have wished for a stronger focus on Meiji himself. A few of them manage to impress themselves strongly on the reader's imagination. There is Japan's last shogun, Tokugawa Yoshinobu, who resigns his powers to the emperor in 1867 only to have a change of heart and take up arms against imperial soldiers in 1868. Defeated, he is treated with uncharacteristic leniency, and allowed to live out his life, to die one year after Meiji in 1913.

Emperor of Japan chronicles both the personal and the political events of Meiji's significant reign. There is Japan's initial opposition to opening the country to Western foreigners, or "barbarians," fiercely hated by Meiji's father Kōmei. The conflict begins with the visit of the American commodore Matthew Calbraith Perry in 1853. Once foreigners are reluctantly allowed into Japan, Western accounts of their adventures in Japan are used by Keene to complement his Japanese sources. The first state visit of a Westerner to see the Japanese emperor personally, for example, leads to a well-documented attack. Two assassins fall upon the procession of Sir Harry Parkes and try to kill the hated British. Defeated with the help of their Japanese escort, one assassin is killed immediately, while the second begs for a speedy execution. Parkes, who is not hurt, has to reschedule his visit, and the emperor apologizes for the attack.

Japan's successful war with China, which leads to the Japanese annexation of Taiwan, is chronicled, as well as the callous murder of Queen Min of Korea. Her resistance to Japanese attempts to colonize Korea had earned Queen Min the hatred of the Japanese already residing in the country, some of whom decided to kill her. In a bold attack on the Korean palace, the invaders search for the queen and brutally assassinate her. Keene's translation of the various accounts of her murder chill the reader, when one assassin recalls how "I swung my sword down on her head . . . so one blow was enough to finish her." The body of Queen Min is stripped naked and burned nearby. In spite of some foreign pressure, Emperor Meiji does not punish the assassins. Eventually, in 1910, Korea was annexed to the Japanese empire and would not regain its independence until 1945.

Japan's triumph over the Russian fleet at Tsushima in May, 1905, when "Admiral . . . Tōgō's fleet annihilated the Russians," is as much part of *Emperor of Japan* as is a focus on the private life of the somewhat enigmatic emperor himself. Keene admits that his biography is not helped by the fact that, apart from his poems, there are no private notes, writings, or diaries in which Meiji recorded his own thoughts and feelings. The official accounts are generally silent about Meiji's personal opinions, and anecdotes occasionally contradict each other. Yet Meiji does emerge from the many pages of Keene's book as a monarch who reflects Japan's substantial changes in the wake of Japan's dramatic encounter with the Western powers.

The reader does learn some facts of Meiji's private life. He appears as a conscientious, diligent ruler who had to face some grief because of the early deaths of most of his children. As Keene points out, the children of Japan's imperial family, curiously, died at a much higher rate than children of the general population. By the time Meiji was thirty-one years old, for example, "six of the emperor's seven children had died in infancy." Even though the official records researched by Keene do not record any personal reaction of Meiji to these tragedies, the author understandably assumes that grief must have struck the emperor.

None of Meiji's children were born by Haruko; all were the children of his concubines and court ladies. Indicative of Japanese cultural attitudes on the subject, Haruko even visited her husband together with two of his favorite concubines in Hiroshima during the war with China in 1895. Eventually, Meiji began to "visit her house . . . every evening, not returning until morning to imperial headquarters." Haruko also asked to see wounded soldiers from the war in the local hospital, where her visit, dressed in Western clothes, was warmly welcomed.

As father, Meiji reserved his personal attention for his boys and "persisted in refusing to see" his daughters. Here he decided not to break ancient customs, as he did in many other instances, and contemporary reaction to this rather cold decision varies from praise to pity.

Haruko "worried about her husband's drinking"; he occasionally consumed two bottles of champagne at dinner, with his aides trying to cover up his inebriated state. She wrote him a poem that begins with the lines, "I hope you will observe/ Moderation when drinking." Meiji did not neglect his duties over saké and champagne, for "as all sources agree, he went early every morning to his office to conduct business," even after a night of heavy drinking.

Later in life, Meiji became unhappy over newspaper accounts that "the emperor weighed more than 170 pounds." He distrusted court physicians, perhaps because they had been notoriously unable to preserve the lives of most of his children. As Keene shows, Meiji always put his official duties above his health. He attended military maneuvers right up to the point of his death of heart failure on July 30, 1912. With him died an emperor who had ruled over one of the most transformative eras in Japanese history.

Characteristic of the huge scope of Keene's book is its account of two nobles who become close executives for Meiji. The lives of Itō Hirobumi and Iwakura Tomomi are followed as they interact with Meiji, and a reader learns to appreciate the complexity and diversity of the men and women seeking to influence the emperor. The illustrations highlight changes in culture and politics. There are two official photos of the emperor, one showing him in traditional Japanese dress, and one in a Western-style uniform. Portraits of Empress Haruko show a kind but determined woman. Paintings illustrating key events from Meiji's reign show the strong artistic license the artists of the time took with historical facts. A case in point is Saigō Takamori, once an ally of Meiji. When his rebellion failed in 1887, he was hunted down until "he had only forty men left." Wounded and facing the defeat, Saigō "bowed his head" and had an aide behead him. This suicide inspired the romantic imagination of Meiji's age. A painting falsely places the event at sea, with Saigō exposing his naked belly in preparation of committing *seppuku*, the ritual suicide beginning with one's self slitting of the belly before a trusted aide beheads the bleeding sufferer.

A reader somewhat familiar with Japanese history, especially of the nineteenth and early twentieth century, will enjoy following Keene's detailed records of political intrigues, wars, assassinations, and constitutional changes. Such a reader will also detect how such practices as *tenchû*, or "divine punishment," which are used as a justification for politically motivated assassinations of opponents, would continue all the way to the early part of the twentieth century, when imperialist officers murdered politicians in the 1920's and 1930's who opposed Japanese military aggression. As Keene shows, Meiji's reign saw its number of such assassinations, when "the conspirators . . . insisted that they were acting in consonance with the emperor's true wishes, that they would rid him of the corrupt officials."

Emperor of Japan requires of its readers either a certain familiarity with modern Japanese history and culture or the patience to sift through a massive, elaborate narrative and discover much knowledge in the process. Apart from the occasional editorial oversight, Keene's book is well researched and documented. It does take some work to keep track of all the players and keep in sight the central figure of Meiji and his family, but the wealth of detail can be very rewarding to the interested reader.

R. C. Lutz

Sources for Further Study

Booklist 98 (May 1, 2002): 1501.
Library Journal 127 (June 1, 2002): 164.
The New York Times Book Review 107 (August 18, 2002): 9.
Publishers Weekly 249 (March 18, 2002): 85.

THE EMPEROR OF OCEAN PARK

Author: Stephen L. Carter (1954-   )
Publisher: Alfred A. Knopf (New York). 657 pp. $26.95
Type of work: Novel
Time: The turn of the twenty-first century
Locale: Martha's Vineyard; Elm Harbor, Connecticut;
Washington, D.C.; Aspen, Colorado

≈

*This first novel by a well-known law professor and so-
cial critic explores the manners, mores, and intrigues of
the African American upper crust, a prestigious law school,
and the corridors of political power as well as other forms
of "clout" in the United States*

≈

Principal characters:

TALCOTT "MISHA" GARLAND, an African American law school profes-
sor
KIMBERLY "KIMMER" GARLAND, his wife, a high-powered attorney
BENTLEY, their son
OLIVER GARLAND, Talcott's father, a judge nominated and ultimately
rejected for the U.S. Supreme Court
MARIAH, Talcott's conspiracy-theorist sister
ADDISON, Talcott's television evangelist brother
"UNCLE" JACK ZIEGLER, a mysterious family friend who may have been
responsible for Oliver's downfall

In *The Emperor of Ocean Park*, Stephen L. Carter blends several literary conventions to produce a unique and highly readable first novel. Part comedy of manners,
part novel of ideas, and part mystery-thriller, the book combines richness of detail with a free-flowing and suspenseful narrative. It is, in short, a page turner with
depth.

Talcott "Misha" Garland, the book's narrator and main character, is a distinguished law school professor at an elite East Coast university. He is also a prosperous
member of "the darker nation" (African Americans). He has an attractive wife,
Kimberly (or "Kimmer"), who is a high-powered attorney under consideration for an
appointment to a federal appellate court. The couple has a healthy young son,
Bentley, just on the cusp of fluid speech and the apple of Talcott's eye. Talcott himself is son of the famous (or infamous, depending on how one looks at it) Oliver Garland, the "emperor" of the book's title. Commonly referred to as "the Judge," Oliver
was once an up-and-coming jurist. Ultimately, he became the subject of painful confirmation hearings which ended disastrously, dashing his hopes for a seat on the U.S.

Supreme Court. Oliver then became a thoroughly embittered front man for conservative and right-wing causes as well as a high-priced public speaker available to sympathetic groups. As a father, Oliver Garland was stoic, distant, and hard to please. A figure of mythic proportions, Oliver is the fount of Talcott's aspirations and accomplishments, but also of his son's deep-seated self-doubt.

The novel opens with Oliver Garland's death. At the funeral the reader is introduced to various family members and friends. Talcott's sister, Mariah, a fabulously wealthy housewife (formerly an investigative reporter), believes her father has been murdered. She proves to be an avid and eclectic conspiracy theorist throughout the novel. Talcott's television evangelist brother, Addison, on the other hand, seems supremely uninterested in any possible murder conspiracy. (A second sister, Abigail, was killed in a hit-and-run accident before the events of the novel take place.) Toward the end of the graveside service, an appearance is made by the mysterious "Uncle" Jack Ziegler, intricately involved with (and possibly the cause of) the Judge's downfall.

Ziegler's bizarre visitation substantially thickens the plot. Much to Talcott's confusion and consternation, Ziegler demands to know about "the arrangements" made by the Judge in the event of his death. Ominously, he tells Talcott that he and his family are in no physical danger as long as Talcott makes every attempt to uncover and share "the arrangements" with Ziegler. The problem is that Talcott has not the foggiest notion of what Ziegler is talking about. Soon afterward, Talcott is interviewed very aggressively by men claiming to be Federal Bureau of Investigation (FBI) agents. He also finds that he is being followed. Hesitantly, clumsily, Talcott begins to unravel the mystery. He speaks with people who knew his father, but no one seems to have all the facts. He seems to be getting nowhere. On the other hand, mysterious clues, including a note from his father and two chess pieces, appear out of thin air.

Meanwhile, Talcott's marriage and professional life are crumbling. Kimberly, whom Talcott already suspects of having an affair, has no patience or sympathy whatsoever with her husband's quest for "the arrangements," particularly in the light of her fragile shot at the much-coveted appeals court nomination. At work, Talcott's job is jeopardized by both Kimberly's situation and his own unorthodox behavior following the death of his father. In time, all these matters are settled. The truth about Kim-

~

Stephen L. Carter is the William Nelson Cromwell Professor of Law at Yale University. He is also a prolific writer who has written more than a half-dozen nonfiction books, including Reflections of an Affirmative Action Baby *(1991),* The Culture of Disbelief: How American Law and Politics Trivializes Religion *(1993),* Integrity *(1996), and* Civility: Manners, Morals, and the Etiquette of Democracy *(1998). Carter lives with his wife and children outside New Haven, Connecticut.*

~

berly's faithfulness and the fate of her potential nomination are revealed. Talcott's career crisis is resolved for better or worse. Talcott finally discovers "the arrangements" and comes to know more about his father than he ever dreamed or wanted to know. Conspiracies are revealed (though not any of the ones imagined by Mariah) and revenge exposed. Villains emerge and are dealt with. Talcott's tale ends—his life never to quite be the same.

The greatest strength of Carter's novel lies in its deft characterization. Talcott Garland comes alive as a prim, proper, awkwardly judgmental, and just slightly hypocritical gentleman. In his combination of gentility and human frailties, Talcott is both an anachronism and an example of the vanities of his era. Readers may blanch at his constant concern with prestige and stature, but they will also recognize this obsession as contemporary and deeply human. Likewise, there is no difficulty feeling Talcott's highly ambiguous emotions with regard to his father's life and death, as well as his wife's possible dalliances. Kimberly also comes alive as an ambitious, spoiled up-and-comer, consumed by job and career, yet also a highly conspicuous consumer, spending to the very limits of the couple's considerable means. Kimberly says that she loves Talcott; it is hard to say whether she really does or not. Posthumously, Oliver Garland also takes on a concrete and unforgettable presence in the novel. Proud, patriarchal, and stoic to the end, the Judge comes across as a formidable and troubled creation, one with more than enough individuality to forestall any all-too-convenient comparisons to real-life conservative Supreme Court Justice Clarence Thomas. In addition, the book's sizable supporting cast is drawn skillfully and memorably.

Carter's novel also deserves praise for its convincing portrayal of the darker nation's upper-class elite, both in Washington, D.C., and in Martha's Vineyard, and for its efficient, stylish prose. Given the preeminence in American society of certain racial stereotypes, many readers will be less than fully familiar with the well-to-do, successful African American subculture presented in Carter's novel. Such readers will come away with an enriched sense of how unmonolithic the African American experience has been. Since Talcott narrates his entire story in the present tense, Carter's writing style may seem jarring at first. This relatively uncommon device, however, soon becomes eminently comfortable for the reader. As a result, the book is easy to follow yet fresh (and even moderately daring) in its stylistic approach.

The Emperor of Ocean Park is less successful in terms of plot. While, throughout the novel, there is a well-wrought motif based on the game of chess (and, more specifically, a chess "problem"), the novel's mystery plot does not come across as particularly convincing or realistic. Key players remain vague in motivation and dramatically undefined. Clues fall out of the sky. Much of the dialogue is drawn-out and contrivedly inconclusive. In short, Carter's story is not nearly as believable as his characters and his descriptions of various places and social milieus.

These plot deficiencies are likely to be forgiven in the light of the fact that Carter's book has a parallel incarnation as a novel of ideas. In his Author's Note at the conclusion of the text, Carter does assert that *The Emperor of Ocean Park* is "just a story." The primary purpose of this claim is to keep overly zealous commentators from mistaking his fictional characters, institutions, and current history for the real things. Carter might also be interpreted to be saying that the book is not a work of social commentary. Nevertheless, it cannot be denied that much of the prepublication interest in the novel is owed to Carter's reputation, earned in his previous books, for offering unconventional analyses and critiques of contemporary American society. More to the point is the fact that Talcott and his fellow characters speak constantly of current cultural, social, and political issues, particularly ones touched upon by Carter in his previous works. For instance, Kimberly has a deep suspicion of affirmative action (*Reflections of an Affirmative Action Baby*, 1991), Talcott often laments the contemporary lack of manners (*Civility*, 1998), and the potency (and appropriateness) of religious belief is on prominent display—amounting, really, to an important subtheme—throughout the novel (*The Culture of Disbelief*, 1993). Carter introduces these concerns into his novel gracefully for the most part, and handles them with considerable clarity. In doing so, he preserves continuity with the overall flavor of his previous books, eschewing conventional orthodoxies of the "right" and the "left" as well as any easily palatable "centrism." He is especially unfriendly to any of the common knee-jerk approaches to the issue of race. A coherent position emerges out of all this, one that calls—in ever-so-civil a way—for independent thinking and liberation from cozy prejudices. On the other hand, Carter, perhaps purposefully, misses chances to address some issues on a more provocative or profound level. For example, he has a character seemingly reach the very precipice of suggesting that the 1965 *Griswold v. Connecticut* case which established the right to privacy also might be seen as removing legal barriers to gay marriage. Just then the character is interrupted by a call to dinner. Likewise, legal case-fixing pops up in the book in a way that cries out for discussion of the law's daunting malleability in this modern lawyer-ridden, interest-group-laden society. Carter passes the moment by.

Carter does achieve genuine depth in his subtly effective rejection of stereotypes. His African Americans are educated and upwardly mobile, yet full of human flaws. They are both profoundly similar to and different from other peoples. No matter what their race, Carter's women are also multifaceted, complex individuals who need not be willowy and paper-thin to be wildly attractive. Carter's other characters may fall into ethnic categories, but they are not ethnic or any other kind of caricature. Once again, Carter helps his readers to shed their prejudices and see the world as it exists, rather than as they have been conditioned to believe it exists.

The Emperor of Ocean Park is, therefore, successful for both its literary merit and the ideas it conveys. Readers are transported into a fictional world of substantial authenticity. At the same time, they learn much about what makes the real world tick.

Ira Smolensky

Sources for Further Study

Black Issues Book Review 4 (May/June, 2002): 28.
Booklist 98 (April 1, 2002): 1283.
Ebony 57 (October, 2002): 24.
Library Journal 127 (April 15, 2002): 123.
The New York Review of Books 49 (June 27, 2002): 4.
The New York Times Book Review 107 (June 9, 2002): 11.
Publishers Weekly 249 (April 22, 2002): 45.
Weekly Standard 7 (June 17, 2002): 43.

THE ENIGMA OF ANGER
Essays on a Sometimes Deadly Sin

Author: Garret Keizer (1953-   )
Publisher: Jossey-Bass (San Francisco). 384 pp. $22.95
Type of work: Essays, religion, and psychology

≈

An exploration from a broadly Christian perspective of the nature of anger and its expression in the church and in the world

≈

Garret Keizer offers two definitions of anger in *The Enigma of Anger*. He calls it "an emotion of extreme frustration . . . poised at the possibility of action"; but it is also "an emotion arising from a refusal to suffer or to permit violation." Anger can be a deadly sin, visiting injustice on others (and on oneself) in its intemperance, yet it can also be a sign of divine justice that refuses to countenance abuse. Keizer's anatomy of anger is an attempt both to come to terms with his own temper ("I am a descendant of angry men") and to limn anger's battle lines in the mind, the home, the church, and in the larger world. In the midst of it all is the conviction that "anger can be redeemed. . . . [A]nger can be controlled without being destroyed, and expressed without necessarily leading to destruction."

The *Enigma of Anger* is decidedly not a self-help book, for one of the things Keizer is angry about is the glibness of the self-help movement in its goal of curing life of every problem, step by step. Instead, the author offers observations from the trenches, with the deftness of novelist and theologian Frederick Buechner and (at times) the acerbity of Samuel Johnson. One of the first headnotes of the book, in fact, is a quotation from Johnson's novel *Rasselas* (1759), in which the wise philosopher Imlac notes the difference between a moralist's exalted pronouncements and his everyday life. Johnson is never far from Keizer and he returns at the end as something of a role model.

"Johnson seemed born to struggle," Keizer observes,

> and not only with his petulance, though that is the main reason for celebrating him here. . . . The inner struggles of Johnson boil down in many cases to the plight of a man who was a Christian by conviction, but not by disposition. . . . Johnson's life is of great interest to me, not only because of a similar tension between my own temperament and my religion, but because I believe that the religion itself is based on a certain inner tension. . . . In Johnson we see a simultaneous insistence on the sinful state of humanity and on the duty of human beings to be better than they are.

Anger has a place in the Christian life, and indeed in the life of every mature adult. At its best it is analogous to God's wrath at injustice and idolatry and to Christ's anger at

Garret Keizer, a high school English teacher for almost twenty years, became the priest of Christ Episcopal Church in Island Pond, Vermont, in 1992. A frequent contributor to The Christian Century, Harper's Magazine, *and other periodicals, his books include the novel* The God of Beer *(2002)*, A Dresser of Sycamore Trees: The Finding of a Ministry *(1991), and* No Place but Here: A Teacher's Vocation in a Rural Community *(1988).*

the money changers in the Temple. The Gospel of Mark also records that Jesus was angry at those who criticized him for healing a man's withered hand on the Sabbath. Sometimes, however, his anger is mysterious. Jesus cursed a fig tree for not bearing fruit, and it withered. For Keizer this is not some safe parable on the importance of faith bearing fruit but vivid expression of the idealism of the creator of life. "I do not understand his cursing of that tree. I do not like what he does. But on some level, in the same deep place that I believe in the resurrection of the dead and believe, also, that I shall one day see John Brown in heaven, I love him for it."

Anger can lead to excess, and there is reason for calling it one of the seven deadly sins. Each of the six other sins (Keizer pairs pride with envy, lust with gluttony, and sloth with avarice) angrily overreaches. Pride and envy are based on a false view of oneself and others. Pride puffs up and is angry at those who do not see but is also angry at those who do. The envious rage at not having what they think they deserve. Lust and gluttony deny bodily boundaries. The glutton binges and then purges so the cycle can be repeated. The lustful does as well: "In its most extreme forms . . . lust attempts to increase its pleasure through the sensation or infliction of pain. Lust never arrives at the throne of grace. Lust never comes." How dare another criticize what lust and gluttony demand? As for avarice and sloth, Keizer points out that they are both death wishes. "The slothful spouse and the avaricious spouse are both absentees. They're no fun. They inspire a sense of bereavement in those who love them. They're as good as dead." Anger is kindled when loved ones step in and try to shake some life into the dying.

Keizer's abiding concern is with anger as a response to an imagined sense of disproportion that usually starts in the mind. The angry person assumes that others are fully aware of his or her deepest thoughts and values and really do intend this or that slight.

Fear fuels anger, especially when one's projects or principles appear to be threatened. There is also the fear of suffering. Keizer relates the story of going to a choral presentation at which his young daughter would be performing, but his enjoyment of the concert was constantly interrupted by a noisy woman behind him. He did not ask the woman to be quiet, reasoning that she would little care for the feelings of a total stranger if she could not even be silent when her child was performing. The author did not move to some other part of the audience but instead chose to suffer in place, remembering that the love engendered by Christ drives away fear and that fear is often the fear of suffering. "If so," he writes, "what must I suffer in order to maintain some semblance of humanity? And is it as unbearable as I fear? . . . Whom do I love, and what does that love require? Sometimes it requires me to wield my anger like a sharp sword. But more often it requires me to suffer, and to do so fearlessly and without complaint." Anger refuses to embrace suffering.

The author identifies himself as an ordinary, middle-aged resident of a small town, a heterosexual, feminist-leaning Episcopalian often struck by the moral ambiguity of anger: "It is possible, for example, to have every right to be angry and still to do something wrong as a result." In his essay on what to teach children about anger he writes: "I can get mad or I cannot get mad, but God is still God, and therefore, why get mad? If that sounds less than clear, it is because I have intuited the truth much more than I have lived it. In a very real sense, I have chosen to write about anger because I did not have enough material to write about faith."

Midway in *The Enigma of Anger* Keizer presents portraits of mythological angry men and women, from Agamemnon in Homer's *Iliad* (750 B.C.E.) and King Saul in the Old Testament to Clytemnestra, Agamemnon's wife and sister of Helen of Troy, and Medea, spurned by the Greek Jason after she helped him obtain the fabled Golden Fleece. The author concludes that "one cannot escape the impression that the men slept in the beds they made, whereas the women merely woke up in the same beds in which they were born, suddenly unable to sleep," aware of their being used by men.

In examining anger in the home, Keizer suggests that the very nature of domestic work enables women to control their anger better than men are able to (which should give men something to think about). Household work calls a person to deal with the material world, a world of cooking and cleaning and making connections with other selves. Domestic chores bring a person away from self-absorbed abstractions to a world of particulars; they are a discipline that puts needs over feelings. Anger puts feelings over needs.

The household of faith, Keizer finds, is also beset with illness, especially as Christian teaching makes faith into feeling and denies the objective covenant relationship with God. "Given what we have already said about anger as a thing in the head, we can readily see the potential for anger in churches organized as loose confederations of subjective sovereign states." In the end, Keizer says, much of the anger some profess at the institutional church is really anger against the mercy of God which reaches down even to the objects of one's so-called righteous anger.

In the world, as well as in the church, there is an unwillingness of some to respect common courtesy. Speech codes help, and Keizer writes that he is frequently angry at himself for violating them. (Certainly "political correctness" can run amuck: "The problem with political correctness," he says, "is that most of us tend to be a good deal more zealous about taking offense than preventing it. . . . If instead of becoming more courteous, each of us labors to become more reflexively fastidious, we may wind up being too diverse even to appreciate diversity.") Keizer offers his own pithy speech code, advising himself "Never [to] use knowledge or vocabulary to exclude another person. This is no different from eating bread in the presence of the hungry." "Be wary of prescribing commandments," he writes at the end of his list. "Break any code for the sake of unsentimental compassion. A noble silence is not always the opposite of noise. Nor is hatred always the opposite of love. Sometimes dogma is."

There are moments, however, when anger comes of grace. Moses was filled with holy wrath and broke the tablets of God's law when he saw the idolatry of the people. Righteous anger moves beyond the mind into the world and in this Keizer sees a parable of the Incarnation in which the power of God was made manifest in a child who was sent to heal the wounds of sin.

Keizer recognizes that, though anger can be full of grace, it most often falls into the categories of selfish excess or misdirected energy. He concludes with a Buddhist sentiment to be more mindful (though he rejects Buddhist nonattachment). It is important, he writes, as one moves out into the world, to recognize oneself, or at least one's sibling, in the angry person and to beware of the certitude anger implies. Emotions are important in God's service and they can be redeemed. "God herself stands as proof that wrath and mercy can coexist. The One who breaks the rocks does not break the bruised reed." There is more: "[T]he Consuming Fire Who Is God allows us our own fire, however much it fumes and stinks at times. We are permitted our share of honest fury."

Written in the shadow of the terrorist attacks on the World Trade Center and the Pentagon on September 11, 2001, Keizer's words suggest that the real danger is not "honest fury" but rather the absence of emotion, the cool calculation of the torturer. Perhaps only the properly angry can call a halt to the actions of those who think they are serving God by suicide. The *Enigma of Anger* is a humane treatment of an emotion that is both dangerous and essential.

Dan Barnett

Sources for Further Study

Booklist 98 (August, 2002): 1891.
Christianity Today 46 (November 18, 2002): 86.
Publishers Weekly 249 (August 12, 2002): 297.
Sojourners Magazine 31 (November/December, 2002): 45.

ESSAYS ON MUSIC

Author: Theodor W. Adorno (1903-1969)
Edited, with notes and introduction, by Richard Leppert
Translated from the German by Susan H. Gillespie and
   others
Publisher: University of California Press (Berkeley). 752
   pp. $75.00; paperback $34.95
Type of work: Fine arts, history, media, philosophy, and
   sociology

∽

These seminal essays on music's relationships to mo-
dernity, media, and society by noted musicologist-social
scientist-philosopher Adorno are greatly enhanced by edi-
tor Richard Leppert's insightful commentaries and by new
translations from the German originals

∽

    The reputation of Theodor W. Adorno continues to grow. A powerful and wide-ranging intellectual whose voluminous writings embraced such seemingly disparate fields as philosophy and political theory, Adorno was in the vanguard of those twentieth century thinkers who seriously examined the place and role of the arts against the backdrop of modern society in both its capitalistic and totalitarian manifestations. Although Adorno wrote at length across the humanities and social sciences, it was music that was his muse, his passion, and the subject to which he returned time and time again.

    Born in Frankfurt, Germany, in 1903, Adorno, an only child, enjoyed the benefits of being raised by loving and prosperous parents. His rigorous intellectual training included tutoring in philosophy by Siegfried Kracauer (who later gained fame as a film theorist). There were also demanding studies of classical piano and composition that extended from his childhood to his early twenties. In 1924, at the age of twenty-one, he completed a doctorate in philosophy at Frankfurt's Johann Wolfgang Goethe University, which encompassed studies in philosophy, sociology, psychology, and music. It was during this period that Adorno formed important and lasting friendships with Max Horkheimer (1895-1973) and Walter Benjamin (1892-1940), the founders of the influential Institute of Social Research (commonly known as the Frankfurt School) in Frankfurt in 1923. During the 1920's, Adorno also became a public intellectual, balancing scholarly work with music journalism, a regimen that continued throughout his life. Adorno's enduring intellectual legacy can be traced through an extensive bibliography which includes hundreds of journalistic commentaries as well as an array of scholarly books and papers, many of which were published by the Institute of Social Research, which he formally joined in 1938 during its American exile.

~

Theodor W. Adorno, the noted German musicologist-sociologist-philosopher, was a principal member of the Institute of Social Research (now best known as the Frankfurt School). His important writings include Ästhetische Theorie *(1970;* Aesthetic Theory, *1984) and, with Max Horkheimer,* Dialektik der Aufklärung *(1969;* The Dialectic of Enlightenment, *1979).*

~

Editor Richard Leppert is a Distinguished Professor of Humanities and Cultural Studies and Literature at the University of Minnesota, and the author of Art and the Committed Eye: The Cultural Functions of Imagery *(1996) and* The Sight of Sound: Music, Representation, and the History of the Body *(1993).*

~

Following his death in 1969, Adorno's influence in music circles diminished. In place of his sophisticated, multilayered expositions which discussed music in its sociological, psychological, political, and technological dimensions, musicologists and music critics of the 1970's practiced a more formalistic approach devoted to internal analyses of individual compositions with little reference to the social conditions that gave rise to them. In short, Adorno was regarded by the formalists as impressionistic. Adorno's influence was further attenuated since much of his work had not been translated into English; moreover, due to often incompetent translations, those works available in English often missed the nuances of Adorno's ideas and style. In the 1980's, as music and humanities scholars increasingly grounded their work within the social and cultural milieus of their subjects, the cross-disciplinary Adorno increasingly came to be seen as an inspiration and, indeed, a model worthy of emulation. There were also fresh reappraisals of Adorno by scholars such as Martin Jay and Rose Rosengard Subotnik, who were crucial in helping position Adorno as central to the development of the discourses in the burgeoning fields of qualitative music sociology and critical theory. These discourses are now further enriched by the publication of *Essays on Music*, which enlarges the historical and contemporary appreciation of Adorno's scholarly and journalistic legacy.

Essays on Music, which includes twenty-seven of Adorno's key pieces (almost half of which appear in English for the first time), is more than an anthology. Indeed, thanks to the erudition and stylistic grace of editor Richard Leppert's copious and insightful annotations, the massive tome reads like a conversation across the years. While allowing a better appreciation of Adorno's often complex ideas and the specific historical moments out of which they appeared, Leppert is equally adept at underscoring the relevance of Adorno's work to the present. The inclusion of Adorno's "The Radio Symphony" (1941) and Leppert's astute commentary on it illustrate the point.

Leppert first paints the historical backdrop. Adorno, having just arrived in the United States from Nazi Germany in 1938, begins work on the Rockefeller Foundation-funded Princeton Radio Research Project, an appointment arranged by his friend Max Horkheimer. After two years, funding for Adorno's radio music division is cut off, largely because of Adorno's unwillingness to adapt to the narrowly empirical social science methods of project director Paul Lazarsfeld. Leppert explains that while Lazarsfeld amassed survey data in order to forecast and control consumer behavior (often at the behest of the broadcasting industry), Adorno pressed for a decidedly qualitative—and, one might add, humanistic—approach that sought to map the larger scale social, cultural, and psychological powers of modern media. As Leppert points out, the fundamental argument between empirical and qualitative approaches to social science still rages. In similar fashion, Leppert effectively parses Adorno's argument against the presumption that radio—and, by extension, later technologies for disseminating art such as television—can democratize high culture works such as a Beethoven symphony, thus calling into question, for example, the high arts agenda of American public television.

The informed "dialogue" between Adorno and Leppert is made even more extraordinary as a result of Leppert's meticulous scholarship, clarity, and cultural breadth and, perhaps most significantly, his empathy with Adorno the intellectual as well as Adorno the man. In addition to his astute commentaries on Adorno's essays, Leppert contributes a lengthy and lucid eighty-two page introduction, a sweeping biography that backgrounds the intellectual streams within which Adorno's thought developed. Leppert's introduction also includes warmly revealing details such as Adorno's admiration for Charlie Chaplin's *Modern Times* (1936), a film that, like much of Adorno's own work, challenged the supposed benefits of modernity. Equally poignant is Leppert's account of Adorno patiently tutoring novelist Thomas Mann in the intricacies of twelve-tone serialism as the great novelist was in the throes of writing *Doctor Faustus: The Life of the German Composer Adrian Leverkühn as Told by a Friend* (1948). Leppert is a well-read and gracious scholar whose informative footnotes brim with citations to secondary sources that pay deserved credit to an impressive number of colleagues. *Essays on Music* also benefits greatly from the new and felicitous translations of Susan H. Gillespie (and others) who catch the cadence as well as the substance of Adorno's notoriously difficult prose.

Following Leppert's introduction, *Essays on Music* is organized into four sections: "Locating Music: Society, Modernity, and the New"; "Culture, Technology, and Listening"; "Music and Mass Culture"; and "Composition, Composers, and Works." Each section is prefaced with an in-depth commentary by Leppert. A comprehensive twenty-eight page bibliography and a useful thirty-one page index add immensely to the book's utility as a key Adorno reference. A listing of the twenty-seven pieces included in *Essays on Music* and their original publication dates provides a useful overview of the range of issues surveyed by Adorno over the course of his five-decade-long career as a public and scholarly commentator on music.

The first group of essays, "Locating Music: Society, Modernity, and the New," sketches Adorno's attempts to situate music in modernity, stressing music's relationship to history in general and to its culturally produced meanings in particular. Included here is the pivotal "On the Contemporary Relationship of Philosophy and Music" (1953), which outlines Adorno's claim that philosophy is basic to musical understanding. Among other evocatively titled essays in this section are "Music, Language, and Composition" (1956); "Why Is the New Art So Hard to Understand?" (1931); "On the Problem of Musical Analysis" (1969); "The Aging of the New Music" (1955); and "The Dialectical Composer" (1934).

The second grouping of essays, "Culture, Technology, and Listening," reveals Adorno's concern with the social and cultural consequences of music consumed through such technologies as the radio and phonograph and his skepticism of the supposed capacity of the media to bring the arts to the masses. Interestingly, Adorno softened this virtually lifelong critique of mediated music in "Opera and the Long Playing Record" (1969), in which he takes a more optimistic view of modern mass media. The other essays in this section are "The Radio Symphony" (1941); "The Curves of the Needle" (1927/1965); "The Form of the Phonograph Record" (1934); "On the Fetish-Character in Music and the Regression of Listening" (1938); and "Little Heresy" (1965).

In the third set of essays, Leppert presents Adorno's most important and controversial critiques of popular music, including what Adorno, writing in the early 1930's, took to be jazz. In aggregate, these essays suggest that music in the modern age, whether highbrow or lowbrow, or whether produced under capitalism or totalitarianism, is organized through a production process increasingly driven by centralization and profit, a process that has inexorably eroded music's traditional role in the service of truth, individuality, and emancipation. Here, one finds "What National Socialism Has Done to the Arts" (1945); "On the Social Situation of Music" (1932); "On Popular Music" (1941); "On Jazz" (1936); "Farewell to Jazz" (1933); "Kitsch" (c. 1932); and "Music in the Background" (1934).

The fourth and concluding section, "Composition, Composers, and Works," brings together essays on the six classical composers—Ludwig von Beethoven, Richard Wagner, Gustav Mahler, Arnold Schoenberg, Alban Berg, and Igor Stravinsky— about whom Adorno wrote most extensively. As Leppert points out, Adorno's musical interests were mostly limited to the study of Western modernity, beginning with the rise of the post-French Revolution bourgeoisie and ending with the music of his own time. An articulate and faithful advocate of the classical avant-garde, Adorno, in his early years, wrote passionately on the serial works of Schoenberg and Berg; after World War II, that passion reappeared in his writings on such postwar composers as John Cage, Pierre Boulez, and Karl-Heinz Stockhausen. In this section, the accomplishments of Adorno's heroes (Beethoven, Mahler, Schoenberg, and Berg) are measured dialectically against the shortcomings of Adorno's flawed antiheroes (Wagner and Stravinsky). The essays constituting this section include "Late Style in Beethoven" (1937); "Alienated Masterpiece: The *Missa Solemnis*" (1959); "Wagner's Relevance for Today" (1963); "Mahler Today" (1930); "Marginalia on Mahler" (1936); "The Opera *Wozzeck*" (1929); "Towards an Understanding of Schoenberg" (1955/ 1967); and "Difficulties" (1964, 1966).

Essays on Music, again in large part due to Leppert's illuminating commentaries and Gillespie's new and nuanced and readable translations, is at once a landmark contribution to Adorno scholarship and a multifaceted prod to serious thinking on music. While *Essays on Music* is essential for scholars working in the areas of qualitative music sociology and critical studies and the general critique of modernity, it is also of substantive use to serious nonspecialist readers seeking insights into such provocative issues as why so little contemporary classical music is performed or loved, and why the art-music tradition seems increasingly less central to contemporary culture. Finally, and in contrast to musicology's formalists, Adorno provides a reminder that music does not exist as sets of hermetically sealed relationships among specified sequences of musical events. Instead, Adorno insists on a fully interactive and interdisciplinary approach. If the creation, dissemination, and reception of music is to be fully understood and appreciated, it must be examined within and against the larger contexts of culture, sociology, psychology, philosophy, politics and, especially in terms of modernity, technology.

Chuck Berg

Sources for Further Study

Los Angeles Times Book Review, August 25, 2002, p. 5.
The New York Times, September 14, 2002, p. B9.

EVERYTHING IS ILLUMINATED

Author: Jonathan Safran Foer (1977-   )
Publisher: Houghton Mifflin (Boston). 288 pp. 24.00
Type of work: Novel
Time: 1791-1998
Locale: Odessa, Lutsk, Lvov, and Trachimbrod, Ukraine

≈

A young American writer visits the Ukraine seeking the woman who saved his grandfather's life during the Holocaust and is guided on his search by a young Ukrainian and his grandfather

≈

Principal characters:
> JONATHAN SAFRAN FOER, a young American writer
> ALEXANDER (ALEX) PERCHOV, Jonathan's guide and translator
> GRANDFATHER, Alex's grandfather
> BROD, Jonathan's great-great-great-great-great-grandmother
> YANKEL, Brod's adoptive father
> SHALOM/SAFRAN (THE KOLKER), Brod's husband
> SAFRAN, Jonathan's grandfather
> ZOSHA, Safran's first wife
> THE GYPSY, Safran's mistress
> LISTA, the last survivor of Trachimbrod
> SAMMY DAVIS JUNIOR JUNIOR, Alex's grandfather's dog

Jonathan Safran Foer's remarkable first novel explores Jewish life in the Ukraine during the late eighteenth and early nineteenth centuries and in the 1930's and 1940's. *Everything Is Illuminated* is, however, much more. It is as much about the nature of storytelling as about the story it tells. Foer's style and narrative technique make the impact of his dramatic, funny, sad story even greater.

Foer is also one of the protagonists, visiting the Ukraine in 1997 seeking Augustine, a woman who saved his grandfather, Safran, during the Holocaust. (The novel is inspired by a real journey for this purpose.) Safran's first wife, Zosha, died during the Holocaust and he met his second wife in a displaced-persons camp. Safran died suddenly shortly after immigrating to the United States. Jonathan's grandmother has given him a photograph of Augustine, and he hopes to find her still alive and also to find Trachimbrod, the shtetl where his grandfather had lived.

Jonathan's guide and translator is Alex, who is curious about America, where he hopes to settle someday. Alex's sometimes distant father works for Heritage Touring, which guides American Jews to locations in their ancestors' homeland. Because Alex does not have a driver's license, they are accompanied on their journey by Alex's grandfather (also named Alex), who drives although he claims to be legally blind, and the grandfather's flatulent dog, Sammy Davis Junior Junior.

The structure of *Everything Is Illuminated* is complicated. There are Alex's letters to Jonathan after the writer has returned to America. In these, Alex talks about his family life with his father, his beloved thirteen-year-old brother (Little Igor), grandfather, and Sammy. He comments on the manuscript in progress that Jonathan has been sending him. Alex also acknowledges Jonathan's observations about his eccentric style of English. Then there are the chapters narrated by Alex describing the search for Augustine.

The other sections of the novel are Jonathan's narratives about two of his ancestors, his great-great-great-great-great grandmother, Brod, and

Born in Washington, D.C., Jonathan Safran Foer attended Princeton University and has worked as a receptionist at a public relations firm, a jewelry salesman, and a morgue assistant. He is the editor of the anthology A Convergence of Birds: Original Fiction and Poetry Inspired by the Work of Joseph Cornell *(2001). His short stories have been published in* Conjunctions *and* Paris Review. *He lives in Queens, New York.*

his grandfather, Safran. In 1791, when Brod is an infant, the wagon of her father, Trachim, tumbles into the river Brod, and only the baby is rescued. The shtetl holds a lottery for her custody, and she is won by the seventy-two-year-old Yankel, who names her for the river where she was found. In a later development, Yankel wins another contest and renames the shtetl Trachimbrod. Brod grows up thinking Yankel is her father.

Brod gives new meaning to Yankel's life. His two children are dead and his wife has left him. Born Safran, he had been a leading citizen in the shtetl until he lost his usurer's license following a scandal and trial. Leaving the shtetl, he returns three years later as Yankel, the name of the bureaucrat who ran away with his wife, and resumes his previous life. The myriad ways in which people are unable to control their destinies and their efforts to do so are one of Foer's many themes. Yankel sees the baby as a chance to live without shame.

The shtetl comes to have an elaborate celebration on Trachimday, reenacting the baby's rescue from the river, but Yankel never tells the young Brod she is the subject of this event. Shielding her from the truth about her origin and himself, he creates stories to distract her, even inventing a perfect wife he lost somewhere in the distant past, composing letters from her to himself. So that he will not lose touch with the truth, Yankel begins writing fragments of his life story on the ceiling of his bedroom. Foer constantly examines the elusiveness of truth, the randomness of memory, and the ways art can be used to capture and control them.

By the age of ten, Brod is the most desirable female in the shtetl, but she is also the most melancholy, discovering 613 unique sadnesses. She loves the idea of love even though she can love no one, not even Yankel. People can live together and care for each other without truly knowing each other, seeing only themselves in the other person. There are gaps of understanding in all relationships in the novel. Brod is not even certain about the truth of her own nature. Eventually, her beauty and enigmatic qualities drive every man in the shtetl, even those already married, to propose to her.

Then, one Trachimday, she meets her future husband Shalom, called the Kolker because he is from Kolki, and after several melodramatic events, including the death of Yankel, everything changes. She continues loving Shalom even after an accident at the flour mill leaves him with a piece of metal in his head that slowly drives him mad. Brod also changes his name to Safran, something she recalls seeing on Yankel's ceiling. Following his death, Safran's body is bronzed by the shtetl, becoming an almost religious totem to which everyone tells their troubles.

The story of Brod's descendant named Safran has many parallels to her story. Jonathan's grandfather has a withered arm that makes him strangely attractive to the women of the shtetl. From the age of ten (the same age at which Brod became desirable), Safran becomes the sexual plaything of the women of the shtetl. At seventeen, he is betrothed to Zosha, whom he barely knows, despite loving the Gypsy and having sex with Zosha's sister: "Wasn't everything that had happened, from his first kiss to this, his first marital infidelity, the inevitable result of circumstances over which he had no control?"

Safran's love life imitates the often chaotic forces at play in the stories of Brod and Yankel. The Gypsy kills herself because of his betrayal. On his wedding night in 1941, Safran finds he has fallen in love with Zosha even as their house rocks from the bombs of the approaching German army. Only a few days later, the Nazis begin rounding up the Jews.

Moving back to 1997, the search for Augustine leads Jonathan, Alex, and Grandfather to an old woman they first think is the object of their quest. She turns out, however, to be Lista, whose husband was killed in a freak accident before their marriage was consummated. She became Safran's lover and gives Jonathan a copy of William Shakespeare's play *Hamlet* which his grandfather had given her. The odd twists and turns of fate are another of Foer's concerns. Lista is the only survivor of Trachimbrod, and her home is filled with boxes containing the remains of the shtetl. The boxes help keep alive the memory of a place that no longer exists.

The modern scenes are relatively lighthearted because of Alex's humor and Sammy's antics, until Lista is found. Then they approach the tragic poignancy of the Brod and Safran sections. Meeting Lista and hearing how the Nazis forced the Jews of Trachimbrod to betray one another forces Grandfather to face his betrayal of his best friend, Herschel, a Jew, during the war.

Grandfather is a compelling character because at first he seems of little consequence, but he grows in complexity during the quest for Augustine. His real or imagined blindness is a metaphor for his refusal to see the truth about himself and the world left in the rubble of Nazi and Soviet domination.

The search makes Alex wonder early on what Grandfather did during the war, because he has never mentioned it. Grandfather has never returned to his native town since the war because he wanted to build a life for his family without difficult choices and shame and death. When he learns about Herschel, Alex concludes that all people are responsible for one another. Alex's inherited guilt resembles Lista's survivor's guilt.

Foer uses Alex's letters and narration to balance the horrors of *Everything Is Illuminated*. In the letters, Alex mixes the ponderously formal with would-be hipness. He describes his fondness for nightlife: "I dig to disseminate very much currency at famous nightclubs in Odessa." He calls the Ukraine "a totally awesome former Soviet republic." The humor is accented by Alex's awareness that "my second tongue is not so premium."

More important is Alex's commentary on his account of the quest for Augustine and on Jonathan's work-in-progress: "I ruminated extricating Grandfather from the story, so that I would be the driver, but if he ever ascertained this, I am certain that he would be injured, and nor [sic] of us desire that, yes?" (Jonathan, who does not like dogs, asks Alex to eliminate Sammy.)

Alex, who sees himself as a collaborator, questions Jonathan about events in the Brod sections and struggles to understand her complex emotions. He begs Jonathan to find a way for Brod to be happy and is appalled at Jonathan's account of his grandfather's sexual adventures. Alex wonders what their obligation to the truth is. He wishes Jonathan could make the story of his family "more premium than life." As writers, he wonders if "there are any limits to how excellent we could make life seem."

Everything Is Illuminated is highly self-conscious in the postmodernist vein. Alex inserts parenthetical comments about why he includes details in his narrative even though he sometimes does not know why: "Here it is almost too forbidding to continue." Jonathan injects first-person intrusions into the Brod and Safran tales. When Yankel is awarded the baby, "We were to be in good hands." Because much of the Brod story has elements of Magical Realism, Jonathan even allows her glimpses of the future and of the Safran to come. On occasion, the two stories merge into one.

Foer plays seductive games with time. Because Alex's letters are written after Jonathan's visit to Ukraine, they often refer to events that have not yet taken place in the narrative. There is a reference to Herschel, with whom the reader is unfamiliar, many pages before Grandfather betrays him, and Grandfather's death is mentioned long before the reasons behind it. Trachimday is celebrated with such outbursts of sexual passion that the resulting glow can be seen from space by astronauts over 150 years later. This is also one of several literal and figurative illuminations throughout the novel.

Foer's method and style provide some necessary distance from the despair in the characters' lives but do not diminish their emotional impact. The scene in which Alex refuses to take no for an answer when Lista says she does not recognize anyone in the photograph of Augustine is wonderfully handled. It ends with her bursting into tears and admitting that she is all that is left of Trachimbrod. In her account of the day the Nazis came, Lista describes a pregnant woman who is shot but crawls away to safety. She lives but not the baby. Only much later does the reader realize that Lista is this woman and learn the identity of the father. The story is devastating the first time, and the realization of the complete truth is another jolt.

Everything Is Illuminated is an amazing debut novel, especially for a twenty-five-year-old writer, because it encompasses so much. Foer makes Trachimbrod a living, breathing place. That such a place could be obliterated is unimaginable. The novel is about guilt and responsibility, love and forgiveness, truth and illusion. It is also a commentary on the nature of art to transform or illuminate reality. Foer is not writing self-reflective fiction to be clever but to show how art and life converge into a hall of mirrors. Everything is not only illuminated but also connected. Despite its brevity, *Everything Is Illuminated* has an epic scope.

Michael Adams

Sources for Further Study

Booklist 98 (March 1, 2002): 1090.
Library Journal 127 (February 1, 2002): 130.
Los Angeles Times Book Review, April 28, 2002, p. 14.
The New York Times, April 22, 2002, p. E6.
The New York Times Book Review 107 (April 14, 2002): 8.
Publishers Weekly 249 (February 4, 2002): 48.
The Washington Post Book World, April 21, 2002, p. 5.

EVERYTHING'S EVENTUAL
Fourteen Dark Tales

Author: Stephen King (1947-   )

Publisher: Charles Scribner's Sons (New York). 459 pp.
$28.00

Type of work: Short fiction

Time: Primarily the twentieth century

Locale: The United States in both real and alternative dimensions

∼

King's first collection of short fiction in nine years gives the reader a little taste of everything, from the literary to standard horror fare

∼

Principal characters:

DINK EARNSHAW, a loser who, because of his special gift, suddenly finds himself working for a secret government agency

ALAN PARKER, a college student who hitchhikes his way home

ALFIE ZIMMER, a traveling salesman who collects graffiti in a beat-up notebook

ROLAND, the gunfighter from King's Dark Tower series

RICHARD KINNELL, a writer who buys a painting from a yard sale with dire consequences

With *Everything's Eventual: Fourteen Dark Tales*, author Stephen King returns again to the short-story collection (his last collection, *Nightmares and Dreamscapes*, was published in 1993). Between 1993 and 2002, King changed publishers, published *Bag of Bones* (1998) to critical acclaim, survived a bizarre near-fatal car accident (recounted in his 2000 memoir *On Writing*), and finally established himself as a literary writer with four stories in *The New Yorker* magazine.

At the same time, however, King had his share of criticism. In a 2002 article in the Internet newspaper *Salon*, critic Richard Blow suggested that King was starting to repeat himself, churning out one or two mediocre books a year, as if King was past caring about the art of writing. King himself had stated in *On Writing* that any writer who could not turn out a book a year should not really consider himself a writer. If that is the case, should readers expect King's work to be consistently interesting each time when King may be publishing material just to meet a self-imposed deadline?

Everything's Eventual is a solid collection for many reasons, primarily because the stories range from the typical cheap-thrills horror story to something very classical. King's stories in this collection fall into three categories: the basic horror stories that King is known for, miscellaneous stories that first appeared in places other than the tradi-

Stephen King is perhaps the best-known and most successful author of all time. Every one of his more than forty books—from Carrie *(1974) to* On Writing *(2000)—has been a best-seller. His other recent books include* Bag of Bones *(1998) and* Hearts in Atlantis *(1999). In 1996, he won an O. Henry Award for "The Man in the Black Suit." He and his wife live in Bangor, Maine.*

tional printed page, and literary stories. The four literary stories are those originally published in *The New Yorker* ("The Man in the Black Suit," "All That You Love Will Be Carried Away," "The Death of Jack Hamilton," and "That Feeling, You Can Only Say What It Is in French"). When "The Man in the Black Suit" furthered King's sudden literary stride by winning an O. Henry Award in 1996, King was seen in a new light.

Ironically, the story for which King won the literary award is actually the weakest of his so-called literary works. "The Man in the Black Suit" is King's homage to Nathaniel Hawthorne (1804-1864) and Hawthorne's story "Young Goodman Brown," but where it fails is in the simplest level of storytelling. While the story is a tribute to Hawthorne, the tale is not truly original; the setting and the plot ("boy meets the devil") are secondhand. While King has before been inspired by stories that others have told time and again, his final products typically feel fresher than this award-winning story.

"All That You Love Will Be Carried Away" is both sad and unique. Alfie Zimmer is a depressed traveling salesman in the winter heartland of Lincoln, Nebraska, on the last night of his life before he commits suicide. The only thing that gives him joy is a beat-up notebook full of obscure and obscene graffiti that Zimmer has collected on his travels through the years. The last one he collects—"All that you love will be carried away"—is one that gives him pause. It is one of the few thoughtful pieces he has ever found, and he does not want to leave it for people to find and interpret as nothing more than a curious suicide note. All the unusual pieces King brings together make this one of his best tales ever.

King is always trying new ways to get his stories to his audience, as well as trying to keep himself amused. In 1996 he serialized six books, one book per month (collected as *The Green Mile*), not giving himself time to ponder or the opportunity to change anything, thereby eliminating his chance to second-guess himself. It was something the literary world had not seen since Charles Dickens's serialized novels in the nineteenth century, and King did it for exactly that reason. By doing this, he opened the door to other options. He published "1408" and "In the Deathroom" as audio books only, while "Lucky Quarter" appeared in the most mainstream of media, the national newspaper *USA Weekend*.

Most famously, he first published "Riding the Bullet" as an electronic book (an eBook) as an inspiration to other writers to try publishing methods other than the traditional print. What is the difference between an eBook and a traditional book in terms of story? Nothing, and that was exactly the point King was trying to make.

King scared the publishing world by self-publishing "Riding the Bullet"—and later his 2000 eBook series *The Plant*—although he was only following a tradition of self-publishing that includes noted authors William Wordsworth (1770-1850) and Oscar Wilde (1854-1900). What made King's book unique was that it was published electronically on the Internet and for a fraction of the cost of a printed book. More important, King wanted to prove that anybody with a minuscule amount of time, money, and computer knowledge could do the same thing. Even though King was not the first person to do this, King single-handedly legitimized the eBook as another mainstream creative outlet for writers.

These challenges to traditional publishing, as well as his literary avenues, brought King even more attention than before. King had been considered a genre writer only, not the author of mainstream works like Saul Bellow (born 1915) or Ernest Hemingway (1899-1961). King may be the most popular genre writer ever, and to readers on both sides of the literary divide this is a problem. For horror fans, King's mainstream image is not frightening enough, and for mainstream readers the fact that King comes from a school in which, they believe, great literature is the last thing on the writer's mind cheapens the established upper-class plateau where literary books reside. For many readers, the only situations in which writers cross over from genre writing to literature occur when the author has been publishing for a very long time, or is dead, as with Edgar Allan Poe (1809-1849).

King published *Roadwork* in 1981 under the pseudonym Richard Bachman for exactly this reason: King was trying to write a literary novel instead of the genre fiction his fans were used to, but it was not a style that he was comfortable writing in at the time; hence, the use of a pseudonym instead of writing under his real name. He wrote "The Body" (in *Different Seasons*) in 1982 to critical acclaim, but because King was considered a horror writer it was hard for people to think of him as anything else. By the end of the 1990's, however, because his work was being published in *The New Yorker* (as opposed to genre magazines such as *Fantasy and Science Fiction*), King was able to reach an even wider audience than before and show readers that he was more than just a horror writer. This time, people noticed.

Literary and eBook stories aside, *Everything's Eventual* also provides some of the typical horror readings one would expect from King. One of the best tales in the collection, the title story, is about teenager Dink Earnshaw and his ability to draw signs and symbols and then make them become real. He is recruited by Mr. Sharpton, who works for a secret government agency that can use Dink's powers (but whether that use is for the good of the world remains to be seen.) King is at his best when he describes the world as seen by Dink and other adolescents, a world where one does not fit in. He has explored this theme repeatedly over the years in novels such as *It* (1986), *Firestarter* (1980) and *The Girl Who Loved Tom Gordon* (1999). Mr. Sharpton's secret agency, while never named, is hauntingly familiar to King readers; in fact, it could be the same organization that was interested in extrasensory perception (ESP) in *Firestarter*.

For fans of King's Dark Tower series, King delivers a mininovel called "The Little Sisters of Eluria." Set in the same cross-pollinated world as previous Dark Tower works (where the world is hauntingly familiar to the reader, yet at the same time very different), this is a prequel to the entire series. Prequels, with rare exceptions, rarely equal or exceed the quality of the original since there is no suspense as to the overall outcome of the story or series, but King builds suspense by blending an Old West storyline with his version of a very familiar horror theme, and it works.

Other stories in the collection include "Autopsy Room Four," about a man who wakes up but cannot move as an autopsy is performed on him (told in first person for extra fright), and "The Road Virus Heads North," which concerns a painting that keeps changing to a scene of horror that has just occurred and is getting closer to its new owner. "L.T.'s Theory of Pets" is the story of L.T. and his tale of woe over his estranged wife, Lulubelle (this is the story King reads to audiences whenever he gets the chance.) While it is King's favorite, the writing is not as convincing as in other King stories. On the other hand, King's version of hell in "That Feeling, You Can Only Say What It Is in French," would stand among the best episodes of the television series *The Twilight Zone.*

The literary and genre classifications of King's writing, while interesting, ultimately do not make any difference. The stories stand or fall on their own merit, and the majority of *Everything's Eventual* stands up very well. Unfortunately, the first two stories—"Autopsy Room Four" and "The Man in the Black Coat"—are the weakest. Also, "The Road Virus Heads North" is similar to King's "The Sun Dog" (published in 1990's *Four Past Midnight*), about a camera which keeps taking pictures of a demonic dog as it gets closer and closer to the camera's owner, making the argument that King is recycling old materials seem more plausible. Even so, three weak stories out of fourteen is not that bad an average to maintain, and to some readers *Everything's Eventual* will read much better than other King collections that drag on far too long (such as *Nightmares and Dreamscapes*).

In the collection's introduction, King says that he writes for the sake of writing, period. While this statement can be interpreted to prove their point equally by people who love or who hate his stories, it ultimately says that King believes it is his stories that are of primary importance, not their genre classification. In 2002, King said that within a few years he would retire from writing for publication and would only publish something if he thought it was worth the effort. Whether this is the last collection from King or not, it is just the right length to be one of his best.

Kelly Rothenberg

Sources for Further Study

Library Journal 127 (April 1, 2002): 144.
The New York Times, March 18, 2002, p. E7.
The New York Times Book Review 107 (April 14, 2002): 6.
Publishers Weekly 249 (March 18, 2002): 73.
The Times, April 6, 2002, p. 13.
USA Today, March 19, 2002, p. D1.

THE EYRE AFFAIR

Author: Jasper Fforde (1961-   )
First published: 2001, in Great Britain
Publisher: Viking (New York). 374 pp. $23.95
Type of work: Novel
Time: 1985
Locale: An alternate-universe Great Britain, particularly
London, Swindon, and the People's Republic of Wales

≈

Thursday Next, a literary detective in the government's Special Operations Network, must foil master criminal Acheron Hades' fiendish plot to kidnap Jane Eyre and hold her for ransom

≈

Principal characters:
    THURSDAY NEXT, veteran of the Crimean War, currently a detective
        charged with investigating cases of literary crime
    COLONEL NEXT, Thursday's father, a time-traveling ChronoGuard on the
        lam for acts he may not yet have committed
    ACHERON HADES, the world's third most-wanted criminal, a fiendish
        mastermind who was formerly Thursday's university English pro-
        fessor
    FELIX TABULARASA, Hades' henchman
    JACK SCHITT, putative head of internal security, actually working for the
        advanced weapons division, of the all-powerful military-industrial
        Goliath Corporation
    "Spike" Stoker, a special operative for Swindon's Vampire and Were-
        wolf Disposal Operations
    MYCROFT NEXT, Thursday's uncle, the inventor of the Prose Portal, a
        machine that allows people to enter works of literature and interact
        with the characters inside
    POLLY NEXT, his wife, Thursday's aunt
    LANDEN PARKE-LAINE, Thursday's former fiancé, now a successful
        author
    VICTOR ANALOGY, head of Swindon's LiteraTec operations
    BOWDEN CABLE, Thursday's partner at the Swindon LiteraTec division
    EDWARD ROCHESTER, hero of the novel *Jane Eyre*

Welsh novelist Jasper Fforde spent fourteen years working as a cameraman in the film industry before turning his ambitions to the printed page. *The Eyre Affair*, featuring LiteraTec Thursday Next, is his first novel (a second, *Lost in a Good Book*, was published in Britain in the summer of 2002 and he is under contract to write two more), and despite its almost compulsively literary frame of reference, the effects of a

Jasper Fforde worked for almost twenty years in the film industry as an assistant cameraman. His film credits include Quills *(2000),* Goldeneye *(1995), and* The Mask of Zorro *(1998). He lives in Wales and has written a sequel to* The Eyre Affair *titled* Lost in a Good Book *(published in Britain in 2002), with more to follow.*

life in the movies are, for better and worse, quite evident.

The Eyre Affair is one of the latest examples of the trend toward the blurring of boundaries between literary genres, a testament to the attenuated influence of Magical Realism, which introduced elements of fantasy into literary fiction. The basic plot structure follows the conventions of the spy thriller, with a main character who is an iconoclastic investigator within a government agency—an agent of the Establishment who is nonetheless her own woman, with all the potential for conflict with not only the villains but also the reactionary forces on her own side that such a position entails. This underlying architecture is overlaid with a facade of alternate-universe elaboration. Although it is 1985, the Crimean War is still in progress, a martial morass that has absorbed the energies and resources of Britain and Russia for over 130 years. (As a result, Russia is still czarist, but Wales has broken away from England to form its own socialist republic; the Iron Curtain lies not between Western and Eastern Europe but along the Welsh Marches.) Cloning is commonplace and the most popular household pets are dodoes. Most importantly, classic literature is the currency of popular culture; movies, television, and rock and roll do not exist.

Thursday Next is an operative for the Literary Detective Division, SO-27, of the labyrinthine Special Operations Network (or SpecOps) in charge of maintaining public order. Since England is essentially a police state, there is a great deal of order to maintain. Thursday's father, for instance, is a rogue ChronoGuard, fighting a temporally incoherent rearguard (or possibly front line) battle against the Office for Special Temporal Stability. Thursday spends her time tracking down forgers and copyright infringers until she is loaned to SO-5, a SpecOps division so secret they will not reveal to her what, precisely, they do.

SO-5 is interested in Thursday because she is one of the few people able to identify master criminal Acheron Hades, the third-most-wanted man in the world. Hades is suspected of having stolen the original manuscript of Charles Dickens's *Martin Chuzzlewit* (1843-1844) for purposes that are no doubt nefarious. A stake-out goes awry, with Thursday's confederates (one of whom is a former lover, Filbert Snood) killed by Hades, Thursday only saved by the mysterious intervention of a figure who bears a strange resemblance to Edward Rochester, the hero of Charlotte Brontë's *Jane Eyre* (1847), and Hades apparently dead in a car crash. In the aftermath of the investigation, Thursday encounters Jack Schitt, the putative head of internal security for the Goliath Corporation, a military-industrial multinational that has used the ongoing Crimean conflict to become the power behind the nominal English government. Goliath is developing a plasma rifle that, it is rumored, will prove to be the key to England's victory. While recovering in the hospital, Thursday is visited by her own time-traveling future self, who advises her to take a job in Swindon, her home town.

When a job at the Swindon branch of LiteraTec opens up, Thursday takes her own advice and transfers.

It seems that Thursday's tour of duty in the Crimea was marked by disaster. In one of the few actual engagements between the English and Russians, Thursday's brother Anton was involved in some kind of military debacle that seems decidedly reminiscent of the charge of the Light Brigade; Thursday's fiancé Landen Parke-Laine, also Anton's best friend, publically blamed Anton for the disaster, a betrayal for which Thursday has never forgiven him. It also seems that in this alternate universe, *Jane Eyre* ends with Jane leaving Mr. Rochester to live in India with her cousins the Riverses.

In Swindon, Thursday visits her mother, Uncle Mycroft, and Aunt Polly. Mycroft is an inventor along the line of James Bond's Q; his latest invention is called the Prose Portal, a device for entering a text by means of its being eaten by genetically modified bookworms. If the worms are presented with a printed copy of a book, the person merely enters that copy; however, if the worms gain access to the original manuscript of a work, the person enters every single copy of the work and any actions the explorer takes within the text immediately manifest in all copies, forever altering the story. While Mycroft is testing the Portal by sending his wife into a copy of William Wordsworth's poem "I Wandered Lonely as a Cloud" (1807, rev. 1815), Hades (not dead after all) steals the copy of the poem with Polly trapped in it and thereby coerces Mycroft into assisting him in his nefarious plans. Hades, who was indeed behind the *Chuzzlewit* heist, uses the Portal to enter the original manuscript, kidnap a character named Mr. Quaverley, and murder him. The chapter devoted to the character thus disappears from every copy of the novel in existence, and Mr. Quaverley is reduced to a passing mention.

Thursday, meanwhile, settles into her new job with her new partner, Bowden Cable; strikes up a friendship with an operative in the Vampire and Werewolf Disposal Unit named Spike, who turns out to be a bit of a vampire himself; becomes reacquainted with Landen, now a highly successful author who still yearns for her but has become engaged to a gold digger named Daisy Mutlar; and is drawn into the search for Acheron Hades (still not dead, despite SpecOps's insistence to the contrary) and her uncle.

Hades steals the original manuscript of *Jane Eyre* and uses it to kidnap Jane and hold her for ransom; if the elimination of Mr. Quaverley resulted in the loss of a chapter, the elimination of Jane, the first-person narrator, would erase an entire novel. Thursday, assisted by Cable and their boss, Victor Analogy, tracks Hades to his lair in the People's Republic of Wales. Hades manages to escape back into the *Eyre* manuscript but Thursday follows him, entering the plot slightly before Hades. She avoids affecting the plot by lying low in the background of the narrative with the connivance of Mr. Rochester. When Hades finally makes his move, Bertha Rochester breaks out of the attic, sets the house on fire, and attacks Hades. Hades throws Bertha to her death from the roof, but Thursday finally manages to kill him with a silver bullet given her by Spike. The novel is saved but the ending has been irreversibly rewritten; with Bertha out of the way, Jane and Mr. Rochester marry.

Back in her own world, Thursday realizes, under the inspiration of Jane and Mr. Rochester, that she must reconcile with Landen and races to the church where he is about to marry Daisy. Much to her amazement, the wedding is actually stopped by Mr. Briggs, the lawyer from *Jane Eyre*, who reveals that Daisy is already married; Landen is left at the altar. Thursday's own happy ending concludes her own novel: Reader, she marries him.

The Eyre Affair is unmistakably clever. The bookworms, for instance, excrete punctuation marks from the source manuscript that turn up on the pages of *The Eyre Affair* ("Any'thing That The Hu'man Imag'ination Can Think Up, We Can Reproduce. I Look At The Port'al as Les's Of A Gateway To A Million Worlds, But More Like a Three Dim'ensional Photocopier. With It We Can Ma'ke Anything We Want; Even Another Portal—A H&held Version.") Most of the fun of the book comes from the puns and literary jokes, particularly the ongoing controversy over the authorship of Shakespeare's plays. One of the funniest scenes takes place at a performance of *Richard III* (1597, rev. 1623), which has turned into an audience participation event along the lines of the fan participation with the film *The Rocky Horror Picture Show*:

> Richard opened his mouth to speak and the whole audience erupted in unison:
> "*When* is the winter of our discontent?"
> "Now," replied Richard with a cruel smile, "is the winter of our discontent . . . made glorious summer by this son of York," continued Richard, limping to the side of the stage. On the word "summer" six hundred people placed sunglasses on and looked up at an imaginary sun.

At the same time, in comparison to the literature spoofed, *The Eyre Affair* is decidedly generic. The characters are flat stereotypes: the egomaniacal criminal mastermind, the tough, traumatized war-veteran-turned-cop, the bureaucratic superior with dubious allegiances, the double agent in the pay of an evil corporation. The literary references become overwhelming and sometimes downright contradictory: It is one thing to have a vampire hunter named Stoker in reference to Bram Stoker, the author of *Dracula* (1897); to nickname him "Spike" and make him a vampire himself, an obvious reference to the morally ambiguous vampire Spike on the current television series *Buffy the Vampire Slayer*, merely confuses the picture. The plot's parallelism with that of *Jane Eyre* eventually becomes contrived, and even in *The Eyre Affair*, Edward Rochester has more depth of character than Landen Parke-Laine, who appears to exist simply so that Thursday has someone to marry at the end.

Perhaps the most intriguing aspect of the novel is the rules that govern the insertion of a living person into the manuscript of a piece of literature. Each work is an entire world unto itself—surely the effect of reading a true work of the imagination—with events going on outside of the awareness of the work's narrator in which the inadvertent traveler may lurk. Thursday indeed runs into a Japanese tourist and his courier observing from the sidelines in *Jane Eyre*. Novels, plays, and poems are not so much works of "unreal" fiction as portals to other worlds. This aspect of his own fictional world is obviously one on which Fforde worked long and hard, an aspect not taken over wholesale from any genre. As a result, it is the aspect that works the best.

Leslie Ellen Jones

Sources for Further Study

The New York Times, February 12, 2002, p. E8.
The New York Times Book Review 107 (February 17, 2002): 17.
Publishers Weekly 248 (December 17, 2001): 69.
USA Today, February 21, 2002, p. B14.
The Washington Post Book World, April 11, 2002, p. 15.

THE FALL OF BERLIN, 1945

Author: Anthony Beevor (1946-   )
Publisher: Viking (New York). Illustrated. 490 pp.
   $29.95
Type of work: History
Time: Winter and spring of 1945
Locale: Berlin, Germany

~

As American, British, and Soviet forces raced toward Berlin in the closing days of World War II, Joseph Stalin decided that the Red Army had to be there first; in capturing Adolf Hitler's capital, he would avenge Nazi crimes and position himself to dominate postwar Germany

~

Principal personages:
   JOSEPH STALIN (1879-1953), first secretary of the Communist Party
   KONSTANTIN ROKOSSOVSKY (1896-1968), marshal of the Soviet Army, hero of the battles at Moscow and Stalingrad, and commander of the advance on Berlin
   GEORGI K. ZHUKOV (1896-1974), marshal of the Soviet Army
   IVAN KONEV (1897-1973), marshal of the Soviet Army
   ADOLF HITLER (1889-1945), chancellor of Germany, head of the Nazi Party
   JOSEPH GOEBBELS (1897-1945), Reichsminister of propaganda
   HEINZ GUDERIAN (1888-1954), commander of the Nazi forces defending the approaches to Berlin
   HEINRICH HIMMLER (1900-1945), head of the Schutzstaffel (SS), the Gestapo, and the concentration and extermination camps
   DWIGHT DAVID EISENHOWER (1890-1969), supreme commander of the Western armies

Only a few years ago, anyone willing to cross the Berlin Wall could easily imagine the desperate fighting that took place in the heart of this city in early 1945. Today this same visitor has to look hard and in the right places to see war damage or locate important sites such as Hitler's underground chancery. Thus, in 2003, as in 1933 or 1943, it is difficult to imagine the terrible fate that befell Berlin in those weeks. It is fitting that Anthony Beevor follows up his widely acclaimed volume on Stalingrad with this story of the equally hard-fought battle for Berlin, one in which the Red Army bled terribly for possession of a symbol rather than a city.

At the time of the Yalta meeting between Franklin D. Roosevelt, Winston Churchill, and Joseph Stalin in early 1945, it appeared that the Red Army would occupy most of Germany and certainly Berlin. Eisenhower was advancing cautiously in the

Rhineland, careful not to expose his flanks to a German counterattack, and he anticipated that his forces would not be able to cross the Rhine until the spring floods had subsided. However, when American troops captured the bridge at Remagen and General Patton forced separate crossings of the great river, it quickly became apparent that he could advance into the heart of Germany almost as fast as he could supply his vehicles with gasoline. Germans were eager to surrender to American and British troops be-

Antony Beevor was educated at Winchester and Sandhurst, then served five years with the 11th Hussars before resigning to become a professional writer. His Stalingrad *(1998) has been translated into nineteen languages and given numerous awards.*

cause both Goebbels and swiftly spreading rumor were telling them that they had to expect terrible retribution for the Nazi crimes in Russia, while offering hope that wonder weapons would reverse the battlefield situation within days or weeks.

Stalin understood the significance of this development. Therefore, while telling Eisenhower that Soviet forces were being directed toward Saxony (and encouraging the bombing of Dresden as part of this campaign), he gave orders to his marshals Zhukov and Konev to take Berlin immediately, no matter what it cost.

The German army, meanwhile, was completely disorganized. Whatever hope Guderian and his generals had of making effective resistance was spoiled by Hitler, who tied down experienced units and equipment in irrelevant fortresses that were soon far behind Soviet lines and diverted the few available reserves to hopeless offensive operations on scattered fronts; in return, Guderian received phantom armies and untrained, almost unarmed militia (Volksturm) units composed of half-grown children and aged men. Even so, Guderian prepared a strong defensive line along the mud flats of the Oder River, forty miles east of Berlin, where Zhukov's troops almost bled to death in their desperate and poorly coordinated assaults on the slippery slopes of the Seelow Heights. Guderian lacked reinforcements, fuel, and ammunition, but Hitler blamed this, as every other failure, on cowardice and treason.

Himmler, whose ineffective leadership on the Vistula River line was obscured somewhat by his theatrical performances at conferences with Hitler, demanded harsh punishment for incompetents and defeatists; meanwhile, despite his putative loyalty to the Führer, he was plotting ways to contact the West in order to negotiate a separate peace that would leave him as leader of Germany; the death camps had not yet been discovered, and he was blind to the reaction that civilized people would have when they learned of them. His SS units, used mainly to enforce his decrees against desertion and defeat, were unable and unwilling to fight alongside the regular army (the Wehrmacht).

As American troops reached the Elbe, Stalin increased the pressure on his marshals to capture Berlin quickly (and with it the scientists, equipment, and uranium involved in the German atomic bomb program). Soon Soviet troops were hitting one another with artillery and small arms fire in their frenzied and chaotic rush through the maze of canals and lakes of the metropolitan region; they soon discovered that massive bomb damage had clogged streets and made buildings into small forts.

Berlin itself had very few regular army forces committed to its defense, and many of those wanted to break out to the west, so as to avoid becoming Soviet prisoners. While Hitler brooded in his underground lair, his medal-covered cronies (known popularly as "golden pheasants") enjoyed one last drunken revel, young women facing rape and perhaps murder gave themselves to young men about to die, and children and old men were rounded up for a suicidal defense of the Führer's bunker. Gangs of SS police and Gestapo were executing deserters and fugitives from broken units. Water and sewage services were disrupted by devastating American and British bombing, and food could hardly be found (except at the Nazi officials' final parties).

Similarly, in the Soviet forces, special NKVD units searched for soldiers shirking their duty, forced released prisoners into front line duties, and executed SS soldiers wherever they found them. They rarely enforced orders against rape and looting, though official reports denied that such crimes ever happened.

The only effective Nazi force was the Waffen SS, composed of volunteers from occupied countries: Russia, Estonia, Denmark, and especially France. These rightwing fanatics had not been cut to pieces in earlier fighting, were well equipped (especially with the few King Tiger tanks that had been produced), and hated communism. Their snipers could take positions in tall buildings where the tank guns could not be elevated sufficiently to hit them and their infantry (together with youthful Volksturm members) could employ the antitank weapons known as Panzerfaust from basement windows with deadly effect.

As the Red Army tore into Berlin, it expressed its rage and frustration in an orgy of rape. Germans and Poles who lived through the experience of being conquered or liberated by Soviet troops vividly remember the sheer horror of these moments. Soviet soldiers wanted watches and women, and they took both whenever they had the chance. The chances were many, because officers understood that terror was a means of warfare, justified by Nazi crimes in Russia, and also understood the need to concentrate on pushing forward into Berlin without being distracted by the need to maintain discipline among the troops. In the long run, this would work strongly against official Soviet hopes for future friendships between the German and Russian peoples. In the short term, however, German highways and roads had been filled with refugees and deserters, long columns of fugitives that hindered convoys, but these masses rarely slowed the Soviet tanks, which would roll right over carts and light vehicles that failed to get out of the way.

Inside Berlin, civilians could hardly be told from combatants. Every bomb shelter was a potential center of resistance. Soviet soldiers could hardly be faulted for throwing grenades into the doorways first and asking questions later. Nurses refused to allow weapons in the hospitals, knowing that Russians would assume the soldiers had fought to the last moment and therefore deserved no pity; women destroyed portraits of Hitler and even pictures of husbands and sons in military uniforms; suicide was common, especially among the victims of gang rape and their families.

Hitler delayed his suicide, thereby guaranteeing that many tens of thousands of his followers would die as well; he ordered beaten commanders executed and broken units stripped of their medals. At last, drugged and perhaps insane, he shot himself, thereby giving his closest comrades the opportunity to quarrel over who now was the new head of state. Nazism, in its closing moments, showed its most perverted and criminal nature.

The storming of the Reichstag was a fitting climax to a relentless combat that had become an orgy of violence. Both armies were exhausted, inebriated, and fearful, but in the end Soviet numbers, weaponry, and determination prevailed. The last stages of the battle became a massacre, as German units fled westward, breaking through here and there, but mostly lost in the woods or hiding from Soviet aircraft and tanks, out of fuel and without food or ammunition. Somehow, in the confusion, many successfully escaped, crossing the Elbe under heavy fire. Those who did not make it went to Siberia for as long as nine years.

Seventy-eight thousand Soviet troops died taking Berlin and a quarter million were wounded in order to capture the German capital before the Americans or British could get there. These losses were unnecessary. Eisenhower saved American lives, not just from the resistance potentially offered by fanatic Nazis, but also from possible confrontations with Soviet troops. He probably saved even more British soldiers, who would have been sacrificed so that General Montgomery could strut about as the victor of Berlin (assuming that his habitually slow advance would have speeded up to reach the capital before Zhukov); Eisenhower diverted him to Denmark, thereby unintentionally saving that nation from Soviet occupation.

Once Berlin was occupied, Stalin took steps to assure that he would not have to deal with future "Decemberists," as the victorious soldiers of the Napoleonic wars were known after 1825, when they attempted to force the czar to make reforms which would turn Russia into a modern nation along the models they had seen in Germany and France. Stalin humiliated Zhukov, exiling him to a remote area; he ordered massive arrests of officers and soldiers, 135,000 in all, who unwisely wrote candid letters home; and he sent 1.5 million Soviet prisoners of war into the gulags or labor camps; then he turned on the Jews. Victory was attributed to Stalin alone. The incompetence of the Nazi leadership was hidden as thoroughly as Hitler's body: Zhukov and the world were allowed to believe that the archcriminal might somehow have escaped, to reappear at some future date and create a new fascist threat. Comrade Stalin had to remain the head of the party and the state, to protect communism against its many enemies, new and old.

William L. Urban

Sources for Further Study

The Atlantic Monthly 289 (June, 2002): 114.
Booklist 98 (May 15, 2002): 1569.
Library Journal 127 (May 15, 2002): 106.
The New York Review of Books 49 (May 23, 2002): 46.
The Washington Post Book World, May 19, 2002), p. 2.

FAMILY MATTERS

Author: Rohinton Mistry (1952-   )
Publisher: Alfred A. Knopf (New York). 448 pp.
  $26.00
Type of work: Novel
Time: The mid-1990's
Locale: Bombay, India

≈

*The story of how the plight of an elderly, bedridden man
affects all the members of his extended family*

≈

Principal characters:

> NARIMAN VAKEEL, a seventy-nine-year-old Parsi, a retired English professor
> COOMY CONTRACTOR, his ill-tempered, middle-aged stepdaughter
> JAL CONTRACTOR, her younger brother, a well-intentioned but easily intimidated man
> ROXANA CHENOY, Nariman Vakeel's kind-hearted daughter
> YEZAD CHENOY, her husband, a clerk at a sporting goods store
> MURAD CHENOY, their thirteen-year-old son
> JEHANGIR CHENOY, their nine-year-old son
> VIKRAM KAPUR, a Punjabi, Yezad's employer
> HUSAIN, a Muslim, Kapur's other employee

From the appearance of his first published work, the short story collection *Tales from Firozsha Baag* (1987), which appeared in the United States as *Swimming Lessons and Other Stories from Firozsha Baag* (1989), Rohinton Mistry has been recognized as an outstanding contemporary writer. His blend of unsentimental compassion and uncompromising realism, his sense of tragedy, and his gift for comedy have led critics to compare him to such other fiction writers as the Irish James Joyce, whose novel *Ulysses* (1922) described the thoughts and interactions of his characters during one day in Dublin; Leo Tolstoy, whose epic novel *War and Peace* (1865-1869) placed generals and aristocrats against the backdrop of Russia during the Napoleonic invasion; and Charles Dickens who, in works such as *David Copperfield* (1849-1850), recreated the England of his youth. Like these authors, Mistry aims at defining a people and a place. The setting and, in a sense, the subject of all of Rohinton Mistry's works is his native Bombay; however, he also uses Bombay as a metaphor for twentieth century India.

In his early works, Mistry sought to achieve his purpose with a small cast of characters functioning in a very limited area within the city. That was his approach in both *Tales from Firozsha Baag* and the novel *Such a Long Journey* (1991). By contrast,

A Fine Balance (1996) was panoramic, much like *War and Peace*, and appropriately so, since the aim of that novel was to show India during Indira Ghandi's national state of emergency in 1975, with its legal, political, and social structures in a shambles and some of its people murdered, others in flight.

With *Family Matters*, Mistry has returned to the narrower focus he used in his first two books. The characters involved in the main plot of this novel are all members of one extended family, along with a few close friends and neighbors, and the two additional characters in the subplot

Rohinton Mistry has won several awards for his novels, including the Governor General's Award, the Commonwealth Writers Prize, and the Smith Books/Books in Canada Award for Such a Long Journey *(1991).* A Fine Balance *(1996) won a Los Angeles Times* Book Award *and the Commonwealth Writers Prize for Best Novel.*

are a fellow employee of one of the family members and his employer. Moreover, this family is made up of Parsis, or Zoroastrians, members of one of India's smallest religious sects. However, the scope of *Family Matters* is much broader than one might assume, for it deals with an increasingly common problem, the care of an aging relative in declining health, and it treats this situation as a test of character. The members of the extended family are seen choosing to be spiteful or forgiving, selfish or selfless, tolerant or intolerant, and suffering the consequences of the choices they have made.

Nariman Vakeel, the patriarch of the family and to some extent the central character in the novel, is a gentle, witty man, a retired English professor, whose former students still have fond memories of him. He has been living in his large home with his stepdaughter, Coomy Contractor, and his stepson, Jal Contractor, both of whom are unmarried. Coomy and Jal both chose to keep the name of their birth father, even though they were adopted legally by Nariman. The atmosphere in "Chateau Felicity," where the three live, is hardly pleasant, primarily because Coomy is constantly finding fault with either Jal or Nariman, whose presence in what was his own house clearly annoys her. She has never forgiven Nariman for his part in her mother's unhappy life and tragic death. Now that he is more or less at her mercy, she can have her revenge, either by making rules that humiliate him, such as setting times when he may go to the bathroom, or by attempting to deny him his few remaining pleasures, such as his customary walk around the neighborhood. At the beginning of the novel, it is obvious that Coomy has long since made her choice as to how she will behave toward others and, unfortunately, Jal has become a passive partner in her self-centered and spiteful conduct since he is too timid to defy his sister.

The moral drama that is at the crux of *Family Matters* is soon transferred to the small apartment where Nariman's daughter Roxana Chenoy lives with her husband Yezad and their two sons, Murad and Jehangir. Even in their cramped quarters, living on a very tight budget, the Chenoys take pleasure in each other's company and generally enjoy life. However, each of them is tested when Coomy and Jal dump Nariman on them, unannounced, his leg in a cast. Supposedly he is to stay only until his broken ankle has mended and he can walk again; however, while he is at

Roxana's, Coomy deliberately damages the ceiling of her stepfather's bedroom so that, pretending that there are structural defects in the house, she can keep him away permanently.

In actuality, Roxana and Yezad are far less able to care for Nariman than Coomy and Jal were. The two Contractors had no outside commitments whatsoever. By contrast, the Chenoys are working every moment, Yezad at his job as a sporting goods salesman and Roxana at her household tasks, which are even more time-consuming because she must function without outside help and with barely enough money to cover the family's expenses. Even Murad and Jehangir have little spare time, for when they are not at school, their parents make sure that they are keeping up with their homework.

It is hardly surprising that the arrival of Nariman, bedridden and helpless, sends Roxana into near panic, although, kind-hearted as she is, she would not say a word to her father about her feelings. However, as the days go by, it becomes increasingly clear to her that his presence threatens not only their happiness but even their very survival. Initially, Roxana has to solve the problem of sleeping arrangements, since there is no second bedroom in the apartment. Therefore Roxana decides to put Nariman on the settee where Jehangir ordinarily sleeps and have the two boys alternate between a cot beside their grandfather and a mattress under an improvised tent on the balcony. However, Nariman's most intimate needs are not so easily managed. Presumably because of his Parsi feelings about cleanliness, Yezad forbids the boys to help their mother with the physical care of her father, leaving Roxana to answer his frequent calls for a urinal and to lift him onto and off of the bedpan. Soon she is both emotionally and physically exhausted, but although she cries in private and sometimes snaps at her husband, she is determined never to let her father feel unwelcome or unloved.

Yezad is not so noble. While he has always enjoyed being around his father-in-law, Yezad can hide neither his annoyance about his daily schedule being disrupted nor his jealousy at being displaced as the most important figure in his wife's life. Since he cannot vent his anger on Coomy and Jal, whom he regards as the real culprits, Yezad finds fault with his sons and lashes out at Roxana, who sometimes argues with him and at other times just weeps.

Murad and Jehangir are much more flexible than their father. They have no problem with the sleeping arrangements. They treat camping out on the balcony as a great adventure, and Jehangir, in particular, likes holding his grandfather's hand when it is his turn to sleep beside him. He does not mind the loss of his mother's attention because now his grandfather is always handy to tell him stories or to play games with him. To Jehangir, taking care of his grandfather is a privilege. At one point, when she sees how tenderly Jehangir spoons food into his grandfather, Roxana cannot help thinking that some good has come out of the situation, after all.

However, the truth is that caring for Nariman has brought their family to the brink of financial disaster. The pittance that Coomy turns over to Roxana, insisting that it is the whole of his pension, is insufficient to meet the cost of his medicines, let alone his meals. As a result, Roxana has to cut back on food, and the time will come, she fears, when she cannot even pay her other bills. Seeing his mother so troubled about money, Jehangir begins taking bribes from some of the classmates, whose work he grades, and sneaks his ill-gotten gains into the envelopes from which Roxana pays her bills. When his teacher tells Jehangir's parents about his dishonesty, Roxana is devastated and Yezad, who had always been so proud of his sons, has yet one more reason to hate Roxana's heartless relatives.

Financial pressures also force Yezad into actions he would never before have considered. First he tries gambling, and though at first he has some success, in the end he loses everything. Yezad's only hope now is to obtain a promotion at work. His employer, Vikram Kapur, has talked about becoming involved in politics and leaving Yezad in charge of the store. Since Kaput is a good-hearted idealist who sees Bombay as a city where people of all backgrounds and all faiths can live together in peace, Yezad reasons that a threat from the Shiv Sena, hoodlums who view themselves as enforcers of strict Hindu doctrine, would certainly send Kaput into public life. However, the plan backfires. When Kaput defies the Shiv Sena, they murder him, leaving Yezad both jobless and consumed by guilt.

This subplot parallels the main action in that it, too, shows characters choosing between good and evil. Despite the fact that he was driven out of his native Punjab by fanatical Muslims, Kaput has taken in Husain, a Muslim who saw his family torched by Hindu extremists. In the sporting goods store, not only do a Punjabi, a Muslim, and a Parsi work together in harmony, but Kaput has his window displays celebrate the festivals of all the peoples of Bombay. Sadly, Kaput's utopian dream is defeated. The forces of intolerance win.

However, some good comes from all this evil. First, a repentant Yezad starts helping Roxana with the care of her father; then, after Coomy is killed as a result of her experiments with the ceiling, Jal persuades Yezad and Roxana to sell their house and move in with him. Mistry seems about to present his readers with a most uncharacteristic happy ending. However, he is too much of a realist to let it go at that. In the epilogue, Nariman is dead, and although Jal seems to be finding true love, Yezad has become so fanatical about his faith that he has broken off with his best friend and is in the process of alienating the members of his own family.

Rohinton Mistry has hinted that, at some point, he may set a work of fiction in Canada, where he now lives, rather in Bombay. The change would be no more than a superficial one, for although Mistry is painstakingly accurate about particulars, his primary concern is with universals. As a realist, he knows that, more often than not, good is defeated by evil. However, he is just idealistic enough to believe that it does not have to be so. Mistry's gentle humor, his compassion, his passion for tolerance, and, above all, the strength with which both he and his characters cling to hope for the future combine to make *Family Matters* his finest work to date.

Rosemary M. Canfield Reisman

Sources for Further Study

The Atlantic Monthly 290 (September, 2002): 165.
Booklist 98 (July, 2002): 1797.
Kirkus Reviews 70 (July 1, 2002): 910.
The New York Times, September 24, 2002, p. E7.
The New York Times Book Review 107 (October 13, 2002): 7.
The New Yorker 78 (September 30, 2002): 140.
Publishers Weekly 249 (July 15, 2002): 51.
The Spectator 288 (March 30, 2002): 41.
Time International 159 (June 10, 2002): 59.
The Times Literary Supplement, April 19, 2002, p. 21.

FIRST GREAT TRIUMPH
How Five Americans Made Their Country a World Power

Author: Warren Zimmermann (1934-   )
Publisher: Farrar, Straus and Giroux (New York). 562 pp. $30.00
Type of work: History
Time: 1838-1937
Locale: Washington, D.C., Cuba, the Philippines, Hawaii, Puerto Rico, and Panama

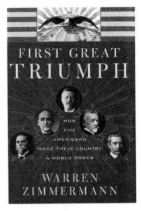

～

A veteran diplomat explains how five American political and military figures guided the process that established the United States as a world power in the late nineteenth and early twentieth centuries

～

Principal personages:
JOHN HAY (1838-1905), diplomat and secretary of state
ALFRED T. MAHAN (1840-1914), naval officer and authority on naval strategy
ELIHU ROOT (1845-1937), corporation lawyer and member of two presidents' cabinets
HENRY CABOT LODGE (1850-1924), United States senator from Massachusetts
GEORGE DEWEY (1837-1917), naval hero of the battle for the Philippines in the Spanish-American War
LEONARD WOOD (1860-1927), military governor of Cuba after that war
WILLIAM MCKINLEY (1843-1901), twenty-fifth president of the United States
THEODORE ROOSEVELT (1858-1919), twenty-sixth president of the United States
WILLIAM HOWARD TAFT (1857-1930), twenty-seventh president of the United States

The lives of the five men Warren Zimmermann credits with engineering the rise of the United States to the status of world power span a century. John Hay, the eldest, was born in 1838, and Elihu Root, who lived the longest, died in 1937. Zimmermann devotes five of the six substantial chapters of part 1 of his study to biographical sketches of the five, before he focuses part 2, "Imperial America," on American foreign policy in the final years of the nineteenth century and the initial years of the twentieth—with the major emphasis on the year 1898, when the United States achieved domination over the Philippines and Hawaii, the islet of Guam, and the Caribbean islands of Cuba and Puerto Rico. Except for Hawaii, all of these islands were

Warren Zimmermann's thirty-three years in the United States Foreign Service included the post of ambassador to Yugoslavia from 1989 to 1992. He has taught at Columbia and Johns Hopkins Universities and written widely on foreign affairs.

garnered as a result of the Spanish-American War of that year. The nature, extent, and subsequent development of American hegemony differed in each case, but in controlling islands on both sides of the North American land mass, the United States joined European nations such as Great Britain, France, and Germany in the ranks of the world's imperial powers.

While conceding the importance of other men—Zimmermann credits the contributions of Admiral George Dewey, General Leonard Wood, and presidents William McKinley and William Howard Taft to the process of empire building—the author contends that Hay and Root, along with Alfred T. Mahan, Henry Cabot Lodge, and Theodore Roosevelt, furnished both the rationale for power and the indomitable energy that effected it. The author agrees with those historians who regard McKinley as more of a reluctant recruit than the presiding officer of the expansion that erupted during his administration.

Zimmermann's plan is an unusual one that could have resulted in disjointedness but proves effective. After setting the scene in his introduction and surveying the earlier history of the American "expansionist impulse," he summarizes in sequence the lives of his five principals up to the point of the 1898 war. First comes John Hay, who attained prominence as half of Abraham Lincoln's White House staff while still in his early twenties and gained considerable fame as poet, novelist, and historian before McKinley named him ambassador to Great Britain and then secretary of state. Zimmermann depicts Hay as the least aggressive of the five but a valuable counterweight to the belligerent Roosevelt, who kept him on as head of the State Department despite strong doubts about his forcefulness.

The naval career of Alfred T. Mahan would not have earned him a significant niche in history, but his *The Influence of Sea Power upon History, 1660-1783* (1890) profoundly impressed students of international affairs, including Theodore Roosevelt, who as President McKinley's assistant secretary of the navy a few years later began to apply its lessons by urging the build up of the heretofore mediocre American navy. Without a great navy and a political leadership that recognized naval power as essential to international potency, the keen ambitions of men such as Roosevelt, Lodge, and Root could not have been fulfilled.

Roosevelt and Lodge became friends in 1884 when the two served as delegates to the Republican National Convention in Chicago and strove vainly to defeat the party's choice of James G. Blaine over the incumbent president, Chester Alan Arthur. Although they decided to support Blaine in the November election, their earlier opposition proved politically inexpedient. Lodge's campaign to represent his Massachusetts district in the House of Representatives failed that year and Roosevelt, with no immediate prospects, retreated to a ranch in the Dakota territory. Nine years and three successful Congressional campaigns later, however, Lodge began a long career as a United States senator and rose quickly to positions of leadership. Drawing heavily upon Mahan's book, he too exhorted his colleagues to enhance the navy and to annex Hawaii, already a long-standing center of American commercial interests.

Although Elihu Root, another of Roosevelt's friends from the 1880's, assumed extraordinarily complex duties as secretary of war in the aftermath of the 1898 victory over Spain and succeeded John Hay as Roosevelt's secretary of state in 1905, perhaps his most important contribution to the nation's rise to the status of world power was his steady promotion of, and shrewd advice to, Roosevelt. A scholarly New York lawyer, Root threw his support to the twenty-three-year-old political neophyte in the latter's successful 1881 bid for a seat in the New York Assembly. Four years later, Root backed his protégé, albeit less successfully, in the race for mayor of New York. As a reformer at heart, Root saw in Roosevelt the kind of energy and determination that could bring to fruition reforms of the sort that the wily lawyer conceptualized so well himself. In 1895 he prepared a legal brief to help Roosevelt, by this time a New York City police commissioner, overcome the obstructionist tactics of a fellow commissioner in Roosevelt's onslaught on municipal graft and corruption. After Roosevelt's exploits in Cuba made him a national celebrity and an instant candidate for governor of New York, opponents attempted to derail him by citing the fact that the idolized Rough Rider had previously declared his residence to be Washington, D.C., to avoid taxes, but Root won over the convention delegates with a disingenuous and diversionary speech. Finally, against the prevailing wisdom which held the vice presidency to be a political graveyard, Root's counsel again prevailed when President McKinley offered to make Roosevelt his second-term running mate. Neither could have foreseen that McKinley would fall to an assassin's bullet a little over a year later, but Root, probably remembering that three vice presidents had gained the presidency as the result of presidential deaths in the preceding sixty years and judging that not even the vice presidency could cast the tempestuous Roosevelt into obscurity, advised him to accept. Roosevelt listened.

Zimmermann's sketch of the best-known member of this quintet efficiently summarizes Roosevelt's first, dynamic forty years and leads into the subsequent account of the rise of American imperialist sway. It should be noted that, except for Admiral Mahan, these men generally avoided the unpopular word "imperialism"; Zimmermann uses the term in Mahan's customary sense of "the extension of national authority over alien communities," a definition that includes forms of authority other than outright ownership. Although Zimmermann examines both the ends and means of American imperialism critically, he takes pains to distinguish it from the typical European model. Even more than the British, the Americans insisted on improving living conditions in possessions such as Hawaii and the Philippines. Even in Cuba, where the record is generally more deplorable, the record of Leonard Wood, its humane military governor from the end of the conflict until 1903, shines in comparison with that of his European counterparts in their Asian and African dependencies.

Zimmermann balances his study by giving due attention to the anti-imperialist opposition of the time, which included such notable Americans as the psychologist and philosopher William James (1842-1910), industrialist Andrew Carnegie (1835-1919), labor leader Samuel Gompers (1850-1924), America's most famous author, Mark Twain (1835-1910), and, in the United States Senate, Lodge's Massachusetts colleague, George Frisbie Hoar (1826-1904). The diversity of these men is a tell-tale sign that anti-imperialist motivation varied considerably. Zimmermann credits Carnegie, for instance, with a largely humanitarian motive, Hoar with a constitutional one, Gompers with the goal of protecting American workers from competition from cheap immigrant labor. Many of these critics of the new American internationalism shared prejudices common to imperialists, especially the conviction that foreigners were inferior beings. Imperialists argued that America was doing a favor to these ineffectual Asian and Latin American subjects in taking over the management of their affairs; anti-imperialists worried that incursions of undesirable immigrants would surely pollute American society. A number of the Anglophiles on both sides in this debate were disturbed by the already increasing immigration from southern and eastern Europe.

The most entertaining of the anti-imperialists was not Twain, whose voice was often shrill, but Peter Finley Dunne (1867-1936), the Irish American humorist whose garrulous bartender, Mr. Dooley, satirized delightfully the deceptions and hypocrisies practiced by the imperialists. Zimmermann sprinkles Dunne's witticisms liberally through his presentation of the case against American expansion overseas. Another literary man, Rudyard Kipling (1865-1936), whose name has become synonymous with imperialism, was living in Vermont when he penned his famous poem "The White Man's Burden" (1899), but both sides misjudged it. The imperialists saw it simply as an endorsement of their aims, the anti-imperialists as the height of jingoism, but Zimmermann points out that a more careful reading of the poem reveals a "cautionary tone." Having grown up in India, Kipling appreciated the sense of duty and responsibility that he viewed as characterizing and justifying the British Empire's accumulation and maintenance of overseas possessions.

A hovering presence in the dispute over empire was a major construction project still years away in 1898—the Panama Canal. It was not known then whether the canal would knife across Panama (a dependency of Colombia) or Nicaragua, but that it would be built no one doubted. Decisions about the size of the navy, the security and effectiveness of both commercial and military shipping, and appropriate responses to foreign initiatives interpreted as challenges to the Monroe Doctrine all hinged on the future canal. It inevitably became a major preoccupation of all advocates of American overseas expansion.

Zimmermann achieves his stated objective of avoiding both the hero-worship that Theodore Roosevelt in particular tends to inspire and the revisionist attempt to depict the United States as an imperial bully. The resulting book is an evenhanded presentation of the emergence of the United States' new role in the world. He frequently reminds the reader of his principals' flaws: Roosevelt's bellicosity, Lodge's contempt for his intellectual opponents, Root's coldly impersonal approach to human affairs.

Their prejudices influenced their decisions; their vision of America's future, often acute, nevertheless required ignoble maneuvers. The tortuous legalistic process by which the United States obtained the rights to its canal, for instance, amounted to a standing insult to Colombia and Panama. Overall, however, high-mindedness predominated in these men.

Zimmermann closes his book with reflections both positive and negative on the legacy of imperial America. The decisive effect of the entrance of the United States into two world conflicts in the twentieth century is only one obvious example of the significance of the new American power. However, the assumption of this role has entailed responsibilities immensely difficult to carry out. He judges that the terrorist events of September 11, 2001, have hastened a deterioration of the power and confidence needed to maintain the nation's status—a deterioration that he dates back to the end of the Cold War in the late 1980's. To reverse this process, he suggests that future statesmen "recall the positive legacies of 1898: the confidence in America's founding principles, the generosity of spirit, the conviction that America is a natural leader in the world, the clear sense of U.S. interests, and, most of all, the understanding that power must be combined with what Theodore Roosevelt called high purpose."

Robert P. Ellis

Sources for Further Study

Foreign Affairs 81 (November/December, 2002): 148.
Library Journal 127 (October 1, 2002): 115.
The New York Times, October 23, 2002, p. E7.
The New York Times Book Review 107 (November 24, 2002): 13.
Publishers Weekly 249 (August 5, 2002): 62.

FLESH AND MACHINES
How Robots Will Change Us

Author: Rodney A. Brooks
Publisher: Pantheon Books (New York). Illustrated. 270
  pp. $26.00
Type of work: Science

∼

Speculations by a professor of artificial intelligence about the relationship between humans and robots, supported by the history and current state of research into artificial intelligence

∼

When most people think about intelligent robots, their images are typically of mechanical simulations of humans, epitomized perhaps by the character C3PO from the *Star Wars* films. In *Flesh and Machines: How Robots Will Change Us*, Rodney A. Brooks reverses that view, showing how humans are essentially machines. He also shows how he has achieved success by negating the basic assumptions of other researchers in the artificial-intelligence community.

Early goals in artificial intelligence were mostly "things that highly educated male scientists found challenging," such as chess, integral calculus, and complex algebra problems. Actions that small children can do effortlessly, such as visually identifying a table or cup or walking from bedroom to living room, were not considered to require intelligence. Walking on two legs and seeing, however, turned out to be harder to accomplish than the loftier-sounding early goals.

In the mid-1980's, Brooks looked anew at the foundation of research up to that time, in which a robot's sensors and motor processes were coordinated by a "cognition box." The best way to build this center of thinking and intelligence, he decided, was to eliminate it. While others worked on how best to have a robot map the world around it and then use that map to move about, Brooks took the contrarian angle and eliminated the map, so his robot would simply sense and use the immediate environment. This is the way real-world animals operate, he reasoned.

This is also Brooks's major approach to problem-solving. Early in his career, he "would look at how everyone else was tackling a certain problem and find the core central thing that they all agreed on so much that they never even talked about it." Then he would throw that thing out and see where it led. For example, when everyone else was working on how to represent certain obstacles, he looked at "where the stuff wasn't."

By looking at the evolution of real insects and other animals, he noted that they started with simple capabilities and gradually developed more sophisticated capabilities. The way to build robots, he reasoned, was to build complex capabilities on top of simpler ones. An early exemplar of this approach was Genghis, an insectlike creature that detected the warmth of any passing person, then used six insectlike legs to walk over anything in its path as it followed the person around like a puppy. It had no large master control program, but a set of fifty-one relatively small programs, each of which sensed a certain thing or actuated a certain motion. In *Flesh and Machines*, Brooks devotes a twelve-page appendix to describing the design and implementation of Genghis.

∽

Rodney A. Brooks is a professor of computer science and engineering at the Massachusetts Institute of Technology, where he is also the director of the Artificial Intelligence Laboratory. He is the chairman and chief technological officer of iRobot Corporation.

∽

Raised in an isolated part of Australia "at the end of the technological Earth," Brooks says he "grew up a nerd in a place that did not know what a nerd was." By age twelve, nevertheless, he had built a machine that could play tick-tack-toe flawlessly. At Flinders University in Adelaide, South Australia, he created a computer language specifically for artificial intelligence and wrote programs that proved mathematical theorems. Joining the Stanford Artificial Intelligence Laboratory in 1977, he worked with Hans Moravec and other pioneers of that nascent field. He later moved across the country to become a professor at the Massachusetts Institute of Technology (MIT), where he also became director of the 230-person Artificial Intelligence Laboratory.

Brooks has published papers and books about model-based computer vision, path planning, uncertainty analysis, robot assembly, active vision, autonomous robots, microrobots, microactuators, planetary exploration, representation, artificial life, humanoid robots, and compiler design. His books include *Model-Based Computer Vision* (1984), *Programming in Common Lisp* (1985), and *Cambrian Intelligence* (1999). A 1997 documentary featuring him was called *Fast, Cheap, and Out of Control*, after one of his papers in the *Journal of the British Interplanetary Society*. The title reflects his controversial idea that robots could be made quickly and inexpensively and allowed to run autonomously, thus "out of control."

Brooks starts *Flesh and Machines* by discussing the things that separate people from animals: syntax and technology. He describes a famously clever African grey parrot that appeared to put words together in new ways; closer analysis, however, showed that the bird did not exhibit syntax. Chimpanzees can appear to have rudimentary technology, but they have been observed for decades without showing any innovations. Brooks finishes the "Dances with Machines" chapter by describing human technological revolutions—the advent of early tools, followed by agricultural, cultural, industrial, informational, and biotechnological revolutions.

He then launches into "The Quest for an Artificial Creature," starting with cave painters of thirty centuries ago. Archeologists have found articulated animals, made of limestone, in Persian sites 3,100 years old. About 1,900 years ago, Hero of Alexandria had built pneumatically operated human forms. In 1688, a French general built a peacock that walked and ate. In 1815, Henri Maillardet built a humanoid that could write script in both French and English and could draw landscapes. The cleverest of these, however, could not respond to their environments. They did exactly the same thing every time.

Early electronic creatures were built by W. Grey Walter, who felt that his study of electroencephalography would be advanced by building and studying electromechanical models of animals that showed spontaneity, autonomy, and self-regulation. In the 1940's, Walter and his wife used relays and vacuum tubes to construct shoebox-sized "tortoises." They could sense light and register bumping and react accordingly. Brook notes that the tortoises' ability to move and react without depending on any outside control made them the first artificial creatures.

The advent of transistors boosted the abilities of robots in the 1950's, but robots still had to be controlled by room-sized computers communicating with the robots through cables. From 1968 through 1972, Nils Nilsson's team at Stanford Research Institute built Shakey, which got its name from the way its camera and television transmitter wobbled as it moved. Shakey could go to a particular room and push a colored block to another room—in six to eight hours, whereas a child could do in just seconds.

Years later, the Genghis project led to a 1988 presentation to the Jet Propulsion Laboratory (JPL) for a planned Mars mission. Engineers there, however, had more traditional ideas. Brooks student Colin Angle interned at JPL in 1989, seeding some ideas among the space scientists, and those efforts eventually led to the Sojourner robot that roved a patch of Mars in 1997.

Many moviegoers are familiar with HAL, the computer in the film *2001: A Space Odyssey* (1968), and with the many robot-based stories and novels written by Isaac Asimov (1920-1992). Brooks explores how current and future robots relate to HAL and to Asimov's famous Three Laws of Robotics. A major roadblock to creating HAL, Brooks notes, lies in the sense of sight. He explains how human eyes implement visual recognition and how currently available video cameras are superior to eyes in some ways and inferior in others. Human perception of what the eyes can see is still beyond laboratory emulation.

Asimov's three laws present different difficulties. Briefly, they entail upon robots protection of humans, obedience to humans, and self-protection. Before 1998, no robot could obey the first law because none could distinguish between humans and other objects. That perception, like vision, is still in a very primitive state. Brooks's discussion of this problem includes fascinating details about how humans use their eyes and perceive the images that their eyes detect.

His Kismet robot mimics a human head, able to move its neck, eyeballs, eyebrows, ears, jaws, and lips, all in response to human speech. It does not recognize specific spoken words but rather their "prosody," or pitch variations. It can also detect where the person's attention lies, just as humans do in normal conversation. Based on these data, Kismet displays an "emotional state" by shifting its face accordingly, and inserts prosodic cues into its own voice.

The ongoing progress in artificial intelligence already has applications outside the laboratory. Brooks mentions several of them, including gate-scheduling at airports, analysis of mortgage applications, and even some video games and toys, such as the

Furby doll and AIBO dog. Brooks cites his own company's efforts at getting such a toy manufactured and marketed, although as an example of the differing viewpoints of futurists and business executives. He speculates on what sorts of robots might make it into homes in the near future but notes that actual predictions are nearly impossible. On one hand, a robotic lawnmower that Brooks bought turned out to be less than successful. On the other hand, in September, 2001, a herd of small robots burrowed nimbly into the World Trade Center debris in search of victims of the terrorist attack.

The last one-third of *Flesh and Machines* is more philosophical in nature, as indicated by the last four chapter titles: "We Are Special," "We Are Not Special," "Them and Us," and "Us as Them." An excellent discussion of "beingness" explores whether a machine could possibly have the status of a being as opposed to a mere object. People gladly grant "beingness" to dogs and horses, but rarely to reptiles or fish. Strict laws prohibit cruelty to dogs, but encourage the killing of rats and insects. As long as robots' physiology remains vastly different from humans' and they do not exhibit convincingly emotional behavior, most people will continue to deny them "beingness." Brooks makes some rather unsettling points in the comparison of "real" and machine-simulated emotions.

A major reason for societal rejection of robotic "beingness" is, Brooks says, humans' psychological need to be special. Historically, acceptance of the Copernican heliocentric universe made this world a little less special. Later, the emerging concept of species evolution further lessened human specialness. The physics theories of relativity, quantum mechanics, and Heisenbergian uncertainty then weakened human certainty of ultimately knowing how the universe works. The discovery of deoxyribonucleic acid (DNA) and thus of the tight similarity of the basic structures of humans, fruit flies, and other creatures were further blows to human specialness, as are the many continuing advances in computer capabilities.

Having established this need for specialness, Brooks then tells the reader that "the body, this mass of biomolecules, is a machine that acts according to a set of specifiable rules." As the hardware and software of robots become more sophisticated and powerful, the differences between "them" and "us" are likely to become smaller and smaller. Brooks describes his startled reaction in 1999 when an elevator door opened and out walked colleague Hugh Herr, a double-leg amputee. Herr had become a cyborg, with metal rods in place of leg bones, circuit boards in place of muscles, batteries taped on, and wires dangling all over. There are also thousands of formerly deaf people who can now hear by means of cochlear implants. Even some blindness is beginning to yield to cybernetic retinal implants, although this field is still in its infancy.

Part of the attraction of robots is that they can work mindlessly as humans' slaves. If future robots look like humans and have actual feelings, however, certain ethical considerations would arise. Brooks notes: "We had better be careful just what we build, because we might end up liking them, and then we will be morally responsible for their well-being. Sort of like children."

J. Edmund Rush

Sources for Further Study

Booklist 98 (January 1-January 15, 2002): 786.
Los Angeles Times Book review, March 31, 2002, p. 6.
New Statesman 131 (April 29, 2002): 49.
The New York Times Book Review 107 (April 14, 2002): 16.
Publishers Weekly 248 (December 24, 2001): 52.
The Times, May 6, 2002, p. 10.

FLOTSAM AND JETSAM

Author: Aidan Higgins (1927-   )
Publisher: Dalkey Archive Press (Chicago). 470 pp.
    $15.95
Type of work: Autobiography, short fiction, and travel

∾

A collection of short fiction, autobiographical excerpts,
and travel pieces, mostly published between 1960 and
1989, by an award-winning Irish memoirist and fiction
writer

∾

This aptly named mélange of fiction and nonfiction
covers thirty years of Aidan Higgins's literary career, be-
ginning with his first book of stories, *Felo de Se,* in 1960. Because Higgins so often
recycles and republishes his work under different titles, it is necessary to identify the
previous publication of the pieces included here. One of Higgins's most famous stories, "North Salt Holdings," has the following history. It was first published as
"Killachter Meadow" in the collection *Felo de Se,* which in turn was republished in
1972 as *Asylum, and Other Stories.* Moreover, the story was worked up and expanded
into the novel *Langrishe, Go Down* in 1966 and appeared again in the collection
Helsingør Station and Other Departures in 1989. Other stories included here that
originally appeared in the *Felo de Se* collection under different names are "In Old
Heidelberg" (originally "Tower and Angels) and "Berlin After Dark" (originally
"Winter Offense"). The excerpt "Catchpole" is a reworked section of Higgins's novel
Balcony of Europe (1972), which was short-listed for the British Booker Prize that
year. The title story of the collection originally appeared as "Nightfall on Cape
Piscator"; it is republished here with the addition of a first-person opening that situ-
ates it in the period when Higgins traveled with his first wife in South Africa.

Another aspect of Higgins's writing practice—his blurring of the line between autobiography and fiction—needs to be recognized in order to understand this book.
Many of his fictions are derived from, or reflected, in his three-volume autobiography: *Donkey's Years* (1995), *Dog Days* (1998), and *The Whole Hog* (2000). For example, when the first volume of the autobiography appeared, Higgins made public
the fact that the "fictional" story of the Langrishe family, featured in "Killachter
Meadow," *Langrishe, Go Down,* and "North Salt Holdings" was really the story of his
own family revealed in *Donkey's Years.* The sisters of the story and the subsequent
novel, he said, were really his brothers and himself "in drag."

Still a third element of Higgins's work reflected in this hefty volume is that he frequently merges fiction and autobiography with his travel writing. For example
"Ronda Gorge" (originally entitled *Sommerspiele*) and "Black September" (origi-

∼

*Born in County Kildare, Ireland,
Higgins writes fiction, travel pieces,
and radio drama. His novel*
Langrishe, Go Down *(1966) won
the James Tait Black Memorial
Prize and the Irish Academy of
Letters Award; his novel* Balcony of
Europe *(1972) was short-listed for
the Booker Prize in 1972.*

∼

nally entitled "The Opposite") were first published in 1989 in *Ronda Gorge and Other Precipices*, which was subtitled *Travel Writing: 1956-1989*. The pieces "Helsingør Station," "Sodden Fields," "The Bird I Fancied," "Frere Jacques, Brüder Hans," "The Other Day I Was Thinking of You," and "Under the Ice Shelf" were all published in 1989 in the collection *Helsingør Station and Other Departures*, which was subtitled *Fictions and Autobiographies, 1956-1989*.

The problem for readers approaching Higgins's writing is that he never really distinguishes which of his works are fictions, which are autobiography, and which are nonfiction travel pieces. The fact that Higgins subtitled the first volume of his autobiography *Memories of a Life as Story Told* suggests that for him the past is not only grist for the fictional mill, but that there is no way to recount the past without making use of the conventions of fiction. He once said that *Donkey's Years*, which he described in the appendix of that book as a "bogus autobiography," was actually closer to a novel because all honest autobiographies must inevitably be bogus. Similarly, when Higgins writes travel pieces, there is no such thing as a simple description of an exotic place; he almost always grounds the locale in a narrative with a human perspective.

Although it is probably a truism that many writers use experience from their own lives as the basis for their fictions, the reader usually expects some measure of concealment and control of such personal material. Higgins, however, makes little effort to conceal the personal source of his fiction and little effort to exert a tight formal control to give them the sense of structured short fiction. As a landlady says of Higgins's writing in the second volume of his autobiography, *Dog Days*, it has no beginning, no middle, and no end. Indeed, one of the frustrating things about reading Higgins is his constant shifting about from event to event, seemingly as memories occur to him. As he said in the opening of *Donkey's Years*, "I am consumed by memories and they form the life of me." However, a loose rendering of such memories seems too often self-indulgent in Higgins's writing. Lacking an overall sense of significance and form, the work must depend almost solely on the reader's appreciation of the writer's individual perceptions and the purity of his prose. Indeed, it is the rhythm of the prose that engages the reader. Higgins is a modern literary example of the classic Irish oral tradition of presenting the sound of a voice talking.

In its emphasis on the sound of a human voice rather than a tightly structured aesthetic form, Higgins's stories will never be mistaken for the work of a painstaking creator of aesthetic form such as William Trevor. Although it could never be said that Aidan Higgins writes conventional short fiction, the three pieces that seem closest to what a reader expects of a short story are the title piece and his two most famous short fictions, "North Salt Holdings" (that is, "Killachter Meadow") and "Asylum."

"Flotsam and Jetsam" focuses on a man on holiday with his unresponsive and overweight wife and her elderly father and bedridden mother. Tormented with regret at being saddled with this "veritable mountain of flesh" who has been disgusted by sex since her wedding night, the man is tortured by dreams of orgies and bestialities. The story moves toward its inevitable conclusion when his dreams begin to feature their black servant, Amalinda Pandova, who walks the Earth as though her clothes were a burden to her. Finally, on a night without dreams, he knows what must happen and goes to her hut and attacks her unresisting, naked body. Although the plot of the story is a conventional one about a man whose life has always been "a marvel of prudence and restraint," but who is increasingly drawn into a primitive heart of darkness, no one is apt to mistake Higgins's story for one by Somerset Maugham (1874-1965), or by Joseph Conrad (1857-1924), for that matter. In its dreamlike rhythms and its sexual suggestiveness, it is more akin to the fiction of Samuel Beckett (1906-1989), although less complex, or J. P. Donleavy (born 1926), albeit more reserved.

Higgins's most famous story, "North Salt Holdings," begins with the funeral of Emily Norton Kervick in March, 1927. When the piece was used in his best-known novel *Langrishe, Go Down*, the dead woman's name was Emily Langrishe and her burial took place on March 3, 1927, which the first volume of Higgins's autobiography *Donkey's Years* indicates is Higgins's birthday. The story focuses primarily on the oldest of four sisters: Emily, Tess, Helen, and Imogen. Emily, who is overweight, goes swimming naked every day in the summer while her activities are recorded by her sister Helen, a potential writer, in a daybook. The serpent in this grotesque garden of spinsters is Joseph the gardener, a man with the stench of advanced decay. The story of these sequestered women, stifled in their own repressed and forestalled desires, ends on a summer day when Emily, on one of her daily bathing rituals, unable to swim, loses footing (whether purposely or accidentally is not clear) and is carried downstream. Her movement in space toward death becomes a movement in time, as she seems to see her sisters as children again. Her last sight is her amanuensis, Helen, whose child's face is overlaid with her adult face in a perverted mask. The story is a haunting, dreamlike portrait of seclusion, repression, and frustration.

The longest fiction in the book, "Asylum," is about the relationship between Eddy Brazill, an Irish working man who goes from unsatisfactory job to unsatisfactory job until he meets Ben Boucher, the alcoholic son of a wealthy landowner, who has been left a large estate on the condition that he stays sober for a year. Boucher hires Brazill as a golfing companion while he tries to "dry out" in a sanatorium. Broken up into chapterlike sections in novelistic fashion, the story focuses primarily on Brazill's courtship of a pantomime performer named Elizabeth Demeter Sted and the gradual mental deterioration of Boucher. The story explores a favorite Higgins's theme—the tension between the dangerous desires of the body and the equally risky obsessions of the mind. As Boucher becomes more and more preoccupied with Christlike parables, trying to make some kind of contact with Brazill, the other man is impervious to the intellectual, maintaining "an almost total blankness" to Boucher's suffering, "such being the birthright of the poor in heart." With Brazill interested only in his sexual relation with Elizabeth Sted, Boucher despairs completely, finally committing suicide by setting fire to his room. The story ends with Brazill, unable to find words to pray, simply repeating over and over that while Boucher has gone to the madhouse, he has come from the poor house, thus indicating the basic tension between the duality the two men represent.

The long selection entitled "Catchpole" is an excerpt from Higgins's novel *Balcony of Europe*, which, during what Higgins calls the "eight constipated years" when it was being written, gave him so much trouble that he withdrew it from publication as a failure. The excerpt here focuses on still another wandering, desire-ridden man on holiday with wife and child. Although Catchpole is physically present with his family, his mind is elsewhere, either in the past, recounting his many homosexual encounters, or else drawn to the young men he sees around him in Spain.

The second half of *Flotsam and Jetsam* is made up primarily of fictionalized nonfiction pieces from Higgins's travel book *Ronda Gorge and Other Precipices* and fictionalized autobiography pieces from his collection *Helsingør Station and Other Departures*. The piece "Helsingør Station," which could be subtitled "Down and Out in Copenhagen," is a romance filled with love and squalor, and with the local color of Tivoli Gardens and the Little Mermaid statue. "Black September" takes place in Munich in 1972 at the time that terrorists killed a number of Israeli athletes competing in the Olympics. The longest autobiographical piece in the collection is "Sodden Fields," which begins in Joycean fashion, as Higgins says he was conceived at the "tail-end" of June in 1926 and then "expelled" the following March "puffing and choking" and wishing to sink back into the warm "uterine depths with a bubbling groan."

Higgins's writing has received a mixed reception from Irish and British critics (he is not well known in the United States), who welcome, on the one hand, his comic ribaldry and rhythmic prose style but are, on the other hand, less than enthusiastic about his indulgent parade of the self. British critics have suggested that often there is no sense of form in his work, in spite of the fact that there is much substance, and some Irish critics have noted that Higgins is an "odd man out," going his own way, more interested in writing books than making up stories. They say he is more concerned with presenting the formlessness of experience than trying to create order and more interested in "tonal values than in compositional development." Indeed, the reader must come to the writing of Higgins in this collection of miscellaneous flotsam and jetsam willing to get lost in the formless song of self that he sings.

Charles E. May

Sources for Further Study

Booklist 98 (March 1, 2002): 1092
Kirkus Reviews 70 (January 2, 2002): 17.
Irish Times, February 22, 1997, p. S9.
Library Journal 127 (February 15, 2002): 180.
The New York Times Book Review 107 (June 16, 2002): 24.
Publishers Weekly 249 (February 18, 2002): 75.

FOOD POLITICS
How the Food Industry Influences Nutrition and Health

Author: Marion Nestle (1936-   )
Publisher: University of California Press (Berkeley). 457
   pp. $29.95
Type of work: Current affairs, economics, and science

~

*Nestle, chair of the Department of Nutrition and Food
Studies at New York University, details and documents the
pervasive and detrimental influence the food industry ex-
erts on consumers' food choices and on government policies regarding nutrition and food safety*

~

Most Americans are familiar with the food pyramid developed by the U.S. Department of Agriculture. It emphasizes the importance of eating more food from the grain,
fruit, and vegetable groups (plant foods); fewer servings from the meat and dairy
groups; and limited intake of animal fats, oils, and sweets. Most Americans also understand that keeping their weight within normal limits is important to good health
and that people who are overweight need to eat less and reduce sugar and foods high
in fat in the diet. Yet the number of people who are overweight (over the ideal weight
for their age and height) nearly doubled between the late 1970's and the early 1990's.
At least 14 percent of children aged six to eleven, 12 percent of adolescents, and 35
percent of adults are overweight. The rate of obesity (having more than 25 percent
body fat in men and 30 percent body fat in women) rose from 12 percent to almost 18
percent among adults in the years between 1991 and 1998 alone.

Compared to the people of other nations, most Americans consume more food in
general, but especially more animal-based foods (meat, fried foods, dairy products,
and grain dishes with high-fat sauces), causing them to be overweight and contributing to cardiovascular disease, diabetes, and many chronic illnesses, which are the major health problems in this society. The medical costs for diet-related conditions was
more than $70 billion in 1995. Obesity in children is associated with health problems
that were formerly seen only in adults, such as "adult-onset" high blood sugar and
high blood pressure. The state of affairs is so bad that, in December of 2001, U.S. surgeon general David Satcher announced that obesity would soon become the Number
1 killer in America. Satcher has urged schools and industries to develop new policies
to deal with this growing epidemic.

In *Food Politics: How the Food Industry Influences Nutrition and Health*, Marion
Nestle, professor and chair of the Department of Nutrition and Food Studies at New
York University and former nutrition policy advisor to the U.S. Department of Health
and Human Services, places the blame for this deplorable state of affairs squarely on

Professor and chair of the Department of Nutrition and Food Studies at New York University, Marion Nestle has served as a nutrition advisor to the Department of Health and Human Services, the Department of Agriculture, and the Food and Drug Administration, and as editor of the 1988 Surgeon General's Report on Nutrition and Health. She is the author of Nutrition in Clinical Practice *(1985).*

the food industry. In this well-organized and well-researched book, she skillfully mounts a carefully documented argument that, to a large extent, the powerful food industry in America determines what people eat. Because more food is produced than is needed in this country, food companies, in fierce competition with one another, must encourage the public to eat large quantities of their products in order to increase sales and profits. Portion sizes have increased markedly in recent years; "super-size" sodas and fries, "jumbo" milkshakes, enormous cookies, and larger muffins and pizzas are the order of the day. Nestle charges that food companies, using clever marketing strategies, "routinely place the needs of stockholders over considerations of public health" and they "will make and market any product that sells, regardless of its nutritional value or its effect on health." Raw food producers receive only about 20 percent of the retail cost of food—the rest goes to labor; processing (such as converting cheap potatoes to expensive potato chips) and additives to increase food value, attractiveness, or convenience; packaging; and advertising. Food companies spend over $33 billion annually on marketing and advertising, including more than $11 billion on direct media advertising in television, magazines, billboards, supermarket displays, and the Internet. Given this kind of intense psychological pressure, most people find it difficult to resist overeating.

School children are increasingly becoming the target of advertising. According to Nestle, "The amount of money spent on marketing directed to children and their parents rose from $6.9 billion in 1992 to $12.7 billion in 1997." Children are especially vulnerable to television advertising because they watch television for many hours, commercials are endlessly repeated, and children are less aware of the difference between commercials and program content. Beyond television, there is Internet marketing, the use of logo items, "educational" counting books and puzzles, and prizes. Companies also target schools. Many schools, hard-pressed for financial assistance, have formed partnerships that allow food companies to advertise under the guise of education. One disturbing example is Channel One: In exchange for television sets and installation hardware, twelve thousand schools have required viewing that includes commercials for products such as soft drinks and candy in most classrooms for twelve minutes per day on 90 percent of school days (or thirty-one hours a year). The programs themselves are of questionable educational value. Another example of blatant advertising to children is "pouring rights" or contract agreements with soft drink companies, whereby a school district receives large payments from a soft drink company in exchange for the company's exclusive rights to sell only its products in the district's schools. Soft drinks are high in calories and caffeine but low in nutrients, and they have replaced milk in the diet of many children. They contribute to obesity, tooth decay, and bone fractures, especially among teenagers. Meanwhile, the U.S. government does not know what to do with a supply of nonfat milk powder worth $1 billion (equal to 1.3 billion gallons of milk) that it has bought and stockpiled over the past three years to support dairy farmers' income. Nestle points out that "the large agricultural corporations that most benefit from federal subsidies spare no effort to persuade Congress and the administration to continue and increase this largesse." It is well documented that early food choices set the pattern for lifelong preferences. Candy, soft drinks, ice cream, and fast food rank high among the preferences of children who use their own money to buy food and beverages. Research indicates that only 1 percent of all American children even come close to eating a diet that resembles the number of serving recommendations of the food pyramid.

The industry manipulates the public by labeling foods high in calories and sugar as nutritious because they are "fortified" with vitamins and minerals. Kellogg spent $20 million trying to convince Americans that sugar-coated cereals are good for children. Nestle complains that Kellogg's Froot Loops cereal

> contains no fruit and no fiber and provides 53 percent of the calories from added sugar. The New Froot Loops ('same great taste with zinc, iron, and now calcium') reduces the sugar to 50 percent of calories and offers all of 1 gram of fiber per serving. Nevertheless, the company advertises Froot Loops as a health food.

In fact, Nestle argues, Froot Loops are more like candy than cereal and belong at the very top of the food pyramid.

People can become aware of the impact of advertising. Few people realize, however, the extent to which the food industry influences politics to gain professional and government support for their products. The food industry spends millions to manipulate public opinion indirectly by lobbying government agencies and members of Congress, making financial contributions to nutrition and health professionals, and intimidating critics with lawsuits. As an expert witness in lawsuits involving the industry, Nestle has seen documentation of lobbying interactions with government officials and Congress, "but such documents are proprietary, subject to sworn confidentiality agreements, and unusable as sources of information." Federal health officials endure "almost constant congressional interference with their dietary recommendations" and it is difficult, if not impossible, for them to recommend restrictions on any food category because of conflicts with the food industry.

Nestle cites many examples of how food companies influence nutrition professionals to endorse their products. It is a deliberate strategy in the industry to gain the support of nutrition experts by hiring them as advisors and consultants, funding research, underwriting publications, and sponsoring professional meetings, similar to the way pharmaceutical companies support some physicians and many activities of the medical profession. Nestle contends that dietitians, nutritionists, scientists, and universities allied with food companies have compromised their objectivity and critical judgment and are no longer in a position to give unbiased information. Studies indicate that research sponsored by industry is more likely to draw conclusions favorable to the industry than nonsponsored research. The American Dietetic Association, which represents seventy thousand registered nutritionists, relies on such sponsorship, and critics say it never criticizes the food industry. As evidence, Nestle points to the association's fact sheets: One that stresses the importance of biotechnology is financed by Monsanto, the leading American producer of genetically engineered crops; one that endorses aspartame is financed by NutraSweet; and one that states that the connection between sodium and high blood pressure is unclear is sponsored by Campbell Soup. University departments concerned with nutrition, food science, and agriculture now actively seek corporate funding, and there are now exclusive public-private partnerships between some food companies and university departments. For example, Novartis, the Swiss company that owns Gerber Products, and the Department of Plant and Microbial Biology at the University of California (UC), Berkeley, have a partnership that gives the company the right to select participating faculty, review research findings before publication, and influence faculty participation on certain projects. What concerns critics, according to Nestle,

is the idea that companies might dictate the direction of research or unduly influence or delay its publication. Although faculty have reported incidents of intimidation and of pressure on students to work on Novartis-funded projects, the dean of the college reportedly termed such concerns "silly."

This book has caused a great deal of controversy and angered critics, who claim that Nestle neglects the complexity of the social and cultural environment that influences food choices, especially the contribution that physical inactivity makes to obesity. Some say the food industry is only giving people what they want and that people resent any efforts to control what they eat—after all, popcorn, salt, alcohol, soft drinks, fast foods, frozen dinners, and sugar substitutes are not harmful to all of their users. They suggest it would be better for public health activists to teach consumers how to select food, read food labels, and choose recommended portion sizes, rather than to attack specific foods and ingredients.

Nevertheless, Nestle's indictment of the food industry is compelling and disturbing. If only to generate discussion of the issues it raises, the book is a must for food and nutrition professionals; government officials who deal with these issues; consumer advocates; students in agriculture, nutrition, and public policy programs; and people who work in the food industry. It is also recommended for the general reader concerned about food, nutrition, and health, although it reads like a textbook. Numerous tables, figures, and comprehensive notes support the text.

Edna B. Quinn

Sources for Further Study

The Economist 363 (May 11, 2002): 78.
Los Angeles Times, April 2, 2002, p. E3.
The Nation 274 (May 6, 2002): 37.
The New York Times, May 15, 2002, p. F6.

THE FOUNDING FISH

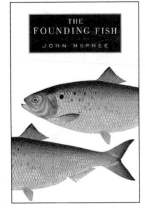

Author: John McPhee (1931-   )
Publisher: Farrar, Straus and Giroux (New York). 358
   pp. $25.00
Type of work: Essays, natural history, and science
Time: 2001
Locale: The Delaware, Pamunkey, Connecticut, St.
   Johns, Hudson, Potomac, Schuylkill, Shubenacadie,
   and other eastern "shad" rivers, and the Bay of Fundy

Seventeen essays explore many aspects of the shad,
Alosa sapidissima, *including its habitats, culture, and mi-*
gration patterns, its function in American history and econ-
omy, its qualities as a sport fish, and especially McPhee's
love for the fish, all developed characteristically from extensive personal research in
the field and extensive interviews with experts and presented in his inimitable style

Principal personages:
   BOYD KYNARD, field biologist and director of the S. O. Conte Anadro-
      mous Fish Research Center, Turners Falls, Massachusetts
   ARMAND CHAREST, maker of shad darts
   ED CERVONE, educator and shad fisher
   BUDDY GRUCELA, expert shad fisher
   GERALD HARTZEL, shad fisher for thirty years
   RICHARD ST. PIERRE, U.S. Fish and Wildlife Service
   SETH GREEN, transplanted shad fingerlings to the Sacramento River, cre-
      ating a West Coast fishery
   WILLY BEMIS, University of Massachusetts fish anatomist
   MIKE DADSWELL, Canadian ichthyologist whose studies of the effects of
      turbine fans on shad helped to kill the proposed Bay of Fundy gener-
      ating plant

   In his twenty-sixth book, John McPhee profiles a species of fish, the American
shad—*Alosa sapidissima*—and dozens of men and women who fish for shad, biologists and ichthyologists who study shad, environmentalists who seek to preserve shad
habitat, and others including several of McPhee's own ancestors. This book, like his
famous "geological" text, *Annals of the Former World* (1998), provides in equal mixture the anecdotal and the technical, the scientific and the affective, a technique that in
McPhee's hand ensures lively and informative, if at times challenging, reading. Many
of its most delightful passages provide detailed, lyrical descriptions of historically
important shad rivers such as the Delaware and the Connecticut, the Hudson, the
Schuylkill, the Susquehanna, and others. Typically, he also provides passages dense

and rich with the important scientific exposition based on work done in the twentieth century by ichthyologists to reveal the details of the species' life cycle and the pernicious effects of dams and pollution on it. Much of the book is likewise devoted to detailed descriptions of McPhee and others in the water catching—or trying to catch—shad and preparing and eating this most savory fish. Some readers may view his confession that he is a "meat" fisherman as paradoxical coming as it does at the end of his love song to the shad. The book as a whole reveals the enormous importance of the shad to the history of the country, and the intriguing complexity of the shad's sensitivity to the ecology and health of rivers.

∽

John McPhee has written for Time *magazine and, since 1965,* The New Yorker. *His first book,* A Sense of Where You Are, *was published in the same year.* Encounters with the Archdruid *(1972) and* The Curve of Binding Energy *(1974) were nominated for National Book Awards in the category of science. In 1977, McPhee received the Award in Literature from the American Academy of Arts and Letters.* Annals of the Former World *(1998) received the Pulitzer Prize in 1999.*

∽

Ever curious about the natural world and humankind's interactions with it, McPhee deepens his (and his readers') understanding of the shad through research, interviews, and participant observation. The chapter titles reveal both their content and McPhee's attitude toward his subject and create a subtle and satisfying rounding of his work. In the first chapter, "They're in the River," McPhee puts his readers in the river, in a johnboat with himself and two companions, Ed Cervone and his son, Edmund Cervone, on the Delaware River between New Hope, Pennsylvania, and Lambertville, New Jersey. Toward the end of winter, shad, which are schooling ocean fish during most of their adult life, begin their run upstream mostly to their birthplaces to spawn and complete the life cycle. As they begin their move, the word goes out by e-mail and telephone, radio and television, that "they're in the river," and fishermen appear on the river in congregating numbers, hoping to catch a share of this delectable, savory if bony, and historical fish. The river is thus crowded below the surface with (in most years) vast numbers of shad. It is also crowded on the surface and along the banks with huge numbers of fishermen, especially at places such as dams or serious rapids that cause the fish to "school up." McPhee memorializes such expert shad fishers as Buddy Grucela and Gerald Hartzel, celebrating (and perhaps envying) their skill at catching shad.

The other chapters continue McPhee's postgraduate course in shad. McPhee buttresses or explains his personal observation of the fish, its history, and its habitats with testimony and analysis from "visiting" scholars and with textual references. For example, chapter 2, "A Selective Advantage," reveals his typical strategy when he allows Boyd Kynard, field biologist and director of the S. O. Conte Anadromous Fish Research Center in Turners Falls, Massachusetts, to explain (between casts and catches) what a shad's scale reveals through chemical analysis. One may learn its age, its specific place of origin, where it did its growing, and why it behaves the way it does, including literally stopping to study a strange riffle or even dying of fright at times. Because they are a schooling fish, when one stops, all (or nearly all) will stop, too. Swimming together in a huge school has hydrodynamic advantages; like bicyclers in a pack, the fish draft each other and thus, as a group, go farther faster using less energy. However, the selective advantage turns out to go, in Kynard's view, to those fish who get farthest upstream to spawn, because their offspring will find more to eat on their way down to the ocean and will therefore be larger and less likely to be eaten on the trip down—genetics plus behavior plus environment.

Because shad are very sensitive to their environment, the populations of various shad fisheries are affected by artificial obstacles (dams) that bar their way to and from their spawning grounds and pollution, including sedimentation and chemical pollution. On some rivers, industrialization in the nineteenth century effectively ended shad spawning runs far short of their normal spawning grounds and nearly eliminated some populations. By building such dams as the one at Holyoke, Massachusetts, the Connecticut River populations were severely affected. Commercial fishing boats off shore overfished other populations by intercepting the large schools and translating them into human food or fertilizer.

Chapter 3, "Amending Nature," reveals how the Pamunkey tribe near Richmond, Virginia, maintained their traditional shad fishery, while other East Coast fisheries were crashing, by setting up a fish hatchery in 1918, later tearing it down and building a much larger one to ensure shad survival on the Pamunkey River. In spawning season, the Pamunkey people will catch as many as eighty female spawners a day, strip the roe into buckets, and strip the milt from male spawners into the same buckets. They let the buckets stand for an hour and then transfer the contents, a hundred thousand fertilized eggs per three liters, to hatching jars attached to tanks. About seven million fingerlings survive per eight-week season and are released through tubes into the Pamunkey River, thereby assisting and "amending" nature. An increasing number of fish hatcheries on other rivers assist the recovery of their shad populations. One of the most important devices for amending the rivers is the Clean Water Act of 1972. It mandated tearing down many nineteenth century dams and removing water pollution, bringing shad (and other species) back from disaster. However, as McPhee points out, seventy-eight dams on major East Coast rivers continue to block shad migrations. Similar problems exist on the West Coast, where Seth Green successfully transplanted shad fingerlings in 1878 to establish what is now a thriving shad fishery, but not without its own problems of pollution and dam blockage. As an anadromous species, shad must spawn in the best fresh water they can find, their progeny returning to the ocean for a period of three to eight years to mature. Then they themselves will return to their natal river to spawn and repeat the cycle—unless stopped by humankind's waste or unthinking industrialization.

McPhee argues in his powerful narratives for much greater ecological activity to preserve and extend shad and other species. The successes of dam removals, fishery restoration with fish hatcheries, as well as the shelving of such destructive and short-sighted plans as damming the Bay of Fundy have brought several species back from near extinction on a number of watersheds. Powering that rebound has been the scholarly work of a number of biologists and ichthyologists such Boyd Kynard, Richard St.

Pierre, Willy Bemis, and Mike Dadswell, whose work McPhee celebrates. Kynard, for instance, thinks that the cooling of the ocean in places that were once good places for shad to overwinter may be causing the formerly abundant food sources to decline, thus contributing to the decline of shad populations.

McPhee is a vast and intelligent reader as well as listener. Consequently, he makes full and effective use of many forms of traditional narrative to enrich and enliven (if not leaven) his prose, celebrating and critiquing the connections between *Homo sapiens* and *Alosa sapidissima*. The book is a treasury of personal and traditional anecdotes about the fish and its hunters. For instance, he relates a number of stories from his own family history, going back several generations to suggest the strong relationship between personal history and community, regional, and national history. In the chapter entitled "The Shad City," for example, McPhee notes that his father was a publisher in Philadelphia who bought shad from a street vendor and carried it home in a newspaper through streets strident with the Philadelphia yodel of "Shad-e-o!" The food traditions of Philadelphia were rich in recipes for shad, and writers of that city avowed that only in Philadelphia was shad properly and truly appreciated. One popular legend has it that General Washington's troops at Valley Forge were saved from starvation by the unseasonable appearance of huge schools of shad in the Schuylkill in the early spring of 1778. McPhee cites historian Wayne Bodle's judgment of the story as nothing less than "the providentialist canard" to support his own assessment of it as "recommended by everything but sources." (Other stories—that the young Washington was a commercial shad fisherman and that Thomas Jefferson had "hauled" seine as a youth—McPhee accepts as historically factual because they are supported by written sources.)

These examples of shad stories circulating in the oral tradition testify to the important place of the shad in American history and culture. Perhaps they also warrant a call to modify some of them by implicitly arguing that recalling and maintaining personal and community oral history and traditions provides an important context for understanding the broader history of community and state. It also suggests a complex and compelling relationship between and among species and the powerful, mythic relationship of the American shad to colonial history from first European settlement to the Revolutionary War and now down to the twenty-first century. McPhee titles the book *The Founding Fish* to suggest these functions as both a literal and a mythic basis of the country's origin and survival and thus to warrant and celebrate the work of restoration and conservation that has brought the shad fishery back from severe "crashes" in a number of eastern rivers. This rich mixture of anecdotes, tall tales, and personal narratives with scientific data and testimony gives McPhee's work its characteristic compelling flavor and tone, making it a fit addition to his oeuvre.

Theodore C. Humphrey

Sources for Further Study

Booklist 98 (July, 2002): 1799.
The New York Times Book Review 107 (December 8, 2002): 16.
Publishers Weekly 249 (August 26, 2002): 57.
Time 160 (November 25, 2002): 94.

THE FUTURE OF LIFE

Author: Edward O. Wilson (1929-   )
Publisher: Alfred A. Knopf (New York). 229 pp. $22.00
Type of work: Natural history

~

*Biologist Wilson examines the status of the planet's bio-
diversity, its startling magnificence, and its underestimated
peril*

~

On the fortieth anniversary of the publication of Rachel
Carson's *Silent Spring* (1962), the distinguished Harvard
biologist Edward O. Wilson has published an important
new book on the state of life on Earth. There is a sense of urgency about Wilson's
book, because half of the world's species may be extinct by the end of the twenty-first
century. In seven carefully reasoned chapters, Wilson describes how the biodiversity crisis has come about and what its implications are. He explains why preserving
biodiversity is essential to human survival for economic, psychological, and aesthetic reasons. In clear and lucid terms, he explains the global implications of the massive human transformations of the planet's ecosystems. The human ecological "foot-
print" has simply become unsustainable in comparison to the rest of the natural
world. Life has flourished with unparalleled abundance since the beginning of the Ce-
nozoic Era about 66.4 million years ago, but human activity now threatens to reverse
this trend with an accelerating rate of human-induced extinctions that will create a
much-impoverished world by the end of the twenty-first century. Humankind is entering a metaphoric bottleneck in its battle between the preservation and extinction of
life.

In his prologue, Wilson uses a cleverly worded open letter to naturalist icon Henry
David Thoreau (1817-1862) to assess the present global environmental state of affairs. Wilson invokes the spirit of Thoreau and their kinship as naturalists to underscore the urgency of the current ecological crisis. His assessment is bleak: "The natural world in the year 2001 is everywhere disappearing before our eyes." A global
Armageddon is approaching—the destruction of the biosphere by humanity. "We are
inside a bottleneck of overpopulation and wasteful consumption," Wilson observes,
that is straining Earth's natural resources to their limits. What is needed, Wilson concludes, is a new global land ethic that will enable humankind to preserve what is left
of Earth's magnificent biodiversity. A more encompassing wisdom is needed to balance the natural economy and the market economy.

Since humans seem to be able to value the natural world only in economic terms,
Wilson raises the intriguing question of the financial worth of the biosphere. The
value of the combined services of the biosphere is estimated to be about $33 trillion,

∾

Edward O. Wilson is a distinguished professor of zoology at Harvard University and author of two Pulitzer Prize-winning books, On Human Nature *(1978) and* The Ants *(1990; with Bert Holldobler), as well as* Consilience *(1998),* In Search of Nature *(1996),* Naturalist *(1994),* The Diversity of Life *(1992), and* Biophilia *(1984). He is a recipient of many of the world's leading prizes in science and conservation, including the 1976 National Medal of Science.*

∾

or twice the 1997 combined Gross National Product (GNP) of all of the world's economies, which is about $18 trillion. These services "include the regulation of the atmosphere and the climate; the purification and retention of fresh water; the formation and enrichment of the soil; nutrient recycling; the detoxification and recirculation of waste; the pollination of crops; and the production of lumber, fodder, and biomass fuel." The true value of a healthy biosphere actually is much greater, because all of these functions are essential for human life and, once the biosphere is destroyed, it almost certainly could not be rebuilt, at least not with current knowledge. Wilson uses the example of the probable extinction of the magnificent ivory-billed woodpecker to underscore his argument that the loss of a species cannot simply be written off as an acceptable cost of progress. Each species is a unique and irreplaceable treasure. Unfortunately, average people simply do not understand the connection between their actions and the destruction of the biosphere.

In "Nature's Last Stand," Wilson reviews the conventional ecological assumptions about the causes of loss of biodiversity. The major threats to biodiversity are expressed in the acronym HIPPO: habitat destruction, invasive species, pollution, population, and overharvesting. The prime mover for all of these incursive forces is human overpopulation—too many people consuming too many natural resources too quickly. The prospects for preserving biodiversity are bleak, but the trajectory of species loss depends on human choice. Humans must find a way to resolve the current impasse between environmentalism and economics, between long-term and short-term values. That means figuring out how to feed billions of new human mouths over the next few decades while saving the rest of life at the same time. Wilson sees potential economic benefits in preserving biodiversity both in terms of new agricultural crops and in bioprospecting for new pharmaceuticals. The preservation of the natural world is essential for long-term material prosperity and health.

Humanity is inflicting on itself and on Earth a mistake in capital investment. Humans are currently spending down Earth's natural resources to make increasingly large payments to the wealthiest industrial nations to improve standards of living. Unfortunately, the key elements of natural capital are not capable of sustaining infinite growth, and they are being rapidly depleted through overuse. The per-capita natural resources left to be harvested are shrinking, and the long-term prospects for finding more are not good. This rapid plundering of Earth's resources has two collateral results: a growing disparity between rich and poor nations and an accelerating extinction of natural ecosystems and species. Why, the present generation's descendants will ask, did humanity permanently impoverish itself by needlessly extinguishing other species? What is to be done?

Any meaningful response, Wilson argues, must begin with ethics. A global conservation ethic is needed that will enable humans to preserve the nonhuman world for future generations. There are three ethical levels of concern for the natural world: the anthropocentric, the pathocentric, and the biocentric. The first views the natural world strictly in human terms, the second acknowledges some limited rights for higher-functioning animals, and the third recognizes the intrinsic right of all organisms to exist. There is obviously some overlap among these views, but in order to protect the biosphere, a more widespread acceptance of the biocentric view must evolve. Wilson finds hope in a greater congruence of environmental concerns between science and religion, particularly in ecospiritual views that emphasize humanity's inescapable involvement in the natural world, epitomized in popular scientific narratives of the evolution of the cosmos and of life on Earth (which Wilson terms the "Epic of Evolution") and of the philosophical movement of Deep Ecology, which attempts to place humankind in a more sustainable relationship with the ecosystem. Humanity's innate biophilia may yet save it from its economic drive to plunder the planet for short-term gains. The public is beginning to realize that if the natural environment is destroyed, nothing else will matter very much.

Wilson acknowledges that, since "the juggernaut of technology-based capitalism cannot be stopped," the best thing to do is redirect its energies to improve the plight of the world's poor and try to save as much of the biosphere as possible. However, meaningful action depends upon reaching political consensus on environmental policies. In order to highlight the conflict between economic development and environmental conservation, Wilson creates a hypothetical dialogue between an environmentalist and a "people-first" advocate in which each caricatures the views of the other. The neoconservative "people-firster" views environmentalists as impractical, probureaucratic "tree-huggers" who would deprive citizens of their legal rights to their private property, while the environmentalist views critics as antigovernment, prodevelopment, right-wing extremists who mask their greed and self-interest in free-market rhetoric. The basic problem is that while the people-first ethicist takes a short-term view of the environment, the environmental ethicist takes a long-term view. To protect the biosphere, it is necessary to find areas of consensus in reconciling these perspectives. In "The Solution," Wilson suggests ten practical steps to be taken: salvage immediately the "hotspots," those ecosystems most at risk; keep intact the five remaining frontier forests; protect lakes and river watershed systems everywhere; finish mapping the world's biodiversity; include all of the world's ecosystems in a global conservation policy; make conservation profitable; seek out the economic benefits of biodiversity; initiate ecological restoration projects; increase the capacity to breed endangered species; and support population planning.

The goal for this century must be to lift a stabilized world population to a decent quality of life while salvaging and restoring as much of the environment as possible. Wilson believes this may just be possible with a new partnership between science and religion in the area of environmental ethics. Wilson concludes by explaining the reasons for his cautious optimism. He estimates that the global environment could be saved for about $30 billion, only a thousandth of the world's annual GNP. Some of these funds could be acquired simply by ending perverse subsidies that are used to aid industries that are depleting the environment, such as fishing, logging, mining, or ranching. Wilson looks to a combination of government, the private sector, and science and technology to find innovative solutions to the biodiversity crisis, but nongovernmental organizations (NGOs) must take the lead in the extinction battle because governments "are too distracted by the necessities of military defense, political intrigue, and the economy to deal effectively with the death of nature."

Wilson points to the evolution of the World Wildlife Fund (WWF) as an example of an NGO that broadened its mandate during the 1990's to find innovative ways to save endangered species and ecosystems. Back in 1984, they were an organization of 100,000 members mainly concerned with raising funds to protect large endangered animals such as tigers and pandas. By 1994, they had grown to over one million members and were concentrating on preserving entire threatened ecosystems. A second change in the WWF was to begin to form partnerships with indigenous peoples living in or around threatened ecosystems. They have worked together to turn targeted ecosystems into economic assets.

Two new approaches that international conservation organizations have recently adopted are the debt-for-nature swap and the conservation concession. With the former, funds are raised to purchase a portion of a country's debt at discount and the resulting equity raised is used for conservation purposes. The latter are long-term leases that can be arranged for large tracts of land, especially in tropical nations where the largest concentrations of biodiversity exist. Here existing reserves can be expanded at a relatively low cost, eventually to create continent-long wildlife corridors to protect even the largest species. Wilson cites recent successes of the Nature Conservancy and Conservation International in Guyana, Suriname, Bolivia, the Palmyra Island in the Pacific, and the Pantanal wetlands between Brazil, Paraguay, and Bolivia. This new kind of international ecosystem conservation requires interplay between biology, economics, and diplomacy. Wilson outlines three stages in the development of nature conservation projects: the creation of individual reserves, the restoration and enlargement of natural reserves, and the establishment of large corridors to connect existing parks and reserves.

More international treaties are also needed to protect the environment and all nations need to put aside their self-interest and ratify existing treaties, such as the Kyoto Protocol. Wilson cites the success of the Montreal Protocol in reducing chlorofluorocarbons (CFCs), and of the Convention on International Trade in Endangered Species of Wild Flora and Fauna (CITES), Convention on Migratory Species (CMS), and Convention on Biological Diversity in preserving species. He also sees great promise in the creation of an international wildlife park along the demilitarized zone between North and South Korea. "The strength of each country's conservation ethic," he affirms, "is measured by the wisdom and effectiveness of its legislation in protecting biological diversity." One such example is the United States' Endangered Species Act. Environmental protest groups or individuals can also help raise public awareness, as in the case of Julia "Butterfly" Hill. Wilson believes that an enlightened and aware public can save the world's biodiversity. The central challenge of the current century will be to raise the standard of living of the world's poor while preserving biological diversity.

Andrew J. Angyal

Sources for Further Study

The American Spectator 35 (March/April, 2002): 54.
Booklist 98 (December 1, 2001): 604.
The Boston Globe, January 13, 2002, p. E7.
Choice 39 (June, 2002): 1793.
Commentary 113 (April, 2002): 65.
The Ecologist 32 (May, 2002): 40.
Library Journal 127 (January 1, 2002): 147.
New Statesman 131 (April 29, 2002): 46.
The New York Times Book Review 107 (February 17, 2002): 11.
The New Yorker 78 (March 4, 2002): 83.
Publishers Weekly 248 (December 17, 2001): 73.

THE GIRL FROM THE COAST

Author: Pramoedya Ananta Toer (1925-   )
First published: Gadis Pantai, 1990, in Indonesia
Translated from the Indonesian by Willem Samuels
Publisher: Hyperion (New York). 280 pp. $22.95
Type of work: Novel
Time: The early twentieth century
Locale: Java, Indonesia

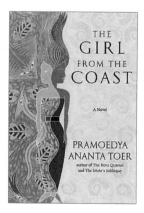

～

   A fictionalized account of the experiences of the author's grandmother as "practice wife" of a Javanese nobleman

～

   Principal characters:
        THE GIRL FROM THE COAST, an unnamed beauty from a poor fisherman's
           family
        THE BENDORO, a Javanese aristocrat who takes the girl as his "practice
           wife"
        MBOK, a servant who tends to the girl
        MARDINAH, another servant who replaces Mbok

    Pramoedya Ananta Toer is Indonesia's best-known writer. A nationalist and social critic, Toer was imprisoned by the government of former Indonesian president Suharto for fourteen years and his books were banned until Suharto's fall from power in 1999. Outside Indonesia, however, translations of his books circulated around the world. His best-known work, the Buru Quartet, consists of four novels—*Bumi Manusia* (1981; *This Earth of Mankind,* 1990) *Anak Semua Bangsa* (1982; *Child of All Nations,* 1993), *Jejak Langkah* (1986; *Footsteps,* 1990), and *Rumah Kaca* (1988; *House of Glass,* 1992)—composed during the author's imprisonment on the eastern Indonesian island of Buru; they follow the development of Indonesian national consciousness. *The Girl from the Coast,* published in the original Indonesian in 1990, is the most recent of his books to be translated into English. Its social and political themes will be familiar to readers who know Toer's earlier work. While the novels of the Buru Quartet are organized around the life history of a nationalist intellectual, however, *The Girl from the Coast* takes the perspective of a heroine from a poor fishing village.
    Much of Toer's writing consists of the fictional investigation of Indonesian history. This latest translated work looks back at the beginning of the twentieth century. Toer tells in a footnote at the end of the book that he had originally meant this to be the first volume of a trilogy about the growth of the nationalist movement in Indonesia, but the two following novels were destroyed by the Indonesian military. This was intended, then, to be the beginning of a much larger epic.

The central character, never identified by name, is a young girl who lives with her parents in a fishing village on the coast of Java. When she is fourteen, word of her beauty reaches the local Bendoro, a Javanese aristocrat in the service of the Dutch colonial overlords. The nobleman sends word to her family that she is to become his wife. Filled with hope for their daughter's future, her mother and father agree to have her married in a ceremony in which the groom is absent and is represented by a dagger. The parents accompany their child to the great man's house in the city. There, they find a disturbing omen of their daughter's future. A servant is caring for a baby, child of a previous wife who had been divorced and dismissed at the Bendoro's whim.

Pramoedya Ananta Toer was born the son of a rural schoolmaster in East Java, Indonesia, when that country was still a Dutch colony. His first novel, Perburuan *(1950), later translated into English as* The Fugitive *(1975), won the Balai Pastaka literary prize in the year it was published. In 1988, he was awarded the Freedom to Write Award in absentia by the international writer's organization* PEN.

The servant, Mbok, becomes the personal servant and caretaker of the girl. The girl grows to depend on Mbok, who tells her stories and gives her advice on adjusting to the strange ways of the aristocracy. Among the stories is Mbok's own tale of how she and her husband were taken away from their village by the Dutch to work on a plantation. After the pregnant Mbok had been kicked in the stomach by a foreman, killing the unborn child, her husband had run amok and had been killed by soldiers. Jailed and then let go to fend for herself, Mbok had eventually ended up in the service of the Bendoro. Mbok is sympathetic to the girl but also aware of her own complete dependence on her employer.

The Bendoro is a devout Muslim and insists that the girl learn her prayers. His religion is largely a matter of the observance of forms and rituals, and it does not give him any sense of charity or fellowship with other people in general. He regards villagers as dirty and lazy. The author of the novel clearly sees no more virtue in organized religion than in the traditions of feudal aristocracy or in colonialism.

Mbok's integrity, courage, and care for the girl lead to the servant's downfall. After some of the male relatives of the Bendoro, who live in the house, help the girl clean her room, the girl's wallet proves to be missing. She is distraught, since this wallet contained money for household expenses. When the relatives respond to Mbok's inquiry with contempt, Mbok brings the matter before the Bendoro. The lord discovers the thief and orders him to leave the house, but Mbok is also dismissed. She had dared to accuse a superior and can no longer remain.

Without Mbok, the girl is alone. A new servant, Mardinah, arrives, but Mardinah is a sinister figure. A relative of the Bendoro, Mardinah, who is the same age as the girl, has already been divorced. Unlike Mbok, Mardinah refuses to treat the girl as a superior and is often rude.

The appearance of Mardinah is the occasion for a strange turn in the novel. The Bendoro encourages the girl to return to her village to visit her parents. Although she does not want to bring Mardinah with her, she does so on the Bendoro's insistence. In the village, the girl finds that the other villagers and even her own parents keep their distance from her and treat her as a member of the nobility. In a bizarre sequence of events, the villagers discover that a woman who has been living in the village is actually a man, and he turns out to be the brother of Mardinah, stationed in the village as a spy. Mardinah's bodyguards are found to be planning to murder the girl on their return from the village. Mardinah herself had planned this improbable murder to help the regent in her town of Demak, who wanted to marry his daughter to the Bendoro. After Mardinah's confession, she is married to the village good-for-nothing storyteller and tambourine player, named Dul. The bodyguards are led out to sea, on the pretense of saving them from attacking pirates, and drowned.

Following this peculiar interlude, the girl returns to the house of the Bendoro. She becomes pregnant and bears a daughter. The daughter, however, is the child of her noble father and the new mother has no right to the baby. Having finally decided to take a real wife of his own social class, the Bendoro orders his practice wife to leave. When she refuses to abandon her child, he beats her and has his servants force her out the gate. For a month afterward, a carriage would pass by the gate and someone would look from behind the carriage curtain at the Bendoro's mansion.

The Indonesian version of the novel ends with the figure in the carriage. For the English language reader, however, Toer has added an epilogue to take the place of the two lost sequels and to give this surviving work a more satisfactory ending. This was a wise move, because the epilogue clarifies the writer's own relation to the work and compensates for the weird sequence of events during the visit to the village by making the tale seem more realistic. Toer tells readers that Sa'idah, the daughter of the girl, grew up in the home of the Bendoro and received an education. At the age of eighteen, almost past marriageable age for an Indonesian woman of her era, Sa'idah became involved with an older schoolmaster who had taken the last name of "Toer" (last names are a fairly recent innovation in Indonesia and many people still do not use them today). After the Bendoro's death, Toer recounts, his noble widow gave Sa'idah the choice of finding a job or marrying the schoolmaster.

As soon as the author mentions the name "Toer," the reader begins to understand the story differently. While this is fiction, Toer is telling a version of his own family history. Mas Toer (the "Mas" is an honorific or title) is the author's own father. Toer briefly touches on the schoolmaster's conflicts with the Dutch, and these conflicts were probably central to at least one of the sequels destroyed by the military. More significantly for ending this book, the adult Sa'idah happens to meet her own mother, the girl from the coast. This is the author's own grandmother. It is difficult to know what parts of the tale are true and what parts have been invented to give the story narrative form or to fill in unknown details in the grandmother's life. Still, this epilogue does give a poignance to the novel that it would otherwise lack.

Toer is at his best in bringing Indonesian history to life and in dramatizing the evils of feudalism and colonialism. He is a skilled storyteller, and readers can easily imagine him recounting tales for his fellow prisoners during his years of imprisonment. Even in his best work, however, characterization is not one of his strong points, and the people in his novels often seem to have no more depth than the puppets in an Indonesian *wayang* play. This is a particular problem with *The Girl from the Coast*. The girl herself is so idealized that only occasionally does she come across as a real character. Most of the other characters remain at the level of symbols or representations of the author's political and social criticisms.

The plot, although entertaining, relies heavily on dramatic artifice in the part in which Mardinah's evil plans are discovered during the visit to the girl's village. Readers might reasonably wonder why the servant would need to go to such elaborate lengths to get rid of the girl. Since the girl was, from the beginning, only a practice wife preceded by other practice wives, it would hardly seem necessary to kill her to get her out of the Bendoro's life. In fact, he does put her out, just as he put out his other practice wives, immediately after the birth of her child. Even if her death would have made it easier for the regent to marry his daughter to the Bendoro, why would Mardinah have made the risky effort to accompany her young mistress to the fishing village, since a much simpler and less risky assassination could have been arranged? Mardinah's acquiescence in her marriage to the lazy village singer Dul strains credulity, as does her sudden change in personality after the marriage.

The translation, by Willem Samuels, is generally good, but it does read like a translation, with stiff sentences and occasionally clumsy syntax. For all of its problems, however, most readers will find *The Girl from the Coast* well worth their time. The story is enjoyable and the short novel is a good place to begin to become familiar with Indonesian literature in general and with the work of Pramoedya Ananta Toer in particular. It offers an intriguing view of Indonesian history and society and provides interesting insights into the role of Indonesian native elites under Dutch colonialism. The portrayal of daily life in the fishing village gives Western readers a window into a culture unfamiliar to them that continues to exist today.

Carl L. Bankston III

Sources for Further Study

Booklist 98 (August, 2002): 1926.
Kirkus Reviews 70 (July 1, 2002): 918.
Library Journal 127 (June 15, 2002): 97.
Los Angeles Times Book Review, August 4, 2002, p. 10.
The New York Times Book Review 107 (August 11, 2002): 15.

GIRL MEETS GOD
On the Path to a Spiritual Life

Author: Lauren F. Winner (1977-   )
Publisher: Algonquin Books (Chapel Hill, N.C.). 314 pp.
    $23.95
Type of work: Autobiography and religion
Time: 1977-2000
Locale: Asheville, North Carolina; Charlottesville, Virginia; New York City; Cambridge, England

Girl Meets God

On the Path to a Spiritual Life

Lauren F. Winner

◇

A spiritual autobiography that recounts Winner's journey from Judaism to Christianity

◇

Principal personages:
LAUREN F. WINNER, a Jewish woman raised in the South
RANDI, her best friend
STEVEN, a former boyfriend
HANNAH, a Christian friend in New York
MILIND SOJWAL, rector of All Angels' Episcopal Church, New York
JO BAILEY WELLS, chaplain of Clare College chapel, Cambridge, England

Religion occupies a unique place in American society. Although separation of church and state assures a secular culture, most Americans identify with some form of religion. Americans take an individualistic view of their religious practices. The result is a virtual "supermarket" of religious options, and Americans are accustomed to "shopping" in this religious marketplace in search of the religious or spiritual path that they feel suits them best. *Girl Meets God*, twenty-five-year-old Lauren Winner's account of her relatively youthful spiritual journey as she seeks to find a religious home first in Judaism and then in Christianity, is both an intensely personal narrative and a representative voice for the situation that her generation faces as they confront the landscape of American religion in the early twenty-first century.

Winner was born in Asheville, North Carolina. Her father was Reform Jewish and her mother was a lapsed Southern Baptist. Lauren and her older sister, Leanne, were raised in the Jewish faith even after her parents divorced and she moved to Charlottesville, Virginia, with her mother. As a teenager, she actively participated in the life of the Reform synagogue in Charlottesville, joining a meditation group and teaching Sunday school with her friend Randi. She read and studied about Judaism. One summer when she was in high school, she took classes at Drisha Institute for Jewish Education in New York, which is one of the few places where women can study the Talmud, and she lived with an Orthodox Jewish family. The summer before she went to college, she participated in a program in Israel.

She concluded that the only way to be true to her Jewish belief was to convert to Orthodox Judaism. She attended Columbia University in New York because of the active Orthodox Jewish life there. She had to undergo a formal conversion process since her mother was not Jewish and Judaism is matrilineal. She prepared for the *bet din*, an examination before a court of three rabbis, by studying with one rabbi in New York and with her special mentor, a rabbi in Boston who was a leader of the group with whom she had traveled to Israel. In December of her freshman year at Columbia, she went through the *bechina* (exam) and the ritual bath, *mikvah*. For most of her four years in college, she endeavored to live as an Orthodox Jew.

During this time, her intellectual interests at Columbia gravitated toward Christianity, and her course work focused on American religious history, especially Protestantism in the South. She

Lauren F. Winner is a doctoral candidate in the history of American religion at Columbia University, a contributing editor for Christianity Today, *and a former book editor for the* Beliefnet *Internet site.*

loved to spend time at the Cloisters, a museum devoted to medieval art. Just a year after her conversion to Orthodox Judaism, she had a dream in which she and some other women were captured by mermaids, spent a year in captivity, and were rescued by a group of graying men, except for one "beautiful, thirtyish, dark Daniel-Day-Lewis-like man" with whom she continued to have conversations about the kidnapping. She believed that "the dream was about Jesus, about how He was real and true and sure."

By her senior year in college, things changed. She explains that "gradually, my Judaism broke," and she became more open to Christianity. As she read novels by Jan Karon, which revolve around an Episcopalian rector in a small town in western North Carolina and depict the Christian faith of these people as they go about their daily lives, she thought: "I want what they have." She confided her attraction to Christianity to a Presbyterian minister on campus, but he told her that she could not divorce Judaism. Soon thereafter, she purchased a Book of Common Prayer and attended a series of "learning services" at an Episcopal church. By the time she graduated she had determined to convert to Christianity. She was baptized and confirmed in the Anglican Church while she was living in England as a fellow at Clare College, Cambridge.

Upon her return to complete doctoral studies at Columbia two years later, she had to confront putting the pieces of her religious life together from the perspective of her newfound Christian faith within an environment where she was known as an Orthodox Jew. One of the ways that she approached this situation was through writing for publications such as *Christianity Today* and the Internet magazine *Beliefnet*. Her book *Girl Meets God* is in some ways an extension of that writing process and, indeed, parts of the book have appeared in other versions in these venues.

Winner presents her reflections by looking at a year in her life, following, for the most part, the Christian liturgical calendar from Advent through Christmas, Epiphany, Lent, Holy Week, Eastertide, Pentecost, and returning full circle to Advent. A strength of the book is that Winner allows the reader to witness how her Christian faith impacts every little corner of her life, from the mundane business of daily living to engagement with theological ideas. In the process, she touches on many concerns that most people encounter, but at times avoid, along their own spiritual journey.

Given her personal history, a crucial issue for Winner is the reconciliation and integration of her Jewish past with her Christian present and future. Although she "divorced" Judaism and divested herself of her Jewish books and religious objects, she finds that Judaism continues to pervade her life. In her personal life, relationships with family and friends have changed. Her conversion adds to the strain between Winner and her father. Some friends such as Randi remain, but in many cases, close ties such as that with her rabbi in Boston and an Orthodox Jewish family who virtually adopted her during her undergraduate years are completely ruptured. In religious terms, her whole being follows the rhythm of the Jewish liturgical calendar as much as the Christian one. On several occasions she tries to integrate the two, with a Christian Passover seder and a Pentecost *leil tikkun Shavuot.* Her Jewish reading habits continue to inform her reading of the Christian Old and New Testaments. A startling shock comes as she hears the Holy Week liturgy in which a passion play taken from gospel readings casts Jews as villains in demanding the crucifixion of Jesus. Although later, upon reflection, Ms. Winner arrives at the private insight that the Jews "didn't kill Him; the weight of our sin killed Him," this difficult incident highlights how all Jews and Christians struggle to balance their common bonds with the reality of their differences.

Within the broad spectrum of theological positions of American Protestantism, Winner identifies herself as an evangelical Episcopalian. The cornerstone of her Christianity and a crucial reason for her conversion resides in the Incarnation, "the idea that God lowered himself and became a man." Winner, along with most evangelicals, values "a personal relationship with Jesus" which includes "walking and talking with their God, about everything from world peace to car insurance." For her, this incarnational God is the one true God. In line with evangelical thinking, she understands that humanity is sinful and she believes that through the redemptive sacrifice of Jesus's crucifixion she is saved. She sees the Bible as the primary authority, but she does not read it literally. She also considers it an obligation to evangelize or spread the Gospel and to witness, but she feels "unhidden, uncloseted . . . embarrassed" when on Ash Wednesday the cross marked with ashes on her forehead forces her visibly to proclaim her faith on the subway and on Columbia's secular campus.

Although person-to-person evangelism is not her forte, she finds comfort in the concept of "lifestyle evangelism" which "just requires living a good, God-fearing, Gospel-exuding life." For someone who believes in and relies on "lifestyle evangelism," some of her life choices are puzzling. She reveals that in her confessions, prayer and sex are the two main topics. "Not enough of one, too much of the other"— not behavior, she admits, that conforms to Paul's admonition to "avoid sexual immorality." She can overindulge with liquor as at a departmental party where she got drunk and "came on . . . wildly" to a "sexy blond professor." Forgiving others does not come easily, especially a former boyfriend, Steven, from whom she wishes she could retrieve a literal debt for plane tickets to visit him in Arkansas.

While everyone makes mistakes in daily life, in religious terms Winner's "lifestyle evangelism" comes to resemble a burden, more forced than spontaneous. She has difficulty with prayer. "Sometimes whole weeks elapse when I hardly bother to pray at all, because prayer is boring; because it feels silly . . . ; but above all because it is unproductive." Although she believes that the Eucharist is the most important thing she does, that this sacrament is "where I most really meet Christ," she says that she has "never felt stirred, or joyful, or peaceful, or sad. . . . I have never felt God at the communion rail." When she goes to confession, she brings a lengthy list of sins in which the same topics recur. Most important, a sense of desolation creeps into her experience of religion. She says that she is coming to know "how we are all running around desperate to make connections with one another, but mostly we are all just estranged. Because I know more and more that this glass here is so very dark, that this really is a long loneliness. . . ."

By the end of the book, as the cycle of the liturgical year comes full circle, Winner feels "a sort of sinking staleness," and she begins to question her faith. What she is discovering from a more mature perspective than when she abandoned Judaism is that the spiritual life requires a long-term commitment. As Canon Dr. Martyn Percy says in *Previous Convictions: Conversion in the Real World* (2000), "It is not possible to hand over 'the whole of our lives' to God at once, because we live, and as we live, we change. . . . To be a Christian is to be a 'becoming person.'"

In *Girl Meets God*, Lauren Winner has openly shared her experience up to this point of being a "becoming person." When she thinks about her Baptist maternal grandmother, she expresses doubt that she "will ever have the unwavering faith that she had. I will always be too embarrassed and too sophisticated and too modern to believe the way she believed." This generational difference is good because with her interfaith background, her intelligence, and her spiritual calling, Winner has the potential to bring fresh perspectives to the experience of religion in the twenty-first century in a world torn by a combination of religious dissension and religious apathy. The reader must take her at her word: "I want God to give me the grace to stick with this, to stay here. And I believe He will."

Karen Gould

Sources for Further Study

Booklist 99 (October 1, 2002): 292.
Books and Culture 8 (November/December, 2002): 9.
The Christian Century 119 (October 9, 2002): 23.
Library Journal 127 (November 1, 2002): 97.
Publishers Weekly 249 (August 12, 2002): 293.

GLOBALIZATION AND ITS DISCONTENTS

Author: Joseph E. Stiglitz (1943-   )
Publisher: W. W. Norton (New York). 282 pp. $24.95
Type of work: Current affairs and economics
Time: The 1990's
Locale: Washington, D.C., and the developing world

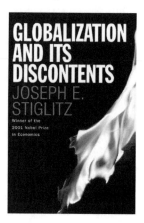

~

A discussion of globalization is highly critical of the role played by the International Monetary Fund in dealing with global financial crises and the transition to market economies in developing nations

~

Popular discontent with the economic process known as globalization is on the rise not only in developing countries, for which globalization has had adverse consequences, but also in the West, as shown by the large street demonstrations that take place whenever the World Trade Organization (WTO), the World Bank, or the International Monetary Fund (IMF) hold a major meeting. These demonstrations can no longer be shrugged off as the work of a small, discontented minority. In *Globalization and Its Discontents*, the critics of globalization and the role of Western financial and trade institutions in promoting it receive some heavyweight support from an insider who knows what he is talking about. This book is a sustained and often devastating critique of the role of the IMF in globalization and is only slightly less critical of the economic policies and assumptions of the U.S. government. Stiglitz relentlessly offers example after example of situations in which the IMF's rigid insistence that its policies were the only correct ones to be pursued, in spite of evidence to the contrary, led to disastrous results across the globe, from East Asia to Latin America and Russia.

Globalization is the process which has led to a closer integration of all the nations of the world by the reduction in costs of transportation and communication and the breaking down of artificial barriers to the movement of goods, services, capital, and people across borders. There is no doubt, as Stiglitz points out, that globalization has brought many benefits. The opening up of international trade has helped many developing countries grow far more quickly than they otherwise would have done. Standards of living have been raised and life expectancy extended. However, in many parts of the world, globalization also has failed to bring the predicted economic improvements. More people live in poverty in 2003 than at the beginning of the 1990's, even though total world income has increased during the same period. Nor has globalization brought economic stability, as crises in Latin America and Asia have shown.

The IMF was created in 1944 with the task of ensuring global economic stability. Stiglitz believes that it has failed in its mission. Not only have economic crises become more frequent over the last twenty-five years, but in many cases, the policies promoted by the IMF have actually made the situation worse, especially for the poor. Nor has the IMF been successful in the task it adopted in the 1990's, to supervise the transition to a market economy in former communist countries.

The basic criticism that Stiglitz makes is that the IMF is attached to a rigid ideological agenda that is not always appropriate for the situation. He calls this the "Washington Consensus." This consensus, which emerged in the Reagan era of the 1980's, values the free market above everything else. It emphasizes fiscal austerity, privatization, and market liberalization. According to Stiglitz, when the consensus first emerged it made considerable sense, but as the years went by it came to be applied as an end in itself rather than

Joseph E. Stiglitz is a leading economist whose work has dealt extensively with growth and development in the Third World. He has also seen global economic policy making at first hand, as a cabinet member in the Clinton administration and chairman of the Council of Economic Advisors and as senior vice president and chief economist of the World Bank. Stiglitz shared the 2001 Nobel Prize in Economic Sciences and is a professor of economics at Columbia University.

as a means to ensure equitable and sustainable growth in the nations concerned. The Washington Consensus was then pushed too far and too fast. Stiglitz calls this "market fundamentalism."

Too often, the approach of the IMF to developing countries is that of a "colonial ruler." Agreements between the IMF and leaders of developing nations are not made between equal partners. The nation in effect hands over its economic sovereignty to the IMF in order to receive IMF-based aid. Stiglitz cites an arrogance at the heart of the IMF culture, the notion (not borne out by the facts) that it always knows best. Little real discussion is permitted, nor are dissenting views. The IMF might claim that it always negotiates the terms of its loans and does not use coercive tactics, but Stiglitz argues that such negotiations are completely one-sided since all the power lies with the IMF. Given the fact that IMF-based economic measures fail as often as they succeed, it is not surprising that the IMF is vilified in most developing countries. In those countries that have had some success in avoiding or recovering from economic crises, such as Uganda, Ethiopia, Botswana, and China, and in a country such as Poland, which has had relative success in making a transition to a market economy, the strategies followed have largely differed from those of the Washington Consensus.

Much of Stiglitz's book focuses on the economic crises in East Asia (in a chapter subtitled "How IMF Policies Brought the World to the Verge of a Global Meltdown") and Russia. The East Asian crisis began in July, 1997, when the Thai currency collapsed. Within months, the crisis had spread to Malaysia, Korea, the Philippines, and Indonesia. Attempting to ride to the rescue, the IMF, in Stiglitz's analysis, merely made things worse. Huge IMF loans came with certain conditions, including higher interest rates, cutbacks in spending, and raising of taxes, as well as the insistence on structural economic and political reforms such as increased openness and improved financial market regulation. These contractionary policies were the opposite of what was needed. High interest rates "strangled" the economy, and the policies also created a "beggar-thy-neighbor" effect: Economic downturns were passed on to neighboring countries as each country reduced its imports.

As exchange rates continued to fall, the IMF then blamed the countries themselves, claiming that they had not taken the necessary reforms seriously enough. This had the further effect of eroding investor confidence, and the result was the flight of capital from the countries concerned. The IMF had become part of the problem, not the solution. The IMF's mishandling of national economies led to social unrest, especially in Indonesia. Although the IMF had provided $23 billion in loans, it had provided nothing directly to help the poor. Even worse, food and fuel subsidies were cut back, and riots broke out the very next day.

Stiglitz argues that the IMF has not learned from its mistakes, and in the next crisis may make exactly the same errors. He believes that an alternative strategy would have worked better. This would have been to maintain the economy as close to full employment as possible, which requires an expansionary rather than contractionary fiscal and monetary policy. The IMF also miscalculated in its dealings with Russia and other former communist countries in Eastern Europe as they struggled to make the transition to a market economy. The Russian economy during the 1990's turned out to be a disaster. In every year after 1989, gross domestic product (GDP) fell. Over the period 1990-1999, GDP fell by 54 percent. Industrial production fell by 60 percent, a greater drop than during World War II. There is no underestimating the task faced by the Russian government during this decade. Nearly seventy years of struggling along under an unrealistic, centrally planned economy had to be wiped out and the economy reshaped so that it responded to market forces.

The mistakes made, according to Stiglitz, were in the IMF's encouragement of a "shock therapy" approach, in which the transition was made too quickly, over a gradualist strategy. For example, too-rapid price liberalizations led to huge inflation. Rapid privatization, carried out on the instructions of the IMF, did not lead to increased efficiency or growth, but to asset stripping and decline. It also led to a loss of confidence in government, democracy, and reform. IMF policies also ignored the social context in which their measures were to be carried out. During the 1990's there was an increase in inequality in Russia. The rich got richer and the poor got very much poorer and more numerous. In 1989, only 2 percent of Russians lived in poverty. By 1998, that figure had soared to 23.8 percent.

Stiglitz also faults U.S. government policy toward Russia and developing countries. On too many occasions, pandering to special economic interests made the United States look hypocritical. For example, although the United States supports free trade, when a poor country tried to export a commodity to the United States, more often than not domestic protectionist interests interfered. Trade laws were exploited to construct barriers to imports. One case Stiglitz cites is when the United States accused Russia of "dumping" (that is, selling below cost) aluminum. Not only was the charge false, but the U.S. response relied on the opposite of the market forces it was supposedly promoting: It created an international cartel that regulated the production and export of aluminum. Prices rose, and consumers lost out. The Russians learned from this, as well as from their attempt to export uranium, that on occasion, the United States preaches one thing but does another.

For Stiglitz, the challenge is not to go back on globalization, but to make it work for everyone, not just the industrialized world. He argues that to accomplish this will require reforms of the international financial system. He proposes several major areas of reform: acceptance of the dangers of capital market liberalization; bankruptcy reforms (a better way of addressing debt than IMF-financed bailouts); improved banking regulations; improved risk management; improved safety nets (unemployment insurance programs, for example); and improved responses to crises. He also notes that the advocates of globalization must become more sensitive to the impact the process has on a culture's traditional values. Urbanization, for example, can have an adverse effect on rural societies; the ascendancy of large national retailers has adverse effects on small town businesses and communities. *Globalization and Its Discontents* is a sobering reminder that despite noble rhetoric, Western-dominated financial interests, as manifested in institutions such as the IMF, often suffer from an intellectual myopia that leads them (and those forced to rely on their prescriptions) astray, and also leads to an unsettling tendency to arrange international economic affairs largely for their own benefit.

Bryan Aubrey

Sources for Further Study

Booklist 98 (May 15, 2002): 1560.
Business Week, June 17, 2002, p. 17.
Foreign Affairs 81 (July/August, 2002): 157.
Library Journal 127 (May 15, 2002): 106.
The New York Times Book Review 107 (June 23, 2002): 12.
The New Yorker 78 (July 15, 2002): 82.
Publishers Weekly 249 (May 13, 2002): 64.

GOULD'S BOOK OF FISH
A Novel in Twelve Fish

Author: Richard Flanagan (1961-   )
First published: 2001, in Australia
Publisher: Grove Press (New York). 404 pp. $27.50
Type of work: Novel
Time: The present and the nineteenth century
Locale: Tasmania

∼

The picaresque narrative of a forger confined to an infamous penal colony, told in a convoluted and hallucinatory style with episodes of Magical Realism

∼

Principal characters:
> SID HAMMET, a shady entrepreneur in modern-day Tasmania
> WILLIAM BUELOW GOULD, a convict imprisoned at the brutal Sarah Island penal colony
> THE COMMANDANT, chief warden of the prison
> TOBIAS ACHILLES LEMPRIERE, the prison doctor
> TWOPENNY SAL, the Commandant's aboriginal mistress, with whom Gould has an affair
> TOM BRADY, a guerrilla rebel
> CAPOIS DEATH, a fellow prisoner to whom Gould is especially close

Nobody can accuse Richard Flanagan of resting on his laurels after his well-received debut novel *The Sound of One Hand Clapping* (1999) and its follow-up, *Death of a River Guide* (2001). Certainly no one can accuse him of retelling, as some authors do, the same basic story again and again in different guises. *Gould's Book of Fish: A Novel in Twelve Fish* is about as different a book as it is possible to imagine in comparison to his previous two works—and for that matter, in comparison to its fiction competitors of this publishing season, as well. Reviewer Caroline Fraser, writing in the *Los Angeles Times*, rightly calls it "surely one of the most eccentric novels to appear in recent years."

Flamboyant, lushly styled, outrageous, dark, funny, cynical, humane, gratuitously violent, byzantine, self-conscious, exuberant, grotesque, graceful, ghoulish, frustrating, cocky, over-reaching, and chaotic are all valid descriptors of the picaresque tall tale within a tall tale that is *Gould's Book of Fish*. If some of those terms seem contradictory, that is because Flanagan's third novel is at its heart, among many other things, such an act of willful—at times joyful—contradiction that its pages at times seem barely capable of containing it. Strangely enough, the pages themselves even

get into the act, with various chapters printed in
different ink colors representing the natural pigments its castaway hero was able to find, steal, or
cajole on a particular day to fuel his makeshift
pens, which are actually spines from sea urchins.
Since any kind of record-keeping by prisoners is
a capital crime, Gould goes to great lengths to
keep his pages hidden in a high crevice of his
cell, which is located below the tide line and fills
twice a day with water.

*Richard Flanagan won several
prizes in his native Australia for
both* Death of a River Guide *(2001)
and* The Sound of One Hand
Clapping *(1999). He adapted the
latter into a film and directed it
himself. He lives in Tasmania.*

The novel's complexity makes a brief overview of its plot difficult to achieve. The story is
set, as are all Flanagan's novels, on the remote
island off the southeast coast of Australia known
as Tasmania. The contemporary narrator of the
thirty-eight-page preface is a ne'er-do-well whose
latest failed scheme was creating fake antiques
for the port's tourist market. One day in a junk
shop he comes across an unusual old volume
(coincidentally titled *The Book of Fish*) with magical and hallucinatory properties, which becomes his sole obsession. Then, one night in a pub, the book inexplicably self-destructs (technically, turns into water) before his eyes. The remainder
of the novel is presented as the antique-forger's attempt to reconstruct, from memory and his own haphazard notes, the journal of a nineteenth century convict named
William Buelow Gould, imprisoned (coincidentally, for forgery) at the infamous
and unspeakably brutal Sarah Island penal colony of Van Diemen's Land, or today's Tasmania. (Gould is based on a real-life character, whose paintings the author first saw at the Allport Library and Museum of Fine Art, Library of Tasmania;
twelve of the paintings are reproduced in full color, one at the beginning of each
chapter.)

The book recounts the drastic ups and downs of Gould's years on Sarah Island, doing the bidding of the bizarre, and likely insane, men (rendered here as caricatures,
alas, but complex and compelling ones) who make up the penal colony's administrators. The novel gets its title from an ongoing project that Gould is assigned when the
prison's doctor, one Tobias Achilles Lempriere, discovers the forger's artistic talents.
Lempriere, an amateur naturalist, dreams of scientific fame and believes that producing an elaborate illustrated taxonomy of the region's unique species of fish (although
ghost-painted, as it were, by the prisoner) will win him election to the Royal Society.
Gould's painting schedule provides him, for a few hours a day, a semblance of normal
life and mobility from which he witnesses the torture and degradation of the colony's
inmates. Gould's arrival on the island provides one of the book's most memorable
passages:

On disembarking, we were to discover all the requisite brutality & squalid circumstances you might expect of such a place. But even before alighting, even before we saw anything up close, our noses were assailed by the effluvium of death. Death was in that heightened smell of raddled bodies & chancre-encrusted souls. Death arose in a miasma from gangrenous limbs and bloody rags of consumptive lungs. Death hid in the rancorous odour of beatings, in the new buildings already falling apart with the insidious damp that invaded everything, was seeping out sphincters rotting from repeated rapes. Death was rising in the overripe smell of mud fermenting, enmities petrifying, waiting in wet brick walls leaning, in the steam of flesh sloughing with the cat falling, so many fetid exhalations of unheard screams, murders, mixed with the brine of a certain wordless horror; collectively those scents of fearful sweat that sour clothes & impregnate whole places & which are said to be impervious to the passage of time, a perfume of spilling blood of which no amount of washing or admission was ever to rid me. And perhaps because everywhere was death, life has perversely never seemed so sweet as what it did when I first came to Sarah Island.

Eventually, Gould's painting skills bring him to the attention of the book's overarching personality, the prison's ominous, unnamed, larger-than-life Commandant. Suffering from syphilis, addicted to laudanum, and concealing his face from underlings by means of a gold mask, the Commandant nonetheless has grandiose fantasies of building the mile-square island into an economic power with tourist attractions the equal of Europe's wonders. He is tormented from afar by his nemesis, a populist guerrilla outlaw named Tom Brady. Reminiscent of the isolated former dictators in the novels of Colombian writer Gabriel García Márquez, the Commandant's madness is at one point described thus:

Of a night he was unable to sleep for want of the sound of a nation. All he could hear echoing up & down the lonely market aisles that were supposed to be full of the noise of bartering, of trade, of people, was that hollow sound of the waves ominously slapping the shore.
Lying awake, terror mounting, he began to wonder whether that one sound was the sea or was it his lungs or was it his destiny calling slap-slap-slap even then, calling him back. . . . No matter how many fine new stone buildings he put between him and his night-time visions, no matter how much of Europe he erected between him and the silence, it was the same nightmare of the sea rising & rising & rising, & Brady coming ever closer & closer & the flames of Hell ever hotter . . .

The Commandant has a much larger canvas in mind for Gould's painting talents. In a rare moment of lucidity, he has realized that, other than tourists, the island's grand new scenic railway is lacking only one thing: scenery. He therefore commissions the convict to paint giant backdrops of famous vistas for the train to pass, Flanagan's homage to Russia's "Potemkin villages" of the previous century.

At times, in fact, Flanagan's novel resembles an immense pastiche of allegory and reference and tribute, rendered in stylistic and tonal indulgences that echo such past masters as Jonathan Swift, Henry Fielding, Herman Melville, Charles Dickens, Joseph Conrad, Isaac Bashevis Singer, William Faulkner—Flanagan's epigraph is from Faulkner's *As I Lay Dying* (1930): "My mother is a fish"—and contemporary writers including García Márquez and Cormac McCarthy. In that sense, *Gould's Book of Fish* is almost flagrantly derivative, but in a way that seems a tribute to, rather than a send-up of, the great picaresque novelists of the past. At Flanagan's best, though, the loving irreverence of his authorial voice sings with a beauty all its own. In fact, the contrast between Gould's devil-may-care brio and his reflections, in quieter moments, on how such transcendent natural beauty and horrific human cruelty can coexist in the same small square of land and ocean is one of the most appealing aspects of the book.

Ultimately, it is the author himself who brings down the entire fantastical edifice he has constructed—brings it down not only in its plot, in an apocalyptic forest fire whose raging momentum inevitably sweeps over the prison colony and its inhabitants with exquisitely described carnage, but through a denouement of literary devices that at first heighten the narrative's hall-of-mirrors construction and then methodically deconstruct the very foundation of reality underneath the tall tales, calling into question the existence of the supporting characters and turning Gould himself not only metaphorically, but literally into a fish:

> I like my fellow fish. They do not whinge about small matters of no import, do not express guilt for their actions, nor do they seek to convey the diseases of kneeling to others, or of getting ahead, or of owning things. They do not make me sick with their discussions about their duties to society or science or whatever God. Their violences to one another—murder, cannibalism—are honest & without evil. . . .
>
> Sometimes I must admit I long once more to have the power of human speech, if only for a few moments, so that I might explain how I once wanted to live as a rainbow of colour exploding, hard sun falling apart in soft rain, but had to be content instead with making grubby marks on cheap cartridge paper.

Likewise, the author has set up the reader, throughout, to realize instinctively that such an extravagant undertaking, defying the gravity of logic and chronology, must end in failure. It is far from an ignominious failure, however—it is a grand fireworks display of the possibilities of human voice and longing, viewed in a crystalline reflecting pool whose depths Flanagan's book, unlike the transcendent moments of García Márquez's Magical Realism in *Cien años de soledad* (1967; *One Hundred Years of Solitude*, 1970) or McCarthy's Goyaesque horrors in *Blood Meridian* (1985), never quite plumbs. In the end, all the narrative's brilliant peregrinations cannot escape the gravitational field of the author's imposing intellect.

At the same time, *Gould's Book of Fish* raises its author into the sparse pantheon of contemporary fiction writers whose gift of language and unique slant of mind make their every new literary effort a storehouse of wonder that no serious reader can afford to ignore.

Carroll Dale Short

Sources for Further Study

The Economist 363 (June 22, 2002): 102.
Entertainment Weekly, May 10, 2002, p. 75.
New Statesman 131 (June 3, 2002): 50.
The New York Times, March 26, 2002, p. E1.
The New York Times Book Review 107 (June 2, 2002): 23.
Publishers Weekly 249 (March 25, 2002): 40.
The Times Literary Supplement, June 7, 2002, p. 21.

GRACEFULLY INSANE
The Rise and Fall of America's Premier Mental Hospital

Author: Alex Beam (1954-   )
Publisher: Public Affairs (New York). 273 pp. $26.00
Type of work: History, psychology, and science
Time: 1817-1999
Locale: Belmont, Massachusetts

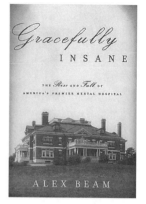

∼

A history of Boston's McLean Hospital, the second-oldest mental hospital in the United States, focusing on its wealthy and privileged clientele and developments in psychiatric medicine as they were played out at McLean

∼

Principal personages:

WILLIAM FOLSOM, diarist, McLean Hospital apothecary in 1825

SIGMUND FREUD (1856-1939), Austrian founder of psychoanalysis

HORACE FRINK, McLean patient in 1924-1925, former patient of Sigmund Freud

WILLIAM JAMES (1842-1910), psychologist, philosopher, "father of American psychiatry," possible McLean patient

SUSANNA KAYSEN, author of *Girl, Interrupted* (1993), an account of her stay at McLean

CARL LIEBMAN, McLean patient from 1935 to the late 1960's, former patient of Sigmund Freud

ROBERT LOWELL (1917-1977), Pulitzer Prize-winning poet, intermittent McLean patient between 1958 and 1962

STANLEY McCORMICK, heir to McCormick Harvest Company (International Harvester), McLean patient in 1906-1907

FREDERICK LAW OLMSTED (1822-1903), landscape architect, designer of New York City's Central Park and McLean Hospital grounds

WALTER PATON (pseudonym), McLean patient since 1948

SYLVIA PLATH (1932-1963), poet, McLean patient in 1953-1954

ANNE SEXTON (1928-1974), Pulitzer Prize-winning poet, McLean poetry seminar instructor in 1968-1969 and McLean patient in 1973

LOUIS AGASSIZ SHAW II, McLean patient from 1964 to 1987

JAMES

KATE, and

LIVINGSTON TAYLOR, musicians, McLean patients in the 1970's

FRANKLIN WOOD, McLean director during the 1940's and 1950's

Newspaper columnist Alex Beam spent years gathering material for *Gracefully Insane: The Rise and Fall of America's Premier Mental Hospital*, initially planning to compile an oral history of McLean Hospital from interviews with past and current doctors, patients, and nurses associated with McLean. Beam saw the Belmont, Massachusetts, hospital's history as a reflection of Boston's history and culture. Established in the late nineteenth century a few miles outside Boston, several of McLean's original buildings were named after wealthy Bostonians, and many prominent figures in New England society and the arts had been patients at McLean.

Although Beam found the oral history unwieldy and abandoned that format, *Gracefully Insane* retains the character of a personal narrative based upon interviews with people who lived in or worked at the hospital. Beam also discovered that McLean had inspired poetry by Robert Lowell, prose by Susanna Kaysen and Sylvia Plath, and songs by James Taylor and Livingston Taylor, in addition to letters and diaries by lesser-known people, and at least one detailed history of the hospital. Beam draws heavily and very effectively on this literary record to bring McLean to life on the page.

McLean also provided Beam with a vehicle for examining the history of treatments for mental illness in the United States. McLean was one of the first mental hospitals to offer the "moral treatment," or "milieu therapy" newly popular in the early nineteenth century. In contrast to the imprisonment and punishments routinely inflicted on mental patients up to that time, moral treatment sought to remove the mentally ill from the stresses of everyday life. However, throughout its history McLean also offered other, less peaceful treatments as they became fashionable in American psychiatry. These included hydrotherapy (spraying patients with hoses or immersing them in baths for long periods), electroshock (briefly running electric current through the brain), psychosurgery (lobotomy, or surgical alteration of the brain) and Freudian analysis.

McLean Hospital opened as the Charlestown Asylum in 1817. Developing his theme of McLean's historical ties to Boston's social elite, Beam notes that the first hospital trustees included a former United States president, a future president, a future Supreme Court judge, and a future president of Harvard University. Shortly after McLean opened its doors, two other hospitals were opened in Boston, both designed to care for the poor, and McLean began to focus on attracting an upscale clientele.

In 1895, the hospital was moved to a new location. The hospital buildings included gymnasiums, bowling alleys, and billiard rooms, and the grounds incorporated a golf course, a stable of horses, tennis courts, an apiary for producing honey, a herd of milk cows, and two orchards. Landscape architect Frederick Law Olmsted designed the new hospital grounds around uncluttered, pastoral spaces where patients could take long nature walks. Olmsted planned wards to house patients with similar illnesses together, a new idea at the time. Wealthy McLean patients stayed in furnished private suites designed to help them feel at home in the hospital. In its new location McLean also offered cottages designed for single patients—a typical McLean "cottage" might be a five-bedroom home, the construction of which was funded by the patient's family.

Critics note that *Gracefully Insane* fails to examine the darker sides of mental illness and treatment. In avoiding serious discussions of psychosis and its effects, the author makes a stay in McLean seem like a pleasant vacation rather than incarceration of individuals whose mental disturbances required their removal from the outside world. Beam was, in fact, drawn to McLean by his personal interest in the concept of the individual's struggle to find shelter from harsh reality. While his descriptions of early treatments such as hydrotherapy and lobotomy are chilling, Beam emphasizes the natural beauty and sumptuous facilities McLean offered in its heyday over the struggles of the mentally ill.

Beam also offers humorous examples of eccentric patient behaviors; Carl Leibman, who had been treated by the best names in the psychoanalytic business before coming to McLean, habitually greeted doctors with the words, "I am my father's penis." Chapters have tongue-in-cheek titles such as "The Mayflower Screwballs," "The Country Clubbers" and "The Mad Poets Society." Beam quotes lyrics from a Broadway-style musical comedy written and performed by McLean patients in 1958, which included songs entitled "The Forty-Day Commitment Blues" and "Diagnostic Tango."

Gracefully Insane does provide frightening descriptions of some of the experimental psychiatric theories and treatments that have been used throughout the years that McLean has been in operation, although these treatments were not necessarily used there. These include violent methods intended to shock mental patients into sanity. Although McLean's emphasis was on the gentle, moral treatment, its doctors dabbled in more radical approaches including, in the 1940's, hypothermia, which involved swaddling patients in special blankets through which a refrigerant was pumped to lower the body temperature. Hydrotherapies were also used at McLean in which patients were wrapped in cold, wet sheets or immersed in baths for hours at a time.

Several shock therapies were also used at McLean. Patients were deliberately given overdoses of insulin to induce a supposedly therapeutic insulin coma; schizophrenic patients were injected with the chemical metrazol to cause convulsions that were believed to cancel out schizophrenic disturbance. Patients were given low-level electric shocks as an alternative to insulin coma and Metrazol treatments; lobotomies were used at McLean in the early 1950's, also with limited success.

Beam notes that McLean physicians were particularly interested in mental illness among society's elite, naturally enough as their clientele was drawn from the wealthiest New England social class. McLean's patient roster included associates and kin of the eminent writer Ralph Waldo Emerson (1803-1882) and the oldest son of physician John Collins Warren (1778-1856), the first physician to use ether as an anesthetic. Beam discusses evidence that William James, the author of the classic text *Principles of Psychology* (1890), was once a patient at McLean and discusses at length the case of patient Stanley McCormick, the heir to the International Harvester fortune.

Gracefully Insane profiles renowned poets who were admitted to McLean in the 1950's. Pulitzer prize-winning poet Robert Lowell suffered from delusions and mania; he checked into McLean four times in eight years and wrote his poem "Waking in the Blue" about living in the men's ward. The poet Sylvia Plath wrote a fictional account of her experience as a McLean patient in her novel *The Bell Jar* (1963). Poet Anne Sexton, also a Pulitzer Prize winner, wanted to check into McLean because Lowell and Plath had been patients there. Sexton taught poetry seminars for McLean patients before being admitted briefly herself in 1973.

Two famous patients of psychoanalyst Sigmund Freud were later admitted to McLean. Dr. Horace Frink, considered one of Freud's great failures, was himself a psychoanalyst but suffered from depression and became Freud's patient in 1921. Dr. Frink, who was having an affair with one of his own patients, divorced his wife and married the patient on Freud's advice. The marriage was disastrous; Frink became suicidal but was later treated with greater success at McLean.

McLean patient Carl Liebman was a "psychiatric celebrity" who had been a patient of several of the most famous psychiatrists of the 1920's and 1930's, including Freud. In addition to psychoanalysis, the paranoid schizophrenic Liebman was treated with insulin shock, electroshock therapy, and hydrotherapy, and received a topectomy (a less radical variety of lobotomy) while at McLean. During his stay in Upham Memorial Hall, young doctors eager to meet one of Freud's few surviving patients often visited him.

Beam devotes a chapter to other elderly and very wealthy McLean patients who checked into the hospital's grand Upham Memorial Hall and lived there comfortably for decades. Among these was the eccentric and snobbish Louis Agassiz Shaw II, committed to McLean in 1964 after strangling one of his maids—an action his aristocratic family considered "highly inappropriate"—remaining there until he was moved to a nursing home in 1987. The gently mad septuagenarian Walter Paton (a pseudonym) was admitted to McLean in 1948 and was still a patient in the late 1990's. Beam notes that the hospital made little effort to treat chronically ill patients whose families could afford to maintain them in the stylish suites of Upham Hall. In the early 1970's, McLean began housing disturbed adolescent patients in Upham, and over the next two decades the once-luxurious building took on a different character and was gradually allowed to fall into ruin. Upham became a homeless shelter in the late 1990's and was locked and abandoned entirely in 1998.

Many teenagers from wealthy New England families became McLean patients during the late 1960's and 1970's. Beam devotes a chapter to these "hippies," among them several well-known musicians, including siblings James, Livingston, and Kate Taylor. James wrote a popular song called "Knockin' 'Round the Zoo" about his stay at McLean. Beam notes that the disturbances from which such young patients suffered may have been nothing more than typical adolescent rebellion. Well-to-do parents taken aback by the social turbulence of the 1960's and 1970's could simply afford to have their children looked after by professionals in a controlled setting.

Beam's task of interweaving the stories of doctors, patients, and treatments can sometimes make for a convoluted read, moving constantly backward and forward through vaguely defined periods of time. This is a history that eschews specifics in favor of anecdotes evoking the personalities inhabiting the hospital, to such a degree that it is difficult to determine what titles were held by particular administrators, when they attained their positions at the hospital, and when they stepped down. McLean director Franklin Wood is referred to frequently throughout the text but placed only vaguely in context as the "World War II era" director whose patients might have driven Packard limousines. Typically, Beam offers a quote from a speech given by McLean's first superintendent, Rufus Wyman, then jumps forward in time to tell an anecdote about Wyman's successor Luther Bell—then moves chronologically backward again to discuss William Folsom, a young druggist who worked under Wyman. The book would benefit from a chronology placing in context the large number of hospital administrators and patients discussed.

Changes in psychiatric medicine eventually brought about McLean's decline as a haven for wealthy, chronic patients. As more hospitals were established to treat mental illness, drug therapies became more common, and the costs of hospital stays increased, the long-term care that was McLean's specialty became obsolete. More and more patients relied on insurance plans to cover their hospital expenses rather than the indulgence of wealthy families, and antipsychotic drugs made extended hospital stays less common for the mentally ill. In 2002, McLean's administration began selling much of McLean's acreage and several buildings to developers in an effort to keep part of the hospital open as a more conventional treatment center.

Maureen J. Puffer-Rothenberg

Sources for Further Study

Library Journal 127 (January 1, 2002): 131.
Los Angeles Times Book Review, January 20, 2002, p. 7.
The New York Times Book Review 107 (February 24, 2002): 8.
Publishers Weekly 248 (December 10, 2001): 61.
The Washington Post, May 22, 2002, p. C9.

THE GREAT MOVIES

Author: Roger Ebert (1942-   )
Publisher: Broadway Books (New York). 511 pp. $29.95
Type of work: Essays and film

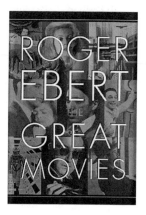

∽

*A collection of one hundred informal essays on individ-
ual films that bear marks of true greatness*

∽

A film critic for the *Chicago Sun-Times* since 1967,
Roger Ebert is best known for his appearances on national
television's long-running *Siskel and Ebert at the Movies*
(later *Ebert and Roeper*). Through three and a half decades,
he has reviewed more than two hundred new films every
year. Many of his newspaper reviews have been collected in books that have become
popular film guides. The present book, however, has nothing to do with these earlier
collections. Its one hundred essays are derived from more than 150 newspaper columns on films of the past that Ebert began writing in the late 1990's. He wrote the essays to help call attention to the history of films, which he believes is badly neglected
in college film courses, and makes the implicit argument that modern films suffer
from a lack of historical perspective among the people who make them.

These essays contrast with Ebert's regular film reviews in having been written after repeated viewings of the films over many years and in being freed of many of the
traditional constraints of film reviewing, such as having to be careful not to reveal too
much plot detail. Here, even more than in his reviews of contemporary films, Ebert's
opinions on what makes films important emerge. In general, he is more interested in
moods and feelings than in facts and details and is not bothered by a lack of story. His
essay on *Lawrence of Arabia* (1962) offers a clear example of his preferences. This
World War I epic is probably best remembered for its larger-than-life characters and
its dramatic battle scenes, but what Ebert most likes about it is its "quiet, empty passages, the sun rising across the desert, the intricate lines traced by the wind in the
sand."

Ebert has a particular love of black-and-white films, which account for 60 percent of the films covered in this book. Similarly, about 60 percent of the films are
American-made, with the rest coming from only eight other countries—most notably
France. Chronologically, the films range from *Broken Blossoms* (1919) to *Fargo*
(1996), with a median year of 1959. About two-thirds of the films were made before
Ebert became a film critic; this is not surprising, since his preferences tend toward
older films. Nevertheless, the chronological distribution of titles is impressively even
between the 1920's and the 1970's. Numbers for the last two decades of the twentieth
century drop off significantly, however. Part of this drop-off must be due to Ebert's

generally lower regard for recent films. However, the very newness of those films also has given him little time to put them in perspective.

One of the chief pleasures of reading *The Great Movies* is being repeatedly challenged to consider what makes any film "great." Ebert himself is not dogmatic on this point, as he recognizes that film viewing is such a highly personal experience that it is foolish to attempt to enumerate "the" greatest films of all time. Moreover, critical views are constantly changing. He points out that three years after *The Bicycle Thief* (1949) was made, an international poll of filmmakers and critics ranked it the greatest film of all time. A decade later, the film had sunk to sixth place on the list, and by the next decade it had dropped off the list altogether. In any case, Ebert's own criteria for movie greatness vary from film to film.

No clear patterns are apparent in the book's selection of films. Virtually every genre is represented by at least a few titles, and there are essays on about a dozen silent films, one animated film (*Pinocchio*, 1940), and several documentaries, including *Hoop Dreams* (1994), a long-term study of young basketball players. Apart from a natural preponderance of films that might be classified as "dramas," one genre that stands out is suspense and thrillers, which account for more than a dozen titles. If any popular film genre is underrepresented, it may be Westerns, whose only representatives here are *My Darling Clementine* (1946), a film about Wyatt Earp; *Red River* (1948), the classic film about a great cattle drive; and Sam Peckinpah's violent *The Wild Bunch* (1969).

The first writer to win a Pulitzer Prize (1975) for film criticism, Roger Ebert is best known as cohost of the long-running television film review series Siskel and Ebert at the Movies *(later* Ebert and Roeper*), which began in 1976. Other collections of Ebert's film reviews include* Roger Ebert's Movie Home Companion *(1986-1993),* Roger Ebert's Video Companion *(1994-1998), and* Roger Ebert's Movie Yearbook *(1999-   ).*

Ebert does not claim that the one hundred films discussed in this book are the greatest films of all time. He sees them merely as important "landmarks" in the first century of cinema history. He is concerned with the question of which films will still be watched a century or two from now. This, in turn, raises the question of what makes some films hold up better than others over time. A first test of his selection of titles, therefore, might be how well they engage the attention of modern audiences.

An interesting case in point is Michelangelo Antonioni's *Blowup* (1966). Regarded as a stylish "swinging London" film during its time, it has long since gone out of fashion. *Blowup* is ostensibly about a trendy London photographer (David Hemmings) who may or may not have witnessed a murder in a park, but Ebert sees it as something quite different—a "hypnotic conjuring act, in which a character is awakened briefly from a deep sleep of bored alienation and then drifts away again." In this regard, the film has a timelessness that should make it worth watching for years to come. *Blowup* came out a few months before Ebert began working as a film critic and evidently played an important role in his subsequent career.

Ebert does a great deal of reminiscing in these essays, with frequent reflections on when he first saw certain films and how he reacted to them. His essay on *La Dolce Vita* (1959), for example, recalls different stages in his life when he saw the film and comments on how differently he reacted to it, almost as if he saw a different film each time. *The Wizard of Oz* (1939)—which opens in black and white, switches to color, and goes back to black and white at the end—he recalls as the film that first made him aware of the difference between black-and-white and color films—a distinction of which he was oblivious up until that moment.

The impressions that most films make, Ebert believes, last no longer than their images remain on the screen. A rare few, however, "penetrate your soul." One such film is Spike Lee's examination of race relations, *Do the Right Thing* (1989), which left Ebert in tears after he first saw it at the Cannes Film Festival. He recalls the moment as one of the most extraordinary filmgoing experiences in his life, as "Lee had done an almost impossible thing. He'd made a movie about race in America that empathized with all the participants." Not all reviewers agreed with that assessment, but Ebert makes such a strong case for his view that one wonders how many of the film's original critics might have different views now.

A point that these essays make over and over is the need to see a film many times in order fully to appreciate its greatness. "Every time you see a great film," he argues, "you find new things in it." He recalls, for example, seeing Stanley Kubrick's antiwar film *Dr. Strangelove* (1964) for perhaps the tenth time and noticing for the first time the incredible facial gyrations performed by George C. Scott, who played a hawkish general.

Ebert has seen many of the films discussed in this book dozens of times, and nearly half of them he has studied one shot at a time—usually while teaching film classes. In this regard, this book is an inspiration to owners of DVD players, who can now easily do the same thing in their own homes. Indeed, DVD technology not only makes possible the same kind of shot-by-shot study that Ebert advocates but also offers a wealth of other possibilities, such as running commentaries and other extra features that are often offered with classic films.

Although Ebert reviews four or five new films a week, his interest in films seems never to flag. One of his most surprising admissions is that he has seen the documentary *Gates of Heaven* (1978) "perhaps thirty times" and still has not fathomed its depths. All he knows, he says, is that "it's about a lot more than pet cemeteries." He goes on to say that the film "has given me more to think about over the past twenty years than most of the other films I've seen," and he once ranked the film among the "ten greatest films ever made."

Less surprising is Ebert's admiration of the romantic Humphrey Bogart-Ingrid Bergman classic, *Casablanca* (1942)—which, not coincidentally, was the subject of the first of these essays that he wrote. Ebert's affection for this film is so palpable that it is difficult to read his essay on it without thinking of Woody Allen's nebbish film reviewer in *Play It Again, Sam* (1972), who dreams of living out the role that Bogart created in *Casablanca*. "Seeing the film over and over again, year after year," Ebert writes, "I find it never grows overfamiliar."

Another pleasure found in reading *The Great Movies* is the fresh perspectives that it offers on many films. For example, most people who have seen Quentin Tarantino's *Pulp Fiction* (1994) probably remember it best for its eccentric characters and shocking moments. Ebert, however, sees the film's greatness in its most quiet dialogue, much of which has little direct bearing on the film's plot. He singles out scenes in which a boxer's petite girlfriend expresses a wish to have a potbelly like a man and in which professional hitmen discuss what hamburgers are called in American restaurants in Europe. In Ebert's opinion, *Pulp Fiction* is great because of the high level to which it raises dialogue—a neglected component of modern films.

Throughout the book, Ebert cites examples of films that initially were ignored or drew negative reviews. A prime example is *Bonnie and Clyde* (1967), which was widely panned on its first release. Another, perhaps more surprising, example is the Christmas film *It's a Wonderful Life* (1946), whose reputation as a classic is now so firmly entrenched that few people remember the years when the film was largely forgotten. Its current reputation, according to Ebert, is the result of a happy accident: After its owners neglected to renew its copyright in 1974, the film fell into the public domain and was consequently shown all over television, where it found appreciative new audiences.

Although this book is meant for casual reading rather than reference, its value could have easily been enhanced by the addition of an index and a list of films by date. Most of the still pictures that illustrate each essay are striking images, but in the absence of explanatory captions, some make no clear point. The most egregious example is the photo illustrating the essay on *The Passion of Joan of Arc* (1928). That piece opens with the bold statement that the reader "cannot know the history of silent film unless you know the face of Renée Maria Falconetti." The photograph illustrating the essay naturally shows Falconetti, the actress who plays Joan; however, since her face is barely a quarter inch high, the chance to reinforce Ebert's statement is lost. In view of the fact that all these essays are readily available for no charge online, it is curious that the book's publisher did not do more to make it an attractive purchase. Nevertheless, it remains a worthy addition to any film library.

R. Kent Rasmussen

Sources for Further Study

Library Journal 127 (February 15, 2002): 145.
The New York Times Book Review 107 (March 10, 2002): 19.
Publishers Weekly 249 (February 4, 2002): 69.

THE HAUNTING OF L.

Author: Howard Norman (1949-   )
Publisher: Farrar, Straus and Giroux (New York). 326
    pp. $24.00
Type of work: Novel
Time: 1926-1927
Locale: Churchill, Manitoba; Halifax, Nova Scotia

~

*Peter Duvett, a photographer's assistant, enters into an
uneasy affair with Kala Murie, the wife of his calculating
and dangerous employer Vienna Linn*

~

Principal characters:
> PETER DUVETT, a twenty-eight-year-old photographer's assistant and
>   caption specialist
> KALA MURIE, the beautiful thirty-eight-year-old wife of Vienna Linn,
>   who lectures on spirit photography and is obsessed with Georgiana
>   Houghton's book on the subject, *The Unclad Spirit*
> VIENNA LINN, husband of Kala Murie, a photographer who arranges
>   catastrophes so that he can sell pictures of them
> RADIN HEUR, a wealthy London man who pays Linn for his photographs
>   of death and disaster
> STEWART BISHOP, a man romantically involved with Peter Duvett's
>   mother, and then with his aunt

The Haunting of L. is the third novel of Howard Norman's Canadian Trilogy,
which began with *The Bird Artist* (1994) and continued with *The Museum Guard*
(1998). In each of these novels, a young man involved in some aspect of the art world
is slowly drawn out of his detachment by the love of a woman; in each case, the path
of this love is difficult to navigate. *The Bird Artist* is narrated by Fabian Vas, a young
Newfoundland man who specializes in naturalist portraits of birds. Fabian kills a man
for his lover, Margaret, and must deal with the legal and moral repercussions of his
act. In *The Museum Guard*, Defoe Russet must steal a painting from his Halifax museum for his lover, Imogen Linney. Twenty-eight-year-old Peter Duvett, the narrator
and protagonist of *The Haunting of L.*, is a photographer's assistant and caption writer
who conducts an affair with his employer's wife.

The themes of detachment and isolation, as well as redemption, are more pronounced in *The Haunting of L.* than the other novels, and as such it is the fitting cap-
stone to an exceptional literary trilogy. Each of these young narrator-protagonists is in
some way incapable of understanding the world and his place in it; in each case, a
form of art serves as a metaphor for the isolation of these individuals. Fabian Vas tries
to gain some comprehension of his life through his paintings of Newfoundland birds.

Defoe Russet's life is centered almost entirely around the museum he serves. His understanding of the world is not immediate; instead, it is filtered through the minds and talents of the artists whose works he guards. Peter Duvett is perhaps the most isolated and distant of the three. While Vas and Russet commit crimes for the women in their lives, Peter Duvett wrestles again and again with his passivity and inability to act.

Although an American, Howard Norman is known for his focus on Canadian culture. He began his literary career as a translator of Native American folk tales. His first two novels, The Northern Lights *(1987) and* The Bird Artist *(1994), were finalists for the National Book Award. His most recent novel prior to* The Haunting of L. *was* The Museum Guard *(1998).*

Much in the way that a developing picture gradually appears on photographic paper, *The Haunting of L.* is slow and deliberate in its unveiling of characters and themes. In September, 1926, Peter Duvett leaves his job as a newspaper developer in Halifax to travel to the frozen, remote town of Churchill, Manitoba, to become a photographer's assistant for Vienna Linn. He arrives on the same day that his employer marries the beautiful Kala Murie; before the wedding night is over, Peter and Kala have begun an affair. Peter is initially a cipher in the novel. He is obviously in retreat from some event, yet the nature of his past and his character are obscure at first. He is given to stepping outside himself at any moment and considering himself as part of a still photograph in need of captioning: "[F]or instance, if I left my raincoat inside on a rainy day, I would immediately think, *Man Who Forgot Raincoat Standing on Street.*" His detachment from the events of his own life is so profound that even when he stands over the bed of his lover, Kala, he thinks "*View of My Employer's Wife.*" Peter wonders why he mentally composes such a caption rather than a more "intimate" one such as "*View of Kala Murie Sleeping,*" but he does not question his need to view himself, his surroundings, and the people in his life from a distance, as through a camera's viewfinder.

Kala Murie, Peter's lover, and her mysterious husband Vienna Linn, his employer, are also characters numbed to their own desires, hopes, and beliefs, separated from their true selves as surely as Peter is. Kala is obsessed with *The Unclad Spirit*, a nineteenth century book on spirit photography by Georgiana Houghton. (Houghton actually did exist, according to prefatory material by Norman, although her book bore a different title and his rendering of her work is largely fictional). Kala not only studies the book as if it were Holy Writ, but lectures on its presentation of spirit photographs. Spirit photographs are those pictures of groups that also include the spirit of a person no longer living, or what Houghton calls an "uninvited guest." As Peter puts it, "On the occasion, say, of a wedding, funeral, birthday, family reunion, baptism, no one actually *sees* or speaks to this person—the person isn't even vaguely recalled. Yet when the official photograph of the event is developed, there *he* is, or there *she* is—the uninvited guest." These ghosts captured on film are again a metaphor for the sundered, divided self, and in Kala the reader finds a woman torn between a practical world where she must marry a man she distrusts and fears—Vienna Linn—while at the same time aspiring to a higher morality.

Kala has good reason to distrust her husband. As she reveals to Peter their first night together, Vienna Linn has a wealthy and powerful patron in London, one Radin Heur, who has paid extravagant sums for Linn to arrange horrific train wrecks so that he may photograph the resulting carnage for Heur's private collection. Having failed in one of his assignments, Linn has retreated to Churchill in fear of Heur's retribution. Although he soon becomes aware of Peter's affair with Kala, he takes no action save to draw his assistant into his scheme to regain his patron's good graces. While his detachment is such that he submits to his wife's infidelity, Vienna Linn is the only one of the three of them who, through manipulation of the train wrecks (and later, a plane crash and street car explosion) actively participates in reality, albeit in a horrific, depraved fashion. Ironically, it is through his prior failure to act—to procure the necessary photographs—that he comes to fear for his life.

Kala and Linn are similar in that each of their lives is tremendously influenced by absent persons: in Kala's case, the late spiritualist Houghton, and in Linn's case, his remote sponsor Heur (who never appears in the novel). In a sense, each is haunted by the specter of these distant mentors just as they are haunted by the victims of the accident in the way Houghton defines it: "Haunting. Wherein a mental image never leaves the person alone with peace-of-mind." Vienna Linn has sacrificed his peace of mind to the people he has allowed to suffer in his arranged accidents, and Kala is disturbed by her silent complicity.

Linn does confront Peter about his affair with Kala but implies that he will allow it to continue so long as Peter does not reveal his employer's actions. Not long after, Peter relates one of his favorite lines from *The Unclad Spirit:* "Now, what a person does with knowledge unpredictably gained either reveals one's most deeply informing dignity, or cowardice." For most of the novel, Peter does nothing with the knowledge of evil he has gained. Although he is warned that Linn will sabotage the small plane of Driscoll Pretchey, killing the pilot, several Eskimos, and very nearly Kala Murie, Peter fails to act. Linn takes pictures of the murdered Eskimos and manipulates the photographs to show hazy smudges rising from the bodies of the two of them who had been baptized—presumably, visible proof of the Christian soul's ascent to Heaven. The separation of soul and physical body describes each member of the triangle, but most of all Peter.

As the novel eventually reveals, Peter Duvett retreated to Churchill because of a tragedy in his life. Peter's widowed mother and aunt had both become romantically involved with the same man, Stewart Bishop. Peter's mother married Bishop, but before long she drowned in the Halifax harbor. Although the police ruled the drowning an accident, Peter was convinced that Bishop and his aunt conspired to kill his mother. A sympathetic police detective implied to Peter that the police likely would not investigate too closely if Peter were to seek revenge for his mother's death in some subtle way. Yet Peter did nothing other than repeatedly write the police the same letter about the situation—which they discarded—and his aunt and former stepfather left town together.

Peter realizes he cannot flee from life forever, however, when Linn informs him and Kala that they must relocate to Halifax so that his doctored photograph of the

Eskino spirits may be verified by David Harp, an expert sent to them by Heur. As his love for Kala deepens and she becomes pregnant with his child, Peter realizes that he can reintegrate himself and become whole. Kala states that she wishes for something to "humanize" herself, which she defines, following Houghton, as "a total dedication to another person." Even as Kala tries and fails to publicly expose Linn, Peter dedicates himself to Kala and their unborn child.

Vienna Linn, on the other hand, slowly dissipates like the souls rising from the dead Eskimos. Haunted by the murder he has committed, he tells Peter in a letter, "You cannot begin to imagine, Duvett, what demons occupy my mind, and they each and every one have a mortal's name. Those many faces float in front of my eyes day and night. They lay siege." Linn's disintegration is shown by his signature in the hotel register in Halifax. He initially signs it "Vienna Linn," then "V. Linn," then "V.L.," and finally, the "L." of the title alone.

As one would expect in a novel of such complexity, the ending is ambiguous. Is Linn's final accident, a self-consuming street-car explosion which he intends for Peter to photograph, an unselfish act which will free Peter and Kala of Heur's influence, or is it an attempt to curse Peter with the same haunting that has inflicted Linn? Does Peter actually sell the photograph of Linn's corpse to Heur or merely to his former newspaper? Is there truly a difference? Norman forces the reader to take a long look at the modern world's love for "hard" news and bloody realism, at society's insatiable appetite for firsthand accounts of tragedy and doom. At what point does the audience become so desensitized that their souls are sundered from their physical corpus? The novel seems to end on a redemptive note, as Kala and Peter set off for England and are married on the ship. However, the reader is left with the knowledge that the couple will be haunted by the memory of Linn in the years to come.

Scott Yarbrough

Sources for Further Study

The Atlantic Monthly 289 (June, 2002): 112.
Booklist 98 (February 15, 2002): 971.
The New York Times Book Review 107 (April 21, 2002): 8.
Publishers Weekly 249 (January 7, 2002): 43.

HEAVEN ON EARTH
The Rise and Fall of Socialism

Author: Joshua Muravchik (1947-   )
Publisher: Encounter Books (San Francisco). 417 pp.
    $27.95
Type of work: History
Time: The late 1700's through the late 1900's

~

A critical history of socialism, presented primarily through a series of biographical portraits, that argues that socialism failed because it held the unrealistic goal of changing human nature

~

Principal personages:

FRANÇOIS NOËL "GRACCHUS" BABEUF (1760-1797), French revolutionary and father of modern socialism

ROBERT OWEN (1801-1877), utopian socialist and founder of the New Harmony commune in Indiana

FRIEDRICH ENGELS (1820-1895), German social theorist and coauthor with Karl Marx of *The Communist Manifesto* (1848)

KARL MARX (1818-1883), German philosopher and founder of communism

EDUARD BERNSTEIN (1850-1932), German socialist, leader of the Social Democratic Party

VLADIMIR ILYICH LENIN (1870-1924), Russian revolutionary and first chairman of the Council of People's Commissars of the Russian Socialist Federative Soviet Republic

JULIUS NYERERE (1922-1999), socialist president of Tanzania

SAMUEL GOMPERS (1850-1924), American socialist and labor leader

GEORGE MEANY (1894-1980), American labor leader and president of the American Federation of Labor and Congress of Industrial Organizations (AFL-CIO)

Visions of an ideal, intentionally designed society are at least as old as the writings of Plato (c. 428-348 B.C.E.), but only in modern times have there been efforts to realize those visions through social movements and political efforts. Following the French Revolution, socialism developed as one of the most inspiring and influential programs of social and economic planning. Socialism, as Joshua Muravchik recognizes in this new history, took on several forms, but all were united by the ideas that cooperation, rather than competition, could and should be the driving force of human productive activity and that all members of a society could and should share equally in the fruits of production.

Muravchik recounts the history of socialism through a series of biographical vignettes. He begins with François Noël "Gracchus" Babeuf, who is justly recognized as the father of modern socialism. Babeuf, a pamphleteer and agitator during the French Revolution, organized a group of plotters known as the Conspiracy of Equals. Their goal was to create a society in which private property and money would be abolished and all people would live in completely equal circumstances. This would not be accomplished merely by changing the social system, but by changing people. Babeuf and his collaborators intended to have the state take control of each individual at birth in order to educate selfless citizens. This plan of remaking society by remaking people, in Muravchik's view, became central to socialism. It was also, as he suggests throughout the book, why socialism fell. Humans beings were not readily redesigned.

Joshua Muravchik is a resident scholar at the American Enterprise Institute. From 1968 to 1973, he was national chairman of the Young People's Socialist League, and he was executive director of the Coalition for a Democratic Majority from 1977 to 1979. Muravchik holds a Ph.D. in international relations from Georgetown University. He has written a number of books, as well as articles for news magazines and newspapers, including The Wall Street Journal, The New York Times, *and* Foreign Affairs.

While Babeuf began a tradition of social change through conspiracy and violence, the Scot Robert Owen pioneered a more humane and voluntary path to utopia. Owen, who reportedly coined the word "socialism," achieved public recognition after he bought a textile mill at New Lanark, Scotland. Reacting against the horrific conditions common in factories in his day, Owen reduced working hours, used authoritarian but gentle methods of evaluating and rewarding works, and attempted to control and direct workers' lives in the company-owned village. Had he ended his reforming career at New Lanark, Owen might today be regarded as an early paternalistic capitalist, a forerunner of Henry Ford and George Pullman. Instead, he moved to America and in 1825 founded the famous communal settlement at New Harmony, Indiana. As a model for idealists, New Harmony became legendary, but as a place where people actually lived and worked, it was a failure. Since no one received any special benefit from production when everything was equally shared, community members did not produce what they needed. Since goods were distributed by committees, there were shortages even of the goods that were available. Muravchik argues that Owen's failed efforts inspired rather than discouraged socialism because his goals seemed so lofty. However, the experiences of communes such as New Harmony suggested that utopia could not be created by forming isolated communities within the existing society. Instead, the whole of society would have to change in order to make an environment favorable to the reshaping of human nature.

Socialists found what appeared to be a practical and realistic program for changing the whole of society in the scientific socialism of Karl Marx and Friedrich Engels. Muravchik's chapter on Marx and Engels is one of his most interesting because he makes a good case for the argument that Engels was the true originator of most of the ideas known as Marxism and was the primary author of *The Communist Manifesto* (1848). Whoever deserves the greater share of the credit, however, Marxist theory became the basis of a systematic ideology for change.

As a scientific theory, Marxism offered predictions as well as interpretation. However, predictions can be dangerous because events may not bear them out. Marx and Engels had maintained that workers in a capitalist society would see their living standards steadily deteriorate and that entrepreneurs who were continually reduced in number by competition would produce more and more goods that could not be sold to the impoverished majority. As a result, workers would take control of industrial society and establish a new communist order. By the early twentieth century, these predictions seemed to be wrong. Workers were better off than they had been in earlier years and most advanced industrial nations showed few signs of collapse into revolution.

Eduard Bernstein, a former colleague of Marx and Engels, argued that capitalism had become less vicious and that gradual reform rather than revolution should be the goal of socialists. This argument angered the true believers, including one living in Russia who assumed the name of Vladimir Ilyich Lenin. When Lenin managed to outmaneuver the reformists in a Russia thrown into upheaval by World War I , he initiated a new era for socialism, one in which socialism seemed to have finally come to power.

Muravchik describes several versions of socialism in power. One of these was the Soviet system, established by Lenin and taken over by Joseph Stalin (1879-1953) after Lenin's death. Another was fascism, under the Italian dictator Benito Mussolini (1883-1945). Muravchik argues persuasively that Mussolini did not abandon his early socialism when he turned to fascism, but simply developed a heretical version of the socialist faith. Another branch of socialism was the social democracy of England initiated by Prime Minister Clement Atlee (1883-1967), which attempted to remake society and its members by means of elected government. Finally came the Third World socialism exemplified by the ideology of *Ujamaa*, or "familyhood," advocated by Julius Nyerere of Tanganyika, which became Tanzania after its 1964 merger with Zanzibar.

By the mid-twentieth century, it seemed that future of the world lay in one form of socialism or another. However, the United States, the world's most prosperous nation by many measures, had never embraced socialism. By looking at the lives of two influential American union leaders, Samuel Gompers and George Meany, Muravchik illustrates the kind of reformist practicality that led American workers to spurn seizing the means of production, concentrating instead on good wages and favorable conditions. In the Soviet Union, birthplace of the Communist state, socialist inefficiency in production became so serious that Soviet leader Mikhail Gorbachev tried to liberalize the system. As a result, the Soviet Union literally fell apart. China, the other major Communist state, maintained the authoritarian rule of the Communist Party. Under the leadership of Deng Xiaoping, however, it adopted a market economy, so that the Chinese system largely became a Communist government without a Communist economy. In the United Kingdom, the social democratic Labour Party, under the direction of Prime Minister Anthony "Tony" Blair, turned away from its program of state ownership and state control and began to forge ties with businesses.

Heaven on Earth departs from its biographical approach in the epilogue, where the book considers an instance of socialism that, in the author's view, was almost a success. The kibbutz movement in Israel, charged with nationalistic idealism, for a time appeared to be providing models of cooperative, communal living, but even the kibbutzim have now been shifting rapidly to cash economies. Two useful appendixes summarize the extent of world socialism in the late twentieth century. The first lists all the countries under communism, social democracy, and Third World socialism in 1985, the year in which the largest number of countries was governed by socialists. The second provides a list of all the nations that are or have been under socialist governments, with the dates that they maintained this type of political and economic system.

Muravchik's strategy of telling his story by focusing on selected individuals and events is an effective one for holding the interest of readers, but this approach necessarily requires him to omit some important parts of socialist history. The lives and work of antisocialist labor leaders Samuel Gompers and George Meany are relevant to the explanation of why socialism never achieved the organized influence in the United States that it did in many other countries. Still, leaders can only lead where followers are willing to go, and the general support of American workers for the market system owes as much to a culture of individualism, to practical and compromising business and governmental leaders, and to the sheer material success of the American marketplace as it does to the ideological preferences of union chiefs. Muravchik largely ignores the anticommunism of the Cold War, which contributed greatly to the distrust that Americans and many people in other nations came to feel for all shades of socialism. Neither the political opportunism of Senator Joseph McCarthy (1908-1957) nor the thoughtful anticommunism of Sidney Hook (1902-1989) play any part in this story of the downfall of socialism.

There are only brief mentions of the Communist Party in the United States, and coverage of European socialism is similarly spotty. There is no reference to the French Communist Party, a major aspect of the French political system into the twenty-first century. Muravchik also ignores the brief but fascinating efflorescence of Eurocommunism, an attempt by Communist leaders in Western Europe during the 1970's and 1980's to create a communism that would be democratic and independent of Soviet control. While he devotes two chapters to social democracy in the United Kingdom, where socialism seems to have failed, he gives only passing attention to social democracy in Sweden, which is often pointed out as socialism's success story.

While it may not provide a comprehensive history of socialism, *Heaven on Earth* is a well-written and thoughtful meditation on some of the fundamental questions of modern political history. It attempts to address the question of how ideas of social organization that seem to be at odds with existing human nature came to be so widely held. It also seeks to say why movements dedicated to creating a better way of life often resulted in brutality and murder. For Muravchik, these two questions have the same answer. Socialism appealed to people because it offered a faith that could give meaning to life. By the same token, commitment to a faith that transcends the realities of the present and the lives of individual people could justify any action. This is not an original observation—socialism has often been accused of being a substitute for religion—but it is an observation that may well be true, and Muravchik supports it with a series of persuasive cases.

Carl L. Bankston III

Sources for Further Study

Booklist 98 (April 1, 2002): 1287.
Commentary 113 (June, 2002): 47.
Library Journal 127 (May 15, 2002): 110.
The Weekly Standard 7 (April 22, 2002): 31.

HELL TO PAY

Author: George P. Pelecanos (1957-   )
Publisher: Little, Brown (Boston). 344 pp. $24.95
Type of work: Novel
Time: Fall, 2000
Locale: Washington, D.C., area

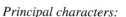

This gritty crime novel immerses readers in the talk, tastes, codes, and personal problems of private investigators and the pimps, prostitutes, players, drug dealers, and killers they are investigating

≈

Principal characters:

DEREK STRANGE, an African American private investigator in his fifties
TERRY QUINN, his younger, white partner, a former police officer
SUE TRACY, a private investigator from a suburban agency
KAREN BAGLEY, her African American partner in the agency
LAMAR WILLIAMS, teenage worker in Strange's office
JOE WILDER, eight-year-old Pee Wee football player
SANDRA WILDER, Joe's mother
LORENZE WILDER, Joe's uncle
GARFIELD "D" POTTER, a drug dealer
CARLTON "DIRTY" LITTLE, Potter's partner
CHARLES "COON" WHITE, Potter's other partner
FRED "WORLDWIDE" WILSON, pimp specializing in young prostitutes
JENNIFER MARSHALL, a white teenage prostitute from the suburbs
STELLA, a white teenage prostitute from Pittsburgh
"ALL-ASS" EVE, black exotic dancer
GRANVILLE OLIVER, a drug kingpin, Joe's father

From the hundreds of crime novels published annually, what is it that makes a few stand out? Undoubtedly the style of the writer makes a difference, and so does the ability to depict memorable characters, especially the main investigator and sometimes a partner, but the ability to capture a particular ambiance or location also seems important. This is the strength of George P. Pelecanos, author of *Hell to Pay*. Pelecanos has been writing about Washington, D.C., for a long time. It was the setting for his previous novel, *Right as Rain* (2001), to which *Hell to Pay* is a loose sequel. Before *Right as Rain*, Pelecanos wrote a series of D.C. novels centered around descendants of Greek immigrants, but in his last two novels, Pelecanos has shifted his focus to D.C.'s majority African American community. He seems to have made the

*George P. Pelecanos is author of a
series of crime novels set in the
Washington, D.C., area, including
the best-selling* Right as Rain
*(2001). He also writes and produces
films. He lives in Washington, D.C.,
with his wife and children.*

shift with remarkable success, based on his close knowledge of the city's ambiance.

Pelecanos hardly mentions the official Washington, D.C., of tourists, government, embassies, and universities; instead, he sets his novels in the mostly run-down, crime-ridden neighborhoods where generations of permanent residents, an increasing number of them African American, have lived. These neighborhoods are a collection of America's worst urban ills, where homegrown terrorists have ruled the streets for decades. Yet, surprisingly, a sense of community exists in these neighborhoods similar to that in a small town. People know each other by first name and the social order reflects close alliances that often go back to childhood or high school (for people who got that far) and that cross the boundaries of the law with ease. Nonetheless, a fairly strict street code operates: Drug dealers stick to their territories, law-abiding residents pretend to be unafraid but do not look punks straight in the eye, the police look the other way at minor offenses (such as smoking marijuana), and "mean dudes" are to be avoided, since they have reputations to uphold.

The need to uphold one's reputation for being mean, and thereby keep one's manhood intact, leads to one of the novel's main plot lines. Petty drug dealer Garfield "D" (short for "Death") Potter has, as his nickname implies, a reputation for being mean. To show how mean he is, he shoots his partner's dog. It does not bother him that the teenage girls with whom he has sex are afraid of him. When Potter and his two partners rob a craps game and Potter pistol-whips an old man who talks back, he even feels it necessary to announce his name to the world: "Can't nobody in this city f—k with Garfield Potter." Naturally Potter feels concern when Lorenze Wilder, who owes him $100 for marijuana, does not pay up. If the word gets around town, Potter's reputation will be ruined. Only one thing can save it: Lorenze Wilder has to be killed; then people will know not to mess with Garfield "D" Potter.

It does not seem to matter to Potter's reputation that he needs the help of his two partners to settle with Wilder, nor that it takes several forays before they finally catch up with him. In the meantime, the threesome interrelate (and the suspense builds). They unconsciously parody a family group, dependent on one another but observing a pecking order, with Potter the leader (or father figure for "his boys"), Carlton Little number two, and Charles White at the bottom. This order is reflected in their seating arrangement within the car—Potter driving, Little in the front passenger seat, and White in back—and in their other activities. Potter makes all the decisions, and, as last in line, White has to go out to fetch the fast food. Generally, however, they share the same tastes in clothes (jeans and Nautica shirts), shoes (Air Maxes, Timberland), music (rap, played loud), girls (dumb teenagers), fast food chains (Popeye's, Taco Bell, and McDonald's, although Potter rejects McDonald's as too greasy), and good times (sitting around the living room watching television and getting high on malt liquor and marijuana).

Eventually, more than halfway through the novel, the threesome catch up with Lorenze Wilder, block his car at a take-out ice cream shop, and spray his windshield full of bullets. Lorenze dies instantly, but so, unfortunately, does his eight-year-old nephew, Joe Wilder, whom he was treating to a chocolate-and-vanilla ice cream cone. As the novel states,

> Because of the numbing consistency of the murder rate, and because lower-class black life held little value in the media's eyes, the violent deaths of young black men and women in the District of Columbia had not been deemed particularly newsworthy for the past fifteen years.

The murder of Joe Wilder, however, makes a splash in the media, brings a crowd to his funeral, and results in a commemorative T-shirt for sale to his friends and relatives. (Pelecanos comments that producing such T-shirts "had become a cottage industry in D.C.").

Joe Wilder's killing also puts Potter and his partners on a collision course with private detective Derek Strange, owner of Strange Investigations and Joe Wilder's coach in the Pee Wee football league. Up until this time, Strange has been seen doing a routine background check, knocking off at noon, and visiting massage parlors. Why he wants to visit massage parlors when he has a sexy secretary who leaves PayDay candy bars on his desk and wants to give him pot roast and good loving every night is hard to say. By coincidence, Strange runs into Potter and his crew in the football field parking lot when they are looking for Lorenze Wilder, and they taunt him with cries of "Yo, Fred Sanford! Fred!" (after the obscene old man in the television show *Sanford and Son*). They are not far off the mark: Strange is an aging African American man with problems.

However, two female investigators from the suburbs, Karen Bagley and Sue Tracy, think more highly of him and hire his agency to help track down runaway suburban teens who have become prostitutes, in particular fourteen-year-old Jennifer Marshall. Strange gives this assignment to his part-time partner, Terry Quinn, a former police officer who also works in a Silver Spring, Maryland, bookstore. Quinn's search for Jennifer Marshall constitutes the second main plot line in *Hell to Pay*. With the help of Stella, a seventeen-year-old prostitute who plays the middle for money, and "All-Ass" Eve, an exotic dancer who became too old to work as a prostitute, Quinn is pointed in the direction of the pimp "Worldwide" Wilson, who specializes in peddling young flesh and is the "meanest dude" in D.C. Together, Quinn and Tracy invade Wilson's apartments and, while Tracy points a gun at Wilson's leering, sneering face, retrieve Jennifer. Later, Jennifer runs away from home again, and "Worldwide" Wilson takes revenge by punching in Stella's ribs and slashing up her face.

Strange and Quinn begin to feel bad about letting down their young charges, Joe Wilder and Stella, and start to plot revenge on the perpetrators. By this time, readers might have begun to think that Strange and Quinn are only a cut or two above the perpetrators themselves. Both seem to be maverick former cops who did not last long on the force because they were too violent, and both eagerly embrace the code of street justice. They both grew up in D.C., know people all around the city, and share the D.C. ambiance with the perpetrators, down to similar tastes in music and sports. Like "Worldwide" Wilson, Strange and Quinn love their old rhythm-and-blues classics and, in a quaint show of community, the whole city stops when the Redskins play (apparently the safest time in D.C. is when surrogate violence is taking place on the football field).

In the end, Quinn carries through with his revenge, climbing into Wilson's apartment and confronting the pimp in his den. While getting beaten and cut up himself, Quinn trashes Wilson's phonograph, beats him up, kicks in his face, and handcuffs him to a radiator. After the police arrive, Quinn is charged with aggravated assault, but the novel ends with Quinn expecting to get off with a suspended sentence. On the other hand, Strange at the last minute changes his mind about taking revenge after setting up Potter and his crew to be slaughtered by Granville Oliver, the drug lord who turns out to be Joe Wilder's father. This twist in the plot near the novel's end is highly unconvincing, but it seems to signal a turning point for Strange, who asks his secretary Janine to marry him on the last page.

Pelecanos ends his novel with this note of social uplift in an apparent attempt to balance its cinematic violence (much in the novel seems more cinematic than literary). There are many such notes in the novel, some subtle, some not, creating an undercurrent of social need throughout this entertaining crime novel. Just as African American novelist Ralph Ellison (1914-1994) saw blacks as living at war with the surrounding white culture, so does Pelecanos. Now, however, the war is not against racist whites; the war on the inner-city streets is against deplorable social conditions. It is no coincidence that both Strange and Quinn are volunteer coaches in the Pee Wee football league, even though these scenes of doing good make dull reading. Strange feels sorry for all the fatherless boys in D.C., from the ranks of which come most of the petty criminals, punks, and lowlifes in the novel.

Strange even feels sorry for the drug kingpin Granville Oliver (whom Strange made fatherless thirty-two years before) and takes on Oliver as a client at the end of the novel. Strange is a social crusader, and so is Pelecanos, but the author also seems to be looking toward the next novel in the series. Will Strange be conflicted in his relationship with Oliver, who after all profited from and helped perpetuate D.C.'s deplorable social conditions? Will Strange actually marry Janine, and will he be faithful to her? Will Janine continue to make good pot roast? Will Quinn get off or go to prison? "Worldwide" Wilson and Jennifer Marshall are still at large, Wilson looking much meaner and Jennifer still innocent and suburban. What will happen next?

Harold Branam

Sources for Further Study

Booklist 98 (December 1, 2001): 606.
Library Journal 127 (August, 2002): 172.
The New York Times Book Review 107 (March 3, 2002): 21.
The New Yorker 78 (April 8, 2002): 90.
Publishers Weekly 248 (December 10, 2001): 50.

A HISTORY OF PHILOSOPHY IN AMERICA, 1720-2000

Author: Bruce Kuklick (1941-   )
Publisher: Oxford University Press (New York). 326 pp.
  $30.00
Type of work: History and philosophy
Time: 1720-2000
Locale: The United States

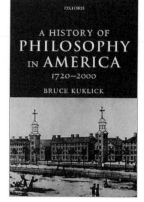

~

Distinguished historian Kuklick examines trends in American philosophy from its roots in Calvinist theology to contemporary trends that demonstrate the fragmentation of the discipline in the late twentieth century

~

Principal personages:
  JONATHAN EDWARDS (1703-1768), eighteenth century preacher and
    theologian
  WILLIAM JAMES (1842-1910), principal proponent of American Pragma-
    tism in the early twentieth century
  JOHN DEWEY (1859-1952), influential early twentieth century American
    philosopher
  JOSIAH ROYCE (1855-1916), influential writer on Pragmatism in early
    twentieth century
  CHARLES SANDERS PEIRCE (1839-1914), philosopher whose work influ-
    enced William James and other Pragmatist philosophers
  THOMAS KUHN (1922-1996), twentieth century scientist and philosopher
  RICHARD RORTY (1931-   ), twentieth century philosopher

It may surprise readers to learn that Bruce Kuklick's *A History of Philosophy in America* is intended to be a textbook. Attempting to "steer between the Scylla of philosophers' suspicion of history and the Charybdis of historians' suspicion of philosophers," Kuklick provides a survey of the development of American thought, a movement he believes demonstrates "the long circuitous march from a religious to a secular vision of the universe."

Kuklick is particularly well qualified to write such a study. The author of more than a half-dozen books on an array of subjects involving American politics and philosophy and the editor of works by Thomas Paine and William James, Kuklick brings his considerable knowledge of American intellectual history to bear on his sweeping examination of the growth of philosophy in the United States. His subject demands that its author be thoroughly familiar with the sometimes obscure writings of dozens of figures who have shaped American thought during three centuries. Fortunately, Kuklick proves capable of handling this task with exceptional skill and clarity.

The task Kuklick sets for himself is a most ambitious one. First, he wishes to trace

the growth of American philosophy from its beginnings in the theological studies of men associated with the Protestant ministries in New England and in the colleges, principally Harvard,
Yale, and Princeton, set up to prepare young men
for those ministries. Early philosophers were concerned with issues of free will versus determinism. They concentrated their efforts on explain-

Bruce Kuklick is a professor of history at the University of Pennsylvania and author of several studies of American philosophical thought.

ing how God is present in the natural world and how the deity relates to man. For
them, the work was no simple academic exercise; ideas mattered, because through
them people could come to understand God's plan for salvation. Kuklick's goal is to
show how the writings of eighteenth and early nineteenth century figures better
known as theologians shaped the thought of those involved in the development of philosophy as a professional discipline at American universities. At the same time, he
summarizes the thought of major figures, providing detailed analysis of their principal works and examining the sources on which they drew for inspiration. As he explains the work of later philosophers, he incorporates commentary on the influence of
earlier American figures as well as that of European giants whose work clearly shaped
American thought from the founding of the colonies.

Along the way, Kuklick provides interesting commentary on the development of
American higher education and the role of philosophy departments in institutions as
diverse as Harvard University, the University of Michigan, and Calvin College. This
book is as much about the way philosophy developed as an academic discipline in
American institutions of higher education as it is about the ideas promulgated by American thinkers. Readers learn from Kuklick's careful analysis of the political dynamics
that shaped postsecondary learning in the United States how personalities had as much
to do with the success of individual philosophers as did the quality of their thought.

A question lying beneath the surface of Kuklick's study surfaces on occasion, providing a theme that links philosophers across the generations: Do philosophers wish
only to study the world and humankind, or do they wish to influence human behavior?
Put another way, do those who practice philosophy—especially those in institutions of
higher education—wish to remain passive commentators on the human condition, or do
they wish to become leaders in their communities and country, shaping moral standards
and social policy to bring about a good and just society? The answer has changed over
generations, but Kuklick is convinced that his contemporaries at the end of the twentieth century elected to remain on the sidelines, writing to and for each other rather than
stepping forward to participate in the process of shaping the future of the country.

Kuklick makes it clear that the influence of European thought shaped American
philosophy from its beginnings in the colonial era until the end of the twentieth century. The work of John Locke (1632-1707), David Hume (1711-1776), and the British
empiricists led philosophers in one direction; the reputations of these giants then suffered when American philosophers fell under the spell of Immanuel Kant (1724-
1804) and his successors, who promoted a form of idealism that appealed to mid-
nineteenth century practitioners and influenced the founding fathers of Pragmatism.

The profound impact of Charles Darwin's *On the Origin of Species* (1859) and *The Descent of Man* (1871) is given a place of prominence in Kuklick's examination of the theories of late nineteenth and early twentieth century philosophers, all of whom struggled to reconcile the discoveries of science with earlier ideas about human nature. The interchange of ideas between American and European philosophers grew exponentially during the twentieth century, when U.S. universities began to invite to their faculties and their lecture halls the members of the Frankfurt School or proponents of logical positivism and existentialism.

Kuklick balances his account of American philosophy by weaving together the story of its development and contributions to thought with brief summaries of the ideas of its principal practitioners. Because he begins with Jonathan Edwards, the fiery Massachusetts preacher better known for his sermon "Sinners in the Hands of an Angry God" (1741), Kuklick is able to establish a continuum that links early colonial thinkers with their nineteenth and twentieth century successors. "From the mid-eighteenth until the end of the nineteenth century the central issue for American thinkers was the connection of God's supremacy to human freedom." In Kuklick's opinion, Edwards's *Freedom of the Will* (1754) "was the most famous philosophical text written in America through the nineteenth century"; therefore, understanding what Edwards thought is crucial to appreciating the writings of nineteenth century figures such as James Marsh (1794-1842), Ralph Waldo Emerson (1803-1882), Horace Bushnell (1802-1876), and Nathaniel Taylor (1786-1858).

If there are heroes in Kuklick's book, they are certainly the American Pragmatists, especially William James and his only real rival for primacy among American philosophers, John Dewey. More attention is paid to the ideas of these two men than to any figure other than Jonathan Edwards. Kuklick is careful to show how both wrestled with the problems of epistemology (and to a lesser extent, metaphysics) in the light of scientific advances. In Kuklick's view, the Golden Age of American philosophy occurred during the forty-year period from 1880 to 1920. Departments of philosophy at Harvard, Chicago, Michigan, Berkeley, Stanford, and other universities provided welcome havens for dozens of philosophers who engaged in spirited dialogue about key questions that had perplexed their predecessors and for which they struggled, individually and collectively, to find answers not only for themselves but for society as a whole.

On the other hand, Kuklick has little good to say about the developments in American philosophy during the second half of the twentieth century. The successors of James and Dewey were pygmies walking in the footsteps of giants; moreover, they abandoned the opportunity, made possible for them by their predecessors, to make an impact on American life. Turning increasingly toward "the philosophy of language," philosophers became ever more marginalized. "The classic pragmatists had thought philosophy might change the world; the interwar generation had worried that it was not changing the world; by the 1950's philosophers had stopped agonizing about their shrunken role, and even embraced it." Characterized by fragmentation in thought and a growing tendency to focus on analytic, technical issues, American philosophers grew increasingly more distant from the mainstream of life within the country.

"At the end of the twentieth century," Kuklick observes, "analytic philosophers trying to make sense of their field regularly worried over their withdrawal from much social contact, but had few resources to explain it." Professional philosophers have trouble attracting an audience. Their dense, jargon-filled prose has failed to garner readers among a wider literate public. Some, such as A. O. Lovejoy (1873-1962) and C. I. Lewis (1883-1964), were truly distinguished; but most have simply retreated to the ivy-covered walls of American universities, content to write books for other philosophers to read.

The two late-twentieth century philosophers on whom he concentrates are exceptions to this trend: Richard Rorty and Thomas Kuhn. Both of these men have consciously written for wider audiences and as a result, Rorty's conclusions on the limitations of analytic philosophy and Kuhn's ideas about the nature of scientific (and philosophical) revolutions have permeated the larger culture. More likely, Kuklick notes, is that Americans who are familiar at all with philosophy have learned about the subject secondhand from practitioners of other disciplines such as literature, history, and the social sciences. Concepts such as existentialism and semiotics have become mainstays of teaching by those who are not trained in philosophy, but who see in their disciplines the need for comprehensive theories of knowing and existence.

Kuklick's book is not simply a summary of the major ideas of major and minor American thinkers, detached from the context in which these men developed their conceptions of reality. Rather, as one might expect of a good historian, Kuklick provides readers with information about the historical, social, political, and cultural background of his subjects. Without derailing his study, he offers succinct biographical sketches that make his philosophers come alive as people whose relationships with parents, spouses, children, colleagues, and communities affect not only what they wrote but how well received their work was by contemporaries. The case of Charles Sanders Peirce is a good example: Kuklick sketches the career of this iconoclastic, sometimes depressed, and often rebellious thinker to illustrate why his version of Pragmatism had less influence on wider audiences than the work of more mainstream figures such as William James and Josiah Royce.

Whether Kuklick's book will live up to its dust-jacket billing as "an American counterpart to Bertrand Russell's *History of Western Philosophy*" (1945) remains to be seen. What is certain, however, is that those interested in the history of American thought will find great pleasure in reading *A History of Philosophy in America*, a fine, if all too brief summary of an oft-neglected field of study.

Laurence W. Mazzeno

Sources for Further Study

Publishers Weekly 249 (April 8, 2002): 222.
The Weekly Standard 7 (May 6, 2002): 39.

HISTORY OF THE SURREALIST MOVEMENT

Author: Gérard Durozoi (1942-   )
First published: Histoire du mouvement surréaliste,
    1997, in France
Translated from the French by Alison Anderson
Publisher: University of Chicago Press (Chicago). Illustrated. 805 pp. $95.00
Type of work: Fine arts, history, literary history, and literary theory
Time: 1919-1969
Locale: France, Belgium, Canada, Czechoslovakia, Mexico, Spain, Switzerland, the United States, and the former Soviet Union

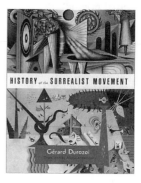

～

An encyclopedic panorama of the surrealist movement, from its origins in and relationship to Dadaism in the 1920's to its decline in the 1960's, underlining, through the discussion of the activities of many writers and artists, its links to major aesthetic, social, and political debates of the twentieth century

～

Principal personages:
    LOUIS ARAGON (1897-1982), French writer, one of the most active and visible intellectuals of the French Communist Party
    ANTONIN ARTAUD (1896-1948), French poet who espoused the need for a spiritual and metaphysical revolution while disagreeing with the surrealists' desire for political commitment
    ANDRÉ BRETON (1896-1966), French poet, one of the founders of the surrealist movement and author of surrealist manifestos
    PAUL ÉLUARD (1895-1952), French poet, principal figure in the surrealist movement and most famous of France's Resistance poets
    PHILIPPE SOUPAULT (1897-1990), French poet, principal figure in the early Paris Dada events
    TRISTAN TZARA (1896-1963), Romanian and French poet, the leading proponent of Dadaism

Surrealism is unarguably one of the most influential and innovative artistic and literary movements of the twentieth century. *History of the Surrealist Movement* provides an in-depth and lavishly illustrated chronological account of its birth, evolution, and decline during a fifty-year period, from 1919 to 1969, through detailed documentation and discussion of its principal figures and events. Gérard Durozoi, a French philosopher, has written extensively on twentieth century French art and philosophy, including the work of André Breton, and is eminently qualified to guide the reader through the fascinating world of surrealism. The artistic, political, literary, and social currents of the time provide a backdrop upon which Durozoi paints scenes, events, and activities that exemplify surrealist aesthetics and objectives while also recounting the rich socio-cultural history of Paris and, to a lesser extent, of Europe. The work provides a chronological history of surrealism, divided into seven periods: 1919 to 1924, 1924 to 1929, 1929 to 1937, 1938 to 1944, 1944 to 1951, 1951 to 1959, and 1959 to 1969. Each period corresponds to significant events having influence on practice, ideology, and personal relations within surrealist circles, from the influence of the Dada movement to André Breton's death in 1966.

Gérard Durozoi is the coauthor, with Bernard Lecherbonnier, of Le Surréalisme: Théories, thèmes, et techniques *(1971) and* André Breton: L'Ecriture surréaliste *(1974), the author of* Le Surréalisme *(2002), the editor of* Dictionnaire de l'art moderne et contemporain *(1992), and coeditor, with André Roussel, of* Dictionnaire de philosophie *(1997). During the 1950's and 1960's, he was associated with the surrealist movement as a philosopher.*

The initial publication in Paris by Philippe Soupault, André Breton, and Louis Aragon of the monthly periodical *Littérature* in 1919 marked the beginning of a rich and groundbreaking collaborative effort. These three young men shared a common interest in the poetry of Guillaume Apollinaire, Arthur Rimbaud, and Isidore Ducasse (known as Lautréamont), as well as in the art of Henri Matisse, Marc Chagall, and Pablo Picasso. In the spring of 1918, Breton had discovered the first two issues of the periodical *Dada*, in which he read some of Tristan Tzara's poetry. Tzara had cofounded the Cabaret Voltaire in Zurich. Here was established the origin of the Dadaist movement, which endeavored to create works built on models inspired by children, madmen, and primitive people and capable of connecting with reality and a life emptied of all convention. Dadaist practices moved easily from one technique or genre to another, from theater, to a parody of dance or music, to the composition of a poem, according to whim and unbound by literary convention. The founders of *Littérature* became fervent converts to Dadaism, and Tzara arrived in Paris in 1920, greeted by Breton, Aragon, and Paul Éluard. Dadaist events took place in Paris over the next months, and during this time, public performances, manifestos, and painting exhibitions were planned in order to give voice to Dadaist ideals. This was indeed an agitated period in Parisian artistic and literary circles. Performers were pelted with decomposing fruits and vegetables, steaks and chops, and bombarded with insults and animal cries. Quite ironically, Dadaism became fashionable entertainment and, to some, an example of highbrow snobbishness. This categorization and such public perception would ultimately thwart further development and cause the movement's decline in the early 1920's. However, with great energy and commitment, Paris Dadaists had, in the end, facilitated the advent of surrealism by eliciting a reexamination of artistic and literary aesthetics, indeed of the very concept of aesthetics.

Thus, in 1924 the existence of a surrealist group in Paris was publicly confirmed by the opening of a Bureau for Surrealist Research, whose goal was to gather all possible information that might express the unconscious activity of the mind. The establishment of a research center underlined the collective nature of the movement as well as the need to avoid the trivialization that befell Dada. During the same period, Breton was preparing to publish his *Manifeste du surréalisme* (1924; *Manifesto of Surrealism*, 1969). The surrealists wished to appeal to the unconscious and to liberate all those interested in expression where thought is freed from intellectual preoccupations. When Breton's manifesto appeared in the same year, it quickly acquired the status of a treatise, delineating the goals and challenges of surrealism while insisting on the supremacy of the poetic image and the need to reevaluate attitudes born of positivistic tradition, which is hostile to the desired intellectual and moral reawakening. The importance of dreams was emphasized as well, since they reinforced the notion that thought has a much wider scope than the traditional positivist image governed by limiting tenets of realism. Areas of research included the possibilities for the continuity of dreams and their application to life's problems; the possibility that dreams contain the causes of human preferences and desires; the natural allure of dreams where everything seems possible; and the possible reconciliation of dreams and reality, as contradictory as this might appear. Breton and the other surrealists gave themselves wholeheartedly to the discussion and analysis of these questions, applications, and objectives, and endeavored to investigate further surrealism as a pure psychic automatism with which one can express the real process of thought, outside any aesthetic or moral constraints, and outside the boundaries of traditional literature. Breton, Artaud, Éluard, Pablo Picasso, Francis Picabia, Giorgio De Chirico, Max Ernst, Salvador Dalí, Man Ray, and Joan Miró are but some of the writers and artists whose participation in the early years of surrealism in Paris is recounted with the support of a vast selection of iconography, ranging from photographs of themselves and of Paris, color images of paintings, copies of pamphlets, letters, and literary excerpts. This aspect of *History of the Surrealist Movement* is indeed its most compelling, as it illuminates visually and intellectually the principal figures, their work, and their specially crafted artistic objects, poetry, and pamphlets. The breadth and variety of this documentation creates an integral picture, in conjunction with Durozoi's comments, of Paris and surrealism. One of the merits of the work lies in the fact that this type of documentation colors the entire work and, in doing so, re-creates a time and a place that for many are so very important to the development of the visual and artistic aesthetics and ideologies of contemporary literature and art.

Second Manifeste du surréalisme (1930; *Second Manifesto of Surrealism*, 1969), authored by Breton and initially published in the last issue of *La Révolution surréaliste* in 1929, professed an interest in social issues as well as an adherence to dialectal materialism and its application to the problems of love, dreams, madness, art, and religion. Breton was not above reproach, however, for he was criticized for making money from the sale of art works and accused of artistic impotence, since his intellectual activity was based primarily on literary or art criticism. Once Durozoi clearly establishes the origins, tenets, and practices of the surrealist group and the fundamental role of Breton, he chronicles the 1930's debate surrounding surrealist objects, whose purpose was to mark a distance from traditional sculpture as defined at the time and which were created by a montage of heterogeneous elements. In this regard, the images of such objects as Meret Oppenheim's "Fur Breakfast" (1938), a teacup, saucer, and spoon covered in fur, provide the necessary material needed to conceptualize the visual intent of the surrealists and underline the importance of creating objects through fantasy and not out of the necessity of function. This type of artistic expression remains one of surrealism's most eloquent and compelling representations.

The political arena, specifically communist ideology and the surrealists' fractious relationships with the French Communist Party, figures prominently in Durozoi's history. The 1947 anticolonialist pamphlet, "Liberté est un mot vietnamien" (freedom is a Vietnamese word) condemned the war in Indochina. It denounced the silence of the press and reiterated that the main demand of surrealists remained the liberation of humankind and a radical transformation of society. Those in Vietnam who opposed imperialist aggression were considered by the surrealists as the incarnation of the evolution of freedom. Political beliefs of the surrealist group developed further into utterances supporting antifascism, anticolonialism, and de-Stalinization. The 1957 pamphlet "Hongrie, soleil levant" (Hungary, rising sun) condemned the fascist repression of the Budapest uprising. These events ultimately led the surrealists to join other intellectuals to launch what they termed an "Appeal in Favor of an International Circle of Revolutionary Intellectuals."

Breton's death in 1966 irrevocably altered the evolution of the surrealist movement. He had been its vital instigator and animator and without him, the Paris group was unable to avoid dissolution shortly thereafter. Although Durozoi points out that surrealism neither succeeded in changing life nor in transforming the world, he does rightly acknowledge that it is the only artistic and literary movement of the twentieth century to espouse an ethic, and that in doing so, it did succeed in reintegrating the artistic process to the very heart of everyday life and in encouraging all individuals to transform life into the free expression of hope, love, and poetry. In this way, surrealism does indeed live on past the twentieth century.

History of the Surrealist Movement provides meticulous documentation surrounding principally the French and European surrealist movement, while also providing short biographical sketches of principal surrealists and their followers. In addition, a detailed bibliography lists works dealing with surrealism and cinema, politics, and photography as well as surrealism in Belgium, Canada, Czechoslovakia, Denmark, Egypt, Great Britain, Japan, Latin America, Portugal, Romania, and Spain. An indispensable and highly readable encyclopedic account of a fascinating period in the artistic and intellectual history of the twentieth century, the work provides a multitude of compelling color illustrations that make of it an object of considerable attraction. In sum, Durozoi is to be most highly commended for assembling one of the most complete and detailed histories of surrealism.

Kenneth W. Meadwell

Sources for Further Study

Library Journal 127 (May 1, 2002): 97.
Publishers Weekly 249 (March 4, 2002): 66.

HOW TO BE ALONE

Author: Jonathan Franzen (1959-   )
Publisher: Farrar, Straus and Giroux (New York). 278
    pp. $24.00
Type of work: Essays
Time: 1994-2002
Locale: New York City, Chicago, Pennsylvania, Colo-
    rado, Washington, D.C., and St. Louis, Missouri

∽

Fourteen miscellaneous nonfiction pieces dealing
rather loosely with the theme of "how to be alone in a noisy
and distracting mass culture," written by a brilliant, rebel-
lious young writer who was catapulted to fame in 2001 by
the publication of his best-selling novel The Corrections

∽

Almost all the selections in this book were written while Jonathan Franzen was in his thirties and still struggling to survive as a writer of what he repeatedly calls "seri-ous fiction." "Scavenging" gives a good picture of his mental and physical state. Not unlike the dedicated writers portrayed in George Gissing's *New Grub Street* (1891) and in Knut Hamsun's *Sult* (1890; *Hunger,* 1899), Franzen lived in cold and squalor, sustained by ideals and ambition. He furnished his transient rooms with orange crates, doors converted to tables, bookshelves made from cinder blocks and raw lumber, chairs and lamps salvaged from trash piles, mismatched dishes, laundry soaking in the bathtub, candles stuck in chianti bottles, and bullfight posters glued to the bare walls. His ancient television set showed nothing but snow unless he kept holding the bare antenna wire between his fingers. His antique typewriters were chronically breaking down. He repaired one using dental floss to replace the nylon cord that supplied ten-sion to advance the carriage. When he acquired a computer, it was more of a challenge to repair, and it made such a racket that he had to wear earmuffs.

It is noteworthy that by 1996 Franzen had already published two novels which had been favorably reviewed. "No doubt about it," wrote Laura Shapiro in her review of *Strong Motion* (1992) for *Newsweek,* "Jonathan Franzen is one of the most extraordi-nary writers around." Richard Eder, covering Franzen's first novel for the *Los An-geles Times* some four years earlier, called *The Twenty-seventh City* (1988) "a novel so imaginatively and expansively of our times that it seems ahead of them." *Succès d'estime* and financial success are not synonymous. Many novelists earn barely enough from one novel to survive to finish the next.

Franzen was not unlike myriad other talented young people who discover a love for one of the arts and vow to dedicate their lives to literature, music, painting, sculp-ture, acting, singing, or dancing without realizing how depressing the hardships and disappointments will ultimately become. They see their erstwhile friends scrambling up the economic ladder, getting promotions and raises just for showing up, getting married, having babies, buying houses. They often remember how their parents advised them to go into medicine, dentistry, law, engineering, accounting, or some other practical profession—anything but art. Anton Chekhov describes three such naïve idealists in a story titled "Talent" (1916):

> Like wolves in a cage, the three friends kept pacing to and fro from one end of the room to the other. They talked without ceasing, talked hotly and genuinely; all three were excited, carried away. To listen to them it would seem they had the future, fame, money, in their hands. And it never occurred to either of them that time was passing, that every day life was nearing its close, that they had lived at other people's expense a great deal and nothing yet was accomplished; that they were all bound by the inexorable law by which of a hundred promising beginners only two or three rise to any position and all the others draw blanks in the lottery, perish playing the part of flesh for the cannon.

Franzen's personal essays reveal his state of mind during his struggle to survive as a freelance writer. He lived in many cities but discovered that a person who moves from one poor neighborhood to another poor neighborhood is virtually living in the same city, no matter where it is. He ranted and raved against consumerism and capitalism until he became one of the few who catch the gold ring. *The Corrections* was a well-deserved turning point in his career. His misunderstanding with Oprah Winfrey was a side issue. His long, autobiographical novel won the National Book Award for fiction without her help, but its selection for her now-defunct book club certainly helped him earn many extra dollars, representing freedom to continue writing without worrying about landlords and bill collectors. Before *The Corrections*, Franzen was an angry (and hungry, lonely, frustrated, anxious) young man, an enfant terrible; after *The Corrections*, the tone of his prose changes dramatically. He is like the back-up quarterback when the starter breaks a leg. Suddenly everybody wants to be near him. He had so many interviews he could hardly keep up with them, and the warm attention was apparently just what was needed to thaw him.

How to Be Alone was obviously pieced together in order to capitalize on the unusual notoriety of *The Corrections* attributable to its critical success, his receipt of the prestigious National Book Award, and the highly publicized misunderstanding with Oprah Winfrey which did him more good than harm. He modestly describes his conflicted feelings during the Winfrey affair in "Meet Me in St. Louis." He may be remembered as the brash young idealist who was "disinvited" to appear on Winfrey's popular television talk show because he told many interviewers that he did not think much of her literary taste.

His public disparagement of Winfrey's club may have been directly responsible for her decision to abolish it. Many critics felt that she may have promoted some mediocre writers but at least was getting couch potatoes to read. Franzen has been called everything from "sensitive" to "arrogant." He unflinchingly quotes some of the strongest epithets in "Meet Me in St. Louis," including "spoiled, whiny little brat" and "ego-blinded snob." In his defense, it should be pointed out that he was not merely

Jonathan Franzen lives in New York City. His novels The Twenty-seventh City *(1988) and* Strong Motion *(1992) received favorable reviews, and* The Corrections *(2001) won the National Book Award in 2001 and brought him fame, fortune, and international recognition.*

idealistic but dealing in his third novel with the most intimate autobiographical matters, including the lingering illness and death of his father, chronicled in the second essay in the collection, "My Father's Brain."

Without *The Corrections*, there would have been no market for a potpourri of essays, articles, and memoirs such as *How to Be Alone*; and since Franzen worked on his big novel for eight years, it would have been too much for his publisher to hope for a quick follow-up in the form of another work of fiction. *How to Be Alone* might be called a Franzen sampler. It shows his intelligence and talent along with some of his faults, perhaps the greatest of which is—or was—an overinflated ego. The pieces are only remotely interrelated. In "Cigarettes," for example, Franzen blames his love-hate addiction to smoking on the big tobacco companies and their advertising agencies. "Lost in the Mail" is a solid piece of reportage about the deplorable deterioration of the postal service in Chicago in the 1990's. "Control Units" reads like more commissioned journalism. It deals sensitively and intelligently with conditions in modern American prisons. Franzen's other faults, pointed out by many critics, are that he tends to overwrite and show off his vocabulary. As a sampler, *How to Be Alone* reveals an exceptionally gifted writer, no longer young, who may or may not have the necessary endurance, creativity, and luck to become one of the most important writers of his generation.

The pièce de résistance of Franzen's collection is "the Harper's essay," revised and shortened (most of what Franzen writes, including *The Corrections*, could stand shortening) and given the revealing new title of "Why Bother?" In "A Word About This Book," Franzen explains what he revised and eliminated from the original Harper's essay, "Perchance to Dream" (1996), which had provoked so much controversy. When he looked at the original, he says,

> I found an essay . . . of such painful stridency and tenuous logic that even *I* couldn't quite follow it. . . . I used to consider it apocalyptically worrisome that Americans watch a lot of TV and don't read much Henry James. . . . I used to think that our American political economy was a vast cabal whose specific aim was to thwart my artistic ambitions, exterminate all that I found lovely in civilization, and also rape and murder the planet in the process. . . . What goes for the *Harper's essay* goes for this collection as a whole. I intend this book, in part, as a record of a movement away from an angry and frightened isolation toward an acceptance—even a celebration—of being a reader and a writer.

Franzen is standing on the pinnacle of success, but as every creative writer knows, that is a slippery pinnacle. Having used up his most intimate family memories in *The*

Corrections, he may have a hard time finding another theme that will suit his aspirations to write in what he calls the "high-art literary tradition." Franzen considers himself a postmodernist and speaks admiringly of Don DeLillo. Novelists, like everyone else, are allowed only one set of biological parents, and after they have killed them off or exorcized them in a work of fiction they are faced with the problem of what to do for an encore. Although Franzen's writings all show his talent and his dedication, he may or may not be able to stick to his principles for the long life he still has ahead; he may or may not run out of ideas; he may or may not become the great social novelist he aspires to be.

There is a remarkable contrast between most of the pieces in *How to Be Alone* that were written during the 1990's and the three pieces written after the turn of the century. Franzen suddenly sounds less like a professional bad boy, less like a fire-eating revolutionary who blames "upbeat techno-corporatism" for his personal troubles. Success has made him serious, modest, chastened, humble, middle-aged. He is conscious that he is no longer addressing a select audience of cognoscenti but is now playing at the big table. Unlike the vast majority of aspiring artists who come out of college every year and encounter the dog-eat-dog competition of the real world, his dreams have come true. His photo on the back flap of the cover shows a man with uncombed hair and a three-day growth of beard, standing in the twilight zone between youth and middle age. He is wearing a denim jacket with the collar rakishly turned up. It is as if he is trying to proclaim that he is still a renegade, but his later essays belie that assertion.

Professor Stephen Cox, who reviewed *How to Be Alone* for the *San Diego Union-Tribune*, wrote that Franzen was "like many other cultural conservatives who mistake themselves for liberals." Franzen's fairy-tale release from poverty and obscurity may not be making him politically conservative so much as revealing his innate conservative values to himself. Success may spoil Franzen. His 1990's essays sound like rumblings of a passing storm; he sounds like Hal denouncing Falstaff on the day of his coronation in William Shakespeare's *King Henry IV, Part II* (pr. 1598). In "Inauguration Day, January, 2001," Franzen seems to be repudiating the radical malcontents of his youth. He tells how, "lacking any better invitation," he participated in a cold, wet, socialist demonstration against George W. Bush "even if [he] didn't actually believe that George Bush was a bigot or that he'd stolen any votes that day." This last entry ends with these words:

> You may still be one version of yourself, the version from the bus, the younger and redder version, as long as you're waiting for the subway and riding home. But then you peel off the thermal layers, still damp, of the long day's costume, and you see a wholly different kind of costume hanging in your closet; and in the shower you're naked and alone.

Bill Delaney

Sources for Further Study

Booklist 99 (September 1, 2002): 47.
The Guardian, October 5, 2002, p. 36.
Kirkus Reviews 70 (August 1, 2002): 1093.
Library Journal 127 (October 1, 2002): 94.
The New York Times Book Review 107 (November 10, 2002): 7.
Publishers Weekly 249 (September 2, 2002): 65.
San Diego Union-Tribune Book Review, October 6, 2002, p. 8.
San Francisco Chronicle Book Review, October 13, 2002, p. 2.

HOW WE BECAME HUMAN
New and Selected Poems, 1975-2001

Author: Joy Harjo (1951-   )
Publisher: W. W. Norton (New York). 192 pp. $26.95
Type of work: Poetry

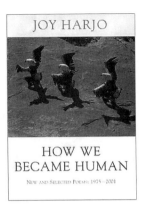

~

Encompassing her entire career, the newest collection of poems from Harjo reveals her growth as a writer, a visionary, and a woman

~

When Joy Harjo published her first chapbook *The Last Song* in 1975, Native American literature was just beginning to gain literary and critical attention. Writers such as Leslie Marmon Silko, Linda Hogan, N. Scott Momaday, and Harjo, once considered pioneers of this important movement, are now viewed as accomplished artists whose work is often included in American literature anthologies. Harjo's poetry, in particular, has gained wide recognition and praise for its political, social, cultural, and spiritual content. A mixed-blood Muskogee Creek, Harjo frequently blends traditional Native American values and myth with images from contemporary life to highlight themes such as the interrelatedness of all things, survival, the power of language and memory, feminist concerns, continuance, and transcendence. Her book *In Mad Love and War* (1990) won the prestigious William Carlos Williams Award from the Poetry Society of America and the Delmore Schwartz Memorial Prize from New York University. *How We Became Human* collects poems from each of seven previous books—two of which are now out of print—and includes thirteen new poems.

The first section of *How We Became Human* features eight of the ten poems originally published in *The Last Song*, which were eventually incorporated into Harjo's second book, *What Moon Drove Me to This?* (1980). Many of the poems are devoid of punctuation and capitalization. Her lack of concern for the "proper" rules of English grammar reflects the influence of other Native American poets Harjo was reading at the time these poems were written and may be a conscious protest against the language of the European colonizers. Largely autobiographical, Harjo's early poems also incorporate many of the images and themes that she would develop in her later work.

The title poem in *The Last Song*, for example, tells the story of Harjo's visit to her childhood home in Oklahoma. Landscape and a sense of place are primary concerns in Harjo's work and spring from her Native American perspective. Her deep connection to her birthplace is reflected in the last lines, "oklahoma will be the last song/ i'll ever sing." Not only is the land an essential part of her personal history, it also pro-

Joy Harjo, an enrolled member of the Muskogee Creek Nation, is the author of seven books of poetry and is also a musician. A former teacher, she now resides in Hawaii and travels with her band, The Real Revolution.

vides a tangible link to her tribal culture and past. The importance of land, memory, and the Native oral tradition is evident in the following lines:

> an ancient chant
> that my mother knew
> came out of a history
> woven from wet tall grass
> in her womb
> and i know of no other way
> than to surround my voice
> with the summer songs of crickets
> in this moist south night air

These lines blend a mythic perspective with feminist and cultural viewpoints, a potent combination upon which Harjo would eventually expand. Her feminist and cultural concerns are also represented in "I Am a Dangerous Woman," which appeared for the first time in *What Moon Drove Me to This?* The setting of the poem, a modern airport surrounded by the Sandia Mountains, illustrates the clash between Native and Anglo values. This conflict is further emphasized when the Native speaker is asked to step into the security guard's "guncatcher machine." The refrain "I am a dangerous woman" is repeated twice in the poem and highlights the speaker's feminine power.

Harjo's next book, *She Had Some Horses* (1983), moved away from the short lyrics of *The Last Song* and *What Moon Drove Me to This?* to include longer poems that weave together more complex themes and images and draw more extensively from American Indian myth and legend. Arranged in a cyclical fashion, the poems not only explore social issues such as racism, injustice, and the destructive effects of colonialism on marginalized peoples, but also examine the detrimental effects of those issues on the speaker's psychological and spiritual landscapes. Beginning and ending with poems about fear, the entire work represents a journey from fragmentation to wholeness.

The best example of this journey is the title poem, "She Had Some Horses." The poem, written in the form of a Native American chant, repeats the phrases "she had some horses" and "she had horses," giving the work a rhythmic quality while reinforcing the speaker's native identity. The speaker's inner landscape has been scarred as a result of her living as a mixed-blood Native American in an alien society. She attempts to heal the wounds within herself by engaging in a ritual that will reconcile conflicting aspects of her personality. By the end of the poem, she realizes her goal when she says, "She had some horses she loved./ She had some horses she hated./ These were the same horses." This ceremony is a necessary predecessor to "I Give

You Back," the last poem of the collection, where the speaker is able to gain mastery over the fear that threatens to overwhelm her.

Secrets from the Center of the World (1989), Harjo's fourth collection, was a departure from her previous work. The original publication was a collaboration between Harjo and astronomer and amateur photographer Stephen Strom and brought together Harjo's short, koanlike responses to Strom's color photographs of the Southwestern landscape. The complementary pictures and poetry are meant to be appreciated as a whole work of art. For example, when Harjo writes, "It is an honor to walk where all around me stands an earth house made of scarlet, of jet, of ochre, of white shell," she is responding to a stunning picture of a red-rock canyon near Medicine Hat, Utah. The poems selected for this section of *How We Became Human* do not include Strom's photographs. Although the pieces can stand on their own, the reader does not experience the full impact of the poems without the accompaniment of the photographs.

Harjo comes away from her desert experience with a fresh vision. Exploring social and political issues more in depth than in her previous work, many of the poems in *In Mad Love and War* touch on concerns of Native, African, and Central Americans, all victims of colonization. The impact of racism is explored in two poems of witness, "For Anna Mae Pictou Aquash, Whose Spirit Is Present Here and in the Dappled Stars (for we remember the story and tell it again so we all may live)" and "Strange Fruit." Both poems are based on the true stories of women activists, one Native American and one African American. Anna Mae Pictou Aquash, an American Indian Movement (AIM) activist at the Pine Ridge Reservation in 1976, was found killed by a bullet fired at close range. "Strange Fruit" memorializes Jacqueline Peters, who was lynched in California in 1986 after she attempted to organize a local chapter of the National Association for the Advancement of Colored People (NAACP) in response to the killing of a young black man by the Ku Klux Klan. "The Real Revolution Is Love" also deals with social and political oppression. Written as a result of Harjo's attendance at a poetry convention in Nicaragua in 1986, the poem explores the erotic interactions of a group of poets at a party. On a deeper level, the poem examines the devastating effects of colonization on indigenous people. Although Harjo frequently addresses the issue of colonization in this collection, she nonetheless holds out hope that love can heal. While the search for wholeness is a major theme in *She Had Some Horses*, transformation through love is the key concept in *In Mad Love and War*.

Transformation continued to be an important theme in *The Woman Who Fell from the Sky* (1996). The title of the poem is taken from an Iroquois creation myth in which a beautiful young woman becomes the bride of the sun. Wrongly accused of adultery, she is flung down a hole in the sky by her husband but is rescued by a flock of ducks. The title work, a long prose poem, is based on this creation myth and tells the story of two Native Americans who experience transformation and redemption through love: Johnny, a homeless Vietnam veteran, and Lila, a woman with two children who has been thrown out of the house by her husband. "The Flood" is another example of Harjo's prose poetry and is also based on Native American myth, this time the story of the water monster. The poem intertwines the story of a Native teenager who died by drowning and the myth of the malevolent water monster who lives at the bottom of the lake. The water monster image became even more prominent in Harjo's next book, as she confronted painful issues that hampered her spiritual and personal growth. Harjo's frequent use of the prose poem in this collection reflects her growing sophistication as a poet as well as a storyteller.

Harjo continued to explore the creation/transformation theme in *A Map to the Next World* (2000). Harjo looked back on her entire experience as she sought a new direction for the twenty-first century. The centerpiece of the book is a long poem that deals with the troubled relationship between Harjo and her father. Now writing in midlife, Harjo confronts the painful relationship that was the cause of her self-hatred and fear. Harjo links her father to the destructive figure of the water monster when she writes that her father "loved the water" just as "the water loved him." Water takes on a variety of meanings in the poem. In addition to its connection with destruction, it also is an instrument of revenge. Expressing her anger at Anglo society, Harjo imagines the colonizer disappearing "in the deep." At the end of the poem, water is an agent of purification, transformation, and rebirth, giving the speaker "the ability to make songs out of the debris of destruction/ as we climb from the watery gut to the stars."

When "Returning from the Enemy" was first published, Harjo alternated autobiographical narrative with poetry that commented on the narrative. The poem was twenty-eight pages long, but in *How We Became Human* the narrative has been deleted. The choice to leave out the narrative is understandable, given that one must make some difficult editorial decisions when publishing a book that embraces over a quarter century of work. Nonetheless, the piece is more enlightening with the inclusion of the narrative, and those who desire to better understand Harjo's work would do well to read the original version.

The last thirteen poems in *How We Became Human* demonstrate how Harjo's poetic vision has matured and in some senses has been tinged by the cynicism and disillusionment that sometimes comes with middle age. Now living in Hawaii instead of the southwestern United States, Harjo identifies with the indigenous people residing on the islands and draws on Hawaiian as well as American Indian myth to emphasize themes in her poems. However, she has lost some of the idealism that characterized her earlier work. In "Morning Prayers," she says "good-bye to the girl/ with her urgent prayers for redemption." The powerful—and timely—poem titled "When the World as We Know It Ended" closes the book. Apparently written in response to the terrorist attacks on the Twin Towers of the World Trade Center on September 11, 2001, Harjo claims that the Indian community "knew it was coming." References to "two towers . . . from the east island of commerce . . ./ Swallowed/ by a fire dragon, by oil and fear" and to "those who would steal to be president" amount to a scathing attack on the economic, political, and social structures of the United States and Western society. Yet it seems that Harjo still holds out some hope for the continuance of the human race in spite of the difficulties it now faces. The birth image in the last lines of the poem highlight the power of language and transcendence to help people move beyond perceived differences between nations and cultures and to recognize that they are all linked as one human family. In spite of minor drawbacks, *How We Became Human* provides an opportunity to follow the personal and professional evolution of one of the most significant voices in contemporary American Indian literature.

Pegge Bochynski

Sources for Further Study

Library Journal 127 (June 15, 2002): 70.
Publishers Weekly 249 (June 17, 2002): 58.

I HAVE LANDED
The End of a Beginning in Natural History

Author: Stephen Jay Gould (1941-2002)
Publisher: Harmony Books (New York). 418 pp. $25.95
Type of work: History of science

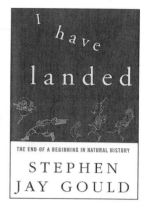

～

The last collection of Gould's previously published essays includes reflections on Charles Darwin, the connections between science and the humanities, continuity, and the tragedy of September 11, 2001

～

For twenty-seven years, from January, 1974, until January, 2001, Stephen Jay Gould, a paleontologist and historian of science at Harvard University best known in scientific circles as the cocreator of the theory of punctuated equilibria, contributed a monthly essay to *Natural History* magazine, a publication of the American Museum of Natural History. In three hundred essays published under the general title "This View of Life," a title derived from a phrase in Charles Darwin's concluding sentence in *On the Origin of Species* (1859), Gould examined science, history, philosophy, art, and literature and the relationships and interactions among these human endeavors. Evolution—its history, scientific implications, and misuse—was his favorite theme. He always attempted to use very specific examples to illuminate very large issues in intellectual history and science. He prided himself in finding new ways to approach old topics. *I Have Landed* is the tenth, and last, collection of these essays, assembled before Gould's death from cancer on May 20, 2002. Unlike the earlier collections, however, almost half (fifteen of thirty-one) of the contributions to this volume were not part of the *Natural History* series. They were originally published in such diverse places as an art exhibition catalog, the proceedings of a scholarly conference, a Canadian newspaper, and *The New York Times*.

The thirty-one essays are organized, as were Gould's earlier collections, into categories or themes rather than by date of publication. (Gould did not provide bibliographic information for his *Natural History* essays, and did so for only some of the pieces taken from other sources, so in many cases the reader has only the vaguest idea of the chronological relationship among the essays.) The first grouping consists of only the title essay, which was the last *Natural History* essay he published. A mixture of sentimentality, history, and the sharp insights into evolution readers have come to expect from Gould, the essay looks at continuity in life, whether in the macrocosm of biological evolution or in the microcosm of a single family. At its core is the story of the immigration of Gould's grandfather to the United States, an event recorded by "Papa Joe," as Gould later knew him, in a grammar book with the words "I have landed." This essay is followed by four that explore the relationship between human-

istic endeavors—literature, history, the performing arts, and painting—and science. The third
grouping consists of three short intellectual biographies, one of Gould's favorite methods of illuminating a point. As was often the case, Gould either looks at familiar figures in a new light—for
example, Sigmund Freud's great failure or E. Ray
Lankester's presence at Karl Marx's funeral—or
resurrects an individual well known to contemporaries but forgotten by history—the popular
science writer Isabelle Duncan, for instance. Next
come three essays in which Gould takes ideas
prevalent in an earlier time, ideas which now
seem at best odd, at worst horribly misguided,
and attempts to place them in their historical
context and to demonstrate their logic within
their own time. With these examples he hoped to
illuminate the great strengths and limitations of
the human mind.

At the time of his death in May, 2002, Stephen Jay Gould was on the faculties of Harvard University and New York University. He published twenty-two books, including monographs in the history of science and technical works in evolutionary biology. The Mismeasure of Man *(1981) received the National Book Critics' Circle Award for 1982.*

The fifth section of *I Have Landed* represents
a change in format. Apparently, there were sim-
ply not enough essays from either *Natural History* or other sources available to fill a book, so
Gould included six short opinion pieces from
newspapers and magazines. These opinion pieces all, in one way or another, defend
Charles Darwin and the theory of evolution. Only a fraction of the length of his other
essays, these opinion pieces lack the well-developed arguments and the multitude of
examples so characteristic of the longer essays.

The next two groupings represent a return to the more standard format and typical
themes of this series. Ten essays, each focusing on different aspects of evolution, are
divided into two sections. The first concerns the basic concepts of evolutionary theory, the second the implications or misuse of that theory.

Gould concludes with four very short pieces revolving around the events of September 11, 2001, and their aftermath. The day of the suicide attacks on the World
Trade Center in New York and the Pentagon in Washington, D.C., coincided with the
centennial of Papa Joe's arrival in New York. Gould had planned to fly into New
York from Italy that day and to go to Ellis Island, where Papa Joe had landed, to commemorate that centennial. Instead, his flight was diverted to Halifax, Nova Scotia,
where he was greeted with compassion and warm-heartedness by the residents of that
Canadian city. In these final pieces, Gould thanks the citizens of Halifax and expresses his optimism in the ultimate good of the human race, the great strength of the
United States, and the future. These pieces serve as a reminder that, although Gould
spent most of his adult life in Boston and Cambridge, Massachusetts, he was New
York City born and bred.

Of the thirty-one essays in *I Have Landed*, there are a number that capture the essence of Gould as historian, scientist, and thinker. One that stands out appears in the fourth grouping, "Essays in the Paleontology of Ideas," and is titled "When Fossils Were Young." In it, Gould argued that certain conventions, originally created for very good reasons, continue long after changes in the situation have rendered the conventions less than useful. Finally, someone realizes that a small alteration in the convention will reform the situation and produce a system much more reflective of, or responsive to, the contemporary situation. Because the reform can be accomplished with relative ease and the result is so obviously an improvement over the old way, the new way of doing things is rapidly accepted as the new convention.

In the essay, Gould provides three examples drawn, as his examples often were, from both everyday life and the history of science, from the familiar and the not-so-familiar, which together demonstrate his erudition, curiosity, and willingness to draw conclusions. All three examples are taxonomies, which he defines as ways of organizing knowledge either to make it easier to retrieve the information or to explain the basis of variation among the items. The first example is the listing of gates for airplane departures. For many years, this information was organized by the time of departure of the flight. This worked well as long as there were relatively few flights (and still works well for trains, because there are many fewer trains leaving a station at any given time than flights leaving an airport). However, as the number of flights grew, it became more difficult to find a particular flight to Chicago among all the other departures at or near the same time. The brilliant solution was to organize departures by city of destination rather than time of departure.

The second example is the organization of scholarly bibliographies in books. The earliest efforts, dating back to the sixteenth century, organized the bibliography alphabetically by the first name of the author. As Gould demonstrated, this made tremendous sense at that time, when almost all the authors listed were scholars from antiquity known by a single name, such as Aristotle. However, this practical idea became a convention, used reflexively and without further examination. It was still the accepted practice well into the seventeenth century, even after the list of sources in science books grew and authors of a single name were joined by contemporary authors with both first and last names. As a result of the continuation of this convention, the reader was confronted with the absurdity of a bibliography containing two dozen authors, all with the first name "John," listed together. Remembering the last name of an author would not be sufficient. By the mid-seventeenth century, however, reform occurred. As readers came to recognize the absurdity of such lists, bibliographies came to be organized by last names.

The last example is drawn from the history of science. Gould argues that outmoded conventions, or as he describes them here, "false taxonomies," hurt the development of science. He examines a late sixteenth century work on fossils and shows how three iconographic conventions developed by this author made sense at the time. However, later scientists blindly followed the conventions, hamstringing themselves and impeding further progress in the field of paleontology. Not until the late eighteenth century were these conventions successfully challenged.

Gould saw his essays as contributions to scholarship, not merely the recycling for general audiences of information already well known to specialists. In some cases—in what he saw as his most important contribution to the state of scholarship—he presented an analysis of a newly discovered document. The documents in question were very often in the form of annotations or marginalia to books. An example in this volume is his analysis of Louis Agassiz's marginalia in his copy of Ernst Haeckel's *Natürliche Schöpfungsgeschichte* (1868; *The History of Creation*, 1876). Gould captured the passion of Agassiz's response to his rival Haeckel's forging of evidence.

Another form of scholarly contribution was the offering of new interpretations of historical actors, publications, or scientific theories. Examples of such new interpretations in *I Have Landed* include Gould's exegesis of Isabelle Duncan's 1860 attempt to reconcile the Biblical account of creation and geology and his analysis of J. F. Blumenbach's classification of humans into five races rather than the four used by Blumenbach's predecessors.

A quite different form of new interpretation was Gould's reinterpretation of published scientific data. With these reinterpretations, Gould set out to prove that scientists were not always as objective in interpreting data as they would like their readers to believe. This reinterpretation was one of the unique aspects of Gould's forays into the history of science. The best known of these reinterpretations was his book-length study of the pseudoscience of racial classification and ranking according to intelligence, *The Mismeasure of Man* (1981).

Gould complained that other scholars have not given due credit and recognition to his contributions to the history of science because he had chosen to present his discoveries and insights in the *Natural History* essays, devoid of footnotes (although not devoid of citations to the scientific literature where appropriate), rather than in peer-reviewed journals. It is difficult to believe, however, that he took the rejection by professional historians too seriously. If he truly wanted the attention of historians, he would have published in the peer-reviewed journals. He has no difficulty crafting history for the historians. His *The Mismeasure of Man*, which does have all the proper scholarly apparatus, is frequently cited and used by the scholarly community. Rather, he loved writing for "millions of folks with a passionate commitment to continuous learning," the folks who might use his essays as bathroom reading.

Marc Rothenberg

Sources for Further Reading

Booklist 98 (March 1, 2002): 1050.
Library Journal 127 (April 15, 2002): 122.
New Scientist 174 (May 18, 2002): 54.
The New York Review of Books 49 (May 23, 2002): 52.
The New York Times Book Review 107 (June 9, 2002): 28.

IF NOT, WINTER
Fragments of Sappho

Author: Sappho (c. 630 B.C.E.-c. 560 B.C.E.)
Translated from the Greek by Anne Carson (1950-   )
Publisher: Alfred A. Knopf (New York). 397 pp. $27.50
Type of work: Poetry

≈

A bilingual edition of fragments surviving from the po-
etry of one of the ancient world's most influential authors

≈

Anne Carson's new translation of Sappho's poetry focuses on the theme of fragmentation. Although Sappho
was one of the ancient world's most influential and celebrated poets, only one of her works has survived intact. The
rest of her poetry is known only from the merest fragments. Ancient authors will
sometimes quote a stanza, line, or individual word and identify it as appearing in one
of the books of Sappho. In addition, a few dried bits of papyrus have survived bearing
several words that can be identified—certainly or at least plausibly—as coming from
the lost poems of Sappho. Other than these scattered remains, however, all of
Sappho's nine books of lyric poems, wedding songs, and odes on various topics have
vanished, apparently forever.

To convey this fragmentary nature of Sappho's surviving works, Carson and her
publishers have given *If Not, Winter* a feel of torn scraps and remnants. The dust
jacket is barren white, broken only by a thin strip of papyrus, laced with gaping holes.
In the text itself, square brackets indicate lost characters, and broad spacing reinforces the sense that the reader has been handed mere shards. In most cases, only the
residue of a single poem—even if this is no more than a few words—stands alone on
each page, surrounded by a vast border of empty space. The Greek text, based on a
1971 transcription by the scholar Eva-Maria Voigt, appears on each left-hand page,
attractively set in a Greek font tinted the same sienna-colored hue as the papyrus fragment on the cover. The English translation appears, broadly spaced, on the right-hand
side of the page. As a result, the sheer emptiness of the book serves as a silent commentary on how much of Sappho's work has been lost or destroyed throughout the
ages.

Carson takes her title for the work from fragment 22 of Sappho, a highly incomplete poem that contains the words "If not, winter . . . no pain." These particular lines
are emblematic of what much of Sappho's poetry has become today: a promise of
great beauty that must ultimately remain elusive. It is impossible to know with any
certainty the original context of these few puzzling words or to understand how the
ancient author developed this image of winter. Nevertheless, the remainder of frag-

ment 22 chronicles many of the recurrent themes of Sappho's work: song, the lyre, longing, unfulfilled desire, the goddess Aphrodite, happiness, the beauty of a gown, and a friend (Abanthis) whose relationship with Sappho is never satisfactorily revealed.

Anne Carson is a classicist and poet at McGill University in Montreal. In 2000, she received a prestigious MacArthur Foundation Fellowship. She has published a wide variety of works, including Eros the Bittersweet *(1986),* Autobiography of Red *(1998),* Plainwater: Essays and Poetry *(2000), and* The Beauty of the Husband: A Fictional Essay in Twenty-nine Tangos *(2001).*

Since antiquity, both the meaning of Sappho's poetry and the sexual orientation of its author have been subject to widely divergent interpretations. Born on the Aegean island of Lesbos and composing her works in the Lesbian form of the Aeolic dialect, Sappho gave the English adjective "lesbian" its connotation of female homosexuality. Writing what appear to be frankly amorous or erotic poems to several companions or girls in her charge, Sappho is commonly assumed by modern readers to have been herself homosexual or at least bisexual. Nevertheless, the evidence to support this assumption is, like Sappho's poetry, fragmentary at best. While it must be understood that ancient biographies are notoriously unreliable, it is significant that very few early accounts of Sappho's life associate her with homoeroticism. She is said to have married a man named Kerkylas and to have given birth to a daughter, Kleis, who was perhaps named after the poet's own mother. Whatever doubts there may be about other aspects of Sappho's life, Kleis certainly existed, called the poet's "beautiful child" in fragment 32. Other ancient sources describe Sappho as committing suicide because her love for another man, Phaon, went unrequited. Nowadays, however, it is generally accepted that the legend of Phaon, like many stories pertaining to the deaths of Greek literary figures, was the invention of some late comic author. On the other hand, it is probably important that Sappho's poetry was intimately known by many ancient readers who found her passionate attraction, first to a husband and then to a male lover, not at all unbelievable. It may be significant, too, that the Roman poet Catullus, who was influenced by Sappho in writing his own heterosexual love poetry, could address his beloved as "Lesbia" and raise no eyebrows.

The uncertainty about Sappho's sexual orientation derives from the frank passion with which she frequently addresses the women of her circle. As early as the tenth century C.E., the medieval lexicon known as the Suda described Sappho as having had amorous relationships with such female companions as Atthis, Telesippa, and Megara and as having been notorious as a result. Since the Suda was itself a compilation of far earlier material, this image of Sappho's homosexuality may be nearly as ancient as her poetry itself. While still living on the island of Lesbos, Sappho maintained a *thiasos*, an establishment attached to the worship of a particular deity, in Sappho's case Aphrodite and the Muses. Since Sappho's *thiasos* seems to have consisted largely of young women, it is sometimes treated by modern authors as though it were some sort of finishing school, salon, or women's college. Despite the uncertainty of the poet's actual sexual orientation, it is clear that she was fond of the young women whom she knew. One of Sappho's nine books consisted entirely of wedding songs composed for these companions. Some scholars believe that each time a member of the *thiasos* was married, Sappho composed a marriage ode. For this reason, the longing and passion that appears in these poems may have been genuine, may have been conventional, or may simply have seemed an appropriate theme for the occasion. In the end, the question of Sappho's sexual orientation, like the meaning of many of her poems, will never be settled to each reader's satisfaction. The evidence is simply too incomplete.

Carson wisely chooses to pass over this vexing issue quickly and to concentrate on the poetry itself. The result is a work in which the words themselves, not the life of the figure who stands behind those words, commands the reader's attention. Nor does the translator seek to intrude on the power of those words. On the last page of the volume, surrounded by the same white space that encompasses so much of the poetry in *If Not, Winter*, stands the bare comment, "A note about the translator: Anne Carson lives in Canada." What is not said here is thus far more significant than what these words reveal. The translator remains faceless, featureless, and figureless. Whoever has translated these words, Carson appears to be saying, should not distract the reader for a moment. It is more important to focus on the words of Sappho. Few though they may be, they are precious.

If the reader heeds Carson's implicit advice, *If Not, Winter* will be a genuine delight. Its very sparseness gives the reader time to pause and savor each exquisite drop, like a rich liqueur. A slow and attentive reading of these fragments reveals that, for all their brevity, they contain an extraordinary richness of imagery. Even today, the island of Lesbos is a setting filled with flowers, and floral or botanical imagery recurs in poem after poem. Sappho refers in a large number of fragments to roses, violets, chervil, and clover. When the Hellenistic poet Meleager (c. 100 B.C.E.) called Sappho's verses "few but roses all," he was struck not merely by their extraordinary beauty but also by the frequency of their floral imagery. Other repeated images include the dew, the color purple and its many implications, honey, gold, dawn, the goddess Aphrodite (who reappears throughout the fragments under a bewildering variety of names), and song itself.

The latter image is particularly important because all the poet's fragments were originally parts of songs. Sappho's poetry was lyric in the truest sense: It was meant to be sung by a solo vocalist to the accompaniment of a lyre. None of Sappho's original melodies have survived. As a result, there is yet another way in which Sappho's poetry has been reduced to the merest fragments. Although the author was said by the philosopher Aristoxenus (c. 370 B.C.E.) to have invented the Mixolydian mode, none of her music has endured to the modern day. Although the poet invented the metrical form that remains known today as "Sapphic," her words are so incomplete that all too few of Sappho's own Sapphic stanzas can be read in their entirety.

In her translation, Carson seeks to preserve the concrete quality of Sappho's language. Sappho preferred the vernacular forms of her own Lesbian/Aeolic dialect to many of the more refined literary forms that had already become established in Greek literature by her own day. Carson seeks equivalently colloquial expressions in her translation. In fragment 48, for example, Carson renders an expression that other translators may have set as "I was driven mad for you" or "I was beside myself because of you" with the more conversational phrase "I was crazy for you." In fragment 179, she translates the word *gruta*, given in standard lexicons as "dressing-case" or "receptacle for vanities," simply as "makeup bag." Only occasionally does Carson's simplicity of language actually distort Sappho's text or subvert her meaning. In one such case, Carson translates fragment 145 as "do not move stones," an intriguing but unnecessarily cryptic injunction. The difficulty is that the Greek word *cherados*, which Carson translates as "stones," is actually an extremely rare word used for silt, rubble, or a heap of pebbles. As a result, Sappho's original image for futility or long and pointless labor is concealed by the deceptive simplicity of Carson's translation.

On a few other occasions, too, readers are likely to gloss over some of their favorite passages from Sappho because Carson has rendered them in an unfamiliar or idiosyncratic way. For instance, in fragment 111, the opening of the wedding hymn that is commonly translated as "Raise high the roof beam, carpenters" is rendered by Carson (more accurately but less familiarly) as "up with the roof! Hymenaios—lift it, carpenters!" Perhaps in cases such as this, poetry has been forced to take second place to a more awkward literalism. More frequently, however, Carson's language captures the very essence of Sappho's ability to keep the images of her world still vivid more than two millennia after her death. Readers familiar with Greek will continually revert to the left-hand side of the page in order to be reacquainted with the precious fragments of one of the world's greatest poets; readers who are not will probably view the strange, umber-colored characters scattered across the left-hand pages with awe and wonder, perhaps feeling that their loss is all the greater.

Jeffrey L. Buller

Sources for Further Study

Library Journal 127 (June 15, 2002): 70.
Los Angeles Times Book Review, August 25, 2002, p. 3.
Publishers Weekly 249 (May 27, 2002): 52.

IGNORANCE

Author: Milan Kundera (1929-   )
First published: La ignorancia, 2000, in Spain, Argentina, Colombia, and Mexico
Translated from the French by Linda Asher
Publisher: HarperCollins (New York). 195 pp. $23.95
Type of work: Novel
Time: The 1950's to the 1990's
Locale: Paris, Prague, and a provincial city in Bohemia

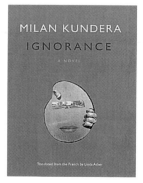

~

A woman and a man who had a brief encounter before they fled Czechoslovakia in 1969 to Paris and Denmark, respectively, meet again when they pay their homeland a visit after the fall of the Communist regime in 1989

~

Principal characters:
IRENA, a forty-something Czech émigré widow in Paris
JOSEF, a sixtyish Czech émigré widower in Denmark
MARTIN, Irena's dead Czech émigré husband
GUSTAF, Irena's married Swedish boyfriend
SYLVIE, Irena's French friend
IRENA'S MOTHER, still living in Prague
JOSEF'S BROTHER, still living in Czechoslovakia
JOSEF'S SISTER-IN-LAW, who holds grudges against Josef
JOSEF'S STEPDAUGHTER, from his brief Czech marriage
MILADA, Josef's high school sweetheart, a spinster
N., Josef's Czech friend, a former Communist commissar

Though first published in a Spanish translation, *Ignorance* is the latest of three novels that Milan Kundera has written in French after making his mark in his native Czech with poetry, plays, criticism, and fiction, most notably the novels *Le Livre du rire et de l'oubli* (1979; *The Book of Laughter and Forgetting,* 1980) and *L'Insoutenable Légèreté de l'être* (1984; *The Unbearable Lightness of Being,* 1984). Like many other Czech artists and intellectuals, Kundera was booted from the Communist Party after the Prague Spring of 1968, and his writings were banned. In 1975 he and his wife were finally allowed to immigrate to France, where they have since lived, mostly in Paris, and become citizens. *Ignorance* seems like a novel by an author who might want to visit his homeland but not live there.

Thematically, *Ignorance* raises the question of where home is anymore in the modern world, not only for émigrés but for anyone who moves around. The place of one's birth no longer seems to qualify, as one grows away from it, moves to more attractive places, or becomes cosmopolitan in tastes. For people in and from formerly communist countries, sudden opportunities to travel and migrate, after decades of restricted opportunities, seem to have raised the question afresh.

Irena, the novel's main character, who lives in Paris, has enjoyed the status of émigré for two decades: Parisians feel sorry for the poor Czech woman and other displaced persons of her ilk. However, after the fall of Czech communism in 1989, they begin to wonder why she is not hurrying back home to help out. Her Parisian friends seem to consider it her patriotic duty. Yet Irena has worked hard to become settled in Paris, where she buried her Czech husband and raised their two daughters, who for all practical matters are French. Now Irena has a job, an apartment, and a boyfriend in Paris, not a bad city in which to make one's home. Only a visit from her mother, who still lives in Prague, persuades Irena to make a return visit to the city of her birth.

Josef, the novel's other main character, likewise fled Czechoslovakia in 1969. He settled in Denmark, where he married a Danish woman,

Milan Kundera was born in Brno, Czechoslovakia, in 1929 and has lived in France, his second homeland, for more than twenty years. In Czech, he is the author of poetry, drama, criticism, and fiction, most notably the novels The Book of Laughter and Forgetting *(1979) and* The Unbearable Lightness of Being *(1984). His recent fiction and criticism have been in French.*

and they lived happily together until she died. Josef, still mourning her death and attached to their home in Denmark, where he keeps everything just as it was when she was alive, is also very slow to return to the land of his birth. Now he is returning for a visit only because he had promised his dying wife that he would. Josef also returns to see friends and close relatives who remained in Czechoslovakia, specifically his brother and brother's family.

On their way to Czechoslovakia, Irena and Josef meet by chance in the Paris airport. Irena remembers Josef from another chance encounter many years before in Prague, before she married. She had joined friends in a bar, and one of them had brought along Josef. There had been some chemistry between the two, but after their meeting they had never seen each other again: "Their love story stopped before it could start." Now Irena introduces herself again, and they agree to get together in Prague. Actually, Josef cannot remember her (he had frequented the Prague bar to pick up women), but now he sees no reason to turn down an opportunity for friendship with a warm, good-looking woman.

Before they rendezvous in Prague, they both have certain rounds to make. Here is where Kundera begins to chip away at the idea of the Great Return. Both Irena and Josef are struck by the strangeness of the spoken Czech language, which seems to have developed an ugly nasal drawl since their departure. They also both notice the hometown diminution effect: Landscapes and city scenes that once seemed impressive have shrunk into insignificance, if they have not disappeared altogether. Worst of all, the whole country has been inundated by tasteless popular culture and crass commercialism; for example, the music on the radio is described as "noise" and "sewage-water music," and the tubercular face of writer Franz Kafka adorns a T-shirt for tourists.

Both Irena and Josef get a glimpse of what they might have become if they had stayed in Czechoslovakia. When the weather turns hot, Irena buys a dowdy Czech dress that makes her look "naïve, provincial, inelegant" and "pitiable, poor, weak, downtrodden." In his high school diary that his brother had saved for him, Josef is able to contemplate the "little snot" he used to be, back in the days of his virginity, when he obsessed about girls but could express his feelings only by torturing his girlfriends emotionally. Both Irena and Josef also get an eyeful of their potential selves in the friends and relatives that they meet, who form a kind of gauntlet for the two visitors but who otherwise have not missed them for twenty years.

Irena consults her old address books and invites some old Prague friends to a party, where she makes the mistake of serving up twelve bottles of old Bordeaux. After an awkward moment, her friends declare their "plain-and-simple" preference for beer. Then, beer in hand, they stand around chatting to each other about local matters, pretty much ignoring Irena. They are totally uninterested in what she has been doing during the twenty years she was away. Irena realizes that they have "amputated twenty years from her life" and no longer have much in common with her. She already misses her Parisian friend Sylvie.

In the provincial hometown that he visits, Josef has to run an even worse gauntlet formed by his sister-in-law, his Czech former wife (to whom he was married for only a few months), and his stepdaughter. Josef's brother is happy enough to see him again, though the brother is somewhat embarrassed because he has taken over the family home and Josef's old belongings. Although she also enjoys his goods, Josef's sister-in-law has not forgiven him for running off and causing them to suffer under the Communist regime. Worse, she calls up his former wife and tells her he is in town. Then his stepdaughter calls him to say she has to see him right away to discuss certain important matters that she cannot talk about on the phone. Later, when he calls back to break their appointment, the stepdaughter says her mother warned her about what "a filthy little egotist" he is.

By the time Irena and Josef meet in Prague, they are ready for some relief and consolation. They share each other's stories over lunch and wine, then head up to his hotel room. Before long, they are making mad love throughout the afternoon. Irena erupts like a woman who has not made love in years and Josef like a man who is doing it for the last time: They enjoy each other thoroughly. However, Josef keeps his eyes on his watch and Irena gets steadily drunker. Eventually she discovers that he does not know her name, protests that she has been treated like a whore, and cries herself to sleep. He leaves to catch his plane back to Denmark.

Thus, the ending of the novel is immensely sad. For both Irena and Josef, the Great Return to their homeland fizzles out and so does their brief romance. Even though Josef realizes that Irena is in love with him, he is still emotionally committed to his dead wife. Irena and Josef have crossed paths again, but again their paths do not match. At this point in his life, Josef's path seems more parallel to that of another character in the novel, the mysterious Milada. Milada was Josef's high school girlfriend who attempted suicide over him, who has remained a spinster all of her life, and who is committed to a memory of love, but Milada might also be a mirror character for Irena, whose heart Josef might also have broken.

Another possibility, however, is that Irena will find the encounter with Josef liberating. Until this encounter, Irena has tended to be dependent in her relationships with other people—first with her mother, then with her husband, Martin, and even with her married boyfriend, Gustaf. Gustaf, who cannot stand his wife and hometown back in Sweden, also cannot commit to a love relationship (or even a memory of one). The encounter with Josef, in which Irena takes the initiative, reminds Irena what love feels like, and she determines to leave Gustaf. Meanwhile, Irena's mother seduces Gustaf, who seems quite happy with their convenient arrangement, so everything works out for them (at least it is nice to know that somebody in this novel is happy).

Throughout the novel, Kundera also draws parallels to and meditates on the ur-myth of the Great Return—the story of Homer's *Odyssey* (c. 725 B.C.E.), which is at the center of *Ignorance* just as the story of Oedipus's sense of moral responsibility is at the center of *The Unbearable Lightness of Being*. Here Kundera seems to draw on the myth of Odysseus's return primarily to show that it no longer applies to the modern world but is a romantic hangover from another time. For Odysseus, the return had tremendous validity, as he struggled to get back to his beloved homeland and wife. Around the time of the Victorian poet Alfred, Lord Tennyson, who wrote a stirring poem about Odysseus's restlessness after his return, the myth started going downhill. Now the myth seems totally meaningless.

Where is home anymore? Where is love? In *Ignorance* Kundera seems to say that in the modern world neither of these is easy to find. The ur-myth no longer works as a guideline. Certainly Kundera demolishes the idea that the place of one's birth has any special significance. Instead, life is full of possibilities. Home and love are out there somewhere, but they have to be compatible with one's identity, which in the modern world is a shifting, developing concept, dependent not just on one's origins but on one's experiences, memories, ideals, and ignorance.

Harold Branam

Sources for Further Study

Booklist 99 (September 1, 2002): 57.
Library Journal 127 (October 15, 2002): 94.
The New York Times Book Review 107 (October 6, 2002): 38.
Publishers Weekly 249 (August 26, 2002): 38.

IMPERFECT GARDEN
The Legacy of Humanism

Author: Tzvetan Todorov (1939-   )
First published: Le Jardin imparfait: La Pensée
  humaniste en France, 1998, in France
Translated from the French by Carol Cosman
Publisher: Princeton University Press (Princeton, N.J.).
  254 pp. $29.95
Type of work: History and philosophy

~

Todorov defends traditional humanism against compet-
ing systems and claims it is the only effective guide for
modern society

~

Imperfect Garden is an unusual book to be published in the early twenty-first century. In a period of deconstruction, new historicism, and poststructuralism, the book is
a very old-fashioned history-of-ideas analysis that looks back to the Renaissance and
the Enlightenment for a guide to the principles people should live by today. The subtitle of the book does not call into question the "legacy of humanism" but celebrates it
as the only coherent philosophy that Western society has. Tzvetan Todorov's primary
sources for humanism are all French thinkers of the sixteenth to the nineteenth centuries. This gives the book a clear focus but an obvious limitation.

Todorov defines humanism primarily from the works of Michel de Montaigne
(1533-1592) and Jean-Jacques Rousseau (1712-1778), although he qualifies and
sharpens that definition by discussing Benjamin Constant de Rebecque (1767-1830),
René Descartes (1596-1650), and a number of other thinkers. Humanism, for Todorov,
is the "doctrines according to which man is the point of departure. . . . The specificity
of human affairs (in contrast to those that relate to God) is therefore the point of departure for humanist doctrine . . . ." Todorov, referring to the tale of Satan offering Christ
all the treasures of the world if he will worship him, compares humanism to Satan's
offer to make humanity autonomous and free; however, for this gift, Satan demands
that a price be paid.

The primary method for analyzing humanism is to compare and, especially, contrast it to related families of thought: conservatism, scientism, and individualism.
Todorov sees an interplay of these families along with humanism rather than a clear
division between them. Often he will acknowledge that some of the thinkers he
discusses represent both humanist and one or more of the other families. For example, Rousseau is often seen as both a humanist and an individualist. The conservatives
feel that the price for human freedom is too great and wish, therefore, to reject the
initial declaration of freedom and return to tradition and the necessity of having a de-

ity. Todorov uses Louis-Gabriel-Ambroise de Bonald (1754-1840) as an example of this position. Bonald desired to turn back the results of the French Revolution because the price for the freedom it created—the rejection of tradition and religion—was too great. The scientists focus on collective sharing rather than individual freedom, since their goal is to discover the essential laws of the universe. Todorov cites biologist Charles Darwin (1809-1882), political philosopher Karl Marx (1818-1883), and psychoanalyst Sigmund Freud (1856-1939) as examples of this view. In direct contrast, the individualists believe that each human being is completely self-

∼

Tzvetan Todorov is Research Director of the Centre National de la Recherche Scientifique in Paris. He is the author of many books of philosophy and literary criticism, including The Fantastic: A Structural Approach to a Literary Genre *(1975),* The Conquest of America: The Question of the Other *(1984), and* Frail Happiness: An Essay on Rousseau *(2001).*

∼

sufficient. Individuals do not need tradition, religion, or even society; their will is supreme. An example of this new perspective would be the Marquis de Sade (1740-1814), according to Todorov.

The "declaration of autonomy" that modern man made in the Renaissance is first seen in Montaigne. He emphasizes people's choice in their personal lives. The mind, above all, must be free to seek and find and not be restricted. However, Montaigne does recognize and submit to the necessity of law and acknowledges the power of custom. He maintains the perspective of autonomy by claiming that people make this submission knowingly, through reason, rather than unthinkingly.

This autonomy is extended by Descartes and Rousseau. Descartes stresses the freedom of the mind and sees knowledge as coming not from tradition or authority but from reason. He also sees limitations in this choice and autonomy, seeing freedom as "compatible with divine omnipotence." Rousseau also stresses the "autonomy of reason," although, like his predecessors, he feels that it is necessary to "remain subject to the prevailing laws." However, he qualifies that view and extends the humanist autonomy by demanding that the laws and political system must be freely chosen by the people and not merely imposed. Constant de Rebecque is a very different thinker. From his position after the French Revolution he was very aware of the social breakdown that accompanied the Terror. In this case, human autonomy led to evil rather than good. Constant de Rebecque warned of allowing such abuses, advocating an awareness of the potential problems of abuse of power.

"Living Alone" is one of the more interesting chapters in the book. Todorov confronts the problems of isolation that can result from autonomy. The new autonomy, according to Todorov, makes as its ideal the solitary person rather than the classic hero. The focus of this chapter is primarily Rousseau. Todorov first pinpoints a number of problems and some contradictions in the thinker's work. For example, Rousseau flees society and its obligations in order to "live freely." Solitariness is both a "dreaded state," and "the ideal to which he aspires." Todorov attempts to heal some of these contradictions by claiming that Rousseau could not have meant what he said. After all, Rousseau was a writer and wished, above all, to communicate with others, and his desire to be loved goes directly against his plea to be a solitary being. Todorov finally attempts to reconcile these opposites by claiming that, while Rousseau may desire a solitary state for himself, he denies it as "his ideal for man." This argument is not completely convincing. The fact that Todorov again and again must search for a way to reconcile divergent views in his authors, especially Rousseau, leads the reader to suspect that the humanist position is not as consistent as Todorov claims.

"The Ways of Love" analyzes the place of love in humanist thought. Todorov's first point is that the beloved is always seen as unique and cannot be substituted by another; this is, as Rousseau makes clear, a direct contrast to the animal world, and is also distinct from the Christian notion of *agape*, which is general rather than particular. However, there is a problem in any love relationship: The lover desires the beloved, but once the lover is successful, love diminishes. Montaigne solves the problem by giving priority to friendship rather than sexual love. However, Rousseau deals more directly with the paradox at the heart of the love relationship. He claims that if the lover does not see the beloved as "instrumental"—that is, as used for the lover's own purposes and desires—then the differences can be reconciled and the impasse overcome. He also acknowledges that love is always tinged with illusion and the lover still loves even while seeing the beloved as another imperfect being.

"The Individual" deals with the interesting problem of how a person can be diverse and still stable. Todorov uses the ideas of Montaigne to attempt, once more, to reconcile this apparent dilemma. Montaigne speaks of his own changeableness and diversity; he is now one man and later another. How can he solve this problem? The first attempt is to claim that there is a "ruling pattern" in humans that provides unity in the midst of diversity. This sounds like a version of individualism. However, he thinks about a dead friend for whom he cared deeply, and "while he has identified his own ruling quality," he also sees "the ideal of his existence in successful human exchange." Montaigne says, "My essential pattern is communication and revelation." This connection enables him, according to Todorov, to reconcile these differences so that "the individual can be universalized." Rousseau seems to be very different, insisting on his difference rather than his connection to other men. He "alone is a 'man of nature,'" the best of men and superior to others. This position may resolve the problem of the diversity of the individual, but it does not seem as close to the humanist ideal as Montaigne's formulation.

"A Morality Made for Humanity" makes the most important claim for the necessity of humanism in the modern era. Todorov sees humanist morality primarily through the works of Rousseau. He begins with another impasse in Rousseau's work: the need to reconcile the autonomy of the individual with society. Being forced to submit to society will "denature" humans. Todorov claims that Rousseau provides a "third way" out of this dilemma, by which education enables people both to be social beings and to retain their individual autonomy. This will not "denature" them, since the "natural man" is made for society. Todorov defends Rousseau from charges that he favors the idea of the "noble savage." Todorov stresses that this morality is based on Christian values rather than those of the ancients. However, Rousseau "reduced the Christian religion to these two formulas, the universality of the self and the love of one's neighbor . . . ." This universalism, according to Todorov, is not abstract but rooted in the specific person.

The last chapter returns to the competing families of conservatism, individualism, and scientism and the wager of Satan. Todorov states that the conservatives would rob people of their autonomy as individuals in favor of the state and an established religion. He claims that individualism has led to human isolation. People now live in a society in which each person is self-sufficient in a suburban castle. The sense of neighborhood and any real social life has been lost. He calls this a "social autism" that now afflicts society. The effects of scientism have been even worse, leading to Nazism and communism. The utopian dream has led to a nightmare in which the individual has become a cog in a totalitarian regime that aims to perfect humanity. The scientific perspective has led society to value only economic prosperity rather than communal values. It attempts to improve human nature through genetic and other dubious research. In contrast, humanism does not reject technology or the individual, but subsumes the individual into a larger whole in which the "I," the "you" and the "they" can be reconciled rather than one dominating the other. Humanism is "allied with love" and democracy in a truly human way of life. Todorov comes back to Montaigne and acknowledges that the "garden" that humanism provides is "imperfect" and indeterminate. However, it remains the best choice available.

Tzvetan Todorov's *Imperfect Garden* is densely argued and clearly written. It is very good in analyzing the problems of the competing philosophies of humanism, individualism, conservatism, and scientism. Todorov uses his sources effectively, especially by directly citing the works of Montaigne and Rousseau. In addition, there is an extensive bibliography of primary sources and more recent commentary on humanism. His argument for humanism may be unfashionable but it is forcefully stated. The only weak part of his argument is his attempt to too easily reconcile the contradictory views in his authors. Montaigne and Rousseau both had long writing careers and there are many contrasting positions within those writings. They are not as consistent as Todorov at times suggests. However, this is a book that is worth reading and contemplating. Modern society certainly has problems that cannot be ignored. Humanism, as old as it is, may be a way to heal some of them.

James Sullivan

Sources for Further Study

The American Scholar 71 (Summer, 2002): 151.
Choice 40 (December, 2002): 645.

IN DARWIN'S SHADOW
The Life and Science of Alfred Russel Wallace

Author: Michael Shermer (1954-   )
Publisher: Oxford University Press (New York). 422 pp.
  $35.00
Type of work: Biography and science
Time: 1823-1913
Locale: England, the Amazon, and the Malay Archipel-
  ago

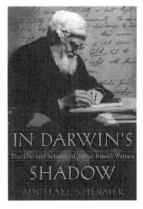

≈

Shermer adopts a psychobiographical approach to as-
sess Wallace's long career, from his independent discov-
ery of the origin of species through his experiences among
the spiritualists

≈

Principal personages:
> ALFRED RUSSEL WALLACE (1823-1913), versatile scientist and social
> thinker who discovered principles of natural selection simultaneously
> with Darwin
> CHARLES DARWIN (1809-1882), student of evolution and author of *On*
> *the Origin of Species*
> JOSEPH HOOKER (1816-1911), friend of both Darwin and Wallace who
> manipulated a "gentleman's agreement" on the priority of their dis-
> coveries
> CHARLES LYELL (1797-1875), author of *Principles of Geology* (1830-
> 1833, 3 vols.) and another friend who helped Hooker with the priority
> problem

Michael Shermer gives his book the sub-subtitle *A Biographical Study on the Psy-*
chology of History, and he organizes it around these five "schemata": Wallace the
Man, including an analysis of his ideas; Wallace and Darwin, focusing on the priority
of the discovery of natural selection and on Darwin's rejection of Wallace's conviction that some higher intelligence beyond natural selection must account for man's intelligence; Wallace the Heretic, arguing that Wallace's "heretic personality" and his
science influenced his spiritualism; Wallace and the Psychology of Biography, drawing on the statistical studies of Frank Sulloway to explain Wallace's intellectual
development; and Wallace and the Nature of History, contending that Wallace's life
reveals "the dynamic interaction of contingencies and necessities."

Shermer's introductory chapter provides a skeleton for the study that he will flesh
out in the following chapters. Shermer's three-dimensional Historical Matrix Model
purports to construct a psychobiography of Wallace that demonstrates the interaction
among five "internal forces" (thoughts) with five "external forces" (culture) across

Michael Shermer lives in Pasadena, California. He is founding publisher of Skeptic *magazine, director of the* Skeptics Society, *and a contributing editor of* Scientific American.

a span of six periods in Wallace's life. In decreasing order of influence, the internal forces are hyperselectionism, the undue emphasis on adaptation in evolution; monopolygenism, the debate over whether humans have a single origin or multiple origins; egalitarianism, Wallace's conviction that all people are born equal; environmental determinism, the tracing of apparent differences to unlike environments; and personality, the personal qualities that influenced Wallace. The external forces ("cultural variables") are spiritualism and phrenology, popular movements in Wallace's day; teleological purpose, the belief that life is directed toward a goal; scientific communal support, in "both the rejection of natural selection to the human mind, as well as for spiritualism and other nonscientific claims"; anthropological experiences, Wallace's years in Amazonia and the Malay Archipelago; and working-class associations, especially Wallace's education in the Mechanics' Institutes and the influence on him of Robert Owen (1771-1858) and Herbert Spencer (1820-1903).

In an excursus on quantitative biography, Shermer further elaborates on the "large-scale themata" that inform his study of Wallace: theory and data, time's arrow and time's cycle, adaptationism and nonadaptationism, punctuationism and gradualism, and contingency and necessity, themes that he asserts "concern most synthetic thinkers" and all of which he later treats more fully. Shermer also classifies Wallace's twenty-two books by subject (evolutionary theory, social commentary, biogeography, natural history, botany, origins of life, and spiritualism) and finds that of Wallace's 747 papers, 29 percent treat biogeography and natural history, 27 percent evolutionary theory, 25 percent social commentary, 12 percent anthropology, and 7 percent spirituality and phrenology.

Shermer and Sulloway asked ten historians of science (most of them were skeptical of the validity and reliability of the project) to rate Wallace on the so-called Big Five personality traits identified by Sulloway in his book *Born to Rebel* (1996), and their combined judgments produced percentile scores of 84 on conscientiousness, 90 on agreeableness, 86 on openness to experience, 58 on extroversion, and 22 on neuroticism. Wallace was the eighth of nine children, and these figures conform closely to Sulloway's analysis of the relationship between these traits and birth order, with both Wallace and Darwin scoring very high on openness to experience, the trait most sensitive to birth order. Shermer concludes that "Wallace was simply far too conciliatory toward almost everyone whose ideas were on the fringe. He had a difficult time discriminating between fact and fiction, reality and fantasy, and he was far too eager to please, whereas his more tough-minded colleagues (Huxley especially) had no qualms about not suffering fools gladly."

With this elaborate outline in place, Shermer turns to Wallace's birth on January 8, 1823, in Usk, Monmouthshire, Wales, to Thomas Vere Wallace and Mary Anne Wallace (née Greenell), a Church of England family. Because of his father's financial setbacks Wallace's only formal schooling was seven years at the Hertford Grammar School. The dominant "research paradigm" for understanding the universe in Wallace's youth was a melding of Sir Isaac Newton's mechanics and the Reverend Thomas Burnet's *Sacred Theory of the Earth* (1684-1690, 2 vols.) into a vision of an orderly creation revealing God's design and purpose. Denied a more prestigious education, Wallace enrolled in the night school at a London Mechanics' Institute, where the ideas of the Socialist Robert Owen had great credence, especially the belief in the superior influence of nurture over nature, a conviction that Wallace maintained throughout his life. The Mechanics' Institute and the Society for the Diffusion of Useful Knowledge fostered many of Wallace's lifelong interests in science and killed any religious faith that he still professed. Among the influences on him at this time were John Lindley's works on botany, which asserted that species did not always have distinct boundaries; Thomas Malthus's *Essay on the Principle of Population* (1798); and Robert Chambers's controversial and often wrong-headed *Vestiges of the Natural History of Creation* (1844). Shermer says that reading Chambers made an "evolutionist" out of Wallace and that he went to the Amazon to find support for his theory.

Wallace's father died in 1843, and the next year Wallace took a teaching position in Leicester, where he became a good friend of Henry Walter Bates (1825-1892), with whom he set sail in 1848 on HMS *Mischief* bound for Pará, Brazil, at the mouth of the Amazon. Life in the Amazon had its dangers (jaguars and snakes) and its new experiences (monkey meat for breakfast), but Wallace paid his way by sending specimens back to England, including 400 butterflies, 450 beetles, and 1,300 other insects in his first consignment. Exhausted by bouts of malaria, dysentery, and yellow fever, he left for home in 1852 on the brig *Helen*, which three weeks into the voyage caught fire and sank. After ten miserable days in lifeboats, Wallace and the crew were rescued by the London-bound *Jordeson*, only to have that ship spring leaks that eventually cost Wallace the rest of his specimens. All told, Wallace and Bates collected 14,712 species (not individuals), about 8,000 of which were previously unknown in Europe. Wallace's papers on his collections helped found the discipline of biogeography.

Financed on his expedition to the Malay Archipelago by the Royal Geographical Society, Wallace arrived in Singapore on the steamer *Bengal* on April 20, 1854. In 1858 he was studying butterfly species on the tiny island of Ternate in the Moluccas when he had his crucial insight, and "there suddenly flashed upon me the idea of *the survival of the fittest*—that the individuals removed by these checks must be, on the whole, *inferior* to those that survived." Two days later he had completed "On the Tendency of Varieties to Depart Indefinitely from the Original Type," which he soon put in a mail pouch addressed to Charles Darwin.

When Darwin received the essay he was stunned: "I never saw a more striking coincidence. If Wallace had my M.S. sketch written out in 1842 he could not have made a better short extract!" This challenge to the first claim of a theory he had worked on for so long distressed Darwin, and he immediately wrote to his friend Charles Lyell, who consulted with Joseph Hooker. These two fellow scientists agreed to read both Wallace's essay and Darwin's preliminary sketches to the Linnean Society of London at a historic meeting on July 1, 1858, fixing Darwin's priority but giving Wallace equal credit for his work and installing him in the front ranks of the scientists of his day. Shermer notes that "In the spring of 1862 he headed for home after compiling an almost unbelievable collection of 125,660 total specimens, including 310 mammals, 100 reptiles, 8,050 birds, 7,500 shells, 13,100 butterflies, 83, 200 beetles, and 13,400 'other insects.'"

Of the disagreements between Wallace and Darwin, none was disputed more intensely than what Shermer calls "the greatest heresy of this heretic scientist"— Wallace's conviction that only some "Overruling Intelligence," not natural selection, could explain humans' highly developed brain. Wallace's firmness on this topic became the centerpiece of his growing spiritualism, but Shermer insists that Wallace's spiritual beliefs did not ensue from the usual religious faith but—at least in Wallace's view—from a rational approach to the phenomena. In Shermer's words, "Natural selection, and the entire Darwinian paradigm, fit snugly into his scientific vision of man evolving into a higher state of physical, intellectual, and spiritual development."

From about 1870 till his death in 1913, Wallace was mainly preoccupied with his spiritualist affiliations. To explain this array of interests in the supernatural, Shermer calls on his historical matrix model and such factors as Wallace's working-class background, his early dabbling in mesmerism and phrenology, his experiences with séances, his insistence on finding a purpose for everything in nature and, finally, "the need to incorporate these experiences into his scientific worldview, and the final leap from the natural to the supernatural when his science failed to explain by the laws of nature what he knew to be true."

Shermer's chapter on "Heretical Thoughts" expands on the internal forces (thoughts) of his historical matrix model. Wallace's absolute commitment to natural selection departed from Darwin's more balanced position, and he insisted that only ignorance prevented understanding of a feature's purpose. On this issue he differed sharply from Darwin, as he did in rejecting Darwin's assignment of a large role in evolution to sexual selection. In opposing vaccination—apparently the smallpox virus had its place in the operation of the Overruling Intelligence—Wallace approached Alexander Pope's naïve proposition in his "Essay on Man" (1733-1734) that "Whatever is, is right." Wallace's stance on monopolygenism was a blurred compromise on whether humans had one origin or several; he was a staunch egalitarian; and he claimed a superior role for nurture and environment over nature and heredity. These beliefs constitute for Shermer convincing evidence for "the genius and eccentricity of Alfred Russel Wallace."

Wallace's faith that everything exists for a reason had roots in the common argument from design of his day, exemplified in the metaphor of God as a clockmaker and the world as his clock, a conceit found in Archdeacon William Paley's *Natural Theology* (1802). Shermer summarizes Wallace's reason for being as "a belief in a purposeful cosmos that under the direction of a higher intelligence inexorably led to the appearance of humans who were capable of perfectibility and would, in time, achieve immortality of the spirit." Darwin disagreed, but Wallace enjoyed support from other scientists such as the naturalists St. George Jackson Mivart and George Henslow. An important element in this philosophy was Wallace's egalitarianism, with its sources in his working-class background and observation of the peoples of the Amazon and the Malay Archipelago.

In Darwin's Shadow would benefit from disciplined compression and some rigorous editing and proofreading. Moreover, many scholars will probably dismiss Shermer's programmatic approach and his musings on "Psychobiography and the Study of History," but his thoroughness (the documentation is excellent) provides a satisfying portrait of "The Last Great Victorian," as he calls him.

Frank Day

Sources for Further Study

Booklist 99 (September 1, 2002): 33.
Library Journal 127 (October, 2002): 124.
Natural History 111 (February, 2002): 74.
The Washington Post Book World, October 13, 2002, p. 5.

IN THE DEVIL'S SNARE
The Salem Witchcraft Crisis of 1692

Author: Mary Beth Norton (1943-   )
Publisher: Alfred A. Knopf (New York). 436 pp. $30.00
Type of work: History
Time: 1675-1693
Locale: Essex County, Massachusetts, and the Maine
frontier

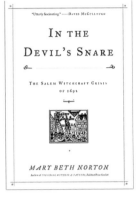

∾

A well-respected historian presents a detailed and schol-
arly account of the Salem witch craze and argues that the
violence and fears associated with King Williams's War
(1689-1699) had a great influence in promoting both the
accusations of witchcraft and the criminal convictions

∾

Principal personages:

COTTON MATHER (1663-1728), Puritan minister who generally defended
the prosecutions of alleged witches
SAMUEL PARRIS (1653-1720), Puritan minister of Salem village, in
whose home the first fits occurred in January, 1692
SAMUEL WILLARD (1639?-1707), Puritan minister of Boston who urged
caution in the use of spectral evidence
SIR WILLIAM PHIPS (1651-1695), governor of Massachusetts during the
witchcraft trials
WILLIAM STOUGHTON (1630?-1701), chief justice of the special Court of
Oyer and Terminer
JOHN HATHORNE (1641-1717), a justice of the peace at Salem who dom-
inated most of the early inquiries
TITUBA, Indian slave who was the first to confess to charges of witch-
craft
GEORGE BURROUGHS, Puritan minister who was executed on charges of
witchcraft even after he repeated the Lord's Prayer without mistake
REBECCA NURSE (1621-1692), one of the few persons with a good repu-
tation to be executed
ANN PUTNAM (1680?-1716), a young accuser who later repented and
asked for forgiveness

For secular Americans of the twenty-first century, everything about the witchcraft
outbreak of 1692 appears extremely bizarre. Within a period of five months, at least
144 persons (38 of them men) were prosecuted as witches, 54 persons confessed to
practicing demoniac witchcraft, 14 women and 5 men were hanged, another man was
pressed to death by heavy stones, and 3 women and 1 man, along with several infants,
died while in jail. Rather than taking place in the Dark Ages, the trials were contem-

~

Mary Beth Norton is a distinguished professor of American history at Cornell University. Since the early 1970's, she has been a pioneer and leader in the feminist approach to historiography. Her several books include Liberty's Daughters: The Revolutionary Experience of American Women, 1750-1800 *(1980) and* Founding Mothers and Fathers: Gendered Power and the Forming of American Society *(1996), which was a Pulitzer Prize finalist. She also served as general editor of* The AHA Guide to Historical Literature *(3d ed., 1995).*

~

poraneous with the Scientific Revolution, when educated persons of Europe and America were familiar with the writings of scientists such as Galileo Galilei (1564-1642) and Sir Isaac Newton (1642-1727). The men who conducted the trials were the elite of colonial Massachusetts. They were intelligent persons with reputations of stability and sobriety. Rather than being a poor backwater, seventeenth century Massachusetts had one of the most educated and prosperous populations to be found anywhere in the world.

Convictions of witchcraft in colonial America were usually impossible without the confessions of impressionable young girls and unstable adults who claimed to see "specters," or ghostly apparitions, of alleged witches tormenting and murdering people as well as consorting with animals and birds. While spectral evidence was essential to most convictions, it was augmented by instances of strange growths on a body, places where the skin was insensitive to pin pricks, unusual strength assumed to indicate demoniac assistance, and the inability to repeat the Lord's Prayer without a mistake. Although the judges and prosecutors preferred to have confessions as proof of guilt, they did not seem to understand the significance of the fact that these accused who claimed innocence were usually condemned to death, while those who confessed to witchcraft were rarely prosecuted and never executed.

With the large and growing literature about the 1692 events, historians will immediately ask whether there is any good reason for yet another book. *In the Devil's Snare* does indeed make a number of valuable contributions. Norton, assisted by several student assistants, has conducted meticulous research in the original sources. As a result, her book clarifies a number of factual details, especially about the accusers and confessors, and it frequently includes perceptive observations that are not available elsewhere. The book's eighty-six pages of notes, moreover, provide a useful guide in locating interesting statements made by the various people involved, and the notes also include succinct and thoughtful comments on the interpretations made by other historians.

The most important contribution of the book is its interpretative thesis: that the violent fighting on the Maine frontier was a major causative factor in producing the witchcraft crisis. When Norton began work on her book, she expected to base her interpretation on a feminist reinterpretation of gender relations. While pursuing her research, however, she writes that she became intrigued that so many of the accusers and accused were from the northern frontier, the location of brutal fighting during both King Philip's War of 1675-1678 (then called the First Indian War) and King William's War of 1689-1699 (called the Second Indian War). Some of the participants had fled Maine during the first war and then returned just in time for the second war, during which flourishing communities were destroyed and numerous families were wiped out. In late January, 1692, just one week after the first instances of witchcraft symptoms in Salem village, a large force of Wabanaki Indians had attacked the town of York, Maine, killing almost fifty settlers and capturing another hundred.

Such experiences, no doubt, were extremely traumatic to the participants, especially to vulnerable women and children who had no real control over their destinies. It appears significant that the descriptions of demoniac torment often sounded similar to the descriptions of bodily tortures and suffering during the two Indian wars. It is also interesting that the accusers referred to Satan as a "dark man," which was a contemporary way of referring to an Indian. Norton discovered that at least ten of the accusers and confessors and twenty-three of the accused had family or personal ties to the embattled frontier region. As Norton became convinced that this was more than a coincidence, her work "evolved into a dual narrative of war and witchcraft." Although never basing her interpretations on psychoanalytic speculations, she cogently observes that "the phenomenon known today as post-traumatic stress disorder" could be "a plausible explanation" for behavior that sometimes appears irrational. Norton acknowledges that previous historical works, including Carol Karlsen's *The Devil in the Shape of a Woman* (1987), touched on a connection between the witchcraft outbreak and the fighting on the Maine frontier, although they did not focus on the linkage in any great detail.

The violence on the frontier, according to Norton, contributed to the witch scare in several ways. Since the Puritans believed so strongly in divine predestination and providence, they found it difficult to understand the military successes of the French-speaking Catholics and the pagan Wabanakis, both of whom were assumed to be enemies of the true religion. Within this worldview, one possible Puritan explanation would be a diabolical fifth column within the community of the elect, an idea that encouraged rumors and suspicions about survivors of violent incidents. Accuser Mercy Lewis, for instance, had lived in Falmouth, Maine, during the first war, and most of her family had been killed, whereas the most famous of the accused, Reverend George Burroughs, had "remarkably escaped unscathed." Since Puritan ministers commonly preached that they were under attack from both demoniac and human enemies, it is perhaps understandable that young children and unstable adults were predisposed to experiencing bewitchment.

Norton also observes that many of the leaders of the prosecution—including John Hathorne, Sir William Phips, and William Stoughton—had been involved in leading military campaigns on the Maine frontier, and that they had made disastrous mistakes that resulted in many deaths and much suffering. Norton goes so far as to argue that "they attempted to shift the responsibility for their own inadequate defense of the frontier to the demons of the invisible world, and as a result they presided over the deaths of many innocent people." These powerful officials, in other words, found it easy to believe in the guilt of the alleged witches because they wanted to believe that they "were not guilty of causing New England's current woes." Although suggesting that the motivation was primarily unconscious, Norton writes that she is convinced that Samuel Parris and others destroyed records that implicated them in dubious decisions.

It does appear that Norton's feminist perspective has some influence on the ways in which she approaches the various persons in the book. When writing about the young girls and women making accusations and confessions, she tends to find sympathetic excuses for their behavior. In contrast, she discusses the male officials as if she were a prosecuting attorney. For example, she accuses Sir William Phips of lying in his report to London, when a more charitable assessment of the letter might be possible.

While emphasizing the impact of the war, Norton does not deny that other causative factors were also at work. Like most historians, she recognizes the importance of the pre-Enlightenment worldview and the precedents of witch trials in Europe, especially in England. Also she takes into account the importance of the local conflicts in Salem Village, as emphasized in Paul Boyer and Stephen Nissenbaum's influential *Salem Possessed: The Social Origins of Witchcraft* (1974). On the possibility of fraud in regard to physical manifestations such as teeth marks, Norton takes no position and writes that she is "an agnostic." She has "no doubt" but that the earliest afflictions of the young girls "were genuine (that is, not deliberately or rationally faked)." At the same time she recognizes the importance of suggestibility as well as later "enhancements" of tales as the girls became the center of attention.

Nonetheless, Norton is highly skeptical about hypotheses suggesting that accusers and confessors were experiencing hallucinations or terrible nightmares as a result of ergot poisoning or diseases such as encephalitis. The major flaws in such hypotheses, she writes, are that they "cannot explain the content of the girls' visions" and that they "cannot explain contemporary observations that the girls appeared healthy whenever the specters were not tormenting them (that is, most of the time)." On this particular point, Norton's firm dismissal appears somewhat unjustified. Almost everyone in the seventeenth century grew up assuming that dreams and visions were means of communicating with the spiritual realm. This belief, after all, was clearly taught in the Bible. It is certainly conceivable that ergot poisoning or any number of undiagnosed illnesses might have increased the frequency of nightmares or produced hallucinations, with their contents simply reflecting the fears and culture of the time. One might also wonder if any of the Salem residents were suffering from epileptic seizures, because it is well known that young children and unstable persons frequently imitate unusual behaviors that they observe.

Norton has written this large book primarily for scholars and those with a special interest in the topic. It would not be a good choice for a general reader who simply wants an introductory treatment of the witchcraft crisis of 1692. The book simply gives more details about obscure persons than general readers will want to know. Another problem is that the narrative tends to shift focus without clear transitions, which can be confusing. For uninitiated and general readers, more compelling and clearer narrative accounts can be found in several other books, most especially Bryan Le Beau's *The Story of the Salem Witch Trials* (1998).

While recognizing the difficulties in trying to determine cause-effect connections in human affairs, Norton sometimes presents hypotheses as if they were well-established facts. For instance, she writes: "Had the Second Indian War on the northeastern frontier somehow been avoided, the Essex County Witchcraft crisis of 1692 would not have occurred. This is not to say that the war 'caused' the witchcraft crisis, but rather that the conflict created the conditions that caused the crisis to develop as rapidly and extensively as it did." Although this hypothesis is interesting and entirely plausible, there is simply no way to be certain about "what might have been" statements of this kind. Historians must be careful to avoid the fallacy of post hoc reasoning or the assumption that an earlier event is necessarily the cause of a later event. Still, most students of the Salem witch scare will agree that Norton has presented a cogent and provocative interpretation that historians will debate for a long time.

Thomas Tandy Lewis

Sources for Further Study

Booklist 98 (August 1, 2002): 1890.
The Boston Globe, October 1, 2002, E8.
Kirkus 70 (July 1, 2002): 938.
Library Journal 127 (September 1, 2002): 193.
The New York Times, October 31, 2002, p. A27.
The New York Times Book Review 107 (November 3, 2002): 12.
Newsweek 140 (October 28, 2002): 56.
Publishers Weekly 249 (July 1, 2002): 63.
The Women's Review of Books 20 (November, 2002): 14.

IN THE FOREST

Author: Edna O'Brien (1936-   )
Publisher: Houghton Mifflin (Boston). 262 pp. $24.00
Type of work: Novel
Time: The 1960's to the 1990's
Locale: The countryside of Western Ireland

∼

A novel located in and around a forest in Western Ireland that imaginatively re-creates the circumstances of a multiple murder committed by a tormented young man who becomes a monster of depravity

∼

Principal characters:
> MICHEN O'KANE, also called the Kinderschreck, who seeks refuge in the forest and in his mind from what he perceives as a brutal and unjust world
> AILEEN O'KANE, his sister, who never entirely loses her familial affection for him
> EILEEN "EILY" RYAN, the woman he fancies as his lover, whom he murders in a confusion of anger, resentment, and perverted desire
> MADDIE, her four-year-old son, also his victim
> CASSANDRA, Eily's sister

During the time that Edna O'Brien was engaged in research for her novel *Wild Decembers* (2000), she was brought to a spot in a forest in the west of Ireland where the bodies of a woman and a child had been found in a shallow grave. In response to this unsettling discovery, O'Brien recalled that she "felt, without a shadow of a doubt, a trigger which said, 'You must tell this story.'" The story, which understandably caused a great deal of pain among the members of the community where the victims lived, concerned events in April, 1994, when Imelda Riney, aged twenty-nine, and her son Liam, aged three, went missing from the isolated cottage in the woods of County Clare where they lived. A search was organized, and several days later a curate in adjoining County Galway, Father Joe Walshe, also was discovered to be missing. Local suspicion was directed toward Brendan O'Donnell, a young man from the region with a previous history of violence and instability, who was home from England on remand from prison. O'Donnell was captured, on the run, six days later, having abducted another young girl. Shortly afterward, although O'Donnell maintained his innocence, the bodies of Imelda Riney, Liam Riney, and Joe Walshe were found in Cregg Wood. They had been shot at close range. O'Donnell was charged with the murders and tried in 1996 in Central Criminal Court, Dublin. Jailed for life, he was found dead by the nursing staff of Dublin's Central Mental Hospital in 1997.

O'Brien has explained that although she found *In the Forest* "hell" to write, the setting in County Clare called to her since "My books are a part of County Clare, the place is as strong in the books as the characters in the story." The opening paragraph of the first chapter, "Cloosh Wood" (O'Brien's name for the forest of the title), introduces the wilderness as a tangible, living presence, with woodland "straddling two counties" and a mountain "brooding" over the entrance of the forest. As the narrative progresses, the dense, tangled network of trails through its terrain becomes a symbol for the troubled mind of Michen O'Kane, the central figure of the novel, who is O'Brien's version of the monster who terrorized a whole community and murdered three people in a final rampage before his capture and incarceration. The linkage between the mind of the tormented young man and the features of the landscape is the foundation for O'Brien's effort to understand and express the psychological condition which could lead to the terrible events that are at the core of the novel's narrative action.

In addition to the numerous novels that Edna O'Brien has published since the initial success of her Country Girls *trilogy (1960-1964), her 1999 biography of James Joyce was highly praised and she received the 2002 Medal of Honor for literature from the National Arts Club. She is also an honorary member of the American Academy of Arts and Letters.*

The problems that this presented were daunting. While never defending his actions, O'Brien recognized the lurid fascination which they aroused in everyone who knew or knew about the killer. To present him as evil incarnate or a monster of depravity would have been a simplistic reduction. On the other hand, to make him sympathetic or to try to rationalize his actions might be seen as an apology of sorts, as well as an insult to his victims. The method that O'Brien developed involves a multiple narrative focus with frequent shifts in tone and mood so that the events gradually emerge as if from sources that are not controlled by any specific authorial point of view. The reader learns about Michen O'Kane both from his perspective as a young boy who is mistreated from his early youth and from the reactions of the people who are caught up in the incidents that eventually culminate in the triple murder. The narrative track is essentially chronological, progressing toward the spasm of viciousness which is its core revelation, but O'Kane's history is mingled with recollection and reflection as the full effect of his life on a small region of Ireland ultimately emerges. As a permeating presence, the forest persists beyond O'Kane's short life as a figure for a dark, primal impulse in a land where O'Brien wants to examine "the darkness that still prevails."

While the actual details of O'Kane's homicidal rampage are not completely delineated until the later chapters of the novel, there is a feeling of dread from the start, as the second paragraph depicts "Ellen, the widow woman"—a minor character who is a part of the numbed local community—subject to a recurring dream in which she is lost in Cloosh Wood, pursued by "Eily, the dead woman with her long hair" who beseeches, "Why, why didn't you help me?" The narrative itself is haunted by this question and by the bewilderment of people who cannot fathom how a youngster from their midst could turn into "The Kinderschreck." This is the title of the second chapter, a word from an alien language that is "what the German man called him when he stole the gun." It is an ominous foreign term that suggests an ogre in tales designed to frighten children, an unworldly creature who has lurched out of a lair in the forest. Yet, as O'Brien puts it, "he had been a child of ten and eleven and twelve years, and then he was not a child." This transformation is crucial in establishing the ruined humanity of O'Kane, and it is deftly depicted. After his first crime, O'Kane tries to explain himself by pleading, "I didn't mean to kill, only to frighten one man," as he is beaten by the police and by his father, but his words are ignored or suppressed, leading to an early experience of anger and aggression. Additional occasions of confusion and misrepresentation occur when he is unable to find anyone who will even consider his side of the story. As injustice and insult are compounded by his miserable treatment at the hands of juvenile authorities and hardened youths in detention facilities, O'Kane becomes more mistrustful, resentful, and enraged by his seemingly hopeless situation, until he turns to the forest as a refuge and begins to construct a new identity as a *Caolite*, an inhabitant of the wilderness, an incarnation of the spirit of the dark wood.

To balance the grim journey O'Kane makes from civilization toward a primal condition of being, O'Brien constructs a counternarrative that follows Eily Ryan, and it is her voice that offers an alternative to O'Kane's desperation. "I would come here for the mornings alone," she proclaims in an expression of her thoughts, "Everything fresh, sparkling, the fields washed after rain, the whole world washed." This is a vision of a vernal paradise, the place which she hopes to claim as the true essence of her heart's spirit. The tragic nature of the novel lies in the contrast between this appealing, if somewhat simplistic conception and the reality of a world in which evil is rampant and unchecked until terrible damage has been done. Eily and her son are emblems of innocence, and O'Brien's description of their life in what they regard as their pleasant pastoral place tends toward the sentimental, to the degree that reviewer Caleb Crain called it "Celtic kitsch." The power of O'Brien's lyric passages that inform the woodland idyll that Eily and her friends pursue rescues this element of the narrative to an extent, but once Eily's life has been introduced, there is little additional development. O'Brien, and the reader, are understandably drawn to the mysterious, frenzied energy of O'Kane, the shape of his mind and the diminution of his soul.

From the moment the teenage O'Kane returns to the region, in the chapter "Homecoming," when Sergeant Wiley is startled to see "a face peering at him from the other side of the gap, the tongue forking in and out in obscene and apish mockery," a pattern of sudden, inexplicable appearances and disappearances characterizes O'Kane's seemingly random movements. O'Kane's disapproving and self-serving father, his loyal if worried sister Aileen (her name echoing Eily's), various local people seen in quick snatches of dialogue, and fumbling, incompetent officials unsure about how to handle a growing menace provide outsider's reactions to O'Kane, while alternate chapters set within his mind express his thoughts and feelings through streams of inner consciousness and bursts of profane, vulgar speech. O'Kane is not without a sardonic wit at times, though it tends to border on the mordant, and he is capable of moments of real self-awareness, at least until he commits murder. In the forest with Eily and Maddie, he reveals something of the ways in which he has been formed by his life to this point. In a typical rant, he declares:

> That's one of the things I missed out on, dancing and scuba diving. You go through them jail gates and you're gutted. They drill a hole in you. Take your balls. I bullshitted them. Couldn't unmask me. Extremely attractive nurse on wing said I was malingering. My grimace was not the prodroma of genuine psychosis. They studied my laugh, my grimace. Jack Palance came by, stole it for *Shane* . . . never paid me a penny.

Defiant, self-pitying, self-promoting, bragging, posturing—O'Kane at this point still wants to impress and draw a positive response from Eily. However, he is consumed by a fantasy that she is somehow his destined lover, and as she desperately tries to deal with his desires, her rejection of his advances seems to drive him past any constraints or limits. Eily Ryan is an archetypal victim—a single mother, sexually adventurous, living foolishly alone in the woods, far too independent for a conventional culture—and her death seems almost ordained.

After the murders, when O'Kane is on the run, the pace of the narrative picks up in a series of action sequences that are vivid, suspenseful, and like the rest of the novel, very compelling even though the eventual outcome of the pursuit has already been made clear. Whatever appeal O'Kane's character may have had is dispersed by the horror of his actions. O'Brien has spoken of "a darkness that still prevails" in contemporary Ireland and has described County Clare, her home ground, as a place "enclosed, fervid, bigoted." O'Kane is not meant to be a representative figure, but it is clear that he is an incarnation of an impulse that O'Brien wants to examine. In response to the fact that "I have had some very barbaric letters, unsigned" about *In the Forest*, she has insisted, "I have not written a voyeuristic or vulgar book. I have written a book to commemorate and perpetuate this almost Greek tragedy that took place in a forest that I happen to know."

In an attempt to ameliorate to some extent the burden of the book, the last line of the novel is, "Magic follows only a few." This sentence has puzzled some commentators, and O'Brien has tried to explain it by admitting, "It's a mystery to me, that little chapter," adding, "I think I meant the magic that story and imagination can, even briefly, create against a bulwark of nightmare, death, and nonresurrection." Perhaps this is an effort to restore some of the mood of her previous novel, *Wild Decembers*, also set in County Clare, which Mira Mataric likened to drinking water from "an endlessly fresh nourishing well." Whatever the last chapter may accomplish, *In the Forest* is more like a voyage along the turbulent course of a very dark river.

Leon Lewis

Sources for Further Study

The Atlantic Monthly 289 (March, 2002): 124.
The New York Times Book Review 107 (April 7, 2002): 11.
Publishers Weekly 249 (January 28, 2002): 267.
The Times Literary Supplement, May 10, 2002, p. 25.

IN THE IMAGE

Author: Dara Horn (1977-   )
Publisher: W. W. Norton (New York). 278 pp. $24.95
Type of work: Novel
Time: The late nineteenth to the early twenty-first century
Locale: New Jersey, New York City, and Europe

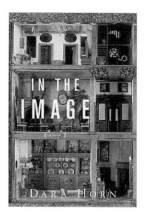

∽

The connections among immigrant Jews and their chil-dren in America are explored in Horn's first novel

∽

Principal characters:
    LEORA, a young Jewish woman
    BILL LANDSMANN, an elderly Jew
    NADAV, his father
    LEAH, his grandmother
    JASON/YEHUDAH, Leora's college boyfriend
    JAKE, her fiancé

In the Image, Dara Horn's first novel, having begun with the grief of the protago-nist Leora over the death of her closest friend in high school, Naomi Landsmann, dis-closes, mostly through images, the connection Leora and other characters in the story have with their significance as Jews. If there is a flaw in the novel, it is not in the char-acterization, which is complex, nor in the story, which is intriguing, but in the abun-dant coincidences which permit predictability and rhetoric to tilt the story a bit like ballast unevenly placed.

Bill Landsmann, Naomi's grandfather, contacts Leora and presents her and her parents with a slide show illustrating early Jewish history. Since her time with Landsmann reanimates her grief over Naomi, Leora only reluctantly returns when he invites her. After several of his slide shows for her, featuring locations of Jewish com-munities around the world, Landsmann takes her to East Mountain, a nature preserve in the New Jersey town in which they live, where he shows her the grave of his father Nadav, who committed suicide in 1946 after emigrating to America with his son. Leora finds herself beginning to be lured by the pictures in Landsmann's windowlike slides.

The first of the novel's many coincidences starts with Jason, Leora's lover in col-lege. His family, it turns out, lives in the same town as Leora's and his father manages the zoo on East Mountain where Landsmann took Leora. Further, Jason's feelings about his Jewish background changed from indifference to a Hassidic commitment after he visited Jerusalem, leading him to change his name to Yehudah, to break up with Leora, and to marry a like-minded woman, Rivka. Leora runs into him and his wife in Costco, where she discovers that Jason has abandoned medical school and his as-

Dara Horn is a graduate student at
Harvard University, where the focus
of her studies in comparative
literature is Hebrew and Yiddish.
She has published articles in
American Heritage, Science, *and*
The Christian Science Monitor.

piration to help the elderly and now works in his father-in-law's diamond business in New York.

To illuminate coincidence as connection, the novel shifts from Leora's point of view to that of Bill Landsmann. His father, a victim of shell shock in World War I whose his business in Vienna failed and whose wife was in a mental hospital, moved to Amsterdam, taking with him his son Wilhelm, as Bill Landsmann was then called. Thrown out of one school, reviled in another, violently neglected by Nadav, and not fluent in Dutch, Wilhelm skulked about as an outsider, no better than a barbarian who peers into the lighted windows of those he lives among. In this way he is like Leora, who does the same thing. He also resembles her in that the elaborately detailed doll cabinets on display in the Rijksmuseum in Amsterdam fascinate him as much as Leora's dollhouse later fascinates her when she shares its pleasures with his granddaughter Naomi.

The story returns to Leora after college. She is writing for a magazine in New York, spending her Friday nights in bars with her itinerant roommates looking for "live-in boyfriends" or at Sabbath dinners with her synagogue acquaintances looking for "live-in husbands." This unappetizing lifestyle results in her enduring weekends alone in her apartment on Amsterdam Avenue, as isolated as Landsmann had been in his father's apartment in Amsterdam itself. She has become an outsider as Landsmann was, and if he equated this with being a "barbarian," Leora might well do the same. In college, Leora found her friend Jessica's excitement over the suicide of a fellow student barbaric, and she begins to wonder whether treating events as an observer rather than a participant is not "much more pleasant"—that is, to be a barbarian may be better than to be an initiate in the pain of others.

Then, while researching the discovery of a skull called "Amsterdam Avenue Man," said to be the "missing link" from an anomalous period fifty thousand years in the past, Leora finds a mousetrap disguised as a dollhouse (suggesting, perhaps, the temptation and danger to her in entering a world she had only looked at from outside before). Immediately afterward, she finds a set of tefillin (several small boxes containing Hebrew prayers on parchment and meant to be strapped on a man's forehead and arms). The tefillin are one hundred years old and were found at the bottom of New York Harbor, thrown overboard by immigrant Jews drawn, as it were, to the dollhouse mousetrap of America.

In Leora's case, the salvaged tefillin may be, like the Amsterdam Avenue skull, a "missing link" to her own past as a Jew. She begins to explore this possibility when, on the pretext of writing an article on the drug culture of Amsterdam for her magazine, she attends a conference on Benedict Spinoza (1632-1677), the philosopher who was expelled from the Jewish community of Amsterdam for his idea that God and his creation were the same. Leora visits the Rijksmuseum, where, like Bill Landsmann before her, she is struck by Rembrandt's *The Prophet Jeremiah Mourning over the Destruction of Jerusalem* (1630), then by Jan Vermeer's *Woman in Blue Reading a Letter* (c. 1633-1634), the one an example of great sorrow, the other of secrecy. While she is regarding the latter painting, she meets Jake, a history professor at Columbia University, whose lecture on Spinoza "excommunicating himself" she had heard at the conference. They come to the doll cabinet collection where Leora, as enchanted by it as Landsmann had been when he was a boy, is moved to tell Jake about Naomi and the dollhouse they shared. She challenges Jake to find the store where she found the missing-link skull and other bones, "to find the thing . . . that interested me the most" in it, and to meet her there when she returns to New York. The coincidence of Leora and Jake's interest in the meaning of God in relation to people foreshadows the intimacy they will share, which seems certain when, having met all the terms of her challenge but unable to meet her at their agreed upon time or to buy the tin dollhouse mousetrap for her, he sends her the tefillin that had so beguiled her.

The novel then tells the story of Leah, Naomi's great-great-grandmother, who emigrated with her family to New York and married and then divorced a Talmudic intellectual, David, who rammed her head against a wall on their wedding day. She finally married Aaron, a clerk at the sewing factory where she worked. He was to her as kind, generous, and loving as Jake will be to Leora. When Aaron dies in a fire, the pregnant Leah returns to Europe, first casting the tefillin her father has given her into New York Harbor. In Europe she gives birth to Nadav Landsmann, whose hatred of his Jewish roots underlies his spiritual isolation and eventual suicide.

This story introduces another coincidence, for Jake tells Leora about seeing a man die in a fire, and it soon becomes clear that Jake is related, through his mother, to Leah's husband Aaron, who died in a similar fashion; he is therefore related to Bill Landsmann and Naomi. Thus the novel continues to enhance the theme of inclusion over exclusion. Moreover, it turns out that Jake went to elementary school with Tony Random, whose uncle owns the shop where Leora found the tefillin that Jake bought for her.

Resuming Bill Landsmann's point of view, the novel considers memory. For Landsmann, memory is not as reliable as the slides he has made in his exploration of Judaic history and his living family. He still hates his father, and this leads him to remember a Jewish New Year in Europe when he was six years old and his Aunt Sarah attacked Nadav, blaming him for her son's death in the war. He also remembers the bits of stale bread symbolizing his sins that he cast into a river. What concerns him most, however, is his wife Anna's loss of memory and her credo that to love is more important than to hate. Although she angers him when she admits to taking from his collection, and then misplacing, all the slides with Naomi in them, he realizes, as she sleeps beside him, that he no longer hates his father, with the implication that his love for Anna and hers for him is all that matters where memory is concerned.

This is the kind of love that brings Jake to the diamond district in New York to find an engagement ring for Leora. The important image in this chapter is diamonds, and the important coincidence is that Jake buys the diamond from Jason, Leora's college boyfriend. The irony is that the ex-boyfriend tutors the fiancé in the meaning of diamonds as a metaphor for relationships, which, "Unlike love . . . involved 'work,' 'struggle,' 'compromise,' 'problems,' and 'issues.'" If the right diamond is an art of such flaws, to Jake the right flaws are "like tiny pieces of soil within the stone, like packed-up treasures buried in a closet." He also understands, when he sees the slides Leora sends him of paintings in the Rijksmuseum, that she "was . . . a light. And he was a square of slide film, and she shined herself through him and made all the things inside him appear."

Uplifted by this insight and by Leora's attention to details easy to overlook, Jake begins to repair her dollhouse in secret, including in it a miniature set of Spinoza's *Ethics* and painting a minuscule *Woman in Blue Reading a Letter*, crowning the doll that most resembles Leora with the diamond engagement ring he plans to present to her. However, a hurricane floods Leora's parents' basement, where Jake has been working on the dollhouse, and ruins it (though Jake saves the Leora-doll and the ring). At the same time Landsmann loses to the storm all of his slides, except the ones that Anna had hidden.

To elaborate on this theme of loss, if not of God's brutality, the narrator reveals that even though part of the reason Nadav killed himself was because of having seen his cousin Isaac killed right in front of him in the war, the destruction of her dollhouse leads Leora to acceptance and hope. Likewise, the destruction of his slides leads Landsmann to accept, like Job, God's challenge "to collect . . . images" as resonant and simple as God himself. With Anna, he visits their son Ben and his family in California and sees in the slides of Naomi—which Anna had sent to Ben—the kind of images that are "worth keeping."

The climax of Leora's own exploration comes when she dreams she visits a city of forgotten people, animals, and books at the bottom of New York Harbor, the road into which is made of tefillin. Its inhabitants speak the forgotten language of the Indians who predated the Dutch in New York and "breathe through gills in their half-severed necks." Here she encounters an avatar of Bill Landsmann, keeper of the aboveground Landsmann's lost slides, which are now blank. He instructs her that her task is to fill these frames with "whatever you like," but that she must "find someone to show them to," which seems to mean that all the outside-looking-in throughout the novel can only become meaningful if it is exchanged for intimacy and belonging.

Mark McCloskey

Sources for Further Study

Booklist 98 (August, 2002): 1921.
Library Journal 127 (September 1, 2002): 214.
The New York Times Book Review 107 (November 24, 2002): 32.
Publishers Weekly 249 (August 26, 2002): 45.

ITALIAN STORIES

Author: Joseph Papaleo (1925-   )
Publisher: Dalkey Archive Press (Chicago). 295 pp.
  $13.95
Type of work: Short fiction
Time: The 1930's to the end of the 1960's
Locale: Mostly the Bronx, but also the boroughs of
  Brooklyn, Queens, Manhattan; Westchester County,
  New York; and the southern Italian province of Calabria
  and cities such as Florence, Rome, and Naples

~

Publishing his first short-story collection at seventy-five, Papaleo dramatizes the stunning interaction of ethnic and personal identities in New York City

~

Principal characters:
> Johnny, youngest of the five Mauro children; often a filter through
>   whom action is conveyed
> Reni, Johnny's sister
> Victor and Al, Johnny's older brothers
> Luigi (Lou) and Rose Mauro, Johnny's parents
> Pasquale, Johnny's uncle
> Fonzi, vulgar buffoon, obnoxious in-law, a "taker" on whom familial
>   kindness is lavished by the Mauros, his would-be victims

At the close of "Prologue for an Ethnic Life," Joseph Papaleo introduces, via parody, an aesthetic which, judging from the stories that follow, has formed him as a writer; namely, the two-faced Janus of stereotypicality. He presents a mock Italian American genealogy that begins with a tall, blond family from Sicily and Naples who moved to New York City in 1907. They did not like spaghetti or tomatoes, nor did they urinate in doorways or go into construction or work on the railroad. What they became, after attending Smith and Harvard, were professionals living on estates in Westchester County, north of the city. In one such abode, Tony Junior tells Tony Senior that he would like to spend a few days with college friends in the Hamptons before starting his senior year at Harvard. The family—Papa Tony, Mama Rosa, and son Junior—enjoy their Chivas until Twombley calls them to supper. Tony raises his small liqueur glass. "Here's to a good senior year." A squad of American-Way-of-Life-Protection hitmen bursts through the doors and shoots all three dead in their chairs. Their leader proclaims "Death To All Those Who Betray the Stereotype."

Joseph Papaleo's dilemma is that many of his stories will be remembered for their enactments of prevailing beliefs about Italian Americans but also be limited by them:

〜

Joseph Papaleo, born in New York City, is the author of two novels, All the Comforts *(1967) and* Out of Place *(1970). Many of the pieces in* Italian Stories *were originally published in* The New Yorker, Harper's Magazine, Commentary, *and* Paris Review. *He is a long-time professor at Sarah Lawrence College.*

〜

Italians are compassionate yet violent; clan-oriented yet capable of betrayal within the family; deeply respectful of their wives yet inclined to stray, especially at first sighting of a sexy blonde. Papaleo best overcomes the paradox of narratives that are at once generated and reduced by stereotypes in "The Kidnap," the opening story. Besides serving as an introduction to the Mauro family of Lorin Place, the Bronx, this story deftly combines the apparent and the real. A seemingly frightening letter—crudely handwritten—threatens the kidnapping of the Mauro children if five hundred dollars is not delivered in a bag according to instructions. Some readers will find more revealing than the abduction threats a subtext that promises an outcome that is "all in the family." All the Mauro men and even Mama Rosa, who wrings her hands in approved Calabrian style, suspect that someone among certain Sicilian in-laws is behind the deal. In the spirit of *I Soliti Ignoti* (1958; *Big Deal on Madonna Street*), the comic Italian film of a botched heist, Fonzi, a pitiful and grossly fat sponger, bungles his own plot but is rewarded by the Mauros, his would-be victims, with the promise of a job. "I give up," the oldest son Victor muses. "Now you're going to get this guy a job. What can you do?" Answer: Nothing.

That question and answer could serve as the coda for all the first nine stories. They go with the cultural territory. In "Nonna" (grandmother), the Mauros treat Lou Mauro's mother with the deference to the very old that is an Italian family trademark. Crazy Nonna, propped up against pillows that seem to have grown around her, is left to languish in a tiny bedroom that is off limits to young Johnny. One day, hearing Nonna's muffled call, the boy dares to enter: "She was like a wooden statue. Her face . . . a cast of green over the many wrinkles; her mouth was stuck open." Fighting fear, he obeys her feeble signals, finds her beads and medallions, fastens them to the bedpost. Directed to her bureau drawers, he removes long-neglected artifacts—a peasant wedding dress, linens and tablecloths, necklaces and bracelets, finally a wedding photo—and arranges them on the bed—splashes of color that relieve the ashen death mask. In death, Johnny has brought his grandmother to life. By titling these first stories "Immigrant Epiphanies," Papaleo reveals a debt to James Joyce's *Dubliners* (1914), perhaps literature's most famous collection of "ethnic" stories. For Joyce, epiphanies were "showings forth"—manifestations—of inner life.

"Mission," the book's second story, follows closely the plot line of "Araby," Joyce's classic story of a boy's first awakening to sex, but falters at the end, offering an accommodation that rings false. A side-by-side look at the two stories may be instructive. In Joyce's story, the unnamed Stephen Dedalus figure determines to bring "Mangan's sister" a gift from a bazaar called Araby. He is thwarted at all points, at first seeing himself "[bearing] my chalice safely through a throng of foes" but finally, left alone after closing time, "a creature driven and derided by vanity . . . eyes burn[ing] with anguish and anger." His has been puppy love, to be sure, but heightened by the power of language.

For young Johnny Mauro of "Mission," it is "Gallarello's sister"—the Gallarellos and the Mauros are neighbors—who is to receive a memento from the array of religious items on sale at what Reni calls "the biggest Mission ever came to the Bronx." Unlike the girl in the shadows of a darkening Dublin street, Gallarello's sister invites Johnny's attentions. Made to feel underage by religious trappings and a priest's insufferable droning, neither of which he comprehends, Johnny pays fifty cents for a medallion, then flees. "His mother was waiting. She had been saying her rosary and marked her place in the beads." At this point an epiphany takes place; the son offers the gift to his mother who places the medallion around her neck ("My first present from my Johnny") and reaches to kiss him. "John had the sudden desire to turn away, but she held her arms out. He leaned down to accept a kiss, turning his cheek slightly aside. Her hair gave off her musty indoor odor." Like "Araby," "Mission" ends in darkness—that of Johnny's room facing the Gallarellos' house. Johnny imagines he sees another person (Gallarello's sister?), nude, poised before him. This juxtaposing of the religious and the sexual echoes Joyce, but an overreliance on dialogue that makes the introspective epilogue seem too abrupt a tonal shift flaws the story.

"Resting Place," the shortest story in the volume, closes out "Immigrant Epiphanies." Fittingly, it describes the funeral of Luigi, the Mauro patriarch, and makes way for part 2, a ten-story segment titled "Losing the Bronx." These are largely saturnine tales of departures from their Bronx home base by two generations of Italian Americans and the fate of these émigrés, often one of disenchantment. In "Leaving Vermont," Tony, who has made a fortune as a dealer in pornography and is returning to the Bronx to bury his father, sums up the bitter tone of these middle stories when he tries to calm his troubled sister about his legal problems: "What the f—k else do I have but money?"

In "The Golden Fleece Returns via Le Havre," Papaleo, a long-time professor at Sarah Lawrence, relates in the first person the experiences aboard ship of a writer and his wife who are returning to New York after two years in Paris. Among many pretentious fellow passengers, a drunken, Hemingwayesque figure named Ryan provides most of the action and confirms the narrator's growing suspicion of expatriates. Roughed up in a brawl with another drunk, Ryan exhorts the narrator to beat him into a bloodier pulp. He responds finally by tossing overboard the novel by an obscure Frenchman whom Ryan extolled.

"Homes and Rooms" is also about a wanderer returning to America—in Lucky's case, to see his best friend. Told by his friend's widow that Jack is dead, Lucky tries to express grief in his usual way—booze and hired girls—but empathy comes to him only when he visits his old neighborhood on 126th Street. In "The Word to Go," Millie, sixty-five and childless, plans to leave with Mario, her husband, the old neighborhood where the newcomers shun the fresh, just-made sausage at Immediato's and ask for ham hocks and chitlins. She will return to Italy where she was born. She is dispersing to her sisters and brothers her furniture, many pieces of which belonged to their mother. The family "auction" turns into a debate over the place they left and the place to which she is returning. "If I can just remember how nice it was over there. . . . I just have to believe it's real over there. . . . Then I'll make it."

"Blendings and Losses" is the title of the final section, the shortest, containing seven stories. Such titles as "The Last Sabbatical," "Hits of the Past," and "Memories Reflected in Palm Springs" hint strongly of the central theme: deja-vu, or looking back. In "Friday Supper," Jack Sarfatti, an older associate of a successful business-man named Tony, advises his boss that it is all right to change his name. His counsel is the closest Papaleo comes to a catechism for Italian Stories:

> . . . don't you see what I'm telling you? It's a nice heritage we saw for a moment in time. And it got buried under another one, a new one, a hip one. And that's the train we happen to be on. . . . So now it's America, and we happen to be Americans. A happy moment of history. And everybody in the world is trying to get on the bandwagon. My cousins in Italy ask me to send them the L. L. Bean catalogue and Timberland shoes. . . .

Later in the story, Anthony, a prototype of Papaleo's Bronx hustlers who have prospered uptown, asks his ailing father if he has decided to accept the son's offer to finance the transplanting of the parents to Florida. The old man remonstrates with the usual litany about how he landed in New York with "five cents in my pocket" and has "worked every day since." The son's response at once defines the generational gap between them and the aesthetic problem of these stories: "Parts of it, in some way, sounded false, a story too old to be true, much too familiar not to be constructed from the typical, like a movie that starts as if new and then gets stale without anybody knowing how."

Joseph Papaleo, despite publication in *The New Yorker*, *Harper's*, *The Paris Review*, and nearly every magazine and journal that features serious fiction, has been quoted as regretting that it is the fate of ethnic writing to be both known and limited by perceived stereotypes rather than by the literary elements and quality of his fiction. He need not worry. Armed with a flawless ear for the voices of the Bronx and a sense of the immigrant experience only given to a participant, he has stopped history, made it turn around and be recognized and honored.

Richard Hauer Costa

Sources for Further Study

Library Journal 127 (January, 2002): 156.
The New York Times, February 10, 2002, p. 5.
Publishers Weekly 249 (January 14, 2002): 42.

JIHAD
The Rise of Militant Islam in Central Asia

Author: Ahmed Rashid (1950-   )
First published: 2001, in Great Britain
Publisher: Yale University Press (New Haven, Conn.).
  2 maps. 272 pp. $24.00
Type of work: Current affairs, history, and religion
Time: 1991-2002
Locale: Turkmenistan, Uzbekistan, Tajikistan, Kyrgyzstan, and Kazakhstan

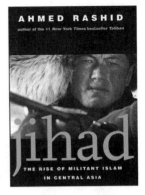

∼

Rashid argues that although militant Islam lost much ground in Central Asia in the aftermath of September 11, 2001, it will revive unless the West can persuade regional strongmen to make political and economic reforms

∼

Principal personages:
  NURSULTAN NAZARBAYEV, president of Kazakhstan since 1991
  ASKAR AKAYEV, president of Kyrgyzstan since 1991
  SAPARMURAD NIYAZOV, president of Turkmenistan since 1991
  ISLAM KARIMOV, president of Uzbekistan since 1991
  RAKHMON NABIEV, president of Tajikistan in 1991-1992 and currently
    head of its coalition government
  EMOMALI RAHMONOV, president of Tajikistan since 1992
  JUMA NAMANGANI, founder of the Islamic Movement of Uzbekistan
  SAYED ABDULLAH NURI, founder of the Tajikistan Islamic Renaissance
    Party

Central Asia has been a political backwater since the end of the "Great Game" between Russia and Great Britain for domination of the Eurasian heartland. It was always an ethnically complex region, but Soviet efforts to divide and rule, combined with suppression of religious expression and free thought, winking at corruption and environmental devastation, left the nations of this huge mountainous and desert region with almost insuperable challenges when the Soviet Union suddenly collapsed in 1991.

Although Central Asians were traditionally tolerant Sunni Muslims who took pride in their ancient Buddhist monuments, since the early 1980's Pakistan and Saudi Arabia had sponsored guerrilla armies in Afghanistan. These holy warriors, many of them Arabs, introduced strict practices associated with the Wahhabi sect of Islam. Encouraged and armed by the United States, they not only forced the Soviet Union to retreat, but encouraged the rise of a variety of Islamic movements in the region. The

Ahmed Rashid is a Pakistani journalist who has been covering Afghan affairs for more than twenty years; he is a correspondent for the Far Eastern Economic Review *and* London's Daily Telegraph *and is a writer for Pakistan's* The Nation *newspaper. In 2000, he published* Taliban: Militant Islam, Oil, and Fundamentalism in Central Asia.

subsequent civil war in Afghanistan, won by the Pakistani-backed Taliban, allowed al-Qaeda to train international terrorists who were soon in action in Chechnya, Bosnia, Algeria, and even the United States. Their goal was a jihad, a holy war against the enemies of Islam.

What was this jihad, however? As understood in the West, by many modern Muslim fundamentalists, and apparently by hot-blooded young Islamic fanatics from time immemorial, it was literally armed conflict, with believers obliged to honor the memory of martyrs and to marry their widows. Intellectuals, in contrast, said that it meant the lifelong struggle for improvement, a complete dedication to God. Obviously, the intellectuals have lost the argument among those discontented with their rulers' current inability to end poverty or crush the enemies of the faith. For the Wahhabi fundamentalists, jihad emphasized overthrowing local corrupt regimes more than attacking Western infidels, and then imposing sharia (Islamic law), which requires men to wear beards and pray in public and women to cover themselves from head to foot in plain clothing and to behave as properly meek and submissive wives and mothers. Unlike most Muslims—certainly those living in Central Asia—the fundamentalists hated the modern world and all regional variations of Islam, particularly the mystical Sufi sects of Tajikistan. Consequently, the Taliban and al-Qaeda made few local converts; they were dependent on Pakistani and Saudi money and volunteers.

Locally born Islamic revolutionaries thrived on the severe economic crises following independence in 1991, on ethnic strife, and on the growing corruption and repressive nature of the new Central Asian regimes. Regional politics had always reflected personal and clan associations, and consequently all concepts associated with governing through representative assemblies were weak, especially the idea of holding fair elections that might require surrendering power to the opposition. Now, however, power was held by dictators who would rank high in any list of history's strangest and least competent rulers. All are former Communist Party leaders.

Kazakhstan, with its large Russian minority, must be aware of the wishes of its powerful northern neighbor, which has revived under the leadership of Vladimir Putin. Russian leaders today, having suffered through the Afghan war and two long conflicts in Chechnya, have no sympathy for any kind of Muslim; on the other hand, they have no interest in assuming the financial and military responsibilities for this or any other region. Khazak president Nursultan Nazarbayev counts on oil exports replacing the country's dependency on ecologically devastating irrigation for cotton, but he is not allowed to build pipelines to the south; instead, he must use Russian pipelines and accept Russian prices. Well on the way to establishing a family dynasty, he has no frontier with Afghanistan and hence has fewer immediate problems with fundamentalism than neighboring despots.

Kyrgyzstan almost escaped economic dependence on a combination of nomadic herding and Soviet subsidies, but was pressed by its more powerful neighbors into abandoning democratic processes and ethnic pluralism. Forced into unwise policies, Kyrgyzstan now suffers from massive unemployment, illegal drug production, and political extremism.

Turkmenistan is entrapped in the bizarre personality cult of President Saparmurad Niyazov, who likes to be called the Father of All Turkmen. This is most homogenous of the states and thus the most stable; nevertheless, it relies on a Russian army presence to protect its likely prospects of becoming a major oil producer and to maintain order in its vast stretches of desert.

Uzbekistan, a largely desert country in the center of the region, is concerned with sizable Uzbek minorities in most of its neighbors' territories. The most powerful of the five states, it is still a poor and relatively lightly populated country. President Islam Karimov runs an authoritarian state, but his only consistency is in a brutal repression of dissent. Still, it is well understood that whatever successes or failures Uzbekistan has will be shared by all the other Central Asian states.

Mountainous Tajikistan has the smallest population, but many Tajiks live in Uzbekistan and Afghanistan. Civil war raged from 1992 to 1997, leaving the country's economy in shambles, with many dead, hundreds of thousands in refugee camps, and drug lords ruling vast areas. President Emomali Rahmanov is working at maintaining an inclusive government coalition, but neighbors interfere with every effort to restore stability.

Each country has ethnic problems, but the prize for greatest complexity and conflict goes to the fertile Fergana valley, the heartland of the entire region. Historically, whoever controls this valley controls Central Asia; hence, the Soviets divided it between Uzbekistan, Kyrgyzstan, and Tajikistan.

As these rulers plotted against one another and gave refuge to each other's minorities and allowed refugees to train as guerrillas, their economies collapsed. Irrigation systems ceased to function, transportation and trade were disrupted, and factories closed; military equipment rusted and training practically ceased. When Putin came to power, he began to reassert Russian influence; meanwhile, China made its presence known and American oil companies appeared. Out of sight, several Islamic parties began organizing. None was interested in being dominated by al-Qaeda or the Taliban, though they share some ideas and common interests in overthrowing the existing party structures in Central Asia. This was a worrisome development, since oil can hardly be produced or shipped in the midst of armed conflict and without oil money, none of these states can compensate for the agricultural losses due to drought and disappearing markets. Moreover, war is a fertile seed bed for religious extremism.

The bloody civil war in Tajikistan brought forth the Islamic Renaissance Party. Far from a carbon copy of the foreign Islamists, it honored ancient traditions of resistance to Russians and Soviets. Led by Sayed Abdullah Nuri, it was weakened by the peace settlement in 1998 that brought about free elections. However, without any coherent plan for economic or political reforms, the Islamic Renaissance Party has slipped into the position of a small minority with few prospects of taking power.

In contrast, in Uzbekistan, President Karimov made no concessions to opposition figures. Consequently, resistance to his erratic and brutal despotism took the form, in part, of potentially erratic and brutal new ideologies. The first, the Hizb ut-Tahir al-Islami (HT; the Party of Islamic Liberation), intends to restore the medieval caliphate. This great state had not been very successful in its original form and would encounter even greater internal challenges today. Still, a superstate uniting all Muslims under one ruler and one law would automatically correct many of the problems associated with local corruption and ambition, and presumably it could deal more effectively with the dislocations that always accompany social and economic change. The present leader of HT, a Palestinian named Sheikh Zaloom, blames Israel and the Jews for all the world's problems, but he has no love for Shia Muslims, either. Nonviolent to date, the HT hopes to take power by a peaceful mass uprising that is simply too powerful to resist. The impressive number of new mosques built by the cult suggest that this might be possible.

The second organization, the Islamic Movement of Uzbekistan, is a guerrilla force led by the brilliant commander known as Juma Namangani. His campaign to overthrow Karimov began with car bombings in 1999 intended to assassinate the president; by 2000, he had established a base in Afghanistan, whence he carried the war into the neighboring states. Karimov was able to retain power by mass arrests, but his military forces seemed helpless against the daring attacks by small guerrilla forces whose members had international training and experience. It was no surprise, therefore, that when the United States announced its intention of pursing the September 11 terrorists into Afghanistan, Karimov offered the use of Uzbek bases and readily accepted American aid and weapons. Putin surprised almost everyone by supporting the American operations that swiftly routed the Taliban. Terrorism, it seems, draws together those it seeks to harm and cannot keep allies who have little in common except their methods.

The overthrow of the Taliban and the pursuit of al-Qaeda thus present a wholly changed set of possible futures for the region. There is abundant money now, both from the Western military operations and from relief missions. More important, with Russia and the United States working together, possibly with Chinese cooperation, there is a united front against any organization perceived as composed of terrorists or likely to support terrorists, and the united front can, if it wishes, require local rulers to institute the kinds of reforms most likely to undermine the Islamic fundamentalists such as freedom to express dissent and free elections, to provide for long-term economic development, and to hinder the elites' efforts to steal everything. Without peace and stability nothing can be done, but without guaranteeing individuals and groups the freedom to garner the results of their talents and hard work, nothing will be done.

Last, if the oil resources can be developed and pipelines built through every country in the region, every ruler will be rich, and presumably each will understand the need to avoid both oppression at home and harboring guerrillas who will attack neighboring countries. Oil can provide the money for schools and hospitals, and once parents see the advantages of a secular education for their children's future, they will cease to send them to the only institutions currently available, the Islamic *madrassahs* that teach fundamentalism and hatred.

None of the three Islamic fundamentalist parties in Central Asia can aspire to taking power soon. Some of their cadres are on the run with al-Qaeda, others have been arrested by the newly invigorated governments, and others are watching and waiting. Watching and waiting is a reasonable policy for locals, but it could be ruinous to long-term Western and Russian interests. The time to develop a policy for future decades is now. The West may be in a war, but it has to plan for peace.

William L. Urban

Sources for Further Study

Choice 39 (June, 2002): 1877.
The New York Review of Books 49 (April 11, 2002): 27.
Publishers Weekly 249 (January 14, 2002): 51.
Studies in Conflict and Terrorism 25 (September/October, 2002): 341.
The Washington Post Book World, February 17, 2002, p. 3.

JIHAD
The Trail of Political Islam

Author: Gilles Kepel (1955-   )
First published: Jihad: Expansion et déclin de
   l'Islamisme, 2000, in France
Translated from the French by Anthony F. Roberts
Publisher: Harvard University Press (Cambridge, Mass.).
   454 pp. $29.95
Type of work: Current affairs, history, and religion
Locale: The Muslim world

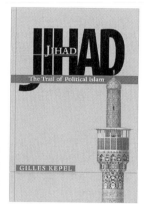

～

Kepel's examination of the growth and the decline of the
Islamist movement, with an optimistic reading of Islamist
violence and terrorism as a sign of the defeat of the mili-
tants

～

In his *Jihad: The Trail of Political Islam*, Gilles Kepel traces the Islamist movement back to Ayatollah Ruhollah Khomeini in Iran, Sayyid Qutb in Egypt, and Mawlana Mawdudi in Egypt, the theorists who in the 1960's provided the rationale for the political movement that he terms Islamism. According to Kepel, their writings dominated Islamist thinking after the Israeli-Arab War of 1973. In 1979, the first successful phase of the movement came with the defeat of the shah of Iran, and since that time the Iran of Khomeini and his successors has contended with the monarchy in Saudi Arabia, loosely allied with the West and intent on preserving its control of the Muslim world. This conflict intensified when the Saudis and the U.S. Central Intelligence Agency (CIA) intervened in Afghanistan, which was controlled by the Soviets. When a jihad, or holy war, was declared against the Russian occupiers, both the Saudis and the Americans supported the rebel Taliban. The ensuing war produced two results: For the Muslims, jihad became more important than the Palestinian cause, and Islamism replaced the nationalism that had preoccupied the Muslim world. For Kepel, the failure of Islamism was indicated by events in Bosnia, where Islamist efforts were thwarted by the Dayton Accords of 1995, and in Algeria and Egypt, where Islamist terrorism and militancy alienated the movement from the general population. According to Kepel, since 1997 the vast majority of Muslims have favored a clean break with armed struggle and an attempt to reconcile their cultural values with democratic ones.

Part 1 of Kepel's book concerns the expansion of Islamism throughout the Middle East, Europe, and the Far East. The Muslim world's allegiance was split between two power blocs: Gamal Abdel Nasser's Egypt, Muammar el-Qaddafi's Libya, Sukarno's Indonesia, Ahmed Ben Bella's Algeria, the Baathist regimes of Syria and Iraq, and

Southern Yemen were allied with the Russians; Turkey and Saudi Arabia were tied to the Americans; and Khomeini's Iran went it alone. Only in Iran did Islamism initially succeed, and then because Khomeini was adept at uniting the disinherited, the middle classes, the intellectuals, and the clerics. In other Muslim countries the radical values of the young urban poor were at odds with those of the bourgeoisie, who became concerned about how the violence would affect their lifestyle and possessions. The other factor that influenced Islamism was the role of the clergy. Nasser and some other political figures were able to coopt the *ulemas* (clergy) by appointing them to positions of power, which then weakened their credibility with the general population. Pakistan, however, was an exception, for there the *madrassahs*

Gilles Kepel, professor of Middle East Studies at the Institute for Political Studies in Paris, is the author of several books on Islam and the Middle East, three of which have been translated into English: Muslim Extremism in Egypt: The Prophet and Pharaoh *(1985),* The Revenge of God: The Resurgence of Islam, Christianity, and Judaism in the Modern World *(1994), and* Allah in the West: Islamic Movements in America and Europe *(1997).*

(religious schools) gave the *ulemas* an extensive network for revolutionary political ideas—Pakistan's secular schools were few and available only to the elite. The *madrassahs* later produced the Taliba (*madrassah* pupils) and the Deobandi militants active in terrorist activity in Kashmir.

The conflict in the Muslim world was essentially between revolutionary Iran and Saudi Arabia, which had the petro-dollars to aid other Muslim countries and to finance banking in Muslim countries. The Saudis also controlled access to Mecca, the most important pilgrimage site for Muslims. Iranian pilgrims flooded Saudi Arabia, which was concerned about Iranian efforts to undermine the legitimacy of the Saudi throne and which feared that the Iranians would attempt to take control of the Grand Mosque. Fighting broke out between the two sides, and the Saudis finally got the power to limit the number of pilgrims who could make the Mecca pilgrimage from each country. Iran had been operating from a position of strength because Iraq's invasion on September 22, 1980, elicited the enlistment of thousands of young Iranians from the urban poor; Khomeini then had support from all sectors of Iranian society. However, when the tide of battle turned against Iran at the same time that the Mecca squabble erupted, Iran's position weakened.

Despite some setbacks, Iran did have a legacy for the Muslim world, particularly in Lebanon and to a lesser extent in Europe: Khomeini issued a *fatwa* (legal opinion) calling for the death of Salman Rushdie, who had published *The Satanic Verses* (1988) in England; and in France there was a battle over the wearing of the *hijab* (veil) in public schools. Even within the Islamist movement there were problems. Yasser Arafat, leader of the Palestine Liberation Organization (PLO), was challenged by the more militant Hamas group, which worked to win the hearts of the Palestinians. Kepel ends part 1 by commenting that Muslims "from Bosnia to Chechnya to Central Asia" appeared to be ready to "join the Community of Believers and become prey to the activists." In part 2, Kepel explores why the "last decade of the twentieth century did not fulfill this abundant promise, despite the ardent hopes of Islamist militants around the globe."

Kepel begins part 2 by discussing how Saudi Arabia's decision to appeal for American aid to combat Iraqi troops affected the Islamic world. While American aid saved the monarchy, it also undermined the leadership the Saudis had exerted through their financial backing of Muslim countries and their control of Mecca. The Saudis had, in fact, invited infidels into the home of Islam. Muslim countries were then pushed into a corner and had to decide which of the Muslim antagonists—the Saudis or the Iraqis—to support. The American presence in Saudi Arabia angered many Islamists, notably Osama bin Laden, whose anti-American views resulted in his ouster from Saudi Arabia.

He and his fellow jihadists went to Afghanistan, where the Taliban, who had been supported by the Americans and Saudis against the Soviets and who had unified the country, welcomed them with open arms. The Taliban's destruction of Buddhist statues in 2001 and the persecution of foreigners in Afghanistan were followed by al-Qaeda's terrorist attacks on the World Trade Center and Pentagon on September 11, 2001. Kepel believes that the subsequent American bombing of Afghanistan has effectively destroyed the Taliban and jihadists in Afghanistan.

Kepel sees similar declines in the Islamist movement in the rest of the world. In Bosnia, despite the intervention of foreign jihadists, Islamism did not succeed, primarily because the secular interests of Bosnia Muslims outweighed their religious interests. In Algeria, the failure of the Islamist movement resulted from a split between the young urban poor and a devout middle class that was turned off by the violence and terrorism, which Kepel repeatedly terms "self-destructive." Similarly, in Egypt, the Islamist terrorism that culminated in the massacre of tourists at Luxor on November 17, 1997, led to government crackdowns and less tolerance for the Islamist movement there. In France, Islamist acts of terrorism met the same fate. Even in the Palestinian separatist movement there were problems. When Arafat and the PLO cast their lots with Iraq in the Gulf War, they lost vital Saudi funding and lost ground to Hamas, which had prudently avoided taking sides; but, according to Kepel, Hamas fell into the "trap of terrorism" and forfeited the support of moderate Muslims. Kepel concludes his discussion of the Jordanian policy of "isolating and repressing the young urban poor" and by "embracing those of the devout middle class who wished to participate in the political system" by claiming that such a policy is "in line with what most other Muslim countries were trying to achieve in the waning months of the twentieth century."

The original title of Kepel's book, which was published in France in 2000, contained a reference to the decline of Islamism; but in the light of the terrorist attacks of September 11, 2001, "decline" no longer seems appropriate. In his revision of the book, however, Kepel does not waver from his original position. In the conclusion, Kepel describes the September 11 attacks as "a desperate symbol of the isolation, fragmentation, and decline of the Islamist movement, not as a sign of its strength and irrepressible might." He repeatedly terms violence as a "death trap" for the Islamist movement, which he believes is doomed to failure. Elections in Muslim countries, particularly in Iran, where reformers have won, demonstrate, for him, that Muslims yearn for prosperity, peace, and democracy. Even the demographics that contributed so much to the rise of Islamism now work against the militants. The high birth rate that produced so many urban poor in Muslim countries has dropped significantly, and Muslim young people now grow up in cities where they have better access to education. As a result, they are more open to change and more prone to question what their predecessors readily accepted. In addition, they have seen that in countries that have adopted Islamism, Iran and Afghanistan, those regimes have not satisfied the desires, needs, and aims of their people. Muslim young people have relatives in the West, where many of them have received educations, watch satellite television programs, and see the technological progress that has been made in the West, and many of them want what they see. Kepel, however, does concede that changes will have to be made to democratize Muslim countries, but he does not appear to acknowledge the difficulty of reconciling democratic values with the Muslim religion. Furthermore, although the jihadists have been largely unsuccessful at winning elections, they have been influential in many Muslim countries.

Kepel's book covers the entire Muslim world as well as Europe, and traces the economic, political, and religious history of Muslim countries through the twentieth century. There is a wealth of detail, strengthened by asides that examine the ripples made by individual events such as the Rushdie affair; and the book contains maps, copious notes, and a dictionary of Arabic words that may be unfamiliar to nonspecialists. As a sociologist, Kepel tends to devote a great deal of attention to social classes, but his explanation for the decline of Islamism is more economic than sociological. Material prosperity, or the fear of losing it, seems to be the antidote to militant jihadism. Kepel's optimistic thesis may reassure readers who regard Islamism as the chief threat to global security, but some readers may have doubts about the destruction of the al-Qaeda organization and about the need for contemporary Islamist theorists to sustain the movement.

Thomas L. Erskine

Sources for Further Study

Booklist 98 (April 1, 2002): 1284.
Choice 40 (November, 2002): 549.
Library Journal 127 (March 15, 2002): 96.
The New York Times Book Review 107 (May 26, 2002): 10.
Publishers Weekly 249 (March 4, 2002): 68.
The Washington Post Book World, April 28, 2002, p. 4.

JOHN MARSHALL AND THE HEROIC AGE
OF THE SUPREME COURT

Author: R. Kent Newmyer (1930-   )
Publisher: Louisiana State University Press (Baton
    Rouge). 511 pp. $39.95
Type of work: Biography and history
Time: 1755-1835
Locale: Virginia and Washington, D.C.

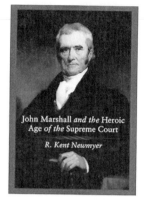

John Marshall *and the* Heroic
Age *of the* Supreme Court

R. *Kent Newmyer*

❦

*A scholarly and readable biography of Marshall, with
an emphasis on how his constitutional thinking developed
during the three decades that he presided over an increasingly divided Supreme Court*

❦

Principal personages:
>   JOHN MARSHALL (1755-1835), chief justice of the United States from
>   1801 to 1835
>   THOMAS JEFFERSON (1743-1826), Republican leader and president who
>   was Marshall's major antagonist for many years
>   JOHN ADAMS (1735-1826), Federalist president (1797-1801) who
>   appointed Marshall as chief justice in 1801
>   ALEXANDER HAMILTON (1755-1804), conservative Federalist leader who
>   anticipated much of Marshall's jurisprudence
>   SPENCER ROANE (1762-1822), appellate judge of Virginia who defended
>   states' rights in published debates with Marshall
>   GEORGE WASHINGTON (1732-1799), first U.S. president, who was the
>   subject of an admiring biography written by Marshall
>   JAMES MADISON (1751-1836), framer of the U.S. Constitution who dis-
>   agreed with Marshall's broad judicial interpretations
>   ANDREW JACKSON (1767-1845), Democratic president (1829-1837) who
>   personified many values that Marshall held in contempt

   John Marshall is usually ranked as the most significant judicial figure in the history
of the United States. Based on the number of recent works devoted to Marshall, there
appears to be a renewed interest in his life and career. These works include a new edition of *The Papers of John Marshall* (ten volumes to date), Jean Edward Smith's 1996
full biography that is especially good on Marshall's private life, and excellent studies
of his jurisprudence by Charles Hobson (1996), Herbert Johnson (1997), G. Edward
White (1991), and Robert Lowry Clinton (1989). Building on this scholarship,
R. Kent Newmyer's objective was to produce an "interpretative biography" that combines a traditional narrative approach with a "study of Marshall's jurisprudence." The
result is the most sophisticated one-volume treatment to date, full of mature insights

and controversial theses about Marshall's judicial ideas and decisions.

The biography begins with an examination of Marshall's early years within the context of the American Revolutionary era. Influenced by a father who supported the revolutionary cause, Marshall at the age of twenty took up arms against the British in the 1775 battle of Great Bridge in Virginia. Even at this time, there is evidence that he was motivated primarily by a concern for the constitutional principles of "rights and liberties." Marshall was already well acquainted with the British legal tradition, especially the common law as summarized in the writings of William Blackstone. Marshall later wrote that the revolution was not a struggle "against actual oppression," but that it was "a war of principle against a system hostile to political liberty." Newmyer finds that the war provided him with an education in constitutional principles and that his decision to participate in the war was his "first great constitutional decision."

Following the war, Marshall was elected a member of Virginia's legislature, where he became highly critical of its narrow localism. Marshall himself wrote that "the general tendency of state politics convinced me that no safe and permanent remedy could be found but in a more efficient and better organized general government." Unhappy with the limited powers of the central government under the Articles of Confederation, he strongly argued in favor of the Constitution at the Virginia ratification, declaring that it would create "a well regulated Democracy." Like other leading Federalists, Marshall acknowledged that the people were the ultimate source of national sovereignty, although he doubted that they had the virtue and wisdom to govern directly. Newmyer observes that the tension between these two ideas would always be a central problem in his jurisprudence.

Large chunks of Newmyer's book are necessarily devoted to Marshall's judicial opinions while serving as chief justice. Newmyer provides detailed analysis of the major cases, especially the three that were the most influential: *Marbury v. Madison* (1803), when the Supreme Court for the first time held that a congressional statute was unconstitutional, *McCulloch v. Maryland* (1819), which upheld the Bank of the United States and overturned a state tax on the bank, and *Gibbons v. Ogden* (1824), which ruled that Congress had the ultimate power to regulate interstate commerce. As an authority in constitutional law, Newmyer does an excellent job in choosing which cases to emphasize. Occasionally, however, he fails to provide sufficient explanation about the background to a few influential cases, such as *Barron v. Balti-*

R. Kent Newmyer is a professor of law and legal history at the University of Connecticut School of Law. A recognized authority in nineteenth century jurisprudence, he is the author of several books, including The Supreme Court Under Marshall and Taney *(1968) and a highly acclaimed biography of John Marshall's closest associate,* Supreme Court Justice Joseph Story: Statesman of the Old Republic *(1984).*

more (1833), which held that the Bill of Rights was not binding on the states.

Newmyer refers to the long debate between Marshall and Jefferson as "A Grand Creative Hatred," in which each man fired the creative genius of the other. Their most fundamental disagreements involved federalism and the role of the courts. The chief justice believed that Jefferson wanted to subvert the rule of law, while Jefferson feared judicial tyranny and subversion of the legitimate powers of the states. Newmyer looks upon the Marbury decision as the chief justice's first victory to put the rule of law over partisan politics, and in the impeachment trial of Samuel Chase and the treason trial of Aaron Burr he finds that Jefferson "came off as impetuous, vindictive, and self-righteous."

Among the numerous components within Marshall's constitutional jurisprudence, Newmyer argues that "none was more important than the distinction he drew between law and politics." By this statement, Newmyer means that Marshall was committed to a "rule of law," and that he tried not to base his judicial decisions on strictly partisan concerns. The term "politics" often refers to political values and public policies, and for this reason Newmyer finds that Marshall was not always able, in practice, to follow a strict separation between law and politics. Even the Constitution itself, he acknowledges, was "supreme law and supremely political as well." In the case of *Marbury v. Madison*, Newmyer admits that Marshall was forced to take into account the possibility that President Jefferson might disobey a court order, which would have seriously weakened the political power of the Supreme Court. In this decision, Marshall's "opinion, like the Constitution itself, was both political and legal."

In interpreting the Constitution, Newmyer argues that Marshall consistently adhered "to the intent of the Framers as expressed in the text of the document." More than any other aspect of Marshall's judicial philosophy, according to Newmyer, his assumption that "the Framers' intent had real meaning" places him "in his own age and distinguishes his jurisprudence from ours." Since Marshall had participated in the ratification of the Constitution, many of his assumptions about the intent of the document were based on his personal memories and perceptions of what had been said and written at the time.

The chief justice's concept of original intent was quite different from that of James Madison, who tended to focus on how the Constitution limited federal powers. Marshall tended to frame his constitutional arguments more in terms of the broad objectives and structural logic of the document, and he tended to think in terms of how the Constitution expanded the powers of the central government. In upholding the constitutionality of the Bank of the United States in *McCulloch*, for instance, he based his argument primarily on an expansive reading of the "necessary and proper" clause, so that the words "necessary and proper" meant broad policies that were generally appropriate to the powers of Congress. In analyzing this decision, Newmyer suggests that "it seems obvious that the doctrine of broad construction" was in large part "a response to Madison's strict construction views."

Rather than being a result-oriented justice attempting to defend his own judicial preferences, Newmyer insists that the chief justice generally "believed what he said." Yet Newmyer admits that his values and policy preferences had at least an unconscious influence on how he decided cases. As an aggressive speculator in land, Marshall was a strong supporter of the value of private property and he believed that the original intent of the Constitution was to promote this value. In some cases, such as *New Jersey v. Wilson* (1812), Newmeyer questions Marshall's claim that precedent controlled the case, and he writes: "What did seem to be controlling, or at least constant, instead, was a general disposition on his part to bend common-law methodology to create uniform, property-protecting rules for the land market."

In a period of developing capitalism, a large percentage of Marshall's decisions dealt with issues of vested property rights. In cases such as *Fletcher v. Peck* (1810) and *Dartmouth College v. Woodward* (1819), he broadly interpreted the contract clause to apply to grants and charters of the state legislatures. Thus, Newmyer observes that the chief justice turned the clause into "an all-purpose instrument for protecting private property from state regulation, even when no contract was involved." Marshall consistently defended the interests of large land speculators, and he "spent his professional life making law serve those who had property and wanted to get more or keep what they had."

During most of his adult life, Marshall owned about a dozen slaves, and he lived with the institution on a daily basis. As a judge and lawmaker, he actively participated in the administration of slave law, recognizing that the Constitution deferred to the states on the issue of slavery. Newmyer finds that his rigorous adherence to slave law is "painful to observe." Although finding that the chief justice "showed little interest in the subject," he places the chief justice in the tradition of southern paternalism, using his influence to soften the harsh realities of the system. Probably Marshall's most revealing opinion concerning slavery was *The Antelope* (1825). Although Marshall wrote that the international slave trade was "contrary to the law of nature" and that "every man has a natural right to the fruit of his own labor," he then held that positive law took priority over natural rights and the personal opinions of judges. In spite of the use of liberal rhetoric, Newmyer writes, "the bottom line was that property trumped freedom again."

However, Marshall never manifested the racist ideas that were so common among his contemporaries. In his decisions relating to Native Americans, for example, he managed to preserve at least some of their rights, especially when the state legislatures tried to subvert federal treaties. His famous opinion *Worcester v. Georgia* (1832), to the distress of Andrew Jackson, established the concept of limited tribal sovereignty. Newmyer writes: "In an age when racism, land greed, and arrogance mingled to destroy an innocent people unnecessarily, he worked to put the Court on the side of justice."

In the years following his controversial *McCulloch* decision of 1819, Marshall was increasingly frustrated by the growth of the states' rights forces, as articulated by Judge Spencer Roane of the Virginia Court of Appeals. Roane criticized Marshall's opinions in print and Marshall answered the attacks under a pseudonym. Marshall believed that the election of Andrew Jackson in 1828 meant the triumph of states' rights and democratic mass participation, two ideas that he opposed. Newmyer argues that the chief justice adopted to the new reality by becoming more pragmatic and less doctrinaire. He writes: "It was flexibility, along with tactical savvy, that permitted Marshall to salvage so much of his constitutional nationalism in an age hostile to it."

The epilogue of the biography consists of an interesting discussion of Marshall's judicial legacy and the reasons for his lasting reputation as the "Great Chief Justice." Although Marshall was a "workhorse" who wrote the majority opinions in 49 percent of the cases heard by the Court during his tenure, Newmyer writes that "only a handful of these opinions were truly memorable." He observes that Marshall was not especially original, but finds that originality was not necessarily a virtue in the work of making judicial decisions and writing opinions. He finds that a major source of Marshall's success was his temperament, especially his "caution and moderation, mixed with a good sense of what the situation allowed."

Thomas Tandy Lewis

Sources for Further Study

Choice 39 (May, 2002): 1664.
Library Journal 126 (November 15, 2001): 80.
The New Republic 225 (December 17, 2001): 36.
The New York Times Book Review 107 (January 13, 2002): 18.
Publishers Weekly 248 (October 29, 2001): 51.
The Washington Post Book World, January 27, 2002, p. 3.

JULY, JULY

Author: Tim O'Brien (1946-   )
Publisher: Houghton Mifflin (Boston). 322 pp. $26.00
Type of work: Novel
Time: 1969-2000
Locale: Minneapolis, Minnesota

~

O'Brien's account of the 2000 reunion of the Darton Hall College class of 1969 moves from present to past, focusing on the characters' former ideals, lived realities, and present hope while probing a changing American culture

~

Principal characters:

DAVID TODD, a veteran who lost a leg in Vietnam
MARLA DEMPSEY, the former wife of David Todd
BILLY MCMANN, a Vietnam draft-dodger who fled to Canada
DOROTHY STIER, a Republican who rejected Billy McMann and who has breast cancer
AMY ROBINSON, recently married and divorced
JAN HUEBNER, recently deserted by her husband
MARV BERTEL, an overweight, married businessman in love with Spook Spinelli
SPOOK SPINELLI, a free-love spirit in the 1960's, now married to two husbands
PAULETTE HASLO, an ordained minister, jobless since robbing a parishioner's home

In *July, July*, the 1969 graduates of Darton Hall College come together in July, 2000, one year late for their thirtieth reunion. During their college years the United States faced conflicts between liberals and conservatives on questions of race, gender, and the Vietnam War. From an omniscient narrator the reader learns of each reunion member's early ideals and dreams and what has become of each. Class member Jan Heubner's early remark, "Maybe that's the trick. Never hope," warns the reader of what is to come.

As was true of O'Brien's earlier novels, such as *Going After Cacciato* (1978) and *The Things They Carried* (1990), this novel's narrative structure is nonlinear, allowing O'Brien to shift from past to present, from story piece to story piece. Some events stray from realism. However, the reunion story as it interweaves with stories from the past is told in chronological order. Throughout the text, dialogue shifts easily from coffee-klatch and barroom small talk and stale clichés to bitter humor and grim honesty. As always, part of O'Brien's style is sprinkling worn clichés into absurd situations.

~

Tim O'Brien won the National Book Award for his first novel, Going After Cacciato, *in 1979. His other works include* The Things They Carried *(1990), winner of France's Prix du Meilleur Livre Etrange, and* In the Lake of the Woods *(1994), winner of the James Fenimore Cooper Prize.*

~

When, in a story from the past, Spook Spinelli asks her first husband to remain married to her while she marries another man, O'Brien writes: "He . . . understood that relationships require fine-tuning, . . . that he wasn't losing a wife but gaining an in-law."

Because of their number, their whiny and somewhat intoxicated voices, and their gossip about each other's weaknesses and failures, the characters are not easy to like, much less to identify with. Yet this odd bunch stay through the reunion and somehow come together, looking into each other but looking more into themselves and, eventually, finding voices in which to speak the secrets of their deepest selves. Although these secrets contain some absurdity, they also contain depth. As the characters tell all, each moves toward some wisdom. The stories all center in broken or rocky relationships, past, present, and future. Perhaps O'Brien is saying that relationships, always risky, are the hope of humanity, or at least what bring about survival. Somehow the characters understand this.

The first chapter introduces the novel's characters gathered at the reunion dance. It soon becomes clear that in the thirty years between 1969 and 1999, and even into 2000, the characters' lives revolved around war—specifically the Vietnam War—and dismemberment. Some of the dismemberments revealed at the reunion are physical, some mental or emotional. Two members of the class have died, and that reality runs as an undertone in the dialogue; near the end of the reunion the events around one of these deaths are told to all, but the narrator reveals the second death story only to the reader.

The stories of David Todd, Dorothy Stier, Billy McMann, and Marla Dempsey, those most affected by war and dismemberment, carry much of the meaning central to the novel. Todd's is a Vietnam story, and the writing style is reminiscent of O'Brien's earlier Vietnam tales where the narrator mixes grim humor with grim horror, bringing the reader closer to the reality of a soldier's life in Vietnam than any reportage. Todd voluntarily enlisted in the army after his junior year at Darton Hall College. He was wounded on July 16, 1969. Alone, severely wounded, barely alive, he moves in and out of a delirium of pain and morphine. With Todd is Johnny Evers, a voice from a transistor radio. This voice taunts Todd, goads him; it never comforts him. The voice knows everything and can even give Todd the choice between life and death, telling him, after four days, that he may either stay and die quickly or live and be in for a life of physical, mental, and emotional pain. Todd chooses life; he retains his hope, primarily the hope that eventually Marla Dempsey will marry him and they will live happily ever after. Sending in the rescue helicopter, the radio voice mocks Todd's decision but calls him brave. For Todd, survival of Vietnam and the dismemberment it caused is possible, but at a great price.

As ghastly as Todd's war wound and war experience were, it is the aftermath—the post-traumatic stress in which he hears the constant sound of Johnny Evers's voice, his addiction to drugs, and his eventual divorce from Marla—that are the real challenges to Todd's survival. For all the characters—those who the Vietnam War radicalized, those who went to Vietnam, those who fled to Canada, those who supported the war—this historical event stayed with them through the next thirty years. It stayed most vividly in the psyches of those who survived the war but it stayed also with the others who came of age in 1969. Marla Dempsey tries to escape the war's effect by divorcing Todd, so traumatized by his experience in Vietnam. However, when she runs away with a rich motorcycle rider, she finds no peace. She comes to the reunion alone, joining the others as they go back over the thirty years since their graduation.

It is actually thirty-one years since their graduation. O'Brien sets the novel not in July, 1999, but because of some errors made by the reunion arranger, in July, 2000, on the cusp of the new century as well as in the age of midlife crises for the characters. This allows the possibility that something new may come out of the tragedy and failures of that war and the tragedy and failures of the characters. At the same time that Darton Hall College invites the class of 1969 to go home to the place Vietnam holds in their lives, past and present, and perhaps to look forward, *July, July* invites the readers to go back to that war and its past effects on them and perhaps look forward.

O'Brien mocks the American public's attitude toward the war when it was happening in July, 1969:

> The war went on. People ate Raisin Bran. There were new orphans and widows and Gold Star mothers. Three thousand and twenty American soldiers died that summer, and more than seven thousand Vietnamese. People took aspirin for their headaches. People requested doggie bags at fancy restaurants. Dow Chemical made a killing.

Is that passivity about the Vietnam War still present in the American public, or did the next thirty years of life force everyone to confront the trauma hidden down deep in them?

Dorothy Stier, another reunion member, stands in contrast to Todd. She was a war supporter and in 1969 had no patience with her classmates' "all you need is love drivel." That explains why, although she was in a relationship with Billy McMann when he fled the Vietnam draft by flying off to Winnipeg, Dorothy chose not to go with him and married McMann's best friend, a husband right out of the American Dream. McMann brings the pain of that rejection to the reunion and Dorothy brings a need for his forgiveness. She brings dismemberment, also: the loss of her breast to cancer. As Todd survived Vietnam with guts, Dorothy has survived "the fires and thirst" of her cancer with "brains and common sense." As Todd learned that survival comes with aftershocks, she has learned also.

Dorothy's cancer makes her a parallel character to Todd. As he, the Vietnam vet, is minus one leg, so she, the cancer victim, is minus one breast. As Marla Dempsey cannot be the wife Todd wants after his dismembering war experience, Ron cannot be the husband Dorothy wants after her dismembering cancer surgery: He cannot look at or touch her scar. From 1969 through 1999, Vietnam was a curse that spread through the nation, crossing all boundaries with its pain; in that same period, cancer was a curse that spread also, crossing all boundaries with its pain. The greatest pain has been in broken relationships. So too, healing and growth will come in relationships.

At the novel's end, a drugged Todd is walking with Marla Dempsey, not into marriage to be sure, but into a relationship. A drugged Dorothy, walking home through the darkened streets to her husband Ron, looks up "at the opulent summer stars." Other characters, too, look forward into new relationships. McMann has fallen in love with classmate Paulette Haslo, the defrocked minister who led the prayers for the dead classmates at the reunion. Another classmate has during the reunion confessed an affair to her husband, and although he has walked out of their hotel room, she is following him, hoping for forgiveness. Amy Robinson and Jan Huebner, both recently divorced, vow to go on searching for someone, but they will search together. The two strangest characters in the novel, Spook Spinelli and Marv Bertel, who have been dancing around their thirty-year-long but as-yet-unconsummated sexual attraction, are flying on the same plane toward someplace unclear to them and the reader. If, indeed, all these newly formed relationships are signs that hope has not died for these Darton Hall College alums, the hope that remains is as crazy and fragile as the characters in this risky novel.

Perhaps O'Brien's reason for the reunion plot device is that time has to go by before adjustments can begin for such large cultural forces as war and cancer and their ugly and painful reality. As the reunion moves toward its close, Dorothy teams up with Todd, moving with him into a narcotic trance. As they comfort each other and listen to each other, the theme comes forward, perhaps too loudly: "'Nam and cancer, it's like. . . . It's not like anything is it? Once you're there, you're there. You don't come home," says Dorothy. Later, looking at her chest, her missing breast, she says, "Purple Stinking Heart."

In pouring a monstrous thunderstorm on the characters' departure, is O'Brien suggesting that the new millennium offers a new baptism, a cleansing of the past? Or is he saying that the tropical rains of Vietnam are still present? As the novel ends, Jan says to Amy, "Follow me, sweetheart. We're golden," seeming to reverse her opening rejection of hope.

Francine A. Dempsey

Sources for Further Study

Booklist 99 (September 1, 2002): 7.
Kirkus Review 70 (July 15, 2002): 984.

Library Journal 127 (July, 2002): 122.
New York 35 (October 21, 2002): 85.
The New York Times Book Review 107 (October 13, 2002): 6.
Publishers Weekly 249 (July 1, 2002): 44.
Texas Monthly 30 (October, 2002): 108.
The Times Literary Supplement, November 1, 2002, p. 27.
The Wall Street Journal 240 (September 27, 2002): W8.

KILN PEOPLE

Author: David Brin (1950-   )
Publisher: Tor (New York). 458 pp. $25.95
Type of work: Novel
Time: The mid-twenty-first century
Locale: Los Angeles

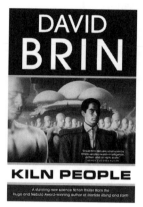

~

The ability to produce disposable multiple selves, or "dittotech," is the scientific breakthrough whose social consequences are explored in this tale of a veteran detective's battle with a clever archenemy

~

Principal characters:
> ALBERT MORRIS, a hard-boiled private eye who specializes in crimes involving the illegal duplication of persons
> BETA, the criminal mastermind Morris has spent years pursuing
> AENEAS KAOLIN, an industrialist whose company controls the dittotech process
> RITU MAHARAL, Kaolin's executive assistant
> DR. YOSIL MAHARAL, Ritu's father and a leading expert in the dittotech field
> CLARA GONZALEZ, the feisty army officer with whom Morris is in love
> MALACHAI "PAL" MONTMORILLIN, Morris's wheelchair-bound colleague
> GINEEN WAMMAKER, a media mogul and porn star who is being illegally duplicated by Beta
> JAMES GADARENE, an antidittotech activist convinced that this technology is morally wrong

Kiln People depicts a society in which the capacity to manufacture inexpensive but short-lived "dittoes" of real people has had far-reaching consequences. Freed of the necessity to work or perform other onerous social tasks, those who can afford the new technology use their dittoed replicas for a variety of purposes. For the average law-abiding individual, dittoes are labor-saving and errand-running devices that can also be employed to experience the vicarious thrills of extreme sex and violence. Those who lead more dangerous lives, however, such as private detective Albert Morris, use these additional selves to investigate situations where bodily harm is a likely occurrence, which significantly expands both the scope of Morris's operations and the probability that at least one of his selves will be in danger at all times.

Unlike those science-fiction authors for whom a faster-than-light drive or time-travel machine offers a quick fix to previously insoluble problems, David Brin presents his technological breakthrough as a somewhat flawed and limited one. Dittoes only have a twenty-four-hour life span, and although they begin their brief careers as an exact copy of their original—or "archie," short for "archetype"—their subsequent experience can only be shared with an archie through downloading or direct communication. Since Morris's dittoes are often in danger of physical destruction, this adds yet another element of suspense to the narrative: Will what his ditto has learned be conveyed to him before it dies either a natural or unnatural death? The existence of different kinds of color-coded dittoes ranging from the intellectually gifted

David Brin has written more than a dozen science-fiction novels, including six titles in the widely acclaimed Uplift series. He won the Hugo, LOCUS, and Nebula Best Novel Awards for Startide Rising *(1983) and the Hugo and LOCUS Best Novel Awards for* The Uplift War *(1987).*

blacks to the office worker grays to the sex toy whites, and the narrative's gradual revelations concerning the ability of some dittoes to develop independent traits also help to make an interestingly complicated concept out of what might, in lesser hands, have been merely a variation on the idea of cloning.

Kiln People begins with Morris in hot pursuit of his old nemesis Beta, a mysterious villain whose illegal dittoing operations Morris has often been able to shut down, but who has himself always eluded capture. The first narrative voice to be encountered is that of one of Morris's dittoes, a green errand runner who has been sent to spy out Beta's latest lair and is fleeing from his homicidal henchmen. The fact that "homicidal" is not quite right here—the green is not really human, even though endowed with a human's thoughts and feelings—points to one of the novel's characteristic strategies, the high-spirited play with concepts of the human and the nonhuman that forces readers to rethink their assumptions about these categories. In the case of the menaced green, for example, the need to follow his archie's dangerous instructions is frequently tempered with a concern for self-preservation, even though the green knows that he has at most one day to live; the conflict between duty and discretion, precisely because it is not a "real" problem, plays out at a more philosophical than usual level that permits Brin to explore the situation at length and without melodramatic overtones.

It would be misleading to imply, however, that *Kiln People*'s concerns are predominantly metaphysical and technological. Although Brin's Uplift series of novels emphasizes the hard science and massive social dislocation involved in admitting dolphins and chimpanzees to equivalent-to-human status, most of his other fiction—particularly *The Postman* (1985) and *Earth* (1990)—feature a more conventional variety of the adventure story in which resolutely heroic protagonists overcome a succession of obstacles on their way to ultimate victory. Thus, *Kiln People*'s generally interesting portrayal of the dittoing process and its societal and philosophical ramifications is periodically interrupted by mass gun battles and other forms of cinematically spectacular violence, which sometimes seem gratuitous rather than either integral or enhancing to the plot. This is not to say that these purple passages are badly written or devoid of a certain degree of febrile excitement, but they do not, on the whole, add a great deal to what is in most other respects an intriguing story of sudden technological breakthrough and its unforeseen consequences.

As Albert Morris wends his way along the trail of clues that he hopes will lead to Beta's capture, he creates several dittoes whose first-person accounts of their activities provide an effective demonstration of the possibilities of multiple selfhood. There are opportunities for humor as well as drama here, and the narrative makes good use of them: An anxious client who contacts Morris and asks, "Could you please send a you over here right away?" is one of many examples of Brin's flair for comic invention. The profusion of multiple but psychically connected narrators will force readers to stay alert for switches in point of view, however, as the complexities of Morris's investigation lead him to ditto green, gray, and black selves who each take turns at pushing the plot forward.

The course of Morris's investigation alters when he begins to pick up indications that Universal Kilns, the corporation that holds all the patents on the dittoing process, is trying to suppress new breakthroughs in the field. In the early days of dittoing technology, it was hoped that refinements in the copying of archies would eventually make it feasible for people to reproduce themselves ad infinitum and thus achieve personal immortality; the brief life span of dittoes and the fact that they cannot themselves be successfully replicated, however, seem to have established that the death of the original archie body still marks the end point of human existence. It turns out, however, that some of Universal Kiln's scientists have been experimenting with the possibility of duplicating human souls, who will survive the demise of their bodily hosts and can be kept alive through complex manipulations of the immaterial forces of which they are composed.

It is at this point that Brin's explanation of the science that underlies his fiction opts for mystification rather than intelligibility. His earlier descriptions of dittoing procedures are so graphically detailed and so supported by credible accounts of the technical processes involved that the reader accepts these developments as a logical consequence of humanity's growing biological expertise. *Kiln People*'s rationale for soul duplication, however, veers off into essentially occult invocations of mysterious forces that are not well grounded in any scientifically valid body of knowledge, and the result is a significant loss of narrative plausibility. Like those episodes of the *Star Trek* television series in which a new basic principle of physics is invented in order to resolve a plot difficulty, Brin here chooses a quick and all-too-easy fix for a concept that requires a much more cogent and comprehensive explanation.

That this does not seriously disrupt the novel's forward momentum says something for its author's ability to keep his cast of characters and their ever-increasing multiple selves in absorbing as well as entertaining motion. In addition to Albert Morris, a worthy addition to the long list of hard-boiled private eyes who star in so much American genre fiction, there are several other characters who add human interest to *Kiln People*'s intriguing technological speculations. Aeneas Kaolin, the founder of Universal Kilns, has accumulated so much power and influence that his ambitions have careened out of control and into areas where mere mortals have usually feared to tread; Clara Gonzalez, the significant other in Morris's life, combines professional soldiering and wide-ranging intellectual curiosity into a career that is refreshingly independent of her partner's; Malachai Montmorillin, the literal "Pal" who serves as

Morris's sidekick on most of his investigations, adds that element of wisecracking repartee without which any story involving male bonding in the face of adversity would seem incomplete.

Although these characters all have their moments, the most interesting personage in the novel is Ritu Maharal, the Universal Kilns executive whose enigmatic presence steals all of her scenes with Morris and whose fate turns out be intimately connected with Aeneas Kaolin's efforts to achieve psychical immortality. Brin sets this up very nicely by introducing Maharal as one of the standard clichés of the hard-boiled detective novel, the distraught young woman who begs the private eye to help her find a missing person—in this case, her father, the scientist Dr. Yosil Maharal. Conventionally, the narrative should now proceed to feature Morris working toward a solution while he gradually falls in love with Maharal, an assumption that is first heightened but then deflated by a hilarious scene in which Morris and Maharal experience coitus interruptus when they confuse their real and dittoed selves. What actually happens, however, is that Ritu herself becomes the focus of Morris's investigation as he follows a complicated trail that eventually leads to a stunning revelation about her involvement with Beta, the evil genius Morris has spent years attempting to apprehend. Since the exact nature of the Maharal-Beta relationship is the key to the narrative's denouement, it will remain unrevealed here, in the expectation that some of the readers of this review will wish to sample *Kiln People*'s pleasures for themselves; rest assured, however, that the novel's conclusion is a powerful and surprising one.

The advent of relatively simple and inexpensive cloning procedures at the end of the twentieth century has made the sort of world that Brin imagines as the near future a readily believable one. Although it is possible to fault the narrative for its over-reliance on mass mayhem and the inadequacy of its treatment of soul duplication, on the whole this is a worthy and entertaining addition to the author's already impressive body of work. In keeping with David Brin's penchant for punning, it seems appropriate to conclude with the observation that *Kiln People* is a tasty science-fiction confection whose consistency is far more than half-baked.

Paul Stuewe

Sources for Further Study

Book: The Magazine for the Reading Life 21 (January/February, 2002): 27.
Booklist 98 (February 1, 2002): 930.
Kirkus Reviews 69 (November 15, 2001): 1588.
Library Journal 126 (November 1, 2001): 99.
Nature 414 (December 20/ December 27, 2001): 848.
New Scientist 173 (January 12, 2002): 45.
Publishers Weekly 248 (December 17, 2001): 69.

KOBA THE DREAD
Laughter and the Twenty Million

Author: Martin Amis (1949-   )
Publisher: Talk Miramax Books (New York). 306 pp.
   $24.95
Type of work: Biography and history
Time: The twentieth century
Locale: Russia and Great Britain

≈

   Amis criticizes western liberals, particularly in Great Britain, who condemned Adolf Hitler's fascism but who were excessively tolerant of Soviet communism under Vladimir Lenin and Joseph Stalin, whose victims were even more numerous than those of Hitler's Germany

≈

         Principal personages:
            MARTIN AMIS, author and prominent British novelist
            KINGSLEY AMIS, his father, a notable novelist
            ROBERT CONQUEST, British historian
            CHRISTOPHER HITCHENS, British political journalist
            ADOLF HITLER, German Nazi leader
            VLADIMIR LENIN, Soviet revolutionary
            ALEKSANDR SOLZHENITSYN, Russian author
            JOSEPH STALIN, Soviet leader, successor to Lenin
            LEON TROTSKY, Soviet revolutionary and rival of Stalin

   Martin Amis is one of England's premier writers. The son of the acclaimed novelist Kingsley Amis, he has received numerous prizes and wide recognition for his novels beginning with *The Rachel Papers* (1973) and including *Money* (1984) and *Time's Arrow* (1991). Among his nonfiction works is *Experience* (2000), an autobiography of growing up as the son of the often difficult and curmudgeonly Kingsley Amis. *Koba the Dread* is also a memoir, but it is something more.
   Koba was a nickname applied to Joseph Stalin, ruler of the Soviet Union from Vladimir Lenin's death in 1923 until Stalin's own death in 1953. One of the most bloodthirsty tyrants in history, he is responsible for upward of twenty million deaths and ranks with Germany's Adolf Hitler and China's Mao Zedong as the twentieth century's monstrous mass murderers. One of Amis's aims is to inform the reader of Koba's crimes, which he does through numerous examples.
   However, the magnitude of Stalin's crimes has been generally known for several decades. Beginning in the 1960's, Robert Conquest, a close friend of both Amises, wrote a series of works on the inhumanity of the Soviet Union and its leaders, nota-

bly Stalin. Admittedly, many persons in the West
are more aware of the atrocities of Hitler and
Nazi Germany, in part because of the fact that the
United States waged a military war against Hitler
while Stalin's Soviet Union was America's ally
in World War II, and in part because of widespread knowledge of the Holocaust against Jews
and others in the death camps of the Third Reich.
The difference in public awareness of the scale
of Stalin's murders would not be a sufficient reason itself for Amis, known to the public mainly
for his novels, to write an objective history of
those who died as the result of decisions made by
the Soviet dictator. Amis makes no pretense of
extensive archival research. Others have done that
and will continue to do so. Amis relies upon commonly recognized experts on Communist Russia,
such as Conquest, Martin Malia, Richard Pipes,
the Nobel Prize-winning Aleksandr Solzhenitsyn,
and the Russian historian Dmitri Volkgonov, and
the stories he tells and the anecdotes he relates are
chilling in the extreme.

Martin Amis, the son of the
celebrated British writer Kingsley
Amis, has written several critically
received novels, including The
Rachel Papers *(1973),* Money
(1984), London Fields *(1989), and*
Time's Arrow *(1991). He has been*
nominated for Britain's prestigious
Booker Prize and has also written a
highly regarded memoir,
Experience *(2000).*

For Amis, however, giving information about
the Soviet atrocities is connected to a more im-
portant question. He also asks why so many Western intellectuals, including his own
father, so long closed their eyes and their minds to evidence which well established
Stalin's complicity in those many horrific events, public events from the 1930's and
even before. Thus *Koba the Dread* is not just dispassionate history but a personal
memoir of intellectuals like his father and those from his own generation, and it is
written with polemical passion. A parallel could be made with the French writer
Émile Zola (1840-1902) who, in his 1898 letter that began "J'accuse," attacked
France's political and military elite at the time of the Dreyfus affair for their overt
anti-Semitism.

Amis notes that while editing Kingsley Amis's letters for publication, he found a
letter, written in 1941 while the elder Amis was a student at Oxford, defending the Soviet Union in spite of public knowledge of Soviet aggression in the late 1930's and of
Stalin's elimination of old Bolsheviks, the upper ranks of the military, intellectuals,
and others in the show trials of that decade. In was only after the death of Stalin that
Kingsley Amis quit the Communist Party. In the following years, the senior Amis, reversing his earlier course, became a staunch anticommunist. Martin Amis was and is
less conservative and differed with his father over the latter's support of the U.S. involvement in Vietnam. In the 1970's Martin Amis was on the staff of the leftist *New
Statesman* weekly and a committed anticommunist, particularly after the publication
of Solzhenitsyn's *Gulag Archipelago* (begun in 1973). Among his fellow young writ-

ers on the magazine was Christopher Hitchens, who was a Trotskyist Communist (Trotsky had been expelled from the Soviet Union in the 1920's and later was murdered on Stalin's orders). In writing *Koba the Dread*, Amis is discussing the same questions which he and Hitchens had debated twenty-five years earlier—whether Stalin was any different from Lenin and whether the Soviet Union under Stalin was any better than Hitler's Nazi Germany. In a very real sense, *Koba the Dread* is written to Hitchens.

One question which Amis asks in *Koba the Dread* is what were the motives which led to the murder of millions in the Soviet Union during the Stalin era. The stated ideology of Marxism, at least as implemented in the Soviet Union, envisioned violent class conflict with the class enemies (the bourgeoisie, the wealthier peasants or *kulaks*, or however "enemies" were defined) being eliminated and destroyed, and Amis traces the murderous violence of the Soviet regime back past Stalin to Lenin himself and the 1917 Bolshevik Revolution. On the other hand, Amis also suggests that Stalin killed and murdered simply for its own sake, noting Stalin's claim that "Death solves all problems. No man, no problem." When arrested, many victims asked "Zachto?" or "What for?" Guilty of nothing, there could be no answer and no answer was needed. As the nineteenth century British historian Lord Acton noted, "Power tends to corrupt and absolute power corrupts absolutely."

Another issue Amis confronts are the differences, if any, between Soviet communism and German fascism or Nazism, or between what Amis calls the Little Mustache (Hitler) and the Big Mustache (Stalin). Many intellectuals, historians, and pundits, while noting that both regimes killed millions of human beings, claim that the Bolshevik ideology of Marx and Lenin descended directly from the eighteenth century Enlightenment in its attempt to establish a society based on social justice. Nazism was its antithesis, with its commitment to the pseudoscience of racial purity and the resulting genocide of the Jews. Thus, the atrocious crimes of the Soviet Union can be characterized as less heinous because their stated goals were enlightened and egalitarian. Amis is not convinced of this ends-justify-the-means argument, arguing that at most the Nazi Holocaust against Jews and others was merely more precise than the holocausts in the Soviet Union (the gulag, the famines, the political trials and executions) which were, he argues, more random but no less deadly. For Amis, both regimes were equally immoral. Yet why have not the twenty million Soviet victims had equivalency with the Holocaust dead in the public mind and record?

Amis believes the answer is a willful failure of Western intellectuals to accept it, claiming that one illustration of this failure is humor. He points out that it has long been acceptable, both within the Soviet Union and elsewhere, to joke about the failures of the Soviet system, such as the fact that exploding television sets was the leading cause of fire in the Soviet Union. Another joke was, why is the Soviet Union the same as America? Because in the Soviet Union one can joke about America and in America one can joke about America. More pointed, for Amis, is not just the humor of the general population but the humor, or lack of it, among intellectuals like himself and Hitchens toward Nazi Germany and the Soviet Union. Amis relates that back in their *New Statesman* days, he questioned Hitchens about the famines of the 1930's in the Soviet Union, and Hitchens responded that there were no famines, only "shortages," a comment that Hitchens denies ever making. Again, in a 1999 London debate over the European Union, Hitchens, addressing the assembly, commented that he knew the venue of the meeting hall well, having been there often with many "an old comrade," a remark that engendered much laughter. Amis questions whether there would have been the same response if Hitchens had identified himself as a former fascist, and doubts it. One laughs at—or ignores—the crimes of the Big Mustache but not those of the Little Mustache.

"Letter to a Friend," the final section of *Koba the Dread*, begins with a long letter to Hitchens (over ten pages in length in the text) written while on a holiday in Uruguay. After humorous references to Gregor Samsa (from Franz Kafka's 1915 novella *Die Verwandlung*, or *The Metamorphosis*, 1936), Hamlet, the novelist Vladimir Nabokov, and Friedrich Nietzsche, Amis, again humorously, addresses Hitchens as Comrade Hitchens. Still continuing the long dialogue between them, he asks "Why you [Hitchens] wouldn't want to put more distance between yourself and these events than you do, with your reverence for Lenin and your unregretted discipleship of Trotsky. These two men did not just precede Stalin. They created a fully functioning police state for his later use." Without disowning them, Amis claims, Hitchens implicitly condones the policy of terror which resulted in the death of millions of innocent victims. The 1917 Bolshevik Revolution, Amis argues, was not a Revolution which ultimately failed; rather, it was a counterrevolution which succeeded only too well.

Koba the Dread begins with a brief description of Amis's life in the 1960's with his father, Kingsley, and the book ends with a postscript addressed to his father: "Afterword: Letter to My Father's Ghost." In it, he tells his father of the recent death of Sally, Kingsley's daughter and Martin's sister. He then compares the novels written by father and son, contrasting the subject matter, which was perhaps due to the generational differences between them. Most significantly, however, Amis notes that his father was ideological and he is not, and "probably to my detriment, I never felt the call of the political faith (and probably one should feel it, one should be zealous, for a while)." The letter and the book concludes, "Your middle child hails you and embraces you."

The postmodernist mixture of the individual and the personal with the historic and the public in *Koba the Dread* can be criticized as overly confessional and self-indulgent or be regarded affecting and involving, depending upon the response of the reader. However, the issues Amis raises about the failure of the intellectuals to condemn the disastrous Soviet experiment might resonate in greater depth with British rather than American readers. The United States differs from Britain in history and culture. There is nothing in American society that quite compares with the power and influence that the Oxford and Cambridge elite and the city of London exert upon political and intellectual Britain, the possible claims of America's Ivy League universities, New York City, and Washington, D.C., to the contrary. Amis is addressing Britain's intellectual community, a community which does not exist in the diverse and largely ahistorical America where Stalinist intellectuals played little role in public policy and perception.

Eugene Larson

Sources for Further Study

The Atlantic Monthly 290 (September, 2002): 144.
Booklist 98 (May 1, 2002): 1442.
Commentary 114 (October, 2002): 71.
Library Journal 127 (June 1, 2002): 169.
London Review of Books 24 (October 17, 2002): 21.
New Statesman 131 (September 2, 2002): 12.
The New York Times Book Review 107 (July 28, 2002): 7.
Publishers Weekly 249 (May 20, 2002): 55.

LANDS OF MEMORY

Author: Felisberto Hernández (1902-1964)
Translated from the Spanish by Esther Allen
Publisher: New Directions (New York). 190 pp. $24.95
Type of work: Short fiction
Time: The early to mid-twentieth century
Locale: Uruguay and Argentina

～

The intricate reflections of a Uruguayan pianist

～

Principal characters:
THE AUTHOR, the narrator/protagonist
CLEMENTE COLLING, his piano teacher
SEÑORA MUÑECA, a widow
FILOMENA (DOLLY), her maid
THE FRIEND, a poet and concert promoter
THE POETRY RECITER, a young woman to whom the narrator is attracted

Esther Allen, the translator of *Lands of Memory*, provides in the prologue a small biography of Felisberto Hernández in which she outlines his peculiar life (he was a concert pianist who began as a piano player for silent films when he was twelve, he recorded the titles of tango music on state radio to protect the composers from theft, he worked as a stenographer, he started a bookstore that failed because he paid no attention to it, and he had four wives) and his humorous and eccentric way of seeing things (for example, "He had a habit of comparing pianos to coffins," and "His purpose, if he has one . . . is to immerse the reader in a shifting sequence of states of being and mysterious mental processes"). Indeed, it is the narrator's eccentricity in perceiving himself and the people and objects around him that define the main character (who is the author himself) of the two short novels and four short stories that compose this collection.

In the first of the short stories, "My First Concert in Montevideo," the narrator, practicing in his family's house for the concert in the title, is dispirited by the violence of his father's creditors, by his separation from his wife and daughter in another city, and by a pessimism about himself which carries over to the concert when he gives it, remembering how the first concert he ever gave brought him little money and no entrance into unfamiliar houses.

In fact, he is so depressed that he dreams of his wife moving toward their wedding by herself, while he is a dog dragged slowly along on her bridal train. As he is about to go on stage for his recital in Montevideo, he imagines his piano as a shark he will have to wrestle in "an illuminated swimming pool." When he starts playing, he begins to feel "a confidence born from madness."

~

Felisberto Hernández was a concert pianist in Uruguay and Argentina in his twenties and a state bureaucrat after that. He had four wives, spent several years in Paris writing, published seven books, and died poor.

~

His dark mood brings up the memory of the one new house he managed to enter after his former recital, when he was hired by a jilted widow to play the piano twice a week for her. Her name is Señora Muñeca, and her maid Filomena (or Dolly) introduces the narrator to the house and reveals things about the widow (especially that her lover, after composing a tango for her on her piano, ran away with another woman), but since Dolly addresses the narrator in the familiar form of "you," smokes cigarettes, and tries to bully him into her bed, she disgusts him, as does Señora Muñeca herself, who is repulsively tiny, wall-eyed, prissy, demanding, and a drunk.

The narrator's memory, on the other hand, does not exclude "moments of happiness," such as his feeling the morning after the concert in Montevideo. It is a mingling of joy, repugnance, and even humor that ends the story: He woke up and saw in the bed he shared with two of his friends "a mouse that had approached the sleeping head of one of the painters and was eating his hair."

"Mistaken Hands" consists of letters the narrator writes to three women (Irene, Inés, and Margarita), in which he writes about the "unknown," mostly the mysterious details of strangers' movements, such as a woman turning her head in a theater, or a woman hiding her laughter with a handkerchief. As he writes to Irene, anguish comes to him from the unknown, while to Inés he writes of her mysteriousness to him—how "Through the loose weave of your hat brim, the light cast arabesques of shadow on the upper part of your face"—and how it makes his memory of her a dream with a space in it for a feeling that will surprise him. Writing to Irene again, he gives her a list of things he wants to happen, the order of which is without the logic of drama, causing him to suspect "that reality is sometimes intrinsically dark and confused," and in tandem with this, when he writes to Margarita, he says he imagines his letters falling "into the abyss of the mystery of extraordinary women." Pausing for a moment to resume writing to Irene, he remarks that the unknown can spring up in the act of unexpectedly comparing the eyes of a dead acquaintance to the eyes of a woman he is talking to—that is, in a collision of the past with the present—then, returning to Margarita, he explains what the "mistaken hands" of the title mean: They are his own hands futilely writing and receiving letters to find "a little mystery," which he admits he probably makes up himself, although he also admits that his pursuit of the unknown is a distraction that pleases him.

In "The Crocodile," the narrator is a traveling salesman for a brand of women's stockings called Illusion; he has made up his own slogan for the brand: "Nowadays, who doesn't cherish their Illusions?" His sales record is dismal (as he says, "a concert pianist who sold stockings made a bad impression"), but then he learns to weep spontaneously in front of shopkeepers and soon his sales improve. Some women try to comfort him when he does this—one of them points out that a secret distress in him causes his tears (he already knows it is at least self-pity)—while other women do not, for when he pulls his stunt of weeping at a concert he is giving, one of them shouts from the audience, "Crooo-co-diiiiile!" At the end of the story, the narrator finds that just as the dingy harp player at the beginning of the story cannot help his blindness, he himself cannot help weeping, and thus his tears, whether he intends to fake them or not, reveal the true condition of his soul.

"The New House" is set in motion by the narrator trying to distract himself from his poverty and from his poet-friend's so-far failed attempt to arrange a concert for him by looking at the houses outside the café in which he is writing. He focuses on a house which gives off a "strident white light" in its desolate newness, and because he feels guilty for manipulating his friend to promote him, he hates this house. Then, aware how pleasurable contradictions are to him, he remembers that he once entered the house at which he is looking. This happened when he and his poet-friend, at the conclusion of a successful performance they had given together, were invited to the house by an elderly poet on the city council and his daughter, "a reciter of poetry." This girl aroused contradictory feelings in the narrator, for though he was infatuated with her, she also repelled him by saying "vulgar things with false emotion." Her house is now the very one to which his poet-friend takes him to propose the concert, for the elderly poet is now the mayor. Caught between his hatred of the house and the sudden likelihood of his concert being funded by its owner, the narrator is presented with the pleasure of contradiction.

Two short novels which begin and end the collection. The first, "Around the Time of Clemente Colling," describes the narrator's piano teacher, and the second, "Lands of Memory," shows how the narrator came to be the way he is. In "Around the Time of Clemente Colling," the narrator reveals that he came to his teacher because his blind cousin Elnene was Colling's student. He concentrates on the mixture of Colling's characteristics as he saw them when he was an adolescent, not the least of which is Colling's own blindness. He describes how one of the teacher's eyes is missing because of a failed operation, and what the other looks like when it moves, and how Colling uses his hands since he cannot see.

In addition, remembering his Aunt Petrona, who is adept at seeing how people show off to hide what they do not want to be seen about themselves, the narrator re- members how Colling, who has lost his fame and has gone to seed, especially in his habits (he sleeps with his shoes on and he is infested with bugs) parades his memories of better times, such as when the composer Camille Saint-Saëns praised him for his ability to improvise on the piano. The narrator sees that the memories of others are less interesting to him than his own memories of them, for when Colling is going on about himself, the narrator is too distracted by other things to keep up with what Colling is saying, nor is he able, though he knows his teacher is a masterful organist and has a "great faculty for memorizing and improvisation," and though he cares about him, to regard Colling's work as anything but sad, as though he were "a child who loves a vulgar toy and clings to it tenderly." In the end, Colling, for the narrator, is an example of the mystery of the human soul exhibited by memories in which "it wasn't only objects that had shadows," but "events . . . and feelings and ideas," mak- ing the remembering observer half-blind to the whole truth of another's character.

"Lands of Memory" details the growth of the author's memory and his perception of what it contains, both of which are the principal vehicle of the other stories. At the start, the narrator thinks that in leaving Montevideo, "I would have to change my life," and this understanding, along with the disgusting presence of Mandolión, a musician on his way to a job with the narrator in another city, impels him to remember a similar train ride nine years earlier when he was fourteen and on his way to Chile on the equivalent of a Boy Scout trip. Since Mandolión is pushy, has grotesque feet in yellow shoes, and "look[s] bloated, like a dead animal," the narrator flees from him through his memory of when "my first acquaintance with life began," which was in a school where one of the two female instructors infatuated him, so that he dreamed of stroking her arms, and he "gaze[d] up at her as if she were a cathedral."

This memory foreshadows another, this one of the young woman he calls the "poetry reciter," whom he encountered in Mendoza, Argentina, on the Scout trip, a girl whose stance he describes as "between the infinite and a sneeze"—the same image he uses for the poetry reciter in "The New House." In order to explain his memory of this woman, he shows how his body intervenes when thoughts disconnected from it are having a secret conference in his head, and how his body also allows him, by making him feel comfortable, to deal with "the mysteries to which my imagination was drawn," such as the poetry reciter. As he regards her, the narrator sees both how pretentious and how physically alluring she is, though she is much heavier and taller than he. Remembering a history lesson about goddesses, he tries to compare her "strides" to the movements of the goddesses as he remembers them, but the poetry reciter collapses his flattery by saying that her strides have "staging," then degrades his romantic words by talking about the future of reciting poetry and what it is currently selling for in "the Buenos Aires theaters."

The narrator realizes that just as his body attacks the piano like a tiger to capture a piece of music new to him, his feeling pursues a woman with the same sort of violence, and he adds that his desire for and clumsiness with an unfamiliar melody compare to his approach to a woman he does not know yet, "who has been sleeping somewhere in a forest," as he puts it. This violence saturates his impression of the poetry reciter when he is surprised to find her telling others at a party for the Scouts that someone her parents had hired for their sausage shop explained to them what "roast cat" was. Not only does he become disappointed in her enough to shift his earlier attraction to her arms (much as he had been attracted to the arms of his teacher in the school) to a picture of her hands "in her sausage shop, wrapping up a thick, pale slab of lard," but he also has a nightmare about three doors which terrifies him enough to scream himself awake. As he falls halfway back to sleep and repossesses the dream, he sees the three doors are from a story he remembers in which the owners of a sausage shop in Europe kill some of their clientele behind one of three doors in it and add this "human flesh and blood" to the pork items which have made them hugely successful. He also connects his scream to the soul of the cat in the poetry reciter's story, seeing its soul "navigating within that sound" toward freedom from the torment of its death. Cleansed of his terror by his memory and of his amorous confusion by connecting the poetry reciter to the violence, he comes to see her "simply as a person who was strange," and to understand, for his own sake, that the mystery of things depends less on his memory than on his ability to imagine them in a new light.

Much of what Felisberto Hernández presents in his stories is comic, for at their center is a narrator/protagonist who behaves like someone making fun of himself and others with a straight face. Behind the humor, however, is a description of his perceptions, memories, and feelings so meticulous and luminous as to be amazing.

Mark McCloskey

Sources for Further Study

Artforum 9 (Summer, 2002): 21.
The Nation 275 (October 7, 2002): 31.
The New York Times Book Review 107 (July 7, 2002): 22.
Publishers Weekly 249 (June 3, 2002): 62.

THE LAST GIRLS

Author: Lee Smith (1944-   )
Publisher: Algonquin Books (Chapel Hill, N.C.). 384 pp.
   $24.95
Type of work: Novel
Time: The early 1960's to 1999
Locale: Mary Scott College, Virginia, and the *Belle of Natchez*, a Mississippi River luxury steamboat

~

Four middle-aged former college roommates take a cruise down the Mississippi to scatter the ashes of a fifth roommate, which provides an opportunity for storytelling and reflection

~

   Principal characters:
   MARGARET "BABY" BALLOU, a charismatic Southern belle who has
      recently died in an "accidental" car crash
   HARRIET HOLDING, an unmarried woman who still holds herself respon-
      sible for her childhood friend Jefferson Carr's accidental death after
      his break-up with Baby
   CATHERINE WILSON, a successful sculptor whose third husband, Russell,
      is having a midlife crisis
   COURTNEY RALSTON, a woman torn between her responsibilities to her
      ailing husband and her lover's demands that she leave her husband for
      him
   ANNA TODD, a successful romance novelist whose early stories of Appa-
      lachian life were deemed "too upsetting" for the reading public

   Lee Smith's tenth novel focuses on five women who were once undergraduate roommates at a Southern women's college. In 1965, inspired by a handsome young instructor's dramatic reading of Mark Twain's *Adventures of Huckleberry Finn* (1884), the five young women joined with six others and sailed down the Mississippi River on a raft, earning some notoriety as local newspapers photographed the spunky college girls and less adventurous, land-bound housewives offered them picnic lunches along the river.

   Thirty-five years later, Harriet Holding, Catherine Wilson, Courtney Ralston, and Anna Todd travel again down the Mississippi, retracing the route of their earlier trip—this time on the *Belle of Natchez*, a luxury cruise ship full of elderly tourists. When the *Belle* docks in New Orleans they will scatter the ashes of a fifth college roommate, Margaret "Baby" Ballou, who drove her car off a bridge—perhaps accidentally, perhaps not—on a beautiful clear day just before Christmas. According to Baby's husband, in the weeks before her death she spoke of reuniting with Harriet,

Anna, Catherine, and Courtney to re-create their youthful trip downriver; now he has contacted each of the women and asked them to make this final voyage with Baby's remains.

Lee Smith's literary awards include an Academy Award in Literature from the American Academy of Arts and Letters (1999), a Robert Penn Warren Prize for Fiction (1991), and a Weatherford Award for Appalachian Literature (1988). The Last Girls *is her tenth novel.*

Baby was a Southern belle, a promiscuous young woman from a wealthy family who could not help behaving badly, rather to Harriet Holding's vicarious delight. Shy Harriet was Baby's roommate in college; on the *Belle of Natchez* trip she brings along several pages of Baby's handwritten poetry from their college days, preserved by Harriet through all the ensuing years. The poems reveal Baby's desperate grief for her deceased mother and younger brother. Baby's mother was apparently a lower-class woman who "drank gin like water/ all day long" and whom her father had forgotten in favor of Baby's more socially acceptable stepmother. Baby's poems also reveal an inner turmoil. A beautiful debutante, she meets social expectations but feels like a "bitch" trapped inside, "locked/ behind [a] chain-link fence/ where she paces/ back and forth."

At Mary Scott College Harriet introduced Baby to her childhood friend Jefferson Carr. It seemed briefly to Harriet that she and Jeff might have become a couple, but instead Jeff and Baby were drawn together and began a passionate romance. Jeff, solid and dependable, was a student at Shenandoah Military Institute and planned a career as an officer, but he jeopardized those plans when he broke several school rules in efforts to entertain Baby. When she broke up with the adoring Jeff ("if you could possibly/ Assist me off this pedestal please/ It's hurting my ass"), Jeff left school in despair, joined the Army, and was killed in a helicopter crash during basic training.

Harriet's friendship with Baby did not survive Jefferson Carr's death, and Harriet actually has no idea how Baby spent the years since college graduation. Harriet felt partly responsible for Carr's death; shortly after Baby ended her relationship with Carr, Harriet went to see him, intending to try and reunite the doomed couple; instead she had sex with the grieving Jeff herself and left without mentioning Baby. Harriet has lived for years with the guilt of having (in her view) allowed the great true love between Baby Ballou and Jefferson Carr to perish; believing her intervention could have saved their romance and thus Jefferson's life, Harriet has never married or even seriously dated, never allowing herself to build the sort of domestic life she thinks Baby and Jeff might have had together.

Courtney Gray Ralston finds herself torn between Hawk Ralston, her philandering husband of thirty-five years, and Gene Minor, her long-time lover. After several years of clandestine meetings, Minor has suddenly demanded that Courtney leave her husband, although Hawk is becoming increasingly confused and forgetful and Courtney feels it would be inappropriate to desert him. Courtney has worked hard to maintain an image of Southern gentility in her marriage to the wealthy Hawk, even while he has been habitually unfaithful to her. Courtney struggles to convince herself that Hawk is fine; during the cruise, however, a series of telephone calls to her daughter, her housekeeper, and her husband's secretary bring home the fact that Hawk's confusion is a serious problem. As Minor presses her to make a final decision between himself and Hawk, Courtney must choose between her personal happiness and the socially correct, conservative course of staying with her husband.

Anna Todd has become a famous romance novelist, with thirty-two steamy novels to her credit. Anna once wrote literary fiction, inspired by her childhood in the backwoods and hollers of Appalachia; when publishers rejected her Appalachian tales as too disturbing for a popular audience, Anna turned to romance. Anna married her college sweetheart, a scholarly graduate student who left her when she surpassed him professionally; realizing she was pregnant, she resolved to bear and raise their child alone, but her baby was stillborn. She then lived with a painter who helped her build a career around romance novels and endorsements, but he died unexpectedly while they were having sex. Anna has since remade herself into a flamboyant, aging diva swathed in layers of chiffon. Although she agrees to accompany the other women on Baby Ballou's final voyage, Anna has worked hard to forget her past and hopes they will not remind her too much of the girl she was in college. She spends most of the cruise alone in her cabin, fantasizing about the cabin boy and writing her thirty-third novel, in which a Louisiana heiress stamps her tiny feet in fury at the swarthy Cajun who will obviously be sweeping her into his powerful arms by the story's end.

Catherine Wilson is accompanied on the *Belle of Natchez* by her third husband, Russell, who is getting on her nerves. Catherine is a successful artist who makes large lawn sculptures from scrap metal; Russell is having a midlife crisis. His comical idiosyncracies include his consuming fear that he will have a heart attack (he actually witnesses another steamboat passenger's death of a heart attack in the steamboat bar) and his obsession with the women meteorologists on the Weather Channel.

The 1965 raft trip forms a disappointingly small part of Smith's story, although it was inspired by an actual raft trip Smith took with her friends in college. Just as Smith and her peers found the river more wild and difficult to travel than expected, the fictional Mary Scott College girls encounter torrential rain, merciless mosquitoes, and an endless diet of tuna sandwiches. The other six college students who traveled down the river on the raft are profiled briefly at the end of the book.

Death plays a greater part in these women's lives than marriages or the births of children; tragic events overtake the women's expectations. Baby Ballou deeply mourned the deaths of her mother and brother; Catherine and Harriet suffered the deaths of younger siblings when they were young; Anna's child was stillborn and her partner died while making love to her; Catherine's second husband was killed in a convenience store robbery. In contrast, births and marriages are barely mentioned— Courtney and Catherine's relationships with their grown children are not close—and seem not to have the same level of impact. These are women who became adults in the early 1960's, when marriages were made out of a sense of obligation and need for respectability.

The Last Girls is a departure for Smith, whose earlier works have told stories of Appalachian life. Challenged to write about women more like herself—educated, successful Southern women—Smith chose to focus on a group of women in their fifties and show that their lives did not follow stereotypical patterns but were rich with comedy, tragedy, and possibilities for change. Harriet, Courtney, Anna, and Catherine are strong characters whose lives embody myriad experiences and challenges met, but in college they were considered "girls" who would need husbands to care for them. The expectation that each would find true love, marry, and live happily ever after proved unrealistic—only Baby, the wild one, appears to have achieved it.

In *The Last Girls* Smith tells a wealth of stories, not only those of the five college roommates, but those of other women and men in their lives. Smith also imbues her characters with their own ideas about, fascination with, and reliance on stories and storytelling. Each of the women protagonists took creative writing classes in college, and each is very creative in ways either directly or indirectly related to telling stories.

Anna writes predictable, comforting genre fiction, compensating for the tragedies she has suffered (Anna notes that romance novels must end just as the lovers unite, before anything can happen to them). Harriet has become a community college English teacher and specializes in helping women write personal stories about their own lives. At one point Anna and Harriet argue about what makes a story a story, Anna insisting that a satisfying, conventional ending is essential to real storytelling. On the *Belle of Natchez* Harriet begins a tentative romance with the ship's official historian, fascinated with his job as a professional storyteller. Even Courtney has created a story of sorts, an image of herself as the perfect Southern lady whose home is a showplace and whose shoes always perfectly match her dress—all carefully documented in voluminous scrapbooks she carries with her on the cruise.

The most poignant story is the one Baby Ballou's husband Charlie Mahan tells in a letter to Harriet. Questions remain about Baby's death. Her story has been told largely through Harriet's memories, and Charlie has the last word as Harriet reads his letter aloud and Baby's ashes are scattered in the Mississippi. Charlie details the devotion Baby (whom he calls "Maggie") felt for her children and grandchildren, and the plans she was making for a traditional family Christmas when she accidentally drove her car off the side of a bridge. Charlie refers obliquely to an ongoing illness of Baby, assuming Harriet will understand, and Harriet, recalling Baby's self-destructive tendencies, believes Baby committed suicide. However, realizing that Baby's life went on after college, Harriet is able to resolve her guilt and move forward in her own.

Maureen J. Puffer-Rothenberg

Sources for Further Study

Atlanta Journal and Constitution, September 22, 2002, p. F1.
Booklist 98 (May 15, 2002): 1555.
Kirkus Reviews 70 (July 1, 2002): 914.
Library Journal 127 (June 15, 2002): 96.
The New York Times Book Review 107 (October 6, 2002): 19.
Publishers Weekly 249 (July 1, 2002): 44.

LAZY B
Growing Up on a Cattle Ranch in the American Southwest

Authors: Sandra Day O'Connor (1930-   ) and H. Alan
   Day
Publisher: Random House (New York). Illustrated. 318
   pp. $24.95
Type of work: Memoir
Time: 1880-1996
Locale: The American Southwest, especially western
   New Mexico and southeastern Arizona

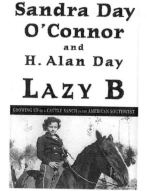

Sandra Day
O'Connor
and
H. Alan Day

LAZY B

GROWING UP on a CATTLE RANCH in the AMERICAN SOUTHWEST

~

*Lazy B, the huge cattle ranch overseen for 113 years by
three generations of the Day family, provides the backdrop
for this intimate memoir by the first woman to be named a
justice in the United States Supreme Court and her brother*

~

Principal personages:
   SANDRA DAY O'CONNOR, the first woman named to the United States
      Supreme Court
   H. ALAN DAY, her brother, nine years her junior
   ANN, her sister, ten years her junior
   HARRY DAY, their father, referred to as DA
   ADA MAE DAY, their mother, referred to as MO
   RAFAEL ESTRADA, nicknamed "Rastus"
   JIM BRISTER,
   CLAUDE TIPPETS, and
   RALPH "BUG" QUINN, all ranch hands on Lazy B

Lazy B began operations in 1880 when the authors' grandfather, H. C. Day, a
transplanted New Englander newly arrived from Wichita, Kansas, decided to claim as
much as he could of the public land made available following the Gadsden Purchase.
The land he was allocated, most of it open range, consisted of 160,000 acres stretch-
ing from western New Mexico well into southeastern Arizona. The total holding,
about one-fifth the size of Rhode Island, made it the largest ranch in the Southwest.
The Lazy B Corporation that H. C. formed owned 8,560 acres. Thirty thousand acres
were leased from Arizona and about twenty-two thousand acres were leased from
New Mexico. The remaining land belonged to the federal government and was overseen by the Bureau of Land Management (BLM), which had a staff of one man and
two secretaries to administer the Safford Grazing District, which totaled some 1.5
million acres.

Although H. Alan Day, Sandra's younger
brother, is listed as coauthor of this book, the
entire text, save possibly for parts of the brief
preface, appears to be written exclusively by
Sandra Day O'Connor, whose intimate memoir is obviously a work of love and of deep
personal commitment. Her sentiments toward
Lazy B and her attachment to it throughout
her lifetime are well expressed toward the end
of the book, where she calls the ranch "a
never-changing anchor in a world of uncer-
tainties." In an interview with Gwen Ifill,
O'Connor credits her brother, who managed

*Sandra Day O'Connor was a lawyer in
private practice and in many branches
of the government, a superior court
judge and a justice of the Arizona
Court of Appeals, as well as an Arizona
state senator, until her appointment by
President Ronald Reagan as the first
female U.S. Supreme Court justice in
1981. H. Alan Day is her younger
brother.*

the Lazy B for many years after their father ceded control to him, with providing details about the ranch and its operations.

In her childhood, living with her parents in this remote outpost some miles southwest of Lordsburg, New Mexico, and a few miles south of Duncan, Arizona, where
some of the ranch children went to school, Sandra enjoyed none of the amenities that
many children in the 1930's took for granted. The Day household did not have electricity, running water, or indoor plumbing. Sandra's parents, although the owners of
vast quantities of land and well over two thousand head of cattle, led a hardscrabble
existence that was proudly self-sufficient but that was generally lacking in ready cash.

During her first decade of life, Sandra was an only child. She was joined by her siblings, H. Alan when she was nine and Ann when she was ten. The family was close.
Its value system was directly influenced by her father, DA, a reasonable but determined man. Some of the ranch hands who helped keep Lazy B going were as close
to the Days as any family members might have been. Rastus, Jim Brister, Bug
Quinn, and others arrived at the ranch with somewhat clouded backgrounds but were
treated so evenhandedly that they felt secure enough to stay on, some for over half a
century.

Citing an old cowboy song, O'Connor writes, "The life of a cowboy was a lot of
hard work, low pay, few female companions, but a great deal of loyalty and pride in
the craft and skill. Most of the time the work went on seven days a week." These
words depict quite well what it was like to be a cowboy in the isolation of the great
southwestern desert. The hands that stayed the longest with the Day family stayed because they were treated fairly and consistently. Many of them had escaped abusive
childhoods from which they had distanced themselves before they reached adolescence. They spoke little of their pasts once they became part of the Days' extended
family. They appreciated the unfailing fairness and consistency they could depend
upon from DA and the obvious concern and understanding of MO.

Sandra O'Connor attributes some of her ease around men to the fact that on the
ranch she was never really treated as a girl. She reports that she "rode occasionally on
the roundup [which] had been an all-male domain. Changing it to accommodate a female was probably my first initiation into joining an all-men's club, something I did

462 Magill's Literary Annual 2003

more than once in my life." She goes on to say that once "the cowboys understood that a girl could hold up her end, it was much easier for my sister, my niece, and the other girls and young women who followed to be accepted in that rough-and-tumble world." O'Connor was never a militant feminist. She never felt the need to be because she was accepted easily within a familial situation in which she interacted with men on a more-or-less equal basis.

The moral values that O'Connor embraced were essentially those of her father, DA, who was reasonable but somewhat absolutist in the areas of morality and values. In Sandra's formative years, her association with DA was close. He and his wife, MO, exemplified in Sandra's mind the ideals of a productive marriage in which each party contributed significantly to the welfare of the other. The Days were upstanding members of their community, which was essentially the large spread of land that comprised the ranch and the areas north and east of it, extending to Duncan and Lordsburg. They were good neighbors, ever ready to come to the rescue of those in need. Sandra learned many lessons in social responsibility from her parents, but particularly from her father, a thoughtful man with a strong sense of right and wrong and a keen appreciation of evenhanded justice.

Through her early life on the ranch, Sandra was exposed to many realities, including death. At times, for the overall good of the ranch, her father, to prevent overgrazing, had to slaughter large numbers of cattle. He did this with regret but with a firm sense of the importance of strengthening the ranch's overall operation through selective slaughtering, particularly at times when water was scarce and when forage was in short supply. One day when Sandra was riding the range with her father, they came upon a calf that had been attacked by a predator that had torn its hind legs to shreds. When DA and Sandra came upon the creature, it was alive but vultures were tearing away its flesh. This was a terrible sight, enough to cause nightmares in one as young as Sandra. She pleaded with her father to take the calf home, hoping that they could nurse it back to health, but DA realized the futility of such an action. Instead, deaf to his daughter's protests, he took his gun from its holster, put it to the calf's head, and pulled the trigger, telling the distraught Sandra that this was the most humane thing he could do for the injured calf.

Knowing that the cow that had given birth to this calf would be looking for her offspring and realizing that some orphan calves in the area did not have a mother from whom they could suckle, DA stripped the outer skin from the dead calf and spread it over an orphaned live calf. He knew that cows identify their offspring mostly through smell and that the mother cow in this instance could probably be deceived into believing that one of the endangered calves was her own. DA's ploy worked. The mother cow, dubious at first, soon accepted the substitute calf as her own and permitted it to suckle. DA saved the life of one small calf by his ingenious tactic, which also taught his daughter a useful lesson about life and death that remained with her throughout her life.

Sandra learned another such lesson from her brother Alan. He was riding Candy, a challenging wild horse that he had been trying to break for a month. The day was very hot, and soon Alan was perspiring fiercely. Candy was also covered with perspiration, her coat glistening and dripping its moisture on the ground. Alan decided that the best course was to go to a watering hole where both he and the horse could cool off. When Alan got Candy to the edge of the water, however, she did not want to go in. Alan cajoled but was wholly unsuccessful in trying to get Candy into the water. Finally, in desperation, he popped his rope between her legs, which caused the startled horse to jump some twenty feet into the water. Only then did Alan discover, to his horror, that Candy could not swim. He had never encountered a horse that could not swim. He did his best to save Candy, but she finally sank irretrievably beneath the surface. A much-chastened Alan realized from that experience that sometimes one must follow the lead of an animal rather then expecting it to follow blindly the lead of a fallible human.

O'Connor demonstrates in this book her significant powers of observation and description. In writing about the dramatic changes a rainstorm can bring about in the parched desert, she writes

> The dry, dusty soil was wet, muddy, brown rivulets of water running down every slope and gully. The grass and plants sparkling with drops of water clinging to them. The greasewood bushes—normally so gray green and dull—releasing their incredible perfume, produced by the rain on their dense oily leaves. The birds chirping frantically, the rabbits peeking out from their burrows. Everything stirring and excited from the rain, and no one more excited than my father. We were saved again—saved from the ever present threat of drought, of starving cattle, of anxious creditors. We would survive for a while longer.

In this passage, O'Connor not only captures the sensual details of what happens in the desert when the long-awaited rain comes, but she also details the practical implications of having the weather change, the drought end. DA always lived in the shadow of those to whom he owed money. He strove ever to be meticulously honest and dependable—a good credit risk—but he, like most ranchers and farmers, was constantly at the mercy of the weather. His daughter well understood the recurrent pressures to which such natural phenomena as a drought could subject him and other ranchers.

Lazy B is arranged as a series of vignettes, each introduced by a set of three or four illustrations. Some of the vignettes are about people, others about the ranch itself or about its activities. Only one of them deals directly with O'Connor's appointment by Ronald Reagan to be a justice of the United States Supreme Court. The book clearly is not about O'Connor as a jurist but about the ranch that produced her and permanently shaped her life. The story unfolds with considerable affection and warmth. *Lazy B* reminds one in many ways of Gladys Taber's *Stillmeadow Seasons* (1950), which, like O'Connor's book, recounts with considerable fondness memories of a locale and of the humans who occupy it.

R. Baird Shuman

Sources for Further Study

Booklist 98 (January 1-15, 2002): 775.
Choice 39 (June, 2002): 1866.
Entertainment Weekly, February 22, 2002, p. 142.
Library Journal 126 (December, 2001): 139.
The New York Times Book Review 107 (February 3, 2002): 10.
Publishers Weekly 248 (December 10, 2001): 62.
The Washington Post Book World, February 3, 2002, p. 2.

LEOPARDS IN THE TEMPLE
The Transformation of American Fiction, 1945-1970

Author: Morris Dickstein (1940-   )
Publisher: Harvard University Press (Cambridge, Mass.).
   242 pp. $15.95
Type of work: Literary criticism

~

Dickstein argues that the American novel was transformed following World War II by Jewish, African American, and other writers outside the mainstream of the nation's culture

~

Principal personages:
   JAMES BALDWIN (1924-1987), African American novelist, playwright, and essayist
   SAUL BELLOW (1915-   ), Nobel Prize-winning Jewish American novelist
   RALPH ELLISON (1914-1994), African American novelist and essayist
   JACK KEROUAC (1922-1969), seminal Beat novelist and poet
   NORMAN MAILER (1923-   ), American novelist and nonfiction writer
   PHILIP ROTH (1933-   ) Jewish American novelist and satirist
   J. D. SALINGER (1919-   ) notoriously reclusive American novelist and short story writer
   JOHN UPDIKE (1932-   ) American novelist and short story writer

A strong case can be made that the period from 1945 to the late 1970's was the golden age of American fiction. More novels likely to be read and studied by future generations were published during this time than any other era. Unlike earlier periods, in which most American writers followed the same schools—Romanticism, realism, naturalism, modernism—the post-World War II era saw a much greater diversity in approaches to the novel and short story. In *Leopards in the Temple: The Transformation of American Fiction, 1945-1970*, Morris Dickstein examines a sizable segment of the writers who created this golden age, focusing primarily on James Baldwin, Saul Bellow, Ralph Ellison, Jack Kerouac, Norman Mailer, Philip Roth, J. D. Salinger, and John Updike.

Dickstein shows how this fiction was heavily influenced by social changes and psychoanalysis and how the jazz, films, and avant-garde painting of the time grew out of similar influences. He is interested in the ways the arts and culture interact and argues that the radicalism associated with the 1960's had firm roots in the 1950's. Disagreeing with most American studies scholars who feel that almost every postwar cultural development was a reflex of Cold War politics, Dickstein sees the baby boom, a

A professor of English at Queens College and the City University of New York Graduate Center, Morris Dickstein is best known for Gates of Eden: American Culture in the Sixties *(1977), which received a National Book Critics Circle nomination for criticism. His other publications include* Double Agent: The Critic and Society *(1992).*

consistently healthy economy, increased educational opportunities, the growing youth culture, and the shifting roles of women, African Americans, and other ethnic minorities as being the major influences.

This changing society was more open to social differences yet still resistant to political dissent and social criticism, creating the necessary tension for literary achievement. Dickstein sees the most significant fiction writers of the time as those who offered commentary about a changing world, especially those who were in some sense outsiders and questioned official values. Such writers can be considered "canaries in the mine, an early warning system whose messages can be understood only in retrospect."

These outsiders included women, African Americans, Jews, Catholics, homosexuals, those with working-class backgrounds, and those who identified with the new youth culture. Dickstein is a bit inconsistent in applying this thesis throughout *Leopards in the Temple*. Flannery O'Connor, for example, is the only woman writer who truly interests him, and he does not discuss any of her works in any detail. Some writers under consideration, such as John Barth, John Cheever, James Jones, Kurt Vonnegut, Jr., and Richard Yates, do not fit into any of Dickstein's outsider categories. This inconsistency does not, however, negate the value of his analyses of the writers included.

Dickstein's title comes from Franz Kafka's *Parables and Paradoxes* (1958): "Leopards break into the temple and drink to the dregs what is in the sacrificial pitchers; this is repeated over and over again; finally it can be calculated in advance, and it becomes part of the ceremony." He sees characters created by many mid-twentieth century American writers as being like these leopards: "implosions of the irrational, children of the Freudian century, sharp-clawed primitives who would somehow be integrated into the once-decorous rites of American literature, who would *become* American literature." Such writers capture the unease of the middle class during the era in which it seemingly triumphed. They also strove to bring sex out into the open for the first time. Dickstein observes that left-wing critics, seeking change in a conventional political form, were blind to the ongoing cultural revolution.

Writers such as Bellow and Roth turned inward, grappling with the problems of ego, identity, anxiety, and alienation, reflecting societal concerns as the white middle class retreated into the protective shell of the suburbs. Mailer is a representative writer because of his evolution from the relatively conventional, realistic approach of *The Naked and the Dead* (1948) to a deeper concern with the self, accompanied by a more surreal technique, in *The Deer Park* (1955) and *An American Dream* (1965). "By cultivating the self," writes Dickstein, "not entirely without a certain narcissism, these writers found new ways of writing the history of their times, an age of prosperity and therapy when the exigent, imperial self became the obsessive concern of many Americans." As fiction was increasingly challenged in the 1960's by journalism and film, it became even more self-conscious.

While writers of the 1930's embraced Marxism, the postwar novelists turned to Freud, existentialism, or, in the case of O'Connor and Updike, theology, looking for answers to the contemporary malaise. In creating self-portraits, Dickstein argues, they accurately portrayed their times. He does not ignore the occasional drawbacks to this approach, acknowledging that writers' self-absorption could be embarrassing, as could their attitudes about race and, particularly, women. The best writers of the 1950's and 1960's are nevertheless admirable for being "faithful to their aesthetic conscience, to the gospel according to James and Joyce, Kafka and Proust, even when the results showed up their own faults of craft or character."

In his chapter on World War II fiction, Dickstein observes that the best of such writing is not primarily about war. Mailer's *The Naked and the Dead* is more about politics and ideas and prefigures the social criticism of writers such as Vance Packard and David Reisman. Mailer depicts an army more concerned with organizational values and social conformity than with patriotic ideals. This view of the military as a soulless bureaucracy reaches its apex in Joseph Heller's *Catch-22* (1961). Dickstein considers Jones's *From Here to Eternity* (1951) the best World War II novel in part because of its focus on the outsider trapped in the unsympathetic social world of the army. Jones makes the military stockade "a metaphor for the mass organization's efforts to stamp out resistance and individual identity" and anticipates the nonconformity of Salinger's *The Catcher in the Rye* (1951) and Kerouac's *On the Road* (1957). With his second war novel, *The Thin Red Line* (1962), Jones demonstrates how the postwar writers were influenced by their times as he incorporates an absurdist view similar to those in *Catch-22* and Vonnegut's *Mother Night* (1961), books that anticipated the tone of the Vietnam War era. The war fiction of the 1960's "reflected a sense of national vulnerability we felt at the peak of our world power, as well as our loss of the moral certainty we had briefly enjoyed."

Dickstein writes sympathetically about the homosexual-as-ultimate-outsider fiction of Baldwin, Paul Bowles, Truman Capote, Gore Vidal, and Tennessee Williams, seeing the latter's short stories as greatly undervalued. Such writers are "bold in exploring a dangerous new terrain, lyrical in evoking both a lost innocence and a utopia of personal freedom." However, he considers this fiction as having less resonance than works by African American and Jewish writers. Dickstein praises Bellow and Ellison for taking "the new style of personal fable in a more social, moral, and ethnic direction, away from the violent aestheticism and lurid primitivism foreshadowed by Capote and Bowles."

Salinger's Holden Caulfield establishes the line of adolescent rebels "whose lives are an epic of thwarted sensitivity," while creating the prototype of counterculture novels with a misfit going on the road while experiencing a degree of mental instability representing his refusal to fit into an unsympathetic society. Kerouac carries Salinger's theme further by presenting subversive rebels more energetically challenging the age's conservative values. As much as Dickstein admires Kerouac's achievement and influence, he realizes that *On the Road* "is somehow a great book without being a good novel. Too much . . . happens mainly because it happened, with little dramatic buildup or consequence." It is ultimately more significant as a cultural icon than as an aesthetic achievement.

Dickstein writes especially passionately about Updike, whose Rabbit Angstrom novels best capture the middle-class disappointment in the prosperity of the postwar period. Like Mailer and Roth, Updike also conveys a sense of male energy and potential hampered by a culture dominated by mediocrity and mindless routine. Rabbit is a central figure because he wants not just personal freedom but something indefinable beyond freedom. Updike stands out for exploring sexual freedom and traditional theological values at the same time.

Deeper into the 1960's, the best American writers offered a much darker perspective than seen in the previous decade. Thus, in *An American Dream*, Mailer drops his earlier realistic stance altogether to present a paranoid hallucination, resembling a vivid merging of Fyodor Dostoyevsky and Jim Thompson. Dickstein, who admires Mailer's nonfiction such as *The Armies of the Night* (1968) even more than his fiction, praises the writer's continuous quest for personal freedom. He calls this larger-than-life figure the "Orson Welles of American literature."

Dickstein seems to find Bellow's ego less enchanting, saying that often the Nobel laureate is really analyzing himself in the guise of depicting his protagonists. In his later fiction, the novelist almost leaves fiction behind in exploring his crankiness, dismissing all points of view but his own. Yet in *Mr. Sammler's Planet* (1970), Bellow still offers a definitive portrait of the moral turmoil of the 1960's, and *Humbolt's Gift* (1975) is his "most purely enjoyable book, tolerant, self-critical, and humane."

Bellow, Bernard Malamud, Baldwin, and Ellison stand out for presenting their portraits of Jews and African Americans more as symbolic than sociological. Unlike Bellow, Baldwin maintains some distance from his emotions, having the ability to step back from his feelings and analyze them objectively. (Dickstein praises varying degrees of this quality in several other writers, establishing it as one of his main criteria for excellence.) Throughout his career, Baldwin struggles to keep his "ironic and prophetic voices in balance." Dickstein sees a moral and aesthetic conservatism underlying Baldwin's fiction and essays.

He interprets the hero of Ellison's *Invisible Man* (1952) as an outsider not just because of his blackness but because of his rejection, like the protagonists of Salinger and Kerouac, of what passes for an ordered life. Like the heroes of the road novels, he must run to survive. Dickstein takes interpreters of *Invisible Man* to task for paying little attention to the Brotherhood sections in which Ellison pulls his many threads together. He especially admires Ellison's insights into cultural pluralism and how he makes his novel emblematic of all aspects of African American life.

Dickstein shows how Roth, like Mailer, gradually progressed from realism to a more distinctively personal, postmodern style. Dickstein can be faulted for paying too little attention to style (the quality above all others that makes great writers great), but he does a good job of explaining how Roth explores a "language closer to speech" while also employing self-conscious metaphors in the vein of his master, Henry James. Roth is notable, says Dickstein, for turning insecurity into art and for rivaling

Bellow as a novelist of ideas. He sees *Sabbath's Theater* (1995) as the last novel of the 1960's, a dark, angry, paranoid book full of surreal fantasies and sexual and verbal excesses.

Dickstein feels passionately about these writers and constantly transmits his excitement over the aesthetic and intellectual qualities in their fiction. This passion, along with his unusually lucid style, and his insight into postwar cultural values and how they and fiction intermingle, make *Leopards in the Temple* a powerful study of its subject.

Michael Adams

Sources for Further Study

Los Angeles Times Book Review, May 26, 2002, p. 13.
The New York Times Book Review 107 (May 19, 2002): 49.
The New Yorker 78 (May 13, 2002): 95.
The Times Literary Supplement, November 15, 2002, p. 21.

LESTER LEAPS IN
The Life and Times of Lester "Pres" Young

Author: Douglas Henry Daniels (1943-   )
Publisher: Beacon Press (Boston). Illustrated. 524 pp.
   $30.00
Type of work: Biography, fine arts, and history
Time: 1909-1959
Locale: The United States, Canada, and Western Europe

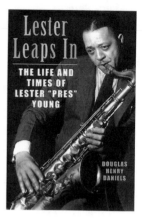

≈

*A sympathetic, revisionist account of the life of a preem-
inent tenor saxophonist whose career illuminates not only
the evolution of jazz but also twentieth century African
American social and cultural life*

≈

   Principal personages:
      LESTER YOUNG, (1909-1959) the most important jazz musician of the
         middle third of the twentieth century, whose revolutionary contribu-
         tions bridged traditional and modern jazz
      COUNT BASIE, (1904-1984) a successful bandleader and pianist who
         helped make Lester Young into an international star
      BILLIE HOLIDAY, (1915-1959) a superlative jazz singer whose empathy
         with Lester Young resulted in a series of influential recordings

   In his film, "Kansas City," director Robert Altman dramatized the most famous
saxophone duel in the history of jazz. In his dramatization, this fabled "cutting contest" between Coleman Hawkins and Lester Young is witnessed by a teenaged Charlie Parker, who would later become pivotal in creating modern jazz. Douglas Daniels
analyzes this much-discussed event in his comprehensive biography of Lester Young,
and his analysis illustrates his underlying mind-set (and heart-set), purposes, and
methods. As an African American, he wants to believe the testimony of such musicians as Count Basie and Mary Lou Williams who claimed they were present when
Lester Young, an unknown saxophonist with an idiosyncratic style and ethereal tone,
outplayed Coleman Hawkins, a renowned saxophonist with a swaggering style and
hefty tone, but their conflicting, even contradictory versions mean that, as a critical
historian, he has to question the veracity of their accounts.

   Such stories about Young were uncritically accepted in previous articles and
books, but Daniels's purpose is to demythologize Young's life and to understand his
career in its African American context. Daniels, who makes use of previous biographies, spent more than twenty years studying materials in archives and libraries and
interviewing many of Young's relatives, friends, and fellow musicians.

   Daniels's reinterpretation of Young begins with his roots. Lester spent much of his youth in southern Louisiana, where he experienced both sacred music in the African Methodist Episcopal Church and secular music in the jazz bands of New Orleans. Willis Handy Young, his father, was an itinerant musician and teacher, and Lizette, his mother, was a religious Creole who instilled such Christian values as honesty and personal responsibility into Lester and his younger sister Irma and brother Lee. However, Daniels's creation of a supportive familial and religious environment for the young Lester is problematic, since it contradicts Young's own memories—admittedly often faulty. He claimed that he did not meet his father until he was ten years old, and he insisted that it was the music of New Orleans bands and not black church music or his father's music that influenced him. This uncertainty also characterizes a momentous event in Lester's youth. In 1919, his father took him and his siblings away from their mother. Willis had married "Sarah," who played saxophone and banjo in his bands. According to his sister, Lester was devastated about leaving his mother, but he characteristically kept his feelings to himself.

In his new family circumstances, Lester learned to play drums, and the rhythmic sensibility he absorbed from this experience later influenced his improvisations on tenor saxophone. The years from 1919 to 1926 were important for Lester's musical education. He switched from drums to alto saxophone in his father's band because he found caring for the drums cumbersome and time-consuming. The Young family settled briefly in Minneapolis, but the family band also toured through Nebraska, Kansas, and the Dakotas. Lester often disliked the music and skits he was forced to perform and sometimes disobeyed his father, who occasionally beat him, causing Lester to run away. When he refused to accompany the family band on a tour of the South, whose racism he despised, Lester Young left his family for good.

The late 1920's and early 1930's constitute what Daniels calls Young's "territorial years." He switched from alto to tenor saxophone and began creating his distinctive style. In his father's bands he had learned to improvise, and his solos were often infused with a feeling for the blues. However, according to Lester himself, the most important influence on how he played the tenor was Frankie Trumbauer, a white musician who was able to produce a light, airy tone on his C-melody saxophone. Lester tried to re-create Trumbauer's sound on the tenor by reducing his vibrato and creating sounds that were much gentler than those of other saxophonists. He was able to refine his tone and develop his improvisational skills while touring with such bands as Wal-

Douglas Henry Daniels received his bachelor's degree from the University of Chicago and his doctorate at the University of California at Berkeley. His first book was Pioneer Urbanites: A Social and Cultural History of Black San Francisco *(1980). Most of his academic career has been spent at the University of California at Santa Barbara, where he is a professor of history and black studies.*

ter Page's Blue Devils. So impressed were his fellow musicians with his seemingly inexhaustible musical imagination that they gave him the honorific "Pres," which was short for "President of the Tenor Saxophone."

Seeking a stability that his nomadic life had denied him, in 1930 Young married Beatrice Toliver, a white woman, in New Mexico, and they settled for a time in Minneapolis. Daniels is unable to explain the details of this relationship, for, in its early years, Young fathered a child with another woman in Minneapolis. This daughter later claimed that Lester had married her mother, who was white, and he had grieved over her early death.

During the 1930's, Young's style ripened into something revolutionary. His carefully chosen processions of notes and silences now seemed to float above the chord changes. He once bragged that he could play a hundred choruses and never repeat himself. Even his way of holding his horn—obliquely away from his body—was unique. His clothing became distinctive, with porkpie hats and ankle-length coats. He started smoking marijuana regularly and preferred the company of musicians who shared his habit. Daniels also credits him with originating many terms that are now part of jazz argot, including "cool" for "controlled."

Young's uncommon behavior extended to his personal life. When he joined Count Basie's band in 1936, he also left his wife. Daniels interprets Young's action as an artist's willingness to sacrifice personal relationships in his search for creative fulfilment, but one wonders about Beatrice's views on the subject. Nevertheless, Young was able to help make Basie's band into one of the greatest ensembles in jazz history, and through tours, radio broadcasts, and recordings Basie helped make Young internationally famous. Evidence of Young's evolution as a storytelling improvisor can be heard in the recordings he made with Basie and as an accompanist to Billie Holiday, the band's female singer in the late 1930's. His rapport with Holiday was deeply empathetic, and whenever she sang with him she was at her best. Young was a "singer-like" player, and he believed that musicians should know the lyrics of the songs they played, since meaningful improvisations involved exploring the emotional intent of a piece. Many writers feel that Pres made his most important contributions through these small groups. For example, his first recording of his signature tune, "Lester Leaps In" was with Basie's Kansas City Seven.

In 1937, Young began a relationship with Mary Dale, an Italian American, and they lived together for a time in Harlem. Some thought they were married, but Daniels could find no record of this. As an interracial couple, Lester and Mary met with disapproval, even rejection, and Young suffered because of these racist attitudes. Daniels also explores the racism that the Basie band encountered. The music business was dominated by whites, and African American bands needed white backing for hotel jobs, tours, radio broadcasts, and recordings, but black bands were often excluded from the most lucrative contracts.

By the end of 1940, the magic of the Basie years had vanished for Lester. The early death of Herschel Evans, his friendly rival on tenor saxophone, darkened his mood, and he also resented how the businessmen behind Basie meddled in music matters. After leaving Basie, he played in small groups around New York before moving to Los Angeles in 1941, when he visited his parents and formed a band with his brother, an excellent jazz drummer. Their band had success both on the West Coast and in New York City, where they were playing when the brothers learned of the final illness of their father. Lee cared for his father until his death and arranged for the funeral, whereas Lester, unwilling to see his father in a coffin, remained in New York.

During World War II Young played for various bands and became romantically involved with a Canadian woman Daniels calls "Teddy Bear." Though both were already married, they began living together. According to her, Young was suffering from epilepsy, and she and others witnessed some of his seizures. He was making heavy use of alcohol and marijuana to assuage his problems, which included the draft board's pursuit of him.

Young passionately feared the military. He hated its institutional racism and he hated its suppression of individuality. Finally, in 1944, federal agents forced Young to comply. His medical examination revealed that he was suffering from neurosyphilis, and he was honest about his alcohol and marijuana use. Nonetheless, Young was accepted for military service. When he was posted to Alabama, his officers could not understand his eccentric language and behavior. In 1945, when he was caught with marijuana, he was court-martialed, convicted, and sentenced to a term of imprisonment. Young tried to escape from the stockade, but he quickly surrendered when he saw "all those cats with guns."

A common interpretation of Young's postwar life has been that his army experiences ruined him as a man and a musician. Daniels disagrees with this interpretation, believing instead that his music became radically innovative during this time. His playing was now incisively economical, but he could say more with a few deeply expressed notes than other musicians could with a hundred. Those who argue for his decline can point to sessions where Young had problems with intonation and breath control and where he relied on cliches instead of new ideas. Those who argue for development can point to sessions where his improvisations exhibited a structural and functional mastery that went beyond anything he had previously achieved.

Unfortunately, the music business was changing in the 1950's, and jazz musicians had few opportunities to exhibit their skills. Norman Granz, a promoter, was able to give work to some talented musicians, including Lester, in his Jazz at the Philharmonic tours. Although Young profited financially from these jazz extravaganzas, he found greater satisfaction by playing ballads in small groups. Though many jazz clubs closed during this period, one—Birdland—survived and became important in Young's later career. He played at this club's opening night and many times thereafter, and he also went on the road with the Birdland All-Stars.

In the late 1950's, Lester's health deteriorated precipitously, largely due to his excessive drinking and his refusal to seek medical help. He moved into the Alvin, a musicians' hotel near Birdland. He still managed to play when opportunities presented themselves and his last "gig" was in Paris, where he exacerbated his problems by drinking brandy and absinthe. He began bleeding internally, and on the plane back to New York, his bleeding worsened. Refusing to enter a hospital, he returned to the

Alvin, where he was cared for by Elaine Swain, a friend who was with him when he died on March 15, 1959.

The circumstances of Young's death present Daniels with a dilemma, since he has created a portrait of a man in love with life and creativity. Some have interpreted Young's death as the "ritual murder" of a black man who knew his own worth but was caught in the quagmire of a racist society. A doctor who took an interest in Young believed that he suffered from schizophrenia, resulting in an overpowering death wish. When some fellow musicians asked Young about his drinking, he responded simply that pain went away when he drank. For the jazz critic Ralph Gleason, Young was a mystical poet, irremediably "hurt that the world was not in actuality as beautiful as he dreamed."

Robert J. Paradowski

Sources for Further Study

Booklist 98 (January 1-15, 2002): 791.
Choice 40 (September, 2002): 108.
The Economist 362 (March 16-22, 2002): 65.
Kirkus Reviews 69 (November 15, 2001): 1593.
Library Journal 127 (January, 2002): 106.
Los Angeles Magazine 47 (February, 2002): 93.
Publishers Weekly 248 (December 24, 2001): 51.

A LIFE IN LETTERS, 1914-1982

Author: Gershom Scholem (1897-1982)
Edited and translated from the German by Anthony Da-
vid Skinner
Publisher: Harvard University Press (Cambridge, Mass.).
547 pp. $35.00
Type of work: Autobiography and letters
Time: 1914-1982
Locale: Germany, Palestine, and Israel

❧

*A collection of letters documenting the life and ideas of
Gershom Scholem, scholar of Jewish mysticism, that in-
cludes correspondence with his family and with important
European intellectuals of the twentieth century*

❧

Principal personages:
> GERSHOM SCHOLEM, German Jewish scholar, author of *Major Trends in
> Jewish Mysticism* (1941)
> BETTY SCHOLEM, his mother
> WERNER SCHOLEM, his brother, a communist political activist
> ARTHUR SCHOLEM, his father
> WALTER BENJAMIN, his friend, a literary critic and philosopher
> HANNAH ARENDT, a political philosopher
> THEODOR ADORNO, a sociologist and philosopher

Anthony David Skinner, a research fellow at the Franz Rosenzweig Center of the
Hebrew University, has gracefully and creatively accomplished a difficult intellectual project in this edition of letters by and to Gershom Scholem. Scholem was a
founding scholar in the field of Jewish mysticism and a key figure in twentieth century Zionism in Palestine/Israel. Skinner has choreographed a sequence of letters in
which Scholem's voice emerges in dialogue with his family and with many of the
most famous European thinkers of his era. These letters, as a dialogic encounter, illuminate not only the key relationships in Scholem's life and his central intellectual
concerns, but also the day-to-day experience of German Jews as the catastrophe of the
Holocaust unfolded across Europe, as well as day-to-day life in Zionist Palestine and,
later, in the newly founded state of Israel.

Skinner composes an introductory section for each cluster of chronologically arranged letters, allowing readers unfamiliar with Scholem's cultural and intellectual
milieu to understand both the historical context and philosophical backdrop to the letters themselves. Especially striking in this collection is the conceptual continuity
among the letters: Each long section pulls readers into a multivoiced conversation,

~

Gershom Scholem was best known for his critical works Major Trends in Jewish Mysticism *(1941),* Shabbatai Sevi veha-tenu ah *(1957;* Sabbatai Sevi: The Mystical Messiah, *1973) and* The Messianic Idea in Judaism, and Other Essays on Jewish Spirituality *(1971). He resided in Jerusalem for most of his adult life.*

~

with the letters linked by both specific ideas as well as a palpable sense of the broader personal and cultural crises facing European Jews in the early and mid-twentieth century. The letters personify both suffering and remarkable intellectual energy. Equally important, given that Scholem emigrated to Palestine in 1923, the collection immerses readers in key debates surrounding the Zionist movement in Palestine and Israel.

Gershom Scholem was born in 1897 into an assimilated family well established in the German middle class. The opening section of letters, entitled "A Jewish Zarathustra, 1914-1918," shows a young and intellectually precocious Scholem debating socialist politics and Zionism with his leftist brother Werner. He explores his initial attraction to the thought of existentialist philosopher Martin Buber (1878-1975), which is followed by his later rejection of Buber's ideas under the influence of Scholem's close friend, critic Walter Benjamin (1892-1940). In these letters, Scholem also discusses his early turn to a philosophy of language and history as the context for his academic study of Judaism. Skinner's introduction examines Scholem's "existentialist philology" as the philosophical context for Scholem's lifelong study of Kabbala and Jewish mysticism. This is especially helpful in situating Scholem's thought within the broader context of Jewish studies.

Skinner also emphasizes the formative influences of war on Scholem's life and work. There are, for example, interesting parallels here with the influence of war on philosopher Franz Rosenzweig (1886-1929), whose classic of Jewish existentialist philosophy, *The Star of Redemption* (1921), was composed during World War I. *A Life in Letters* contains correspondence between Scholem and Rosenzweig; through his juxtaposition of letters, Skinner raises important questions about the formative influences of war (and of "chaos," and "exile") on Jewish thought more generally.

In part 2 of *A Life in Letters*, "Unlocking the Gates, 1919-1932," the unfolding post-World War I economic and political collapse in Germany sets the stage for Scholem's emigration to Palestine and his growing preoccupation with his own scholarly work, a preoccupation supported by his family and friends, but also clearly the source of some impatience in those of his correspondents left struggling with the impending rise of National Socialism in Germany.

There are many letters in this section between Scholem and his mother Betty, who remained in Berlin and reported developments there to her son in Palestine. These letters are haunting in retrospect: Betty Scholem's seemingly casual observations regarding outbursts of anti-Semitism in postwar Germany and calm reports that social unrest is increasingly channeled into scapegoat tactics aimed at German Jews create an undercurrent of inevitable horror and grief. Betty Scholem's letters at the end of this section contain the first specific references to Hitler. Skillful editing by Skinner allows the broader historical scale of the impending catastrophe to become apparent in personal letters between mother and son.

Also in this section, readers will find Scholem's impatient assessment of the famous German translation of the Hebrew Bible produced in the early 1920's by Franz Rosenzweig and Martin Buber, as well as correspondence with Walter Benjamin that reveals Benjamin's long and ambivalent—and never realized—plan to travel to Palestine. Gershom Scholem compiled a collection of his own voluminous correspondence with Walter Benjamin (*The Correspondence of Walter Benjamin and Gershom Scholem: 1932-1940*, 1980) and Skinner draws from some of those previously published letters in this collection. Readers familiar with the Scholem-Benjamin correspondence will see the relationship between the two men in a new light here, as Skinner orchestrates their conversation from his vantage point as interpretive third party. Throughout the early sections of *A Life in Letters*, readers can follow the evolution of their dialogue regarding the nature of Judaism, their differing approaches to philosophy (especially regarding language and aesthetics), their arguments about Zionism and the idea and reality of an eventual state of Israel, and their personal tensions regarding the realities of money and livelihood. Skinner also includes in this section Scholem's letters explaining and analyzing events in Palestine in the late 1920's. Hebrew University opens in Jerusalem in 1925, with Scholem on the faculty. Conflict between Palestinian Arabs and Zionist Jews intensifies, with Scholem seemingly committed to both the Zionist project and some sort of political rapprochement with Palestinians and the Arab world.

The third section of *A Life in Letters*, "Redemption Through Sin, 1933-1947," titled after Scholem's famous 1936 essay, builds for readers both an immediate and a retrospective sense of deep loss, as Betty Scholem's letters continue to document Nazi ascendency through the lens of daily events. Other letters cover Werner Scholem's long imprisonment by German authorities for his political activities, followed by his eventual murder in the Buchenwald concentration camp. This section also includes Scholem's continued back-and-forth with Benjamin, as Scholem extends sometimes transparently ambivalent invitations to Palestine and Benjamin begins a desperate and delayed attempt to escape impending doom in Europe, an attempt that will end tragically with Benjamin's 1940 suicide when it appears that he will not be able to escape Germany after all. Letters in this section also reveal Scholem's effort to coax Martin Buber to Palestine and his own ever-increasing preoccupation with scholarly projects and academic issues.

Skinner's analysis in the introduction to part 3 is especially productive. His interpretive thesis is that Scholem's work increasingly expressed a "fusion of scholar and political-social ventriloquist," a between-the-lines method of inquiry and writing: "In the midst of a world turned suicidal, his work became more esoteric and hence more personal, with his deep, humane convictions camouflaged behind an exacting philological apparatus." As Skinner's subsequent letter sequence shows, Scholem's ability to spend the late 1930's and the war years in the relative safety of Palestine (and for a brief time, New York City) allowed him to concentrate his mental energies on crystalizing a sophisticated theory of Jewish mysticism, especially in terms of mysticism's role within the dialectics of Jewish history. Quoting Scholem, Jewish mysticism is "the attempt to discover the hidden life beneath the external shapes of reality." Skinner goes on to suggest that Scholem's study of Jewish messianism illustrates the way that Scholem actually constructed an analysis of the present (at this point, the 1930's) by embarking on scholarly explication of key texts of the past. Again, according to Scholem, "Jewish messianism is, in its origins and by its nature—this cannot be sufficiently emphasized—a theory of catastrophe. This theory stresses the revolutionary, cataclysmic element in the transition from every historical present to the messianic future." Skinner argues that Scholem's study of the "Lurianic Kabbala" and his comparison of this messianic movement (which followed Jewish expulsion from Spain in 1492) with events in 1933, demonstrates that Scholem tried "to apply the [scholarly] principles he articulated to the tragedies of his time."

The final section of *A Life in Letters*, "Master Magician Emeritus, 1948-1982," succeeds as do the earlier sections in linking the trajectory of ideas in the letters with overarching historical events. Scholem recounts in several letters his trips to recover Jewish texts and libraries from the rubble of Europe, a matter-of-fact portrayal of cultural devastation and survival. The theme of book recovery works in tandem with Skinner's analysis of Scholem's place in "post-Catastrophe" Judaism:

> In the postwar years Gershom Scholem became the living embodiment of German Jewry—of its formidable talents, as well as its tragedy and its determined survival. His prolific scholarship buoyed a world still sunk in disbelief at the monstrous effects of Nazi anti-Semitism. Against this bleak backdrop, Scholem portrayed Judaism as a living, dynamic tradition equal in power and profundity to any other. Scholem himself came to resemble many of the great exegetes he discussed in his work; his peculiarly allusive method, and the terrible context in which this allusive writing appeared, fostered a new Jewish historical consciousness that was able to absorb and overcome disaster.

This concluding section of letters includes Scholem's sharp, eventually friendship-ending debate with social philosopher Hannah Arendt (1906-1975), whose analysis of the Eichmann trials of 1961 and assertions of the "banality of evil" infuriated Scholem. Also interesting in these letters is correspondence to, and about, Swiss psychoanalyst Carl Jung (1875-1961), as well as Mircea Eliade (1907-1986), the Romanian scholar of comparative religion. Scholem maintained communications with both men, despite serious questions raised by others about their stances vis-à-vis anti-Semitism and fascism. Readers will also encounter a letter from Jewish theologian Emil Fackenheim, applauding Scholem's refusal to meet with philosopher Martin Heidegger (1889-1976), whose cooperation with National Socialism was revealed during the postwar years.

The complexity of Scholem's (and others') thought regarding the war-torn formation of the state of Israel is clearly revealed in several letters in the last section of the book. Also in sharp relief is ongoing debate among Jews about the subsequent role of Israel within Judaism. For Scholem, Jewish identity had carried existential primacy since his decision to live in Palestine; this philosophical commitment conditions his analysis of postwar German-Jewish dialogue (about which he is skeptical), Zionism, and scholarly method.

A Life in Letters stands as a collaborative philosophical collage of sorts, assembled by Anthony David Skinner in posthumous conversation with not only Gershom Scholem but also an array of Jewish thinkers of the twentieth century. The collection is highly interpretive, both in terms of Skinner's contextual analysis and in the montage effect of his chosen letter sequences. Skinner's own method seems to replicate the allusive quality he ascribes to Scholem's scholarship. Rather than building a particular strong thesis about Scholem's life and work, Skinner's analysis-by-inference skillfully raises important questions for readers: What is Jewish identity, and how have a range of thinkers addressed this? What is the relationship between scholarship and political life, living in community? How does one human voice develop within an intricate web of conversations with others? How does intellectual life dialectically unfold within the crosscurrents of history? In good dialectic fashion, *A Life in Letters* sparks further inquiry and further conversation.

Sharon Carson

Sources for Further Study

Library Journal 127 (January, 2002): 111.
The New York Times Book Review 107 (April 7, 2002): 12.
Publishers Weekly 249 (January 28, 2002): 280.
The Times Literary Supplement, March 1, 2002, p. 10.

A LIFE IN PIECES
The Making and Unmaking of Binjamin Wilkomirski

Author: Blake Eskin
Publisher: W. W. Norton (New York). 251 pp. $25.95
Type of work: Biography, history, and memoir
Time: 1941-2000
Locales: Israel, Los Angeles, Latvia, New York, Poland,
　　Prague, and Switzerland

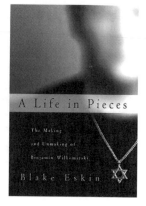

≈

*Spurred by the German writer Daniel Ganzfried's 1997
announcement that Binjamin Wilkomirski's award-winning
Holocaust memoir was a fraud, Eskin investigates the authenticity of the counterfeit memoirist to whom his family
at one time believed they were related*

≈

Principal personages:
　　BINJAMIN WILKOMIRSKI (BRUNO DOESSEKKER; née Grosjean), Swiss
　　　　clarinetist, Jewish archivist, and writer
　　BLAKE ESKIN, American journalist
　　EDEN FORCE ESKIN, Blake Eskin's mother
　　DANIEL GANZFRIED, Swiss novelist and reporter
　　VERENA PILLER, Bruno Doessekker's longtime companion
　　ELITSUR BERNSTEIN, Israeli psychologist and Bruno Doessekker's close
　　　　friend
　　LEA BALINT, Israeli Holocaust researcher and documentarian
　　RAUL HILBERG, Holocaust historian
　　SARAH MOSKOVITZ, psychologist and founder of Child Holocaust Survi-
　　　　vors Group of Los Angeles
　　LAUREN GRABOWSKI (LAUREN STRATFORD; née Laurel Willson), Holo-
　　　　caust survivor impersonator and faux child-survivor memoirist
　　HARVEY PESKIN, clinical psychologist and traumatic memory scholar
　　RUDOLPH ZEHNDER, Bruno Doessekker's uncle

　　The Polish artist and writer Bruno Schulz, who was shot and killed by a Gestapo
officer in the Polish ghetto of Drohobycz in 1942, once worried about what should be
done about events that have no place of their own in historical time, and he wrote that
time might be "too narrow for all events." Furthermore, he believed that when "one is
burdened with a contraband of supernumerary events that cannot be registered, one
cannot be too fussy"—they can simply be placed into one of time's many parallel
branching streams. However, as Blake Eskin's book more than amply demonstrates,
what is good for the artist is not always good for the memoirist. Schulz's comments
were made in the context of one of his fictions, *Sanatorium pod klepsydrą, (1937;*

Sanatorium Under the Sign of the Hourglass, 1978), in which he argued that some things in life are "too big and too magnificent to be contained in mere facts," and the only way to fully understand these moments is through "the phenomenon of imagination and vicarious being." The artist, in other words—whether painter or writer—is best suited to render what is in excess of history and chronological time. Conversely, Eskin's book is about a man, the Swiss Bruno Doessekker, who invented a vicarious being for himself, the Latvian Jew Binjamin Wilkomirski, then placed himself in the eye of one of the worst catastrophes of the twentieth century, the Holocaust, and published the account of his suffering there as autobiography, thereby eliding the boundaries between art and history and calling into question the ethics of memory.

≈

Blake Eskin is a writer and journalist who first covered the Binjamin Wilkomirski saga for the Forward, *where he was arts editor, and also for the syndicated Public Radio International program* This American Life. *He has written articles for* The New Yorker, The Washington Post Magazine, Newsday, ARTnews, *and other publications.*

≈

When Binjamin Wilkomirski's book *Bruchstücke* first appeared in Germany in 1995 and in English translation as *Fragments: Memories of a Wartime Childhood* in 1996, it was greeted with broad and wild acclaim and netted such prestigious awards as the National Jewish Book Award and the Prix de Mémoire de la Shoah. Although it was certainly not the first Holocaust memoir to create such a sensation, it was considered by many to be one of the most singularly arresting pieces of nonfiction literature on the Holocaust ever written, mainly due to the book's narrative persona: a naïve child who was only a toddler when the Nazis came to Riga, emptied out the ghetto, and deported the Jews to the death camps in Poland. In the camps, the young Binjamin has absolutely no sense of time or place, or even of his own identity in relation to that time and place, and his recollections of the horrors and cruelties he experienced there before being smuggled into Switzerland after the war are rendered by Wilkomirski with a raw, unfiltered immediacy. In *The New Yorker* in 1999, Philip Gourevitch wrote that "Wilkomirski was held in awe for his ability to evoke the existential predicament of being frozen inside the uncomprehending yet too knowing mind of a traumatized child."

Four years after Wilkomirski's book was first published, and after Wilkomirski spent years traveling around the world promoting his story as well as the causes of Holocaust testimony and recovered traumatic memory, he was exposed as a fraud in 1998 in the Zurich weekly *Die Weltwoche* by the Swiss writer Daniel Ganzfried. Binjamin Wilkomirski, it turned out, was not the Latvian Jewish Holocaust survivor he claimed to be, but Bruno Doessekker, a Swiss music teacher and clarinet maker who had been born Bruno Grosjean in Switzerland in 1941 to an unmarried Christian woman and later adopted in the mid-1940's by the affluent Protestant Doessekker family. Eskin has both a personal and professional stake in Wilkomirski's story; nevertheless, his book does not simply accept and elaborate upon Ganzfried's conclusions, and Eskin is even willing to take into serious consideration Doessekker's own claim that "The reader was always free to conceive of my book as either literature or as a personal document." Eskin explores every side and facet of the case, not to finally settle the matter, but to pose the more provocative question of whether or not it is ever possible to unravel the tenuous lines that knit together memory and history.

Eskin first noticed *Fragments* in 1997 in a catalog he was browsing and was struck by the name Wilkomirski, because his mother had told him throughout his childhood that her family had come to New York from Riga, Latvia, where their name was Wilkomirski. This led both him and his mother to read the book, which in turn inspired his mother to contact the author and ask him if he would like to explore their possible family connections. "Wilkomirski" replied enthusiastically and after an extended correspondence with Eskin's mother, there was finally an actual meeting with twenty Eskin family members in New York in September, 1997. Eskin himself decided to report on this reunion for the public radio program *This American Life*. One of the defining characteristics of *Fragments* is that its author has practically no recollection whatsoever of his original birthplace or family, and because of the emotionally powerful nature of both the writing and the subject matter, there were many readers who believed they might be related to Binjamin Wilkomirski and wanted to meet him. For some, such as Eskin's family, Wilkomirski was seen as an important link with a hidden and painful past, and his story as well as his existence became a kind of site upon which the hopes of reclaiming family members lost during the maelstrom of the Holocaust could be realized. As Eskin himself writes, while he and his family waited in his parents' living room for the man who called himself Wilkomirski to arrive, they imagined that in his presence "a childhood can be restored, a family can be reunited, history can be rewritten." *Fragments* and its author also had a profound effect upon the field of recovered memory, especially in relation to the traumatic memories of children, who are generally thought incapable of retaining their earliest experiences in the kind of detail which "Wilkomirski" provided in his book. "Binjamin Wilkomirski" even went so far as to coauthor a scholarly paper with the psychologist Elitsur Bernstein on new therapeutic treatments for child survivors of the Holocaust without identity.

Eskin felt lucky, as a reporter, to have such a story fall into his lap, but after meeting "Binjamin," he was also a little wary of whether or not there were enough facts to prove definitively that his family was related to the author of *Fragments*. He also had his doubts as to whether or not "Binjamin can remember anything from such a young age, whether he can reconstruct so specifically what happened to him with so little data after such a long interval, whether he is such a good historian." In his story for public radio, Eskin expressed these doubts as well as the range of his family's reactions to "Binjamin," which varied from his mother claiming him as a cousin to one aunt's skeptical indifference. At the same time, Eskin explains in his book that part of the appeal and power of *Fragments* lay in the fact that the book set aside "the ordering logic of grown-ups" and, because its narrator continually points to his own uncertainty, it was difficult for readers to insist upon factual corroboration of events. Eskin also points out that the anxiety that has historically accompanied Holocaust testimony ("what if no one believes my story?") gave "Wilkomirski" the higher ground when the veracity of his story was questioned. Finally, Eskin himself, for all of his skepticism, never believed that "Wilkomirski" was not, at the very least, a Holocaust survivor.

After his public radio piece, Eskin might have turned away from the Wilkomirski story to other writing projects except for Daniel Ganzfried's exposé of Wilkomirski, "The Borrowed Holocaust Biography," which ran in the August 27, 1998, issue of *Die Weltwoche*. Ganzfried, who himself had written a novel about his father's experiences in the Holocaust, had uncovered a wealth of legal documents and photographs and even persons connected to "Binjamin's" early years that revealed the author of *Fragments* to be, not Binjamin Wilkomirski from Riga, but Bruno Doessekker from Zürichberg. Ganzfried went further in his reporting to also pan Doessekker's book, which he felt had "no place in the realm of literature." He also accused the author and his editors at the German publishing house Suhrkamp-Verlag of the worst kind of ethical misconduct and abuse of history. "Binjamin" responded quickly to Ganzfried's accusations in an interview in the Zurich *Tages-Anzeiger* where, according to Eskin, he argued that "Ganzfried's findings are old news, just another stumbling block in his ongoing struggle to escape the identity imposed upon him." In addition, "Binjamin" denied completely that he was Yvonne Grosjean's illegitimate son, regardless of the birth certificate that said otherwise. Finally, and perhaps most shockingly, "Binjamin" told the *Tages-Anzeiger* that his readers had always been free to interpret his book as either a personal account or as literature.

After that interview, Wilkomirski retreated from public view and would not speak to Eskin when he approached him, more than once, in order to clear up some of the confusion. What fascinated Eskin most and led him to undertake the research that comprises the bulk of *A Life in Pieces* is that Ganzfried's exposé, even with its strong documentary evidence, was not able to shake the public's sympathy for "Binjamin" and, if anything, only fueled that sympathy even more. What Eskin discovered was that vocal skepticism toward *Fragments* had touched deep nerves in many circles, ranging from child survivor support groups to Holocaust historians who have worked to debunk Holocaust deniers. Although Eskin had his doubts about Wilkomirski's real identity, he wanted to give him the benefit of the doubt, and in a story he wrote for the *Forward* on Ganzfried's allegations he purposefully left the conclusion open-ended: "If Mr. Ganzfried's allegations fall apart, this may be the story of a Salieri trying to sabotage a Mozart. If not, Mr. Wilkomirski's greatest work of fiction may not be *Fragments*, but his own construction of himself."

Rather than attempting to simply respond to Ganzfried's research and conclusions on "Binjamin" and *Fragments*, *A Life in Pieces* attends instead to exploring the many layers—personal, political, and otherwise—of the complex relationships between memory, history, art, and identity, and to illustrating that the "Binjamin Wilkomirski" story had roots that extended deep into the collective cultural psyche. In addition to relating the story of *Fragments*—its narrative content and initial reception, his family's and his early encounters with the author, and the later debates about the book's authenticity—Eskin also talked to founders and members of support groups for child survivors of the Holocaust, psychologists working in the field of recovered traumatic memory, Holocaust historians, recovered memory scholars and their skeptics, and Holocaust archivists and documentarians. Eskin also traveled to Riga with his mother and to Israel on his own to investigate his own personal family history. While Eskin finally agrees with Ganzfried that "Wilkomirski" was a fraudulent creation on the part of Bruno Doessekker, he also concludes that, ultimately, "Binjamin was a cipher" who "offered himself up time and again as a universal placeholder for inexpressible and unappeasable absences," and to a certain degree, "the impulse that drove Bruno to become Binjamin is an impulse shared by many of us . . . who identified with Binjamin and saw our own stories through his."

Eileen A. Joy

Sources for Further Study

Booklist 98 (February 1, 2002): 916.
Library Journal 127 (January, 2002): 122.
New Statesman 131 (May 20, 2002): 54.
The New York Times Book Review 107 (February 24, 2002): 22.
The New Yorker 77 (February 4, 2002): 81.
Publishers Weekly 248 (December 24, 2001): 53.
The Times Literary Supplement, May 17, 2002, p. 33.

LIFE OF PI

Author: Yann Martel (1963-   )
First published: 2001, in Canada
Publisher: Harcourt (New York). 336 pp. $25.00; paperback $14.00
Type of work: Novel
Time: 1961 to the present
Locale: Pondicherry, the Pacific Ocean, Mexico, and Toronto

≈

A novel of more than physical survival, in which a sixteen-year-old boy and a Bengal tiger share a lifeboat for seven months

≈

Principal characters:
> PISCINE "PI" MOLITOR PATEL, an Indian boy emigrating to Canada with his family
> RICHARD PARKER, a Bengal tiger
> THE AUTHOR, who is and is not Yann Martel

"In *Life of Pi* we have chosen an audacious book in which inventiveness explores belief," said Lisa Jardine, chair of the committee which selected Yann Martel's novel for the 2002 Man Booker Prize, Britain's most publicized and arguably most prestigious literary award. The choice was surprising given the competition; the shortlist comprised Sarah Waters, Tim Winton, the venerable William Trevor, and three Canadians: Carol Shields, dying of breast cancer; Rohinton Mistry, all three of whose novels have been shortlisted for the Booker, and Martel. Although the dark horse, *Life of Pi* was much admired by reviewers, including fellow Canadian and former Booker winner Margaret Atwood: "a terrific book . . . fresh, original, smart, devious, and crammed with absorbing lore . . . a far-fetched story you can't quite swallow whole, but can't dismiss outright." The power of Martel's novel may be gauged by how well it survived a tabloid-style attack, following the Man Booker ceremony, for not being original enough, borrowing too freely from an obscure 1956 Brazilian novel, Moacyr Scliar's *Max and the Cats*. Set in 1933, Scliar's novel concerns a young Jew who, fleeing Nazi Germany, survives shipwreck by sharing a lifeboat with a panther. That Martel acknowledges Scliar's novel in his "Author's Note" as having provided the "spark of life" to *Life of Pi* hardly mattered, least of all at a time when accusations of plagiarism in high places (against historians Stephen Ambrose and Doris Kearns Goodwin) and the debate over intellectual property rights in the global economy were all the rage.

Martel's "Author's Note," a playful mélange of fact and fantasy (the "author" here is and is not Martel), puts the novel in a more autobiographical context. Born in Spain

~

Yann Martel was born in Spain. He has lived in Costa Rica, Mexico, France, Alaska, Canada, Iran, Turkey, and India, and he resides in Montreal. He is the author of one previous novel, Self (1996), and a collection of short stories.

~

to French Canadian parents (his father a diplomat and poet), the well-traveled Martel grew up wherever his father was posted. After studying philosophy at Trent University in Peterborough, Ontario, he published a collection of short stories, *The Facts Behind the Helsinki Roccamantos* (1993), and a novel, *Self* (1996). Both received good notices but were commercially unsuccessful. Martel went to India where, depending on whether one believes the author or the "Author's Note," one (or both) of two things happened. Either the writer who had planned to write a novel set in Portugal in 1939 suffered writer's block until he ran into an elderly man, Mr. Adirubaswamy, who told him "a story that will make you believe in God," the story that became *Life of Pi*, or the writer, this time speaking *ex cathedra* rather than from within the factoidal "Author's Note," had a vision. The north Indian plain before him became in his imagination an ocean with a lone lifeboat floating upon it. He began researching his novel while still in India, visiting zoos in the south, then returned to Canada where he read extensively in zoology and animal psychology, Hinduism, Christianity, and Islam; he even started attending Catholic mass. Over the course of writing his novel, he became what his protagonist is, a believer, albeit a believer of an odd and oddly inviting kind.

That protagonist is Piscine Molitor Patel, from Pondicherry, a former French colonial city that is now part of the modern Indian state of Tamil Nadu. Named for a Parisian swimming pool but later saddled with the moniker Pissing Patel by a classmate, he reinvents himself as Pi. "And so, in that Greek letter that looks like a shack with a corrugated roof, in that elusive irrational number with which scientists try to understand the universe, I found refuge." The son of secularized parents (as is Martel), Pi becomes as enamored of religion (or religions) as he is of science, but when priest, pandit, and imam each tries to claim him as his own, as his atheist science teacher previously tried, Pi balks, critical of their small-mindedness. When a short time later Prime Minister Indira Gandhi, proving similarly small-minded and territorial, brings down the local government, Pi's father, owner of the local zoo, decides that the family will immigrate to Canada.

On July 2, 1977, just eleven days after leaving Madras, the ship goes down. After 277 days in a 26-foot lifeboat, Pi and Richard Parker, a 450 pound Bengal tiger, arrive in Mexico, the sole survivors. At first, however, the lifeboat is a bit more crowded, its "ecosystem" more complex. The hyena eats the zebra and then the orangutan, before being eaten in turn by Richard Parker, who does not eat Pi. That he does not is as improbable as the tiger's name, only more ambiguously explained. The simple explanation is that Pi, the zookeeper's son, manages to master the beast. However, nothing is ever quite so simple in this artful fable, in which simplicity is invariably a means, not an end in itself. Man (or boy) and tiger, Pi and Parker, become dependent on each other: the tiger on Pi for food and water, Pi on the tiger for a strange kind of companionship that is as much spiritual as psychological.

Pi's "I" is omnipresent but unpretentious in this not-quite-first-person story-within-a-story of a novel, and it is his voice that delights and beguiles. At times he sounds like a fortune cookie, at others like a mini-Salman Rushdie, practicing an art of restrained excess. The humor is all the more effective for being understated and the despair made more poignant, more real, because it is so rarely and reticently expressed. Fantastical and ultimately metaphysical as his story is, Pi grounds it in the details of his severely circumscribed everyday reality. Precise descriptions of butchering a turtle, operating a solar water still, and taming a tiger alternate with brilliantly wrought comic scenes, skits, and shaggy dog stories: the arrival of the three not-so-wise men (pandit, priest, and imam), for example, and Martel's version of how the leopard got its spots (how the tiger got his name). There is the scene, reminiscent of silent film comedy, in which Pi frantically encourages Richard Parker to save himself from drowning by swimming to the lifeboat only to realize, as the tiger climbs aboard, what he has just done, and then leaping into the ocean to save himself from the tiger he has just saved. Best of all is the lengthy Beckett-like scene (five times longer in manuscript) in which a temporarily blind Pi crosses nautical paths with a blind French cannibal, a hallucination that turns out to be real (or as real as anything else in this fabulous, faux-factual novel): The whilom companion-turned-killer is himself killed and eaten by Richard Parker, Pi's hungry savior. Differently funny, more blackly humorous is the floating island which Pi first believes is his salvation and only later realizes is carnivorous. Mistaken first, and second, impressions are common in the novel, for the reader no less than for Pi, who steps on to a Crusoe-like island and right into a Swiftian satire.

This leisurely told tall tale wears its meanings on its sleeve. Martel may be an allegorist, but he is no José Saramago, nor does he wish to be. "In a novel, you must amuse as you elevate," Martel has said, preferring the accessible and amusing Pi not only to the "complicated and dense" fiction of writers such as Salman Rushdie and Gunther Grass but to his own earlier fiction as well, with its "stylistic excesses." Even Pi's extensive intertextuality proves inviting rather than off-putting. Instead of demanding that readers play (and lose) a game of literary trivial pursuit, Martel allows them to make connections and find resemblances without making the reader's pleasure dependent on either: Noah's ark, Edward Hick's painting *The Peaceable Kingdom* (c. 1833), Daniel Defoe's *Robinson Crusoe* (1719), Jonathan Swift's *Gulliver's Travels* (1726), Mark Twain's *Adventures of Huckleberry Finn* (1844), Herman Melville's *Moby Dick* (1851), Rudyard Kipling's *The Jungle Book* (1894), Stephen Crane's "The Open Boat" (1898), Samuel Taylor Coleridge's *The Rime of the Ancient Mariner* (1798), Ernest Hemingway's *The Old Man and the Sea* (1952), and *Max and the Cats*, as well as (unfortunately) the Tom Hanks film *Cast Away* (2000), Michael Ende's *Die Unendliche Geschichte* (1979; *The Neverending Story*, 1983), and (even more worrisome) Richard Bach's *Jonathan Livingston Seagull* (1970).

Martel's intertextual range contributes to his larger purpose, turning either/or into both/and, undermining all forms of exclusivity (religious in particular but secular humanist as well) by positing a more inclusive alternative. In the Peaceable Kingdom of *Life of Pi*, realism lies down with fabulation, the mundane with the miraculous, humor with despair, science with religion, past with present, storyteller with novelist. As Pi says two decades after his ordeal, "My suffering left me sad and lonely. Academic study and the steady, mindful practice of religion brought me back to life." At the University of Toronto, he majors in zoology and religious studies, writing theses on the sixteenth century Kabbalist Isaac Luria and on the thyroid function of the three-toed sloth. "Sometimes I got my majors mixed up."

"Life in a lifeboat isn't much," he says, any more than it is in any confined space, whether an academic discipline or a specific religion or, in Martel's telling, Pi's account of survival on the high seas. Thus, Martel prefaces that story not only with his or a surrogate's "Author's Note," but with Pi's account of his early years, and he intersperses the "author's" italicized remarks on hearing the story from Pi, including glimpses into Pi's later life (his marriage and children). He follows it with "excerpts from the verbatim transcript" of a tape made by two representatives of the Japanese Ministry of Transportation who had interviewed Pi years before in Mexico as part of their investigation into the sinking of the *Tsimtsum*. That transcript includes the very account that has just been read, or some version of it; chapter 96 reads in its entirety, "The story." His Japanese listeners find Pi's account both unhelpful (because it does not explain why the *Tsimtsum* sank—Pi thinks he may have heard an explosion—a big bang) and unbelievable. So Pi tells them a much shorter story in which, instead of Pi, hyena, tiger, zebra, and orangutan, there is Pi, a monstrous cook, Pi's mother, and a young sailor (both of whom the cook kills before being killed in turn by Pi). Why does Pi begin crying at this point? Because this brutal story is painfully true, his fable patently false? Perhaps, but the more likely explanation is that *Life of Pi* is not just a story about salvation, one with a happy ending (Pi saved, his formal studies completed, his family settled and secure). It is also a story about the loss of Pi's other home and other family: mother, father, and older brother, as well as Richard Parker. As soon as they reach Mexico, "Richard Parker, companion of my torment, awful, fierce thing that kept me alive, moved forward and disappeared forever from my life," like a dream, one is tempted to say: a recurring dream, for Richard Parker continues "to prey" on his mind.

Released in Canada on the same day as the September 11, 2001, terrorist attacks on the World Trade Center and the Pentagon, *Life of Pi* is the perfect "literary novel" for the postironic age: earnest, uplifting, global (translated into at least sixteen languages). It is, as the *Nation*'s Charlotte Innes has noted, "a religious book that makes sense to a nonreligious person" and restores the reader's "faith in literature." True enough, but *Life of Pi* is more than that. As the "Author's Note" points out, "They speak a funny English in India. They like the word bamboozle." The novel's charm derives in part from Martel's capturing that slightly stilted, slightly dated Indian colonial English so perfectly and uncondescendingly and in part from its "bamboozling" readers with its metafictional embedding of stories within stories. *Life of Pi* bamboozles most, however, in pretending to cover up and overcome what it exposes and illuminates: that sense of loss upon which *Life of Pi* and the life of Pi are founded. In this, novelist Martel is engaged in an activity surprisingly similar to his volunteer work at a Montreal hospital: palliative care.

Robert A. Morace

Sources for Further Study

Booklist 98 (May 15, 2002): 1576.
Library Journal 127 (June 15, 2002): 95.
The Nation 275 (August 19, 2002): 25.
The New York Times Book Review 107 (July 7, 2002): 5.
Publishers Weekly 249 (April 8, 2002): 200.

LINCOLN'S VIRTUES
An Ethical Biography

Author: William Lee Miller (1926-   )
Publisher: Alfred A. Knopf (New York). 515 pp. $30.00
Type of work: Biography and ethics
Time: 1809-1861
Locale: Kentucky, Indiana, Illinois, and Washington, D.C.

Lincoln's
Virtues

AN ETHICAL BIOGRAPHY

William Lee Miller

～

A thoughtful biography about Abraham Lincoln's ethical and moral beliefs before his inauguration as president of the United States in March, 1861

～

Principal personages:
ABRAHAM LINCOLN (1809-1865), sixteenth president of the United States
MARY TODD LINCOLN (1818-1882), his wife
STEPHEN A. DOUGLAS (1813-1861), U.S. senator from Illinois and Lincoln's major political rival
WILLIAM HERNDON (1818-1891), Lincoln's law partner and his biographer
ZACHARY TAYLOR (1784-1850), twelfth president of the United States
HENRY CLAY (1777-1852), leading Whig politician and Lincoln's mentor
EDWIN STANTON (1814-1869), Lincoln's secretary of war
WILLIAM SEWARD (1801-1872), Lincoln's secretary of state
LYMAN TRUMBULL (1813-1896), U.S. senator from Illinois who strongly supported Lincoln

This book's subtitle, *An Ethical Biography*, describes very well what distinguishes William Miller's approach from the hundreds of books that have been written on Abraham Lincoln since his assassination in April, 1865. His focus is not on Lincoln's service as a war president but rather on Lincoln's moral convictions, which many commentators have badly misunderstood. Miller argues persuasively that Abraham Lincoln is still the most admired American president for a variety of reasons. Lincoln combined political skill with strong ethical beliefs, but Miller also shows that his strong opposition to slavery and his commitment to complete equality between whites and African Americans began long before his election to the presidency in November, 1860, and his declaration of the Emancipation Proclamation on January 1, 1863.

Miller points out that although Lincoln is held in incredible esteem not only in the United States but also in other countries, it is difficult to separate myth and reality. He succeeds admirably in presenting an objective and historically accurate description of

Lincoln's moral positions. Miller does not present an ideal person lacking character faults. He readily admits that Lincoln may have been somewhat harsh in his treatment of his father, whom he never forgave for his alcoholism, and perhaps somewhat too submissive to his wife, Mary Todd. He explains clearly that Lincoln never belonged to a specific church either in Illinois or in Washington, D.C., but indicates that Lincoln knew the Bible better than most clergymen and

William Lee Miller earned his doctorate at Yale University in 1958. He teaches ethics and history at the University of Virginia. He has published extensively on slavery and the Civil War.

also accepted the core Christian beliefs of charity and forgiveness that transcend specific religious denominations. It is significant that both practicing believers and those who do not attend religious services on a regular basis have great admiration for Lincoln. He did not criticize any religion, and he never questioned the sincerity of others's religious beliefs. Miller points out that such tolerance and respect for other religions was exceptional in the 1840's and the 1850's in the United States, when the powerful Know-Nothing Party argued that the United States should consist only of white Protestants, and that Catholics and Jews should be denied American citizenship. Lincoln had nothing to gain politically with white Protestant male voters in Illinois by arguing that Americans should respect the religious freedom of minorities such as Catholics and Jews, but he reaffirmed his commitment to religious tolerance even when he was speaking to prejudiced listeners. It is significant that Lincoln never tailored his message to his audience. He was totally consistent both in his support of full religious freedom for all Americans and in his opposition to slavery.

Miller shows that, even in personal matters, Lincoln adhered to a very strict moral code. He did not smoke, drink alcohol, or gamble, and he did not consider himself superior to others just because he chose not to smoke, drink alcohol, or gamble. In his 1842 speech to the Temperance Organization in Springfield, Illinois, he argued that abstainers like themselves should not condemn those who drank alcoholic beverages, but should rather encourage those who drank alcoholic beverages to recognize the destructive effects of alcohol on their lives and the lives of their family members. This clearly did not make a favorable impression on certain temperance advocates who considered themselves morally superior to those who saw no problem with the moderate consumption of alcohol.

Although Lincoln was consistent in his ethics, he was nevertheless a sensitive politician. He realized that the constituents in the seventh district of Illinois, whom he represented in the U.S. House of Representatives from 1847 to 1849, and the citizens of Illinois whom he wanted to represent as a U.S. senator were racially prejudiced against African Americans, but this did not stop him from arguing that slaves possessed the same constitutional rights as white Americans. Unlike Stephen Douglas, he did not curry favor with racists in order to win elections.

Some historians have claimed that Lincoln's active opposition to slavery did not begin until shortly before his series of debates with Stephen Douglas during the 1858 senatorial campaign in Illinois, but Miller demonstrates that this is simply not true. In early 1849, as he was completing his term as a U.S. congressman, he presented a bill to outlaw slavery in the nation's capital. The Speaker of the House prevented a vote on this proposal, but this represented Lincoln's first effort to end or at least to stop the expansion of slavery. Miller points out that this attempt to end slavery in Washington, D.C., would not have helped Lincoln either with incoming president Zachary Taylor, who was a slaveholder, or with Illinois voters, who were very prejudiced against African Americans. Lincoln took this stand because he firmly believed that slavery was morally wrong and incompatible with Thomas Jefferson's statement in the Declaration of Independence that "all men are created equal." Lincoln interpreted this comment literally and concluded that all Americans, regardless of race or gender, had the same rights. Lincoln's moral opposition to slavery never wavered, although it clearly resulted in his defeat by Stephen Douglas in the 1858 Illinois U.S. senate race.

Between 1849 and 1854, Abraham Lincoln withdrew from politics and practiced law. In 1854, Stephen Douglas led the Senate in approving the Kansas-Nebraska Act, which granted each territory the authority to decide whether it would permit slavery. Douglas used blatantly racist terms to ridicule opponents of this bill. Lincoln correctly understood that the effect of this law would be to extend slavery throughout the United States. Lincoln was offended by Douglas's overt racism and by his vile slander of Senators Chase and Seward, who would later serve in Lincoln's cabinet. Soon thereafter he reentered politics. For the next six years he became the most eloquent opponent of slavery.

Miller argues correctly that the central focus of Lincoln's moral arguments between 1854 and 1860 was his opposition to slavery. Lincoln took on Stephen Douglas, the most feared American debater of his day, and he proceeded systematically to argue that the Kansas-Nebraska Act constituted a clear rejection of the Declaration of Independence and the moral foundation of American democracy. Lincoln argued that if the United States was not based on a love of justice, it would be no better than a dictatorship. With much humor and with effective allusions to the Bible and the Declaration of Independence, Lincoln argued that support for slavery not only violated the basic justification of American democracy by its founders, but also offended the sense of right and wrong. When Douglas responded with the claim that God intended whites to dominate African Americans, his overt racism became abundantly clear to the people in Illinois. They could either support the racist ideology of Stephen Douglas or accept Lincoln's belief that slavery was a "monstrous injustice" and a "great moral wrong." Lincoln described slavery in these terms as early as 1854.

At first, Lincoln's antislavery efforts seemed to be very effective. In the 1854 Illinois election, the Democratic Party lost its majority in both houses of the state legislature. At that time, U.S. senators were elected by state legislatures. When Lincoln realized that he would not be elected himself, he asked his delegates to vote for Lyman Trumbull, an anti-Douglas Democrat, so that Douglas's preferred candidate, Joel Matteson, would not be elected. Trumbull opposed slavery whereas Matteson was as racist as Douglas. Lincoln sacrificed his own ambition so that at least one of the U.S. senators from Illinois would be antislavery. Lyman Trumbull remained staunchly antislavery, and he eventually changed his party affiliation to the Republican Party.

Encouraged by this defeat of Douglas's candidate, Lincoln continued to denounce slavery and began planning for the 1858 senatorial campaign against Douglas himself. He realized that the Whig Party would soon disappear, but he wanted to remain politically active and recognized the need to create a new, antislavery party. In early 1856, he played a central role in creating the Republican Party of Illinois. The Republican Party Convention designated Lincoln as its only candidate for the 1858 senatorial campaign. Before the November, 1858, state legislative election, Douglas and Lincoln participated in seven debates that established Lincoln as a national political leader, although he did lose this election to Douglas.

Miller points out that, although numerous historians have examined the Lincoln-Douglas debates, they have generally overlooked the fact that the two basic themes of these debates were slavery and racism. Douglas was overtly racist and supported slavery, whereas Lincoln condemned slavery and favored equality for all races. Douglas played the "race card" in each debate and pandered to the racial prejudice of white male voters. He repeatedly argued that whites should control the U.S. government and should not share any power with African Americans. In his response to each speech by Douglas, Lincoln's ethical argument never varied. He constantly affirmed his belief that since "all men are created equal," white and African Americans possess the same legal rights. The moral positions of Douglas and Lincoln were totally incompatible. Although Douglas did win this election, his was a Pyrrhic victory. He had permanently alienated moderate Northerners, who would never vote for such an avowed racist in the 1860 Presidential election.

In 1859 and early 1860, Lincoln gave numerous speeches in northern states against slavery. On February 27, 1860, he gave his famous Cooper Union speech in New York City. In this speech, he carefully marshaled his arguments to show that slavery was incompatible with the Declaration of Independence, the American Constitution, and the moral foundation of American democracy. He spoke with such clarity and persuasion that his listeners, who knew him only by reputation, rose to their feet and interrupted his speech several times with applause. He gave similar speeches throughout New England, and audiences responded very positively to his arguments. Voters came to realize that, unlike most politicians, Abraham Lincoln did not change his moral positions. People knew exactly where he stood on slavery.

At its May, 1860, convention in Chicago, Republican delegates nominated Lincoln on the third ballot. In November, he easily defeated the National Democratic candidate, Stephen Douglas, and two Southern candidates, John Bull and John Breckinridge. Despite overtly racist campaigns by his three opponents, Lincoln won this election by telling American voters exactly where he stood against slavery and for the equality of people.

Between his election in November and his inauguration on March 4, 1861, Lincoln made it abundantly clear to all Americans that he would neither modify his opposition to slavery nor allow Southern states to secede. For him, the Union was indivisible. Miller ends this fascinating book with Lincoln's inauguration.

Edmund J. Campion

Sources for Further Study

Booklist 98 (January 1-January 15, 2002): 798.
Library Journal 127 (February 1, 2002): 115.
Los Angeles Times Book Review, February 17, 2002, p. 5.
The New York Times Book Review 107 (February 10, 2002): 11.
Publishers Weekly 248 (December 24, 2001): 55.
The Wall Street Journal, February 8, 2002, p. W9.

THE LITTLE FRIEND

Author: Donna Tartt (1963-   )
Publisher: Alfred A. Knopf (New York). 555 pp. $26.00
Type of work: Novel
Time: The 1970's
Locale: Alexandria, Mississippi

~

Tartt's second novel concerns a Mississippi family that must deal with the unsolved murder of its only son, and the sister who is determined to solve the murder twelve years later

~

Principal personages:
> HARRIET CLEVE DUFRESNES, a twelve-year-old girl who is determined to discover who killed her brother
> ROBIN CLEVE, Harriet's nine-year-old brother who is killed by a stranger on Mother's Day
> ALLISON CLEVE, Harriet's sixteen-year-old sister who blocks out the memory of Robin's murder by sleeping all the time
> CHARLOTTE CLEVE, Harriet's mother, who withdraws from her family after the murder
> HELY HULL, Harriet's young friend and confidant
> DANNY RATLIFF, the man Harriet believes is responsible for Robin's death
> IDA, Cleve family housekeeper who is the only adult Harriet truly loves

In 1992, Donna Tartt took the publishing world by storm with her debut novel, *The Secret History*. So enthusiastic were both her fans and her publisher that they all waited breathlessly for her next novel. Finally, ten years later, Tartt has published *The Little Friend*, with readers and the publishing world looking to see if it is worth the wait.

At the heart of Tartt's *The Little Friend* is a mystery and the effect it has on one family. Set in Alexandria, Mississippi, during the 1970's, the novel recounts the death of Robin, nine years old and left hanging from a tree by an unknown murderer twelve years earlier. His family is devastated; in the intervening years his mother, Charlotte, has withdrawn from everybody and leaves the daily care of her two daughters to Ida, the family maid; his father, Dix, abandons the family entirely except for holiday visits. Allison, now sixteen, sleeps as much as possible and cannot remember anything about the murder. That leaves Harriet, twelve years old and book smart, as the only family member who still wants to know who killed Robin.

Harriet is fascinated by the characters she reads about in books by Robert Louis Stevenson and Arthur Conan Doyle and by the real-life magician Harry Houdini, who

~

Donna Tartt's first novel, The
Secret History, *was published in
1992 to critical acclaim worldwide
and was translated into twenty-four
languages. A native Mississippian,
Tartt is also a critic and essayist.*

~

later in life was committed to revealing the spiritualists of his day for the con artists they really
were. Harriet is compelled to solve the murder
both because solving her brother's murder is the
right thing to do and because her overactive
imagination tells her that it is. Harriet wants to
solve it so she can be like one of those people she
reads about who do great and heroic things. Furthermore, while practicing Houdini's trick of
holding her breath for long periods of time, she
hallucinates yet another person she read about, Arctic explorer Captain Robert Scott,
who tells Harriet that she is the only one who can solve Robin's mystery.

All of these ideas begin to percolate in Harriet's mind until she convinces herself that she can reveal who killed her brother. She questions Allison, who was four
at the time of Robin's death and was in the yard when it happened. She thinks that
Allison may remember something in her dreams; Harriet tries to get Allison to keep
a dream diary by writing down everything as soon as she wakes up, but Allison, like
everyone else, is not interested. Finally, because of something Ida says, it hits her
out of the blue: The killer is Robin's playmate, Danny Ratliff, who is now twenty
years old and a drug user. The fact that she does not have any proof of Danny's involvement does nothing to her determination to seek out revenge on Danny. Her
revenge is the Old Testament version—an eye for an eye—and she is determined that
Danny must die, proof or no. With her friend Hely at her side, Harriet sets out to kill
Danny any way she can. At first, her attempts to kill him come across as nothing
more than little-kid schemes that go awry, but soon they become very serious and
deadly.

To everybody of Harriet's social class, the Ratliffs are the lowest form of life
around, and Tartt does everything in her writing power to make that point come
across. Danny's family, with the exception of his youngest brother Curtis (who is
simple-minded) are all drug runners and other assorted lowlifes. The fact that Danny
is from the poorer side of town makes him stand out even more, even though Harriet
herself is of the same social stature financially, if not socially. If Harriet is poor,
though, Danny is dirt-poor, a lower class of poor; in a place where social stature is everything, even these little differences are important to everybody Harriet knows, and
even to Harriet herself.

Tartt fills in the rest of Harriet's world with grandmothers, aunts, housekeepers,
and other people and places. Setting is one thing that Tartt sets out to establish with
great detail, and for the most part it works. Tartt introduces many supporting characters and gets inside their heads through her use of the third-person omniscient point of
view. Tartt seems to be implying is that, in the South, everybody has an opinion about
everything (including who killed Robin); Tartt gives the reader each character's opinion about whatever is happening to him or her at the time. This omniscient point of
view at first seems fine, but then characters the reader has become interested in are no
longer that important. For example, Allison is the primary character in the first chap-

ter, but for the remaining six chapters she is barely mentioned, as if Tartt herself suddenly realized that Harriet was the true main character.

Tartt's distinctive writing style is both the strength and the weakness of the novel. Her command of language and her novel's unconventional ending confirms that her work deserves the praise it receives. However, some elements of Tartt's writing style may also put off potential readers. Tartt's use of the dash to set off parenthetical explanatory comments is overused, on average once or twice per descriptive paragraph. For example, Tartt writes:

> Except for Curtis—who loved everything in the world, even bees and wasps and the leaves that fell from the trees—all the Ratliffs had an uneasy relationship with Eugene. He was the second brother; he'd been Farish's field marshal in the family business (which was larceny) after their father died. In this he was dutiful, if not particularly energetic or inspired, but then—while in Parchman Penitentiary for Grand Theft Auto in the late 1960's—he had received a vision instructing him to go forth and exalt Jesus. Relations between Eugene and the rest of the family had been somewhat strained ever since. He refused to dirty his hands any longer with what he called the Devil's work, though—as Gum often pointed out, shrilly enough—he was happy enough to eat the food and live under the roof which the Devil and his works provided.

In addition to the three sets of dashes in that one paragraph, at least three more appear on that page. A sentence with dashes requires more work to understand than does a sentence without. In a novel that is over five hundred pages long, this writing technique becomes tedious rather than unique, and the story itself takes second place to the technique that relates it.

Tartt used the same dash-writing style (although not as forcefully) in *The Secret History*, but in her first novel there is a big difference: *The Secret History* is written in the first person. Her narrator, Richard Papen, is a student at Hampden College, an exclusive New England school. The fact that Papen describes things and events in a way that sounds educated is exactly right because he attends a prestigious college. In *The Little Friend*, though, Tartt has chosen to tell Harriet's story in the same fashion. This book's third-person omniscient point of view, combined with Tartt's extensive use of dashes on almost every page, makes it work to read the novel, wearying to the reader rather than a pleasure. For those who have read both books, it is evident that the earlier work is more natural in its storytelling.

Along with the main plot involving the murder, Tartt also includes several subplots that weave their way into the main story, all tied together by the thread of a person's place in society. If there are social structures between Harriet's family and others, there is also the very obvious one between whites and African Americans. This is Mississippi, and even though it is the 1970's, integration still has a long way to go. The Cleve's family housekeeper, Ida, is fired one evening after many years of loyal service because she did not prepare dinner for Harriet. Odean, the housekeeper for Harriet's aunt Libby, does not attend Libby's funeral because nobody thought to invite her, even though she had worked for Libby for over fifty years. Even Hely's family fires housekeepers whenever they feel like it just because they can.

These things affect Harriet in different ways. Harriet knows Odean should have been invited but says nothing about it, which makes her feel worse. When her mother fires Ida, Harriet not only witnesses the separation between cultures but is deeply hurt when Ida shuts Harriet out of her life completely. Along with all this, Harriet must deal with the death of her aunt Libby as a result of an automobile accident caused by her grandmother, Edie. Libby was Harriet's favorite relative and her death is especially shocking; this event seems to follow a pattern of bad things happening one after another. At Libby's funeral, it all seems to crash together as Danny sees Harriet and realizes (wrongly) that he recognizes her, and the fact that their paths are destined to run together is inevitable.

Critics were divided on how well Tartt's writing served her story. Some said that *The Little Friend* was as fine a book as *The Secret History*, while others believed that Tartt actually confused the narrative with her writing style. Tartt tries to give her book a sense of style but fails miserably. Her writing does not flow; the overabundance of dashes, Tartt's way of spelling colloquial slang terms without an apostrophe (such as "yall" instead of "y'all"), and other stylistic quirks leave the reader trying to figure out what Tartt is doing instead of just enjoying her story. Every time a reader may think that he or she has figured out Tartt's style, something else comes around that is jarring.

The ending of the book raises almost as many questions as the book set out to answer. Tartt does not tie up everything neatly, which may leave readers either pleased because she did not follow the traditional path or disappointed for exactly the same reason. Most of the conflicts Tartt sets up throughout the book, from Allison's dreams to who killed Robin, are not resolved. Instead, the plot points become simply a series of things that have happened. Tartt's realism may work for some readers, but setting up the expectation that these questions will be answered and then not resolving them will leave other readers frustrated. Ultimately, Tartt's effort at literary realism is overwrought at the expense of her story.

Kelly Rothenberg

Sources for Further Study

Booklist 99 (September 1, 2002): 8.
Entertainment Weekly, November 1, 2001, p. 72.
Kirkus Reviews 70 (September 1, 2002): 1262.
Library Journal 127 (October 15, 2002): 96.
The New York Times Book Review 107 (October 17, 2001): 1.
Publishers Weekly 249 (September 9, 2002): 40.
U.S. News & World Report, October 21, 2002, p. D16.

THE LOVELY BONES

Author: Alice Sebold (1963-   )
Publisher: Little, Brown (Boston). 336 pp. $21.95
Type of work: Novel
Time: 1973-1983
Locale: Norristown, Pennsylvania, and the eastern United
    States

$\backsim$

A raped and murdered fourteen-year-old girl observes
the effects of the crime on her family and reveals the web of
connections existing between the living and the dead

$\backsim$

Principal characters:
> SUSIE SALMON, raped and murdered at age fourteen
> ABIGAIL SALMON, Susie's mother
> JACK SALMON, Susie's father
> LINDSEY SALMON, Susie's sister
> BUCKLEY SALMON, Susie's brother
> RAY SINGH, wrongly suspected in Susie's disappearance
> RUANA SINGH, Ray's mother
> RUTH CONNORS, a poet whom Susie "touches" as she is passing
> LEN FENERMAN, the detective investigating Susie's murder and Abi-
>   gail's lover
> BRIAN NELSON, "the scarecrow," a classmate of Susie
> "GEORGE HARVEY," a man of many names, the serial killer who mur-
>   dered Susie
> SAMUEL HECKLER, who marries Lindsey Salmon
> HAL HECKLER, Samuel's brother
> GRANDMA LYNN, Abigail's mother
> HOLLY, Susie's Chinese roommate in her heaven
> FRANNY, Susie's intake counselor in her heaven

Drawing on folkloric and religious motifs and ideas, Alice Sebold presents a remarkable, complex, and comforting vision of heaven as the platform from which
Susie Salmon, raped and murdered by a neighbor at the age of fourteen, tells her story.
It is a heaven that indeed has many "mansions," one of which is the "wide wide
Heaven," which can provide one's every desire. It also grants omniscience to the narrator. The word Susie's grandfather has for the dominant quality of this heaven is
"comfort," and oddly comforting, indeed, is Alice Sebold's novel because it postu-
lates a vision of heaven that begins with an "intake" level of simplicity that matches
the experience level of the fourteen-year-old victim and becomes increasingly complex as Susie watches the changes her death effects on her family and friends over a

Alice Sebold studied at Syracuse University and the University of Houston before earning an M.F.A. from the University of California, Irvine. Lucky (1999) is a memoir of her rape as an eighteen-year-old college freshman. The Lovely Bones *is her second book. She lived for ten years in New York City.*

dozen or so years following her death. Sebold's conception of heaven is a complex and progressive spirit world in which the departed continue to grow and develop; thus, those individuals who die while children "mature" over the years as they would have done had they not died prematurely. Found in a number of formal religions, this progressive conception of the afterlife is, in the hands of Alice Sebold, a moving yet unsentimental perspective from which to tell the story of every parent's worst nightmare.

Sebold has asked the unthinkable question, yet one writ large in every day's news headlines: What if one's young daughter does not come home for dinner one evening? How do parents and siblings, friends and neighbors, police and the rest of the community react to the growing conviction that the child has been murdered? How do they react when a dog brings home "a body part," an elbow that, for the police at least, confirms her murder? How do they react to the failure of the police investigation to find the body, despite finding convincing quantities of blood in the dirt of the cornfield? How do they react to the failure to find the killer, to bring him to justice? Only gradually and painfully can the family and the police conclude that the investigation is a murder investigation, that Susie Salmon had been abducted, murdered, and forever obliterated from the face of this Earth. Although other evidence is accumulated, the killer is never arrested, tried, convicted, and executed.

Sebold's choice to have Susie Salmon tell her story from heaven as the first-person narrator in charge of her own story works brilliantly to satisfy the reader of the truth of her vision of heaven as a complex, multidimensioned spiritual reality, a wide place, a place fashioned after the dearest wishes of departed souls. To support her conception of this story, Sebold weaves together cultural myths, Christian scripture, and deeply embedded folk ideas about revenants (souls who return, usually in corporeal form, to the scenes of their lives and their deaths), who may communicate successfully but rarely clearly with those they have left behind, and who sometimes even exact vengeance upon their murderers. Thus, this novel is a wonderful ghost story. However, because it also embodies a vision of a secular heaven to which spirits journey in stages from the moment of their death and are granted in some way the righteous desires of their hearts, the novel is also a complex meditation on those desires, including the desire for retribution.

In Susie's case, the desire for knowledge is paramount. She wants to learn all that she had not been able to learn in her short time on Earth, the knowledge that living brings of love, sex, work, thought, and family, to grow fully through the whole range of life's experiences. Franny, her intake counselor, herself murdered by a wife abuser, assures her that that option is not available (an assertion that Susie will later test with startling consequences). At first, her heaven is that mansion to which female murder victims go, shaped in the familiar forms of school grounds and buildings where her heavenly growth begins. She and Holly, her best friend in heaven, discover that just about anything one can desire is available if desired enough and if one understands why one desires it. She and Holly realize, for instance, that Franny reminds them both very much of their mothers because they miss their mothers intensely. Susie's second desire is to observe, at least, the whole lives she has left behind on Earth so that she and her companion can pretend better, a wish that is granted, thus making the omniscient possibilities of this narrative point of view credible as well as functional.

The ultimate embodiment of Susie's wish is to return in physical form, at least for a few moments, to permit her to make love with Ray Singh years after her murder. She does so, "borrowing" the body of Ruth Connors, a classmate against whom she had "brushed" on her way out of life. That connection gives Ruth her life's calling to write the lives of female victims and suggests also the power of love to transcend mortality. Sebold's conception of heaven is not a place of "gritty reality" but a place where one has fun. It is also a place from which Susie can continue to see how, sometimes at great cost, the relationships and the sometimes tenuous connections among her friends and family are made and developed in the years following her disappearance and the ongoing consequences of her life and death for those still living. These relationships are the "lovely bones" of the novel's title, the armature on which Susie herself grows in knowledge and acceptance to develop the figures of Sebold's themes.

Sebold avoids the pitfall of sentimentality by managing the tone and focusing on Susie's reports of the psychological and physical effects of her murder on her family, on her classmates, on Detective Fenerman, and on the killer. For instance, in the character of Ruth Connors, poet and fearless and compulsive walker throughout Manhattan, Sebold focuses on identifying and commemorating all those women and children who were murdered or abused. Ruth is compelled to locate the places where these crimes occurred and to write the names of all such victims in her journal, doing "important work," Susie tells us, "work that most people on Earth were too frightened even to contemplate" but which her "fans in heaven" cheer on. As Susie watches the lives she left behind, she also remembers when she and Ray Singh nearly but not quite kissed and they secretly witnessed Ruth Connors being scolded for drawing nudes that were too realistic for her art teacher's comfort and that revealed her talent to be much greater than that of her art teacher.

Susie's family members remember her in various ways as they deal with the intense pain, implacable and pervasive, that her murder generates. Susie's mother Abigail in her pain withdraws from her husband, has a brief affair with Fenerman, and flees to the West Coast, working in a winery for several years and returning only when she learns of her husband's stress-induced heart attack, thus reuniting with him eight years later. Jack is overcome by the loss of his daughter and obsessed with finding proof that Mr. Harvey is a viable suspect. Each day, when his consciousness wakes him, Jack's guilt seeps in, poisoning his relationship with his wife and his other children, Lindsey and Buckley. His actions are those of a father deeply attached to his daughter and overwhelmed by loss and guilt. Thus, he is acutely sensible to "intimations" of her presence and of his culpability. The visions, sightings, and intuitions that Jack, Buckley, Ruth, Ray, and Lindsey experience are the results of Susie's efforts to communicate with them. The police, however, require "hard evidence," and Jack's attempts to find it are interpreted as irrational at best and illegal in law, marking him in the minds of some as a dangerous and suspicious person. He pesters Fenerman to treat Mr. Harvey as a suspect to such an extent that the beleaguered detective orders him to quit calling and to cease in his attempts to investigate the case himself.

Susie also watches as Lindsey works hard to develop her identity as a young woman in her own right, not merely a living version of her dead sister. Helping her along this path are the attentions of Samuel Heckler, who gives Lindsay a present on the first Christmas after Susie's death and receives a kiss from Lindsey in return. Susie in her heaven feels the electricity of the kiss and is "almost alive again." Buckley, her four-year-old brother, is kept from the truth, so he continues to ask, "Where is Susie?" As Sam and Lindsey exchange presents, kiss, and begin their healing and life-long connection, Susie's father finds a way to tell Buckley that his sister is dead. Taken during the first Christmas after Susie's death (Christmas being the commemoration of the birth of Christ and thus a subtle promise of immortality), each of these moves begins the healing for Susie's siblings and her father, but it will be a lengthy process and different for each person.

Learning that Mr. Harvey is her father's prime suspect, Lindsey conspires with Jack to enter Harvey's house and find evidence to support their suspicions. She is nearly caught by Harvey, who sees her escaping into the trees and knows he is discovered. Although Harvey immediately leaves town, Lindsey's daring effort causes Harvey's life to spin out of control and enables her to reunite with her father so that they can get on with their own lives after a fashion. Buckley, for instance, will, when he is in the seventh grade, develop a garden near the house, not exactly a "secret garden" but one that allows Susie to signal him by making the entire garden bloom. At the end, years later, through Susie's omniscient witness, readers get to see Mr. Harvey, the serial rapist and her murderer, tumbled into deep snow, not to be found for several months. Nonetheless, justice so long delayed and achieved anonymously is denied for his victims and their families.

Sebold's vision of how the healing process progresses in different ways for each life relies upon a body of traditional belief, customs, and images, including newborns being given the names of the dead and the seasonal resurrections of gardens. Susie continues on her own journey of progression and exploration, returning occasionally to look in on the family members who are now reunited in her absence but who find her manifested in whatever way they want her to be.

Theodore C. Humphrey

Sources for Further Study

Book: The Magazine for the Reading Life 21 (July/August, 2002): 64.
Booklist 98 (May 1, 2002): 1510.
Library Journal 127 (May 15, 2002): 127.
New Statesman 15 (August 19, 2002): 39.
The New York Times Book Review 107 (July 14, 2002): 14.
Publishers Weekly 249 (June 17, 2002): 40.
Seventeen 61 (July, 2002): 152.
Time 160 (July 1, 2002): 62.

LOVING MONSTERS

Author: James Hamilton-Paterson (1941-   )
First published: 2001, in Great Britain
Publisher: Granta Books (London). 308 pp. $24.95
Type of work: Novel
Time: 1918-1999
Locale: Egypt, Italy, and Great Britain

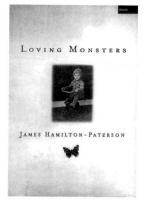

～

The fraught relationship between a professional author
and the mysterious neighbor whose biography he agrees to
write lies at the heart of a novel fascinated by the essential
singularity of human nature

～

Principal characters:
> RAYMOND JERNINGHAM "JAYJAY" JEBB, an English expatriate in his late
> seventies whose reminiscences constitute the balance of the novel's
> content
> JAMES, the narrator, a professional writer
> MARCELLA, the domestic servant who runs Jayjay's Italian home
> DARIO, her son and an intimate friend of Jayjay
> CLAUDIO, Marcella's father, a small farmer who assists in Jayjay's
> household
> RICHARDS, an English clerk whose sexual humiliation Jayjay witnesses
> as a young man
> MANSUR, the Egyptian pornography seller who is Jayjay's first same-sex
> lover
> MILO, an English expatriate who introduces Jayjay to Cairo's criminal
> world
> AGNES MAUNSELL, a married woman twice Jayjay's age and his first
> heterosexual lover
> MIRELLA BOSCHETTI, an Italian consular official who employs Jayjay to
> tutor her son
> ADELIO BOSCHETTI, her son, who on his death leaves Jayjay the family
> home in Tuscany
> PHILIP, the fellow schoolboy for whom Jayjay has a lifelong, but unspo-
> ken and unrequited passion

    Although *Loving Monsters* is presented as a work of fiction, it also plays with the
conventions of biography in recounting the story of an elderly Englishman's progress
from callow youth to world-wise adult. The text includes what purport to be photographs of several of its characters and settings, and the author's "Acknowledge-
ments" refer to Jayjay as if he were an actual person. The otherwise unidentified nar-

rator's first name, "James," is the same as that of his putative creator, James Hamilton-Paterson, and there are a number of other similarities between the careers of "James" and James. This blurring of the boundaries between fiction and nonfiction is one of the major themes of *Loving Monsters* and has particularly significant implications for the novel's many considerations of the nature of biography.

Jayjay's story is part of a complex narrative framework bounded by James's career as a professional writer. It is his familiarity with the latter's books that leads Jayjay to suggest himself as a potentially rewarding biographical subject, and one of the many intriguing strands of this deftly constructed work is James's uncertainty as to whether there is a publishable book here; Jayjay's initial autobiographical recollections, although both exotic and erotic, strike James as

James Hamilton-Paterson is a graduate of Oxford University and a prolific author of fiction, children's fiction, nonfiction, and poetry. He won the Whitbread First Novel Award for Gerontius *(1992).*

lacking the fundamental human interest that would justify a formal biography. The result is a fascinatingly tense situation in which Jayjay's unwillingness to reveal his deepest secrets is gradually overcome by his need to convince James that he is worthy of the writer's time and attention, as both men move toward the revelation of matters that they have long chosen to repress.

The first section of Jayjay's memoirs concerns his childhood in England and his young adulthood in Egypt. The English material seems a conventional account of a sensitive youth's upbringing in an apparently stable if somewhat materialistic middle-class family, but a discordant note is sounded when Jayjay vehemently rejects the idea that his mother was a formative influence in his development. The narrative pauses here to register James's thought that this is probably an evasion rather than a truth, as *Loving Monsters* sets up a running commentary of biographer on subject that accomplishes two important purposes: the inclusion of James's responses amid Jayjay's discourse, an important aspect of the text's overall strategy of bringing their respective stories together, and the establishment of an attitude of suspicion toward Jayjay's veracity, which adds a strong element of suspense to recollections that, if taken at face value, would often seem rather mundane.

The outwardly prosaic nature of Jayjay's English background is enlivened by one episode that foreshadows much of his subsequent life. Taken to the funeral of one of his father's friends, Jayjay is moping around by himself when he encounters an affable stranger who turns out to be a professional gate-crasher. The stranger introduces Jayjay to the idea that it is possible to live one's life as an "imposter," adopting the appropriate behavior and mannerisms for each social situation as a means of enjoying the benefits that accrue to acceptance by the more affluent. Jayjay, who has always assumed that adults were in fact the staid, boring personages they appeared to be, is bowled over by the idea that it is possible to achieve by deception what has been withheld by accident of birth, and his career will be strongly influenced by this revelation as to how private cleverness can create public character.

Jayjay's own career as an imposter gets underway when, at the age of eighteen, he travels to Cairo to work in the offices of a shipping company. Bored by the monotony of the job and the insufferable dullness of his colleagues, he begins to explore the shadier side of the city's nightlife and discovers a nether realm of sexual experimentation that soon draws him into its promiscuous pleasures. It is his encounters with homosexuality, personally in his relationship with the Egyptian pornographer Mansur and voyeuristically when he watches the multiple buggering of his coworker Richards, that are pivotal for both Jayjay's knowledge of himself and his understanding of how society operates. His new awareness of his sexual proclivities is initially disturbing but is soon tempered by the realization that he is able to control this aspect of his erotic life and can even use it as a negotiating device; his knowledge of what Richards practices in secret, on the other hand, alerts him to the hidden desires that may lie under even the most conventional public persona and is a major factor is his decision to become involved in the world of professional pornography.

One of the most compelling aspects of *Loving Monsters* is its clever interweaving of the stories of Jayjay and James, and the former's revelations about his time in Cairo spark some thoughtful reflections on the part of his biographer. James is disturbed by the realization that he is being drawn into Jayjay's past in a way that arouses dormant memories of his own youthful experiences, and this recounting of similar, if less colorful, events serves as an effective textual counterpoint to his subject's lurid revelations. The narrative's representation of James as attracted by, and yet at the same time resentful of, Jayjay's exotic background is an effective source of dramatic tension and also keeps the reader constantly aware that the biographer is a complex human being rather than a self-effacing blank slate upon whose consciousness Jayjay's life will be inscribed.

Jayjay's subsequent years in Egypt are spent in expanding the scope of his pornography business, reveling in the joys of sexuality in all its guises, and then moving to the port city of Alexandria in search of new worlds to conquer. Here he becomes involved with Mirella Boschetti and her son Adelio, whose status as Italian citizens in a period of pre-World War II tensions draws Jayjay into a politically charged milieu that contrasts sharply with the hedonistic life he has led up to this point. The imminent threat of war forces adult responsibilities upon him and his previously uninhibited promiscuity is tempered by the awareness that sex has implications beyond the mere satisfaction of bodily urges; offered the opportunity to take advantage of Adelio's teenage infatuation with him, Jayjay declines because this would violate the position of trust that he occupies in the Boschetti household. His subsequent rescue of the family from a German air raid after hostilities have commenced sets the seal on his new maturity, and he soon finds a productive role for himself in the British Army's propaganda services.

Jayjay's World War II career is punctuated by James's account of his experiences in Southeast Asia during the final years of the twentieth century. Here he leads a life very different from that of an English resident in Tuscany and participates actively in the affairs of a small village that accepts him as an unusual but valuable member of the community. Drawn to this region by his deep sympathy for what its inhabitants have endured under corrupt governments and often malign foreign influences, James too, has undergone a kind of unanticipated personal growth in his involvement with people whom he has chosen to help rather than exploit. The parallel with Jayjay's recollections continues *Loving Monsters*'s pattern of making the biographer and his subject the twin foci of a complex and gripping story, as the text fashions a joint memoir that permits this Boswell to costar with his Johnson.

As Jayjay and James become more comfortable with and trusting of each other, each reveals secrets that they have long hidden from the outside world and, to a large extent, from themselves. For Jayjay, it is his mother and his childhood friend Philip who are the sources of his difficulties in establishing lasting connections with others; he confesses that his mother was certifiably insane and the immediate cause of his decision to move to Egypt, and he also admits to a still-passionate yet never-before-expressed desire for Philip, whom he has thought about daily ever since their first meeting. In James's case, it is the breakdown of his marriage and the distancing of his relationship with his daughter that have blunted his ability to form close personal ties, and his poignant memories of affections lost constitute one of the most moving sections of *Loving Monsters*. It is here that the title's use of "monsters," which has up to this point appeared to apply only to Jayjay's sexual transgressions and consummate egotism, becomes appropriate for biographer as well as subject: Both have become monsters in the sense that, although they have outwardly come to terms with society and even manage to function effectively within it, they nonetheless see themselves as condemned to marginality because of their respective decisions to face life alone.

Hamilton-Paterson's evocative portrayal of this unusual and engrossing relationship is a most impressive accomplishment and will particularly appeal to those interested in the issues that arise when lives are written as biography, autobiography, and/or fiction. Although there is a slight falling off of narrative interest during Jayjay's account of his much more conventionally respectable later years, the novel has by now depicted him as such a fascinating character that readers who have journeyed this far will need to know how his story ends. That it does end, and with profound respect for Jayjay's personal dignity rather than either a bang or a whimper, is a final confirmation that *Loving Monsters* has performed the remarkable feat of touching readers' emotions while engaging their intellects.

Paul Stuewe

Sources for Further Study

Booklist 98 (January 1-15, 2002): 809.
The Boston Globe, June 4, 2002, p. C3.
Los Angeles Times Book Review, March 24, 2002, p. 11.
Publishers Weekly 248 (December 3, 2001): 41.
The Spectator 286 (May 12, 2001): 37.
The Times Literary Supplement, May 25, 2001, p. 21.
The Washington Post Book World, February 24, 2002, p. 15.

MAKING STORIES
Law, Literature, Life

Author: Jerome Bruner (1915-   )
Publisher: Farrar, Straus and Giroux (New York). 130
  pp. $18.00
Type of work: Law, literary theory, and psychology

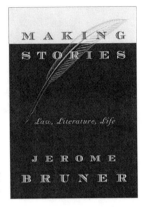

~

*Three lectures by the eminent psychologist on the uses
of story in literature, the law, and autobiography*

~

Based on a series of lectures given at the University of
Bologna, this modest little book breaks no new ground for
cognitive psychologist Jerome Bruner. He covered the ma-
terial in chapter 1, "The Uses of Story," in much more detail in *Actual Minds, Possible
Worlds* (1987). The ideas in chapter 2, "The Legal and the Literary," are derived
largely from the more complex book he cowrote with professor of law Anthony Amsterdam, *Minding the Law* (2000). Chapter 3, "The Narrative Creation of Self," is
based on current theories of a number of thinkers, primarily James Olney (*Memory
and Narrative: The Weave of Life Writing*, 1998), and Paul John Eakin (*How Our
Lives Become Stories*, 1999). The final chapter, "So Why Narrative?" is a brief sum-
mation, reemphasizing the seriousness of narrative in law, literature, and life.

Bruner begins by justifying still another book about stories by reminding readers
that intuitions about how stories are made or understood are so implicit that people do
not know how to explain them. The purpose of his present book, he says, is to get beyond implicitness, something he says most theorists have previously failed to do.
However, when he begins his explanation, he returns to the earliest known effort to
explain the structure of narrative, Aristotle's concept of peripeteia, elucidated in the
Poetics (c. 334-323 B.C.E.)—that sudden reversal in circumstances that turns a routine
sequence of events into story.

Bruner's list of the characteristics of story have been discussed by narratologists
ever since Aristotle. First of all, "story" differs from a sequence of actual events by
having a sense of ulteriority, some purpose or intentionality frequently concealed beneath the mere sequence of events. An important implication of this characteristic of
story is that, contrary to common sense, story is not merely a transparent glass
through which the reader perceives external reality, but rather a highly convention-
bound, thematic form that shapes and alters external reality.

One of the most important theoretical sources of Bruner's theories are the Russian
formalists of the 1920's, who argued that the purpose of story was to make strange or
defamiliarize ordinary reality by transmuting the declarative into the subjunctive, focusing not on what is, but on what might be or could be. Narrative is a dialectic be-

Jerome Bruner, a professor of psychology at the New York University School of Law, is the author of several important works on education and cognitive psychology, including On Knowing: Essays for the Left Hand *(1962) and* The Process of Education *(1961). During the Kennedy and Johnson administrations, he served on the President's Science and Advisory Committee and helped to found the Head Start program.*

tween what is expected and what actually happens, for without something unforeseen taking place, there is no story. Consequently, one of the chief purposes of story is to forewarn the reader, to prepare the reader for the unexpected, give the reader the ability to cope with the new. Echoing the Russian formalists and the literary theorist Morse Peckham in *Man's Rage for Chaos: Biology, Behavior, and the Arts* (1965), Bruner says that story is thus a way to "domesticate" human error and surprise by conventionalizing the common forms of human mishap into genres, such as comedy, tragedy, irony, romance, and so on.

Bruner begins his chapter on the relationship between the law and literature by comparing the formalist literary notion of conventions clustering together to create genres with the legal concept of precedent, for tradition is embodied in both literary conventions and legal precedent. Lawyers (whom Bruner likes to call legal storytellers) appeal to a similarity between their own interpretation of the facts in the present case to similar cases in the past, much the same way a writer or reader creates or interprets a present literary work within the context of previous similar works. A law story therefore prevails not just by its rhetoric, but also by making it clear that there are precedents that match it. Another important element common both to literature and law, says Bruner, is ritualization, for ritual makes the message seem incontestable, suggesting that the message is inherent in the way things are and is therefore beyond debate. Rituals are so deeply embedded in a culture as to seem completely at one with common sense.

Although law often seems to be based on logic and reason, with lawyers and judges trying hard to make their stories seem factual rather than storylike, by "pleading" their case, lawyers often create drama. Moreover, law stories are more like literary stories than logical arguments in that they focus on the particular. Common law, says Bruner, looks for continuity in particulars rather than for universality by deduction from abstract rules, and this, he says, is why law cannot do without narrative.

As an example of how literature finds its way into law, Bruner cites the famous 1954 U.S. Supreme Court case of *Brown v. Board of Education,* in which the court had to decide if the equal-protection guarantee of the Constitution was violated by the practice of racial segregation in local school districts even if the schools could be shown to be equal otherwise. Bruner discusses how American culture's changed narrative about racial discrimination interacted with earlier precedent-setting cases. He ends his chapter on the legal and the literary by reminding the reader that whereas literature looks to the possible and the figurative, law looks to the actual, the literal, and the record of the past. Consequently, while literature errs toward the fantastic, law errs toward the banality of the habitual.

In his third lecture, Bruner tackles the puzzling issue of self, asking the age-old question of whether there is some essential self inside us or whether self is in a constant state of creation. Bruner quickly aligns himself with the latter, stating categorically that there is no such thing as an essential self, but rather that the self is constantly constructed as a narrative to meet the needs of situations human beings encounter. Bruner begins his comparison between self-making and narrative with another reminder of the importance of precedent, tradition, and implicit cultural models. Autobiographies conform to a tacit set of conventions governing what constitutes appropriate public storytelling, he points out. Both self-making and self-telling are about as public as any private act can be, for selfhood involves a commitment to others as well as a commitment to be true to the self.

Bruner lists twelve characteristics of the self, derived from a number of psychologists: The self has intentions and aspirations; it is sensitive to obstacles and responsive to success; it alters aspirations in response to success or failure; it engages in selective remembering; it is oriented to "significant others"; it adopts beliefs and values without losing continuity; it is continuous over time and circumstances; it is sensitive to where and with whom it finds itself; it formulates itself in words; it is moody; and it tries to maintain coherence. He then compares these characteristics to twelve characteristics of narrative: A story needs a plot; a plot needs obstacles; obstacles make people rethink; stories are only concerned with the relevant past; characters have to have allies; characters must grow; characters have to maintain their identities and manifest their continuities; characters have to exist in a world of people; characters have to explain themselves; they inevitably have moods; and characters must make sense.

Selfhood, says Bruner, is a kind of verbalized event that makes the chaos of experience into a coherent and continuous whole. It is not just language that accomplishes this, but narrative in a delicate balancing act in which the self must create a sense of autonomy with a will of its own, while at the same time it must make a commitment to the world of others. Commitment is similar to the legal concept of precedent, for it embodies the cultural expectations and traditions within which individuality can be maintained. Sigmund Freud discussed this concept in terms of the radically autonomous id struggling to keep balance with the culturally demanding superego. In literary criticism, T. S. Eliot (1888-1965) defined the balancing act as that between tradition and the individual talent, for new literary works cannot escape the controls of the traditions within which they are created.

Bruner concludes his third lecture by emphasizing the importance of being able to make stories about the self, citing a neurological disorder called "dysnarrativia," an inability to tell or understand stories associated with such problems as Alzheimer's disease. As one psychologist says, people who cannot construct narratives lose their concept of self. The concept of dysnarrativia seems related to a recent study of Alzheimer's by scientist David Snowdon called the Nun Study. Charting the personal and medical histories of several hundred nuns, even dissecting their brains after death,

Snowdon discovered that the way people express themselves in language has an effect on whether they might develop Alzheimer's in later life. Examining autobiographies of almost two hundred nuns, Snowdon found that those nuns who expressed themselves in complex narrative ways, packing a great number of ideas into their sentences, were less likely to develop Alzheimer's than those who has less "idea density" in their writing.

In his short summary chapter, entitled simply, "So Why Narrative?" Bruner reiterates what he stated in the introductory chapter—that narrative is not only a human delight, it is also a serious business, the essential means by which human aspirations are expressed. Stories are important because they impose a structure on experience. Stories help people cope with surprises by making them less surprising. This "domestication" of unexpectedness that story makes possible is a crucial way culture maintains its coherence.

Bruner refers to common characteristics of language in general in the concluding chapter to suggest that narrative constitutes a kind of language itself. He discusses the two basic features of language—its remoteness of reference, that is, its ability to refer to things not present either to speaker or listener, and its arbitrariness of reference, which frees it from pure mimesis in which signs have to resemble what they refer to. The third essential feature of language is its syntax, or case grammar, which reflects the relationships between agent, action, and recipient of action.

Bruner concludes this series of lectures by referring to his influential 1962 book *On Knowing: Essays for the Left Hand*, which argued that to understand human cognition, one needed an approach that went beyond that provided by the conceptual tools of the psychologist, an approach whose primary medium of exchange was the way of the poet, whose hunches and intuitions create a grammar of their own. He now says that his youthful belief that there were two mutually translatable worlds of mind—the narrative and the paradigmatic—was "profoundly mistaken." Narrative and factuality cannot so easily be isolated from each other. However, as Bruner concludes, reason alone is never adequate; a shared narrative is what matters.

Although Bruner makes no original contribution here to the study of literature, law, or the self, nor introduces any new ideas about their interrelationships—for other literary theorists, psychologists, and culture critics have explored all these issues before—this little book is worth reading. Bruner's voice is a well-known one that commands respect. Consequently, here he can perform the valuable function of introducing important ideas about the seriousness of story to a larger audience more effectively than more academic studies from which he draws.

Charles E. May

Sources for Further Study

The Columbus Dispatch, July 21, 2002, p. 7G.
Los Angeles Times Book Review, May 5, 2002, p. 9.
Publishers Weekly 249 (March 18, 2002): 89.

MASTERS OF DEATH
The SS-Einsatzgruppen and the Invention of the Holocaust

Author: Richard Rhodes (1937-   )
Publisher: Alfred A. Knopf (New York). 336 pp. $27.50
Type of work: History
Time: 1933-1945
Locale: Germany, Poland, the Czech Republic, Romania,
the Slovak Republic, Lithuania, Estonia, Latvia, and
areas of Western Russia occupied by the Nazis

∽

*This well-researched historical study explains in detail
the systematic killing of over 1.5 million people by mobile
execution squads that were called Einsatzgruppen in German*

∽

Principal personages:

ADOLF HITLER (1889-1945), dictator of Germany

HEINRICH HIMMLER (1900-1945), head of the German police forces

REINHARD HEYDRICH (1904-1942), Einsatzgruppen leader and organizer
of the January, 1942, Wannsee Conference, where plans were made
for the systematic extermination of Jews in Nazi concentration camps

HERMANN GÖRING (1893-1946), Nazi military leader who cooperated
with Himmler and Heydrich in exterminating Jews and other groups
hated by Nazis

ODILO GLOBOCNIK (1904-1945), Austrian who first participated in
mobile execution squads and then performed sadistic experiments to
demonstrate the effectiveness of using poisonous gases to kill people
in crematoria

ADOLF EICHMANN (1906-1962), war criminal executed in Israel for his
crimes against humanity

HEINRICH MÜLLER (d. 1945), head of the Gestapo

JOSEF STALIN (1879-1953), Soviet dictator whose Red Army repulsed
the Nazi invasion of the Soviet Union

BENJAMIN FERENCZ (1920-   ), American lawyer who was the chief
prosecutor at the 1947 trial of Einsatzgruppen murderers for crimes
against humanity

MICHAEL MUSMANNO (1897-1968), chief judge at the 1947 trial of
Einsatzgruppen murderers for crimes against humanity

Much of substance has been written on the horrendous death camps such as
Auschwitz, Sobibor, Treblinka, and Dachau, where millions of Jews and other groups
hated by Nazis were killed and then cremated, but scholars have not written extensively on the Einsatzgruppen, or mobile extermination squads, that murdered at least

Richard Rhodes is a historian and the author of nineteen books. His major publications have dealt with World War II and with the development of the atomic and hydrogen bombs.

1.5 million people in Eastern Europe, the Baltic states, and western regions of the former Soviet Union between 1939 and 1942. In this extremely well-researched book, Richard Rhodes explains that although the existence of these mobile extermination squads has been known for decades, the extent of their murders was not fully understood because so many documents now located in Poland, Eastern European countries, and the former Soviet Union were largely unavailable to Western historians until the end of Soviet colonialism starting in 1989 and the implosion of the Soviet Union in 1991. Rhodes carried out extensive archival research in Eastern Europe and personally interviewed numerous Jews who managed to escape death at the hands of the Einsatzgruppen criminals. The quality of his research is superb.

In a comment printed on this book's back cover, Elie Wiesel, the Nobel Prize-winning writer and Holocaust survivor, praises Rhodes for his effective portrayal of "absolute evil and its cold, calculated, and blood-chilling brutality." Wiesel's remark is insightful because it acknowledges Rhodes's attempts to describe both the incredible planning that went into these mass executions and the complete arrogance and immorality of these criminals, who saw nothing wrong with personally murdering innocent men, women, children, and infants.

Rhodes correctly identifies Adolf Hitler and Heinrich Himmler as the two people most responsible for implementing the Holocaust or Shoah, a Hebrew word meaning extermination that Jewish historians prefer to use for the event. Unlike some modern writers who attempted to psychoanalyze these two war criminals, both of whom committed suicide before they could be tried by war crimes tribunals, Rhodes wisely avoids such offensive speculation, which only serves to diminish the personal guilt of leading Nazis. Rhodes does, however, explain that both Hitler and Himmler were brutal, sadistic, and viciously anti-Semitic as early as their late adolescence. He argues persuasively these essentially violent aspects of their character suffice to explain both their sadistic cruelty toward others and their refusal to accept responsibility for their crimes. Hitler had his body burned and Himmler bit down on a cyanide capsule while in British custody. British soldiers buried him in an unmarked grave. Rhodes remarks with wonderful sarcasm, "It was no killing pit, but it would do."

Soon after Hitler became chancellor in 1933, he asked Himmler to eliminate all opponents to his absolute rule. This included Nazis such as Ernst Röhm—whom Hitler no longer trusted—clergymen, judges, and legislators who dared to criticize Hitler's policies. Rhodes argues persuasively that Hitler wanted to eliminate quickly the system of checks and balances that prevents dictatorial rule and protects individual rights. Hitler rewarded Himmler for his loyalty by designating him as the chief of all police forces in Germany. Since Hitler quickly reduced judges to subservience and stripped them of their independence, the actions of Himmler's secret police officers were not subject to judicial review. They acted with complete impunity.

Himmler concluded that the most effective means of killing people was through the use of execution squads. Executions could occur in the basement of police stations, prisons, or concentration camps. At first, Himmler had the executions performed by groups of his "police" officers for very practical reasons. He did not want his officers to believe that they were personally responsible for murdering innocent people. He did not want them to become depressed by the daily drudgery of killing people. It is emotionally draining for prison officials to execute criminals who have been lawfully sentenced to death after objective trials and exhaustive judicial review. Hitler had problems with this approach because he realized that not enough Jews and members of other groups whom he despised could be killed if Einsatzgruppen murderers executed victims in a leisurely manner. He wanted to exterminate European Jews, and for this reason he insisted that Himmler and Reinhard Heydrich devise methods for killing large numbers of people at once.

Hitler asked them to create special forces of trained and callous killers who would not hesitate to execute hundreds of innocent men, women, and children daily. Himmler and Heydrich were arrogant and did not believe that non-Aryan Germans deserved to live, but it was difficult for them to find enough executioners. At first they relied upon similarly fanatic anti-Semites, but eventually they recognized the need to empty German prisons of pathological criminals who had already committed violent crimes. Himmler and Heydrich correctly concluded that such thugs would enjoy having the opportunity to kill people with apparent impunity. Rhodes explains that Himmler and Heydrich kept these sociopaths in line by means of horrendous punishments for those who committed crimes not ordered by their superiors. Himmler and Heydrich wanted these executioners to realize that they could yield to their sadistic tendencies as long as they only killed designated enemies of the Nazis while blindly obeying orders from the Einsatzgruppen officers.

Before the invasion of Poland in 1939 and invasion of the Soviet Union in 1941, Himmler and Heydrich coordinated their efforts with those of the Wehrmacht, the German army. When the German army invaded Poland in September, 1939, and quickly occupied this unfortunate country, more than three thousand Einsatzgruppen soldiers moved into occupied areas and began the systematic execution of Jews and others who protected Jews. Himmler, Heydrich, and their thugs did not want to engage in battle.

They viewed themselves as nothing more than executioners. Himmler and Heydrich implemented plans so that all the Jews could be executed in town after town throughout Poland. At first, only adult men were shot, but soon Himmler and Heydrich presented the obviously specious argument that it was necessary to kill women and children lest avengers rise up against Nazis in later generations. They presented this lie so that Einsatzgruppen killers would not hesitate to shoot women, children, and infants.

Einsatzgruppen murderers were very efficient in shooting to death Jews, communists, and others who opposed their invasion of the Soviet Union, but they also carried out horrendous massacres such as the killing at Babi Yar near Kiev, where well over 100,000 were executed and buried in a single ravine. The Einsatzgruppen also used

German doctors to give lethal injections to another 100,000 victims in Kiev. Similar mass murders occurred throughout the Ukraine, Byelorussia, Lithuania, Latvia, and Estonia. An Einsatzgruppen thug named Karl Jäger bragged in a report dated December 1, 1941, that the soldiers in a single Einsatzgruppen had executed 137,346 people in the area of Kaunas, Lithuania, in the previous five months.

Even mass murders on this scale were not enough for Hitler, Heydrich, and Himmler. They wanted to exterminate all Jews in Nazi-occupied countries. At Hitler's request, Heydrich called the infamous Wannsee Conference of January 20, 1942, just outside Berlin. As a result of this conference, the Nazis began constructing huge concentration camps, with gas chambers and crematoria, in places such as Sobibor, Treblinka, and Auschwitz. Einsatzgruppen soldiers under the command of Odilo Globocnik had already demonstrated the effectiveness of using poisonous gas to murder Jews in mobile killing vans. Adolf Eichmann learned from Globocnik how to use poisonous gas to execute people in stationary buildings such as gas chambers. Einsatzgruppen officers thus provided the technical expertise that Eichmann and other concentration camp commanders needed to murder large numbers of Jews simultaneously. Einsatzgruppen criminals also taught Schützstaffeln (SS) murderers that different gases could be used. In addition, they worked with death camp commandants and architects to help design gas chambers and crematoria. Carbon monoxide and Zylkon B, a prussic acid insecticide, were most frequently used to exterminate people in gas chambers. Staring in early 1942, the main task of the Einsatzgruppen changed. Henceforth, their responsibility would be to round up Jews and ship them by train to death camps for extermination.

The subtitle of this book is *The Einsatzgruppen and the Invention of the Holocaust.* Rhodes chose these words very carefully. The Einsatzgruppen carried out the first systematic killing of European Jews by shooting them, but they also taught concentration camp commanders how to murder Jews in gas chambers on a massive scale and how to destroy the corpses in crematoria. Although the Einsatzgruppen soldiers had no qualms about killing innocent people, they always tried to hide the evidence of their crimes by burning or cremating corpses. Rhodes demonstrates convincingly that Hitler's infamous Final Solution could not have been implemented without the eager cooperation of Himmler, Heydrich, Globocnik, and numerous other war criminals from the SS-Einsatzgruppen.

In the final chapter of this book, Richard Rhodes describes what happened to the Einsatzgruppen criminals after the Allied victory over Germany. Like so many other Nazi war criminals, far too many Einsatzgruppen members were not sentenced in open court for their murders. Czech patriots assassinated Heydrich in 1942. Hitler killed himself in August, 1945, and Himmler committed suicide the next month. Both criminals chose the easy way out and did not have to appear in court. Heinrich Müller, the head of the Gestapo, was never seen after April, 1945. There probably never would have been war crimes trials for Einsatzgruppen soldiers had it not been for an American Jewish lawyer named Benjamin Ferencz, who was then serving in the American army. He went through thousands of SS documents that had been seized in Gestapo headquarters in Berlin by liberating American soldiers and discovered clear proof of the atrocities committed by the Einsatzgruppen. He obtained from Telford Taylor, chief prosecutor at the first Nuremberg trials, permission to prosecute Einsatzgruppen leaders for murder and crimes against humanity. Through his efforts, fourteen Einsatzgruppen leaders were sentenced to death. Four other Einsatzgruppen criminals were hanged in other countries.

Edmund J. Campion

Sources for Further Study

Booklist 98 (April 15, 2002): 1379.
Library Journal 127 (May 1, 2002): 117.
Los Angeles Times Book Review, July 7, 2002, p. 12.
The New York Times Book Review 107 (June 30, 2002): 7.
Publishers Weekly 249 (April 8, 2002): 216.

ME AND SHAKESPEARE
Adventures with the Bard

Author: Herman Gollob (1930-   )
Publisher: Doubleday (New York). 341 pp. $26.00
Type of work: Memoir
Time: 1997-2001
Locale: New Jersey, New York, and Oxford, England

~

*A retired book editor indulges his love of Shakespeare
by reading books, traveling to London and Oxford, interviewing actors and directors, and teaching continuing education classes at a small college in New Jersey*

~

Principal personages:
  HERMAN GOLLOB, retired book editor
  BARBARA, his wife
  BOB, one of Gollob's students
  LOU, a class clown
  EMMA SMITH, Oxford tutor

Herman Gollob spent some time as a theatrical agent for MCA and the William
Morris Agency in California before moving to the East Coast to work as a book editor
for Little, Brown; Atheneum; Doubleday; Simon & Schuster; and other publishing
companies. He edited James Clavell's first book, *King Rat* (1962), and set Clavell's
career in motion. He was the first to edit Dan Jenkins, author of *Semi-Tough* (1972)
and *Rude Behavior* (1998), and Bill Moyers of *Listening to America* (1971) fame. He
was a friend and early editor of the short-story writer David Barthelme, whom he had
met at the University of Houston in the early 1950's. Gollob attended parties with
Hollywood celebrities such as Frank Sinatra and had lunches with legendary directors
such as Orson Welles and Peter Bogdanovich. These relationships and experiences
make for a colorful memoir, but it is his career after retirement that Gollob focuses on
in *Me and Shakespeare: Adventures with the Bard*. In July, 1995, Gollob retired to his
home in Montclair, New Jersey, and soon embarked on a second career as a teacher of
William Shakespeare's plays. His 341-page book is a chronicle of his later-life obsession with all things Shakespeare.

Gollob's pursuit of Shakespeare is at least partly motivated by his desire to understand himself and his past. In this respect *Me and Shakespeare* is similar to Bob
Smith's *Hamlet's Dresser: A Memoir* (2002), in which Smith uses passages from
Shakespeare's plays to understand and explain his own life. At several points Gollob
quotes passages from Shakespeare's plays, particularly *Hamlet* (pr. c. 1600-1601, pb.
1603), to explain the people and events in his life:

> Returning from his journey, Hamlet appears, spiritually, a changed man. From the vantage point of my sixty-fifth year [1995], I could track the changes in my own character following each of my journeys, as I groped to find my particular niche in the scheme of things.

Gollob had always attributed his success to "Timing, luck, connections," but as he explores the Bard's works he begins to suspect the presence of a shaping "divinity" in his own life. Gollob likens his newfound interest in Shakespeare—sparked by seeing Ralph Fiennes in a Broadway production of *Hamlet*—to his "conversion" back to Judaism in later life. In fact, his religion becomes the unifying motif of his study of Shakespeare, culminating in a paper on the Judaic qualities of *King Lear* (pr. c. 1605-1606, pb. 1608). He even toys with the notion that Shakespeare's plays may have been a midrash (or commentary) on the Torah. Gollob's rediscoveries of Shakespeare and Judaism seem to be connected to his memories of his father, who helped to foster his pride in their Jewish heritage and his love of literature.

Although his father died in 1982, Gollob mentions him frequently in his memoir and recalls their relationship with fondness. A lawyer by profession, Abraham Gollob taught his son sports, took him to boxing matches, bought him books, and gave him history lessons. For example, he talked about the founding of Israel in terms of the founding of Texas: "Imagine those first settlers as Hebrews, the Mexicans as Canaanites, Texas as Israel." He pointed to the Jewish presence in motion pictures (actors such as Paul Muni and Kirk Douglas), literature (especially playwright Clifford Odets), and sports (boxer Barney Ross, quarterback Sid Luckman, and baseball player Hank Greenberg), suggesting that his son could do anything he wanted. He made a profound impression on the boy. Like Shakespeare's father, Abraham Gollob had "endured financial setbacks" during the Depression, and those setbacks may have motivated his son to make good in the world. Herman Gollob as Shakespeare? Gollob writes, "Perhaps that particular wound—a father enduring pecuniary misfortune—is the driving force behind the Young Men from the Provinces." Gollob remembers his father being Lear-like in old age—fiercely independent, disdainfully proud, and sharp-tongued. He died of cancer at the age of 83. At his father's funeral Gollob, though not yet a Bardologist, reads lines from *Julius Caesar* (pr. c. 1599-1600, pb. 1601) and *Hamlet*. In one moving scene, in 1997, Gollob visits his father's grave and tells him about his obsession with Shakespeare.

Gollob's relationship with his mother was the antithesis of his relationship with his father. Discussing Hamlet's mother in one chapter, Gollob slips into a digression about his own mother, who had serious psychological problems. He recalls a time when she brandished a knife and threatened to kill herself, only to be talked out of the deed by her son. A chain smoker and chronic coffee drinker, she would sit in front of the television and yell obscenities at soap opera characters. Part of his hostility toward his mother apparently stemmed from her criticism of his father, a "lousy provider." While Gollob was away at college, his mother started hearing voices encouraging her to hurt members of the family, and she was promptly sent to a hospital where she underwent shock treatment and eventually a lobotomy. When Gollob heard about the lo-

Born in Houston in 1930, Herman Gollob attended Texas A&M and the University of Houston, taking courses in English literature and acting. He eventually became a successful book editor on the East Coast. In 1995, he retired to his home in New Jersey, only to embark on a career as a Bardologist in 1997.

botomy, he called to check on her, but could not stop crying long enough to hold a conversation. During the last ten years of her life, "Miss Rubye" as she was called by her husband—lived in relative comfort, becoming a model grandmother before dying in 1970.

Gollob seems to find some peace from these ghosts in his study of Shakespeare's plays. After his retirement he immerses himself in the plays and in Shakespeare criticism, preferring the wisdom of "old farts" such as Harold Goddard and Maynard Mack to more recent critics. He seems particularly attracted to Goddard's and Mack's ideas and uses them to organize several of his lectures on Shakespeare. Whenever he sees a reference to an interesting book, he goes out and buys it. One wonders why he does not use the library (or interlibrary loan) more often. Fortunately he has the money in his retirement to support these urges. He also buys expensive instructional videos, such as John Barton's series *Playing Shakespeare* (1979-1984), which he describes and praises extensively in the book. His memoir is punctuated by enthusiastic summaries of these sources; as his confidence and knowledge grow, he begins to assert his agreement or disagreement with them. Even though he describes himself as an amateur—always "an undergraduate at heart"—he benefits from years of voracious reading and a willingness to keep on reading. Without the crutch of other critics, he is able to draw parallels between Shakespeare and Herman Melville (1819-1891) and Nathaniel Hawthorne (1804-1864). He is able to compare Shakespeare's *Julius Caesar* to his source in Plutarch, offering explanations for the discrepancies. He reads books on Jewish philosophy and theology and uses them to understand Shakespeare's works.

Gollob is not merely content with reading books or viewing videos; sometimes he feels compelled to seek out and interview the authors, actors, and directors in his sources. His former career as a high-powered book editor gives him access to people and places that he would not have access to otherwise. For example, when he sees a photograph in the Bantam Classic edition of *Titus Andronicus* (pr., pb. 1594), he calls up actress Olympia Dukakis—who played Tamora in that production—and asks her whether the director had actually blocked the scene a certain way, because the photograph seemed to confirm his interpretation. He writes to the Folger Shakespeare Library in Washington, D.C., and asks for permission to visit there. Not only is he given special access to the collection, but he also gets a guided tour of the library. While in Oxford he talks his way into an acting workshop taught by John Barton. In New York he manages to get a private interview with Shakespearean actor David Suchet in his dressing room at the Music Box Theater.

To put all this research and experience to good use, Gollob teaches a continuing education course on Shakespeare at Caldwell College in New Jersey. His first twenty-two students—senior citizens in the Lifelong Learning Institute—are justifiably impressed by him, and Gollob is not shy about revealing this. His students stand up and applaud after his first lecture, lavishing him with compliments, many of them quoted in the book. One student, however, complains about the speed of his talking. His reply: "Listen faster." He has a no-bathroom-break policy because he wants to make full use of his two hours a week. No one challenges this policy until the following semester when a retired nun—a former Shakespeare teacher herself—insists on a break; Gollob grudgingly relinquishes five of his minutes. Over time he learns to moderate his authoritarian approach to teaching, but he never allows his classes to degenerate into bull sessions. In fact, he has a strong distaste for open discussions in the classroom. Later, when he travels to Oxford to take a Shakespeare course, he criticizes the unstructured format of the course and shows an odd mixture of disdain and respect for his tutor, Emma Smith.

The chapter about his first semester of teaching at Caldwell is the most useful and entertaining one in the book. It is organized around his syllabus of the six Roman, Greek, and Trojan plays. The first half of the chapter covers *Titus Andronicus*, *Julius Caesar*, and *Antony and Cleopatra* (pr. c. 1606-1607, pb. 1623). His interpretations of the plays are succinct but insightful. A common theme running through his analysis is the trouble that arises from the development of the mind over the heart. He compares Titus and Aaron as fathers, discusses the motives of Brutus and Cassius, and treats Enobarbus as another one of Shakespeare's wise fools. Gollob then takes a coffee break in midchapter—a humorous violation of his no-break policy?—and gives brief biographical information about several of his students, including Bob and Lou, two of his most devoted groupies. After this brief interruption Gollob resumes the "class" with his explications of *Coriolanus* (pr. 1607-1608, pb. 1623), *Timon of Athens* (wr. c. 1607-1608, pb. 1623), and *Troilus and Cressida* (pr. 1601-1602, pb. 1609). Eighty-year-old Lou, ever the class clown, offers an inspired comparison between Coriolanus and James Cagney's character Cody Jarrett ("Top of the world, Ma!") in the film *White Heat* (1949), and Gollob counters with a less inspired comparison between Coriolanus and World War II general Douglas MacArthur. It is obvious from these exchanges, however, that Gollob and his students are thoroughly enjoying the class and one another.

Gollob's memoir is not for everyone. It requires a greater interest in Shakespeare than in celebrities, for example. The reader is tantalized by Gollob's name dropping, but nothing ever comes of it; instead he relates everything in one way or another to Shakespeare. James Clavell is an Elizabethan; Donald Barthelme is Hamlet; Dan Jenkins is a cross between Hotspur and Hal; Willie Morris is a cross between Hal and Falstaff; and Orson Welles is Falstaff (though Gollob was not familiar with Welles's 1965 film *Chimes at Midnight*, in which he plays Falstaff, when he met the actor). In general, Gollob's criticism is well informed and interesting and his scholarship sound, though he does slip in one or two places. For example, he writes, "The early sixteenth century produced two enduring classics of Western culture: the collected works of Shakespeare and the King James translation of the Bible" (these works were produced in the early seventeenth century), and he writes that "I hadn't considered *Troilus and Cressida* a romance, scholarly consensus notwithstanding" (usually the play is classified as a comedy). His opinions are sometimes hard to bear, such as his dismissal of films that update the settings of the plays, his panning of Julie Taymor's film *Titus* (1999), and his unromantic rejection of Falstaff, that lovable coward. Nevertheless, the book has a great deal to offer because of its genuine enthusiasm for the Bard and its affirmation of Shakespeare's continued relevance to the contemporary world.

Edward A. Malone

Sources for Further Study

The Houston Chronicle, June 2, 2002, p. 19.
Kirkus Reviews 70 (February 15, 2002): 236.
Library Journal 127 (April 1, 2002): 106.
Los Angeles Times, April 30, 2002, p. E3.
The New York Times Book Review 107 (June 9, 2002): 28.
Publishers Weekly 249 (April 1, 2002): 67.
The Washington Post Book World, June 16, 2002, p. 5.

MEDIA UNLIMITED
How the Torrent of Images and Sounds Overwhelms Our Lives

Author: Todd Gitlin (1943-   )
Publisher: Metropolitan Books (New York). 261 pp.
  $25.00
Type of work: Media
Time: The present
Locale: Worldwide, but especially the United States

∿

A thoughtful and sometimes impassioned examination
of the overwhelming influence that the various media have
on modern society and on individuals by a noted commen-
tator and social thinker

∿

During the 1960's, the communication theorist Marshall McLuhan famously proclaimed that "The medium is the message." No one (perhaps not even McLuhan himself) was quite sure at the time exactly what this resonant phrase meant, and since then the debate has continued without resolution, but for all the obscurity of explications and multiplicity of explanations, the famous phrase is clearly saying something very important about the media.

Todd Gitlin is among the most recent, and certainly one of the most perceptive observers to follow McLuhan's trail, and in *Media Unlimited* he takes up where McLuhan left off in *Understanding Media: The Extensions of Man* (1964). As its subtitle proclaims, *Media Unlimited* is about the "torrent" of media which are sweeping across cultures and individuals alike from Siberia to San Francisco. While the intensity (perhaps "ferocity" would be the more appropriate word, given some of Gitlin's examples) of the media torrent has increased in recent decades, it has existed in various forms for centuries—for Western culture, certainly as far back as the Middle Ages and perhaps even longer. The differences now are the ever-increasing speed and pervasiveness of the media and their exponentially growing ability to transform not only the human environment but human beings as well.

Gitlin's central point is that the media (plural) have become the Media (singular). While there may be many components involved in this transformation, they refuse to remain discrete and instead fuse into a single entity, difficult to define but as pervasive and uniform as the sky or the ocean. The dozens of facets of many media have merged: Television, music, film, print, billboards, radio, the Internet, and others not named here and not yet named have transformed themselves in a fashion so that they remain many and yet are one. They no longer assault the senses individually and sequentially (if they ever did) but collectively and simultaneously. It is not uncommon for a news report on television to have, in addition to the "talking head" of the

⁓

Todd Gitlin is a professor of culture, journalism, and sociology whose books on the media, politics, and contemporary culture include The Whole World Is Watching *(1977),* Inside Prime Time *(1983), and* The Twilight of Common Dreams *(1995). He is a frequent contributor to the* Los Angeles Times, The Washington Post, *and* The New York Times.

⁓

news reader, lines of stock market quotations flowing along the bottom of the screen, sport scores flashing along the edges of the picture, the local time, temperature, and weather forecast boxed in an upper corner, and other information lodged elsewhere in the frame. Music videos mix more than songs and image to contain words, advertising, and quick-cut references to print, photography, and outdoor advertising.

The list of mergers and meltings-together goes on. It could be disputed whether such richness of information constitutes a cornucopia or a trash heap, but its presence cannot be denied. As the media have become the Media, they have retained their individual natures while assuming a new, unified, and collective nature, an entity as mysterious in its way as that of the Holy Ghost and, like the Holy Ghost, able to fill the faithful with the spirit—and, while the precise nature of the spirit is anyone's guess, it seems to have a great deal to do with ever-increasing consumption of material goods and the instant gratification of immediate needs and manufactured desires.

These needs and desires are framed by kinetic images. Thanks in large part to the Media, Western society has become a culture of images rather than one of thought; a society of feelings and emotions rather than one of intellect and judgment. In contrast to more conventional and less perceptive critics, Gitlin points out that this is no new phenomenon: As early as the 1830's, Alexis de Tocqueville had noted the tendency in the relatively young United States to prefer the sensationalistic, the emotional, the melodramatic, and the informal in its popular entertainments—and, for Americans, there could be no entertainment that was not, in the root sense of the word, "popular." Art was for the people and its purpose was to entertain and ease, rather than inform and uplift. Rather than discriminate and restrict, such art naturally welcomed and embraced, accepting content that broadened its popular appeal while utilizing all new technologies that widened its reach. More efficient printing methods, cheaper paper, greater literacy, growing urban centers, concentrated audiences, improved transportation networks, and a populist democracy helped produce the penny press, the best-selling novel, the advertising broadside (and later the billboard), the minstrel show, the side show, the freak show, and the circus. P. T. Barnum and William Randolph Hearst were creators of (and to some extent, created by) the media, as were their exhibitions and newspapers. The result, as Gitlin terms it, was the "panoply of media," a term aptly chosen, since the literal meaning of the word "panoply" is the armor of a warrior—but, by extension, a panoply is also defined as a "glittering display that covers and protects." This was exactly what the sprawling new media were: a glittering, multifaceted display that covered everyday life with a gaudy pattern and protected the spectator-participants from harsh realities by distracting and beguiling them. Years pass, new technologies evolve, but the panoply remains. The torrent of media may have swollen immensely in recent years, but it has been rushing furiously for quite a while. It is a long time since people noticed their loss of innocence; even longer since the actual loss itself.

One of the paradoxical qualities of this media torrent is that while it catches everyone in its flood, it also separates them even as it unites them. The isolating effects of the media (granting, if only for a temporary time, all individuals the "right to leave society" as the French writer Charles Baudelaire phrased it) have become a more pronounced phenomenon perhaps, but hardly a novel one. The subway commuter's protective cocoon of the daily newspaper is now joined by the personal CD player, the handheld video game, and the miniature personal computer wirelessly linked to the Internet. In the midst of even the largest crowd in the most populous cities, people can be alone—and not just alone in this world, but isolated in a separate reality of their own choosing, idiosyncratically mixed and matched from the superabundance of images, sounds, effects, flavors, and fashions offered by the omnipresent media. People are, Gitlin affirms, supersaturated by the Media.

The Media grows steadily faster. Speed is the essence of the modern world: the assembly line, the automated teller machine, convenience stores, microwaves, instant dinners, fast food. However, Gitlin reminds his readers that this great speed-up has not arisen recently. The English word "speed" once had the primary meaning "to prosper." Thus, "speed the plow" was a wish for an abundant harvest rather than a command to engage in a rapid planting season. By the late Middle Ages this meaning was changing, and "speed" was associated not with the positive outcome of an action but with its pace. "Go fast" was the new meaning of "speed" and going fast, and then ever faster, was considered a good thing in and of itself. The acceleration has never stopped and seldom slackened, especially for the introduction and spread of new technology, much of it media or media-related. For example, it took sixty-seven years for the telephone to reach three-quarters of American households; television accomplished the same conquest in just seven years. People are still grappling with the results of both.

What do human beings do when faced with this overwhelming torrent? How do they handle the supersaturation of the Media and the ever-increasing speed of modern life? Gitlin examines the various "strategies of navigation" people use to negotiate the media torrent and develops a taxonomy of types: fans, critics, paranoids, exhibitionists, ironists, jammers, secessionists, and abolitionists. These cover the whole spectrum of response, from the fans who eagerly embrace the latest media advances and revel in them to the abolitionists who propose a neo-Luddite response of turning back the technological clock and who would force society to "free" itself of its pervasive but largely unnoticed media shackles. Perhaps the only truth shared by all of these styles is that none of them, in the long run, really works. It is no more possible to surrender oneself completely to the Media than to banish it totally from modern society; all of these strategies and styles are at best, as Robert Frost once said of poetry, "momentary stays against confusion."

It is not only America's confusion but the world's, because the American media torrent has gone global, capturing markets and seducing audiences everywhere, as

Gitlin puts it, "Under the Sign of Mickey Mouse & Co." Out of Hollywood have come the three modern archetypes of visual narrative: the Western, the action movie, and the cartoon. So adaptable have these genres proven that some of their classic examples are not, literally, from Hollywood at all: The "spaghetti westerns" of Sergio Leone and the stylized kung fu films of the Hong Kong masters come immediately to mind. Of those films which are actually made in Hollywood, even the most "American" of them, such as *Independence Day* (1996), are likely to be the works of European or Asian directors. As for television, for every highly cultured but barely watched BBC import that arrives on the U.S. airwaves, dozens of American sitcoms, melodramas, crime dramas, and reality shows conquer viewers around the world. There is a new international style in entertainment, and it is American—and the Media is at once the cause, vehicle, and result of the spread of this style.

If such is the power and extent of the Media, then what is to be done? If none of the earlier responses he cataloged is adequate to deal with the torrent, what does Gitlin propose? In many ways, the conclusion of *Media Unlimited* is the weakest aspect of the work: Having established the sweep and extent of the Media's power, Gitlin advances no unified response, no call to a culture war to meet the onslaught. The thoughtful reader, however, will note that diagnosis, rather than prescription, was always Gitlin's purpose with this work. He has presented his readers with the case; now he suggests that they must respond. To Gitlin's credit, he is honest enough not to propose a facile or superficial answer; instead, he admits that there can be no answer, at least now, because the Media is simply not yet understood well enough. Like fish immersed in the ocean, unaware of the water all around them, modern Americans hardly notice the all-pervasive media surrounding them. To carry Marshal McLuhan's observation to its latest, logical, and perhaps inevitable conclusion, "the media is the environment." Difficult as it is, some way must be found to step back from the Media, to find an external viewpoint so that the environment can be seen unfiltered, unmediated, and undistorted. It is only then, Gitlin proposes, that the Media and its effect on society can be understood. He does not pretend that this will be an easy or quickly accomplished task; he does insist that it is a vitally necessary one. With *Media Unlimited* he has taken the first step and shown his readers a path to follow.

Michael Witkoski

Sources for Further Study

Kirkus Reviews 69 (December 15, 2002): 1736.
Los Angeles Times Book Review, March 3, 2002, p. 4.
The New York Review of Books 49 (July 18, 2002): 4.
Publishers Weekly 249 (February 4, 2002): 66.
The Washington Post Book World, February 24, 2002, p. 7.
Wired 10 (March, 2002): 122.

MIDDLESEX

Author: Jeffrey Eugenides (1960-   )
Publisher: Farrar, Straus and Giroux (New York). 544
   pp. $27.00
Type of work: Novel
Time: 1922-2001
Locale: Detroit

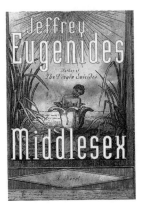

~

A hermaphrodite narrator describes his childhood, in which he was raised as a girl; his discovery of his hermaphroditism; and his decision to live as a male, also relating his family background to explain situations in his own life

~

Principal characters:
   CALLIOPE (CALLIE, later CAL) STEPHANIDES, a pseudohermaphrodite
   DESDEMONA STEPHANIDES, Cal's grandmother
   ELEUTHERIOS "LEFTY" STEPHANIDES, Desdemona's spouse and brother
   MILTON STEPHANIDES, Cal's father
   THEODORA "TESSIE" STEPHANIDES, Cal's mother
   SOURMELINA ZIZMO, Desdemona and Lefty's cousin
   JIMMY ZIZMO, her husband
   MICHAEL ANTONIOU, a Greek Orthodox priest

   Middlesex, the long-awaited and Pulitzer Prize-winning second novel by Jeffrey Eugenides, unfolds like a Greek drama, with a sense of inevitability and of underlying purpose in what might be seen as random and coincidental occurrences. Characters suffer from flaws that the reader knows will somehow be their undoing but act according to their seemingly free will, even when taking actions that they suspect will prove ruinous. The moral lessons, barring an admonition against incest, are not as obvious as in Greek drama, but the reader leaves the book feeling that the gods do in fact have plans for mortal beings.
   Cal Stephanides, a pseudohermaphrodite (he has external female genitalia but male XY chromosomes, rather than female XX), narrates the novel. The opening sentence hints at inevitability: Cal states that he was born twice, as a baby girl in Detroit in 1960, then as a teenage boy in an emergency room in Petoskey, Michigan, in 1974. Readers thus know that Cal will discover his identity, but through many chapters, Calliope (his young female self) remains confused by her feelings and by her body. Cal believes that he breaks from predestination by deciding to live as a man, but one could argue that because he is genetically male (with XY chromosomes), albeit with female genitalia, the choice to be a man is not his.

∽

Jeffrey Eugenides published his first novel, The Virgin Suicides *(1993), to great acclaim, and his short fiction has appeared in such publications as* The New Yorker, The Paris Review, *and* The Yale Review. *Awards for his work include a Guggenheim Fellowship and a fellowship from the National Endowment for the Arts.*

∽

Cal's grandparents are more firmly attached to the idea of life as inevitable tragedy. Shortly before fleeing their tiny Greek village during the Turkish invasion of 1922, they realize that although they are brother and sister, they love each other as man and woman. Thus is rooted another theme of the book, that of transformation—Cal's from female to male identification and his grandparents' reinvention of themselves as husband and wife rather than brother and sister. The latter choice sets Cal's story in motion, for it is through his grandparents' mating that a rare recessive gene is passed to Cal's father.

That is getting ahead of the story, but the narrator does the same. Early chapters begin with snippets of the narrator's current life. He relates that he dates women and is good at chatting up and front-door kisses, even groping and the first stages of undressing, but when a relationship gets to that point, he abandons it. He is compelled to engage in the chase, but he has no real interest in bagging the quarry. These glimpses let readers know early on how Cal has turned out, at least in outline, but how he gets there nevertheless makes for fascinating reading.

The book contains two main stories, one acting as prelude to the other, and a third that is neglected. The prelude, about one third of the book, tells how Cal's grandparents came to the United States, set themselves up as a family, and had a child, Cal's father. The second is Callie's tale of growing up as a girl, increasingly confused about her identity, and her discovery of her dual self. It climaxes with her decision to defy her upbringing and live as a man, then shows the process of breaking away from the past and discovering how to be a different person. The tentative and painful first steps of that process are related poignantly.

The neglected story is what happened to the teenage Cal and how he became the forty-one-year-old narrator: Eugenides reveals only the barest outline of more than two decades of Cal's life. At the age of forty-one, Cal meets a young woman, then abruptly shuts her out of his life when the relationship becomes too serious. He meets her again by chance—but in this novel, what is chance and what is predestination is open to question—and decides for the first time to tell the truth about himself to someone other than a family member. This end fits, for it shows Cal's willingness to move to a new stage in his life.

Cal begins by telling readers about his dual birth, relates a bit about his present circumstances, and then goes back to the roots of his story in the lives of his grandparents. His grandmother, Desdemona, knows that something bad would come from marrying her brother and tries to avoid becoming pregnant. Greek myth enters here. Desdemona and her cousin Sourmelina, with whom Desdemona and Lefty live, become pregnant on the same night after watching an Americanized performance of a Greek tragedy. The double impregnation is doubly ominous, as Sourmelina, a lesbian, had not had sexual intercourse with her husband, Jimmy Zizmo, for five months, putting him off with various excuses.

The primary reason for Cal to tell so much about his grandparents as part of his own story is to reveal how the rare recessive gene for Cal's form of hermaphroditism was passed to his father, Desdemona and Lefty's child Milton. Milton marries Tessie, the daughter of Sourmelina and Jimmy Zizmo. Such intermarrying among close families was common in their home village, but Desdemona comes to learn of the medical reasons against it.

Eugenides has a second reason for telling so much about Desdemona and Lefty: to draw their environment into the story. Like *The Virgin Suicides*, the book is set primarily in Detroit. Desdemona refuses to assimilate; having changed her life once, to become her brother's wife, she remains steadfast in her desire to remain a Greek wife. Lefty, through the assistance of Jimmy, gets a job at Ford Motor Company; he attends classes in English there, and at home he adheres to Henry Ford's strict rules about personal hygiene and behavior. It is also through Jimmy that he loses the job—Ford's Sociological Department objects to Lefty's association with Jimmy, who is a bootlegger.

Jimmy's bootlegging provides the material for a key scene: As he and Lefty drive across a frozen lake into Canada to obtain liquor, Jimmy accuses Lefty of being the father of Sourmelina's child. Lefty jumps out of the car, fearing for his life, and the car crashes through the ice. Desdemona later takes a job at what she finds out is the first Nation of Islam temple. She listens through air vents to the charismatic temple leader, W. D. Fard. The historical Fard, known by a variety of names, has a sketchy past. Eugenides here has a bit of fun with history, revealing Fard to be none other than Jimmy Zizmo, who survived the car crash and chose to reinvent himself as a religious leader—surely in it for the money, the same impetus behind his marriage to Sourmelina. Like the historical Fard, Zizmo is chased from Detroit and vanishes. As one more example of integration of setting into plot, Eugenides describes the Detroit race riots of 1967, in which Milton Stephanides' overinsured restaurant is burned. Milton uses the insurance windfall to begin a chain of restaurants, the success of which allows his daughter Callie to grow up with a privileged lifestyle. Unlike his mother, Milton pursues the American Dream and even supports U.S. policy favoring Turkey, long the enemy of Greeks.

The story bridges fairly quickly to that of Cal. Cousins Milton and Tessie, living next door to each other, fall in love. At one point, Tessie is engaged to marry Michael Antoniou, who is to become a priest in the Greek Orthodox Church, but instead she marries Milton.

Callie's story begins with mistakes. Desdemona, known for her skill at predicting the sex of unborn children, seemingly breaks her string of more than twenty correct guesses by predicting that Milton and Tessie's second child will be a boy. The doctor who delivers Callie, chosen because he is an old family friend (and delivered Milton), fails to notice signs of Callie's hermaphroditism, and thus Callie is set on course to be reared as a girl. A mistake glossed over by the author is Tessie's failure to notice Callie's unusually prominent clitoris (which contains the child's urethra) while bathing and dressing her, even though she has an older boy, referred to by Cal only as "Chapter Eleven" (yet more inevitability—late in the book, Chapter Eleven runs Hercules Hot Dogs, the family business, into bankruptcy).

Callie has a relatively normal girlhood, but as an adolescent she becomes troubled by her attraction to a female classmate, referred to only as the Obscure Object, and by her failure to develop physically or to menstruate. Eugenides here prolongs suspense, providing a series of episodes hinting to Callie that something is wrong and leaving the reader to wonder just how and when she will discover her genetic identity. Her secret comes out while on a vacation with the Obscure Object. They engage in quasi-sexual exploration, each pretending that it is not really happening. The Object's brother accuses them of being lesbians, and Callie runs away, only to be hit by a tractor. The emergency room doctor who treats her discovers her physical abnormality.

Milton and Tessie take Callie to a specialist in gender identity, who tells them that multiple factors determine gender, and in his opinion Callie should receive hormone treatments and surgery to allow her to live as a woman. Callie, however, reads his records and sees that genetically she is male. She leaves her parents a note saying that she really is a boy and that the doctor had lied to them, then runs away. She buys a suit, adopts the name Cal, hitchhikes to California, and lives briefly in a camp of other runaways. After being beaten there by several homeless men, in desperation Cal calls a man he met on the road. Cal works in the man's strip club, revealing his body to peep show customers. He states that the experience, though horrible, allowed him to become comfortable with his body. When the club is raided by police, the underage Cal is taken into custody. He calls home, setting the scene for reconciliation several months after he ran away.

In the meantime, however, Milton has died. He believed a series of telephone calls from a man who claimed to have kidnapped Callie. He delivered ransom money, only to discover that the supposed kidnapper is Father Mike Antoniou. In his Cadillac, he chases Father Mike in his Gremlin. The chase ends when Milton rear-ends the Gremlin, dying in the crash. This scene is notable as the most flagrant example of a problem in the narration: As narrator, Cal relates the thoughts of both Father Mike (envious of Milton's marriage to Tessie and of his money) and Milton. This is only the most obvious case of Cal relating things that he cannot or probably does not know. Here, he tries to get around the problem by stating "I have to be honest and record Milton's thoughts as they occurred to him."

The Greek tragedy thus reaches its climax. Father Mike goes to prison, Chapter Eleven ruins the family business, and Cal moves on to his life as a man. Eugenides treats his characters as people, not as freaks, and tells a story with many insights.

A. J. Sobczak

Sources for Further Study

Booklist 98 (June 1-15, 2002): 1644.
Library Journal 127 (July, 2002): 116.
Los Angeles Times Book Review, September 1, 2002, p. 3.
The New York Times Book Review 107 (September 15, 2002): 9.
Publishers Weekly 249 (July 1, 2002): 46.